# Principles of Macroeconomics 2e

SENIOR CONTRIBUTING AUTHORS

**STEVEN A. GREENLAW, UNIVERSITY OF MARY WASHINGTON**
**DAVID SHAPIRO, PENNSYLVANIA STATE UNIVERSITY**

Based on the 2nd edition of *Principles of
Economics, Economics and the Economy, 2e*
by Timothy Taylor, published in 2011.

ISBN: 978-1-947172-38-8

**OpenStax**
Rice University
6100 Main Street MS-375
Houston, Texas 77005

To learn more about OpenStax, visit https://openstax.org.
Individual print copies and bulk orders can be purchased through our website.

Portions of the Demand and Supply chapter were derived from "Why It Matters: Government in Action by Steve Greenlaw and Lumen Learning." Located at: https://courses.lumenlearning.com/waymakermacroxmasterfall2016/chapter/why-it-matters-government-action/. License: CC BY 4.0.

| | |
|---|---|
| **HARDCOVER BOOK ISBN-13** | 978-1-947172-38-8 |
| **PAPERBACK BOOK ISBN-13** | 978-1-951693-10-7 |
| **B&W PAPERBACK BOOK ISBN-13** | 978-1-50669-988-2 |
| **DIGITAL VERSION ISBN-13** | 978-1-947172-39-5 |
| **ENHANCED TEXTBOOK ISBN-13** | 978-1-947172-50-0 |
| **Revision Number** | MA2-2017-001-(03/18)-LC |
| **Original Publication Year** | 2017 |

Printed by

XanEdu

4750 Venture Drive, Suite 400
Ann Arbor, MI 48108
800-562-2147
www.xanedu.com

## OPENSTAX

OpenStax provides free, peer-reviewed, openly licensed textbooks for introductory college and Advanced Placement® courses and low-cost, personalized courseware that helps students learn. A nonprofit ed tech initiative based at Rice University, we're committed to helping students access the tools they need to complete their courses and meet their educational goals.

## RICE UNIVERSITY

OpenStax, OpenStax CNX, and OpenStax Tutor are initiatives of Rice University. As a leading research university with a distinctive commitment to undergraduate education, Rice University aspires to path-breaking research, unsurpassed teaching, and contributions to the betterment of our world. It seeks to fulfill this mission by cultivating a diverse community of learning and discovery that produces leaders across the spectrum of human endeavor.

## FOUNDATION SUPPORT

OpenStax is grateful for the tremendous support of our sponsors. Without their strong engagement, the goal of free access to high-quality textbooks would remain just a dream.

Laura and John Arnold Foundation (LJAF) actively seeks opportunities to invest in organizations and thought leaders that have a sincere interest in implementing fundamental changes that not only yield immediate gains, but also repair broken systems for future generations. LJAF currently focuses its strategic investments on education, criminal justice, research integrity, and public accountability.

The William and Flora Hewlett Foundation has been making grants since 1967 to help solve social and environmental problems at home and around the world. The Foundation concentrates its resources on activities in education, the environment, global development and population, performing arts, and philanthropy, and makes grants to support disadvantaged communities in the San Francisco Bay Area.

Calvin K. Kazanjian was the founder and president of Peter Paul (Almond Joy), Inc. He firmly believed that the more people understood about basic economics the happier and more prosperous they would be. Accordingly, he established the Calvin K. Kazanjian Economics Foundation Inc, in 1949 as a philanthropic, nonpolitical educational organization to support efforts that enhanced economic understanding.

Guided by the belief that every life has equal value, the Bill & Melinda Gates Foundation works to help all people lead healthy, productive lives. In developing countries, it focuses on improving people's health with vaccines and other life-saving tools and giving them the chance to lift themselves out of hunger and extreme poverty. In the United States, it seeks to significantly improve education so that all young people have the opportunity to reach their full potential. Based in Seattle, Washington, the foundation is led by CEO Jeff Raikes and Co-chair William H. Gates Sr., under the direction of Bill and Melinda Gates and Warren Buffett.

The Maxfield Foundation supports projects with potential for high impact in science, education, sustainability, and other areas of social importance.

Our mission at The Michelson 20MM Foundation is to grow access and success by eliminating unnecessary hurdles to affordability. We support the creation, sharing, and proliferation of more effective, more affordable educational content by leveraging disruptive technologies, open educational resources, and new models for collaboration between for-profit, nonprofit, and public entities.

The Bill and Stephanie Sick Fund supports innovative projects in the areas of Education, Art, Science and Engineering.

# Table of Contents

# PREFACE

Welcome to *Principles of Macroeconomics 2e* (2nd Edition), an OpenStax resource. This textbook was written to increase student access to high-quality learning materials, maintaining highest standards of academic rigor at little to no cost.

## About OpenStax

OpenStax is a nonprofit based at Rice University, and it's our mission to improve student access to education. Our first openly licensed college textbook was published in 2012, and our library has since scaled to over 25 books for college and AP® courses used by hundreds of thousands of students. OpenStax Tutor, our low-cost personalized learning tool, is being used in college courses throughout the country. Through our partnerships with philanthropic foundations and our alliance with other educational resource organizations, OpenStax is breaking down the most common barriers to learning and empowering students and instructors to succeed.

## About OpenStax resources

### Customization

*Principles of Macroeconomics 2e* is licensed under a Creative Commons Attribution 4.0 International (CC BY) license, which means that you can distribute, remix, and build upon the content, as long as you provide attribution to OpenStax and its content contributors.

Because our books are openly licensed, you are free to use the entire book or pick and choose the sections that are most relevant to the needs of your course. Feel free to remix the content by assigning your students certain chapters and sections in your syllabus, in the order that you prefer. You can even provide a direct link in your syllabus to the sections in the web view of your book.

Instructors also have the option of creating a customized version of their OpenStax book. The custom version can be made available to students in low-cost print or digital form through their campus bookstore. Visit the Instructor Resources section of your book page on OpenStax.org for more information.

### Errata

All OpenStax textbooks undergo a rigorous review process. However, like any professional-grade textbook, errors sometimes occur. Since our books are web based, we can make updates periodically when deemed pedagogically necessary. If you have a correction to suggest, submit it through the link on your book page on OpenStax.org. Subject matter experts review all errata suggestions. OpenStax is committed to remaining transparent about all updates, so you will also find a list of past errata changes on your book page on OpenStax.org.

### Format

You can access this textbook for free in web view or PDF through OpenStax.org, and for a low cost in print.

## About *Principles of Macroeconomics 2e*

*Principles of Macroeconomics 2e* (2nd edition) covers the scope and sequence requirements of most introductory macroeconomics courses. The text includes many current examples, which are handled in a politically equitable way. The outcome is a balanced approach to both Keynesian and classical views, and to the theory and application of economics concepts. The second edition has been thoroughly revised to increase clarity, update data and current event impacts, and incorporate the feedback from many reviewers and adopters.

### Coverage and scope

To develop the first edition of *Principles of Macroeconomics*, we acquired the rights to Timothy Taylor's *Principles of Economics* and solicited ideas from economics instructors at all levels of higher education, from community colleges to PhD-granting universities. For the second edition, we received even more expansive and actionable feedback from hundreds of adopters who had used the book for several academic terms. These knowledgeable instructors informed the pedagogical courses, learning objective development and fulfillment, and the chapter arrangements. Faculty who taught from the material provided critical and detailed commentary.

The result is a book that covers the breadth of economics topics and also provides the necessary depth to ensure the course is manageable for instructors and students alike. We strove to balance theory and application, as well as the amount of calculation and mathematical examples.

The book is organized into seven main parts:

**What is Economics?** The first two chapters introduce students to the study of economics with a focus on making choices in a world of scarce resources.

**Supply and Demand**, Chapters 3 and 4, introduces and explains the first analytical model in economics: supply, demand, and equilibrium, before showing applications in the markets for labor and finance.

**Elasticity and Price**, Chapter 5, introduces and explains elasticity and price, two key concepts in economics.

**The Macroeconomic Perspective and Goals**, Chapters 6 through 10, introduces a number of key concepts in macro: economic growth, unemployment and inflation, and international trade and capital flows.

**A Framework for Macroeconomic Analysis**, Chapters 11 through 13, introduces the principal analytic model in macro, namely the aggregate demand/aggregate supply Model. The model is then applied to the Keynesian and Neoclassical perspectives. The expenditure-output model is fully explained in a stand-alone appendix.

**Monetary and Fiscal Policy**, Chapters 14 through 18, explains the role of money and the banking system, as well as monetary policy and financial regulation. Then the discussion switches to government deficits and fiscal policy.

**International Economics**, Chapters 19 through 21, the final part of the text, introduces the international dimensions of economics, including international trade and protectionism.

## Alternate Sequencing

*Principles of Macroeconomics 2e* was conceived and written to fit a particular topical sequence, but it can be used flexibly to accommodate other course structures. One such potential structure, which will fit reasonably well with the textbook content, is provided below. Please consider, however, that the chapters were not written to be completely independent, and that the proposed alternate sequence should be carefully considered for student preparation and textual consistency.

Chapter 1 Welcome to Economics!
Chapter 2 Choice in a World of Scarcity
Chapter 3 Demand and Supply
Chapter 4 Labor and Financial Markets
Chapter 5 Elasticity
Chapter 20 International Trade
Chapter 6 The Macroeconomic Perspective
Chapter 7 Economic Growth
Chapter 8 Unemployment
Chapter 9 Inflation
Chapter 10 The International Trade and Capital Flows
Chapter 12 The Keynesian Perspective
Chapter 13 The Neoclassical Perspective
Chapter 14 Money and Banking
Chapter 15 Monetary Policy and Bank Regulation
Chapter 16 Exchange Rates and International Capital Flows
Chapter 17 Government Budgets and Fiscal Policy
Chapter 11 The Aggregate Demand/Aggregate Supply Model
Chapter 18 The Impacts of Government Borrowing
Chapter 19 Macroeconomic Policy Around the World
Chapter 21 Globalization and Protectionism

Appendix A The Use of Mathematics in Principles of Economics
Appendix B The Expenditure-Output Model

## Changes to the second edition

OpenStax only undertakes revisions when significant modifications to a text are necessary. In the case of *Principles of Macroeconomics*, we received a wealth of constructive feedback. Many of the book's users felt that consequential movement in economic data, coupled with the impacts of national and global events, warranted a full revision. We also took advantage of the opportunity to improve the writing and sequencing of the text, as well as many of the calculation examples. The major changes are summarized below.

> Augmented explanations in chapters one through four provide a more comprehensive and informative foundation for the book.

> A clearer explanation, using a numerical example, has been given for finding the utility maximizing combination of goods and services a consumer should choose.

> The Theory of Production has been added to the chapter on costs & industry structure.

> A more complete treatment has been given to labor markets, including the theories of competitive and monopsonistic labor markets, and bilateral monopoly; and the labor markets chapter and the poverty and economic inequality chapter have been resequenced.

> Substantial revisions to the AD/AS model in chapters 11-13 present the core concepts of macroeconomics in a clearer, more dynamic manner.

> Case studies and examples have been revised and, in some cases, replaced to provide more relevant and useful information for students.

> Economic data, tables, and graphs, as well as discussion and analysis around that data, have been thoroughly updated.

Wherever possible, data from the Federal Reserve Economic Database (FRED) was included and referenced. In most of these uses, links to the direct source of the FRED data are provided, and students are encouraged to explore the information and the overall FRED resources more thoroughly.

Additional updates and revisions appear throughout the book. They reflect changes to economic realities and policies regarding international trade, taxation, insurance, and other topics. For issues that may change in the months or years following the textbook's publication, the authors often provided a more open-ended explanation, but we will update the text annually to address further changes.

The revision of *Principles of Macroeconomics* was undertaken by Steven Greenlaw (University of Mary Washington) and David Shapiro (Pennsylvania State University), with significant input by lead reviewer Daniel MacDonald (California State University, San Bernardino).

## Pedagogical foundation

Throughout *Principles of Macroeconomics 2e*, you will find features that engage the students in economic inquiry and support their learning. Our features include:

> **Bring It Home:** This added feature is a brief case study, specific to each chapter, which connects the chapter's main topic to the real word. It is broken up into two parts: the first at the beginning of the chapter (in the intro module) and the second at chapter's end, when students have learned what's necessary to understand the case and "bring home" the chapter's core concepts.

> **Work It Out:** This added feature asks students to work through a generally analytical or computational problem, and guides them step by step to find out how its solution is derived.

> **Clear It Up:** This boxed feature, which includes pre-existing features from Taylor's text, addresses common student misconceptions about the content. Clear It Ups are usually deeper explanations of something in the main body of the text. Each CIU starts with a question. The rest of the feature explains the answer.

> **Link It Up:** This added feature is a very brief introduction to a website that is pertinent to students' understanding and enjoyment of the topic at hand.

## Questions for each level of learning

*Principles of Macroeconomics 2e* offers four types of end-of-module questions for students:

> **Self-Checks** are analytical self-assessment questions that appear at the end of each module. They "click to

reveal" an answer in the web view so students can check their understanding before moving on to the next module. Self-Check questions are not simple look-up questions. They push the student to think beyond what is said in the text. Self-Check questions are designed for formative (rather than summative) assessment. The questions and answers are explained so that students feel like they are being walked through the problem.

**Review Questions** have been retained from Taylor's version, and are simple recall questions from the chapter in open-response format (<u>not</u> multiple choice or true/false). The answers can be looked up in the text.

**Critical Thinking Questions** are new higher-level, conceptual questions that ask students to *demonstrate their understanding by applying* what they have learned in different contexts. They ask for outside-the-box thinking, for *reasoning* about the concepts. They push the student to places they wouldn't have thought of going themselves.

**Problems** are exercises that give students additional practice working with the analytic and computational concepts in the module.

## Updated art

*Principles of Macroeconomics 2e* includes an updated art program to better inform today's student, providing the latest data on covered topics.

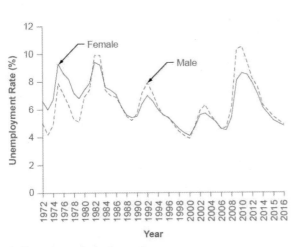

(a) Unemployment rates by gender

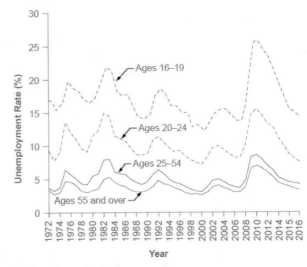

(b) Unemployment rates for women, by age

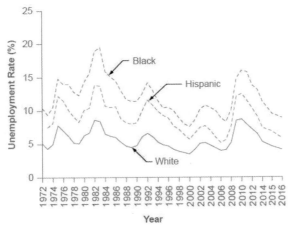

(c) Unemployment rates by race and ethnicity

## Additional resources

### Student and instructor resources

We've compiled additional resources for both students and instructors, including Getting Started Guides, an instructor solution manual, test bank, and PowerPoint slides. Instructor resources require a verified instructor account, which you can apply for when you log in or create your account on OpenStax.org. Take advantage of these resources to supplement your OpenStax book.

### Community Hubs

OpenStax partners with the Institute for the Study of Knowledge Management in Education (ISKME) to offer Community Hubs on OER Commons – a platform for instructors to share community-created resources that support OpenStax books, free of charge. Through our Community Hubs, instructors can upload their own materials or download resources to use in their own courses, including additional ancillaries, teaching material, multimedia, and relevant course content. We encourage instructors to join the hubs for the subjects most relevant to your teaching and research as an opportunity both to enrich your courses and to engage with other faculty.

To reach the Community Hubs, visit www.oercommons.org/hubs/OpenStax.

## Technology partners

As allies in making high-quality learning materials accessible, our technology partners offer optional low-cost tools that are integrated with OpenStax books. To access the technology options for your text, visit your book page on OpenStax.org.

# About the authors
## Senior contributing authors

**Steven A. Greenlaw, University of Mary Washington**

Steven Greenlaw has been teaching principles of economics for more than 30 years. In 1999, he received the Grellet C. Simpson Award for Excellence in Undergraduate Teaching at the University of Mary Washington. He is the author of *Doing Economics: A Guide to Doing and Understanding Economic Research*, as well as a variety of articles on economics pedagogy and instructional technology, published in the *Journal of Economic Education*, the *International Review of Economic Education*, and other outlets. He wrote the module on Quantitative Writing for *Starting Point: Teaching and Learning Economics*, the web portal on best practices in teaching economics. Steven Greenlaw lives in Alexandria, Virginia with his wife Kathy and their three children.

**David Shapiro, Pennsylvania State University**

David Shapiro is Professor Emeritus of Economics, Demography, and Women's, Gender, and Sexuality Studies at the Pennsylvania State University. He received a BA in economics and political science from the University of Michigan, and an MA as well as a PhD in economics from Princeton University. He began his academic career at Ohio State University in 1971, and moved to Penn State in 1980. His early research focused on women and youth in the United States labor market. Following a 1978-79 stint as a Fulbright professor at the University of Kinshasa in the Democratic Republic of the Congo, his research shifted focus to fertility in Kinshasa and more broadly, in sub-Saharan Africa. He has also received the top prize for teaching at both Ohio State and Penn State.

Special thanks to Christian Potter from University of Mary Washington, who thoroughly researched and applied many of the data updates and provided the foundation for many new and revised illustrations.

## Development editor

Thomas Sigel

## Contributing authors

Eric Dodge, Hanover College
Cynthia Gamez, University of Texas at El Paso
Andres Jauregui, Columbus State University
Diane Keenan, Cerritos College
Dan MacDonald, California State University, San Bernardino
Amyaz Moledina, The College of Wooster
Craig Richardson, Winston-Salem State University
David Shapiro, Pennsylvania State University
Ralph Sonenshine, American University

## Reviewers

Bryan Aguiar, Northwest Arkansas Community College
Basil Al Hashimi, Mesa Community College
Emil Berendt, Mount St. Mary's University
Zena Buser, Adams State University
Douglas Campbell, The University of Memphis
Sanjukta Chaudhuri, University of Wisconsin-Eau Claire
Xueyu Cheng, Alabama State University

Robert Cunningham, Alma College
Rosa Lea Danielson, College of DuPage
Steven Deloach, Elon University
Michael Enz, Framingham State University
Debbie Evercloud, University of Colorado Denver
Reza Ghorashi, Richard Stockton College of New Jersey
Robert Gillette, University of Kentucky
Shaomin Huang, Lewis-Clark State College
George Jones, University of Wisconsin-Rock County
Charles Kroncke, College of Mount St. Joseph
Teresa Laughlin, Palomar Community College
Carlos Liard-Muriente, Central Connecticut State University
Heather Luea, Kansas State University
Steven Lugauer, University of Notre Dame
William Mosher, Nashua Community College
Michael Netta, Hudson County Community College
Nick Noble, Miami University
Joe Nowakowski, Muskingum University
Shawn Osell, University of Wisconsin-Superior
Mark Owens, Middle Tennessee State University
Sonia Pereira, Barnard College
Jennifer Platania, Elon University
Robert Rycroft, University of Mary Washington
Adrienne Sachse, Florida State College at Jacksonville
Hans Schumann, Texas A&M University
Gina Shamshak, Goucher College
Chris Warburton, John Jay College of Criminal Justice, CUNY
Mark Witte, Northwestern University

# 1 | Welcome to Economics!

**Figure 1.1 Do You Use Facebook?** Economics is greatly impacted by how well information travels through society. Today, social media giants Twitter, Facebook, and Instagram are major forces on the information super highway. (Credit: Johan Larsson/Flickr)

## Bring it Home

### Decisions ... Decisions in the Social Media Age

To post or not to post? Every day we are faced with a myriad of decisions, from what to have for breakfast, to which route to take to class, to the more complex—"Should I double major and add possibly another semester of study to my education?" Our response to these choices depends on the information we have available at any given moment. Economists call this "imperfect" because we rarely have all the data we need to make perfect decisions. Despite the lack of perfect information, we still make hundreds of decisions a day.

Now we have another avenue in which to gather information—social media. Outlets like Facebook and Twitter are altering the process by which we make choices, how we spend our time, which movies we see, which products we buy, and more. How many of you chose a university without checking out its Facebook page or Twitter stream first for information and feedback?

As you will see in this course, what happens in economics is affected by how well and how fast information disseminates through a society, such as how quickly information travels through Facebook. "Economists love nothing better than when deep and liquid markets operate under conditions of perfect information," says Jessica Irvine, National Economics Editor for News Corp Australia.

This leads us to the topic of this chapter, an introduction to the world of making decisions, processing information, and understanding behavior in markets —the world of economics. Each chapter in this book will start with a discussion about current (or sometimes past) events and revisit it at chapter's end—to "bring home" the concepts in play.

# Introduction

In this chapter, you will learn about:

- What Is Economics, and Why Is It Important?

- Microeconomics and Macroeconomics

- How Economists Use Theories and Models to Understand Economic Issues

- How Economies Can Be Organized: An Overview of Economic Systems

What is economics and why should you spend your time learning it? After all, there are other disciplines you could be studying, and other ways you could be spending your time. As the Bring it Home feature just mentioned, making choices is at the heart of what economists study, and your decision to take this course is as much as economic decision as anything else.

Economics is probably not what you think. It is not primarily about money or finance. It is not primarily about business. It is not mathematics. What is it then? It is both a subject area and a way of viewing the world.

# 1.1 | What Is Economics, and Why Is It Important?

By the end of this section, you will be able to:
- Discuss the importance of studying economics
- Explain the relationship between production and division of labor
- Evaluate the significance of scarcity

**Economics** is the study of how humans make decisions in the face of scarcity. These can be individual decisions, family decisions, business decisions or societal decisions. If you look around carefully, you will see that scarcity is a fact of life. **Scarcity** means that human wants for goods, services and resources exceed what is available. Resources, such as labor, tools, land, and raw materials are necessary to produce the goods and services we want but they exist in limited supply. Of course, the ultimate scarce resource is time- everyone, rich or poor, has just 24 expendable hours in the day to earn income to acquire goods and services, for leisure time, or for sleep. At any point in time, there is only a finite amount of resources available.

Think about it this way: In 2015 the labor force in the United States contained over 158 million workers, according to the U.S. Bureau of Labor Statistics. The total land area was 3,794,101 square miles. While these are certainly large numbers, they are not infinite. Because these resources are limited, so are the numbers of goods and services we produce with them. Combine this with the fact that human wants seem to be virtually infinite, and you can see why scarcity is a problem.

## Introduction to FRED

Data is very important in economics because it describes and measures the issues and problems that economics seek to understand. A variety of government agencies publish economic and social data. For this course, we will generally use data from the St. Louis Federal Reserve Bank's FRED database. FRED is very user friendly. It allows you to display data in tables or charges, and you can easily download it into spreadsheet form if you want to use the data for other purposes. The **FRED website (https://openstax.org/l/FRED/)** includes data on nearly 400,000 domestic and international variables over time, in the following broad categories:

- Money, Banking & Finance

- Population, Employment, & Labor Markets (including Income Distribution)

- National Accounts (Gross Domestic Product & its components), Flow of Funds, and International Accounts
- Production & Business Activity (including Business Cycles)
- Prices & Inflation (including the Consumer Price Index, the Producer Price Index, and the Employment Cost Index)
- International Data from other nations
- U.S. Regional Data
- Academic Data (including Penn World Tables & NBER Macrohistory database)

For more information about how to use FRED, see the variety of **videos (https://openstax.org/l/FRED_intro)** on YouTube starting with this introduction.

**Figure 1.2 Scarcity of Resources** Homeless people are a stark reminder that scarcity of resources is real. (Credit: "daveynin"/Flickr Creative Commons)

If you still do not believe that scarcity is a problem, consider the following: Does everyone require food to eat? Does everyone need a decent place to live? Does everyone have access to healthcare? In every country in the world, there are people who are hungry, homeless (for example, those who call park benches their beds, as **Figure 1.2** shows), and in need of healthcare, just to focus on a few critical goods and services. Why is this the case? It is because of scarcity. Let's delve into the concept of scarcity a little deeper, because it is crucial to understanding economics.

## The Problem of Scarcity

Think about all the things you consume: food, shelter, clothing, transportation, healthcare, and entertainment. How do you acquire those items? You do not produce them yourself. You buy them. How do you afford the things you buy? You work for pay. If you do not, someone else does on your behalf. Yet most of us never have enough income to buy all the things we want. This is because of scarcity. So how do we solve it?

## Link It Up ⚭

Visit this website (http://openstax.org/l/drought) to read about how the United States is dealing with scarcity in resources.

Every society, at every level, must make choices about how to use its resources. Families must decide whether to spend their money on a new car or a fancy vacation. Towns must choose whether to put more of the budget into police and fire protection or into the school system. Nations must decide whether to devote more funds to national defense or to protecting the environment. In most cases, there just isn't enough money in the budget to do everything. How do we use our limited resources the best way possible, that is, to obtain the most goods and services we can? There are a couple of options. First, we could each produce everything we each consume. Alternatively, we could each produce some of what we want to consume, and "trade" for the rest of what we want. Let's explore these options. Why do we not each just produce all of the things we consume? Think back to pioneer days, when individuals knew how to do so much more than we do today, from building their homes, to growing their crops, to hunting for food, to repairing their equipment. Most of us do not know how to do all—or any—of those things, but it is not because we could not learn. Rather, we do not have to. The reason why is something called *the division and specialization of labor*, a production innovation first put forth by Adam Smith (**Figure 1.3**) in his book, *The Wealth of Nations*.

**Figure 1.3 Adam Smith**  Adam Smith introduced the idea of dividing labor into discrete tasks. (Credit: Wikimedia Commons)

## The Division of and Specialization of Labor

The formal study of economics began when Adam Smith (1723–1790) published his famous book *The Wealth of Nations* in 1776. Many authors had written on economics in the centuries before Smith, but he was the first to address the subject in a comprehensive way. In the first chapter, Smith introduces the concept of **division of labor**, which means that the way one produces a good or service is divided into a number of tasks that different workers perform, instead of all the tasks being done by the same person.

To illustrate division of labor, Smith counted how many tasks went into making a pin: drawing out a piece of wire, cutting it to the right length, straightening it, putting a head on one end and a point on the other, and packaging pins for sale, to name just a few. Smith counted 18 distinct tasks that different people performed—all for a pin, believe it or not!

Modern businesses divide tasks as well. Even a relatively simple business like a restaurant divides the task of serving meals into a range of jobs like top chef, sous chefs, less-skilled kitchen help, servers to wait on the tables, a greeter at the door, janitors to clean up, and a business manager to handle paychecks and bills—not to mention the economic connections a restaurant has with suppliers of food, furniture, kitchen equipment, and the building where it is located. A complex business like a large manufacturing factory, such as the shoe factory (**Figure 1.4**), or a hospital can have hundreds of job classifications.

**Figure 1.4 Division of Labor** Workers on an assembly line are an example of the divisions of labor. (Credit: Nina Hale/Flickr Creative Commons)

## Why the Division of Labor Increases Production

When we divide and subdivide the tasks involved with producing a good or service, workers and businesses can produce a greater quantity of output. In his observations of pin factories, Smith noticed that one worker alone might make 20 pins in a day, but that a small business of 10 workers (some of whom would need to complete two or three of the 18 tasks involved with pin-making), could make 48,000 pins in a day. How can a group of workers, each specializing in certain tasks, produce so much more than the same number of workers who try to produce the entire good or service by themselves? Smith offered three reasons.

First, **specialization** in a particular small job allows workers to focus on the parts of the production process where they have an advantage. (In later chapters, we will develop this idea by discussing comparative advantage.) People have different skills, talents, and interests, so they will be better at some jobs than at others. The particular advantages may be based on educational choices, which are in turn shaped by interests and talents. Only those with medical degrees qualify to become doctors, for instance. For some goods, geography affects specialization. For example, it is easier to be a wheat farmer in North Dakota than in Florida, but easier to run a tourist hotel in Florida than in North Dakota. If you live in or near a big city, it is easier to attract enough customers to operate a successful dry cleaning business or movie theater than if you live in a sparsely populated rural area. Whatever the reason, if people specialize in the production of what they do best, they will be more effective than if they produce a combination of things, some of which they are good at and some of which they are not.

Second, workers who specialize in certain tasks often learn to produce more quickly and with higher quality. This pattern holds true for many workers, including assembly line laborers who build cars, stylists who cut hair, and doctors who perform heart surgery. In fact, specialized workers often know their jobs well enough to suggest innovative ways to do their work faster and better.

A similar pattern often operates within businesses. In many cases, a business that focuses on one or a few products (sometimes called its "core competency") is more successful than firms that try to make a wide range of products.

Third, specialization allows businesses to take advantage of **economies of scale**, which means that for many goods, as the level of production increases, the average cost of producing each individual unit declines. For example, if a factory produces only 100 cars per year, each car will be quite expensive to make on average. However, if a factory produces 50,000 cars each year, then it can set up an assembly line with huge machines and workers performing specialized tasks, and the average cost of production per car will be lower. The ultimate result of workers who can focus on their preferences and talents, learn to do their specialized jobs better, and work in larger organizations is that society as a whole can produce and consume far more than if each person tried to produce all of his or her own goods and services. The division and specialization of labor has been a force against the problem of scarcity.

## Trade and Markets

Specialization only makes sense, though, if workers can use the pay they receive for doing their jobs to purchase the other goods and services that they need. In short, specialization requires trade.

You do not have to know anything about electronics or sound systems to play music—you just buy an iPod or MP3 player, download the music, and listen. You do not have to know anything about artificial fibers or the construction of sewing machines if you need a jacket—you just buy the jacket and wear it. You do not need to know anything about internal combustion engines to operate a car—you just get in and drive. Instead of trying to acquire all the knowledge and skills involved in producing all of the goods and services that you wish to consume, the market allows you to learn a specialized set of skills and then use the pay you receive to buy the goods and services you need or want. This is how our modern society has evolved into a strong economy.

## Why Study Economics?

Now that you have an overview on what economics studies, let's quickly discuss why you are right to study it. Economics is not primarily a collection of facts to memorize, although there are plenty of important concepts to learn. Instead, think of economics as a collection of questions to answer or puzzles to work. Most importantly, economics provides the tools to solve those puzzles. If the economics "bug" has not bitten you yet, there are other reasons why you should study economics.

- Virtually every major problem facing the world today, from global warming, to world poverty, to the conflicts in Syria, Afghanistan, and Somalia, has an economic dimension. If you are going to be part of solving those problems, you need to be able to understand them. Economics is crucial.

- It is hard to overstate the importance of economics to good citizenship. You need to be able to vote intelligently on budgets, regulations, and laws in general. When the U.S. government came close to a standstill at the end of 2012 due to the "fiscal cliff," what were the issues? Did you know?

- A basic understanding of economics makes you a well-rounded thinker. When you read articles about economic issues, you will understand and be able to evaluate the writer's argument. When you hear classmates, co-workers, or political candidates talking about economics, you will be able to distinguish between common sense and nonsense. You will find new ways of thinking about current events and about personal and business decisions, as well as current events and politics.

The study of economics does not dictate the answers, but it can illuminate the different choices.

# 1.2 | Microeconomics and Macroeconomics

By the end of this section, you will be able to:
- Describe microeconomics
- Describe macroeconomics
- Contrast monetary policy and fiscal policy

Economics is concerned with the well-being of *all* people, including those with jobs and those without jobs, as well as those with high incomes and those with low incomes. Economics acknowledges that production of useful goods and services can create problems of environmental pollution. It explores the question of how investing in education helps to develop workers' skills. It probes questions like how to tell when big businesses or big labor unions are operating in a way that benefits society as a whole and when they are operating in a way that benefits their owners or members at the expense of others. It looks at how government spending, taxes, and regulations affect decisions about production and consumption.

It should be clear by now that economics covers considerable ground. We can divide that ground into two parts: **Microeconomics** focuses on the actions of individual agents within the economy, like households, workers, and businesses. **Macroeconomics** looks at the economy as a whole. It focuses on broad issues such as growth of production, the number of unemployed people, the inflationary increase in prices, government deficits, and levels of exports and imports. Microeconomics and macroeconomics are not separate subjects, but rather complementary perspectives on the overall subject of the economy.

To understand why both microeconomic and macroeconomic perspectives are useful, consider the problem of studying a biological ecosystem like a lake. One person who sets out to study the lake might focus on specific topics: certain kinds of algae or plant life; the characteristics of particular fish or snails; or the trees surrounding the lake. Another person might take an overall view and instead consider the lake's ecosystem from top to bottom; what eats what, how the system stays in a rough balance, and what environmental stresses affect this balance. Both approaches are useful, and both examine the same lake, but the viewpoints are different. In a similar way, both microeconomics and macroeconomics study the same economy, but each has a different viewpoint.

Whether you are scrutinizing lakes or economics, the micro and the macro insights should blend with each other. In studying a lake, the micro insights about particular plants and animals help to understand the overall food chain, while the macro insights about the overall food chain help to explain the environment in which individual plants and animals live.

In economics, the micro decisions of individual businesses are influenced by whether the macroeconomy is healthy. For example, firms will be more likely to hire workers if the overall economy is growing. In turn, macroeconomy's performance ultimately depends on the microeconomic decisions that individual households and businesses make.

## Microeconomics

What determines how households and individuals spend their budgets? What combination of goods and services will best fit their needs and wants, given the budget they have to spend? How do people decide whether to work, and if so, whether to work full time or part time? How do people decide how much to save for the future, or whether they should borrow to spend beyond their current means?

What determines the products, and how many of each, a firm will produce and sell? What determines the prices a firm will charge? What determines how a firm will produce its products? What determines how many workers it will hire? How will a firm finance its business? When will a firm decide to expand, downsize, or even close? In the microeconomics part of this book, we will learn about the theory of consumer behavior, the theory of the firm, how markets for labor and other resources work, and how markets sometimes fail to work properly.

## Macroeconomics

What determines the level of economic activity in a society? In other words, what determines how many goods and services a nation actually produces? What determines how many jobs are available in an economy? What determines a nation's standard of living? What causes the economy to speed up or slow down? What causes firms to hire more workers or to lay them off? Finally, what causes the economy to grow over the long term?

We can determine an economy's macroeconomic health by examining a number of goals: growth in the standard of living, low unemployment, and low inflation, to name the most important. How can we use government macroeconomic policy to pursue these goals? A nation's central bank conducts **monetary policy**, which involves policies that affect bank lending, interest rates, and financial capital markets. For the United States, this is the Federal Reserve. A nation's legislative body determines **fiscal policy**, which involves government spending and taxes. For the United States, this is the Congress and the executive branch, which originates the federal budget. These are the government's main tools. Americans tend to expect that government can fix whatever economic problems we encounter, but to what extent is that expectation realistic? These are just some of the issues that we will explore in the macroeconomic chapters of this book.

# 1.3 | How Economists Use Theories and Models to Understand Economic Issues

By the end of this section, you will be able to:
- Interpret a circular flow diagram
- Explain the importance of economic theories and models
- Describe goods and services markets and labor markets

**Figure 1.5 John Maynard Keynes** One of the most influential economists in modern times was John Maynard Keynes. (Credit: Wikimedia Commons)

John Maynard Keynes (1883–1946), one of the greatest economists of the twentieth century, pointed out that economics is not just a subject area but also a way of thinking. Keynes (**Figure 1.5**) famously wrote in the introduction to a fellow economist's book: "[Economics] is a method rather than a doctrine, an apparatus of the mind, a technique of thinking, which helps its possessor to draw correct conclusions." In other words, economics teaches you how to think, not what to think.

# Link It Up ⟳

Watch this video (http://openstax.org/l/Keynes) about John Maynard Keynes and his influence on economics.

Economists see the world through a different lens than anthropologists, biologists, classicists, or practitioners of any other discipline. They analyze issues and problems using economic theories that are based on particular assumptions about human behavior. These assumptions tend to be different than the assumptions an anthropologist or psychologist might use. A **theory** is a simplified representation of how two or more variables interact with each other. The purpose of a theory is to take a complex, real-world issue and simplify it down to its essentials. If done well, this enables the analyst to understand the issue and any problems around it. A good theory is simple enough to understand, while complex enough to capture the key features of the object or situation you are studying.

Sometimes economists use the term **model** instead of theory. Strictly speaking, a theory is a more abstract representation, while a model is a more applied or empirical representation. We use models to test theories, but for this course we will use the terms interchangeably.

For example, an architect who is planning a major office building will often build a physical model that sits on a tabletop to show how the entire city block will look after the new building is constructed. Companies often build models of their new products, which are more rough and unfinished than the final product, but can still demonstrate how the new product will work.

A good model to start with in economics is the **circular flow diagram** (**Figure 1.6**). It pictures the economy as consisting of two groups—households and firms—that interact in two markets: the **goods and services market** in which firms sell and households buy and the **labor market** in which households sell labor to business firms or other employees.

## Circular Flow Diagram

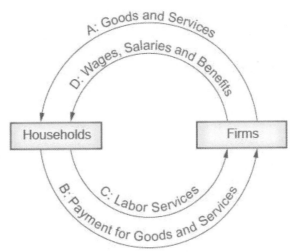

**Figure 1.6 The Circular Flow Diagram** The circular flow diagram shows how households and firms interact in the goods and services market, and in the labor market. The direction of the arrows shows that in the goods and services market, households receive goods and services and pay firms for them. In the labor market, households provide labor and receive payment from firms through wages, salaries, and benefits.

Firms produce and sell goods and services to households in the market for goods and services (or product market). Arrow "A" indicates this. Households pay for goods and services, which becomes the revenues to firms. Arrow "B" indicates this. Arrows A and B represent the two sides of the product market. Where do households obtain the income to buy goods and services? They provide the labor and other resources (e.g. land, capital, raw materials) firms need to produce goods and services in the market for inputs (or factors of production). Arrow "C" indicates this. In return, firms pay for the inputs (or resources) they use in the form of wages and other factor payments. Arrow "D" indicates this. Arrows "C" and "D" represent the two sides of the factor market.

Of course, in the real world, there are many different markets for goods and services and markets for many different types of labor. The circular flow diagram simplifies this to make the picture easier to grasp. In the diagram, firms produce goods and services, which they sell to households in return for revenues. The outer circle shows this, and represents the two sides of the product market (for example, the market for goods and services) in which households demand and firms supply. Households sell their labor as workers to firms in return for wages, salaries, and benefits. The inner circle shows this and represents the two sides of the labor market in which households supply and firms demand.

This version of the circular flow model is stripped down to the essentials, but it has enough features to explain how the product and labor markets work in the economy. We could easily add details to this basic model if we wanted to introduce more real-world elements, like financial markets, governments, and interactions with the rest of the globe (imports and exports).

Economists carry a set of theories in their heads like a carpenter carries around a toolkit. When they see an economic issue or problem, they go through the theories they know to see if they can find one that fits. Then they use the theory to derive insights about the issue or problem. Economists express theories as diagrams, graphs, or even as mathematical equations. (Do not worry. In this course, we will mostly use graphs.) Economists do not figure out the answer to the problem first and then draw the graph to illustrate. Rather, they use the graph of the theory to help them figure out the answer. Although at the introductory level, you can sometimes figure out the right answer without applying a model, if you keep studying economics, before too long you will run into issues and problems that you will need to graph to solve. We explain both micro and macroeconomics in terms of theories and models. The most well-known theories are probably those of supply and demand, but you will learn a number of others.

# 1.4 | How To Organize Economies: An Overview of Economic Systems

By the end of this section, you will be able to:
- Contrast traditional economies, command economies, and market economies
- Explain gross domestic product (GDP)
- Assess the importance and effects of globalization

Think about what a complex system a modern economy is. It includes all production of goods and services, all buying and selling, all employment. The economic life of every individual is interrelated, at least to a small extent, with the economic lives of thousands or even millions of other individuals. Who organizes and coordinates this system? Who insures that, for example, the number of televisions a society provides is the same as the amount it needs and wants? Who insures that the right number of employees work in the electronics industry? Who insures that televisions are produced in the best way possible? How does it all get done?

There are at least three ways that societies organize an economy. The first is the **traditional economy**, which is the oldest economic system and is used in parts of Asia, Africa, and South America. Traditional economies organize their economic affairs the way they have always done (i.e., tradition). Occupations stay in the family. Most families are farmers who grow the crops using traditional methods. What you produce is what you consume. Because tradition drives the way of life, there is little economic progress or development.

**Figure 1.7 A Command Economy** Ancient Egypt was an example of a command economy. (Credit: Jay Bergesen/ Flickr Creative Commons)

Command economies are very different. In a **command economy**, economic effort is devoted to goals passed down from a ruler or ruling class. Ancient Egypt was a good example: a large part of economic life was devoted to building pyramids, like those in **Figure 1.7**, for the pharaohs. Medieval manor life is another example: the lord provided the land for growing crops and protection in the event of war. In return, vassals provided labor and soldiers to do the lord's bidding. In the last century, communism emphasized command economies.

In a command economy, the government decides what goods and services will be produced and what prices it will charge for them. The government decides what methods of production to use and sets wages for workers. The government provides many necessities like healthcare and education for free. Currently, Cuba and North Korea have command economies.

**Figure 1.8 A Market Economy** Nothing says "market" more than The New York Stock Exchange. (Credit: Erik Drost/ Flickr Creative Commons)

Although command economies have a very centralized structure for economic decisions, market economies have a very decentralized structure. A **market** is an institution that brings together buyers and sellers of goods or services, who may be either individuals or businesses. The New York Stock Exchange (**Figure 1.8**) is a prime example of a market which brings buyers and sellers together. In a **market economy**, decision-making is decentralized. Market economies are based on **private enterprise**: the private individuals or groups of private individuals own and operate the means of production (resources and businesses). Businesses supply goods and services based on demand. (In a command economy, by contrast, the government owns resources and businesses.) Supply of goods and services depends on what the demands. A person's income is based on his or her ability to convert resources (especially labor) into something that society values. The more society values the person's output, the higher the income (think Lady Gaga or LeBron James). In this scenario, market forces, not governments, determine economic decisions.

Most economies in the real world are mixed. They combine elements of command and market (and even traditional) systems. The U.S. economy is positioned toward the market-oriented end of the spectrum. Many countries in Europe and Latin America, while primarily market-oriented, have a greater degree of government involvement in economic decisions than the U.S. economy. China and Russia, while over the past several decades have moved more in the direction of having a market-oriented system, remain closer to the command economy end of the spectrum. The Heritage Foundation provides information about how free and thus market-oriented different countries' are, as the following Clear It Up feature discusses. For a similar ranking, but one that defines freedom more broadly, see the Cato Foundation's Human Freedom **Index (https://openstax.org/l/cato)** .

# Clear It Up

## What countries are considered economically free?

Who is in control of economic decisions? Are people free to do what they want and to work where they want? Are businesses free to produce when they want and what they choose, and to hire and fire as they wish? Are banks free to choose who will receive loans, or does the government control these kinds of choices? Each year, researchers at the Heritage Foundation and the *Wall Street Journal* look at 50 different categories of economic freedom for countries around the world. They give each nation a score based on the extent of economic freedom in each category.

The 2016 Heritage Foundation's Index of Economic Freedom report ranked 178 countries around the world: **Table 1.1** lists some examples of the most free and the least free countries. Several additional countries were not ranked because of extreme instability that made judgments about economic freedom impossible. These countries include Afghanistan, Iraq, Libya, Syria, Somalia, and Yemen.

The assigned rankings are inevitably based on estimates, yet even these rough measures can be useful for discerning trends. In 2015, 101 of the 178 included countries shifted toward greater economic freedom, although 77 of the countries shifted toward less economic freedom. In recent decades, the overall trend has been a *higher level of economic freedom around the world*.

| Most Economic Freedom | Least Economic Freedom |
|---|---|
| 1. Hong Kong | 167. Timor-Leste |
| 2. Singapore | 168. Democratic Republic of Congo |
| 3. New Zealand | 169. Argentina |
| 4. Switzerland | 170. Equatorial Guinea |
| 5. Australia | 171. Iran |
| 6. Canada | 172. Republic of Congo |
| 7. Chile | 173. Eritrea |
| 8. Ireland | 174. Turkmenistan |
| 9. Estonia | 175. Zimbabwe |
| 10. United Kingdom | 176. Venezuela |
| 11. United States | 177. Cuba |
| 12. Denmark | 178. North Korea |

**Table 1.1 Economic Freedoms, 2016** (Source: The Heritage Foundation, 2016 Index of Economic Freedom, Country Rankings, http://www.heritage.org/index/ranking)

## Regulations: The Rules of the Game

Markets and government regulations are always entangled. There is no such thing as an absolutely free market. Regulations always define the "rules of the game" in the economy. Economies that are primarily market-oriented have fewer regulations—ideally just enough to maintain an even playing field for participants. At a minimum, these laws govern matters like safeguarding private property against theft, protecting people from violence, enforcing legal contracts, preventing fraud, and collecting taxes. Conversely, even the most command-oriented economies operate using markets. How else would buying and selling occur? The government heavily regulates decisions of what to produce and prices to charge. Heavily regulated economies often have **underground economies** (or black markets), which are markets where the buyers and sellers make transactions without the government's approval.

The question of how to organize economic institutions is typically not a black-or-white choice between all market or all government, but instead involves a balancing act over the appropriate combination of market freedom and government rules.

**Figure 1.9 Globalization** Cargo ships are one mode of transportation for shipping goods in the global economy. (Credit: Raul Valdez/Flickr Creative Commons)

## The Rise of Globalization

Recent decades have seen a trend toward **globalization**, which is the expanding cultural, political, and economic connections between people around the world. One measure of this is the increased buying and selling of goods, services, and assets across national borders—in other words, international trade and financial capital flows.

Globalization has occurred for a number of reasons. Improvements in shipping, as illustrated by the container ship in **Figure 1.9**, and air cargo have driven down transportation costs. Innovations in computing and telecommunications have made it easier and cheaper to manage long-distance economic connections of production and sales. Many valuable products and services in the modern economy can take the form of information—for example: computer software; financial advice; travel planning; music, books and movies; and blueprints for designing a building. These products and many others can be transported over telephones and computer networks at ever-lower costs. Finally, international agreements and treaties between countries have encouraged greater trade.

**Table 1.2** presents one measure of globalization. It shows the percentage of domestic economic production that was exported for a selection of countries from 2010 to 2015, according to an entity known as The World Bank. **Exports** are the goods and services that one produces domestically and sells abroad. **Imports** are the goods and services that one produces abroad and then sells domestically. **Gross domestic product (GDP)** measures the size of total production in an economy. Thus, the ratio of exports divided by GDP measures what share of a country's total economic production is sold in other countries.

| Country | 2010 | 2011 | 2012 | 2013 | 2014 | 2015 |
|---|---|---|---|---|---|---|
| Higher Income Countries | | | | | | |
| United States | 12.4 | 13.6 | 13.6 | 13.5 | 13.5 | 12.6 |
| Belgium | 76.2 | 81.4 | 82.2 | 82.8 | 84.0 | 84.4 |
| Canada | 29.1 | 30.7 | 30.0 | 30.1 | 31.7 | 31.5 |
| France | 26.0 | 27.8 | 28.1 | 28.3 | 29.0 | 30.0 |
| Middle Income Countries | | | | | | |
| Brazil | 10.9 | 11.9 | 12.6 | 12.6 | 11.2 | 13.0 |
| Mexico | 29.9 | 31.2 | 32.6 | 31.7 | 32.3 | 35.3 |
| South Korea | 49.4 | 55.7 | 56.3 | 53.9 | 50.3 | 45.9 |

**Table 1.2 The Extent of Globalization (exports/GDP)**   (Source: http://databank.worldbank.org/data/)

| Country | 2010 | 2011 | 2012 | 2013 | 2014 | 2015 |
|---------|------|------|------|------|------|------|
| **Lower Income Countries** | | | | | | |
| Chad | 36.8 | 38.9 | 36.9 | 32.2 | 34.2 | 29.8 |
| China | 29.4 | 28.5 | 27.3 | 26.4 | 23.9 | 22.4 |
| India | 22.0 | 23.9 | 24.0 | 24.8 | 22.9 | - |
| Nigeria | 25.3 | 31.3 | 31.4 | 18.0 | 18.4 | - |

**Table 1.2 The Extent of Globalization (exports/GDP)** (Source: http://databank.worldbank.org/data/)

In recent decades, the export/GDP ratio has generally risen, both worldwide and for the U.S. economy. Interestingly, the share of U.S. exports in proportion to the U.S. economy is well below the global average, in part because large economies like the United States can contain more of the division of labor inside their national borders. However, smaller economies like Belgium, Korea, and Canada need to trade across their borders with other countries to take full advantage of division of labor, specialization, and economies of scale. In this sense, the enormous U.S. economy is less affected by globalization than most other countries.

**Table 1.2** indicates that many medium and low income countries around the world, like Mexico and China, have also experienced a surge of globalization in recent decades. If an astronaut in orbit could put on special glasses that make all economic transactions visible as brightly colored lines and look down at Earth, the astronaut would see the planet covered with connections.

Despite the rise in globalization over the last few decades, in recent years we've seen significant pushback against globalization from people across the world concerned about loss of jobs, loss of political sovereignty, and increased economic inequality. Prominent examples of this pushback include the 2016 vote in Great Britain to exit the European Union (i.e. Brexit), and the election of Donald J. Trump for President of the United States.

Hopefully, you now have an idea about economics. Before you move to any other chapter of study, be sure to read the very important appendix to this chapter called **The Use of Mathematics in Principles of Economics**. It is essential that you learn more about how to read and use models in economics.

# Bring it Home

## Decisions ... Decisions in the Social Media Age

The world we live in today provides nearly instant access to a wealth of information. Consider that as recently as the late 1970s, the *Farmer's Almanac*, along with the Weather Bureau of the U.S. Department of Agriculture, were the primary sources American farmers used to determine when to plant and harvest their crops. Today, farmers are more likely to access, online, weather forecasts from the National Oceanic and Atmospheric Administration or watch the Weather Channel. After all, knowing the upcoming forecast could drive when to harvest crops. Consequently, knowing the upcoming weather could change the amount of crop harvested.

Some relatively new information forums, such as Facebook, are rapidly changing how information is distributed; hence, influencing decision making. In 2014, the Pew Research Center reported that 71% of online adults use Facebook. This social media forum posts topics ranging from the National Basketball Association, to celebrity singers and performers, to farmers.

Information helps us make decisions as simple as what to wear today to how many reporters the media should send to cover a crash. Each of these decisions is an economic decision. After all, resources are scarce. If the media send ten reporters to cover an accident, they are not available to cover other stories or complete other tasks. Information provides the necessary knowledge to make the best possible decisions on how to utilize scarce resources. Welcome to the world of economics!

# KEY TERMS

**circular flow diagram** a diagram that views the economy as consisting of households and firms interacting in a goods and services market and a labor market

**command economy** an economy where economic decisions are passed down from government authority and where the government owns the resources

**division of labor** the way in which different workers divide required tasks to produce a good or service

**economics** the study of how humans make choices under conditions of scarcity

**economies of scale** when the average cost of producing each individual unit declines as total output increases

**exports** products (goods and services) made domestically and sold abroad

**fiscal policy** economic policies that involve government spending and taxes

**globalization** the trend in which buying and selling in markets have increasingly crossed national borders

**goods and services market** a market in which firms are sellers of what they produce and households are buyers

**gross domestic product (GDP)** measure of the size of total production in an economy

**imports** products (goods and services) made abroad and then sold domestically

**labor market** the market in which households sell their labor as workers to business firms or other employers

**macroeconomics** the branch of economics that focuses on broad issues such as growth, unemployment, inflation, and trade balance

**market** interaction between potential buyers and sellers; a combination of demand and supply

**market economy** an economy where economic decisions are decentralized, private individuals own resources, and businesses supply goods and services based on demand

**microeconomics** the branch of economics that focuses on actions of particular agents within the economy, like households, workers, and business firms

**model** see theory

**monetary policy** policy that involves altering the level of interest rates, the availability of credit in the economy, and the extent of borrowing

**private enterprise** system where private individuals or groups of private individuals own and operate the means of production (resources and businesses)

**scarcity** when human wants for goods and services exceed the available supply

**specialization** when workers or firms focus on particular tasks for which they are well-suited within the overall production process

**theory** a representation of an object or situation that is simplified while including enough of the key features to help us understand the object or situation

**traditional economy** typically an agricultural economy where things are done the same as they have always been done

**underground economy** a market where the buyers and sellers make transactions in violation of one or more government regulations

# KEY CONCEPTS AND SUMMARY

### 1.1 What Is Economics, and Why Is It Important?

Economics seeks to solve the problem of scarcity, which is when human wants for goods and services exceed the available supply. A modern economy displays a division of labor, in which people earn income by specializing in what they produce and then use that income to purchase the products they need or want. The division of labor allows individuals and firms to specialize and to produce more for several reasons: a) It allows the agents to focus on areas of advantage due to natural factors and skill levels; b) It encourages the agents to learn and invent; c) It allows agents to take advantage of economies of scale. Division and specialization of labor only work when individuals can purchase what they do not produce in markets. Learning about economics helps you understand the major problems facing the world today, prepares you to be a good citizen, and helps you become a well-rounded thinker.

### 1.2 Microeconomics and Macroeconomics

Microeconomics and macroeconomics are two different perspectives on the economy. The microeconomic perspective focuses on parts of the economy: individuals, firms, and industries. The macroeconomic perspective looks at the economy as a whole, focusing on goals like growth in the standard of living, unemployment, and inflation. Macroeconomics has two types of policies for pursuing these goals: monetary policy and fiscal policy.

### 1.3 How Economists Use Theories and Models to Understand Economic Issues

Economists analyze problems differently than do other disciplinary experts. The main tools economists use are economic theories or models. A theory is not an illustration of the answer to a problem. Rather, a theory is a tool for determining the answer.

### 1.4 How To Organize Economies: An Overview of Economic Systems

We can organize societies as traditional, command, or market-oriented economies. Most societies are a mix. The last few decades have seen globalization evolve as a result of growth in commercial and financial networks that cross national borders, making businesses and workers from different economies increasingly interdependent.

# SELF-CHECK QUESTIONS

**1.** What is scarcity? Can you think of two causes of scarcity?

**2.** Residents of the town of Smithfield like to consume hams, but each ham requires 10 people to produce it and takes a month. If the town has a total of 100 people, what is the maximum amount of ham the residents can consume in a month?

**3.** A consultant works for $200 per hour. She likes to eat vegetables, but is not very good at growing them. Why does it make more economic sense for her to spend her time at the consulting job and shop for her vegetables?

**4.** A computer systems engineer could paint his house, but it makes more sense for him to hire a painter to do it. Explain why.

**5.** What would be another example of a "system" in the real world that could serve as a metaphor for micro and macroeconomics?

**6.** Suppose we extend the circular flow model to add imports and exports. Copy the circular flow diagram onto a sheet of paper and then add a foreign country as a third agent. Draw a rough sketch of the flows of imports, exports, and the payments for each on your diagram.

**7.** What is an example of a problem in the world today, not mentioned in the chapter, that has an economic dimension?

**8.** The chapter defines *private enterprise* as a characteristic of market-oriented economies. What would *public enterprise* be? *Hint*: It is a characteristic of command economies.

**9.** Why might Belgium, France, Italy, and Sweden have a higher export to GDP ratio than the United States?

## REVIEW QUESTIONS

**10.** Give the three reasons that explain why the division of labor increases an economy's level of production.

**11.** What are three reasons to study economics?

**12.** What is the difference between microeconomics and macroeconomics?

**13.** What are examples of individual economic agents?

**14.** What are the three main goals of macroeconomics?

**15.** How did John Maynard Keynes define economics?

**16.** Are households primarily buyers or sellers in the goods and services market? In the labor market?

**17.** Are firms primarily buyers or sellers in the goods and services market? In the labor market?

**18.** What are the three ways that societies can organize themselves economically?

**19.** What is globalization? How do you think it might have affected the economy over the past decade?

## CRITICAL THINKING QUESTIONS

**20.** Suppose you have a team of two workers: one is a baker and one is a chef. Explain why the kitchen can produce more meals in a given period of time if each worker specializes in what they do best than if each worker tries to do everything from appetizer to dessert.

**21.** Why would division of labor without trade not work?

**22.** Can you think of any examples of *free* goods, that is, goods or services that are not scarce?

**23.** A balanced federal budget and a balance of trade are secondary goals of macroeconomics, while growth in the standard of living (for example) is a primary goal. Why do you think that is so?

**24.** Macroeconomics is an aggregate of what happens at the microeconomic level. Would it be possible for what happens at the macro level to differ from how economic agents would react to some stimulus at the micro level? *Hint:* Think about the behavior of crowds.

**25.** Why is it unfair or meaningless to criticize a theory as "unrealistic?"

**26.** Suppose, as an economist, you are asked to analyze an issue unlike anything you have ever done before. Also, suppose you do not have a specific model for analyzing that issue. What should you do? *Hint:* What would a carpenter do in a similar situation?

**27.** Why do you think that most modern countries' economies are a mix of command and market types?

**28.** Can you think of ways that globalization has helped you economically? Can you think of ways that it has not?

# 2 | Choice in a World of Scarcity

**Figure 2.1 Choices and Tradeoffs** In general, the higher the degree, the higher the salary, so why aren't more people pursuing higher degrees? The short answer: choices and tradeoffs. (Credit: modification of work by "Jim, the Photographer"/Flickr Creative Commons)

## Bring it Home

### Choices ... To What Degree?

In 2015, the median income for workers who hold master's degrees varies from males to females. The average of the two is $2,951 weekly. Multiply this average by 52 weeks, and you get an average salary of $153,452. Compare that to the median weekly earnings for a full-time worker over 25 with no higher than a bachelor's degree: $1,224 weekly and $63,648 a year. What about those with no higher than a high school diploma in 2015? They earn just $664 weekly and $34,528 over 12 months. In other words, says the Bureau of Labor Statistics (BLS), earning a bachelor's degree boosted salaries 54% over what you would have earned if you had stopped your education after high school. A master's degree yields a salary almost double that of a high school diploma.

Given these statistics, we might expect many people to choose to go to college and at least earn a bachelor's degree. Assuming that people want to improve their material well-being, it seems like they would make those choices that provide them with the greatest opportunity to consume goods and services. As it turns out, the analysis is not nearly as simple as this. In fact, in 2014, the BLS reported that while almost 88% of the population in the United States had a high school diploma, only 33.6% of 25–65 year olds had bachelor's degrees, and only 7.4% of 25–65 year olds in 2014 had earned a master's.

This brings us to the subject of this chapter: why people make the choices they make and how economists explain those choices.

# Introduction to Choice in a World of Scarcity

In this chapter, you will learn about:

- How Individuals Make Choices Based on Their Budget Constraint
- The Production Possibilities Frontier and Social Choices
- Confronting Objections to the Economic Approach

You will learn quickly when you examine the relationship between economics and scarcity that choices involve tradeoffs. Every choice has a cost.

In 1968, the Rolling Stones recorded "You Can't Always Get What You Want." Economists chuckled, because they had been singing a similar tune for decades. English economist Lionel Robbins (1898–1984), in his *Essay on the Nature and Significance of Economic Science* in 1932, described not always getting what you want in this way:

> The time at our disposal is limited. There are only twenty-four hours in the day. We have to choose between the different uses to which they may be put. ... Everywhere we turn, if we choose one thing we must relinquish others which, in different circumstances, we would wish not to have relinquished. Scarcity of means to satisfy given ends is an almost ubiquitous condition of human nature.

Because people live in a world of scarcity, they cannot have all the time, money, possessions, and experiences they wish. Neither can society.

This chapter will continue our discussion of scarcity and the economic way of thinking by first introducing three critical concepts: opportunity cost, marginal decision making, and diminishing returns. Later, it will consider whether the economic way of thinking accurately describes either how we *make* choices and how we *should* make them.

# 2.1 | How Individuals Make Choices Based on Their Budget Constraint

By the end of this section, you will be able to:
- Calculate and graph budget constraints
- Explain opportunity sets and opportunity costs
- Evaluate the law of diminishing marginal utility
- Explain how marginal analysis and utility influence choices

Consider the typical consumer's budget problem. Consumers have a limited amount of income to spend on the things they need and want. Suppose Alphonso has $10 in spending money each week that he can allocate between bus tickets for getting to work and the burgers that he eats for lunch. Burgers cost $2 each, and bus tickets are 50 cents each. We can see Alphonso's budget problem in **Figure 2.2**.

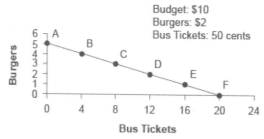

**Figure 2.2 The Budget Constraint: Alphonso's Consumption Choice Opportunity Frontier**   Each point on the budget constraint represents a combination of burgers and bus tickets whose total cost adds up to Alphonso's budget of $10. The relative price of burgers and bus tickets determines the slope of the budget constraint. All along the budget set, giving up one burger means gaining four bus tickets.

The vertical axis in the figure shows burger purchases and the horizontal axis shows bus ticket purchases. If Alphonso spends all his money on burgers, he can afford five per week. ($10 per week/$2 per burger = 5 burgers per week.) However, if he does this, he will not be able to afford any bus tickets. Point A in the figure shows the choice (zero bus tickets and five burgers). Alternatively, if Alphonso spends all his money on bus tickets, he can afford 20 per week. ($10 per week/$0.50 per bus ticket = 20 bus tickets per week.) Then, however, he will not be able to afford any burgers. Point F shows this alternative choice (20 bus tickets and zero burgers).

If we connect all the points between A and F, we get Alphonso's **budget constraint**. This indicates all the combination of burgers and bus tickets Alphonso can afford, given the price of the two goods and his budget amount.

If Alphonso is like most people, he will choose some combination that includes both bus tickets and burgers. That is, he will choose some combination on the budget constraint that is between points A and F. Every point on (or inside) the constraint shows a combination of burgers and bus tickets that Alphonso can afford. Any point outside the constraint is not affordable, because it would cost more money than Alphonso has in his budget.

The budget constraint clearly shows the tradeoff Alphonso faces in choosing between burgers and bus tickets. Suppose he is currently at point D, where he can afford 12 bus tickets and two burgers. What would it cost Alphonso for one more burger? It would be natural to answer $2, but that's not the way economists think. Instead they ask, how many bus tickets would Alphonso have to give up to get one more burger, while staying within his budget? Since bus tickets cost 50 cents, Alphonso would have to give up four to afford one more burger. That is the true cost to Alphonso.

## The Concept of Opportunity Cost

Economists use the term **opportunity cost** to indicate what one must give up to obtain what he or she desires. The idea behind opportunity cost is that the cost of one item is the lost opportunity to do or consume something else. In short, opportunity cost is the value of the next best alternative. For Alphonso, the opportunity cost of a burger is the four bus tickets he would have to give up. He would decide whether or not to choose the burger depending on whether the value of the burger exceeds the value of the forgone alternative—in this case, bus tickets. Since people must choose, they inevitably face tradeoffs in which they have to give up things they desire to obtain other things they desire more.

# Link It Up

View this website (http://openstaxcollege.org/l/linestanding) for an example of opportunity cost—paying someone else to wait in line for you.

A fundamental principle of economics is that every choice has an opportunity cost. If you sleep through your economics class, the opportunity cost is the learning you miss from not attending class. If you spend your income on video games, you cannot spend it on movies. If you choose to marry one person, you give up the opportunity to marry anyone else. In short, opportunity cost is all around us and part of human existence.

The following Work It Out feature shows a step-by-step analysis of a budget constraint calculation. Read through it to understand another important concept—slope—that we further explain in the appendix **The Use of Mathematics in Principles of Economics**.

# Work It Out ─O─O─O

## Understanding Budget Constraints

Budget constraints are easy to understand if you apply a little math. The appendix **The Use of Mathematics in Principles of Economics** explains all the math you are likely to need in this book. Therefore, if math is not your strength, you might want to take a look at the appendix.

Step 1: The equation for any budget constraint is:

$$\text{Budget} = P_1 \times Q_1 + P_2 \times Q_2$$

where P and Q are the price and quantity of items purchased (which we assume here to be two items) and Budget is the amount of income one has to spend.

Step 2. Apply the budget constraint equation to the scenario. In Alphonso's case, this works out to be:

$$\begin{aligned}
\text{Budget} &= P_1 \times Q_1 + P_2 \times Q_2 \\
\$10 \text{ budget} &= \$2 \text{ per burger} \times \text{quantity of burgers} + \$0.50 \text{ per bus ticket} \times \text{quantity of bus tickets} \\
\$10 &= \$2 \times Q_{\text{burgers}} + \$0.50 \times Q_{\text{bus tickets}}
\end{aligned}$$

Step 3. Using a little algebra, we can turn this into the familiar equation of a line:

$$y = b + mx$$

For Alphonso, this is:

$$\$10 = \$2 \times Q_{\text{burgers}} + \$0.50 \times Q_{\text{bus tickets}}$$

Step 4. Simplify the equation. Begin by multiplying both sides of the equation by 2:

$$\begin{aligned}
2 \times 10 &= 2 \times 2 \times Q_{\text{burgers}} + 2 \times 0.5 \times Q_{\text{bus tickets}} \\
20 &= 4 \times Q_{\text{burgers}} + 1 \times Q_{\text{bus tickets}}
\end{aligned}$$

Step 5. Subtract one bus ticket from both sides:

$$20 - Q_{\text{bus tickets}} = 4 \times Q_{\text{burgers}}$$

Divide each side by 4 to yield the answer:

$$5 - 0.25 \times Q_{\text{bus tickets}} = Q_{\text{burgers}}$$
$$\text{or}$$
$$Q_{\text{burgers}} = 5 - 0.25 \times Q_{\text{bus tickets}}$$

Step 6. Notice that this equation fits the budget constraint in **Figure 2.2**. The vertical intercept is 5 and the slope is –0.25, just as the equation says. If you plug 20 bus tickets into the equation, you get 0 burgers. If you plug other numbers of bus tickets into the equation, you get the results (see **Table 2.1**), which are the points on Alphonso's budget constraint.

| Point | Quantity of Burgers (at $2) | Quantity of Bus Tickets (at 50 cents) |
|-------|------------------------------|----------------------------------------|
| A | 5 | 0 |
| B | 4 | 4 |
| C | 3 | 8 |
| D | 2 | 12 |

Table 2.1

| Point | Quantity of Burgers (at $2) | Quantity of Bus Tickets (at 50 cents) |
|-------|-----------------------------|----------------------------------------|
| E | 1 | 16 |
| F | 0 | 20 |

**Table 2.1**

Step 7. Notice that the slope of a budget constraint always shows the opportunity cost of the good which is on the horizontal axis. For Alphonso, the slope is −0.25, indicating that for every bus ticket he buys, he must give up 1/4 burger. To phrase it differently, for every four tickets he buys, Alphonso must give up 1 burger.

There are two important observations here. First, the algebraic sign of the slope is negative, which means that the only way to get more of one good is to give up some of the other. Second, we define the slope as the price of bus tickets (whatever is on the horizontal axis in the graph) divided by the price of burgers (whatever is on the vertical axis), in this case $0.50/$2 = 0.25. If you want to determine the opportunity cost quickly, just divide the two prices.

## Identifying Opportunity Cost

In many cases, it is reasonable to refer to the opportunity cost as the price. If your cousin buys a new bicycle for $300, then $300 measures the amount of "other consumption" that he has forsaken. For practical purposes, there may be no special need to identify the specific alternative product or products that he could have bought with that $300, but sometimes the price as measured in dollars may not accurately capture the true opportunity cost. This problem can loom especially large when costs of time are involved.

For example, consider a boss who decides that all employees will attend a two-day retreat to "build team spirit." The out-of-pocket monetary cost of the event may involve hiring an outside consulting firm to run the retreat, as well as room and board for all participants. However, an opportunity cost exists as well: during the two days of the retreat, none of the employees are doing any other work.

Attending college is another case where the opportunity cost exceeds the monetary cost. The out-of-pocket costs of attending college include tuition, books, room and board, and other expenses. However, in addition, during the hours that you are attending class and studying, it is impossible to work at a paying job. Thus, college imposes both an out-of-pocket cost and an opportunity cost of lost earnings.

## What is the opportunity cost associated with increased airport security measures?

After the terrorist plane hijackings on September 11, 2001, many steps were proposed to improve air travel safety. For example, the federal government could provide armed "sky marshals" who would travel inconspicuously with the rest of the passengers. The cost of having a sky marshal on every flight would be roughly $3 billion per year. Retrofitting all U.S. planes with reinforced cockpit doors to make it harder for terrorists to take over the plane would have a price tag of $450 million. Buying more sophisticated security equipment for airports, like three-dimensional baggage scanners and cameras linked to face recognition software, could cost another $2 billion.

However, the single biggest cost of greater airline security does not involve spending money. It is the opportunity cost of additional waiting time at the airport. According to the United States Department of Transportation (DOT), there were 895.5 million systemwide (domestic and international) scheduled service passengers in 2015. Since the 9/11 hijackings, security screening has become more intensive, and consequently, the procedure takes longer than in the past. Say that, on average, each air passenger spends an extra 30 minutes in the airport per trip. Economists commonly place a value on time to convert an opportunity cost in time into a monetary figure. Because many air travelers are relatively high-paid business people, conservative estimates set the average price of time for air travelers at $20 per hour. By these back-of-the-envelope calculations, the opportunity cost of delays in airports could be as much as 800 million × 0.5 hours × $20/hour, or $8 billion per year. Clearly, the opportunity costs of waiting time can be just as important as costs that involve direct spending.

In some cases, realizing the opportunity cost can alter behavior. Imagine, for example, that you spend $8 on lunch every day at work. You may know perfectly well that bringing a lunch from home would cost only $3 a day, so the opportunity cost of buying lunch at the restaurant is $5 each day (that is, the $8 buying lunch costs minus the $3 your lunch from home would cost). Five dollars each day does not seem to be that much. However, if you project what that adds up to in a year—250 days a year × $5 per day equals $1,250, the cost, perhaps, of a decent vacation. If you describe the opportunity cost as "a nice vacation" instead of "$5 a day," you might make different choices.

## Marginal Decision-Making and Diminishing Marginal Utility

The budget constraint framework helps to emphasize that most choices in the real world are not about getting all of one thing or all of another; that is, they are not about choosing either the point at one end of the budget constraint or else the point all the way at the other end. Instead, most choices involve **marginal analysis**, which means examining the benefits and costs of choosing a little more or a little less of a good. People naturally compare costs and benefits, but often we look at total costs and total benefits, when the optimal choice necessitates comparing how costs and benefits change from one option to another. You might think of marginal analysis as "change analysis." Marginal analysis is used throughout economics.

We now turn to the notion of **utility**. People desire goods and services for the satisfaction or utility those goods and services provide. Utility, as we will see in the chapter on **Consumer Choices (http://cnx.org/content/m63895/latest/)**, is subjective but that does not make it less real. Economists typically assume that the more of some good one consumes (for example, slices of pizza), the more utility one obtains. At the same time, the utility a person receives from consuming the first unit of a good is typically more than the utility received from consuming the fifth or the tenth unit of that same good. When Alphonso chooses between burgers and bus tickets, for example, the first few bus rides that he chooses might provide him with a great deal of utility—perhaps they help him get to a job interview or a doctor's appointment. However, later bus rides might provide much less utility—they may only serve to kill time on a rainy day. Similarly, the first burger that Alphonso chooses to buy may be on a day when he missed breakfast and is ravenously hungry. However, if Alphonso has a burger every single day, the last few burgers may taste pretty boring. The general pattern that consumption of the first few units of any good tends to bring a higher level of utility to a person than consumption of later units is a common pattern. Economists refer to this pattern as the **law of diminishing marginal utility**, which means that as a person receives more of a good, the additional (or marginal) utility from each additional unit of the good declines. In other words, the first slice of pizza brings more satisfaction than the sixth.

The law of diminishing marginal utility explains why people and societies rarely make all-or-nothing choices. You would not say, "My favorite food is ice cream, so I will eat nothing but ice cream from now on." Instead, even if you get a very high level of utility from your favorite food, if you ate it exclusively, the additional or marginal utility from those last few servings would not be very high. Similarly, most workers do not say: "I enjoy leisure, so I'll never work." Instead, workers recognize that even though some leisure is very nice, a combination of all leisure and no income is not so attractive. The budget constraint framework suggests that when people make choices in a world of scarcity, they will use marginal analysis and think about whether they would prefer a little more or a little less.

A rational consumer would only purchase additional units of some product as long as the marginal utility exceeds the opportunity cost. Suppose Alphonso moves down his budget constraint from Point A to Point B to Point C and further. As he consumes more bus tickets, the marginal utility of bus tickets will diminish, while the opportunity cost, that is, the marginal utility of foregone burgers, will increase. Eventually, the opportunity cost will exceed the marginal utility of an additional bus ticket. If Alphonso is rational, he won't purchase more bus tickets once the marginal utility just equals the opportunity cost. While we can't (yet) say exactly how many bus tickets Alphonso will buy, that number is unlikely to be the most he can afford, 20.

## Sunk Costs

In the budget constraint framework, all decisions involve what will happen next: that is, what quantities of goods will you consume, how many hours will you work, or how much will you save. These decisions do not look back to past choices. Thus, the budget constraint framework assumes that **sunk costs**, which are costs that were incurred in the past and cannot be recovered, should not affect the current decision.

Consider the case of Selena, who pays $8 to see a movie, but after watching the film for 30 minutes, she knows that it is truly terrible. Should she stay and watch the rest of the movie because she paid for the ticket, or should she leave? The money she spent is a sunk cost, and unless the theater manager is sympathetic, Selena will not get a refund. However, staying in the movie still means paying an opportunity cost in time. Her choice is whether to spend the next 90 minutes suffering through a cinematic disaster or to do something—anything—else. The lesson of sunk costs is to forget about the money and time that is irretrievably gone and instead to focus on the marginal costs and benefits of current and future options.

For people and firms alike, dealing with sunk costs can be frustrating. It often means admitting an earlier error in judgment. Many firms, for example, find it hard to give up on a new product that is doing poorly because they spent so much money in creating and launching the product. However, the lesson of sunk costs is to ignore them and make decisions based on what will happen in the future.

### From a Model with Two Goods to One of Many Goods

The budget constraint diagram containing just two goods, like most models used in this book, is not realistic. After all, in a modern economy people choose from thousands of goods. However, thinking about a model with many goods is a straightforward extension of what we discussed here. Instead of drawing just one budget constraint, showing the tradeoff between two goods, you can draw multiple budget constraints, showing the possible tradeoffs between many different pairs of goods. In more advanced classes in economics, you would use mathematical equations that include many possible goods and services that can be purchased, together with their quantities and prices, and show how the total spending on all goods and services is limited to the overall budget available. The graph with two goods that we presented here clearly illustrates that every choice has an opportunity cost, which is the point that does carry over to the real world.

# 2.2 | The Production Possibilities Frontier and Social Choices

By the end of this section, you will be able to:
- Interpret production possibilities frontier graphs
- Contrast a budget constraint and a production possibilities frontier
- Explain the relationship between a production possibilities frontier and the law of diminishing returns
- Contrast productive efficiency and allocative efficiency
- Define comparative advantage

Just as individuals cannot have everything they want and must instead make choices, society as a whole cannot have everything it might want, either. This section of the chapter will explain the constraints society faces, using a model called the **production possibilities frontier (PPF)**. There are more similarities than differences between individual choice and social choice. As you read this section, focus on the similarities.

Because society has limited resources (e.g., labor, land, capital, raw materials) at any point in time, there is a limit to the quantities of goods and services it can produce. Suppose a society desires two products, healthcare and education. The production possibilities frontier in **Figure 2.3** illustrates this situation.

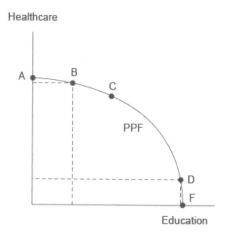

**Figure 2.3 A Healthcare vs. Education Production Possibilities Frontier**  This production possibilities frontier shows a tradeoff between devoting social resources to healthcare and devoting them to education. At A all resources go to healthcare and at B, most go to healthcare. At D most resources go to education, and at F, all go to education.

**Figure 2.3** shows healthcare on the vertical axis and education on the horizontal axis. If the society were to allocate all of its resources to healthcare, it could produce at point A. However, it would not have any resources to produce education. If it were to allocate all of its resources to education, it could produce at point F. Alternatively, the society could choose to produce any combination of healthcare and education on the production possibilities frontier. In effect, the production possibilities frontier plays the same role for society as the budget constraint plays for Alphonso. Society can choose any combination of the two goods on or inside the PPF. However, it does not have enough resources to produce outside the PPF.

Most importantly, the production possibilities frontier clearly shows the tradeoff between healthcare and education. Suppose society has chosen to operate at point B, and it is considering producing more education. Because the PPF is downward sloping from left to right, the only way society can obtain more education is by giving up some healthcare. That is the tradeoff society faces. Suppose it considers moving from point B to point C. What would the opportunity cost be for the additional education? The opportunity cost would be the healthcare society has to forgo. Just as with Alphonso's budget constraint, the **slope** of the production possibilities frontier shows the opportunity cost. By now you might be saying, "Hey, this PPF is sounding like the budget constraint." If so, read the following Clear It Up feature.

# Clear It Up $

## What's the difference between a budget constraint and a PPF?

There are two major differences between a budget constraint and a production possibilities frontier. The first is the fact that the budget constraint is a straight line. This is because its slope is given by the relative prices of the two goods, which from the point of view of an individual consumer, are fixed, so the slope doesn't change. In contrast, the PPF has a curved shape because of the law of the diminishing returns. Thus, the slope is different at various points on the PPF. The second major difference is the absence of specific numbers on the axes of the PPF. There are no specific numbers because we do not know the exact amount of resources this imaginary economy has, nor do we know how many resources it takes to produce healthcare and how many resources it takes to produce education. If this were a real world example, that data would be available.

Whether or not we have specific numbers, conceptually we can measure the opportunity cost of additional education as society moves from point B to point C on the PPF. We measure the additional education by the horizontal distance between B and C. The foregone healthcare is given by the vertical distance between B and C. The slope of the PPF between B and C is (approximately) the vertical distance (the "rise") over the horizontal distance (the "run"). This is the opportunity cost of the additional education.

## The Shape of the PPF and the Law of Diminishing Returns

The budget constraints that we presented earlier in this chapter, showing individual choices about what quantities of goods to consume, were all straight lines. The reason for these straight lines was that the relative prices of the two goods in the **consumption budget constraint** determined the slope of the budget constraint. However, we drew the production possibilities frontier for healthcare and education as a curved line. Why does the PPF have a different shape?

To understand why the PPF is curved, start by considering point A at the top left-hand side of the PPF. At point A, all available resources are devoted to healthcare and none are left for education. This situation would be extreme and even ridiculous. For example, children are seeing a doctor every day, whether they are sick or not, but not attending school. People are having cosmetic surgery on every part of their bodies, but no high school or college education exists. Now imagine that some of these resources are diverted from healthcare to education, so that the economy is at point B instead of point A. Diverting some resources away from A to B causes relatively little reduction in health because the last few marginal dollars going into healthcare services are not producing much additional gain in health. However, putting those marginal dollars into education, which is completely without resources at point A, can produce relatively large gains. For this reason, the shape of the PPF from A to B is relatively flat, representing a relatively small drop-off in health and a relatively large gain in education.

Now consider the other end, at the lower right, of the production possibilities frontier. Imagine that society starts at choice D, which is devoting nearly all resources to education and very few to healthcare, and moves to point F, which is devoting *all* spending to education and none to healthcare. For the sake of concreteness, you can imagine that in the movement from D to F, the last few doctors must become high school science teachers, the last few nurses must become school librarians rather than dispensers of vaccinations, and the last few emergency rooms are turned into kindergartens. The gains to education from adding these last few resources to education are very small. However, the opportunity cost lost to health will be fairly large, and thus the slope of the PPF between D and F is steep, showing a large drop in health for only a small gain in education.

The lesson is not that society is likely to make an extreme choice like devoting no resources to education at point A or no resources to health at point F. Instead, the lesson is that the gains from committing additional marginal resources to education depend on how much is already being spent. If on the one hand, very few resources are currently committed to education, then an increase in resources used can bring relatively large gains. On the other hand, if a large number of resources are already committed to education, then committing additional resources will bring relatively smaller gains.

This pattern is common enough that economists have given it a name: the **law of diminishing returns**, which holds that as additional increments of resources are added to a certain purpose, the marginal benefit from those additional increments will decline. (The law of diminishing marginal utility that we introduced in the last section is a more specific case of the law of diminishing returns.) When government spends a certain amount more on reducing crime, for example, the original gains in reducing crime could be relatively large. However, additional increases typically cause relatively smaller reductions in crime, and paying for enough police and security to reduce crime to nothing at all would be tremendously expensive.

The curvature of the production possibilities frontier shows that as we add more resources to education, moving from left to right along the horizontal axis, the original gains are fairly large, but gradually diminish. Thus, the slope of the PPF is relatively flat. By contrast, as we add more resources to healthcare, moving from bottom to top on the vertical axis, the original gains are fairly large, but again gradually diminish. Thus, the slope of the PPF is relatively steep. In this way, the law of diminishing returns produces the outward-bending shape of the production possibilities frontier.

## Productive Efficiency and Allocative Efficiency

The study of economics does not presume to tell a society what choice it should make along its production possibilities frontier. In a market-oriented economy with a democratic government, the choice will involve a mixture of decisions by individuals, firms, and government. However, economics can point out that some choices are unambiguously better than others. This observation is based on the concept of efficiency. In everyday usage, efficiency refers to lack of waste. An inefficient machine operates at high cost, while an efficient machine operates at lower cost, because it is not wasting energy or materials. An inefficient organization operates with long delays and high costs, while an efficient organization meets schedules, is focused, and performs within budget.

The production possibilities frontier can illustrate two kinds of efficiency: productive efficiency and allocative efficiency. **Figure 2.4** illustrates these ideas using a production possibilities frontier between healthcare and education.

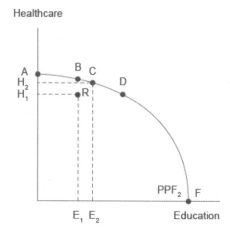

**Figure 2.4 Productive and Allocative Efficiency**   Productive efficiency means it is impossible to produce more of one good without decreasing the quantity that is produced of another good. Thus, all choices along a given PPF like B, C, and D display productive efficiency, but R does not. Allocative efficiency means that the particular mix of goods being produced—that is, the specific choice along the production possibilities frontier—represents the allocation that society most desires.

**Productive efficiency** means that, given the available inputs and technology, it is impossible to produce more of one good without decreasing the quantity that is produced of another good. All choices on the PPF in **Figure 2.4**, including A, B, C, D, and F, display productive efficiency. As a firm moves from any one of these choices to any other, either healthcare increases and education decreases or vice versa. However, any choice inside the production possibilities frontier is productively inefficient and wasteful because it is possible to produce more of one good, the other good, or some combination of both goods.

For example, point R is productively inefficient because it is possible at choice C to have more of both goods: education on the horizontal axis is higher at point C than point R ($E_2$ is greater than $E_1$), and healthcare on the vertical axis is also higher at point C than point R ($H_2$ is great than $H_1$).

We can show the particular mix of goods and services produced—that is, the specific combination of selected healthcare and education along the production possibilities frontier—as a ray (line) from the origin to a specific point on the PPF. Output mixes that had more healthcare (and less education) would have a steeper ray, while those with more education (and less healthcare) would have a flatter ray.

**Allocative efficiency** means that the particular combination of goods and services on the production possibility curve that a society produces represents the combination that society most desires. How to determine what a society desires can be a controversial question, and is usually a discussion in political science, sociology, and philosophy classes as well as in economics. At its most basic, allocative efficiency means producers supply the quantity of each product that consumers demand. Only one of the productively efficient choices will be the allocatively efficient choice for society as a whole.

## Why Society Must Choose

In **Welcome to Economics!** we learned that every society faces the problem of scarcity, where limited resources conflict with unlimited needs and wants. The production possibilities curve illustrates the choices involved in this dilemma.

Every economy faces two situations in which it may be able to expand consumption of all goods. In the first case, a society may discover that it has been using its resources inefficiently, in which case by improving efficiency and producing on the production possibilities frontier, it can have more of all goods (or at least more of some and less of none). In the second case, as resources grow over a period of years (e.g., more labor and more capital), the economy grows. As it does, the production possibilities frontier for a society will tend to shift outward and society will be able to afford more of all goods.

However, improvements in productive efficiency take time to discover and implement, and economic growth happens only gradually. Thus, a society must choose between tradeoffs in the present. For government, this process often involves trying to identify where additional spending could do the most good and where reductions in spending would do the least harm. At the individual and firm level, the market economy coordinates a process in which firms seek to produce goods and services in the quantity, quality, and price that people want. However, for both the government and the market economy in the short term, increases in production of one good typically mean offsetting decreases somewhere else in the economy.

## The PPF and Comparative Advantage

While every society must choose how much of each good or service it should produce, it does not need to produce every single good it consumes. Often how much of a good a country decides to produce depends on how expensive it is to produce it versus buying it from a different country. As we saw earlier, the curvature of a country's PPF gives us information about the tradeoff between devoting resources to producing one good versus another. In particular, its slope gives the opportunity cost of producing one more unit of the good in the x-axis in terms of the other good (in the y-axis). Countries tend to have different opportunity costs of producing a specific good, either because of different climates, geography, technology, or skills.

Suppose two countries, the US and Brazil, need to decide how much they will produce of two crops: sugar cane and wheat. Due to its climatic conditions, Brazil can produce quite a bit of sugar cane per acre but not much wheat. Conversely, the U.S. can produce large amounts of wheat per acre, but not much sugar cane. Clearly, Brazil has a lower opportunity cost of producing sugar cane (in terms of wheat) than the U.S. The reverse is also true: the U.S. has a lower opportunity cost of producing wheat than Brazil. We illustrate this by the PPFs of the two countries in **Figure 2.5**.

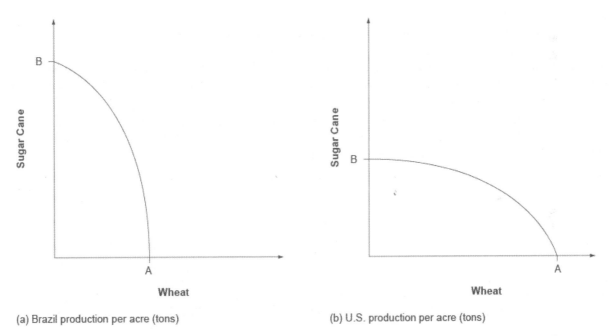

(a) Brazil production per acre (tons)　　　　(b) U.S. production per acre (tons)

**Figure 2.5 Production Possibility Frontier for the U.S. and Brazil** The U.S. PPF is flatter than the Brazil PPF implying that the opportunity cost of wheat in terms of sugar cane is lower in the U.S. than in Brazil. Conversely, the opportunity cost of sugar cane is lower in Brazil. The U.S. has comparative advantage in wheat and Brazil has comparative advantage in sugar cane.

When a country can produce a good at a lower opportunity cost than another country, we say that this country has a **comparative advantage** in that good. Comparative advantage is not the same as absolute advantage, which is when a country can produce more of a good. Comparative advantage is not the same as absolute advantage, which is when a country can produce more of a good. In our example, Brazil has an absolute advantage in sugar cane and the U.S. has an absolute advantage in wheat. One can easily see this with a simple observation of the extreme production points in the PPFs of the two countries. If Brazil devoted all of its resources to producing wheat, it would be producing at point A. If however it had devoted all of its resources to producing sugar cane instead, it would be producing a much larger amount than the U.S., at point B.

The slope of the PPF gives the opportunity cost of producing an additional unit of wheat. While the slope is not constant throughout the PPFs, it is quite apparent that the PPF in Brazil is much steeper than in the U.S., and therefore the opportunity cost of wheat generally higher in Brazil. In the chapter on **International Trade** you will learn that countries' differences in comparative advantage determine which goods they will choose to produce and trade. When countries engage in trade, they specialize in the production of the goods in which they have comparative advantage, and trade part of that production for goods in which they do not have comparative advantage. With trade, manufacturers produce goods where the opportunity cost is lowest, so total production increases, benefiting both trading parties.

# 2.3 | Confronting Objections to the Economic Approach

By the end of this section, you will be able to:
- Analyze arguments against economic approaches to decision-making
- Interpret a tradeoff diagram
- Contrast normative statements and positive statements

It is one thing to understand the economic approach to decision-making and another thing to feel comfortable applying it. The sources of discomfort typically fall into two categories: that people do not act in the way that fits the economic way of thinking, and that even if people did act that way, they should try not to. Let's consider these arguments in turn.

## First Objection: People, Firms, and Society Do Not Act Like This

The economic approach to decision-making seems to require more information than most individuals possess and more careful decision-making than most individuals actually display. After all, do you or any of your friends draw a budget constraint and mutter to yourself about maximizing utility before you head to the shopping mall? Do members of the U.S. Congress contemplate production possibilities frontiers before they vote on the annual budget? The messy ways in which people and societies operate somehow doesn't look much like neat budget constraints or smoothly curving production possibilities frontiers.

However, the economics approach can be a useful way to analyze and understand the tradeoffs of economic decisions. To appreciate this point, imagine for a moment that you are playing basketball, dribbling to the right, and throwing a bounce-pass to the left to a teammate who is running toward the basket. A physicist or engineer could work out the correct speed and trajectory for the pass, given the different movements involved and the weight and bounciness of the ball. However, when you are playing basketball, you do not perform any of these calculations. You just pass the ball, and if you are a good player, you will do so with high accuracy.

Someone might argue: "The scientist's formula of the bounce-pass requires a far greater knowledge of physics and far more specific information about speeds of movement and weights than the basketball player actually has, so it must be an unrealistic description of how basketball passes actually occur." This reaction would be wrongheaded. The fact that a good player can throw the ball accurately because of practice and skill, without making a physics calculation, does not mean that the physics calculation is wrong.

Similarly, from an economic point of view, someone who shops for groceries every week has a great deal of practice with how to purchase the combination of goods that will provide that person with utility, even if the shopper does not phrase decisions in terms of a budget constraint. Government institutions may work imperfectly and slowly, but in general, a democratic form of government feels pressure from voters and social institutions to make the choices that are most widely preferred by people in that society. Thus, when thinking about the economic actions of groups of people, firms, and society, it is reasonable, as a first approximation, to analyze them with the tools of economic analysis. For more on this, read about behavioral economics in the chapter on **Consumer Choices (http://cnx.org/content/m63895/latest/)** .

## Second Objection: People, Firms, and Society Should Not Act This Way

The economics approach portrays people as self-interested. For some critics of this approach, even if self-interest is an accurate description of how people behave, these behaviors are not moral. Instead, the critics argue that people should be taught to care more deeply about others. Economists offer several answers to these concerns.

First, economics is not a form of moral instruction. Rather, it seeks to describe economic behavior as it actually exists. Philosophers draw a distinction between **positive statements**, which describe the world as it is, and **normative statements**, which describe how the world should be. Positive statements are factual. They may be true or false, but we can test them, at least in principle. Normative statements are subjective questions of opinion. We cannot test them since we cannot prove opinions to be true or false. They just are opinions based on one's values. For example, an economist could analyze a proposed subway system in a certain city. If the expected benefits exceed the costs, he concludes that the project is worthy—an example of positive analysis. Another economist argues for extended unemployment compensation during the Great Depression because a rich country like the United States should take care of its less fortunate citizens—an example of normative analysis.

Even if the line between positive and normative statements is not always crystal clear, economic analysis does try to remain rooted in the study of the actual people who inhabit the actual economy. Fortunately however, the assumption that individuals are purely self-interested is a simplification about human nature. In fact, we need to look no further than to Adam Smith, the very father of modern economics to find evidence of this. The opening sentence of his book, *The Theory of Moral Sentiments*, puts it very clearly: "How selfish soever man may be supposed, there are evidently some principles in his nature, which interest him in the fortune of others, and render their happiness necessary to him, though he derives nothing from it except the pleasure of seeing it." Clearly, individuals are both self-interested and altruistic.

Second, we can label self-interested behavior and profit-seeking with other names, such as personal choice and freedom. The ability to make personal choices about buying, working, and saving is an important personal freedom. Some people may choose high-pressure, high-paying jobs so that they can earn and spend considerable amounts of money on themselves. Others may allocate large portions of their earnings to charity or spend it on their friends and family. Others may devote themselves to a career that can require much time, energy, and expertise but does not offer high financial rewards, like being an elementary school teacher or a social worker. Still others may choose a job that does consume much of their time or provide a high level of income, but still leaves time for family, friends, and contemplation. Some people may prefer to work for a large company; others might want to start their own business. People's freedom to make their own economic choices has a moral value worth respecting.

## Clear It Up

### Is a diagram by any other name the same?

When you study economics, you may feel buried under an avalanche of diagrams. Your goal should be to recognize the common underlying logic and pattern of the diagrams, not to memorize each one.

This chapter uses only one basic diagram, although we present it with different sets of labels. The consumption budget constraint and the production possibilities frontier for society, as a whole, are the same basic diagram. **Figure 2.6** shows an individual budget constraint and a production possibilities frontier for two goods, Good 1 and Good 2. The tradeoff diagram always illustrates three basic themes: scarcity, tradeoffs, and economic efficiency.

The first theme is scarcity. It is not feasible to have unlimited amounts of both goods. Even if the budget constraint or a PPF shifts, scarcity remains—just at a different level. The second theme is tradeoffs. As depicted in the budget constraint or the production possibilities frontier, it is necessary to forgo some of one good to gain more of the other good. The details of this tradeoff vary. In a budget constraint we determine, the tradeoff is determined by the relative prices of the goods: that is, the relative price of two goods in the consumption choice budget constraint. These tradeoffs appear as a straight line. However, a curved line represents the tradeoffs in many production possibilities frontiers because the law of diminishing returns holds that as we add resources to an area, the marginal gains tend to diminish. Regardless of the specific shape, tradeoffs remain.

The third theme is economic efficiency, or getting the most benefit from scarce resources. All choices on the production possibilities frontier show productive efficiency because in such cases, there is no way to increase the quantity of one good without decreasing the quantity of the other. Similarly, when an individual makes a choice along a budget constraint, there is no way to increase the quantity of one good without decreasing the quantity of the other. The choice on a production possibilities set that is socially preferred, or the choice on an individual's budget constraint that is personally preferred, will display allocative efficiency.

The basic budget constraint/production possibilities frontier diagram will recur throughout this book. Some examples include using these tradeoff diagrams to analyze trade, environmental protection and economic output, equality of incomes and economic output, and the macroeconomic tradeoff between consumption and investment. Do not allow the different labels to confuse you. The budget constraint/production possibilities frontier diagram is always just a tool for thinking carefully about scarcity, tradeoffs, and efficiency in a particular situation.

**Figure 2.6 The Tradeoff Diagram**   Both the individual opportunity set (or budget constraint) and the social production possibilities frontier show the constraints under which individual consumers and society as a whole operate. Both diagrams show the tradeoff in choosing more of one good at the cost of less of the other.

Third, self-interested behavior can lead to positive social results. For example, when people work hard to make a living, they create economic output. Consumers who are looking for the best deals will encourage businesses to offer goods and services that meet their needs. Adam Smith, writing in *The Wealth of Nations*, named this property the **invisible hand**. In describing how consumers and producers interact in a market economy, Smith wrote:

> Every individual…generally, indeed, neither intends to promote the public interest, nor knows how much he is promoting it. By preferring the support of domestic to that of foreign industry, he intends only his own security; and by directing that industry in such a manner as its produce may be of the greatest value, he intends only his own gain. And he is in this, as in many other cases, led by an invisible hand to promote an end which was no part of his intention…By pursuing his own interest he frequently promotes that of the society more effectually than when he really intends to promote it.

The metaphor of the invisible hand suggests the remarkable possibility that broader social good can emerge from selfish individual actions.

Fourth, even people who focus on their own self-interest in the economic part of their life often set aside their own narrow self-interest in other parts of life. For example, you might focus on your own self-interest when asking your employer for a raise or negotiating to buy a car. Then you might turn around and focus on other people when you volunteer to read stories at the local library, help a friend move to a new apartment, or donate money to a charity. Self-interest is a reasonable starting point for analyzing many economic decisions, without needing to imply that people never do anything that is not in their own immediate self-interest.

# Bring it Home

## Choices ... To What Degree?

What have we learned? We know that scarcity impacts all the choices we make. An economist might argue that people do not obtain a bachelor's or master's degree because they do not have the resources to make those choices or because their incomes are too low and/or the price of these degrees is too high. A bachelor's or a master's degree may not be available in their opportunity set.

The price of these degrees may be too high not only because the actual price, college tuition (and perhaps room and board), is too high. An economist might also say that for many people, the full opportunity cost of a bachelor's or a master's degree is too high. For these people, they are unwilling or unable to make the tradeoff of forfeiting years of working, and earning an income, to earn a degree.

Finally, the statistics we introduced at the start of the chapter reveal information about intertemporal choices. An economist might say that people choose not to obtain a college degree because they may have to borrow money to attend college, and the interest they have to pay on that loan in the future will affect their decisions today. Also, it could be that some people have a preference for current consumption over future consumption, so they choose to work now at a lower salary and consume now, rather than postponing that consumption until after they graduate college.

## KEY TERMS

**allocative efficiency**  when the mix of goods produced represents the mix that society most desires

**budget constraint**  all possible consumption combinations of goods that someone can afford, given the prices of goods, when all income is spent; the boundary of the opportunity set

**comparative advantage**  when a country can produce a good at a lower cost in terms of other goods; or, when a country has a lower opportunity cost of production

**invisible hand**  Adam Smith's concept that individuals' self-interested behavior can lead to positive social outcomes

**law of diminishing marginal utility**  as we consume more of a good or service, the utility we get from additional units of the good or service tends to become smaller than what we received from earlier units

**law of diminishing returns**  as we add additional increments of resources to producing a good or service, the marginal benefit from those additional increments will decline

**marginal analysis**  examination of decisions on the margin, meaning a little more or a little less from the status quo

**normative statement**  statement which describes how the world should be

**opportunity cost**  measures cost by what we give up/forfeit in exchange; opportunity cost measures the value of the forgone alternative

**opportunity set**  all possible combinations of consumption that someone can afford given the prices of goods and the individual's income

**positive statement**  statement which describes the world as it is

**production possibilities frontier (PPF)**  a diagram that shows the productively efficient combinations of two products that an economy can produce given the resources it has available.

**productive efficiency**  when it is impossible to produce more of one good (or service) without decreasing the quantity produced of another good (or service)

**sunk costs**  costs that we make in the past that we cannot recover

**utility**  satisfaction, usefulness, or value one obtains from consuming goods and services

## KEY CONCEPTS AND SUMMARY

### 2.1 How Individuals Make Choices Based on Their Budget Constraint

Economists see the real world as one of scarcity: that is, a world in which people's desires exceed what is possible. As a result, economic behavior involves tradeoffs in which individuals, firms, and society must forgo something that they desire to obtain things that they desire more. Individuals face the tradeoff of what quantities of goods and services to consume. The budget constraint, which is the frontier of the opportunity set, illustrates the range of available choices. The relative price of the choices determines the slope of the budget constraint. Choices beyond the budget constraint are not affordable.

Opportunity cost measures cost by what we forgo in exchange. Sometimes we can measure opportunity cost in money, but it is often useful to consider time as well, or to measure it in terms of the actual resources that we must forfeit.

Most economic decisions and tradeoffs are not all-or-nothing. Instead, they involve marginal analysis, which means they are about decisions on the margin, involving a little more or a little less. The law of diminishing marginal utility points out that as a person receives more of something—whether it is a specific good or another resource—the additional marginal gains tend to become smaller. Because sunk costs occurred in the past and cannot be recovered, they should be disregarded in making current decisions.

## 2.2 The Production Possibilities Frontier and Social Choices

A production possibilities frontier defines the set of choices society faces for the combinations of goods and services it can produce given the resources available. The shape of the PPF is typically curved outward, rather than straight. Choices outside the PPF are unattainable and choices inside the PPF are wasteful. Over time, a growing economy will tend to shift the PPF outwards.

The law of diminishing returns holds that as increments of additional resources are devoted to producing something, the marginal increase in output will become increasingly smaller. All choices along a production possibilities frontier display productive efficiency; that is, it is impossible to use society's resources to produce more of one good without decreasing production of the other good. The specific choice along a production possibilities frontier that reflects the mix of goods society prefers is the choice with allocative efficiency. The curvature of the PPF is likely to differ by country, which results in different countries having comparative advantage in different goods. Total production can increase if countries specialize in the goods in which they have comparative advantage and trade some of their production for the remaining goods.

## 2.3 Confronting Objections to the Economic Approach

The economic way of thinking provides a useful approach to understanding human behavior. Economists make the careful distinction between positive statements, which describe the world as it is, and normative statements, which describe how the world should be. Even when economics analyzes the gains and losses from various events or policies, and thus draws normative conclusions about how the world should be, the analysis of economics is rooted in a positive analysis of how people, firms, and governments actually behave, not how they should behave.

# SELF-CHECK QUESTIONS

**1.** Suppose Alphonso's town raised the price of bus tickets to $1 per trip (while the price of burgers stayed at $2 and his budget remained $10 per week.) Draw Alphonso's new budget constraint. What happens to the opportunity cost of bus tickets?

**2.** Return to the example in **Figure 2.4**. Suppose there is an improvement in medical technology that enables more healthcare with the same amount of resources. How would this affect the production possibilities curve and, in particular, how would it affect the opportunity cost of education?

**3.** Could a nation be producing in a way that is allocatively efficient, but productively inefficient?

**4.** What are the similarities between a consumer's budget constraint and society's production possibilities frontier, not just graphically but analytically?

**5.** Individuals may not act in the rational, calculating way described by the economic model of decision making, measuring utility and costs at the margin, but can you make a case that they behave approximately that way?

**6.** Would an op-ed piece in a newspaper urging the adoption of a particular economic policy be a positive or normative statement?

**7.** Would a research study on the effects of soft drink consumption on children's cognitive development be a positive or normative statement?

# REVIEW QUESTIONS

**8.** Explain why scarcity leads to tradeoffs.

**9.** Explain why individuals make choices that are directly on the budget constraint, rather than inside the budget constraint or outside it.

**10.** What is comparative advantage?

**11.** What does a production possibilities frontier illustrate?

**12.** Why is a production possibilities frontier typically drawn as a curve, rather than a straight line?

**13.** Explain why societies cannot make a choice above their production possibilities frontier and should not make a choice below it.

**14.** What are diminishing marginal returns?

**15.** What is productive efficiency? Allocative efficiency?

**16.** What is the difference between a positive and a normative statement?

**17.** Is the economic model of decision-making intended as a literal description of how individuals, firms, and the governments actually make decisions?

**18.** What are four responses to the claim that people should not behave in the way described in this chapter?

## CRITICAL THINKING QUESTIONS

**19.** Suppose Alphonso's town raises the price of bus tickets from $0.50 to $1 and the price of burgers rises from $2 to $4. Why is the opportunity cost of bus tickets unchanged? Suppose Alphonso's weekly spending money increases from $10 to $20. How is his budget constraint affected from all three changes? Explain.

**20.** During the Second World War, Germany's factories were decimated. It also suffered many human casualties, both soldiers and civilians. How did the war affect Germany's production possibilities curve?

**21.** It is clear that productive inefficiency is a waste since resources are used in a way that produces less goods and services than a nation is capable of. Why is allocative inefficiency also wasteful?

**22.** What assumptions about the economy must be true for the invisible hand to work? To what extent are those assumptions valid in the real world?

**23.** Do economists have any particular expertise at making normative arguments? In other words, they have expertise at making positive statements (i.e., what *will* happen) about some economic policy, for example, but do they have special expertise to judge whether or not the policy *should* be undertaken?

## PROBLEMS

Use this information to answer the following 4 questions: Marie has a weekly budget of $24, which she likes to spend on magazines and pies.

**24.** If the price of a magazine is $4 each, what is the maximum number of magazines she could buy in a week?

**25.** If the price of a pie is $12, what is the maximum number of pies she could buy in a week?

**26.** Draw Marie's budget constraint with pies on the horizontal axis and magazines on the vertical axis. What is the slope of the budget constraint?

**27.** What is Marie's opportunity cost of purchasing a pie?

# 3 | Demand and Supply

**Figure 3.1 Farmer's Market** Organic vegetables and fruits that are grown and sold within a specific geographical region should, in theory, cost less than conventional produce because the transportation costs are less. That is not, however, usually the case. (Credit: Modification of work by Natalie Maynor/Flickr Creative Commons)

## Bring it Home

### Why Can We Not Get Enough of Organic?

Organic food is increasingly popular, not just in the United States, but worldwide. At one time, consumers had to go to specialty stores or farmers' markets to find organic produce. Now it is available in most grocery stores. In short, organic is part of the mainstream.

Ever wonder why organic food costs more than conventional food? Why, say, does an organic Fuji apple cost $1.99 a pound, while its conventional counterpart costs $1.49 a pound? The same price relationship is true for just about every organic product on the market. If many organic foods are locally grown, would they not take less time to get to market and therefore be cheaper? What are the forces that keep those prices from coming down? Turns out those forces have quite a bit to do with this chapter's topic: demand and supply.

## Introduction to Demand and Supply

In this chapter, you will learn about:

- Demand, Supply, and Equilibrium in Markets for Goods and Services

- Shifts in Demand and Supply for Goods and Services

- Changes in Equilibrium Price and Quantity: The Four-Step Process

- Price Ceilings and Price Floors

An auction bidder pays thousands of dollars for a dress Whitney Houston wore. A collector spends a small fortune for a few drawings by John Lennon. People usually react to purchases like these in two ways: their jaw drops because they think these are high prices to pay for such goods or they think these are rare, desirable items and the amount paid seems right.

# Link It Up

Visit this website (http://openstaxcollege.org/l/celebauction) to read a list of bizarre items that have been purchased for their ties to celebrities. These examples represent an interesting facet of demand and supply.

When economists talk about prices, they are less interested in making judgments than in gaining a practical understanding of what determines prices and why prices change. Consider a price most of us contend with weekly: that of a gallon of gas. Why was the average price of gasoline in the United States $3.71 per gallon in June 2014? Why did the price for gasoline fall sharply to $1.96 per gallon by January 2016? To explain these price movements, economists focus on the determinants of what gasoline buyers are willing to pay and what gasoline sellers are willing to accept.

As it turns out, the price of gasoline in June of any given year is nearly always higher than the price in January of that same year. Over recent decades, gasoline prices in midsummer have averaged about 10 cents per gallon more than their midwinter low. The likely reason is that people drive more in the summer, and are also willing to pay more for gas, but that does not explain how steeply gas prices fell. Other factors were at work during those 18 months, such as increases in supply and decreases in the demand for crude oil.

This chapter introduces the economic model of demand and supply—one of the most powerful models in all of economics. The discussion here begins by examining how demand and supply determine the price and the quantity sold in markets for goods and services, and how changes in demand and supply lead to changes in prices and quantities.

# 3.1 | Demand, Supply, and Equilibrium in Markets for Goods and Services

By the end of this section, you will be able to:

- Explain demand, quantity demanded, and the law of demand
- Identify a demand curve and a supply curve
- Explain supply, quantity supplied, and the law of supply
- Explain equilibrium, equilibrium price, and equilibrium quantity

First let's first focus on what economists mean by demand, what they mean by supply, and then how demand and supply interact in a market.

# Demand for Goods and Services

Economists use the term **demand** to refer to the amount of some good or service consumers are willing and able to purchase at each price. Demand is fundamentally based on needs and wants—if you have no need or want for something, you won't buy it. While a consumer may be able to differentiate between a need and a want, but from an economist's perspective they are the same thing. Demand is also based on ability to pay. If you cannot pay for it, you have no effective demand. By this definition, a homeless person probably has no effective demand for shelter.

What a buyer pays for a unit of the specific good or service is called **price**. The total number of units that consumers would purchase at that price is called the **quantity demanded**. A rise in price of a good or service almost always decreases the quantity demanded of that good or service. Conversely, a fall in price will increase the quantity demanded. When the price of a gallon of gasoline increases, for example, people look for ways to reduce their consumption by combining several errands, commuting by carpool or mass transit, or taking weekend or vacation trips closer to home. Economists call this inverse relationship between price and quantity demanded the **law of demand**. The law of demand assumes that all other variables that affect demand (which we explain in the next module) are held constant.

We can show an example from the market for gasoline in a table or a graph. Economist call a table that shows the quantity demanded at each price, such as **Table 3.1**, a **demand schedule**. In this case we measure price in dollars per gallon of gasoline. We measure the quantity demanded in millions of gallons over some time period (for example, per day or per year) and over some geographic area (like a state or a country). A **demand curve** shows the relationship between price and quantity demanded on a graph like **Figure 3.2**, with quantity on the horizontal axis and the price per gallon on the vertical axis. (Note that this is an exception to the normal rule in mathematics that the independent variable (x) goes on the horizontal axis and the dependent variable (y) goes on the vertical. Economics is not math.)

**Table 3.1** shows the demand schedule and the graph in **Figure 3.2** shows the demand curve. These are two ways to describe the same relationship between price and quantity demanded.

| Price (per gallon) | Quantity Demanded (millions of gallons) |
|---|---|
| $1.00 | 800 |
| $1.20 | 700 |
| $1.40 | 600 |
| $1.60 | 550 |
| $1.80 | 500 |
| $2.00 | 460 |
| $2.20 | 420 |

Table 3.1 Price and Quantity Demanded of Gasoline

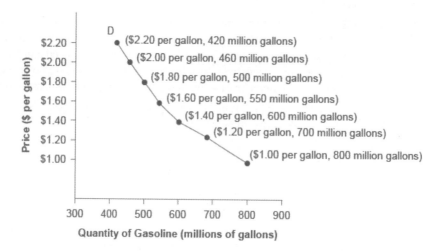

**Figure 3.2 A Demand Curve for Gasoline** The demand schedule shows that as price rises, quantity demanded decreases, and vice versa. We graph these points, and the line connecting them is the demand curve (D). The downward slope of the demand curve again illustrates the law of demand—the inverse relationship between prices and quantity demanded.

Demand curves will appear somewhat different for each product. They may appear relatively steep or flat, or they may be straight or curved. Nearly all demand curves share the fundamental similarity that they slope down from left to right. Demand curves embody the law of demand: As the price increases, the quantity demanded decreases, and conversely, as the price decreases, the quantity demanded increases.

Confused about these different types of demand? Read the next Clear It Up feature.

## Is demand the same as quantity demanded?

In economic terminology, demand is not the same as quantity demanded. When economists talk about demand, they mean the relationship between a range of prices and the quantities demanded at those prices, as illustrated by a demand curve or a demand schedule. When economists talk about quantity demanded, they mean only a certain point on the demand curve, or one quantity on the demand schedule. In short, demand refers to the curve and quantity demanded refers to the (specific) point on the curve.

## Supply of Goods and Services

When economists talk about **supply**, they mean the amount of some good or service a producer is willing to supply at each price. Price is what the producer receives for selling one unit of a good or service. A rise in price almost always leads to an increase in the **quantity supplied** of that good or service, while a fall in price will decrease the quantity supplied. When the price of gasoline rises, for example, it encourages profit-seeking firms to take several actions: expand exploration for oil reserves; drill for more oil; invest in more pipelines and oil tankers to bring the oil to plants for refining into gasoline; build new oil refineries; purchase additional pipelines and trucks to ship the gasoline to gas stations; and open more gas stations or keep existing gas stations open longer hours. Economists call this positive relationship between price and quantity supplied—that a higher price leads to a higher quantity supplied and a lower price leads to a lower quantity supplied—the **law of supply**. The law of supply assumes that all other variables that affect supply (to be explained in the next module) are held constant.

Still unsure about the different types of supply? See the following Clear It Up feature.

## Is supply the same as quantity supplied?

In economic terminology, supply is not the same as quantity supplied. When economists refer to supply, they mean the relationship between a range of prices and the quantities supplied at those prices, a relationship that we can illustrate with a supply curve or a supply schedule. When economists refer to quantity supplied, they mean only a certain point on the supply curve, or one quantity on the supply schedule. In short, supply refers to the curve and quantity supplied refers to the (specific) point on the curve.

**Figure 3.3** illustrates the law of supply, again using the market for gasoline as an example. Like demand, we can illustrate supply using a table or a graph. A **supply schedule** is a table, like **Table 3.2**, that shows the quantity supplied at a range of different prices. Again, we measure price in dollars per gallon of gasoline and we measure quantity supplied in millions of gallons. A **supply curve** is a graphic illustration of the relationship between price, shown on the vertical axis, and quantity, shown on the horizontal axis. The supply schedule and the supply curve are just two different ways of showing the same information. Notice that the horizontal and vertical axes on the graph for the supply curve are the same as for the demand curve.

**Figure 3.3 A Supply Curve for Gasoline** The supply schedule is the table that shows quantity supplied of gasoline at each price. As price rises, quantity supplied also increases, and vice versa. The supply curve (S) is created by graphing the points from the supply schedule and then connecting them. The upward slope of the supply curve illustrates the law of supply—that a higher price leads to a higher quantity supplied, and vice versa.

| Price (per gallon) | Quantity Supplied (millions of gallons) |
|---|---|
| $1.00 | 500 |
| $1.20 | 550 |
| $1.40 | 600 |
| $1.60 | 640 |
| $1.80 | 680 |
| $2.00 | 700 |

**Table 3.2 Price and Supply of Gasoline**

| Price (per gallon) | Quantity Supplied (millions of gallons) |
|---|---|
| $2.20 | 720 |

Table 3.2 Price and Supply of Gasoline

The shape of supply curves will vary somewhat according to the product: steeper, flatter, straighter, or curved. Nearly all supply curves, however, share a basic similarity: they slope up from left to right and illustrate the law of supply: as the price rises, say, from $1.00 per gallon to $2.20 per gallon, the quantity supplied increases from 500 gallons to 720 gallons. Conversely, as the price falls, the quantity supplied decreases.

## Equilibrium—Where Demand and Supply Intersect

Because the graphs for demand and supply curves both have price on the vertical axis and quantity on the horizontal axis, the demand curve and supply curve for a particular good or service can appear on the same graph. Together, demand and supply determine the price and the quantity that will be bought and sold in a market.

Figure 3.4 illustrates the interaction of demand and supply in the market for gasoline. The demand curve (D) is identical to Figure 3.2. The supply curve (S) is identical to Figure 3.3. Table 3.3 contains the same information in tabular form.

Figure 3.4 Demand and Supply for Gasoline   The demand curve (D) and the supply curve (S) intersect at the equilibrium point E, with a price of $1.40 and a quantity of 600. The equilibrium is the only price where quantity demanded is equal to quantity supplied. At a price above equilibrium like $1.80, quantity supplied exceeds the quantity demanded, so there is excess supply. At a price below equilibrium such as $1.20, quantity demanded exceeds quantity supplied, so there is excess demand.

| Price (per gallon) | Quantity demanded (millions of gallons) | Quantity supplied (millions of gallons) |
|---|---|---|
| $1.00 | 800 | 500 |
| $1.20 | 700 | 550 |
| **$1.40** | **600** | **600** |
| $1.60 | 550 | 640 |
| $1.80 | 500 | 680 |

Table 3.3 Price, Quantity Demanded, and Quantity Supplied

| Price (per gallon) | Quantity demanded (millions of gallons) | Quantity supplied (millions of gallons) |
|---|---|---|
| $2.00 | 460 | 700 |
| $2.20 | 420 | 720 |

**Table 3.3 Price, Quantity Demanded, and Quantity Supplied**

Remember this: When two lines on a diagram cross, this intersection usually means something. The point where the supply curve (S) and the demand curve (D) cross, designated by point E in **Figure 3.4**, is called the **equilibrium**. The **equilibrium price** is the only price where the plans of consumers and the plans of producers agree—that is, where the amount of the product consumers want to buy (quantity demanded) is equal to the amount producers want to sell (quantity supplied). Economists call this common quantity the **equilibrium quantity**. At any other price, the quantity demanded does not equal the quantity supplied, so the market is not in equilibrium at that price.

In **Figure 3.4**, the equilibrium price is $1.40 per gallon of gasoline and the equilibrium quantity is 600 million gallons. If you had only the demand and supply schedules, and not the graph, you could find the equilibrium by looking for the price level on the tables where the quantity demanded and the quantity supplied are equal.

The word "equilibrium" means "balance." If a market is at its equilibrium price and quantity, then it has no reason to move away from that point. However, if a market is not at equilibrium, then economic pressures arise to move the market toward the equilibrium price and the equilibrium quantity.

Imagine, for example, that the price of a gallon of gasoline was above the equilibrium price—that is, instead of $1.40 per gallon, the price is $1.80 per gallon. The dashed horizontal line at the price of $1.80 in **Figure 3.4** illustrates this above equilibrium price. At this higher price, the quantity demanded drops from 600 to 500. This decline in quantity reflects how consumers react to the higher price by finding ways to use less gasoline.

Moreover, at this higher price of $1.80, the quantity of gasoline supplied rises from the 600 to 680, as the higher price makes it more profitable for gasoline producers to expand their output. Now, consider how quantity demanded and quantity supplied are related at this above-equilibrium price. Quantity demanded has fallen to 500 gallons, while quantity supplied has risen to 680 gallons. In fact, at any above-equilibrium price, the quantity supplied exceeds the quantity demanded. We call this an **excess supply** or a **surplus**.

With a surplus, gasoline accumulates at gas stations, in tanker trucks, in pipelines, and at oil refineries. This accumulation puts pressure on gasoline sellers. If a surplus remains unsold, those firms involved in making and selling gasoline are not receiving enough cash to pay their workers and to cover their expenses. In this situation, some producers and sellers will want to cut prices, because it is better to sell at a lower price than not to sell at all. Once some sellers start cutting prices, others will follow to avoid losing sales. These price reductions in turn will stimulate a higher quantity demanded. Therefore, if the price is above the equilibrium level, incentives built into the structure of demand and supply will create pressures for the price to fall toward the equilibrium.

Now suppose that the price is below its equilibrium level at $1.20 per gallon, as the dashed horizontal line at this price in **Figure 3.4** shows. At this lower price, the quantity demanded increases from 600 to 700 as drivers take longer trips, spend more minutes warming up the car in the driveway in wintertime, stop sharing rides to work, and buy larger cars that get fewer miles to the gallon. However, the below-equilibrium price reduces gasoline producers' incentives to produce and sell gasoline, and the quantity supplied falls from 600 to 550.

When the price is below equilibrium, there is **excess demand**, or a **shortage**—that is, at the given price the quantity demanded, which has been stimulated by the lower price, now exceeds the quantity supplied, which had been depressed by the lower price. In this situation, eager gasoline buyers mob the gas stations, only to find many stations running short of fuel. Oil companies and gas stations recognize that they have an opportunity to make higher profits by selling what gasoline they have at a higher price. As a result, the price rises toward the equilibrium level. Read **Demand, Supply, and Efficiency** for more discussion on the importance of the demand and supply model.

# 3.2 | Shifts in Demand and Supply for Goods and

# Services

By the end of this section, you will be able to:

- Identify factors that affect demand
- Graph demand curves and demand shifts
- Identify factors that affect supply
- Graph supply curves and supply shifts

The previous module explored how price affects the quantity demanded and the quantity supplied. The result was the demand curve and the supply curve. Price, however, is not the only factor that influences demand, nor is it the only thing that influences supply. For example, how is demand for vegetarian food affected if, say, health concerns cause more consumers to avoid eating meat? How is the supply of diamonds affected if diamond producers discover several new diamond mines? What are the major factors, in addition to the price, that influence demand or supply?

# Link It Up ⌬

Visit this website (http://openstaxcollege.org/l/toothfish) to read a brief note on how marketing strategies can influence supply and demand of products.

## What Factors Affect Demand?

We defined demand as the amount of some product a consumer is willing and able to purchase at each price. That suggests at least two factors in addition to price that affect demand. Willingness to purchase suggests a desire, based on what economists call tastes and preferences. If you neither need nor want something, you will not buy it. Ability to purchase suggests that income is important. Professors are usually able to afford better housing and transportation than students, because they have more income. Prices of related goods can affect demand also. If you need a new car, the price of a Honda may affect your demand for a Ford. Finally, the size or composition of the population can affect demand. The more children a family has, the greater their demand for clothing. The more driving-age children a family has, the greater their demand for car insurance, and the less for diapers and baby formula.

These factors matter for both individual and market demand as a whole. Exactly how do these various factors affect demand, and how do we show the effects graphically? To answer those questions, we need the *ceteris paribus* assumption.

## The *Ceteris Paribus* Assumption

A demand curve or a supply curve is a relationship between two, and only two, variables: quantity on the horizontal axis and price on the vertical axis. The assumption behind a demand curve or a supply curve is that no relevant economic factors, other than the product's price, are changing. Economists call this assumption **ceteris paribus**, a Latin phrase meaning "other things being equal." Any given demand or supply curve is based on the *ceteris paribus* assumption that all else is held equal. A demand curve or a supply curve is a relationship between two, and only two, variables when all other variables are kept constant. If all else is not held equal, then the laws of supply and demand will not necessarily hold, as the following Clear It Up feature shows.

# Clear It Up

## When does *ceteris paribus* apply?

We typically apply *ceteris paribus* when we observe how changes in price affect demand or supply, but we can apply *ceteris paribus* more generally. In the real world, demand and supply depend on more factors than just price. For example, a consumer's demand depends on income and a producer's supply depends on the cost of producing the product. How can we analyze the effect on demand or supply if multiple factors are changing at the same time—say price rises and income falls? The answer is that we examine the changes one at a time, assuming the other factors are held constant.

For example, we can say that an increase in the price reduces the amount consumers will buy (assuming income, and anything else that affects demand, is unchanged). Additionally, a decrease in income reduces the amount consumers can afford to buy (assuming price, and anything else that affects demand, is unchanged). This is what the *ceteris paribus* assumption really means. In this particular case, after we analyze each factor separately, we can combine the results. The amount consumers buy falls for two reasons: first because of the higher price and second because of the lower income.

## How Does Income Affect Demand?

Let's use income as an example of how factors other than price affect demand. **Figure 3.5** shows the initial demand for automobiles as $D_0$. At point Q, for example, if the price is $20,000 per car, the quantity of cars demanded is 18 million. $D_0$ also shows how the quantity of cars demanded would change as a result of a higher or lower price. For example, if the price of a car rose to $22,000, the quantity demanded would decrease to 17 million, at point R.

The original demand curve $D_0$, like every demand curve, is based on the *ceteris paribus* assumption that no other economically relevant factors change. Now imagine that the economy expands in a way that raises the incomes of many people, making cars more affordable. How will this affect demand? How can we show this graphically?

Return to **Figure 3.5**. The price of cars is still $20,000, but with higher incomes, the quantity demanded has now increased to 20 million cars, shown at point S. As a result of the higher income levels, the demand curve shifts to the right to the new demand curve $D_1$, indicating an increase in demand. **Table 3.4** shows clearly that this increased demand would occur at every price, not just the original one.

**Figure 3.5 Shifts in Demand: A Car Example** Increased demand means that at every given price, the quantity demanded is higher, so that the demand curve shifts to the right from $D_0$ to $D_1$. Decreased demand means that at every given price, the quantity demanded is lower, so that the demand curve shifts to the left from $D_0$ to $D_2$.

| Price | Decrease to $D_2$ | Original Quantity Demanded $D_0$ | Increase to $D_1$ |
|---|---|---|---|
| $16,000 | 17.6 million | 22.0 million | 24.0 million |
| $18,000 | 16.0 million | 20.0 million | 22.0 million |
| $20,000 | 14.4 million | 18.0 million | 20.0 million |
| $22,000 | 13.6 million | 17.0 million | 19.0 million |
| $24,000 | 13.2 million | 16.5 million | 18.5 million |
| $26,000 | 12.8 million | 16.0 million | 18.0 million |

**Table 3.4 Price and Demand Shifts: A Car Example**

Now, imagine that the economy slows down so that many people lose their jobs or work fewer hours, reducing their incomes. In this case, the decrease in income would lead to a lower quantity of cars demanded at every given price, and the original demand curve $D_0$ would shift left to $D_2$. The shift from $D_0$ to $D_2$ represents such a decrease in demand: At any given price level, the quantity demanded is now lower. In this example, a price of $20,000 means 18 million cars sold along the original demand curve, but only 14.4 million sold after demand fell.

When a demand curve shifts, it does not mean that the quantity demanded by every individual buyer changes by the same amount. In this example, not everyone would have higher or lower income and not everyone would buy or not buy an additional car. Instead, a shift in a demand curve captures a pattern for the market as a whole.

In the previous section, we argued that higher income causes greater demand at every price. This is true for most goods and services. For some—luxury cars, vacations in Europe, and fine jewelry—the effect of a rise in income can be especially pronounced. A product whose demand rises when income rises, and vice versa, is called a **normal good**. A few exceptions to this pattern do exist. As incomes rise, many people will buy fewer generic brand groceries and more name brand groceries. They are less likely to buy used cars and more likely to buy new cars. They will be less likely to rent an apartment and more likely to own a home. A product whose demand falls when income rises, and vice versa, is called an **inferior good**. In other words, when income increases, the demand curve shifts to the left.

## Other Factors That Shift Demand Curves

Income is not the only factor that causes a shift in demand. Other factors that change demand include tastes and preferences, the composition or size of the population, the prices of related goods, and even expectations. A change in any one of the underlying factors that determine what quantity people are willing to buy at a given price will cause a shift in demand. Graphically, the new demand curve lies either to the right (an increase) or to the left (a decrease) of the original demand curve. Let's look at these factors.

### Changing Tastes or Preferences

From 1980 to 2014, the per-person consumption of chicken by Americans rose from 48 pounds per year to 85 pounds per year, and consumption of beef fell from 77 pounds per year to 54 pounds per year, according to the U.S. Department of Agriculture (USDA). Changes like these are largely due to movements in taste, which change the quantity of a good demanded at every price: that is, they shift the demand curve for that good, rightward for chicken and leftward for beef.

### Changes in the Composition of the Population

The proportion of elderly citizens in the United States population is rising. It rose from 9.8% in 1970 to 12.6% in 2000, and will be a projected (by the U.S. Census Bureau) 20% of the population by 2030. A society with relatively more children, like the United States in the 1960s, will have greater demand for goods and services like tricycles and day care facilities. A society with relatively more elderly persons, as the United States is projected to have by 2030, has a higher demand for nursing homes and hearing aids. Similarly, changes in the size of the population can affect the demand for housing and many other goods. Each of these changes in demand will be shown as a shift in the demand curve.

Changes in the prices of related goods such as substitutes or complements also can affect the demand for a product. A

**substitute** is a good or service that we can use in place of another good or service. As electronic books, like this one, become more available, you would expect to see a decrease in demand for traditional printed books. A lower price for a substitute decreases demand for the other product. For example, in recent years as the price of tablet computers has fallen, the quantity demanded has increased (because of the law of demand). Since people are purchasing tablets, there has been a decrease in demand for laptops, which we can show graphically as a leftward shift in the demand curve for laptops. A higher price for a substitute good has the reverse effect.

Other goods are **complements** for each other, meaning we often use the goods together, because consumption of one good tends to enhance consumption of the other. Examples include breakfast cereal and milk; notebooks and pens or pencils, golf balls and golf clubs; gasoline and sport utility vehicles; and the five-way combination of bacon, lettuce, tomato, mayonnaise, and bread. If the price of golf clubs rises, since the quantity demanded of golf clubs falls (because of the law of demand), demand for a complement good like golf balls decreases, too. Similarly, a higher price for skis would shift the demand curve for a complement good like ski resort trips to the left, while a lower price for a complement has the reverse effect.

### Changes in Expectations about Future Prices or Other Factors that Affect Demand

While it is clear that the price of a good affects the quantity demanded, it is also true that expectations about the future price (or expectations about tastes and preferences, income, and so on) can affect demand. For example, if people hear that a hurricane is coming, they may rush to the store to buy flashlight batteries and bottled water. If people learn that the price of a good like coffee is likely to rise in the future, they may head for the store to stock up on coffee now. We show these changes in demand as shifts in the curve. Therefore, a **shift in demand** happens when a change in some economic factor (other than price) causes a different quantity to be demanded at every price. The following Work It Out feature shows how this happens.

# Work It Out

## Shift in Demand

A shift in demand means that at any price (and at every price), the quantity demanded will be different than it was before. Following is an example of a shift in demand due to an income increase.

Step 1. Draw the graph of a demand curve for a normal good like pizza. Pick a price (like $P_0$). Identify the corresponding $Q_0$. See an example in **Figure 3.6**.

**Figure 3.6 Demand Curve** We can use the demand curve to identify how much consumers would buy at any given price.

Step 2. Suppose income increases. As a result of the change, are consumers going to buy more or less pizza? The answer is more. Draw a dotted horizontal line from the chosen price, through the original quantity demanded, to the new point with the new $Q_1$. Draw a dotted vertical line down to the horizontal axis and label the new $Q_1$. **Figure 3.7** provides an example.

**Figure 3.7 Demand Curve with Income Increase** With an increase in income, consumers will purchase larger quantities, pushing demand to the right.

Step 3. Now, shift the curve through the new point. You will see that an increase in income causes an upward (or rightward) shift in the demand curve, so that at any price the quantities demanded will be higher, as Figure 3.8 illustrates.

**Figure 3.8 Demand Curve Shifted Right** With an increase in income, consumers will purchase larger quantities, pushing demand to the right, and causing the demand curve to shift right.

## Summing Up Factors That Change Demand

Figure 3.9 summarizes six factors that can shift demand curves. The direction of the arrows indicates whether the demand curve shifts represent an increase in demand or a decrease in demand. Notice that a change in the price of the good or service itself is not listed among the factors that can shift a demand curve. A change in the price of a good or service causes a movement along a specific demand curve, and it typically leads to some change in the quantity demanded, but it does not shift the demand curve.

**Figure 3.9 Factors That Shift Demand Curves** (a) A list of factors that can cause an increase in demand from $D_0$ to $D_1$. (b) The same factors, if their direction is reversed, can cause a decrease in demand from $D_0$ to $D_1$.

When a demand curve shifts, it will then intersect with a given supply curve at a different equilibrium price and quantity. We are, however, getting ahead of our story. Before discussing how changes in demand can affect equilibrium price and quantity, we first need to discuss shifts in supply curves.

## How Production Costs Affect Supply

A supply curve shows how quantity supplied will change as the price rises and falls, assuming *ceteris paribus* so that no other economically relevant factors are changing. If other factors relevant to supply do change, then the entire supply curve will shift. Just as we described a shift in demand as a change in the quantity demanded at every price, a **shift in supply** means a change in the quantity supplied at every price.

In thinking about the factors that affect supply, remember what motivates firms: profits, which are the difference between revenues and costs. A firm produces goods and services using combinations of labor, materials, and machinery, or what we call **inputs** or **factors of production**. If a firm faces lower costs of production, while the prices for the good or service the firm produces remain unchanged, a firm's profits go up. When a firm's profits increase, it is more motivated to produce output, since the more it produces the more profit it will earn. When costs of production fall, a firm will tend to supply a larger quantity at any given price for its output. We can show this by the supply curve shifting to the right.

Take, for example, a messenger company that delivers packages around a city. The company may find that buying gasoline is one of its main costs. If the price of gasoline falls, then the company will find it can deliver messages more cheaply than before. Since lower costs correspond to higher profits, the messenger company may now supply more of its services at any given price. For example, given the lower gasoline prices, the company can now serve a greater area, and increase its supply.

Conversely, if a firm faces higher costs of production, then it will earn lower profits at any given selling price for its products. As a result, a higher cost of production typically causes a firm to supply a smaller quantity at any given price. In this case, the supply curve shifts to the left.

Consider the supply for cars, shown by curve $S_0$ in **Figure 3.10**. Point J indicates that if the price is $20,000, the quantity supplied will be 18 million cars. If the price rises to $22,000 per car, *ceteris paribus*, the quantity supplied will rise to 20 million cars, as point K on the $S_0$ curve shows. We can show the same information in table form, as in **Table 3.5**.

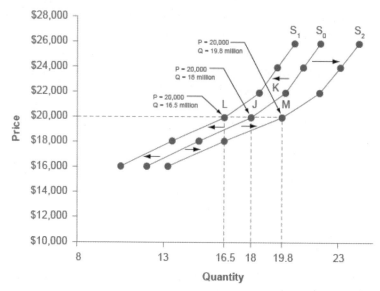

**Figure 3.10 Shifts in Supply: A Car Example** Decreased supply means that at every given price, the quantity supplied is lower, so that the supply curve shifts to the left, from $S_0$ to $S_1$. Increased supply means that at every given price, the quantity supplied is higher, so that the supply curve shifts to the right, from $S_0$ to $S_2$.

| Price | Decrease to $S_1$ | Original Quantity Supplied $S_0$ | Increase to $S_2$ |
|---|---|---|---|
| $16,000 | 10.5 million | 12.0 million | 13.2 million |
| $18,000 | 13.5 million | 15.0 million | 16.5 million |
| $20,000 | 16.5 million | 18.0 million | 19.8 million |
| $22,000 | 18.5 million | 20.0 million | 22.0 million |
| $24,000 | 19.5 million | 21.0 million | 23.1 million |
| $26,000 | 20.5 million | 22.0 million | 24.2 million |

**Table 3.5 Price and Shifts in Supply: A Car Example**

Now, imagine that the price of steel, an important ingredient in manufacturing cars, rises, so that producing a car has become more expensive. At any given price for selling cars, car manufacturers will react by supplying a lower quantity. We can show this graphically as a leftward shift of supply, from $S_0$ to $S_1$, which indicates that at any given price, the quantity supplied decreases. In this example, at a price of $20,000, the quantity supplied decreases from 18 million on the original supply curve ($S_0$) to 16.5 million on the supply curve $S_1$, which is labeled as point L.

Conversely, if the price of steel decreases, producing a car becomes less expensive. At any given price for selling cars, car manufacturers can now expect to earn higher profits, so they will supply a higher quantity. The shift of supply to the right, from $S_0$ to $S_2$, means that at all prices, the quantity supplied has increased. In this example, at a price of $20,000, the quantity supplied increases from 18 million on the original supply curve ($S_0$) to 19.8 million on the supply curve $S_2$, which is labeled M.

## Other Factors That Affect Supply

In the example above, we saw that changes in the prices of inputs in the production process will affect the cost of production and thus the supply. Several other things affect the cost of production, too, such as changes in weather or other natural conditions, new technologies for production, and some government policies.

Changes in weather and climate will affect the cost of production for many agricultural products. For example, in

2014 the Manchurian Plain in Northeastern China, which produces most of the country's wheat, corn, and soybeans, experienced its most severe drought in 50 years. A drought decreases the supply of agricultural products, which means that at any given price, a lower quantity will be supplied. Conversely, especially good weather would shift the supply curve to the right.

When a firm discovers a new technology that allows the firm to produce at a lower cost, the supply curve will shift to the right, as well. For instance, in the 1960s a major scientific effort nicknamed the Green Revolution focused on breeding improved seeds for basic crops like wheat and rice. By the early 1990s, more than two-thirds of the wheat and rice in low-income countries around the world used these Green Revolution seeds—and the harvest was twice as high per acre. A technological improvement that reduces costs of production will shift supply to the right, so that a greater quantity will be produced at any given price.

Government policies can affect the cost of production and the supply curve through taxes, regulations, and subsidies. For example, the U.S. government imposes a tax on alcoholic beverages that collects about $8 billion per year from producers. Businesses treat taxes as costs. Higher costs decrease supply for the reasons we discussed above. Other examples of policy that can affect cost are the wide array of government regulations that require firms to spend money to provide a cleaner environment or a safer workplace. Complying with regulations increases costs.

A government subsidy, on the other hand, is the opposite of a tax. A subsidy occurs when the government pays a firm directly or reduces the firm's taxes if the firm carries out certain actions. From the firm's perspective, taxes or regulations are an additional cost of production that shifts supply to the left, leading the firm to produce a lower quantity at every given price. Government subsidies reduce the cost of production and increase supply at every given price, shifting supply to the right. The following Work It Out feature shows how this shift happens.

# Work It Out ─○─○─○

## Shift in Supply

We know that a supply curve shows the minimum price a firm will accept to produce a given quantity of output. What happens to the supply curve when the cost of production goes up? Following is an example of a shift in supply due to a production cost increase.

Step 1. Draw a graph of a supply curve for pizza. Pick a quantity (like $Q_0$). If you draw a vertical line up from $Q_0$ to the supply curve, you will see the price the firm chooses. **Figure 3.11** provides an example.

**Figure 3.11 Supply Curve**   You can use a supply curve to show the minimum price a firm will accept to produce a given quantity of output.

Step 2. Why did the firm choose that price and not some other? One way to think about this is that the price is composed of two parts. The first part is the cost of producing pizzas at the margin; in this case, the cost of producing the pizza, including cost of ingredients (e.g., dough, sauce, cheese, and pepperoni), the cost of the pizza oven, the shop rent, and the workers' wages. The second part is the firm's desired profit, which is determined, among other factors, by the profit margins in that particular business. If you add these two parts together, you get the price the firm wishes to charge. The quantity Q0 and associated price P0 give you one point on the firm's supply curve, as **Figure 3.12** illustrates.

**Figure 3.12 Setting Prices** The cost of production and the desired profit equal the price a firm will set for a product.

Step 3. Now, suppose that the cost of production increases. Perhaps cheese has become more expensive by $0.75 per pizza. If that is true, the firm will want to raise its price by the amount of the increase in cost ($0.75). Draw this point on the supply curve directly above the initial point on the curve, but $0.75 higher, as **Figure 3.13** shows.

**Figure 3.13 Increasing Costs Leads to Increasing Price** Because the cost of production and the desired profit equal the price a firm will set for a product, if the cost of production increases, the price for the product will also need to increase.

Step 4. Shift the supply curve through this point. You will see that an increase in cost causes an upward (or a leftward) shift of the supply curve so that at any price, the quantities supplied will be smaller, as **Figure 3.14** illustrates.

**Figure 3.14 Supply Curve Shifts** When the cost of production increases, the supply curve shifts upwardly to a new price level.

## Summing Up Factors That Change Supply

Changes in the cost of inputs, natural disasters, new technologies, and the impact of government decisions all affect the cost of production. In turn, these factors affect how much firms are willing to supply at any given price.

**Figure 3.15** summarizes factors that change the supply of goods and services. Notice that a change in the price of the product itself is not among the factors that shift the supply curve. Although a change in price of a good or service typically causes a change in quantity supplied or a movement along the supply curve for that specific good or service, it does not cause the supply curve itself to shift.

(a) Factors that increase supply        (b) Factors that decrease supply

**Figure 3.15 Factors That Shift Supply Curves** (a) A list of factors that can cause an increase in supply from $S_0$ to $S_1$. (b) The same factors, if their direction is reversed, can cause a decrease in supply from $S_0$ to $S_1$.

Because demand and supply curves appear on a two-dimensional diagram with only price and quantity on the axes, an unwary visitor to the land of economics might be fooled into believing that economics is about only four topics: demand, supply, price, and quantity. However, demand and supply are really "umbrella" concepts: demand covers all the factors that affect demand, and supply covers all the factors that affect supply. We include factors other than price that affect demand and supply are included by using shifts in the demand or the supply curve. In this way, the two-dimensional demand and supply model becomes a powerful tool for analyzing a wide range of economic circumstances.

# 3.3 | Changes in Equilibrium Price and Quantity: The Four-Step Process

By the end of this section, you will be able to:

- Identify equilibrium price and quantity through the four-step process
- Graph equilibrium price and quantity
- Contrast shifts of demand or supply and movements along a demand or supply curve
- Graph demand and supply curves, including equilibrium price and quantity, based on real-world examples

Let's begin this discussion with a single economic event. It might be an event that affects demand, like a change in income, population, tastes, prices of substitutes or complements, or expectations about future prices. It might be an event that affects supply, like a change in natural conditions, input prices, or technology, or government policies that affect production. How does this economic event affect equilibrium price and quantity? We will analyze this question using a four-step process.

Step 1. Draw a demand and supply model before the economic change took place. To establish the model requires four standard pieces of information: The law of demand, which tells us the slope of the demand curve; the law of supply, which gives us the slope of the supply curve; the shift variables for demand; and the shift variables for supply. From this model, find the initial equilibrium values for price and quantity.

Step 2. Decide whether the economic change you are analyzing affects demand or supply. In other words, does the event refer to something in the list of demand factors or supply factors?

Step 3. Decide whether the effect on demand or supply causes the curve to shift to the right or to the left, and sketch the new demand or supply curve on the diagram. In other words, does the event increase or decrease the amount consumers want to buy or producers want to sell?

Step 4. Identify the new equilibrium and then compare the original equilibrium price and quantity to the new equilibrium price and quantity.

Let's consider one example that involves a shift in supply and one that involves a shift in demand. Then we will consider an example where both supply and demand shift.

## Good Weather for Salmon Fishing

Supposed that during the summer of 2015, weather conditions were excellent for commercial salmon fishing off the California coast. Heavy rains meant higher than normal levels of water in the rivers, which helps the salmon to breed. Slightly cooler ocean temperatures stimulated the growth of plankton, the microscopic organisms at the bottom of the ocean food chain, providing everything in the ocean with a hearty food supply. The ocean stayed calm during fishing season, so commercial fishing operations did not lose many days to bad weather. How did these climate conditions affect the quantity and price of salmon? **Figure 3.16** illustrates the four-step approach, which we explain below, to work through this problem. **Table 3.6** also provides the information to work the problem.

**Figure 3.16 Good Weather for Salmon Fishing: The Four-Step Process**   Unusually good weather leads to changes in the price and quantity of salmon.

| Price per Pound | Quantity Supplied in 2014 | Quantity Supplied in 2015 | Quantity Demanded |
|---|---|---|---|
| $2.00 | 80 | 400 | 840 |
| $2.25 | 120 | 480 | 680 |
| $2.50 | 160 | 550 | 550 |
| $2.75 | 200 | 600 | 450 |
| $3.00 | 230 | 640 | 350 |
| $3.25 | 250 | 670 | 250 |

**Table 3.6 Salmon Fishing**

| Price per Pound | Quantity Supplied in 2014 | Quantity Supplied in 2015 | Quantity Demanded |
|---|---|---|---|
| $3.50 | 270 | 700 | 200 |

Table 3.6 Salmon Fishing

Step 1. Draw a demand and supply model to illustrate the market for salmon in the year before the good weather conditions began. The demand curve $D_0$ and the supply curve $S_0$ show that the original equilibrium price is $3.25 per pound and the original equilibrium quantity is 250,000 fish. (This price per pound is what commercial buyers pay at the fishing docks. What consumers pay at the grocery is higher.)

Step 2. Did the economic event affect supply or demand? Good weather is an example of a natural condition that affects supply.

Step 3. Was the effect on supply an increase or a decrease? Good weather is a change in natural conditions that increases the quantity supplied at any given price. The supply curve shifts to the right, moving from the original supply curve $S_0$ to the new supply curve $S_1$, which **Figure 3.16** and **Table 3.6** show.

Step 4. Compare the new equilibrium price and quantity to the original equilibrium. At the new equilibrium $E_1$, the equilibrium price falls from $3.25 to $2.50, but the equilibrium quantity increases from 250,000 to 550,000 salmon. Notice that the equilibrium quantity demanded increased, even though the demand curve did not move.

In short, good weather conditions increased supply of the California commercial salmon. The result was a higher equilibrium quantity of salmon bought and sold in the market at a lower price.

## Newspapers and the Internet

According to the Pew Research Center for People and the Press, increasingly more people, especially younger people, are obtaining their news from online and digital sources. The majority of U.S. adults now own smartphones or tablets, and most of those Americans say they use them in part to access the news. From 2004 to 2012, the share of Americans who reported obtaining their news from digital sources increased from 24% to 39%. How has this affected consumption of print news media, and radio and television news? **Figure 3.17** and the text below illustrates using the four-step analysis to answer this question.

**Figure 3.17 The Print News Market: A Four-Step Analysis** A change in tastes from print news sources to digital sources results in a leftward shift in demand for the former. The result is a decrease in both equilibrium price and quantity.

Step 1. Develop a demand and supply model to think about what the market looked like before the event. The demand curve $D_0$ and the supply curve $S_0$ show the original relationships. In this case, we perform the analysis without specific numbers on the price and quantity axis.

Step 2. Did the described change affect supply or demand? A change in tastes, from traditional news sources (print, radio, and television) to digital sources, caused a change in demand for the former.

Step 3. Was the effect on demand positive or negative? A shift to digital news sources will tend to mean a lower quantity demanded of traditional news sources at every given price, causing the demand curve for print and other traditional news sources to shift to the left, from $D_0$ to $D_1$.

Step 4. Compare the new equilibrium price and quantity to the original equilibrium price. The new equilibrium ($E_1$) occurs at a lower quantity and a lower price than the original equilibrium ($E_0$).

The decline in print news reading predates 2004. Print newspaper circulation peaked in 1973 and has declined since then due to competition from television and radio news. In 1991, 55% of Americans indicated they received their news from print sources, while only 29% did so in 2012. Radio news has followed a similar path in recent decades, with the share of Americans obtaining their news from radio declining from 54% in 1991 to 33% in 2012. Television news has held its own over the last 15 years, with a market share staying in the mid to upper fifties. What does this suggest for the future, given that two-thirds of Americans under 30 years old say they do not obtain their news from television at all?

## The Interconnections and Speed of Adjustment in Real Markets

In the real world, many factors that affect demand and supply can change all at once. For example, the demand for cars might increase because of rising incomes and population, and it might decrease because of rising gasoline prices (a complementary good). Likewise, the supply of cars might increase because of innovative new technologies that reduce the cost of car production, and it might decrease as a result of new government regulations requiring the installation of costly pollution-control technology.

Moreover, rising incomes and population or changes in gasoline prices will affect many markets, not just cars. How can an economist sort out all these interconnected events? The answer lies in the *ceteris paribus* assumption. Look at how each economic event affects each market, one event at a time, holding all else constant. Then combine the analyses to see the net effect.

## A Combined Example

The U.S. Postal Service is facing difficult challenges. Compensation for postal workers tends to increase most years due to cost-of-living increases. At the same time, increasingly more people are using email, text, and other digital message forms such as Facebook and Twitter to communicate with friends and others. What does this suggest about the continued viability of the Postal Service? **Figure 3.18** and the text below illustrate this using the four-step analysis to answer this question.

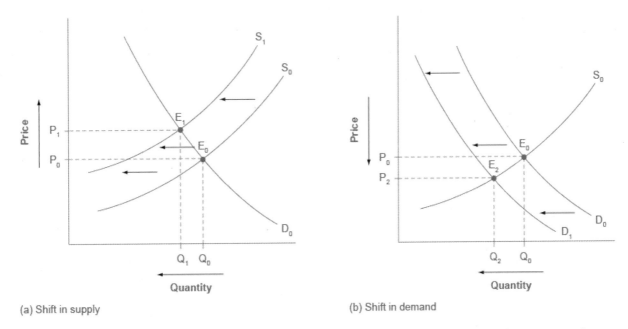

(a) Shift in supply

(b) Shift in demand

**Figure 3.18 Higher Compensation for Postal Workers: A Four-Step Analysis** (a) Higher labor compensation causes a leftward shift in the supply curve, a decrease in the equilibrium quantity, and an increase in the equilibrium price. (b) A change in tastes away from Postal Services causes a leftward shift in the demand curve, a decrease in the equilibrium quantity, and a decrease in the equilibrium price.

Since this problem involves two disturbances, we need two four-step analyses, the first to analyze the effects of higher compensation for postal workers, the second to analyze the effects of many people switching from "snail mail" to email and other digital messages.

**Figure 3.18** (a) shows the shift in supply discussed in the following steps.

Step 1. Draw a demand and supply model to illustrate what the market for the U.S. Postal Service looked like before this scenario starts. The demand curve $D_0$ and the supply curve $S_0$ show the original relationships.

Step 2. Did the described change affect supply or demand? Labor compensation is a cost of production. A change in production costs caused a change in supply for the Postal Service.

Step 3. Was the effect on supply positive or negative? Higher labor compensation leads to a lower quantity supplied of postal services at every given price, causing the supply curve for postal services to shift to the left, from $S_0$ to $S_1$.

Step 4. Compare the new equilibrium price and quantity to the original equilibrium price. The new equilibrium ($E_1$) occurs at a lower quantity and a higher price than the original equilibrium ($E_0$).

**Figure 3.18** (b) shows the shift in demand in the following steps.

Step 1. Draw a demand and supply model to illustrate what the market for U.S. Postal Services looked like before this scenario starts. The demand curve $D_0$ and the supply curve $S_0$ show the original relationships. Note that this diagram is independent from the diagram in panel (a).

Step 2. Did the change described affect supply or demand? A change in tastes away from snail mail toward digital messages will cause a change in demand for the Postal Service.

Step 3. Was the effect on demand positive or negative? A change in tastes away from snailmail toward digital messages causes lower quantity demanded of postal services at every given price, causing the demand curve for postal services to shift to the left, from $D_0$ to $D_1$.

Step 4. Compare the new equilibrium price and quantity to the original equilibrium price. The new equilibrium ($E_2$) occurs at a lower quantity and a lower price than the original equilibrium ($E_0$).

The final step in a scenario where both supply and demand shift is to combine the two individual analyses to determine what happens to the equilibrium quantity and price. Graphically, we superimpose the previous two diagrams one on top of the other, as in **Figure 3.19**.

**Figure 3.19 Combined Effect of Decreased Demand and Decreased Supply**   Supply and demand shifts cause changes in equilibrium price and quantity.

Following are the results:

Effect on Quantity: The effect of higher labor compensation on Postal Services because it raises the cost of production is to decrease the equilibrium quantity. The effect of a change in tastes away from snail mail is to decrease the equilibrium quantity. Since both shifts are to the left, the overall impact is a decrease in the equilibrium quantity of Postal Services ($Q_3$). This is easy to see graphically, since $Q_3$ is to the left of $Q_0$.

Effect on Price: The overall effect on price is more complicated. The effect of higher labor compensation on Postal Services, because it raises the cost of production, is to increase the equilibrium price. The effect of a change in tastes away from snail mail is to decrease the equilibrium price. Since the two effects are in opposite directions, unless we know the magnitudes of the two effects, the overall effect is unclear. This is not unusual. When both curves shift, typically we can determine the overall effect on price or on quantity, but not on both. In this case, we determined the overall effect on the equilibrium quantity, but not on the equilibrium price. In other cases, it might be the opposite.

The next Clear It Up feature focuses on the difference between shifts of supply or demand and movements along a curve.

# Clear It Up

## What is the difference between shifts of demand or supply versus movements along a demand or supply curve?

One common mistake in applying the demand and supply framework is to confuse the shift of a demand or a supply curve with movement along a demand or supply curve. As an example, consider a problem that asks whether a drought will increase or decrease the equilibrium quantity and equilibrium price of wheat. Lee, a student in an introductory economics class, might reason:

"Well, it is clear that a drought reduces supply, so I will shift back the supply curve, as in the shift from the original supply curve $S_0$ to $S_1$ on the diagram (Shift 1). The equilibrium moves from $E_0$ to $E_1$, the equilibrium quantity is lower and the equilibrium price is higher. Then, a higher price makes farmers more likely to supply the good, so the supply curve shifts right, as shows the shift from $S_1$ to $S_2$, shows on the diagram (Shift 2), so that the equilibrium now moves from $E_1$ to $E_2$. The higher price, however, also reduces demand and so causes demand to shift back, like the shift from the original demand curve, $D_0$ to $D_1$ on the diagram (labeled

Shift 3), and the equilibrium moves from $E_2$ to $E_3$."

**Figure 3.20 Shifts of Demand or Supply versus Movements along a Demand or Supply Curve** A shift in one curve never causes a shift in the other curve. Rather, a shift in one curve causes a movement along the second curve.

At about this point, Lee suspects that this answer is headed down the wrong path. Think about what might be wrong with Lee's logic, and then read the answer that follows.

*Answer:* Lee's first step is correct: that is, a drought shifts back the supply curve of wheat and leads to a prediction of a lower equilibrium quantity and a higher equilibrium price. This corresponds to a movement along the original demand curve ($D_0$), from $E_0$ to $E_1$. The rest of Lee's argument is wrong, because it mixes up shifts in supply with quantity supplied, and shifts in demand with quantity demanded. A higher or lower price never shifts the supply curve, as suggested by the shift in supply from $S_1$ to $S_2$. Instead, a price change leads to a movement along a given supply curve. Similarly, a higher or lower price never shifts a demand curve, as suggested in the shift from $D_0$ to $D_1$. Instead, a price change leads to a movement along a given demand curve. Remember, a change in the price of a good never causes the demand or supply curve for that good to shift.

Think carefully about the timeline of events: What happens first, what happens next? What is cause, what is effect? If you keep the order right, you are more likely to get the analysis correct.

In the four-step analysis of how economic events affect equilibrium price and quantity, the movement from the old to the new equilibrium seems immediate. As a practical matter, however, prices and quantities often do not zoom straight to equilibrium. More realistically, when an economic event causes demand or supply to shift, prices and quantities set off in the general direction of equilibrium. Even as they are moving toward one new equilibrium, a subsequent change in demand or supply often pushes prices toward another equilibrium.

# 3.4 | Price Ceilings and Price Floors

By the end of this section, you will be able to:
- Explain price controls, price ceilings, and price floors
- Analyze demand and supply as a social adjustment mechanism

To this point in the chapter, we have been assuming that markets are free, that is, they operate with no government intervention. In this section, we will explore the outcomes, both anticipated and otherwise, when government does intervene in a market either to prevent the price of some good or service from rising "too high" or to prevent the price of some good or service from falling "too low".

Economists believe there are a small number of fundamental principles that explain how economic agents respond in different situations. Two of these principles, which we have already introduced, are the laws of demand and supply.

Governments can pass laws affecting market outcomes, but no law can negate these economic principles. Rather, the principles will become apparent in sometimes unexpected ways, which may undermine the intent of the government policy. This is one of the major conclusions of this section.

Controversy sometimes surrounds the prices and quantities established by demand and supply, especially for products that are considered necessities. In some cases, discontent over prices turns into public pressure on politicians, who may then pass legislation to prevent a certain price from climbing "too high" or falling "too low."

The demand and supply model shows how people and firms will react to the incentives that these laws provide to control prices, in ways that will often lead to undesirable consequences. Alternative policy tools can often achieve the desired goals of price control laws, while avoiding at least some of their costs and tradeoffs.

## Price Ceilings

Laws that government enact to regulate prices are called **price controls**. Price controls come in two flavors. A **price ceiling** keeps a price from rising above a certain level (the "ceiling"), while a **price floor** keeps a price from falling below a given level (the "floor"). This section uses the demand and supply framework to analyze price ceilings. The next section discusses price floors.

A price ceiling is a legal maximum price that one pays for some good or service. A government imposes price ceilings in order to keep the price of some necessary good or service affordable. For example, in 2005 during Hurricane Katrina, the price of bottled water increased above $5 per gallon. As a result, many people called for price controls on bottled water to prevent the price from rising so high. In this particular case, the government did not impose a price ceiling, but there are other examples of where price ceilings did occur.

In many markets for goods and services, demanders outnumber suppliers. Consumers, who are also potential voters, sometimes unite behind a political proposal to hold down a certain price. In some cities, such as Albany, renters have pressed political leaders to pass rent control laws, a price ceiling that usually works by stating that landlords can raise rents by only a certain maximum percentage each year. Some of the best examples of rent control occur in urban areas such as New York, Washington D.C., or San Francisco.

Rent control becomes a politically hot topic when rents begin to rise rapidly. Everyone needs an affordable place to live. Perhaps a change in tastes makes a certain suburb or town a more popular place to live. Perhaps locally-based businesses expand, bringing higher incomes and more people into the area. Such changes can cause a change in the demand for rental housing, as **Figure 3.21** illustrates. The original equilibrium ($E_0$) lies at the intersection of supply curve $S_0$ and demand curve $D_0$, corresponding to an equilibrium price of $500 and an equilibrium quantity of 15,000 units of rental housing. The effect of greater income or a change in tastes is to shift the demand curve for rental housing to the right, as the data in **Table 3.7** shows and the shift from $D_0$ to $D_1$ on the graph. In this market, at the new equilibrium $E_1$, the price of a rental unit would rise to $600 and the equilibrium quantity would increase to 17,000 units.

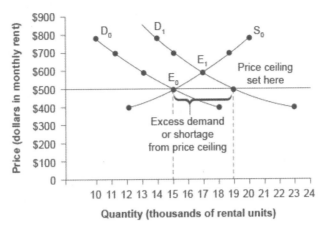

**Figure 3.21 A Price Ceiling Example—Rent Control** The original intersection of demand and supply occurs at $E_0$. If demand shifts from $D_0$ to $D_1$, the new equilibrium would be at $E_1$—unless a price ceiling prevents the price from rising. If the price is not permitted to rise, the quantity supplied remains at 15,000. However, after the change in demand, the quantity demanded rises to 19,000, resulting in a shortage.

| Price | Original Quantity Supplied | Original Quantity Demanded | New Quantity Demanded |
|-------|---------------------------|----------------------------|------------------------|
| $400 | 12,000 | 18,000 | 23,000 |
| $500 | 15,000 | 15,000 | 19,000 |
| $600 | 17,000 | 13,000 | 17,000 |
| $700 | 19,000 | 11,000 | 15,000 |
| $800 | 20,000 | 10,000 | 14,000 |

**Table 3.7 Rent Control**

Suppose that a city government passes a rent control law to keep the price at the original equilibrium of $500 for a typical apartment. In **Figure 3.21**, the horizontal line at the price of $500 shows the legally fixed maximum price set by the rent control law. However, the underlying forces that shifted the demand curve to the right are still there. At that price ($500), the quantity supplied remains at the same 15,000 rental units, but the quantity demanded is 19,000 rental units. In other words, the quantity demanded exceeds the quantity supplied, so there is a shortage of rental housing. One of the ironies of price ceilings is that while the price ceiling was intended to help renters, there are actually fewer apartments rented out under the price ceiling (15,000 rental units) than would be the case at the market rent of $600 (17,000 rental units).

Price ceilings do not simply benefit renters at the expense of landlords. Rather, some renters (or potential renters) lose their housing as landlords convert apartments to co-ops and condos. Even when the housing remains in the rental market, landlords tend to spend less on maintenance and on essentials like heating, cooling, hot water, and lighting. The first rule of economics is you do not get something for nothing—everything has an opportunity cost. Thus, if renters obtain "cheaper" housing than the market requires, they tend to also end up with lower quality housing.

Price ceilings are enacted in an attempt to keep prices low for those who need the product. However, when the market price is not allowed to rise to the equilibrium level, quantity demanded exceeds quantity supplied, and thus a shortage occurs. Those who manage to purchase the product at the lower price given by the price ceiling will benefit, but sellers of the product will suffer, along with those who are not able to purchase the product at all. Quality is also likely to deteriorate.

## Price Floors

A price floor is the lowest price that one can legally pay for some good or service. Perhaps the best-known example of a price floor is the minimum wage, which is based on the view that someone working full time should be able to afford a basic standard of living. The federal minimum wage in 2016 was $7.25 per hour, although some states and localities have a higher minimum wage. The federal minimum wage yields an annual income for a single person of $15,080, which is slightly higher than the Federal poverty line of $11,880. As the cost of living rises over time, the Congress periodically raises the federal minimum wage.

Price floors are sometimes called "price supports," because they support a price by preventing it from falling below a certain level. Around the world, many countries have passed laws to create agricultural price supports. Farm prices and thus farm incomes fluctuate, sometimes widely. Even if, on average, farm incomes are adequate, some years they can be quite low. The purpose of price supports is to prevent these swings.

The most common way price supports work is that the government enters the market and buys up the product, adding to demand to keep prices higher than they otherwise would be. According to the Common Agricultural Policy reform passed in 2013, the European Union (EU) will spend about 60 billion euros per year, or 67 billion dollars per year (with the November 2016 exchange rate), or roughly 38% of the EU budget, on price supports for Europe's farmers from 2014 to 2020.

**Figure 3.22** illustrates the effects of a government program that assures a price above the equilibrium by focusing on the market for wheat in Europe. In the absence of government intervention, the price would adjust so that the quantity supplied would equal the quantity demanded at the equilibrium point $E_0$, with price $P_0$ and quantity $Q_0$. However, policies to keep prices high for farmers keeps the price above what would have been the market equilibrium level—the price Pf shown by the dashed horizontal line in the diagram. The result is a quantity supplied in excess of the quantity demanded (Qd). When quantity supplied exceeds quantity demanded, a surplus exists.

Economists estimate that the high-income areas of the world, including the United States, Europe, and Japan, spend roughly $1 billion per day in supporting their farmers. If the government is willing to purchase the excess supply (or to provide payments for others to purchase it), then farmers will benefit from the price floor, but taxpayers and consumers of food will pay the costs. Agricultural economists and policy makers have offered numerous proposals for reducing farm subsidies. In many countries, however, political support for subsidies for farmers remains strong. This is either because the population views this as supporting the traditional rural way of life or because of industry's lobbying power of the agro-business.

**Figure 3.22 European Wheat Prices: A Price Floor Example**   The intersection of demand (D) and supply (S) would be at the equilibrium point $E_0$. However, a price floor set at Pf holds the price above $E_0$ and prevents it from falling. The result of the price floor is that the quantity supplied Qs exceeds the quantity demanded Qd. There is excess supply, also called a surplus.

# 3.5 | Demand, Supply, and Efficiency

By the end of this section, you will be able to:

- Contrast consumer surplus, producer surplus, and social surplus
- Explain why price floors and price ceilings can be inefficient
- Analyze demand and supply as a social adjustment mechanism

The familiar demand and supply diagram holds within it the concept of economic efficiency. One typical way that economists define efficiency is when it is impossible to improve the situation of one party without imposing a cost on another. Conversely, if a situation is inefficient, it becomes possible to benefit at least one party without imposing costs on others.

Efficiency in the demand and supply model has the same basic meaning: The economy is getting as much benefit as possible from its scarce resources and all the possible gains from trade have been achieved. In other words, the optimal amount of each good and service is produced and consumed.

## Consumer Surplus, Producer Surplus, Social Surplus

Consider a market for tablet computers, as **Figure 3.23** shows. The equilibrium price is $80 and the equilibrium quantity is 28 million. To see the benefits to consumers, look at the segment of the demand curve above the equilibrium point and to the left. This portion of the demand curve shows that at least some demanders would have been willing to pay more than $80 for a tablet.

For example, point J shows that if the price were $90, 20 million tablets would be sold. Those consumers who would have been willing to pay $90 for a tablet based on the utility they expect to receive from it, but who were able to pay the equilibrium price of $80, clearly received a benefit beyond what they had to pay. Remember, the demand curve traces consumers' willingness to pay for different quantities. The amount that individuals would have been willing to pay, minus the amount that they actually paid, is called **consumer surplus**. Consumer surplus is the area labeled F—that is, the area above the market price and below the demand curve.

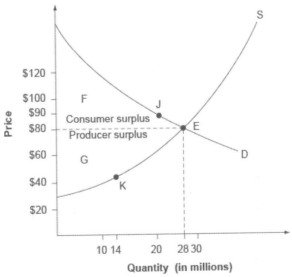

**Figure 3.23 Consumer and Producer Surplus**   The somewhat triangular area labeled by F shows the area of consumer surplus, which shows that the equilibrium price in the market was less than what many of the consumers were willing to pay. Point J on the demand curve shows that, even at the price of $90, consumers would have been willing to purchase a quantity of 20 million. The somewhat triangular area labeled by G shows the area of producer surplus, which shows that the equilibrium price received in the market was more than what many of the producers were willing to accept for their products. For example, point K on the supply curve shows that at a price of $45, firms would have been willing to supply a quantity of 14 million.

The supply curve shows the quantity that firms are willing to supply at each price. For example, point K in **Figure**

3.23 illustrates that, at $45, firms would still have been willing to supply a quantity of 14 million. Those producers who would have been willing to supply the tablets at $45, but who were instead able to charge the equilibrium price of $80, clearly received an extra benefit beyond what they required to supply the product. The amount that a seller is paid for a good minus the seller's actual cost is called **producer surplus**. In **Figure 3.23**, producer surplus is the area labeled G—that is, the area between the market price and the segment of the supply curve below the equilibrium.

The sum of consumer surplus and producer surplus is **social surplus**, also referred to as **economic surplus** or **total surplus**. In **Figure 3.23** we show social surplus as the area F + G. Social surplus is larger at equilibrium quantity and price than it would be at any other quantity. This demonstrates the economic efficiency of the market equilibrium. In addition, at the efficient level of output, it is impossible to produce greater consumer surplus without reducing producer surplus, and it is impossible to produce greater producer surplus without reducing consumer surplus.

## Inefficiency of Price Floors and Price Ceilings

The imposition of a price floor or a price ceiling will prevent a market from adjusting to its equilibrium price and quantity, and thus will create an inefficient outcome. However, there is an additional twist here. Along with creating inefficiency, price floors and ceilings will also transfer some consumer surplus to producers, or some producer surplus to consumers.

Imagine that several firms develop a promising but expensive new drug for treating back pain. If this therapy is left to the market, the equilibrium price will be $600 per month and 20,000 people will use the drug, as shown in **Figure 3.24** (a). The original level of consumer surplus is T + U and producer surplus is V + W + X. However, the government decides to impose a price ceiling of $400 to make the drug more affordable. At this price ceiling, firms in the market now produce only 15,000.

As a result, two changes occur. First, an inefficient outcome occurs and the total surplus of society is reduced. The loss in social surplus that occurs when the economy produces at an inefficient quantity is called **deadweight loss**. In a very real sense, it is like money thrown away that benefits no one. In **Figure 3.24** (a), the deadweight loss is the area U + W. When deadweight loss exists, it is possible for both consumer and producer surplus to be higher, in this case because the price control is blocking some suppliers and demanders from transactions they would both be willing to make.

A second change from the price ceiling is that some of the producer surplus is transferred to consumers. After the price ceiling is imposed, the new consumer surplus is T + V, while the new producer surplus is X. In other words, the price ceiling transfers the area of surplus (V) from producers to consumers. Note that the gain to consumers is less than the loss to producers, which is just another way of seeing the deadweight loss.

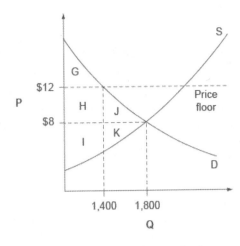

(a) Reduced social surplus from a price ceiling

(b) Reduced social surplus from a price floor

**Figure 3.24 Efficiency and Price Floors and Ceilings** (a) The original equilibrium price is $600 with a quantity of 20,000. Consumer surplus is T + U, and producer surplus is V + W + X. A price ceiling is imposed at $400, so firms in the market now produce only a quantity of 15,000. As a result, the new consumer surplus is T + V, while the new producer surplus is X. (b) The original equilibrium is $8 at a quantity of 1,800. Consumer surplus is G + H + J, and producer surplus is I + K. A price floor is imposed at $12, which means that quantity demanded falls to 1,400. As a result, the new consumer surplus is G, and the new producer surplus is H + I.

**Figure 3.24** (b) shows a price floor example using a string of struggling movie theaters, all in the same city. The current equilibrium is $8 per movie ticket, with 1,800 people attending movies. The original consumer surplus is G + H + J, and producer surplus is I + K. The city government is worried that movie theaters will go out of business, reducing the entertainment options available to citizens, so it decides to impose a price floor of $12 per ticket. As a result, the quantity demanded of movie tickets falls to 1,400. The new consumer surplus is G, and the new producer surplus is H + I. In effect, the price floor causes the area H to be transferred from consumer to producer surplus, but also causes a deadweight loss of J + K.

This analysis shows that a price ceiling, like a law establishing rent controls, will transfer some producer surplus to consumers—which helps to explain why consumers often favor them. Conversely, a price floor like a guarantee that farmers will receive a certain price for their crops will transfer some consumer surplus to producers, which explains why producers often favor them. However, both price floors and price ceilings block some transactions that buyers and sellers would have been willing to make, and creates deadweight loss. Removing such barriers, so that prices and quantities can adjust to their equilibrium level, will increase the economy's social surplus.

## Demand and Supply as a Social Adjustment Mechanism

The demand and supply model emphasizes that prices are not set only by demand or only by supply, but by the interaction between the two. In 1890, the famous economist Alfred Marshall wrote that asking whether supply or demand determined a price was like arguing "whether it is the upper or the under blade of a pair of scissors that cuts a piece of paper." The answer is that both blades of the demand and supply scissors are always involved.

The adjustments of equilibrium price and quantity in a market-oriented economy often occur without much government direction or oversight. If the coffee crop in Brazil suffers a terrible frost, then the supply curve of coffee shifts to the left and the price of coffee rises. Some people—call them the coffee addicts—continue to drink coffee and pay the higher price. Others switch to tea or soft drinks. No government commission is needed to figure out how to adjust coffee prices, which companies will be allowed to process the remaining supply, which supermarkets in which cities will get how much coffee to sell, or which consumers will ultimately be allowed to drink the brew. Such adjustments in response to price changes happen all the time in a market economy, often so smoothly and rapidly that we barely notice them.

Think for a moment of all the seasonal foods that are available and inexpensive at certain times of the year, like fresh corn in midsummer, but more expensive at other times of the year. People alter their diets and restaurants alter their menus in response to these fluctuations in prices without fuss or fanfare. For both the U.S. economy and the world economy as a whole, markets—that is, demand and supply—are the primary social mechanism for answering the basic questions about what is produced, how it is produced, and for whom it is produced.

## Bring it Home

### Why Can We Not Get Enough of Organic?

Organic food is grown without synthetic pesticides, chemical fertilizers or genetically modified seeds. In recent decades, the demand for organic products has increased dramatically. The Organic Trade Association reported sales increased from $1 billion in 1990 to $35.1 billion in 2013, more than 90% of which were sales of food products.

Why, then, are organic foods more expensive than their conventional counterparts? The answer is a clear application of the theories of supply and demand. As people have learned more about the harmful effects of chemical fertilizers, growth hormones, pesticides and the like from large-scale factory farming, our tastes and preferences for safer, organic foods have increased. This change in tastes has been reinforced by increases in income, which allow people to purchase pricier products, and has made organic foods more mainstream. This has led to an increased demand for organic foods. Graphically, the demand curve has shifted right, and we have moved up the supply curve as producers have responded to the higher prices by supplying a greater quantity.

In addition to the movement along the supply curve, we have also had an increase in the number of farmers converting to organic farming over time. This is represented by a shift to the right of the supply curve. Since both demand and supply have shifted to the right, the resulting equilibrium quantity of organic foods is definitely higher, but the price will only fall when the increase in supply is larger than the increase in demand. We may need more time before we see lower prices in organic foods. Since the production costs of these foods may remain higher than conventional farming, because organic fertilizers and pest management techniques are more expensive, they may never fully catch up with the lower prices of non-organic foods.

As a final, specific example: The Environmental Working Group's "Dirty Dozen" list of fruits and vegetables, which test high for pesticide residue even after washing, was released in April 2013. The inclusion of strawberries on the list has led to an increase in demand for organic strawberries, resulting in both a higher equilibrium price and quantity of sales.

# KEY TERMS

**ceteris paribus**  other things being equal

**complements**  goods that are often used together so that consumption of one good tends to enhance consumption of the other

**consumer surplus**  the extra benefit consumers receive from buying a good or service, measured by what the individuals would have been willing to pay minus the amount that they actually paid

**deadweight loss**  the loss in social surplus that occurs when a market produces an inefficient quantity

**demand**  the relationship between price and the quantity demanded of a certain good or service

**demand curve**  a graphic representation of the relationship between price and quantity demanded of a certain good or service, with quantity on the horizontal axis and the price on the vertical axis

**demand schedule**  a table that shows a range of prices for a certain good or service and the quantity demanded at each price

**economic surplus**  see social surplus

**equilibrium**  the situation where quantity demanded is equal to the quantity supplied; the combination of price and quantity where there is no economic pressure from surpluses or shortages that would cause price or quantity to change

**equilibrium price**  the price where quantity demanded is equal to quantity supplied

**equilibrium quantity**  the quantity at which quantity demanded and quantity supplied are equal for a certain price level

**excess demand**  at the existing price, the quantity demanded exceeds the quantity supplied; also called a shortage

**excess supply**  at the existing price, quantity supplied exceeds the quantity demanded; also called a surplus

**factors of production**  the resources such as labor, materials, and machinery that are used to produce goods and services; also called inputs

**inferior good**  a good in which the quantity demanded falls as income rises, and in which quantity demanded rises and income falls

**inputs**  the resources such as labor, materials, and machinery that are used to produce goods and services; also called factors of production

**law of demand**  the common relationship that a higher price leads to a lower quantity demanded of a certain good or service and a lower price leads to a higher quantity demanded, while all other variables are held constant

**law of supply**  the common relationship that a higher price leads to a greater quantity supplied and a lower price leads to a lower quantity supplied, while all other variables are held constant

**normal good**  a good in which the quantity demanded rises as income rises, and in which quantity demanded falls as income falls

**price**  what a buyer pays for a unit of the specific good or service

**price ceiling**  a legal maximum price

**price control**  government laws to regulate prices instead of letting market forces determine prices

**price floor**  a legal minimum price

**producer surplus**  the extra benefit producers receive from selling a good or service, measured by the price the producer actually received minus the price the producer would have been willing to accept

**quantity demanded**  the total number of units of a good or service consumers are willing to purchase at a given price

**quantity supplied**  the total number of units of a good or service producers are willing to sell at a given price

**shift in demand**  when a change in some economic factor (other than price) causes a different quantity to be demanded at every price

**shift in supply**  when a change in some economic factor (other than price) causes a different quantity to be supplied at every price

**shortage**  at the existing price, the quantity demanded exceeds the quantity supplied; also called excess demand

**social surplus**  the sum of consumer surplus and producer surplus

**substitute**  a good that can replace another to some extent, so that greater consumption of one good can mean less of the other

**supply**  the relationship between price and the quantity supplied of a certain good or service

**supply curve**  a line that shows the relationship between price and quantity supplied on a graph, with quantity supplied on the horizontal axis and price on the vertical axis

**supply schedule**  a table that shows a range of prices for a good or service and the quantity supplied at each price

**surplus**  at the existing price, quantity supplied exceeds the quantity demanded; also called excess supply

**total surplus**  see social surplus

## KEY CONCEPTS AND SUMMARY

### 3.1 Demand, Supply, and Equilibrium in Markets for Goods and Services

A demand schedule is a table that shows the quantity demanded at different prices in the market. A demand curve shows the relationship between quantity demanded and price in a given market on a graph. The law of demand states that a higher price typically leads to a lower quantity demanded.

A supply schedule is a table that shows the quantity supplied at different prices in the market. A supply curve shows the relationship between quantity supplied and price on a graph. The law of supply says that a higher price typically leads to a higher quantity supplied.

The equilibrium price and equilibrium quantity occur where the supply and demand curves cross. The equilibrium occurs where the quantity demanded is equal to the quantity supplied. If the price is below the equilibrium level, then the quantity demanded will exceed the quantity supplied. Excess demand or a shortage will exist. If the price is above the equilibrium level, then the quantity supplied will exceed the quantity demanded. Excess supply or a surplus will exist. In either case, economic pressures will push the price toward the equilibrium level.

### 3.2 Shifts in Demand and Supply for Goods and Services

Economists often use the *ceteris paribus* or "other things being equal" assumption: while examining the economic impact of one event, all other factors remain unchanged for analysis purposes. Factors that can shift the demand curve for goods and services, causing a different quantity to be demanded at any given price, include changes in tastes, population, income, prices of substitute or complement goods, and expectations about future conditions and prices. Factors that can shift the supply curve for goods and services, causing a different quantity to be supplied at any given price, include input prices, natural conditions, changes in technology, and government taxes, regulations, or subsidies.

### 3.3 Changes in Equilibrium Price and Quantity: The Four-Step Process

When using the supply and demand framework to think about how an event will affect the equilibrium price and quantity, proceed through four steps: (1) sketch a supply and demand diagram to think about what the market looked like before the event; (2) decide whether the event will affect supply or demand; (3) decide whether the effect on supply or demand is negative or positive, and draw the appropriate shifted supply or demand curve; (4) compare the new equilibrium price and quantity to the original ones.

### 3.4 Price Ceilings and Price Floors

Price ceilings prevent a price from rising above a certain level. When a price ceiling is set below the equilibrium price, quantity demanded will exceed quantity supplied, and excess demand or shortages will result. Price floors prevent a price from falling below a certain level. When a price floor is set above the equilibrium price, quantity supplied will exceed quantity demanded, and excess supply or surpluses will result. Price floors and price ceilings often lead to unintended consequences.

### 3.5 Demand, Supply, and Efficiency

Consumer surplus is the gap between the price that consumers are willing to pay, based on their preferences, and the market equilibrium price. Producer surplus is the gap between the price for which producers are willing to sell a product, based on their costs, and the market equilibrium price. Social surplus is the sum of consumer surplus and producer surplus. Total surplus is larger at the equilibrium quantity and price than it will be at any other quantity and price. Deadweight loss is loss in total surplus that occurs when the economy produces at an inefficient quantity.

## SELF-CHECK QUESTIONS

**1.** Review **Figure 3.4**. Suppose the price of gasoline is $1.60 per gallon. Is the quantity demanded higher or lower than at the equilibrium price of $1.40 per gallon? What about the quantity supplied? Is there a shortage or a surplus in the market? If so, how much?

**2.** Why do economists use the *ceteris paribus* assumption?

**3.** In an analysis of the market for paint, an economist discovers the facts listed below. State whether each of these changes will affect supply or demand, and in what direction.
   a.  There have recently been some important cost-saving inventions in the technology for making paint.
   b.  Paint is lasting longer, so that property owners need not repaint as often.
   c.  Because of severe hailstorms, many people need to repaint now.
   d.  The hailstorms damaged several factories that make paint, forcing them to close down for several months.

**4.** Many changes are affecting the market for oil. Predict how each of the following events will affect the equilibrium price and quantity in the market for oil. In each case, state how the event will affect the supply and demand diagram. Create a sketch of the diagram if necessary.
   a.  Cars are becoming more fuel efficient, and therefore get more miles to the gallon.
   b.  The winter is exceptionally cold.
   c.  A major discovery of new oil is made off the coast of Norway.
   d.  The economies of some major oil-using nations, like Japan, slow down.
   e.  A war in the Middle East disrupts oil-pumping schedules.
   f.  Landlords install additional insulation in buildings.
   g.  The price of solar energy falls dramatically.
   h.  Chemical companies invent a new, popular kind of plastic made from oil.

**5.** Let's think about the market for air travel. From August 2014 to January 2015, the price of jet fuel increased roughly 47%. Using the four-step analysis, how do you think this fuel price increase affected the equilibrium price and quantity of air travel?

**6.** A tariff is a tax on imported goods. Suppose the U.S. government cuts the tariff on imported flat screen televisions. Using the four-step analysis, how do you think the tariff reduction will affect the equilibrium price and quantity of flat screen TVs?

**7.** What is the effect of a price ceiling on the quantity demanded of the product? What is the effect of a price ceiling on the quantity supplied? Why exactly does a price ceiling cause a shortage?

**8.** Does a price ceiling change the equilibrium price?

**9.** What would be the impact of imposing a price floor below the equilibrium price?

**10.** Does a price ceiling increase or decrease the number of transactions in a market? Why? What about a price floor?

**11.** If a price floor benefits producers, why does a price floor reduce social surplus?

## REVIEW QUESTIONS

**12.** What determines the level of prices in a market?

**13.** What does a downward-sloping demand curve mean about how buyers in a market will react to a higher price?

**14.** Will demand curves have the same exact shape in all markets? If not, how will they differ?

**15.** Will supply curves have the same shape in all markets? If not, how will they differ?

**16.** What is the relationship between quantity demanded and quantity supplied at equilibrium? What is the relationship when there is a shortage? What is the relationship when there is a surplus?

**17.** How can you locate the equilibrium point on a demand and supply graph?

**18.** If the price is above the equilibrium level, would you predict a surplus or a shortage? If the price is below the equilibrium level, would you predict a surplus or a shortage? Why?

**19.** When the price is above the equilibrium, explain how market forces move the market price to equilibrium. Do the same when the price is below the equilibrium.

**20.** What is the difference between the demand and the quantity demanded of a product, say milk? Explain in words and show the difference on a graph with a demand curve for milk.

**21.** What is the difference between the supply and the quantity supplied of a product, say milk? Explain in words and show the difference on a graph with the supply curve for milk.

**22.** When analyzing a market, how do economists deal with the problem that many factors that affect the market are changing at the same time?

**23.** Name some factors that can cause a shift in the demand curve in markets for goods and services.

**24.** Name some factors that can cause a shift in the supply curve in markets for goods and services.

**25.** How does one analyze a market where both demand and supply shift?

**26.** What causes a movement along the demand curve? What causes a movement along the supply curve?

**27.** Does a price ceiling attempt to make a price higher or lower?

**28.** How does a price ceiling set below the equilibrium level affect quantity demanded and quantity supplied?

**29.** Does a price floor attempt to make a price higher or lower?

**30.** How does a price floor set above the equilibrium level affect quantity demanded and quantity supplied?

**31.** What is consumer surplus? How is it illustrated on a demand and supply diagram?

**32.** What is producer surplus? How is it illustrated on a demand and supply diagram?

**33.** What is total surplus? How is it illustrated on a demand and supply diagram?

**34.** What is the relationship between total surplus and economic efficiency?

**35.** What is deadweight loss?

# CRITICAL THINKING QUESTIONS

**36.** Review **Figure 3.4**. Suppose the government decided that, since gasoline is a necessity, its price should be legally capped at $1.30 per gallon. What do you anticipate would be the outcome in the gasoline market?

**37.** Explain why the following statement is false: "In the goods market, no buyer would be willing to pay more than the equilibrium price."

**38.** Explain why the following statement is false: "In the goods market, no seller would be willing to sell for less than the equilibrium price."

**39.** Consider the demand for hamburgers. If the price of a substitute good (for example, hot dogs) increases and the price of a complement good (for example, hamburger buns) increases, can you tell for sure what will happen to the demand for hamburgers? Why or why not? Illustrate your answer with a graph.

**40.** How do you suppose the demographics of an aging population of "Baby Boomers" in the United States will affect the demand for milk? Justify your answer.

**41.** We know that a change in the price of a product causes a movement along the demand curve. Suppose consumers believe that prices will be rising in the future. How will that affect demand for the product in the present? Can you show this graphically?

**42.** Suppose there is a soda tax to curb obesity. What should a reduction in the soda tax do to the supply of sodas and to the equilibrium price and quantity? Can you show this graphically? *Hint*: Assume that the soda tax is collected from the sellers.

**43.** Use the four-step process to analyze the impact of the advent of the iPod (or other portable digital music players) on the equilibrium price and quantity of the Sony Walkman (or other portable audio cassette players).

## PROBLEMS

**52.** Review **Figure 3.4** again. Suppose the price of gasoline is $1.00. Will the quantity demanded be lower or higher than at the equilibrium price of $1.40 per gallon? Will the quantity supplied be lower or higher? Is there a shortage or a surplus in the market? If so, of how much?

**44.** Use the four-step process to analyze the impact of a reduction in tariffs on imports of iPods on the equilibrium price and quantity of Sony Walkman-type products.

**45.** Suppose both of these events took place at the same time. Combine your analyses of the impacts of the iPod and the tariff reduction to determine the likely impact on the equilibrium price and quantity of Sony Walkman-type products. Show your answer graphically.

**46.** Most government policy decisions have winners and losers. What are the effects of raising the minimum wage? It is more complex than simply producers lose and workers gain. Who are the winners and who are the losers, and what exactly do they win and lose? To what extent does the policy change achieve its goals?

**47.** Agricultural price supports result in governments holding large inventories of agricultural products. Why do you think the government cannot simply give the products away to poor people?

**48.** Can you propose a policy that would induce the market to supply more rental housing units?

**49.** What term would an economist use to describe what happens when a shopper gets a "good deal" on a product?

**50.** Explain why voluntary transactions improve social welfare.

**51.** Why would a free market never operate at a quantity greater than the equilibrium quantity? *Hint*: What would be required for a transaction to occur at that quantity?

**53.** **Table 3.8** shows information on the demand and supply for bicycles, where the quantities of bicycles are measured in thousands.

| Price | Qd | Qs |
|-------|-----|-----|
| $120 | 50 | 36 |
| $150 | 40 | 40 |
| $180 | 32 | 48 |
| $210 | 28 | 56 |
| $240 | 24 | 70 |

Table 3.8

a.  What is the quantity demanded and the quantity supplied at a price of $210?
b.  At what price is the quantity supplied equal to 48,000?
c.  Graph the demand and supply curve for bicycles. How can you determine the equilibrium price and quantity from the graph? How can you determine the equilibrium price and quantity from the table? What are the equilibrium price and equilibrium quantity?
d.  If the price was $120, what would the quantities demanded and supplied be? Would a shortage or surplus exist? If so, how large would the shortage or surplus be?

**54.** The computer market in recent years has seen many more computers sell at much lower prices. What shift in demand or supply is most likely to explain this outcome? Sketch a demand and supply diagram and explain your reasoning for each.
a.  A rise in demand
b.  A fall in demand
c.  A rise in supply
d.  A fall in supply

**55.** **Table 3.9** illustrates the market's demand and supply for cheddar cheese. Graph the data and find the equilibrium. Next, create a table showing the change in quantity demanded or quantity supplied, and a graph of the new equilibrium, in each of the following situations:

a.  The price of milk, a key input for cheese production, rises, so that the supply decreases by 80 pounds at every price.
b.  A new study says that eating cheese is good for your health, so that demand increases by 20% at every price.

| Price per Pound | Qd | Qs |
|-----------------|-----|-----|
| $3.00 | 750 | 540 |
| $3.20 | 700 | 600 |
| **$3.40** | **650** | **650** |
| $3.60 | 620 | 700 |
| $3.80 | 600 | 720 |
| $4.00 | 590 | 730 |

Table 3.9

**56.** **Table 3.10** shows the supply and demand for movie tickets in a city. Graph demand and supply and identify the equilibrium. Then calculate in a table and graph the effect of the following two changes.

a. Three new nightclubs open. They offer decent bands and have no cover charge, but make their money by selling food and drink. As a result, demand for movie tickets falls by six units at every price.

b. The city eliminates a tax that it placed on all local entertainment businesses. The result is that the quantity supplied of movies at any given price increases by 10%.

| Price per Pound | Qd | Qs |
|---|---|---|
| $5.00 | 26 | 16 |
| $6.00 | 24 | 18 |
| $7.00 | 22 | 20 |
| $8.00 | 21 | 21 |
| $9.00 | 20 | 22 |

Table 3.10

**57.** A low-income country decides to set a price ceiling on bread so it can make sure that bread is affordable to the poor. **Table 3.11** provides the conditions of demand and supply. What are the equilibrium price and equilibrium quantity before the price ceiling? What will the excess demand or the shortage (that is, quantity demanded minus quantity supplied) be if the price ceiling is set at $2.40? At $2.00? At $3.60?

| Price | Qd | Qs |
|---|---|---|
| $1.60 | 9,000 | 5,000 |
| $2.00 | 8,500 | 5,500 |
| $2.40 | 8,000 | 6,400 |
| **$2.80** | **7,500** | **7,500** |
| $3.20 | 7,000 | 9,000 |
| $3.60 | 6,500 | 11,000 |
| $4.00 | 6,000 | 15,000 |

Table 3.11

# 4 | Labor and Financial Markets

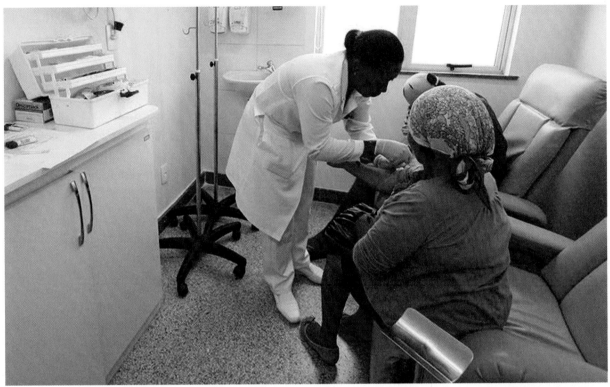

**Figure 4.1** People often think of demand and supply in relation to goods, but labor markets, such as the nursing profession, can also apply to this analysis. (Credit: modification of work by "Fotos GOVBA"/Flickr Creative Commons)

## Bring it Home

### Baby Boomers Come of Age

The Census Bureau reports that as of 2013, 20% of the U.S. population was over 60 years old, which means that almost 63 million people are reaching an age when they will need increased medical care.

The baby boomer population, the group born between 1946 and 1964, is comprised of approximately 74 million people who have just reached retirement age. As this population grows older, they will be faced with common healthcare issues such as heart conditions, arthritis, and Alzheimer's that may require hospitalization, long-term, or at-home nursing care. Aging baby boomers and advances in life-saving and life-extending technologies will increase the demand for healthcare and nursing. Additionally, the Affordable Care Act, which expands access to healthcare for millions of Americans, has further increase the demand, although with the election of Donald J. Trump, this increase may not be sustained.

According to the Bureau of Labor Statistics, registered nursing jobs are expected to increase by 16% between 2014 and 2024. The median annual wage of $67,490 (in 2015) is also expected to increase. The BLS forecasts that 439,000 new nurses will be in demand by 2022.

These data tell us, as economists, that the market for healthcare professionals, and nurses in particular, will face several challenges. Our study of supply and demand will help us to analyze what might happen in the labor market for nursing and other healthcare professionals, as we will discuss in the second half of this case at the end of the chapter.

# Introduction to Labor and Financial Markets

In this chapter, you will learn about:

- Demand and Supply at Work in Labor Markets

- Demand and Supply in Financial Markets

- The Market System as an Efficient Mechanism for Information

The theories of supply and demand do not apply just to markets for goods. They apply to any market, even markets for things we may not think of as goods and services like labor and financial services. Labor markets are markets for employees or jobs. Financial services markets are markets for saving or borrowing.

When we think about demand and supply curves in goods and services markets, it is easy to picture the demanders and suppliers: businesses produce the products and households buy them. Who are the demanders and suppliers in labor and financial service markets? In labor markets job seekers (individuals) are the suppliers of labor, while firms and other employers who hire labor are the demanders for labor. In financial markets, any individual or firm who saves contributes to the supply of money, and any who borrows (person, firm, or government) contributes to the demand for money.

As a college student, you most likely participate in both labor and financial markets. Employment is a fact of life for most college students: According to the National Center for Educational Statistics, in 2013 40% of full-time college students and 76% of part-time college students were employed. Most college students are also heavily involved in financial markets, primarily as borrowers. Among full-time students, about half take out a loan to help finance their education each year, and those loans average about $6,000 per year. Many students also borrow for other expenses, like purchasing a car. As this chapter will illustrate, we can analyze labor markets and financial markets with the same tools we use to analyze demand and supply in the goods markets.

# 4.1 | Demand and Supply at Work in Labor Markets

By the end of this section, you will be able to:
- Predict shifts in the demand and supply curves of the labor market
- Explain the impact of new technology on the demand and supply curves of the labor market
- Explain price floors in the labor market such as minimum wage or a living wage

Markets for labor have demand and supply curves, just like markets for goods. The law of demand applies in labor markets this way: A higher **salary** or **wage**—that is, a higher price in the labor market—leads to a decrease in the quantity of labor demanded by employers, while a lower salary or wage leads to an increase in the quantity of labor demanded. The law of supply functions in labor markets, too: A higher price for labor leads to a higher quantity of labor supplied; a lower price leads to a lower quantity supplied.

## Equilibrium in the Labor Market

In 2015, about 35,000 registered nurses worked in the Minneapolis-St. Paul-Bloomington, Minnesota-Wisconsin metropolitan area, according to the BLS. They worked for a variety of employers: hospitals, doctors' offices, schools, health clinics, and nursing homes. **Figure 4.2** illustrates how demand and supply determine equilibrium in this labor market. The demand and supply schedules in **Table 4.1** list the quantity supplied and quantity demanded of nurses at different salaries.

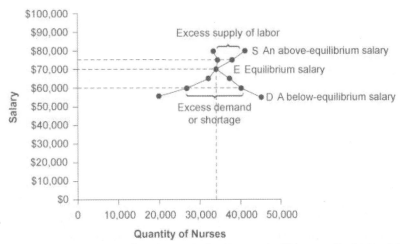

**Figure 4.2 Labor Market Example: Demand and Supply for Nurses in Minneapolis-St. Paul-Bloomington** The demand curve (D) of those employers who want to hire nurses intersects with the supply curve (S) of those who are qualified and willing to work as nurses at the equilibrium point (E). The equilibrium salary is $70,000 and the equilibrium quantity is 34,000 nurses. At an above-equilibrium salary of $75,000, quantity supplied increases to 38,000, but the quantity of nurses demanded at the higher pay declines to 33,000. At this above-equilibrium salary, an excess supply or surplus of nurses would exist. At a below-equilibrium salary of $60,000, quantity supplied declines to 27,000, while the quantity demanded at the lower wage increases to 40,000 nurses. At this below-equilibrium salary, excess demand or a shortage exists.

| Annual Salary | Quantity Demanded | Quantity Supplied |
|---|---|---|
| $55,000 | 45,000 | 20,000 |
| $60,000 | 40,000 | 27,000 |
| $65,000 | 37,000 | 31,000 |
| $70,000 | 34,000 | 34,000 |
| $75,000 | 33,000 | 38,000 |
| $80,000 | 32,000 | 41,000 |

Table 4.1 Demand and Supply of Nurses in Minneapolis-St. Paul-Bloomington

The horizontal axis shows the quantity of nurses hired. In this example we measure labor by number of workers, but another common way to measure the quantity of labor is by the number of hours worked. The vertical axis shows the price for nurses' labor—that is, how much they are paid. In the real world, this "price" would be total labor compensation: salary plus benefits. It is not obvious, but benefits are a significant part (as high as 30 percent) of labor compensation. In this example we measure the price of labor by salary on an annual basis, although in other cases we could measure the price of labor by monthly or weekly pay, or even the wage paid per hour. As the salary for nurses rises, the quantity demanded will fall. Some hospitals and nursing homes may reduce the number of nurses they hire, or they may lay off some of their existing nurses, rather than pay them higher salaries. Employers who face higher nurses' salaries may also try to replace some nursing functions by investing in physical equipment, like computer monitoring and diagnostic systems to monitor patients, or by using lower-paid health care aides to reduce the number of nurses they need.

As the salary for nurses rises, the quantity supplied will rise. If nurses' salaries in Minneapolis-St. Paul-Bloomington are higher than in other cities, more nurses will move to Minneapolis-St. Paul-Bloomington to find jobs, more people will be willing to train as nurses, and those currently trained as nurses will be more likely to pursue nursing as a full-time job. In other words, there will be more nurses looking for jobs in the area.

At **equilibrium**, the quantity supplied and the quantity demanded are equal. Thus, every employer who wants to hire a nurse at this equilibrium wage can find a willing worker, and every nurse who wants to work at this equilibrium salary can find a job. In **Figure 4.2**, the supply curve (S) and demand curve (D) intersect at the equilibrium point (E). The equilibrium quantity of nurses in the Minneapolis-St. Paul-Bloomington area is 34,000, and the equilibrium salary is $70,000 per year. This example simplifies the nursing market by focusing on the "average" nurse. In reality, of course, the market for nurses actually comprises many smaller markets, like markets for nurses with varying degrees of experience and credentials. Many markets contain closely related products that differ in quality. For instance, even a simple product like gasoline comes in regular, premium, and super-premium, each with a different price. Even in such cases, discussing the average price of gasoline, like the average salary for nurses, can still be useful because it reflects what is happening in most of the submarkets.

When the price of labor is not at the equilibrium, economic incentives tend to move salaries toward the equilibrium. For example, if salaries for nurses in Minneapolis-St. Paul-Bloomington were above the equilibrium at $75,000 per year, then 38,000 people want to work as nurses, but employers want to hire only 33,000 nurses. At that above-equilibrium salary, excess supply or a surplus results. In a situation of excess supply in the **labor market**, with many applicants for every job opening, employers will have an incentive to offer lower wages than they otherwise would have. Nurses' salary will move down toward equilibrium.

In contrast, if the salary is below the equilibrium at, say, $60,000 per year, then a situation of excess demand or a shortage arises. In this case, employers encouraged by the relatively lower wage want to hire 40,000 nurses, but only 27,000 individuals want to work as nurses at that salary in Minneapolis-St. Paul-Bloomington. In response to the shortage, some employers will offer higher pay to attract the nurses. Other employers will have to match the higher pay to keep their own employees. The higher salaries will encourage more nurses to train or work in Minneapolis-St. Paul-Bloomington. Again, price and quantity in the labor market will move toward equilibrium.

## Shifts in Labor Demand

The demand curve for labor shows the quantity of labor employers wish to hire at any given salary or wage rate, under the *ceteris paribus* assumption. A change in the wage or salary will result in a change in the quantity demanded of labor. If the wage rate increases, employers will want to hire fewer employees. The quantity of labor demanded will decrease, and there will be a movement upward along the demand curve. If the wages and salaries decrease, employers are more likely to hire a greater number of workers. The quantity of labor demanded will increase, resulting in a downward movement along the demand curve.

Shifts in the demand curve for labor occur for many reasons. One key reason is that the demand for labor is based on the demand for the good or service that is produced. For example, the more new automobiles consumers demand, the greater the number of workers automakers will need to hire. Therefore the demand for labor is called a "derived demand." Here are some examples of derived demand for labor:

- The demand for chefs is dependent on the demand for restaurant meals.

- The demand for pharmacists is dependent on the demand for prescription drugs.

- The demand for attorneys is dependent on the demand for legal services.

As the demand for the goods and services increases, the demand for labor will increase, or shift to the right, to meet employers' production requirements. As the demand for the goods and services decreases, the demand for labor will decrease, or shift to the left. **Table 4.2** shows that in addition to the derived demand for labor, demand can also increase or decrease (shift) in response to several factors.

| Factors | Results |
|---------|---------|
| Demand for Output | When the demand for the good produced (output) increases, both the output price and profitability increase. As a result, producers demand more labor to ramp up production. |

**Table 4.2 Factors That Can Shift Demand**

| Factors | Results |
|---|---|
| Education and Training | A well-trained and educated workforce causes an increase in the demand for that labor by employers. Increased levels of productivity within the workforce will cause the demand for labor to shift to the right. If the workforce is not well-trained or educated, employers will not hire from within that labor pool, since they will need to spend a significant amount of time and money training that workforce. Demand for such will shift to the left. |
| Technology | Technology changes can act as either substitutes for or complements to labor. When technology acts as a substitute, it replaces the need for the number of workers an employer needs to hire. For example, word processing decreased the number of typists needed in the workplace. This shifted the demand curve for typists left. An increase in the availability of certain technologies may increase the demand for labor. Technology that acts as a complement to labor will increase the demand for certain types of labor, resulting in a rightward shift of the demand curve. For example, the increased use of word processing and other software has increased the demand for information technology professionals who can resolve software and hardware issues related to a firm's network. More and better technology will increase demand for skilled workers who know how to use technology to enhance workplace productivity. Those workers who do not adapt to changes in technology will experience a decrease in demand. |
| Number of Companies | An increase in the number of companies producing a given product will increase the demand for labor resulting in a shift to the right. A decrease in the number of companies producing a given product will decrease the demand for labor resulting in a shift to the left. |
| Government Regulations | Complying with government regulations can increase or decrease the demand for labor at any given wage. In the healthcare industry, government rules may require that nurses be hired to carry out certain medical procedures. This will increase the demand for nurses. Less-trained healthcare workers would be prohibited from carrying out these procedures, and the demand for these workers will shift to the left. |
| Price and Availability of Other Inputs | Labor is not the only input into the production process. For example, a salesperson at a call center needs a telephone and a computer terminal to enter data and record sales. If prices of other inputs fall, production will become more profitable and suppliers will demand more labor to increase production. This will cause a rightward shift in the demand curve for labor. The opposite is also true. Higher prices for other inputs lower demand for labor. |

Table 4.2 Factors That Can Shift Demand

# Link It Up 🔗

Click here (http://openstaxcollege.org/l/Futurework) to read more about "Trends and Challenges for Work in the 21$^{st}$ Century."

## Shifts in Labor Supply

The supply of labor is upward-sloping and adheres to the law of supply: The higher the price, the greater the quantity supplied and the lower the price, the less quantity supplied. The supply curve models the tradeoff between supplying labor into the market or using time in leisure activities at every given price level. The higher the wage, the more labor is willing to work and forego leisure activities. Table 4.3 lists some of the factors that will cause the supply to increase or decrease.

| Factors | Results |
| --- | --- |
| Number of Workers | An increased number of workers will cause the supply curve to shift to the right. An increased number of workers can be due to several factors, such as immigration, increasing population, an aging population, and changing demographics. Policies that encourage immigration will increase the supply of labor, and vice versa. Population grows when birth rates exceed death rates. This eventually increases supply of labor when the former reach working age. An aging and therefore retiring population will decrease the supply of labor. Another example of changing demographics is more women working outside of the home, which increases the supply of labor. |
| Required Education | The more required education, the lower the supply. There is a lower supply of PhD mathematicians than of high school mathematics teachers; there is a lower supply of cardiologists than of primary care physicians; and there is a lower supply of physicians than of nurses. |
| Government Policies | Government policies can also affect the supply of labor for jobs. Alternatively, the government may support rules that set high qualifications for certain jobs: academic training, certificates or licenses, or experience. When these qualifications are made tougher, the number of qualified workers will decrease at any given wage. On the other hand, the government may also subsidize training or even reduce the required level of qualifications. For example, government might offer subsidies for nursing schools or nursing students. Such provisions would shift the supply curve of nurses to the right. In addition, government policies that change the relative desirability of working versus not working also affect the labor supply. These include unemployment benefits, maternity leave, child care benefits, and welfare policy. For example, child care benefits may increase the labor supply of working mothers. Long term unemployment benefits may discourage job searching for unemployed workers. All these policies must therefore be carefully designed to minimize any negative labor supply effects. |

Table 4.3 Factors that Can Shift Supply

A change in salary will lead to a movement along labor demand or labor supply curves, but it will not shift those curves. However, other events like those we have outlined here will cause either the demand or the supply of labor to shift, and thus will move the labor market to a new equilibrium salary and quantity.

## Technology and Wage Inequality: The Four-Step Process

Economic events can change the equilibrium salary (or wage) and quantity of labor. Consider how the wave of new information technologies, like computer and telecommunications networks, has affected low-skill and high-skill workers in the U.S. economy. From the perspective of employers who demand labor, these new technologies are often a substitute for low-skill laborers like file clerks who used to keep file cabinets full of paper records of transactions. However, the same new technologies are a complement to high-skill workers like managers, who benefit from the technological advances by having the ability to monitor more information, communicate more easily, and juggle a wider array of responsibilities. How will the new technologies affect the wages of high-skill and low-skill workers? For this question, the four-step process of analyzing how shifts in supply or demand affect a market (introduced in **Demand and Supply**) works in this way:

Step 1. What did the markets for low-skill labor and high-skill labor look like before the arrival of the new technologies? In **Figure 4.3** (a) and **Figure 4.3** (b), $S_0$ is the original supply curve for labor and $D_0$ is the original demand curve for labor in each market. In each graph, the original point of equilibrium, $E_0$, occurs at the price $W_0$ and the quantity $Q_0$.

(a) Technological change and low-skill labor

(b) Technological change and high-skill labor

**Figure 4.3 Technology and Wages: Applying Demand and Supply** (a) The demand for low-skill labor shifts to the left when technology can do the job previously done by these workers. (b) New technologies can also increase the demand for high-skill labor in fields such as information technology and network administration.

Step 2. Does the new technology affect the supply of labor from households or the demand for labor from firms? The technology change described here affects demand for labor by firms that hire workers.

Step 3. Will the new technology increase or decrease demand? Based on the description earlier, as the substitute for low-skill labor becomes available, demand for low-skill labor will shift to the left, from $D_0$ to $D_1$. As the technology complement for high-skill labor becomes cheaper, demand for high-skill labor will shift to the right, from $D_0$ to $D_1$.

Step 4. The new equilibrium for low-skill labor, shown as point $E_1$ with price $W_1$ and quantity $Q_1$, has a lower wage and quantity hired than the original equilibrium, $E_0$. The new equilibrium for high-skill labor, shown as point $E_1$ with price $W_1$ and quantity $Q_1$, has a higher wage and quantity hired than the original equilibrium ($E_0$).

Thus, the demand and supply model predicts that the new computer and communications technologies will raise the pay of high-skill workers but reduce the pay of low-skill workers. From the 1970s to the mid-2000s, the wage gap widened between high-skill and low-skill labor. According to the National Center for Education Statistics, in 1980, for example, a college graduate earned about 30% more than a high school graduate with comparable job experience, but by 2014, a college graduate earned about 66% more than an otherwise comparable high school graduate. Many economists believe that the trend toward greater wage inequality across the U.S. economy is due to improvements in technology.

## Link It Up

Visit this website (http://openstaxcollege.org/l/oldtechjobs) to read about ten tech skills that have lost relevance in today's workforce.

## Price Floors in the Labor Market: Living Wages and Minimum Wages

In contrast to goods and services markets, price ceilings are rare in labor markets, because rules that prevent people from earning income are not politically popular. There is one exception: boards of trustees or stockholders, as an example, propose limits on the high incomes of top business executives.

The labor market, however, presents some prominent examples of price floors, which are an attempt to increase the wages of low-paid workers. The U.S. government sets a **minimum wage**, a price floor that makes it illegal for an employer to pay employees less than a certain hourly rate. In mid-2009, the U.S. minimum wage was raised to $7.25 per hour. Local political movements in a number of U.S. cities have pushed for a higher minimum wage, which they call a **living wage**. Promoters of living wage laws maintain that the minimum wage is too low to ensure a reasonable standard of living. They base this conclusion on the calculation that, if you work 40 hours a week at a minimum wage of $7.25 per hour for 50 weeks a year, your annual income is $14,500, which is less than the official U.S. government definition of what it means for a family to be in poverty. (A family with two adults earning minimum wage and two young children will find it more cost efficient for one parent to provide childcare while the other works for income. Thus the family income would be $14,500, which is significantly lower than the federal poverty line for a family of four, which was $24,250 in 2015.)

Supporters of the living wage argue that full-time workers should be assured a high enough wage so that they can afford the essentials of life: food, clothing, shelter, and healthcare. Since Baltimore passed the first living wage law in 1994, several dozen cities enacted similar laws in the late 1990s and the 2000s. The living wage ordinances do not apply to all employers, but they have specified that all employees of the city or employees of firms that the city hires be paid at least a certain wage that is usually a few dollars per hour above the U.S. minimum wage.

**Figure 4.4** illustrates the situation of a city considering a living wage law. For simplicity, we assume that there is no federal minimum wage. The wage appears on the vertical axis, because the wage is the price in the labor market. Before the passage of the living wage law, the equilibrium wage is $10 per hour and the city hires 1,200 workers at this wage. However, a group of concerned citizens persuades the city council to enact a living wage law requiring employers to pay no less than $12 per hour. In response to the higher wage, 1,600 workers look for jobs with the city. At this higher wage, the city, as an employer, is willing to hire only 700 workers. At the price floor, the quantity supplied exceeds the quantity demanded, and a surplus of labor exists in this market. For workers who continue to have a job at a higher salary, life has improved. For those who were willing to work at the old wage rate but lost their jobs with the wage increase, life has not improved. **Table 4.4** shows the differences in supply and demand at different wages.

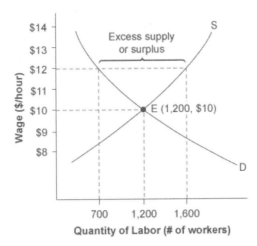

**Figure 4.4 A Living Wage: Example of a Price Floor** The original equilibrium in this labor market is a wage of $10/hour and a quantity of 1,200 workers, shown at point E. Imposing a wage floor at $12/hour leads to an excess supply of labor. At that wage, the quantity of labor supplied is 1,600 and the quantity of labor demanded is only 700.

| Wage | Quantity Labor Demanded | Quantity Labor Supplied |
|---|---|---|
| $8/hr | 1,900 | 500 |
| $9/hr | 1,500 | 900 |
| $10/hr | 1,200 | 1,200 |
| $11/hr | 900 | 1,400 |
| $12/hr | 700 | 1,600 |
| $13/hr | 500 | 1,800 |
| $14/hr | 400 | 1,900 |

**Table 4.4 Living Wage: Example of a Price Floor**

## The Minimum Wage as an Example of a Price Floor

The U.S. minimum wage is a price floor that is set either very close to the equilibrium wage or even slightly below it. About 1% of American workers are actually paid the minimum wage. In other words, the vast majority of the U.S. labor force has its wages determined in the labor market, not as a result of the government price floor. However, for workers with low skills and little experience, like those without a high school diploma or teenagers, the minimum wage is quite important. In many cities, the federal minimum wage is apparently below the market price for unskilled labor, because employers offer more than the minimum wage to checkout clerks and other low-skill workers without any government prodding.

Economists have attempted to estimate how much the minimum wage reduces the quantity demanded of low-skill labor. A typical result of such studies is that a 10% increase in the minimum wage would decrease the hiring of unskilled workers by 1 to 2%, which seems a relatively small reduction. In fact, some studies have even found no effect of a higher minimum wage on employment at certain times and places—although these studies are controversial.

Let's suppose that the minimum wage lies just slightly *below* the equilibrium wage level. Wages could fluctuate according to market forces above this price floor, but they would not be allowed to move beneath the floor. In this situation, the price floor minimum wage is *nonbinding* —that is, the price floor is not determining the market outcome. Even if the minimum wage moves just a little higher, it will still have no effect on the quantity of employment in the economy, as long as it remains below the equilibrium wage. Even if the government increases minimum wage by enough so that it rises slightly above the equilibrium wage and becomes binding, there will be only a small excess supply gap between the quantity demanded and quantity supplied.

These insights help to explain why U.S. minimum wage laws have historically had only a small impact on employment. Since the minimum wage has typically been set close to the equilibrium wage for low-skill labor and sometimes even below it, it has not had a large effect in creating an excess supply of labor. However, if the minimum wage increased dramatically—say, if it doubled to match the living wages that some U.S. cities have considered—then its impact on reducing the quantity demanded of employment would be far greater. As of 2017, many U.S. states are set to increase their minimum wage to $15 per hour. We will see what happens. The following Clear It Up feature describes in greater detail some of the arguments for and against changes to minimum wage.

### What's the harm in raising the minimum wage?

Because of the law of demand, a higher required wage will reduce the amount of low-skill employment either in terms of employees or in terms of work hours. Although there is controversy over the numbers, let's say for the sake of the argument that a 10% rise in the minimum wage will reduce the employment of low-skill workers by 2%. Does this outcome mean that raising the minimum wage by 10% is bad public policy? Not necessarily.

If 98% of those receiving the minimum wage have a pay increase of 10%, but 2% of those receiving the minimum wage lose their jobs, are the gains for society as a whole greater than the losses? The answer is not clear, because job losses, even for a small group, may cause more pain than modest income gains for others. For one thing, we need to consider which minimum wage workers are losing their jobs. If the 2% of minimum wage workers who lose their jobs are struggling to support families, that is one thing. If those who lose their job are high school students picking up spending money over summer vacation, that is something else.

Another complexity is that many minimum wage workers do not work full-time for an entire year. Imagine a minimum wage worker who holds different part-time jobs for a few months at a time, with bouts of unemployment in between. The worker in this situation receives the 10% raise in the minimum wage when working, but also ends up working 2% fewer hours during the year because the higher minimum wage reduces how much employers want people to work. Overall, this worker's income would rise because the 10% pay raise would more than offset the 2% fewer hours worked.

Of course, these arguments do not prove that raising the minimum wage is necessarily a good idea either. There may well be other, better public policy options for helping low-wage workers. (The **Poverty and Economic Inequality (http://cnx.org/content/m63897/latest/)** chapter discusses some possibilities.) The lesson from this maze of minimum wage arguments is that complex social problems rarely have simple answers. Even those who agree on how a proposed economic policy affects quantity demanded and quantity supplied may still disagree on whether the policy is a good idea.

# 4.2 | Demand and Supply in Financial Markets

By the end of this section, you will be able to:
- Identify the demanders and suppliers in a financial market
- Explain how interest rates can affect supply and demand
- Analyze the economic effects of U.S. debt in terms of domestic financial markets
- Explain the role of price ceilings and usury laws in the U.S.

United States' households, institutions, and domestic businesses saved almost $1.3 trillion in 2015. Where did that savings go and how was it used? Some of the savings ended up in banks, which in turn loaned the money to individuals or businesses that wanted to borrow money. Some was invested in private companies or loaned to government agencies that wanted to borrow money to raise funds for purposes like building roads or mass transit. Some firms reinvested their savings in their own businesses.

In this section, we will determine how the demand and supply model links those who wish to supply **financial capital** (i.e., savings) with those who demand financial capital (i.e., borrowing). Those who save money (or make financial investments, which is the same thing), whether individuals or businesses, are on the supply side of the financial market. Those who borrow money are on the demand side of the financial market. For a more detailed treatment of the different kinds of financial investments like bank accounts, stocks and bonds, see the **Financial Markets (http://cnx.org/content/m63860/latest/)** chapter.

## Who Demands and Who Supplies in Financial Markets?

In any market, the price is what suppliers receive and what demanders pay. In financial markets, those who supply financial capital through saving expect to receive a rate of return, while those who demand financial capital by receiving funds expect to pay a rate of return. This rate of return can come in a variety of forms, depending on the type of investment.

The simplest example of a rate of return is the **interest rate**. For example, when you supply money into a savings account at a bank, you receive interest on your deposit. The interest the bank pays you as a percent of your deposits is the interest rate. Similarly, if you demand a loan to buy a car or a computer, you will need to pay interest on the money you borrow.

Let's consider the market for borrowing money with credit cards. In 2015, almost 200 million Americans were cardholders. Credit cards allow you to borrow money from the card's issuer, and pay back the borrowed amount plus interest, although most allow you a period of time in which you can repay the loan without paying interest. A typical credit card interest rate ranges from 12% to 18% per year. In May 2016, Americans had about $943 billion outstanding in credit card debts. About half of U.S. families with credit cards report that they almost always pay the full balance on time, but one-quarter of U.S. families with credit cards say that they "hardly ever" pay off the card in full. In fact, in 2014, 56% of consumers carried an unpaid balance in the last 12 months. Let's say that, on average, the annual interest rate for credit card borrowing is 15% per year. Thus, Americans pay tens of billions of dollars every year in interest on their credit cards—plus basic fees for the credit card or fees for late payments.

**Figure 4.5** illustrates demand and supply in the financial market for credit cards. The horizontal axis of the financial market shows the quantity of money loaned or borrowed in this market. The vertical or price axis shows the rate of return, which in the case of credit card borrowing we can measure with an interest rate. **Table 4.5** shows the quantity of financial capital that consumers demand at various interest rates and the quantity that credit card firms (often banks) are willing to supply.

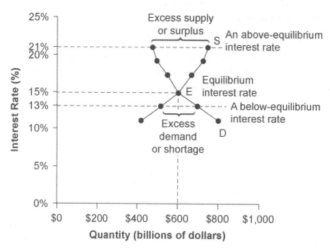

**Figure 4.5 Demand and Supply for Borrowing Money with Credit Cards**  In this market for credit card borrowing, the demand curve (D) for borrowing financial capital intersects the supply curve (S) for lending financial capital at equilibrium E. At the equilibrium, the interest rate (the "price" in this market) is 15% and the quantity of financial capital loaned and borrowed is $600 billion. The equilibrium price is where the quantity demanded and the quantity supplied are equal. At an above-equilibrium interest rate like 21%, the quantity of financial capital supplied would increase to $750 billion, but the quantity demanded would decrease to $480 billion. At a below-equilibrium interest rate like 13%, the quantity of financial capital demanded would increase to $700 billion, but the quantity of financial capital supplied would decrease to $510 billion.

| Interest Rate (%) | Quantity of Financial Capital Demanded (Borrowing) ($ billions) | Quantity of Financial Capital Supplied (Lending) ($ billions) |
|---|---|---|
| 11 | $800 | $420 |
| 13 | $700 | $510 |
| 15 | $600 | $600 |
| 17 | $550 | $660 |
| 19 | $500 | $720 |
| 21 | $480 | $750 |

Table 4.5 Demand and Supply for Borrowing Money with Credit Cards

The laws of demand and supply continue to apply in the financial markets. According to the **law of demand**, a higher rate of return (that is, a higher price) will decrease the quantity demanded. As the interest rate rises, consumers will reduce the quantity that they borrow. According to the law of supply, a higher price increases the quantity supplied. Consequently, as the interest rate paid on credit card borrowing rises, more firms will be eager to issue credit cards and to encourage customers to use them. Conversely, if the interest rate on credit cards falls, the quantity of financial capital supplied in the credit card market will decrease and the quantity demanded will fall.

## Equilibrium in Financial Markets

In the financial market for credit cards in **Figure 4.5**, the supply curve (S) and the demand curve (D) cross at the equilibrium point (E). The equilibrium occurs at an interest rate of 15%, where the quantity of funds demanded and the quantity supplied are equal at an equilibrium quantity of $600 billion.

If the interest rate (remember, this measures the "price" in the financial market) is above the equilibrium level, then an excess supply, or a surplus, of financial capital will arise in this market. For example, at an interest rate of 21%, the quantity of funds supplied increases to $750 billion, while the quantity demanded decreases to $480 billion. At this above-equilibrium interest rate, firms are eager to supply loans to credit card borrowers, but relatively few people or businesses wish to borrow. As a result, some credit card firms will lower the interest rates (or other fees) they charge to attract more business. This strategy will push the interest rate down toward the equilibrium level.

If the interest rate is below the equilibrium, then excess demand or a shortage of funds occurs in this market. At an interest rate of 13%, the quantity of funds credit card borrowers demand increases to $700 billion, but the quantity credit card firms are willing to supply is only $510 billion. In this situation, credit card firms will perceive that they are overloaded with eager borrowers and conclude that they have an opportunity to raise interest rates or fees. The interest rate will face economic pressures to creep up toward the equilibrium level.

The FRED database publishes some two dozen measures of interest rates, including interest rates on credit cards, automobile loans, personal loans, mortgage loans, and more. You can find these at the FRED website (https://openstax.org/l/FRED_stlouis) .

## Shifts in Demand and Supply in Financial Markets

Those who supply financial capital face two broad decisions: how much to save, and how to divide up their savings among different forms of financial investments. We will discuss each of these in turn.

Participants in financial markets must decide when they prefer to consume goods: now or in the future. Economists call this **intertemporal decision making** because it involves decisions across time. Unlike a decision about what to buy from the grocery store, people make investment or savings decisions across a period of time, sometimes a long period.

Most workers save for retirement because their income in the present is greater than their needs, while the opposite will be true once they retire. Thus, they save today and supply financial markets. If their income increases, they save more. If their perceived situation in the future changes, they change the amount of their saving. For example, there is some evidence that Social Security, the program that workers pay into in order to qualify for government checks after retirement, has tended to reduce the quantity of financial capital that workers save. If this is true, Social Security has shifted the supply of financial capital at any interest rate to the left.

By contrast, many college students need money today when their income is low (or nonexistent) to pay their college expenses. As a result, they borrow today and demand from financial markets. Once they graduate and become employed, they will pay back the loans. Individuals borrow money to purchase homes or cars. A business seeks financial investment so that it has the funds to build a factory or invest in a research and development project that will not pay off for five years, ten years, or even more. Thus, when consumers and businesses have greater confidence that they will be able to repay in the future, the quantity demanded of financial capital at any given interest rate will shift to the right.

For example, in the technology boom of the late 1990s, many businesses became extremely confident that investments in new technology would have a high rate of return, and their demand for financial capital shifted to the right. Conversely, during the 2008 and 2009 Great Recession, their demand for financial capital at any given interest rate shifted to the left.

To this point, we have been looking at saving in total. Now let us consider what affects saving in different types of financial investments. In deciding between different forms of financial investments, suppliers of financial capital will have to consider the rates of return and the risks involved. Rate of return is a positive attribute of investments, but risk is a negative. If Investment A becomes more risky, or the return diminishes, then savers will shift their funds to Investment B—and the supply curve of financial capital for Investment A will shift back to the left while the supply curve of capital for Investment B shifts to the right.

## The United States as a Global Borrower

In the global economy, trillions of dollars of financial investment cross national borders every year. In the early 2000s, financial investors from foreign countries were investing several hundred billion dollars per year more in the U.S. economy than U.S. financial investors were investing abroad. The following Work It Out deals with one of the macroeconomic concerns for the U.S. economy in recent years.

# Work It Out ⊶⊶⊷

## The Effect of Growing U.S. Debt

Imagine that foreign investors viewed the U.S. economy as a less desirable place to put their money because of fears about the growth of the U.S. public debt. Using the four-step process for analyzing how changes in supply and demand affect equilibrium outcomes, how would increased U.S. public debt affect the equilibrium price and quantity for capital in U.S. financial markets?

Step 1. Draw a diagram showing demand and supply for financial capital that represents the original scenario in which foreign investors are pouring money into the U.S. economy. **Figure 4.6** shows a demand curve, D, and a supply curve, S, where the supply of capital includes the funds arriving from foreign investors. The original equilibrium $E_0$ occurs at interest rate $R_0$ and quantity of financial investment $Q_0$.

**Figure 4.6 The United States as a Global Borrower Before U.S. Debt Uncertainty**   The graph shows the demand for financial capital from and supply of financial capital into the U.S. financial markets by the foreign sector before the increase in uncertainty regarding U.S. public debt. The original equilibrium ($E_0$) occurs at an equilibrium rate of return ($R_0$) and the equilibrium quantity is at $Q_0$.

Step 2. Will the diminished confidence in the U.S. economy as a place to invest affect demand or supply of financial capital? Yes, it will affect supply. Many foreign investors look to the U.S. financial markets to store their money in safe financial vehicles with low risk and stable returns. Diminished confidence means U.S. financial assets will be seen as more risky.

Step 3. Will supply increase or decrease? When the enthusiasm of foreign investors' for investing their money in the U.S. economy diminishes, the supply of financial capital shifts to the left. **Figure 4.7** shows the supply curve shift from $S_0$ to $S_1$.

**Figure 4.7 The United States as a Global Borrower Before and After U.S. Debt Uncertainty** The graph shows the demand for financial capital and supply of financial capital into the U.S. financial markets by the foreign sector before and after the increase in uncertainty regarding U.S. public debt. The original equilibrium ($E_0$) occurs at an equilibrium rate of return ($R_0$) and the equilibrium quantity is at $Q_0$.

Step 4. Thus, foreign investors' diminished enthusiasm leads to a new equilibrium, $E_1$, which occurs at the higher interest rate, $R_1$, and the lower quantity of financial investment, $Q_1$. In short, U.S. borrowers will have to pay more interest on their borrowing.

The economy has experienced an enormous inflow of foreign capital. According to the U.S. Bureau of Economic Analysis, by the third quarter of 2015, U.S. investors had accumulated $23.3 trillion of foreign assets, but foreign investors owned a total of $30.6 trillion of U.S. assets. If foreign investors were to pull their money out of the U.S. economy and invest elsewhere in the world, the result could be a significantly lower quantity of financial investment in the United States, available only at a higher interest rate. This reduced inflow of foreign financial investment could impose hardship on U.S. consumers and firms interested in borrowing.

In a modern, developed economy, financial capital often moves invisibly through electronic transfers between one bank account and another. Yet we can analyze these flows of funds with the same tools of demand and supply as markets for goods or labor.

## Price Ceilings in Financial Markets: Usury Laws

As we noted earlier, about 200 million Americans own credit cards, and their interest payments and fees total tens of billions of dollars each year. It is little wonder that political pressures sometimes arise for setting limits on the interest rates or fees that credit card companies charge. The firms that issue credit cards, including banks, oil companies, phone companies, and retail stores, respond that the higher interest rates are necessary to cover the losses created by those who borrow on their credit cards and who do not repay on time or at all. These companies also point out that cardholders can avoid paying interest if they pay their bills on time.

Consider the credit card market as **Figure 4.8** illustrators. In this financial market, the vertical axis shows the interest rate (which is the price in the financial market). Demanders in the credit card market are households and businesses. Suppliers are the companies that issue credit cards. This figure does not use specific numbers, which would be hypothetical in any case, but instead focuses on the underlying economic relationships. Imagine a law imposes a price ceiling that holds the interest rate charged on credit cards at the rate Rc, which lies below the interest rate $R_0$ that would otherwise have prevailed in the market. The horizontal dashed line at interest rate $R_c$ in **Figure 4.8** shows the price ceiling. The demand and supply model predicts that at the lower price ceiling interest rate, the quantity demanded of credit card debt will increase from its original level of $Q_0$ to Qd; however, the quantity supplied of credit card debt will decrease from the original $Q_0$ to Qs. At the price ceiling (Rc), quantity demanded will exceed quantity supplied. Consequently, a number of people who want to have credit cards and are willing to pay the prevailing interest rate will find that companies are unwilling to issue cards to them. The result will be a credit shortage.

**Figure 4.8 Credit Card Interest Rates: Another Price Ceiling Example**  The original intersection of demand D and supply S occurs at equilibrium $E_0$. However, a price ceiling is set at the interest rate Rc, below the equilibrium interest rate $R_0$, and so the interest rate cannot adjust upward to the equilibrium. At the price ceiling, the quantity demanded, Qd, exceeds the quantity supplied, Qs. There is excess demand, also called a shortage.

Many states do have **usury laws**, which impose an upper limit on the interest rate that lenders can charge. However, in many cases these upper limits are well above the market interest rate. For example, if the interest rate is not allowed to rise above 30% per year, it can still fluctuate below that level according to market forces. A price ceiling that is set at a relatively high level is nonbinding, and it will have no practical effect unless the equilibrium price soars high enough to exceed the price ceiling.

# 4.3 | The Market System as an Efficient Mechanism for Information

By the end of this section, you will be able to:
- Apply demand and supply models to analyze prices and quantities
- Explain the effects of price controls on the equilibrium of prices and quantities

Prices exist in markets for goods and services, for labor, and for financial capital. In all of these markets, prices serve as a remarkable social mechanism for collecting, combining, and transmitting information that is relevant to the market—namely, the relationship between demand and supply—and then serving as messengers to convey that information to buyers and sellers. In a market-oriented economy, no government agency or guiding intelligence oversees the set of responses and interconnections that result from a change in price. Instead, each consumer reacts according to that person's preferences and budget set, and each profit-seeking producer reacts to the impact on its expected profits. The following Clear It Up feature examines the **demand and supply models**.

## Why are demand and supply curves important?

The demand and supply model is the second fundamental diagram for this course. (The opportunity set model that we introduced in the Choice in a World of Scarcity chapter was the first.) Just as it would be foolish to try to learn the arithmetic of long division by memorizing every possible combination of numbers that can be divided by each other, it would be foolish to try to memorize every specific example of demand and supply in this chapter, this textbook, or this course. Demand and supply is not primarily a list of examples. It is a model to analyze prices and quantities. Even though demand and supply diagrams have many labels, they are fundamentally the same in their logic. Your goal should be to understand the underlying model so you can use it to analyze *any* market.

**Figure 4.9** displays a generic demand and supply curve. The horizontal axis shows the different measures of quantity: a quantity of a good or service, or a quantity of labor for a given job, or a quantity of financial capital. The vertical axis shows a measure of price: the price of a good or service, the wage in the labor market, or the rate of return (like the interest rate) in the financial market.

The demand and supply model can explain the existing levels of prices, wages, and rates of return. To carry out such an analysis, think about the quantity that will be demanded at each price and the quantity that will be supplied at each price—that is, think about the shape of the demand and supply curves—and how these forces will combine to produce equilibrium.

We can also use demand and supply to explain how economic events will cause changes in prices, wages, and rates of return. There are only four possibilities: the change in any single event may cause the demand curve to shift right or to shift left, or it may cause the supply curve to shift right or to shift left. The key to analyzing the effect of an economic event on equilibrium prices and quantities is to determine which of these four possibilities occurred. The way to do this correctly is to think back to the list of factors that shift the demand and supply curves. Note that if more than one variable is changing at the same time, the overall impact will depend on the degree of the shifts. When there are multiple variables, economists isolate each change and analyze it independently.

**Figure 4.9 Demand and Supply Curves** The figure displays a generic demand and supply curve. The horizontal axis shows the different measures of quantity: a quantity of a good or service, a quantity of labor for a given job, or a quantity of financial capital. The vertical axis shows a measure of price: the price of a good or service, the wage in the labor market, or the rate of return (like the interest rate) in the financial market. We can use the demand and supply curves explain how economic events will cause changes in prices, wages, and rates of return.

An increase in the price of some product signals consumers that there is a shortage; therefore, they may want to economize on buying this product. For example, if you are thinking about taking a plane trip to Hawaii, but the ticket turns out to be expensive during the week you intend to go, you might consider other weeks when the ticket might be cheaper. The price could be high because you were planning to travel during a holiday when demand for traveling is high. Maybe the cost of an input like jet fuel increased or the airline has raised the price temporarily to see how many people are willing to pay it. Perhaps all of these factors are present at the same time. You do not need to analyze the market and break down the price change into its underlying factors. You just have to look at the ticket price and decide whether and when to fly.

In the same way, price changes provide useful information to producers. Imagine the situation of a farmer who grows oats and learns that the price of oats has risen. The higher price could be due to an increase in demand caused by a new scientific study proclaiming that eating oats is especially healthful. Perhaps the price of a substitute grain, like corn, has risen, and people have responded by buying more oats. The oat farmer does not need to know the details. The farmer only needs to know that the price of oats has risen and that it will be profitable to expand production as a result.

The actions of individual consumers and producers as they react to prices overlap and interlock in markets for goods, labor, and financial capital. A change in any single market is transmitted through these multiple interconnections to other markets. The vision of the role of flexible prices helping markets to reach equilibrium and linking different markets together helps to explain why price controls can be so counterproductive. Price controls are government laws that serve to regulate prices rather than allow the various markets to determine prices. There is an old proverb: "Don't kill the messenger." In ancient times, messengers carried information between distant cities and kingdoms. When they brought bad news, there was an emotional impulse to kill the messenger. However, killing the messenger did not kill the bad news. Moreover, killing the messenger had an undesirable side effect: Other messengers would refuse to bring news to that city or kingdom, depriving its citizens of vital information.

Those who seek price controls are trying to kill the messenger—or at least to stifle an unwelcome message that prices are bringing about the equilibrium level of price and quantity. However, price controls do nothing to affect the underlying forces of demand and supply, and this can have serious repercussions. During China's "Great Leap Forward" in the late 1950s, the government kept food prices artificially low, with the result that 30 to 40 million people died of starvation because the low prices depressed farm production. This was communist party leader Mao Zedong's social and economic campaign to rapidly transform the country from an agrarian economy to a socialist society through rapid industrialization and collectivization. Changes in demand and supply will continue to reveal themselves through consumers' and producers' behavior. Immobilizing the price messenger through price controls will deprive everyone in the economy of critical information. Without this information, it becomes difficult for everyone—buyers and sellers alike—to react in a flexible and appropriate manner as changes occur throughout the economy.

# Bring it Home

## Baby Boomers Come of Age

The theory of supply and demand can explain what happens in the labor markets and suggests that the demand for nurses will increase as healthcare needs of baby boomers increase, as **Figure 4.10** shows. The impact of that increase will result in an average salary higher than the $67,490 earned in 2015 referenced in the first part of this case. The new equilibrium ($E_1$) will be at the new equilibrium price ($Pe_1$).Equilibrium quantity will also increase from $Qe_0$ to $Qe_1$.

**Figure 4.10 Impact of Increasing Demand for Nurses 2014-2024** In 2014, the median salary for nurses was $67,490. As demand for services increases, the demand curve shifts to the right (from $D_0$ to $D_1$) and the equilibrium quantity of nurses increases from $Qe_0$ to $Qe_1$. The equilibrium salary increases from $Pe_0$ to $Pe_1$.

Suppose that as the demand for nurses increases, the supply shrinks due to an increasing number of nurses entering retirement and increases in the tuition of nursing degrees. The leftward shift of the supply curve in **Figure 4.11** captures the impact of a decreasing supply of nurses. The shifts in the two curves result in higher salaries for nurses, but the overall impact in the quantity of nurses is uncertain, as it depends on the relative shifts of supply and demand.

**Figure 4.11 Impact of Decreasing Supply of Nurses between 2014 and 2024** The increase in demand for nurses shown in Figure 4.10 leads to both higher prices and higher quantities demanded. As nurses retire from the work force, the supply of nurses decreases, causing a leftward shift in the supply curve and higher salaries for nurses at $Pe_2$. The net effect on the equilibrium quantity of nurses is uncertain, which in this representation is less than $Qe_1$, but more than the initial $Qe_0$.

While we do not know if the number of nurses will increase or decrease relative to their initial employment, we know they will have higher salaries.

# KEY TERMS

**interest rate** the "price" of borrowing in the financial market; a rate of return on an investment

**minimum wage** a price floor that makes it illegal for an employer to pay employees less than a certain hourly rate

**usury laws** laws that impose an upper limit on the interest rate that lenders can charge

# KEY CONCEPTS AND SUMMARY

## 4.1 Demand and Supply at Work in Labor Markets

In the labor market, households are on the supply side of the market and firms are on the demand side. In the market for financial capital, households and firms can be on either side of the market: they are suppliers of financial capital when they save or make financial investments, and demanders of financial capital when they borrow or receive financial investments.

In the demand and supply analysis of labor markets, we can measure the price by the annual salary or hourly wage received. We can measure the quantity of labor various ways, like number of workers or the number of hours worked.

Factors that can shift the demand curve for labor include: a change in the quantity demanded of the product that the labor produces; a change in the production process that uses more or less labor; and a change in government policy that affects the quantity of labor that firms wish to hire at a given wage. Demand can also increase or decrease (shift) in response to: workers' level of education and training, technology, the number of companies, and availability and price of other inputs.

The main factors that can shift the supply curve for labor are: how desirable a job appears to workers relative to the alternatives, government policy that either restricts or encourages the quantity of workers trained for the job, the number of workers in the economy, and required education.

## 4.2 Demand and Supply in Financial Markets

In the demand and supply analysis of financial markets, the "price" is the rate of return or the interest rate received. We measure the quantity by the money that flows from those who supply financial capital to those who demand it.

Two factors can shift the supply of financial capital to a certain investment: if people want to alter their existing levels of consumption, and if the riskiness or return on one investment changes relative to other investments. Factors that can shift demand for capital include business confidence and consumer confidence in the future—since financial investments received in the present are typically repaid in the future.

## 4.3 The Market System as an Efficient Mechanism for Information

The market price system provides a highly efficient mechanism for disseminating information about relative scarcities of goods, services, labor, and financial capital. Market participants do not need to know why prices have changed, only that the changes require them to revisit previous decisions they made about supply and demand. Price controls hide information about the true scarcity of products and thereby cause misallocation of resources.

# SELF-CHECK QUESTIONS

1. In the labor market, what causes a movement along the demand curve? What causes a shift in the demand curve?

2. In the labor market, what causes a movement along the supply curve? What causes a shift in the supply curve?

3. Why is a living wage considered a price floor? Does imposing a living wage have the same outcome as a minimum wage?

4. In the financial market, what causes a movement along the demand curve? What causes a shift in the demand curve?

5. In the financial market, what causes a movement along the supply curve? What causes a shift in the supply curve?

**6.** If a usury law limits interest rates to no more than 35%, what would the likely impact be on the amount of loans made and interest rates paid?

**7.** Which of the following changes in the financial market will lead to a decline in interest rates:
   a. a rise in demand
   b. a fall in demand
   c. a rise in supply
   d. a fall in supply

**8.** Which of the following changes in the financial market will lead to an increase in the quantity of loans made and received:
   a. a rise in demand
   b. a fall in demand
   c. a rise in supply
   d. a fall in supply

**9.** Identify the most accurate statement. A price floor will have the largest effect if it is set:
   a. substantially above the equilibrium price
   b. slightly above the equilibrium price
   c. slightly below the equilibrium price
   d. substantially below the equilibrium price

Sketch all four of these possibilities on a demand and supply diagram to illustrate your answer.

**10.** A price ceiling will have the largest effect:
   a. substantially below the equilibrium price
   b. slightly below the equilibrium price
   c. substantially above the equilibrium price
   d. slightly above the equilibrium price

Sketch all four of these possibilities on a demand and supply diagram to illustrate your answer.

**11.** Select the correct answer. A price floor will usually shift:
   a. demand
   b. supply
   c. both
   d. neither

Illustrate your answer with a diagram.

**12.** Select the correct answer. A price ceiling will usually shift:
   a. demand
   b. supply
   c. both
   d. neither

## REVIEW QUESTIONS

**13.** What is the "price" commonly called in the labor market?

**14.** Are households demanders or suppliers in the goods market? Are firms demanders or suppliers in the goods market? What about the labor market and the financial market?

**15.** Name some factors that can cause a shift in the demand curve in labor markets.

**16.** Name some factors that can cause a shift in the supply curve in labor markets.

**17.** How do economists define equilibrium in financial markets?

**18.** What would be a sign of a shortage in financial markets?

**19.** Would usury laws help or hinder resolution of a shortage in financial markets?

## CRITICAL THINKING QUESTIONS

**21.** Other than the demand for labor, what would be another example of a "derived demand?"

**22.** Suppose that a 5% increase in the minimum wage causes a 5% reduction in employment. How would this affect employers and how would it affect workers? In your opinion, would this be a good policy?

**23.** Under what circumstances would a minimum wage be a nonbinding price floor? Under what circumstances would a living wage be a binding price floor?

**24.** Suppose the U.S. economy began to grow more rapidly than other countries in the world. What would be the likely impact on U.S. financial markets as part of the global economy?

**25.** If the government imposed a federal interest rate ceiling of 20% on all loans, who would gain and who would lose?

**26.** Why are the factors that shift the demand for a product different from the factors that shift the demand for labor? Why are the factors that shift the supply of a product different from those that shift the supply of labor?

## PROBLEMS

**28.** Identify each of the following as involving either demand or supply. Draw a circular flow diagram and label the flows A through F. (Some choices can be on both sides of the goods market.)
   a. Households in the labor market
   b. Firms in the goods market
   c. Firms in the financial market
   d. Households in the goods market
   e. Firms in the labor market
   f. Households in the financial market

**20.** Whether the product market or the labor market, what happens to the equilibrium price and quantity for each of the four possibilities: increase in demand, decrease in demand, increase in supply, and decrease in supply.

**27.** During a discussion several years ago on building a pipeline to Alaska to carry natural gas, the U.S. Senate passed a bill stipulating that there should be a guaranteed minimum price for the natural gas that would flow through the pipeline. The thinking behind the bill was that if private firms had a guaranteed price for their natural gas, they would be more willing to drill for gas and to pay to build the pipeline.
   a. Using the demand and supply framework, predict the effects of this price floor on the price, quantity demanded, and quantity supplied.
   b. With the enactment of this price floor for natural gas, what are some of the likely unintended consequences in the market?
   c. Suggest some policies other than the price floor that the government can pursue if it wishes to encourage drilling for natural gas and for a new pipeline in Alaska.

**29.** Predict how each of the following events will raise or lower the equilibrium wage and quantity of oil workers in Texas. In each case, sketch a demand and supply diagram to illustrate your answer.
   a. The price of oil rises.
   b. New oil-drilling equipment is invented that is cheap and requires few workers to run.
   c. Several major companies that do not drill oil open factories in Texas, offering many well-paid jobs outside the oil industry.
   d. Government imposes costly new regulations to make oil-drilling a safer job.

**30.** Predict how each of the following economic changes will affect the equilibrium price and quantity in the financial market for home loans. Sketch a demand and supply diagram to support your answers.

   a. The number of people at the most common ages for home-buying increases.

   b. People gain confidence that the economy is growing and that their jobs are secure.

   c. Banks that have made home loans find that a larger number of people than they expected are not repaying those loans.

   d. Because of a threat of a war, people become uncertain about their economic future.

   e. The overall level of saving in the economy diminishes.

   f. The federal government changes its bank regulations in a way that makes it cheaper and easier for banks to make home loans.

**31.** Table 4.6 shows the amount of savings and borrowing in a market for loans to purchase homes, measured in millions of dollars, at various interest rates. What is the equilibrium interest rate and quantity in the capital financial market? How can you tell? Now, imagine that because of a shift in the perceptions of foreign investors, the supply curve shifts so that there will be $10 million less supplied at every interest rate. Calculate the new equilibrium interest rate and quantity, and explain why the direction of the interest rate shift makes intuitive sense.

| Interest Rate | Qs | Qd |
|---|---|---|
| 5% | 130 | 170 |
| 6% | 135 | 150 |
| 7% | 140 | 140 |
| 8% | 145 | 135 |
| 9% | 150 | 125 |
| 10% | 155 | 110 |

Table 4.6

**32.** Imagine that to preserve the traditional way of life in small fishing villages, a government decides to impose a price floor that will guarantee all fishermen a certain price for their catch.

   a. Using the demand and supply framework, predict the effects on the price, quantity demanded, and quantity supplied.

   b. With the enactment of this price floor for fish, what are some of the likely unintended consequences in the market?

   c. Suggest some policies other than the price floor to make it possible for small fishing villages to continue.

**33.** What happens to the price and the quantity bought and sold in the cocoa market if countries producing cocoa experience a drought and a new study is released demonstrating the health benefits of cocoa? Illustrate your answer with a demand and supply graph.

# 5 | Elasticity

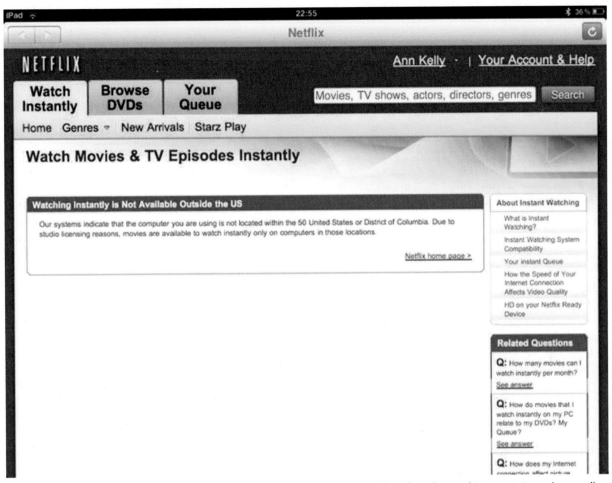

**Figure 5.1 Netflix On-Demand Media**  Netflix, Inc. is an American provider of on-demand Internet streaming media to many countries around the world, including the United States, and of flat rate DVD-by-mail in the United States. (Credit: modification of work by Traci Lawson/Flickr Creative Commons)

## Bring it Home

### That Will Be How Much?

Imagine going to your favorite coffee shop and having the waiter inform you the pricing has changed. Instead of $3 for a cup of coffee, you will now be charged $2 for coffee, $1 for creamer, and $1 for your choice of sweetener. If you pay your usual $3 for a cup of coffee, you must choose between creamer and sweetener. If you want both, you now face an extra charge of $1. Sound absurd? Well, that is similar to the situation Netflix customers found themselves in—they faced a 60% price hike to retain the same service in 2011.

In early 2011, Netflix consumers paid about $10 a month for a package consisting of streaming video and DVD rentals. In July 2011, the company announced a packaging change. Customers wishing to retain both streaming video and DVD rental would be charged $15.98 per month, a price increase of about 60%. In 2014, Netflix also raised its streaming video subscription price from $7.99 to $8.99 per month for new U.S. customers. The company also changed its policy of 4K streaming content from $9.00 to $12.00 per month that year.

How would customers of the 18-year-old firm react? Would they abandon Netflix? Would the ease of access to other venues make a difference in how consumers responded to the Netflix price change? We will explore the answers to those questions in this chapter, which focuses on the change in quantity with respect to a change in price, a concept economists call elasticity.

# Introduction to Elasticity

In this chapter, you will learn about:

- Price Elasticity of Demand and Price Elasticity of Supply

- Polar Cases of Elasticity and Constant Elasticity

- Elasticity and Pricing

- Elasticity in Areas Other Than Price

Anyone who has studied economics knows the law of demand: a higher price will lead to a lower quantity demanded. What you may not know is how much lower the quantity demanded will be. Similarly, the law of supply states that a higher price will lead to a higher quantity supplied. The question is: How much higher? This chapter will explain how to answer these questions and why they are critically important in the real world.

To find answers to these questions, we need to understand the concept of elasticity. **Elasticity** is an economics concept that measures responsiveness of one variable to changes in another variable. Suppose you drop two items from a second-floor balcony. The first item is a tennis ball. The second item is a brick. Which will bounce higher? Obviously, the tennis ball. We would say that the tennis ball has greater elasticity.

Consider an economic example. Cigarette taxes are an example of a "sin tax," a tax on something that is bad for you, like alcohol. Governments tax cigarettes at the state and national levels. State taxes range from a low of 17 cents per pack in Missouri to $4.35 per pack in New York. The average state cigarette tax is $1.69 per pack. The 2014 federal tax rate on cigarettes was $1.01 per pack, but in 2015 the Obama Administration proposed raising the federal tax nearly a dollar to $1.95 per pack. The key question is: How much would cigarette purchases decline?

Taxes on cigarettes serve two purposes: to raise tax revenue for government and to discourage cigarette consumption. However, if a higher cigarette tax discourages consumption considerably, meaning a greatly reduced quantity of cigarette sales, then the cigarette tax on each pack will not raise much revenue for the government. Alternatively, a higher cigarette tax that does not discourage consumption by much will actually raise more tax revenue for the government. Thus, when a government agency tries to calculate the effects of altering its cigarette tax, it must analyze how much the tax affects the quantity of cigarettes consumed. This issue reaches beyond governments and taxes. Every firm faces a similar issue. When a firm considers raising the sales price, it must consider how much a price increase will reduce the quantity demanded of what it sells. Conversely, when a firm puts its products on sale, it must expect (or hope) that the lower price will lead to a significantly higher quantity demanded.

# 5.1 | Price Elasticity of Demand and Price Elasticity of Supply

By the end of this section, you will be able to:
- Calculate the price elasticity of demand
- Calculate the price elasticity of supply

Both the demand and supply curve show the relationship between price and the number of units demanded or supplied. **Price elasticity** is the ratio between the percentage change in the quantity demanded (Qd) or supplied (Qs) and the corresponding percent change in price. The **price elasticity of demand** is the percentage change in the quantity *demanded* of a good or service divided by the percentage change in the price. The **price elasticity of supply** is the percentage change in quantity *supplied* divided by the percentage change in price.

We can usefully divide elasticities into three broad categories: elastic, inelastic, and unitary. An **elastic demand** or **elastic supply** is one in which the elasticity is greater than one, indicating a high responsiveness to changes in price. Elasticities that are less than one indicate low responsiveness to price changes and correspond to **inelastic demand** or **inelastic supply**. **Unitary elasticities** indicate proportional responsiveness of either demand or supply, as **Table 5.1** summarizes.

| If . . . | Then . . . | And It Is Called . . . |
|---|---|---|
| % change in quantity > % change in price | $\dfrac{\% \text{ change in quantity}}{\% \text{ change in price}} > 1$ | Elastic |
| % change in quantity = % change in price | $\dfrac{\% \text{ change in quantity}}{\% \text{ change in price}} = 1$ | Unitary |
| % change in quantity < % change in price | $\dfrac{\% \text{ change in quantity}}{\% \text{ change in price}} < 1$ | Inelastic |

**Table 5.1** Elastic, Inelastic, and Unitary: Three Cases of Elasticity

# Link It Up

Before we delve into the details of elasticity, enjoy this article (http://openstaxcollege.org/l/Super_Bowl) on elasticity and ticket prices at the Super Bowl.

To calculate elasticity along a demand or supply curve economists use the average percent change in both quantity and price. This is called the Midpoint Method for Elasticity, and is represented in the following equations:

$$\% \text{ change in quantity} = \frac{Q_2 - Q_1}{(Q_2 + Q_1)/2} \times 100$$

$$\% \text{ change in price} = \frac{P_2 - P_1}{(P_2 + P_1)/2} \times 100$$

The advantage of the Midpoint Method is that one obtains the same elasticity between two price points whether there is a price increase or decrease. This is because the formula uses the same base (average quantity and average price) for both cases.

## Calculating Price Elasticity of Demand

Let's calculate the elasticity between points A and B and between points G and H as **Figure 5.2** shows.

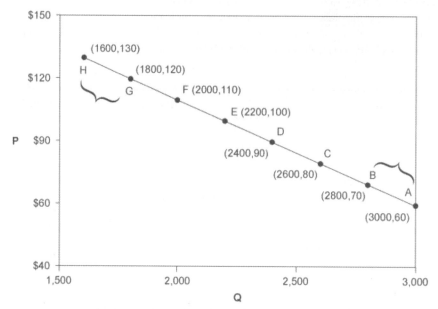

**Figure 5.2 Calculating the Price Elasticity of Demand**  We calculate the price elasticity of demand as the percentage change in quantity divided by the percentage change in price.

First, apply the formula to calculate the elasticity as price decreases from $70 at point B to $60 at point A:

$$\% \text{ change in quantity} = \frac{3{,}000 - 2{,}800}{(3{,}000 + 2{,}800)/2} \times 100$$

$$= \frac{200}{2{,}900} \times 100$$

$$= 6.9$$

$$\% \text{ change in price} = \frac{60 - 70}{(60 + 70)/2} \times 100$$

$$= \frac{-10}{65} \times 100$$

$$= -15.4$$

$$\text{Price Elasticity of Demand} = \frac{6.9\%}{-15.4\%}$$

$$= 0.45$$

Therefore, the elasticity of demand between these two points is $\frac{6.9\%}{-15.4\%}$ which is 0.45, an amount smaller than one, showing that the demand is inelastic in this interval. Price elasticities of demand are *always* negative since price and quantity demanded always move in opposite directions (on the demand curve). By convention, we always talk about elasticities as positive numbers. Mathematically, we take the absolute value of the result. We will ignore this detail from now on, while remembering to interpret elasticities as positive numbers.

This means that, along the demand curve between point B and A, if the price changes by 1%, the quantity demanded will change by 0.45%. A change in the price will result in a smaller percentage change in the quantity demanded. For example, a 10% *increase* in the price will result in only a 4.5% *decrease* in quantity demanded. A 10% *decrease* in the price will result in only a 4.5% *increase* in the quantity demanded. Price elasticities of demand are negative numbers indicating that the demand curve is downward sloping, but we read them as absolute values. The following Work It Out feature will walk you through calculating the price elasticity of demand.

# Work It Out

## Finding the Price Elasticity of Demand

Calculate the price elasticity of demand using the data in **Figure 5.2** for an increase in price from G to H. Has the elasticity increased or decreased?

Step 1. We know that:

$$\text{Price Elasticity of Demand} = \frac{\% \text{ change in quantity}}{\% \text{ change in price}}$$

Step 2. From the Midpoint Formula we know that:

$$\% \text{ change in quantity} = \frac{Q_2 - Q_1}{(Q_2 + Q_1)/2} \times 100$$

$$\% \text{ change in price} = \frac{P_2 - P_1}{(P_2 + P_1)/2} \times 100$$

Step 3. So we can use the values provided in the figure in each equation:

$$\% \text{ change in quantity} = \frac{1,600 - 1,800}{(1,600 + 1,800)/2} \times 100$$

$$= \frac{-200}{1,700} \times 100$$

$$= -11.76$$

$$\% \text{ change in price} = \frac{130 - 120}{(130 + 120)/2} \times 100$$

$$= \frac{10}{125} \times 100$$

$$= 8.0$$

Step 4. Then, we can use those values to determine the price elasticity of demand:

$$\text{Price Elasticity of Demand} = \frac{\% \text{ change in quantity}}{\% \text{ change in price}}$$

$$= \frac{-11.76}{8}$$

$$= 1.47$$

Therefore, the elasticity of demand from G to is H 1.47. The magnitude of the elasticity has increased (in absolute value) as we moved up along the demand curve from points A to B. Recall that the elasticity between these two points was 0.45. Demand was inelastic between points A and B and elastic between points G and H. This shows us that price elasticity of demand changes at different points along a straight-line demand curve.

## Calculating the Price Elasticity of Supply

Assume that an apartment rents for $650 per month and at that price the landlord rents 10,000 units are rented as **Figure 5.3** shows. When the price increases to $700 per month, the landlord supplies 13,000 units into the market. By what percentage does apartment supply increase? What is the price sensitivity?

**Figure 5.3 Price Elasticity of Supply**  We calculate the price elasticity of supply as the percentage change in quantity divided by the percentage change in price.

Using the Midpoint Method,

$$\% \text{ change in quantity} = \frac{13,000 - 10,000}{(13,000 + 10,000)/2} \times 100$$

$$= \frac{3,000}{11,500} \times 100$$

$$= 26.1$$

$$\% \text{ change in price} = \frac{\$700 - \$650}{(\$700 + \$650)/2} \times 100$$

$$= \frac{50}{675} \times 100$$

$$= 7.4$$

$$\text{Price Elasticity of Supply} = \frac{26.1\%}{7.4\%}$$

$$= 3.53$$

Again, as with the elasticity of demand, the elasticity of supply is not followed by any units. Elasticity is a ratio of one percentage change to another percentage change—nothing more—and we read it as an absolute value. In this case, a 1% rise in price causes an increase in quantity supplied of 3.5%. The greater than one elasticity of supply means that the percentage change in quantity supplied will be greater than a one percent price change. If you're starting to wonder if the concept of slope fits into this calculation, read the following Clear It Up box.

## Is the elasticity the slope?

It is a common mistake to confuse the slope of either the supply or demand curve with its elasticity. The slope is the rate of change in units along the curve, or the rise/run (change in y over the change in x). For example, in **Figure 5.2**, at each point shown on the demand curve, price drops by $10 and the number of units demanded increases by 200 compared to the point to its left. The slope is –10/200 along the entire demand curve and does not change. The price elasticity, however, changes along the curve. Elasticity between points A and B was 0.45 and increased to 1.47 between points G and H. Elasticity is the *percentage* change, which is a different calculation from the slope and has a different meaning.

When we are at the upper end of a demand curve, where price is high and the quantity demanded is low, a small change in the quantity demanded, even in, say, one unit, is pretty big in percentage terms. A change in price of, say, a dollar, is going to be much less important in percentage terms than it would have been at the bottom of the demand curve. Likewise, at the bottom of the demand curve, that one unit change when the quantity demanded is high will be small as a percentage.

Thus, at one end of the demand curve, where we have a large percentage change in quantity demanded over a small percentage change in price, the elasticity value would be high, or demand would be relatively elastic. Even with the same change in the price and the same change in the quantity demanded, at the other end of the demand curve the quantity is much higher, and the price is much lower, so the percentage change in quantity demanded is smaller and the percentage change in price is much higher. That means at the bottom of the curve we'd have a small numerator over a large denominator, so the elasticity measure would be much lower, or inelastic.

As we move along the demand curve, the values for quantity and price go up or down, depending on which way we are moving, so the percentages for, say, a $1 difference in price or a one unit difference in quantity, will change as well, which means the ratios of those percentages and hence the elasticity will change.

# 5.2 | Polar Cases of Elasticity and Constant Elasticity

By the end of this section, you will be able to:
- Differentiate between infinite and zero elasticity
- Analyze graphs in order to classify elasticity as constant unitary, infinite, or zero

There are two extreme cases of elasticity: when elasticity equals zero and when it is infinite. A third case is that of constant unitary elasticity. We will describe each case. **Infinite elasticity** or **perfect elasticity** refers to the extreme case where either the quantity demanded (Qd) or supplied (Qs) changes by an infinite amount in response to any change in price at all. In both cases, the supply and the demand curve are horizontal as **Figure 5.4** shows. While perfectly elastic supply curves are for the most part unrealistic, goods with readily available inputs and whose production can easily expand will feature highly elastic supply curves. Examples include pizza, bread, books, and pencils. Similarly, perfectly elastic demand is an extreme example. However, luxury goods, items that take a large share of individuals' income, and goods with many substitutes are likely to have highly elastic demand curves. Examples of such goods are Caribbean cruises and sports vehicles.

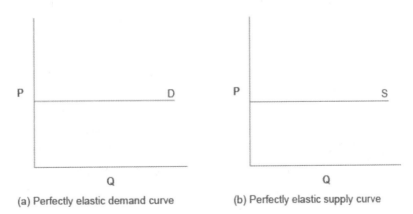

(a) Perfectly elastic demand curve          (b) Perfectly elastic supply curve

**Figure 5.4 Infinite Elasticity** The horizontal lines show that an infinite quantity will be demanded or supplied at a specific price. This illustrates the cases of a perfectly (or infinitely) elastic demand curve and supply curve. The quantity supplied or demanded is extremely responsive to price changes, moving from zero for prices close to P to infinite when prices reach P.

**Zero elasticity** or **perfect inelasticity**, as **Figure 5.5** depicts, refers to the extreme case in which a percentage change in price, no matter how large, results in zero change in quantity. While a perfectly inelastic supply is an extreme example, goods with limited supply of inputs are likely to feature highly inelastic supply curves. Examples include diamond rings or housing in prime locations such as apartments facing Central Park in New York City. Similarly, while perfectly inelastic demand is an extreme case, necessities with no close substitutes are likely to have highly inelastic demand curves. This is the case of life-saving drugs and gasoline.

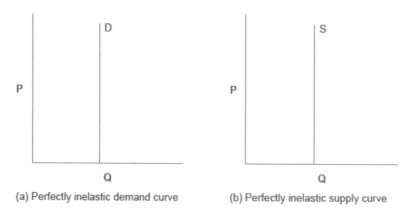

(a) Perfectly inelastic demand curve          (b) Perfectly inelastic supply curve

**Figure 5.5 Zero Elasticity**  The vertical supply curve and vertical demand curve show that there will be zero percentage change in quantity (a) demanded or (b) supplied, regardless of the price.

Constant unitary elasticity, in either a supply or demand curve, occurs when a price change of one percent results in a quantity change of one percent. **Figure 5.6** shows a demand curve with constant unit elasticity. Constant unitary elasticity, in either a supply or demand curve, occurs when a price change of one percent results in a quantity change of one percent. Figure 5.6 shows a demand curve with constant unit elasticity. Using the midpoint method, you can calculate that between points A and B on the demand curve, the price changes by 28.6% and quantity demanded also changes by 28.6%. Hence, the elasticity equals 1. Between points B and C, price again changes by 28.6% as does quantity, while between points C and D the corresponding percentage changes are 22.2% for both price and quantity. In each case, then, the percentage change in price equals the percentage change in quantity, and consequently elasticity equals 1. Notice that in absolute value, the declines in price, as you step down the demand curve, are not identical. Instead, the price falls by $2.00 from A to B, by a smaller amount of $1.50 from B to C, and by a still smaller amount of $0.90 from C to D. As a result, a demand curve with constant unitary elasticity moves from a steeper slope on the left and a flatter slope on the right—and a curved shape overall. Notice that in absolute value, the declines in price, as you step down the demand curve, are not identical. Instead, the price falls by $23 from A to B, by a smaller amount of $1.50 from B to C, and by a still smaller amount of $.90 from C to D. As a result, a demand curve with constant unitary elasticity has a steeper slope on the left and a flatter slope on the right—and a curved shape overall.

**Figure 5.6 A Constant Unitary Elasticity Demand Curve**  A demand curve with constant unitary elasticity will be a curved line. Notice how price and quantity demanded change by an identical percentage amount between each pair of points on the demand curve.

Unlike the demand curve with unitary elasticity, the supply curve with unitary elasticity is represented by a straight line, and that line goes through the origin. In each pair of points on the supply curve there is an equal difference in quantity of 30. However, in percentage value, using the midpoint method, the steps are decreasing as one moves from left to right, from 28.6% to 22.2% to 18.2%, because the quantity points in each percentage calculation are getting increasingly larger, which expands the denominator in the elasticity calculation of the percentage change in quantity.

Consider the price changes moving up the supply curve in **Figure 5.7**. From points D to E to F and to G on the supply curve, each step of $1.50 is the same in absolute value. However, if we measure the price changes in percentage change terms, using the midpoint method, they are also decreasing, from 28.6% to 22.2% to 18.2%, because the original price points in each percentage calculation are getting increasingly larger in value, increasing the denominator in the calculation of the percentage change in price. Along the constant unitary elasticity supply curve, the percentage quantity increases on the horizontal axis exactly match the percentage price increases on the vertical axis—so this supply curve has a constant unitary elasticity at all points.

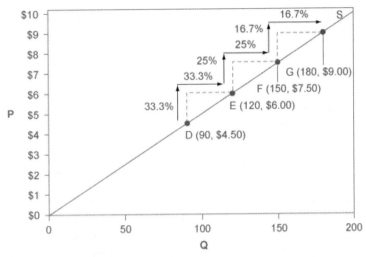

**Figure 5.7 A Constant Unitary Elasticity Supply Curve**  A constant unitary elasticity supply curve is a straight line reaching up from the origin. Between each pair of points, the percentage increase in quantity supplied is the same as the percentage increase in price.

# 5.3 | Elasticity and Pricing

By the end of this section, you will be able to:

- Analyze how price elasticities impact revenue
- Evaluate how elasticity can cause shifts in demand and supply
- Predict how the long-run and short-run impacts of elasticity affect equilibrium
- Explain how the elasticity of demand and supply determine the incidence of a tax on buyers and sellers

Studying elasticities is useful for a number of reasons, pricing being most important. Let's explore how elasticity relates to revenue and pricing, both in the long and short run. First, let's look at the elasticities of some common goods and services.

**Table 5.2** shows a selection of demand elasticities for different goods and services drawn from a variety of different studies by economists, listed in order of increasing elasticity.

| Goods and Services | Elasticity of Price |
|---|---|
| Housing | 0.12 |
| Transatlantic air travel (economy class) | 0.12 |
| Rail transit (rush hour) | 0.15 |
| Electricity | 0.20 |
| Taxi cabs | 0.22 |
| Gasoline | 0.35 |
| Transatlantic air travel (first class) | 0.40 |
| Wine | 0.55 |
| Beef | 0.59 |
| Transatlantic air travel (business class) | 0.62 |
| Kitchen and household appliances | 0.63 |
| Cable TV (basic rural) | 0.69 |
| Chicken | 0.64 |
| Soft drinks | 0.70 |
| Beer | 0.80 |
| New vehicle | 0.87 |
| Rail transit (off-peak) | 1.00 |
| Computer | 1.44 |
| Cable TV (basic urban) | 1.51 |
| Cable TV (premium) | 1.77 |
| Restaurant meals | 2.27 |

Table 5.2 Some Selected Elasticities of Demand

Note that demand for necessities such as housing and electricity is inelastic, while items that are not necessities such as restaurant meals are more price-sensitive. If the price of a restaurant meal increases by 10%, the quantity demanded will decrease by 22.7%. A 10% increase in the price of housing will cause only a slight decrease of 1.2% in the quantity of housing demanded.

# Link It Up ⚭

Read this article (http://openstaxcollege.org/l/Movietickets) for an example of price elasticity that may have affected you.

## Does Raising Price Bring in More Revenue?

Imagine that a band on tour is playing in an indoor arena with 15,000 seats. To keep this example simple, assume that the band keeps all the money from ticket sales. Assume further that the band pays the costs for its appearance, but that these costs, like travel, and setting up the stage, are the same regardless of how many people are in the audience. Finally, assume that all the tickets have the same price. (The same insights apply if ticket prices are more expensive for some seats than for others, but the calculations become more complicated.) The band knows that it faces a downward-sloping demand curve; that is, if the band raises the ticket price and, it will sell fewer seats. How should the band set the ticket price to generate the most total revenue, which in this example, because costs are fixed, will also mean the highest profits for the band? Should the band sell more tickets at a lower price or fewer tickets at a higher price?

The key concept in thinking about collecting the most revenue is the price elasticity of demand. Total revenue is price times the quantity of tickets sold. Imagine that the band starts off thinking about a certain price, which will result in the sale of a certain quantity of tickets. The three possibilities are in **Table 5.3**. If demand is elastic at that price level, then the band should cut the price, because the percentage drop in price will result in an even larger percentage increase in the quantity sold—thus raising total revenue. However, if demand is inelastic at that original quantity level, then the band should raise the ticket price, because a certain percentage increase in price will result in a smaller percentage decrease in the quantity sold—and total revenue will rise. If demand has a unitary elasticity at that quantity, then an equal percentage change in quantity will offset a moderate percentage change in the price—so the band will earn the same revenue whether it (moderately) increases or decreases the ticket price.

| If Demand Is . . . | Then . . . | Therefore . . . |
|---|---|---|
| Elastic | % change in Qd > % change in P | A given % rise in P will be more than offset by a larger % fall in Q so that total revenue (P × Q) falls. |
| Unitary | % change in Qd = % change in P | A given % rise in P will be exactly offset by an equal % fall in Q so that total revenue (P × Q) is unchanged. |
| Inelastic | % change in Qd < % change in P | A given % rise in P will cause a smaller % fall in Q so that total revenue (P × Q) rises. |

Table 5.3 Will the Band Earn More Revenue by Changing Ticket Prices?

What if the band keeps cutting price, because demand is elastic, until it reaches a level where it sells all 15,000 seats in the available arena? If demand remains elastic at that quantity, the band might try to move to a bigger arena, so that it could slash ticket prices further and see a larger percentage increase in the quantity of tickets sold. However, if the 15,000-seat arena is all that is available or if a larger arena would add substantially to costs, then this option may not work.

Conversely, a few bands are so famous, or have such fanatical followings, that demand for tickets may be inelastic right up to the point where the arena is full. These bands can, if they wish, keep raising the ticket price. Ironically, some of the most popular bands could make more revenue by setting prices so high that the arena is not full—but those who buy the tickets would have to pay very high prices. However, bands sometimes choose to sell tickets for less than the absolute maximum they might be able to charge, often in the hope that fans will feel happier and spend more on recordings, T-shirts, and other paraphernalia.

## Can Businesses Pass Costs on to Consumers?

Most businesses face a day-to-day struggle to figure out ways to produce at a lower cost, as one pathway to their goal of earning higher profits. However, in some cases, the price of a key input over which the firm has no control may rise. For example, many chemical companies use petroleum as a key input, but they have no control over the world market price for crude oil. Coffee shops use coffee as a key input, but they have no control over the world market price of coffee. If the cost of a key input rises, can the firm pass those higher costs along to consumers in the form of higher prices? Conversely, if new and less expensive ways of producing are invented, can the firm keep the benefits in the form of higher profits, or will the market pressure them to pass the gains along to consumers in the form of lower prices? The price elasticity of demand plays a key role in answering these questions.

Imagine that as a consumer of legal pharmaceutical products, you read a newspaper story that a technological breakthrough in the production of aspirin has occurred, so that every aspirin factory can now produce aspirin more cheaply. What does this discovery mean to you? **Figure 5.8** illustrates two possibilities. In **Figure 5.8** (a), the demand curve is highly inelastic. In this case, a technological breakthrough that shifts supply to the right, from $S_0$ to $S_1$, so that the equilibrium shifts from $E_0$ to $E_1$, creates a substantially lower price for the product with relatively little impact on the quantity sold. In **Figure 5.8** (b), the demand curve is highly elastic. In this case, the technological breakthrough leads to a much greater quantity sold in the market at very close to the original price. Consumers benefit more, in general, when the demand curve is more inelastic because the shift in the supply results in a much lower price for consumers.

 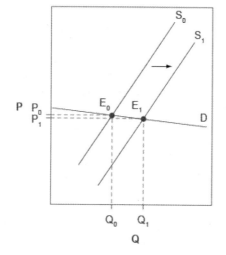

(a) Cost-saving with inelastic demand                (b) Cost-saving with elastic demand

**Figure 5.8 Passing along Cost Savings to Consumers**   Cost-saving gains cause supply to shift out to the right from $S_0$ to $S_1$; that is, at any given price, firms will be willing to supply a greater quantity. If demand is inelastic, as in (a), the result of this cost-saving technological improvement will be substantially lower prices. If demand is elastic, as in (b), the result will be only slightly lower prices. Consumers benefit in either case, from a greater quantity at a lower price, but the benefit is greater when demand is inelastic, as in (a).

Aspirin producers may find themselves in a nasty bind here. The situation in **Figure 5.8**, with extremely inelastic demand, means that a new invention may cause the price to drop dramatically while quantity changes little. As a result, the new production technology can lead to a drop in the revenue that firms earn from aspirin sales. However, if strong competition exists between aspirin producer, each producer may have little choice but to search for and implement any breakthrough that allows it to reduce production costs. After all, if one firm decides not to implement such a cost-saving technology, other firms that do can drive them out of business.

Since demand for food is generally inelastic, farmers may often face the situation in **Figure 5.8** (a). That is, a surge in production leads to a severe drop in price that can actually decrease the total revenue that farmers receive. Conversely, poor weather or other conditions that cause a terrible year for farm production can sharply raise prices so that the total revenue that the farmer receives increases. The Clear It Up box discusses how these issues relate to coffee.

## How do coffee prices fluctuate?

Coffee is an international crop. The top five coffee-exporting nations are Brazil, Vietnam, Colombia, Indonesia, and Ethiopia. In these nations and others, 20 million families depend on selling coffee beans as their main source of income. These families are exposed to enormous risk, because the world price of coffee bounces up and down. For example, in 1993, the world price of coffee was about 50 cents per pound. In 1995 it was four times as high, at $2 per pound. By 1997 it had fallen by half to $1.00 per pound. In 1998 it leaped back up to $2 per pound. By 2001 it had fallen back to 46 cents a pound. By early 2011 it rose to about $2.31 per pound. By the end of 2012, the price had fallen back to about $1.31 per pound.

The reason for these price fluctuations lies in a combination of inelastic demand and shifts in supply. The elasticity of coffee demand is only about 0.3; that is, a 10% rise in the price of coffee leads to a decline of about 3% in the quantity of coffee consumed. When a major frost hit the Brazilian coffee crop in 1994, coffee supply shifted to the left with an inelastic demand curve, leading to much higher prices. Conversely, when Vietnam entered the world coffee market as a major producer in the late 1990s, the supply curve shifted out to the right. With a highly inelastic demand curve, coffee prices fell dramatically. **Figure 5.8** (a) illustrates this situation.

Elasticity also reveals whether firms can pass higher costs that they incur on to consumers. Addictive substances, for which demand is inelastic, are products for which producers can pass higher costs on to consumers. For example, the demand for cigarettes is relatively inelastic among regular smokers who are somewhat addicted. Economic research suggests that increasing cigarette prices by 10% leads to about a 3% reduction in the quantity of cigarettes that adults smoke, so the elasticity of demand for cigarettes is 0.3. If society increases taxes on companies that produce cigarettes, the result will be, as in **Figure 5.9** (a), that the supply curve shifts from $S_0$ to $S_1$. However, as the equilibrium moves from $E_0$ to $E_1$, governments mainly pass along these taxes to consumers in the form of higher prices. These higher taxes on cigarettes will raise tax revenue for the government, but they will not much affect the quantity of smoking.

If the goal is to reduce the quantity of cigarettes demanded, we must achieve it by shifting this inelastic demand back to the left, perhaps with public programs to discourage cigarette use or to help people to quit. For example, anti-smoking advertising campaigns have shown some ability to reduce smoking. However, if cigarette demand were more elastic, as in **Figure 5.9** (b), then an increase in taxes that shifts supply from $S_0$ to $S_1$ and equilibrium from $E_0$ to $E_1$ would reduce the quantity of cigarettes smoked substantially. Youth smoking seems to be more elastic than adult smoking—that is, the quantity of youth smoking will fall by a greater percentage than the quantity of adult smoking in response to a given percentage increase in price.

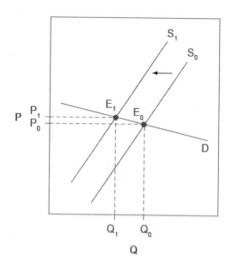

(a) Higher costs with inelastic demand    (b) Higher costs with elastic demand

**Figure 5.9 Passing along Higher Costs to Consumers**  Higher costs, like a higher tax on cigarette companies for the example we gave in the text, lead supply to shift to the left. This shift is identical in (a) and (b). However, in (a), where demand is inelastic, companies largely can pass the cost increase along to consumers in the form of higher prices, without much of a decline in equilibrium quantity. In (b), demand is elastic, so the shift in supply results primarily in a lower equilibrium quantity. Consumers suffer in either case, but in (a), they suffer from paying a higher price for the same quantity, while in (b), they suffer from buying a lower quantity (and presumably needing to shift their consumption elsewhere).

## Elasticity and Tax Incidence

The example of cigarette taxes demonstrated that because demand is inelastic, taxes are not effective at reducing the equilibrium quantity of smoking, and they mainly pass along to consumers in the form of higher prices. The analysis, or manner, of how a tax burden is divided between consumers and producers is called **tax incidence**. Typically, the tax incidence, or burden, falls both on the consumers and producers of the taxed good. However, if one wants to predict which group will bear most of the burden, all one needs to do is examine the elasticity of demand and supply. In the tobacco example, the tax burden falls on the most inelastic side of the market.

If demand is more inelastic than supply, consumers bear most of the tax burden, and if supply is more inelastic than demand, sellers bear most of the tax burden.

The intuition for this is simple. When the demand is inelastic, consumers are not very responsive to price changes, and the quantity demanded reduces only modestly when the tax is introduced. In the case of smoking, the demand is inelastic because consumers are addicted to the product. The government can then pass the tax burden along to consumers in the form of higher prices, without much of a decline in the equilibrium quantity.

Similarly, when a government introduces a tax in a market with an inelastic supply, such as, for example, beachfront hotels, and sellers have no alternative than to accept lower prices for their business, taxes do not greatly affect the equilibrium quantity. The tax burden now passes on to the sellers. If the supply was elastic and sellers had the possibility of reorganizing their businesses to avoid supplying the taxed good, the tax burden on the sellers would be much smaller. The tax would result in a much lower quantity sold instead of lower prices received. **Figure 5.10** illustrates this relationship between the tax incidence and elasticity of demand and supply.

(a) Elastic demand and inelastic supply

(b) Elastic supply and inelastic demand

**Figure 5.10 Elasticity and Tax Incidence** An excise tax introduces a wedge between the price paid by consumers (Pc) and the price received by producers (Pp). The vertical distance between Pc and Pp is the amount of the tax per unit. Pe is the equilibrium price prior to introduction of the tax. (a) When the demand is more elastic than supply, the tax incidence on consumers Pc – Pe is lower than the tax incidence on producers Pe – Pp. (b) When the supply is more elastic than demand, the tax incidence on consumers Pc – Pe is larger than the tax incidence on producers Pe – Pp. The more elastic the demand and supply curves, the lower the tax revenue.

In **Figure 5.10** (a), the supply is inelastic and the demand is elastic, such as in the example of beachfront hotels. While consumers may have other vacation choices, sellers can't easily move their businesses. By introducing a tax, the government essentially creates a wedge between the price paid by consumers Pc and the price received by producers Pp. In other words, of the total price paid by consumers, part is retained by the sellers and part is paid to the government in the form of a tax. The distance between Pc and Pp is the tax rate. The new market price is Pc, but sellers receive only Pp per unit sold, as they pay Pc-Pp to the government. Since we can view a tax as raising the costs of production, this could also be represented by a leftward shift of the supply curve, where the new supply curve would intercept the demand at the new quantity Qt. For simplicity, **Figure 5.10** omits the shift in the supply curve.

The tax revenue is given by the shaded area, which we obtain by multiplying the tax per unit by the total quantity sold Qt. The tax incidence on the consumers is given by the difference between the price paid Pc and the initial equilibrium price Pe. The tax incidence on the sellers is given by the difference between the initial equilibrium price Pe and the price they receive after the tax is introduced Pp. In **Figure 5.10** (a), the tax burden falls disproportionately on the sellers, and a larger proportion of the tax revenue (the shaded area) is due to the resulting lower price received by the sellers than by the resulting higher prices paid by the buyers. **Figure 5.10** (b) describes the example of the tobacco excise tax where the supply is more elastic than demand. The tax incidence now falls disproportionately on consumers, as shown by the large difference between the price they pay, Pc, and the initial equilibrium price, Pe. Sellers receive a lower price than before the tax, but this difference is much smaller than the change in consumers' price. From this analysis one can also predict whether a tax is likely to create a large revenue or not. The more elastic the demand curve, the more likely that consumers will reduce quantity instead of paying higher prices. The more elastic the supply curve, the more likely that sellers will reduce the quantity sold, instead of taking lower prices. In a market where both the demand and supply are very elastic, the imposition of an excise tax generates low revenue.

Some believe that excise taxes hurt mainly the specific industries they target. For example, the medical device excise tax, in effect since 2013, has been controversial for it can delay industry profitability and therefore hamper start-ups and medical innovation. However, whether the tax burden falls mostly on the medical device industry or on the patients depends simply on the elasticity of demand and supply.

## Long-Run vs. Short-Run Impact

Elasticities are often lower in the short run than in the long run. On the demand side of the market, it can sometimes be difficult to change Qd in the short run, but easier in the long run. Consumption of energy is a clear example. In the short run, it is not easy for a person to make substantial changes in energy consumption. Maybe you can carpool to work sometimes or adjust your home thermostat by a few degrees if the cost of energy rises, but that is about all.

However, in the long run you can purchase a car that gets more miles to the gallon, choose a job that is closer to where you live, buy more energy-efficient home appliances, or install more insulation in your home. As a result, the elasticity of demand for energy is somewhat inelastic in the short run, but much more elastic in the long run.

**Figure 5.11** is an example, based roughly on historical experience, for the responsiveness of Qd to price changes. In 1973, the price of crude oil was $12 per barrel and total consumption in the U.S. economy was 17 million barrels per day. That year, the nations who were members of the Organization of Petroleum Exporting Countries (OPEC) cut off oil exports to the United States for six months because the Arab members of OPEC disagreed with the U.S. support for Israel. OPEC did not bring exports back to their earlier levels until 1975—a policy that we can interpret as a shift of the supply curve to the left in the U.S. petroleum market. **Figure 5.11** (a) and **Figure 5.11** (b) show the same original equilibrium point and the same identical shift of a supply curve to the left from $S_0$ to $S_1$.

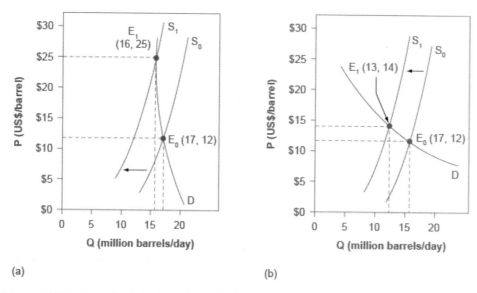

**Figure 5.11 How a Shift in Supply Can Affect Price or Quantity**   The intersection ($E_0$) between demand curve D and supply curve $S_0$ is the same in both (a) and (b). The shift of supply to the left from $S_0$ to $S_1$ is identical in both (a) and (b). The new equilibrium ($E_1$) has a higher price and a lower quantity than the original equilibrium ($E_0$) in both (a) and (b). However, the shape of the demand curve D is different in (a) and (b), being more elastic in (b) than in (a). As a result, the shift in supply can result either in a new equilibrium with a much higher price and an only slightly smaller quantity, as in (a), with more inelastic demand, or in a new equilibrium with only a small increase in price and a relatively larger reduction in quantity, as in (b), with more elastic demand.

**Figure 5.11** (a) shows inelastic demand for oil in the short run similar to that which existed for the United States in 1973. In **Figure 5.11** (a), the new equilibrium ($E_1$) occurs at a price of $25 per barrel, roughly double the price before the OPEC shock, and an equilibrium quantity of 16 million barrels per day. **Figure 5.11** (b) shows what the outcome would have been if the U.S. demand for oil had been more elastic, a result more likely over the long term. This alternative equilibrium ($E_1$) would have resulted in a smaller price increase to $14 per barrel and larger reduction in equilibrium quantity to 13 million barrels per day. In 1983, for example, U.S. petroleum consumption was 15.3 million barrels a day, which was lower than in 1973 or 1975. U.S. petroleum consumption was down even though the U.S. economy was about one-fourth larger in 1983 than it had been in 1973. The primary reason for the lower quantity was that higher energy prices spurred conservation efforts, and after a decade of home insulation, more fuel-efficient cars, more efficient appliances and machinery, and other fuel-conserving choices, the demand curve for energy had become more elastic.

On the supply side of markets, producers of goods and services typically find it easier to expand production in the long term of several years rather than in the short run of a few months. After all, in the short run it can be costly or difficult to build a new factory, hire many new workers, or open new stores. However, over a few years, all of these are possible.

In most markets for goods and services, prices bounce up and down more than quantities in the short run, but quantities often move more than prices in the long run. The underlying reason for this pattern is that supply and demand are often inelastic in the short run, so that shifts in either demand or supply can cause a relatively greater change in prices. However, since supply and demand are more elastic in the long run, the long-run movements in prices are more muted, while quantity adjusts more easily in the long run.

# 5.4 | Elasticity in Areas Other Than Price

By the end of this section, you will be able to:
- Calculate the income elasticity of demand and the cross-price elasticity of demand
- Calculate the elasticity in labor and financial capital markets through an understanding of the elasticity of labor supply and the elasticity of savings
- Apply concepts of price elasticity to real-world situations

The basic idea of elasticity—how a percentage change in one variable causes a percentage change in another variable—does not just apply to the responsiveness quantity supplied and quantity demanded to changes in the price of a product. Recall that quantity demanded (Qd) depends on income, tastes and preferences, the prices of related goods, and so on, as well as price. Similarly, quantity supplied (Qs) depends on factors such as the cost of production, as well as price. We can measure elasticity for any determinant of quantity supplied and quantity demanded, not just the price.

## Income Elasticity of Demand

The income elasticity of demand is the percentage change in quantity demanded divided by the percentage change in income.

$$\text{Income elasticity of demand} \ = \ \frac{\%\text{ change in quantity demanded}}{\%\text{ change in income}}$$

For most products, most of the time, the income elasticity of demand is positive: that is, a rise in income will cause an increase in the quantity demanded. This pattern is common enough that we refer to these goods as normal goods. However, for a few goods, an increase in income means that one might purchase less of the good. For example, those with a higher income might buy fewer hamburgers, because they are buying more steak instead, or those with a higher income might buy less cheap wine and more imported beer. When the income elasticity of demand is negative, we call the good an inferior good.

We introduced the concepts of normal and inferior goods in **Demand and Supply**. A higher level of income causes a demand curve to shift to the right for a normal good, which means that the income elasticity of demand is positive. How far the demand shifts depends on the income elasticity of demand. A higher income elasticity means a larger shift. However, for an inferior good, that is, when the income elasticity of demand is negative, a higher level of income would cause the demand curve for that good to shift to the left. Again, how much it shifts depends on how large the (negative) income elasticity is.

## Cross-Price Elasticity of Demand

A change in the price of one good can shift the quantity demanded for another good. If the two goods are complements, like bread and peanut butter, then a drop in the price of one good will lead to an increase in the quantity demanded of the other good. However, if the two goods are substitutes, like plane tickets and train tickets, then a drop in the price of one good will cause people to substitute toward that good, and to reduce consumption of the other good. Cheaper plane tickets lead to fewer train tickets, and vice versa.

The **cross-price elasticity of demand** puts some meat on the bones of these ideas. The term "cross-price" refers to the idea that the price of one good is affecting the quantity demanded of a different good. Specifically, the cross-price elasticity of demand is the percentage change in the quantity of good A that is demanded as a result of a percentage change in the price of good B.

$$\text{Cross-price elasticity of demand} \ = \ \frac{\%\text{ change in Qd of good A}}{\%\text{ change in price of good B}}$$

Substitute goods have positive cross-price elasticities of demand: if good A is a substitute for good B, like coffee and tea, then a higher price for B will mean a greater quantity consumed of A. Complement goods have negative cross-price elasticities: if good A is a complement for good B, like coffee and sugar, then a higher price for B will mean a lower quantity consumed of A.

## Elasticity in Labor and Financial Capital Markets

The concept of elasticity applies to any market, not just markets for goods and services. In the labor market, for example, the **wage elasticity of labor supply**—that is, the percentage change in hours worked divided by the percentage change in wages—will reflect the shape of the labor supply curve. Specifically:

$$\text{Elasticity of labor supply} \quad = \quad \frac{\text{\% change in quantity of labor supplied}}{\text{\% change in wage}}$$

The wage elasticity of labor supply for teenage workers is generally fairly elastic: that is, a certain percentage change in wages will lead to a larger percentage change in the quantity of hours worked. Conversely, the wage elasticity of labor supply for adult workers in their thirties and forties is fairly inelastic. When wages move up or down by a certain percentage amount, the quantity of hours that adults in their prime earning years are willing to supply changes but by a lesser percentage amount.

In markets for financial capital, the **elasticity of savings**—that is, the percentage change in the quantity of savings divided by the percentage change in interest rates—will describe the shape of the supply curve for financial capital. That is:

$$\text{Elasticity of savings} \quad = \quad \frac{\text{\% change in quantity of financial savings}}{\text{\% change in interest rate}}$$

Sometimes laws are proposed that seek to increase the quantity of savings by offering tax breaks so that the return on savings is higher. Such a policy will have a comparatively large impact on increasing the quantity saved if the supply curve for financial capital is elastic, because then a given percentage increase in the return to savings will cause a higher percentage increase in the quantity of savings. However, if the supply curve for financial capital is highly inelastic, then a percentage increase in the return to savings will cause only a small increase in the quantity of savings. The evidence on the supply curve of financial capital is controversial but, at least in the short run, the elasticity of savings with respect to the interest rate appears fairly inelastic.

## Expanding the Concept of Elasticity

The elasticity concept does not even need to relate to a typical supply or demand curve at all. For example, imagine that you are studying whether the Internal Revenue Service should spend more money on auditing tax returns. We can frame the question in terms of the elasticity of tax collections with respect to spending on tax enforcement; that is, what is the percentage change in tax collections derived from a given percentage change in spending on tax enforcement?

With all of the elasticity concepts that we have just described, some of which are in **Table 5.4**, the possibility of confusion arises. When you hear the phrases "elasticity of demand" or "elasticity of supply," they refer to the elasticity with respect to price. Sometimes, either to be extremely clear or because economists are discussing a wide variety of elasticities, we will call the elasticity of demand or the demand elasticity the price elasticity of demand or the "elasticity of demand with respect to price." Similarly, economists sometimes use the term elasticity of supply or the supply elasticity, to avoid any possibility of confusion, the price elasticity of supply or "the elasticity of supply with respect to price." However, in whatever context, the idea of elasticity always refers to percentage change in one variable, almost always a price or money variable, and how it causes a percentage change in another variable, typically a quantity variable of some kind.

| | |
|---|---|
| Income elasticity of demand $\quad = \quad \dfrac{\text{\% change in Qd}}{\text{\% change in income}}$ | |
| Cross-price elasticity of demand $\quad = \quad \dfrac{\text{\% change in Qd of good A}}{\text{\% change in price of good B}}$ | |

**Table 5.4** Formulas for Calculating Elasticity

| Wage elasticity of labor supply | $=$ | $\dfrac{\text{\% change in quantity of labor supplied}}{\text{\% change in wage}}$ |
|---|---|---|
| Wage elasticity of labor demand | $=$ | $\dfrac{\text{\% change in quantity of labor demanded}}{\text{\% change in wage}}$ |
| Interest rate elasticity of savings | $=$ | $\dfrac{\text{\% change in quantity of savings}}{\text{\% change in interest rate}}$ |
| Interest rate elasticity of borrowing | $=$ | $\dfrac{\text{\% change in quantity of borrowing}}{\text{\% change in interest rate}}$ |

Table 5.4 Formulas for Calculating Elasticity

# Bring it Home

## That Will Be How Much?

How did the 60% price increase in 2011 end up for Netflix? It has been a very bumpy ride.

Before the price increase, there were about 24.6 million U.S. subscribers. After the price increase, 810,000 infuriated U.S. consumers canceled their Netflix subscriptions, dropping the total number of subscribers to 23.79 million. Fast forward to June 2013, when there were 36 million streaming Netflix subscribers in the United States. This was an increase of 11.4 million subscribers since the price increase—an average per quarter growth of about 1.6 million. This growth is less than the 2 million per quarter increases Netflix experienced in the fourth quarter of 2010 and the first quarter of 2011.

During the first year after the price increase, the firm's stock price (a measure of future expectations for the firm) fell from about $33.60 per share per share to just under $7.80. By the end of 2016, however, the stock price was at $123 per share. Today, Netflix has more than 86 million subscribers million subscribers in fifty countries.

What happened? Obviously, Netflix company officials understood the law of demand. Company officials reported, when announcing the price increase, this could result in the loss of about 600,000 existing subscribers. Using the elasticity of demand formula, it is easy to see company officials expected an inelastic response:

$$= \frac{-600{,}000/[(24 \text{ million} + 24.6 \text{ million})/2]}{\$6/[(\$10 + \$16)/2]}$$

$$= \frac{-600{,}000/24.3 \text{ million}}{\$6/\$13}$$

$$= \frac{-0.025}{0.46}$$

$$= -0.05$$

In addition, Netflix officials had anticipated the price increase would have little impact on attracting new customers. Netflix anticipated adding up to 1.29 million new subscribers in the third quarter of 2011. It is true this was slower growth than the firm had experienced—about 2 million per quarter.

Why was the estimate of customers leaving so far off? In the more than two decades since Netflix had been founded, there was an increase in the number of close, but not perfect, substitutes. Consumers now had choices ranging from Vudu, Amazon Prime, Hulu, and Redbox, to retail stores. Jaime Weinman reported in *Maclean's* that Redbox kiosks are "a five-minute drive for less from 68 percent of Americans, and it seems that many people still find a five-minute drive more convenient than loading up a movie online." It seems that in 2012, many consumers still preferred a physical DVD disk over streaming video.

What missteps did the Netflix management make? In addition to misjudging the elasticity of demand, by failing to account for close substitutes, it seems they may have also misjudged customers' preferences and tastes. Yet, as the population increases, the preference for streaming video may overtake physical DVD disks. Netflix, the source of numerous late night talk show laughs and jabs in 2011, may yet have the last laugh.

# KEY TERMS

**constant unitary elasticity**  when a given percent price change in price leads to an equal percentage change in quantity demanded or supplied

**cross-price elasticity of demand**  the percentage change in the quantity of good A that is demanded as a result of a percentage change in good B

**elastic demand**  when the elasticity of demand is greater than one, indicating a high responsiveness of quantity demanded or supplied to changes in price

**elastic supply**  when the elasticity of either supply is greater than one, indicating a high responsiveness of quantity demanded or supplied to changes in price

**elasticity**  an economics concept that measures responsiveness of one variable to changes in another variable

**elasticity of savings**  the percentage change in the quantity of savings divided by the percentage change in interest rates

**inelastic demand**  when the elasticity of demand is less than one, indicating that a 1 percent increase in price paid by the consumer leads to less than a 1 percent change in purchases (and vice versa); this indicates a low responsiveness by consumers to price changes

**inelastic supply**  when the elasticity of supply is less than one, indicating that a 1 percent increase in price paid to the firm will result in a less than 1 percent increase in production by the firm; this indicates a low responsiveness of the firm to price increases (and vice versa if prices drop)

**infinite elasticity**  the extremely elastic situation of demand or supply where quantity changes by an infinite amount in response to any change in price; horizontal in appearance

**perfect elasticity**  see infinite elasticity

**perfect inelasticity**  see zero elasticity

**price elasticity**  the relationship between the percent change in price resulting in a corresponding percentage change in the quantity demanded or supplied

**price elasticity of demand**  percentage change in the quantity *demanded* of a good or service divided the percentage change in price

**price elasticity of supply**  percentage change in the quantity *supplied* divided by the percentage change in price

**tax incidence**  manner in which the tax burden is divided between buyers and sellers

**unitary elasticity**  when the calculated elasticity is equal to one indicating that a change in the price of the good or service results in a proportional change in the quantity demanded or supplied

**wage elasticity of labor supply**  the percentage change in hours worked divided by the percentage change in wages

**zero inelasticity**  the highly inelastic case of demand or supply in which a percentage change in price, no matter how large, results in zero change in the quantity; vertical in appearance

# KEY CONCEPTS AND SUMMARY

### 5.1 Price Elasticity of Demand and Price Elasticity of Supply

Price elasticity measures the responsiveness of the quantity demanded or supplied of a good to a change in its price. We compute it as the percentage change in quantity demanded (or supplied) divided by the percentage change in price. We can describe elasticity as elastic (or very responsive), unit elastic, or inelastic (not very responsive). Elastic demand or supply curves indicate that quantity demanded or supplied respond to price changes in a greater than proportional manner. An inelastic demand or supply curve is one where a given percentage change in price will cause a smaller percentage change in quantity demanded or supplied. A unitary elasticity means that a given percentage change in price leads to an equal percentage change in quantity demanded or supplied.

### 5.2 Polar Cases of Elasticity and Constant Elasticity

Infinite or perfect elasticity refers to the extreme case where either the quantity demanded or supplied changes by an infinite amount in response to any change in price at all. Zero elasticity refers to the extreme case in which a percentage change in price, no matter how large, results in zero change in quantity. Constant unitary elasticity in either a supply or demand curve refers to a situation where a price change of one percent results in a quantity change of one percent.

### 5.3 Elasticity and Pricing

In the market for goods and services, quantity supplied and quantity demanded are often relatively slow to react to changes in price in the short run, but react more substantially in the long run. As a result, demand and supply often (but not always) tend to be relatively inelastic in the short run and relatively elastic in the long run. A tax incidence depends on the relative price elasticity of supply and demand. When supply is more elastic than demand, buyers bear most of the tax burden, and when demand is more elastic than supply, producers bear most of the cost of the tax. Tax revenue is larger the more inelastic the demand and supply are.

### 5.4 Elasticity in Areas Other Than Price

Elasticity is a general term, that reflects responsiveness. It refers to the change of one variable divided by the percentage change of a related variable that we can apply to many economic connections. For instance, the income elasticity of demand is the percentage change in quantity demanded divided by the percentage change in income. The cross-price elasticity of demand is the percentage change in the quantity demanded of a good divided by the percentage change in the price of another good. Elasticity applies in labor markets and financial capital markets just as it does in markets for goods and services. The wage elasticity of labor supply is the percentage change in the quantity of hours supplied divided by the percentage change in the wage. The elasticity of savings with respect to interest rates is the percentage change in the quantity of savings divided by the percentage change in interest rates.

## SELF-CHECK QUESTIONS

**1.** From the data in **Table 5.5** about demand for smart phones, calculate the price elasticity of demand from: point B to point C, point D to point E, and point G to point H. Classify the elasticity at each point as elastic, inelastic, or unit elastic.

| Points | P | Q |
|--------|-----|-------|
| A | 60 | 3,000 |
| B | 70 | 2,800 |
| C | 80 | 2,600 |
| D | 90 | 2,400 |
| E | 100 | 2,200 |
| F | 110 | 2,000 |
| G | 120 | 1,800 |
| H | 130 | 1,600 |

Table 5.5

**2.** From the data in **Table 5.6** about supply of alarm clocks, calculate the price elasticity of supply from: point J to point K, point L to point M, and point N to point P. Classify the elasticity at each point as elastic, inelastic, or unit elastic.

| Point | Price | Quantity Supplied |
|-------|-------|-------------------|
| J | $8 | 50 |
| K | $9 | 70 |
| L | $10 | 80 |
| M | $11 | 88 |
| N | $12 | 95 |
| P | $13 | 100 |

Table 5.6

**3.** Why is the demand curve with constant unitary elasticity concave?

**4.** Why is the supply curve with constant unitary elasticity a straight line?

**5.** The federal government decides to require that automobile manufacturers install new anti-pollution equipment that costs $2,000 per car. Under what conditions can carmakers pass almost all of this cost along to car buyers? Under what conditions can carmakers pass very little of this cost along to car buyers?

**6.** Suppose you are in charge of sales at a pharmaceutical company, and your firm has a new drug that causes bald men to grow hair. Assume that the company wants to earn as much revenue as possible from this drug. If the elasticity of demand for your company's product at the current price is 1.4, would you advise the company to raise the price, lower the price, or to keep the price the same? What if the elasticity were 0.6? What if it were 1? Explain your answer.

**7.** What would the gasoline price elasticity of supply mean to UPS or FedEx?

**8.** The average annual income rises from $25,000 to $38,000, and the quantity of bread consumed in a year by the average person falls from 30 loaves to 22 loaves. What is the income elasticity of bread consumption? Is bread a normal or an inferior good?

**9.** Suppose the cross-price elasticity of apples with respect to the price of oranges is 0.4, and the price of oranges falls by 3%. What will happen to the demand for apples?

## REVIEW QUESTIONS

**10.** What is the formula for calculating elasticity?

**11.** What is the price elasticity of demand? Can you explain it in your own words?

**12.** What is the price elasticity of supply? Can you explain it in your own words?

**13.** Describe the general appearance of a demand or a supply curve with zero elasticity.

**14.** Describe the general appearance of a demand or a supply curve with infinite elasticity.

**15.** If demand is elastic, will shifts in supply have a larger effect on equilibrium quantity or on price?

**16.** If demand is inelastic, will shifts in supply have a larger effect on equilibrium price or on quantity?

**17.** If supply is elastic, will shifts in demand have a larger effect on equilibrium quantity or on price?

**18.** If supply is inelastic, will shifts in demand have a larger effect on equilibrium price or on quantity?

**19.** Would you usually expect elasticity of demand or supply to be higher in the short run or in the long run? Why?

**20.** Under which circumstances does the tax burden fall entirely on consumers?

**21.** What is the formula for the income elasticity of demand?

**22.** What is the formula for the cross-price elasticity of demand?

**23.** What is the formula for the wage elasticity of labor supply?

**24.** What is the formula for elasticity of savings with respect to interest rates?

## CRITICAL THINKING QUESTIONS

**25.** Transatlantic air travel in business class has an estimated elasticity of demand of 0.62, while transatlantic air travel in economy class has an estimated price elasticity of 0.12. Why do you think this is the case?

**26.** What is the relationship between price elasticity and position on the demand curve? For example, as you move up the demand curve to higher prices and lower quantities, what happens to the measured elasticity? How would you explain that?

**27.** Can you think of an industry (or product) with near infinite elasticity of supply in the short term? That is, what is an industry that could increase Qs almost without limit in response to an increase in the price?

**28.** Would you expect supply to play a more significant role in determining the price of a basic necessity like food or a luxury like perfume? Explain. *Hint*: Think about how the price elasticity of demand will differ between necessities and luxuries.

**29.** A city has built a bridge over a river and it decides to charge a toll to everyone who crosses. For one year, the city charges a variety of different tolls and records information on how many drivers cross the bridge. The city thus gathers information about elasticity of demand. If the city wishes to raise as much revenue as possible from the tolls, where will the city decide to charge a toll: in the inelastic portion of the demand curve, the elastic portion of the demand curve, or the unit elastic portion? Explain.

**30.** In a market where the supply curve is perfectly inelastic, how does an excise tax affect the price paid by consumers and the quantity bought and sold?

## PROBLEMS

**33.** The equation for a demand curve is $P = 48 - 3Q$. What is the elasticity in moving from a quantity of 5 to a quantity of 6?

**34.** The equation for a demand curve is $P = 2/Q$. What is the elasticity of demand as price falls from 5 to 4? What is the elasticity of demand as the price falls from 9 to 8? Would you expect these answers to be the same?

**35.** The equation for a supply curve is $4P = Q$. What is the elasticity of supply as price rises from 3 to 4? What is the elasticity of supply as the price rises from 7 to 8? Would you expect these answers to be the same?

**36.** The equation for a supply curve is $P = 3Q - 8$. What is the elasticity in moving from a price of 4 to a price of 7?

**37.** The supply of paintings by Leonardo Da Vinci, who painted the *Mona Lisa* and *The Last Supper* and died in 1519, is highly inelastic. Sketch a supply and demand diagram, paying attention to the appropriate elasticities, to illustrate that demand for these paintings will determine the price.

**31.** Economists define normal goods as having a positive income elasticity. We can divide normal goods into two types: Those whose income elasticity is less than one and those whose income elasticity is greater than one. Think about products that would fall into each category. Can you come up with a name for each category?

**32.** Suppose you could buy shoes one at a time, rather than in pairs. What do you predict the cross-price elasticity for left shoes and right shoes would be?

**38.** Say that a certain stadium for professional football has 70,000 seats. What is the shape of the supply curve for tickets to football games at that stadium? Explain.

**39.** When someone's kidneys fail, the person needs to have medical treatment with a dialysis machine (unless or until they receive a kidney transplant) or they will die. Sketch a supply and demand diagram, paying attention to the appropriate elasticities, to illustrate that the supply of such dialysis machines will primarily determine the price.

**40.** Assume that the supply of low-skilled workers is fairly elastic, but the employers' demand for such workers is fairly inelastic. If the policy goal is to expand employment for low-skilled workers, is it better to focus on policy tools to shift the supply of unskilled labor or on tools to shift the demand for unskilled labor? What if the policy goal is to raise wages for this group? Explain your answers with supply and demand diagrams.

# 6 | The Macroeconomic Perspective

**Figure 6.1 The Great Depression** At times, such as when many people having trouble making ends meet, it is easy to tell how the economy is doing. This photograph shows people lined up during the Great Depression, waiting for relief checks. At other times, when some are doing well and others are not, it is more difficult to ascertain how the economy of a country is doing. (Credit: modification of work by the U.S. Library of Congress/Wikimedia Commons)

## Bring it Home

### How is the Economy Doing? How Does One Tell?

The 1990s were boom years for the U.S. economy. Beginning in the late 2000s, from 2007 to 2014 economic performance in in the U.S. was poor. What causes the economy to expand or contract? Why do businesses fail when they are making all the right decisions? Why do workers lose their jobs when they are hardworking and productive? Are bad economic times a failure of the market system? Are they a failure of the government? These are all questions of macroeconomics, which we will begin to address in this chapter. We will not be able to answer all of these questions here, but we will start with the basics: How is the economy doing? How can we tell?

The macro economy includes all buying and selling, all production and consumption; everything that goes on in every market in the economy. How can we get a handle on that? The answer begins more than 80 years ago, during the Great Depression. President Franklin D. Roosevelt and his economic advisers knew things were bad—but how could they express and measure just how bad it was? An economist named Simon Kuznets, who later won the Nobel Prize for his work, came up with a way to track what the entire economy is producing. In this chapter, you will learn how the government constructs GDP, how we use it, and why it is so important.

# Introduction to the Macroeconomic Perspective

In this chapter, you will learn about:

- Measuring the Size of the Economy: Gross Domestic Product

- Adjusting Nominal Values to Real Values

- Tracking Real GDP over Time

- Comparing GDP among Countries

- How Well GDP Measures the Well-Being of Society

Macroeconomics focuses on the economy as a whole (or on whole economies as they interact). What causes recessions? What makes unemployment stay high when recessions are supposed to be over? Why do some countries grow faster than others? Why do some countries have higher standards of living than others? These are all questions that macroeconomics addresses. Macroeconomics involves adding up the economic activity of all households and all businesses in all markets to obtain the overall demand and supply in the economy. However, when we do that, something curious happens. It is not unusual that what results at the macro level is different from the sum of the microeconomic parts. What seems sensible from a microeconomic point of view can have unexpected or counterproductive results at the macroeconomic level. Imagine that you are sitting at an event with a large audience, like a live concert or a basketball game. A few people decide that they want a better view, and so they stand up. However, when these people stand up, they block the view for other people, and the others need to stand up as well if they wish to see. Eventually, nearly everyone is standing up, and as a result, no one can see much better than before. The rational decision of some individuals at the micro level—to stand up for a better view—ended up as self-defeating at the macro level. This is not macroeconomics, but it is an apt analogy.

Macroeconomics is a rather massive subject. How are we going to tackle it? **Figure 6.2** illustrates the structure we will use. We will study macroeconomics from three different perspectives:

1. What are the macroeconomic goals? (Macroeconomics as a discipline does not have goals, but we do have goals for the macro economy.)

2. What are the frameworks economists can use to analyze the macroeconomy?

3. Finally, what are the policy tools governments can use to manage the macroeconomy?

**Figure 6.2 Macroeconomic Goals, Framework, and Policies**   This chart shows what macroeconomics is about. The box on the left indicates a consensus of what are the most important goals for the macro economy, the middle box lists the frameworks economists use to analyze macroeconomic changes (such as inflation or recession), and the box on the right indicates the two tools the federal government uses to influence the macro economy.

## Goals

In thinking about the macroeconomy's overall health, it is useful to consider three primary goals: economic growth, low unemployment, and low inflation.

- Economic growth ultimately determines the prevailing standard of living in a country. Economists measure growth by the percentage change in real (inflation-adjusted) gross domestic product. A growth rate of more than 3% is considered good.

- Unemployment, as measured by the unemployment rate, is the percentage of people in the labor force who do not have a job. When people lack jobs, the economy is wasting a precious resource-labor, and the result is lower goods and services produced. Unemployment, however, is more than a statistic—it represents people's livelihoods. While measured unemployment is unlikely to ever be zero, economists consider a measured unemployment rate of 5% or less low (good).

- Inflation is a sustained increase in the overall level of prices, and is measured by the consumer price index. If many people face a situation where the prices that they pay for food, shelter, and healthcare are rising much faster than the wages they receive for their labor, there will be widespread unhappiness as their standard of living declines. For that reason, low inflation—an inflation rate of 1–2%—is a major goal.

## Frameworks

As you learn in the micro part of this book, principal tools that economists use are theories and models (see **Welcome to Economics!** for more on this). In microeconomics, we used the theories of supply and demand. In macroeconomics, we use the theories of aggregate demand (AD) and aggregate supply (AS). This book presents two perspectives on macroeconomics: the Neoclassical perspective and the Keynesian perspective, each of which has its own version of AD and AS. Between the two perspectives, you will obtain a good understanding of what drives the macroeconomy.

## Policy Tools

National governments have two tools for influencing the macroeconomy. The first is monetary policy, which involves managing the money supply and interest rates. The second is fiscal policy, which involves changes in government spending/purchases and taxes.

We will explain each of the items in **Figure 6.2** in detail in one or more other chapters. As you learn these things, you will discover that the goals and the policy tools are in the news almost every day.

# 6.1 | Measuring the Size of the Economy: Gross Domestic Product

By the end of this section, you will be able to:
- Identify the components of GDP on the demand side and on the supply side
- Evaluate how economists measure gross domestic product (GDP)
- Contrast and calculate GDP, net exports, and net national product

Macroeconomics is an empirical subject, so the first step toward understanding it is to measure the economy.

How large is the U.S. economy? Economists typically measure the size of a nation's overall economy by its **gross domestic product (GDP)**, which is the value of all final goods and services produced within a country in a given year. Measuring GDP involves counting the production of millions of different goods and services—smart phones, cars, music downloads, computers, steel, bananas, college educations, and all other new goods and services that a country produced in the current year—and summing them into a total dollar value. This task is straightforward: take the quantity of everything produced, multiply it by the price at which each product sold, and add up the total. In 2016, the U.S. GDP totaled $18.6 trillion, the largest GDP in the world.

Each of the market transactions that enter into GDP must involve both a buyer and a seller. We can measure an economy's GDP either by the total dollar value of what consumers purchase in the economy, or by the total dollar value of what is the country produces. There is even a third way, as we will explain later.

## GDP Measured by Components of Demand

Who buys all of this production? We can divide this demand into four main parts: consumer spending (consumption), business spending (investment), government spending on goods and services, and spending on net exports. (See the following Clear It Up feature to understand what we mean by investment.) **Table 6.1** shows how these four components added up to the GDP in 2016. **Figure 6.4** (a) shows the levels of consumption, investment, and government purchases over time, expressed as a percentage of GDP, while **Figure 6.4** (b) shows the levels of exports and imports as a percentage of GDP over time. A few patterns about each of these components are worth noticing. **Table 6.1** shows the components of GDP from the demand side.

| Components of GDP on the Demand Side (in trillions of dollars) | | Percentage of Total |
| --- | --- | --- |
| Consumption | $12.8 | 68.8% |
| Investment | $3.0 | 16.1% |
| Government | $3.3 | 17.7% |
| Exports | $2.2 | 11.8% |
| Imports | −$2.7 | −14.5% |
| **Total GDP** | **$18.6** | **100%** |

Table 6.1 Components of U.S. GDP in 2016: From the Demand Side   (Source: http://bea.gov/iTable/index_nipa.cfm)

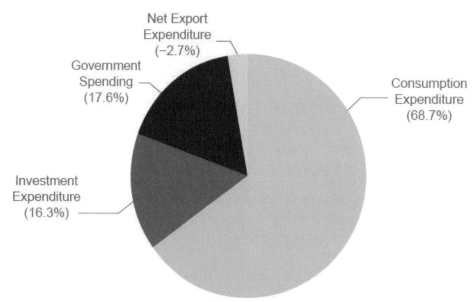

Figure 6.3 Percentage of Components of U.S. GDP on the Demand Side  Consumption makes up over half of the demand side components of the GDP. (Source: http://bea.gov/iTable/index_nipa.cfm)

## What does the word "investment" mean?

What do economists mean by investment, or business spending? In calculating GDP, investment does not refer to purchasing stocks and bonds or trading financial assets. It refers to purchasing new capital goods, that is, new commercial real estate (such as buildings, factories, and stores) and equipment, residential housing construction, and inventories. Inventories that manufacturers produce this year are included in this year's GDP—even if they are not yet sold. From the accountant's perspective, it is as if the firm invested in its own inventories. Business investment in 2016 was $3 trillion, according to the Bureau of Economic Analysis.

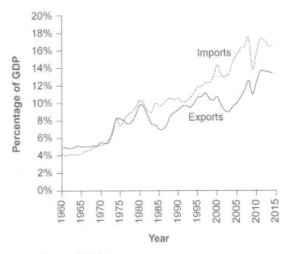

(a) Demand from consumption, investment, and government

(b) Imports and exports

**Figure 6.4 Components of GDP on the Demand Side** (a) Consumption is about two-thirds of GDP, and it has been on a slight upward trend over time. Business investment hovers around 15% of GDP, but it fluctuates more than consumption. Government spending on goods and services is slightly under 20% of GDP and has declined modestly over time. (b) Exports are added to total demand for goods and services, while imports are subtracted from total demand. If exports exceed imports, as in most of the 1960s and 1970s in the U.S. economy, a trade surplus exists. If imports exceed exports, as in recent years, then a trade deficit exists. (Source: http://bea.gov/iTable/index_nipa.cfm)

Consumption expenditure by households is the largest component of GDP, accounting for about two-thirds of the GDP in any year. This tells us that consumers' spending decisions are a major driver of the economy. However, consumer spending is a gentle elephant: when viewed over time, it does not jump around too much, and has increased modestly from about 60% of GDP in the 1960s and 1970s.

Investment expenditure refers to purchases of physical plant and equipment, primarily by businesses. If Starbucks builds a new store, or Amazon buys robots, they count these expenditures under business investment. Investment demand is far smaller than consumption demand, typically accounting for only about 15–18% of GDP, but it is very important for the economy because this is where jobs are created. However, it fluctuates more noticeably than consumption. Business investment is volatile. New technology or a new product can spur business investment, but then confidence can drop and business investment can pull back sharply.

If you have noticed any of the infrastructure projects (new bridges, highways, airports) launched during the 2009 recession, you have seen how important government spending can be for the economy. Government expenditure in the United States is close to 20% of GDP, and includes spending by all three levels of government: federal, state, and local. The only part of government spending counted in demand is government purchases of goods or services produced in the economy. Examples include the government buying a new fighter jet for the Air Force (federal government spending), building a new highway (state government spending), or a new school (local government spending). A significant portion of government budgets consists of transfer payments, like unemployment benefits, veteran's benefits, and Social Security payments to retirees. The government excludes these payments from GDP because it does not receive a new good or service in return or exchange. Instead they are transfers of income from taxpayers to others. If you are curious about the awesome undertaking of adding up GDP, read the following Clear It Up feature.

# Clear It Up

## How do statisticians measure GDP?

Government economists at the Bureau of Economic Analysis (BEA), within the U.S. Department of Commerce, piece together estimates of GDP from a variety of sources.

Once every five years, in the second and seventh year of each decade, the Bureau of the Census carries out a detailed census of businesses throughout the United States. In between, the Census Bureau carries out a monthly survey of retail sales. The government adjusts these figures with foreign trade data to account for exports that are produced in the United States and sold abroad and for imports that are produced abroad and sold here. Once every ten years, the Census Bureau conducts a comprehensive survey of housing and residential finance. Together, these sources provide the main basis for figuring out what is produced for consumers.

For investment, the Census Bureau carries out a monthly survey of construction and an annual survey of expenditures on physical capital equipment.

For what the federal government purchases, the statisticians rely on the U.S. Department of the Treasury. An annual Census of Governments gathers information on state and local governments. Because the government spends a considerable amount at all levels hiring people to provide services, it also tracks a large portion of spending through payroll records that state governments and the Social Security Administration collect.

With regard to foreign trade, the Census Bureau compiles a monthly record of all import and export documents. Additional surveys cover transportation and travel, and make adjustments for financial services that are produced in the United States for foreign customers.

Many other sources contribute to GDP estimates. Information on energy comes from the U.S. Department of Transportation and Department of Energy. The Agency for Health Care Research and Quality collects information on healthcare. Surveys of landlords find out about rental income. The Department of Agriculture collects statistics on farming.

All these bits and pieces of information arrive in different forms, at different time intervals. The BEA melds them together to produce GDP estimates on a quarterly basis (every three months). The BEA then "annualizes" these numbers by multiplying by four. As more information comes in, the BEA updates and revises these estimates. BEA releases the GDP "advance" estimate for a certain quarter one month after a quarter. The "preliminary" estimate comes out one month after that. The BEA publishes the "final" estimate one month later, but it is not actually final. In July, the BEA releases roughly updated estimates for the previous calendar year. Then, once every five years, after it has processed all the results of the latest detailed five-year business census, the BEA revises all of the past GDP estimates according to the newest methods and data, going all the way back to 1929.

# Link It Up

Visit this website (http://openstaxcollege.org/l/beafaq) to read FAQs on the BEA site. You can even email your own questions!

When thinking about the demand for domestically produced goods in a global economy, it is important to count spending on exports—domestically produced goods that a country sells abroad. Similarly, we must also subtract spending on imports—goods that a country produces in other countries that residents of this country purchase. The GDP net export component is equal to the dollar value of exports (X) minus the dollar value of imports (M), (X − M). We call the gap between exports and imports the **trade balance**. If a country's exports are larger than its imports, then a country has a **trade surplus**. In the United States, exports typically exceeded imports in the 1960s and 1970s, as **Figure 6.4**(b) shows.

Since the early 1980s, imports have typically exceeded exports, and so the United States has experienced a **trade**

**deficit** in most years. The trade deficit grew quite large in the late 1990s and in the mid-2000s. **Figure 6.4** (b) also shows that imports and exports have both risen substantially in recent decades, even after the declines during the Great Recession between 2008 and 2009. As we noted before, if exports and imports are equal, foreign trade has no effect on total GDP. However, even if exports and imports are balanced overall, foreign trade might still have powerful effects on particular industries and workers by causing nations to shift workers and physical capital investment toward one industry rather than another.

Based on these four components of demand, we can measure GDP as:

$$GDP = \text{Consumption} + \text{Investment} + \text{Government} + \text{Trade balance}$$
$$GDP = C + I + G + (X - M)$$

Understanding how to measure GDP is important for analyzing connections in the macro economy and for thinking about macroeconomic policy tools.

## GDP Measured by What is Produced

Everything that we purchase somebody must first produce. **Table 6.2** breaks down what a country produces into five categories: **durable goods**, **nondurable goods**, **services**, **structures**, and the change in **inventories**. Before going into detail about these categories, notice that total GDP measured according to what is produced is exactly the same as the GDP measured by looking at the five components of demand. **Figure 6.5** provides a visual representation of this information.

|  | Components of GDP on the Supply Side (in trillions of dollars) | Percentage of Total |
|---|---|---|
| Goods |  |  |
| Durable goods | $3.0 | 16.1% |
| Nondurable goods | $2.5 | 13.4% |
| Services | $11.6 | 62.4% |
| Structures | $1.5 | 8.1% |
| Change in inventories | $0.0 | 0.0% |
| **Total GDP** | **$18.6** | **100%** |

**Table 6.2 Components of U.S. GDP on the Production Side, 2016**   (Source: http://bea.gov/iTable/index_nipa.cfm)

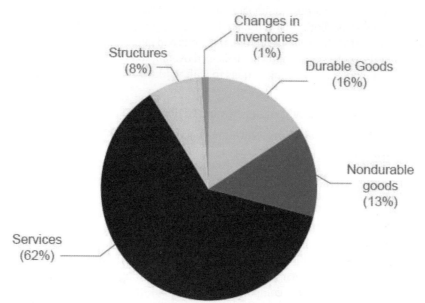

**Figure 6.5 Percentage of Components of GDP on the Production Side**  Services make up over 60 percent of the production side components of GDP in the United States.

Since every market transaction must have both a buyer and a seller, GDP must be the same whether measured by what is demanded or by what is produced. **Figure 6.6** shows these components of what is produced, expressed as a percentage of GDP, since 1960.

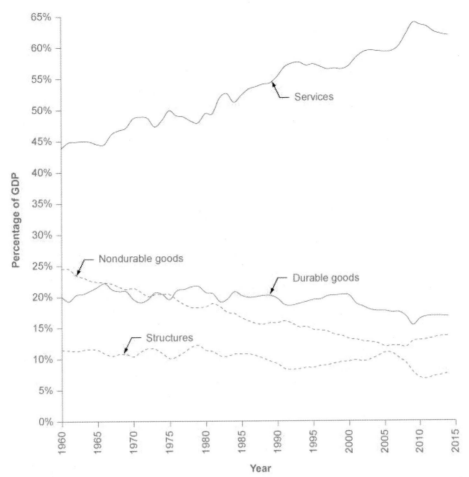

**Figure 6.6 Types of Production**   Services are the largest single component of total supply, representing over 60 percent of GDP, up from about 45 perent in the early 1960s. Durable and nondurable goods constitute the manufacturing sector, and they have declined from 45 percent of GDP in 1960 to about 30 percent in 2016. Nondurable goods used to be larger than durable goods, but in recent years, nondurable goods have been dropping to below the share of durable goods, which is less than 20% of GDP. Structures hover around 10% of GDP. We do not show here the change in inventories, the final component of aggregate supply. It is typically less than 1% of GDP.

In thinking about what is produced in the economy, many non-economists immediately focus on solid, long-lasting goods, like cars and computers. By far the largest part of GDP, however, is services. Moreover, services have been a growing share of GDP over time. A detailed breakdown of the leading service industries would include healthcare, education, and legal and financial services. It has been decades since most of the U.S. economy involved making solid objects. Instead, the most common jobs in a modern economy involve a worker looking at pieces of paper or a computer screen; meeting with co-workers, customers, or suppliers; or making phone calls.

Even within the overall category of goods, long-lasting durable goods like cars and refrigerators are about the same share of the economy as short-lived nondurable goods like food and clothing. The category of structures includes everything from homes, to office buildings, shopping malls, and factories. Inventories is a small category that refers to the goods that one business has produced but has not yet sold to consumers, and are still sitting in warehouses and on shelves. The amount of inventories sitting on shelves tends to decline if business is better than expected, or to rise if business is worse than expected.

## Another Way to Measure GDP: The National Income Approach

GDP is a measure of what is produced in a nation. The primary way GDP is estimated is with the Expenditure Approach we discussed above, but there is another way. Everything a firm produces, when sold, becomes revenues to the firm. Businesses use revenues to pay their bills: Wages and salaries for labor, interest and dividends for capital, rent for land, profit to the entrepreneur, etc. So adding up all the income produced in a year provides a second way of measuring GDP. This is why the terms GDP and **national income** are sometimes used interchangeably. The total value of a nation's output is equal to the total value of a nation's income.

## The Problem of Double Counting

We define GDP as the current value of all final goods and services produced in a nation in a year. What are final goods? They are goods at the furthest stage of production at the end of a year. Statisticians who calculate GDP must avoid the mistake of **double counting**, in which they count output more than once as it travels through the production stages. For example, imagine what would happen if government statisticians first counted the value of tires that a tire manufacturer produces, and then counted the value of a new truck that an automaker sold that contains those tires. In this example, the statisticians would have counted the value of the tires twice-because the truck's price includes the value of the tires.

To avoid this problem, which would overstate the size of the economy considerably, government statisticians count just the value of **final goods and services** in the chain of production that are sold for consumption, investment, government, and trade purposes. Statisticians exclude intermediate **intermediate goods**, which are goods that go into producing other goods, from GDP calculations. From the example above, they will only count the Ford truck's value. The value of what businesses provide to other businesses is captured in the final products at the end of the production chain.

The concept of GDP is fairly straightforward: it is just the dollar value of all final goods and services produced in the economy in a year. In our decentralized, market-oriented economy, actually calculating the more than $18 trillion-dollar U.S. GDP—along with how it is changing every few months—is a full-time job for a brigade of government statisticians.

| What is Counted in GDP | What is not included in GDP |
|---|---|
| Consumption | Intermediate goods |
| Business investment | Transfer payments and non-market activities |
| Government spending on goods and services | Used goods |
| Net exports | Illegal goods |

**Table 6.3 Counting GDP**

Notice the items that are not counted into GDP, as **Table 6.3** outlines. The sales of used goods are not included because they were produced in a previous year and are part of that year's GDP. The entire underground economy of services paid "under the table" and illegal sales should be counted, but is not, because it is impossible to track these sales. In Friedrich Schneider's recent study of shadow economies, he estimated the underground economy in the United States to be 6.6% of GDP, or close to $2 trillion dollars in 2013 alone. Transfer payments, such as payment by the government to individuals, are not included, because they do not represent production. Also, production of some goods—such as home production as when you make your breakfast—is not counted because these goods are not sold in the marketplace.

# Link It Up 

Visit this website (http://openstaxcollege.org/l/undergroundecon) to read about the "New Underground Economy."

## Other Ways to Measure the Economy

Besides GDP, there are several different but closely related ways of measuring the size of the economy. We mentioned above that we can think of GDP as total production and as total purchases. We can also think of it as total income since anything one produces and sells yields income.

One of the closest cousins of GDP is the **gross national product (GNP)**. GDP includes only what country produces within its borders. GNP adds what domestic businesses and labor abroad produces, and subtracts any payments that foreign labor and businesses located in the United States send home to other countries. In other words, GNP is based more on what a country's citizens and firms produce, wherever they are located, and GDP is based on what happens within a certain county's geographic boundaries. For the United States, the gap between GDP and GNP is relatively small; in recent years, only about 0.2%. For small nations, which may have a substantial share of their population working abroad and sending money back home, the difference can be substantial.

We calculate **net national product (NNP)** by taking GNP and then subtracting the value of how much physical capital is worn out, or reduced in value because of aging, over the course of a year. The process by which capital ages and loses value is called **depreciation**. We can further subdivide NNP into **national income**, which includes all income to businesses and individuals, and personal income, which includes only income to people.

For practical purposes, it is not vital to memorize these definitions. However, it is important to be aware that these differences exist and to know what statistic you are examining, so that you do not accidentally compare, say, GDP in one year or for one country with GNP or NNP in another year or another country. To get an idea of how these calculations work, follow the steps in the following Work It Out feature.

## Work It Out ──○──○──○

### Calculating GDP, Net Exports, and NNP

Based on the information in **Table 6.4**:

 a.  What is the value of GDP?

 b.  What is the value of net exports?

 c.  What is the value of NNP?

| | |
|---|---|
| Government purchases | $120 billion |
| Depreciation | $40 billion |
| Consumption | $400 billion |
| Business Investment | $60 billion |
| Exports | $100 billion |

**Table 6.4**

| Imports | $120 billion |
| Income receipts from rest of the world | $10 billion |
| Income payments to rest of the world | $8 billion |

**Table 6.4**

Step 1. To calculate GDP use the following formula:

$$\text{GDP} = \text{Consumption} + \text{Investment} + \text{Government spending} + (\text{Exports} - \text{Imports})$$
$$= C + I + G + (X - M)$$
$$= \$400 + \$60 + \$120 + (\$100 - \$120)$$
$$= \$560 \text{ billion}$$

Step 2. To calculate net exports, subtract imports from exports.

$$\text{Net exports} = X - M$$
$$= \$100 - \$120$$
$$= -\$20 \text{ billion}$$

Step 3. To calculate NNP, use the following formula:

$$\text{NNP} = \text{GDP} + \text{Income receipts from the rest of the world}$$
$$- \text{Income payments to the rest of the world} - \text{Depreciation}$$
$$= \$560 + \$10 - \$8 - \$40$$
$$= \$522 \text{ billion}$$

# 6.2 | Adjusting Nominal Values to Real Values

By the end of this section, you will be able to:
- Contrast nominal GDP and real GDP
- Explain GDP deflator
- Calculate real GDP based on nominal GDP values

When examining economic statistics, there is a crucial distinction worth emphasizing. The distinction is between nominal and real measurements, which refer to whether or not inflation has distorted a given statistic. Looking at economic statistics without considering inflation is like looking through a pair of binoculars and trying to guess how close something is: unless you know how strong the lenses are, you cannot guess the distance very accurately. Similarly, if you do not know the inflation rate, it is difficult to figure out if a rise in GDP is due mainly to a rise in the overall level of prices or to a rise in quantities of goods produced. The **nominal value** of any economic statistic means that we measure the statistic in terms of actual prices that exist at the time. The **real value** refers to the same statistic after it has been adjusted for inflation. Generally, it is the real value that is more important.

## Converting Nominal to Real GDP

**Table 6.5** shows U.S. GDP at five-year intervals since 1960 in nominal dollars; that is, GDP measured using the actual market prices prevailing in each stated year. **Figure 6.7** also reflects this data in a graph.

| Year | Nominal GDP (billions of dollars) | GDP Deflator (2005 = 100) |
|------|-----------------------------------|---------------------------|
| 1960 | 543.3 | 19.0 |
| 1965 | 743.7 | 20.3 |
| 1970 | 1,075.9 | 24.8 |
| 1975 | 1,688.9 | 34.1 |
| 1980 | 2,862.5 | 48.3 |
| 1985 | 4,346.7 | 62.3 |
| 1990 | 5,979.6 | 72.7 |
| 1995 | 7,664.0 | 81.7 |
| 2000 | 10,289.7 | 89.0 |
| 2005 | 13,095.4 | 100.0 |
| 2010 | 14,958.3 | 110.0 |

Table 6.5 U.S. Nominal GDP and the GDP Deflator   (Source: www.bea.gov)

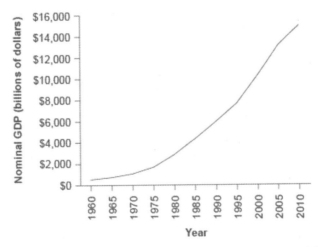

Figure 6.7 U.S. Nominal GDP, 1960–2010   Nominal GDP values have risen exponentially from 1960 through 2010, according to the BEA.

If an unwary analyst compared nominal GDP in 1960 to nominal GDP in 2010, it might appear that national output had risen by a factor of more than twenty-seven over this time (that is, GDP of $14,958 billion in 2010 divided by GDP of $543 billion in 1960 = 27.5). This conclusion would be highly misleading. Recall that we define nominal GDP as the quantity of every good or service produced multiplied by the price at which it was sold, summed up for all goods and services. In order to see how much production has actually increased, we need to extract the effects of higher prices on nominal GDP. We can easily accomplish this using the GDP deflator.

The GDP deflator is a price index measuring the average prices of all goods and services included in the economy. We explore price indices in detail and how we compute them in **Inflation**, but this definition will do in the context of this chapter. **Table 6.5** provides the GDP deflator data and **Figure 6.8** shows it graphically.

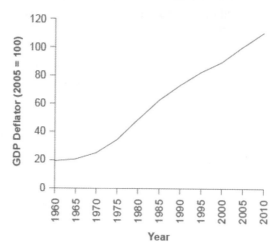

**Figure 6.8 U.S. GDP Deflator, 1960–2010** Much like nominal GDP, the GDP deflator has risen exponentially from 1960 through 2010. (Source: BEA)

**Figure 6.8** shows that the price level has risen dramatically since 1960. The price level in 2010 was almost six times higher than in 1960 (the deflator for 2010 was 110 versus a level of 19 in 1960). Clearly, much of the growth in nominal GDP was due to inflation, not an actual change in the quantity of goods and services produced, in other words, not in real GDP. Recall that nominal GDP can rise for two reasons: an increase in output, and/or an increase in prices. What is needed is to extract the increase in prices from nominal GDP so as to measure only changes in output. After all, the dollars used to measure nominal GDP in 1960 are worth more than the inflated dollars of 1990—and the price index tells exactly how much more. This adjustment is easy to do if you understand that nominal measurements are in value terms, where

$$\text{Value} \quad = \quad \text{Price} \times \text{Quantity}$$
$$\text{or}$$
$$\text{Nominal GDP} \quad = \quad \text{GDP Deflator} \times \text{Real GDP}$$

Let's look at an example at the micro level. Suppose the t-shirt company, Coolshirts, sells 10 t-shirts at a price of $9 each.

$$\begin{aligned} \text{Coolshirt's nominal revenue from sales} \quad &= \quad \text{Price} \times \text{Quantity} \\ &= \quad \$9 \times 10 \\ &= \quad \$90 \end{aligned}$$

Then,

$$\begin{aligned} \text{Coolshirt's real income} \quad &= \quad \frac{\text{Nominal revenue}}{\text{Price}} \\ &= \quad \frac{\$90}{\$9} \\ &= \quad 10 \end{aligned}$$

In other words, when we compute "real" measurements we are trying to obtain actual quantities, in this case, 10 t-shirts.

With GDP, it is just a tiny bit more complicated. We start with the same formula as above:

$$\text{Real GDP} \quad = \quad \frac{\text{Nominal GDP}}{\text{Price Index}}$$

For reasons that we will explain in more detail below, mathematically, a price index is a two-digit decimal number like 1.00 or 0.85 or 1.25. Because some people have trouble working with decimals, when the price index is published, it has traditionally been multiplied by 100 to get integer numbers like 100, 85, or 125. What this means is that when we "deflate" nominal figures to get real figures (by dividing the nominal by the price index). We also need to remember to divide the published price index by 100 to make the math work. Thus, the formula becomes:

$$\text{Real GDP} = \frac{\text{Nominal GDP}}{\text{Price Index} / 100}$$

Now read the following Work It Out feature for more practice calculating real GDP.

# Work It Out ○──○──○

## Computing GDP

It is possible to use the data in Table 6.5 to compute real GDP.

Step 1. Look at Table 6.5, to see that, in 1960, nominal GDP was $543.3 billion and the price index (GDP deflator) was 19.0.

Step 2. To calculate the real GDP in 1960, use the formula:

$$
\begin{aligned}
\text{Real GDP} &= \frac{\text{Nominal GDP}}{\text{Price Index} / 100} \\
&= \frac{\$543.3 \text{ billion}}{19 / 100} \\
&= \$2{,}859.5 \text{ billion}
\end{aligned}
$$

We'll do this in two parts to make it clear. First adjust the price index: 19 divided by 100 = 0.19. Then divide into nominal GDP: $543.3 billion / 0.19 = $2,859.5 billion.

Step 3. Use the same formula to calculate the real GDP in 1965.

$$
\begin{aligned}
\text{Real GDP} &= \frac{\text{Nominal GDP}}{\text{Price Index} / 100} \\
&= \frac{\$743.7 \text{ billion}}{20.3 / 100} \\
&= \$3{,}663.5 \text{ billion}
\end{aligned}
$$

Step 4. Continue using this formula to calculate all of the real GDP values from 1960 through 2010. The calculations and the results are in Table 6.6.

| Year | Nominal GDP (billions of dollars) | GDP Deflator (2005 = 100) | Calculations | Real GDP (billions of 2005 dollars) |
|------|-----------------------------------|---------------------------|--------------|-------------------------------------|
| 1960 | 543.3 | 19.0 | 543.3 / (19.0/100) | 2859.5 |
| 1965 | 743.7 | 20.3 | 743.7 / (20.3/100) | 3663.5 |
| 1970 | 1075.9 | 24.8 | 1,075.9 / (24.8/100) | 4338.3 |
| 1975 | 1688.9 | 34.1 | 1,688.9 / (34.1/100) | 4952.8 |
| 1980 | 2862.5 | 48.3 | 2,862.5 / (48.3/100) | 5926.5 |
| 1985 | 4346.7 | 62.3 | 4,346.7 / (62.3/100) | 6977.0 |
| 1990 | 5979.6 | 72.7 | 5,979.6 / (72.7/100) | 8225.0 |

Table 6.6 Converting Nominal to Real GDP   (Source: Bureau of Economic Analysis, www.bea.gov)

| Year | Nominal GDP (billions of dollars) | GDP Deflator (2005 = 100) | Calculations | Real GDP (billions of 2005 dollars) |
|------|-----------------------------------|---------------------------|--------------|-------------------------------------|
| 1995 | 7664.0 | 82.0 | 7,664 / (82.0/100) | 9346.3 |
| 2000 | 10289.7 | 89.0 | 10,289.7 / (89.0/100) | 11561.5 |
| 2005 | 13095.4 | 100.0 | 13,095.4 / (100.0/100) | 13095.4 |
| 2010 | 14958.3 | 110.0 | 14,958.3 / (110.0/100) | 13598.5 |

**Table 6.6 Converting Nominal to Real GDP** (Source: Bureau of Economic Analysis, www.bea.gov)

There are a couple things to notice here. Whenever you compute a real statistic, one year (or period) plays a special role. It is called the base year (or base period). The base year is the year whose prices we use to compute the real statistic. When we calculate real GDP, for example, we take the quantities of goods and services produced in each year (for example, 1960 or 1973) and multiply them by their prices in the base year (in this case, 2005), so we get a measure of GDP that uses prices that do not change from year to year. That is why real GDP is labeled "Constant Dollars" or, in this example, "2005 Dollars," which means that real GDP is constructed using prices that existed in 2005. While the example here uses 2005 as the base year, more generally, you can use any year as the base year. The formula is:

$$\text{GDP deflator} = \frac{\text{Nominal GDP}}{\text{Real GDP}} \times 100$$

Rearranging the formula and using the data from 2005:

$$\text{Real GDP} = \frac{\text{Nominal GDP}}{\text{Price Index} / 100}$$
$$= \frac{\$13,095.4 \text{ billion}}{100 / 100}$$
$$= \$13,095.4 \text{ billion}$$

Comparing real GDP and nominal GDP for 2005, you see they are the same. This is no accident. It is because we have chosen 2005 as the "base year" in this example. Since the price index in the base year always has a value of 100 (by definition), nominal and real GDP are always the same in the base year.

Look at the data for 2010.

$$\text{Real GDP} = \frac{\text{Nominal GDP}}{\text{Price Index} / 100}$$
$$= \frac{\$14,958.3 \text{ billion}}{110 / 100}$$
$$= \$13,598.5 \text{ billion}$$

Use this data to make another observation: As long as inflation is positive, meaning prices increase on average from year to year, real GDP should be less than nominal GDP in any year after the base year. The reason for this should be clear: The value of nominal GDP is "inflated" by inflation. Similarly, as long as inflation is positive, real GDP should be greater than nominal GDP in any year before the base year.

**Figure 6.9** shows the U.S. nominal and real GDP since 1960. Because 2005 is the base year, the nominal and real values are exactly the same in that year. However, over time, the rise in nominal GDP looks much larger than the rise in real GDP (that is, the nominal GDP line rises more steeply than the real GDP line), because the presence of inflation, especially in the 1970s exaggerates the rise in nominal GDP.

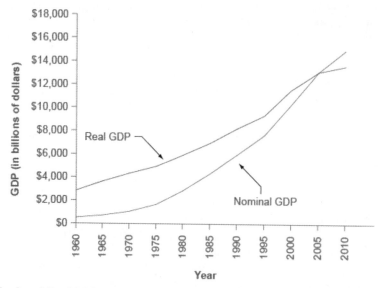

**Figure 6.9 U.S. Nominal and Real GDP, 1960–2012** The red line measures U.S. GDP in nominal dollars. The black line measures U.S. GDP in real dollars, where all dollar values are converted to 2005 dollars. Since we express real GDP in 2005 dollars, the two lines cross in 2005. However, real GDP will appear higher than nominal GDP in the years before 2005, because dollars were worth less in 2005 than in previous years. Conversely, real GDP will appear lower in the years after 2005, because dollars were worth more in 2005 than in later years.

Let's return to the question that we posed originally: How much did GDP increase in real terms? What was the real GDP growth rate from 1960 to 2010? To find the real growth rate, we apply the formula for percentage change:

$$\frac{2010 \text{ real GDP} - 1960 \text{ real GDP}}{1960 \text{ real GDP}} \times 100 = \% \text{ change}$$

$$\frac{13,598.5 - 2,859.5}{2,859.5} \times 100 = 376\%$$

In other words, the U.S. economy has increased real production of goods and services by nearly a factor of four since 1960. Of course, that understates the material improvement since it fails to capture improvements in the quality of products and the invention of new products.

There is a quicker way to answer this question approximately, using another math trick. Because:

$$\begin{aligned} \text{Nominal} &= \text{Price} \times \text{Quantity} \\ \% \text{ change in Nominal} &= \% \text{ change in Price} + \% \text{ change in Quantity} \\ &\quad\quad\quad\quad \text{OR} \\ \% \text{ change in Quantity} &= \% \text{ change in Nominal} - \% \text{ change in Price} \end{aligned}$$

Therefore, real GDP growth rate (% change in quantity) equals the growth rate in nominal GDP (% change in value) minus the inflation rate (% change in price).

Note that using this equation provides an approximation for small changes in the levels. For more accurate measures, one should use the first formula.

# 6.3 | Tracking Real GDP over Time

By the end of this section, you will be able to:
- Explain recessions, depressions, peaks, and troughs
- Evaluate the importance of tracking real GDP over time

When news reports indicate that "the economy grew 1.2% in the first quarter," the reports are referring to the percentage change in real GDP. By convention, governments report GDP growth is at an annualized rate: Whatever the calculated growth in real GDP was for the quarter, we multiply it by four when it is reported as if the economy were growing at that rate for a full year.

**Figure 6.10 U.S. GDP, 1900–2016** Real GDP in the United States in 2016 (in 2009 dollars) was about $16.7 trillion. After adjusting to remove the effects of inflation, this represents a roughly 20-fold increase in the economy's production of goods and services since the start of the twentieth century. (Source: bea.gov)

**Figure 6.10** shows the pattern of U.S. real GDP since 1900. Short term declines have regularly interrupted the generally upward long-term path of GDP. We call a significant decline in real GDP a **recession**. We call an especially lengthy and deep recession a **depression**. The severe drop in GDP that occurred during the 1930s Great Depression is clearly visible in the figure, as is the 2008–2009 Great Recession.

Real GDP is important because it is highly correlated with other measures of economic activity, like employment and unemployment. When real GDP rises, so does employment.

The most significant human problem associated with recessions (and their larger, uglier cousins, depressions) is that a slowdown in production means that firms need to lay off or fire some of their workers. Losing a job imposes painful financial and personal costs on workers, and often on their extended families as well. In addition, even those who keep their jobs are likely to find that wage raises are scanty at best—or their employers may ask them to take pay cuts.

**Table 6.7** lists the pattern of recessions and expansions in the U.S. economy since 1900. We call the highest point of the economy, before the recession begins, the **peak**. Conversely, the lowest point of a recession, before a recovery begins, is the **trough**. Thus, a recession lasts from peak to trough, and an economic upswing runs from trough to peak. We call the economy's movement from peak to trough and trough to peak the **business cycle**. It is intriguing to notice that the three longest trough-to-peak expansions of the twentieth century have happened since 1960. The most recent recession started in December 2007 and ended formally in June 2009. This was the most severe recession since the 1930s Great Depression. The ongoing expansion since the June 2009 trough will also be quite long, comparatively, having already reached 90 months at the end of 2016.

| Trough | Peak | Months of Contraction | Months of Expansion |
|---|---|---|---|
| December 1900 | September 1902 | 18 | 21 |
| August 1904 | May 1907 | 23 | 33 |
| June 1908 | January 1910 | 13 | 19 |
| January 1912 | January 1913 | 24 | 12 |
| December 1914 | August 1918 | 23 | 44 |
| March 1919 | January 1920 | 7 | 10 |
| July 1921 | May 1923 | 18 | 22 |
| July 1924 | October 1926 | 14 | 27 |

**Table 6.7 U.S. Business Cycles since 1900** (Source: http://www.nber.org/cycles/main.html)

| Trough | Peak | Months of Contraction | Months of Expansion |
|---|---|---|---|
| November 1927 | August 1929 | 23 | 21 |
| March 1933 | May 1937 | 43 | 50 |
| June 1938 | February 1945 | 13 | 80 |
| October 1945 | November 1948 | 8 | 37 |
| October 1949 | July 1953 | 11 | 45 |
| May 1954 | August 1957 | 10 | 39 |
| April 1958 | April 1960 | 8 | 24 |
| February 1961 | December 1969 | 10 | 106 |
| November 1970 | November 1973 | 11 | 36 |
| March 1975 | January 1980 | 16 | 58 |
| July 1980 | July 1981 | 6 | 12 |
| November 1982 | July 1990 | 16 | 92 |
| March 1991 | March 2001 | 8 | 120 |
| November 2001 | December 2007 | 8 | 73 |

**Table 6.7 U.S. Business Cycles since 1900**   (Source: http://www.nber.org/cycles/main.html)

A private think tank, the National Bureau of Economic Research (NBER), tracks business cycles for the U.S. economy. However, the effects of a severe recession often linger after the official ending date assigned by the NBER.

# 6.4 | Comparing GDP among Countries

By the end of this section, you will be able to:
- Explain how we can use GDP to compare the economic welfare of different nations
- Calculate the conversion of GDP to a common currency by using exchange rates
- Calculate GDP per capita using population data

It is common to use GDP as a measure of economic welfare or standard of living in a nation. When comparing the GDP of different nations for this purpose, two issues immediately arise. First, we measure a country's GDP in its own currency: the United States uses the U.S. dollar; Canada, the Canadian dollar; most countries of Western Europe, the euro; Japan, the yen; Mexico, the peso; and so on. Thus, comparing GDP between two countries requires converting to a common currency. A second issue is that countries have very different numbers of people. For instance, the United States has a much larger economy than Mexico or Canada, but it also has almost three times as many people as Mexico and nine times as many people as Canada. Thus, if we are trying to compare standards of living across countries, we need to divide GDP by population.

## Converting Currencies with Exchange Rates

To compare the GDP of countries with different currencies, it is necessary to convert to a "common denominator" using an **exchange rate**, which is the value of one currency in terms of another currency. We express exchange rates either as the units of country A's currency that need to be traded for a single unit of country B's currency (for example, Japanese yen per British pound), or as the inverse (for example, British pounds per Japanese yen). We can use two types of exchange rates for this purpose, market exchange rates and purchasing power parity (PPP) equivalent exchange rates. Market exchange rates vary on a day-to-day basis depending on supply and demand in foreign exchange markets. PPP-equivalent exchange rates provide a longer run measure of the exchange rate. For this reason, economists typically use PPP-equivalent exchange rates for GDP cross country comparisons. We will discuss exchange rates in more detail in **Exchange Rates and International Capital Flows**. The following Work It Out feature explains how to convert GDP to a common currency.

# Work It Out

## Converting GDP to a Common Currency

Using the exchange rate to convert GDP from one currency to another is straightforward. Say that the task is to compare Brazil's GDP in 2013 of 4.8 trillion reals with the U.S. GDP of $16.6 trillion for the same year.

Step 1. Determine the exchange rate for the specified year. In 2013, the exchange rate was 2.230 reals = $1. (These numbers are realistic, but rounded off to simplify the calculations.)

Step 2. Convert Brazil's GDP into U.S. dollars:

$$\text{Brazil's GDP in \$ U.S.} = \frac{\text{Brazil's GDP in reals}}{\text{Exchange rate (reals/\$ U.S.)}}$$

$$= \frac{\text{4.8 trillion reals}}{\text{2.230 reals per \$ U.S.}}$$

$$= \text{\$2.2 trillion}$$

Step 3. Compare this value to the GDP in the United States in the same year. The U.S. GDP was $16.6 trillion in 2013, which is nearly eight times that of GDP in Brazil in 2012.

Step 4. View **Table 6.8** which shows the size of and variety of GDPs of different countries in 2013, all expressed in U.S. dollars. We calculate each using the process that we explained above.

| Country | GDP in Billions of Domestic Currency | | Domestic Currency/U.S. Dollars (PPP Equivalent) | GDP (in billions of U.S. dollars) |
|---|---|---|---|---|
| Brazil | 4,844.80 | reals | 2.157 | 2,246.00 |
| Canada | 1,881.20 | dollars | 1.030 | 1,826.80 |
| China | 58,667.30 | yuan | 6.196 | 9,469.10 |
| Egypt | 1,753.30 | pounds | 6.460 | 271.40 |
| Germany | 2,737.60 | euros | 0.753 | 3,636.00 |
| India | 113,550.70 | rupees | 60.502 | 1,876.80 |
| Japan | 478,075.30 | yen | 97.596 | 4,898.50 |
| Mexico | 16,104.40 | pesos | 12.772 | 1,260.90 |
| South Korea | 1,428,294.70 | won | 1,094.925 | 1,304.467 |
| United Kingdom | 1,612.80 | pounds | 0.639 | 2,523.20 |

**Table 6.8 Comparing GDPs Across Countries, 2013**   (Source: http://www.imf.org/external/pubs/ft/weo/2013/01/weodata/index.aspx)

| Country | GDP in Billions of Domestic Currency | | Domestic Currency/U.S. Dollars (PPP Equivalent) | GDP (in billions of U.S. dollars) |
|---|---|---|---|---|
| United States | 16,768.10 | dollars | 1.000 | 16,768.10 |

**Table 6.8 Comparing GDPs Across Countries, 2013**  (Source: http://www.imf.org/external/pubs/ft/weo/2013/01/weodata/index.aspx)

## GDP Per Capita

The U.S. economy has the largest GDP in the world, by a considerable amount. The United States is also a populous country; in fact, it is the third largest country by population in the world, although well behind China and India. Is the U.S. economy larger than other countries just because the United States has more people than most other countries, or because the U.S. economy is actually larger on a per-person basis? We can answer this question by calculating a country's **GDP per capita**; that is, the GDP divided by the population.

$$\text{GDP per capita} \ = \ \text{GDP/population}$$

The second column of **Table 6.9** lists the GDP of the same selection of countries that appeared in the previous **Tracking Real GDP over Time** and **Table 6.8**, showing their GDP as converted into U.S. dollars (which is the same as the last column of the previous table). The third column gives the population for each country. The fourth column lists the GDP per capita. We obtain GDP per capita in two steps: First, by multiplying column two (GDP, in billions of dollars) by 1000 so it has the same units as column three (Population, in millions). Then divide the result (GDP in millions of dollars) by column three (Population, in millions).

| Country | GDP (in billions of U.S. dollars) | Population (in millions) | Per Capita GDP (in U.S. dollars) |
|---|---|---|---|
| Brazil | 2,246.00 | 199.20 | 11,275.10 |
| Canada | 1,826.80 | 35.10 | 52,045.58 |
| China | 9,469.10 | 1,360.80 | 6,958.48 |
| Egypt | 271.40 | 83.70 | 3,242.90 |
| Germany | 3,636.00 | 80.80 | 44,999.50 |
| India | 1,876.80 | 1,243.30 | 1,509.50 |
| Japan | 4,898.50 | 127.3 | 38,479.97 |
| Mexico | 1,260.90 | 118.40 | 10,649.90 |
| South Korea | 1,304.47 | 50.20 | 25,985.46 |
| United Kingdom | 2,523.20 | 64.10 | 39,363.50 |
| United States | 16,768.10 | 316.30 | 53,013.28 |

**Table 6.9 GDP Per Capita, 2013**  (Source: http://www.imf.org/external/pubs/ft/weo/2013/01/weodata/index.aspx)

Notice that the ranking by GDP is different from the ranking by GDP per capita. India has a somewhat larger GDP than Germany, but on a per capita basis, Germany has more than 10 times India's standard of living. Will China soon have a better standard of living than the U.S.? Read the following Clear It Up feature to find out.

### Is China going to surpass the United States in terms of standard of living?

As **Table 6.9** shows, China has the second largest GDP of the countries: $9.5 trillion compared to the United States' $16.8 trillion. Perhaps it will surpass the United States, but probably not any time soon. China has a much larger population so that in per capita terms, its GDP is less than one fifth that of the United States ($6,958.48 compared to $53,013). The Chinese people are still quite poor relative to the United States and other developed countries. One caveat: For reasons we will discuss shortly, GDP per capita can give us only a rough idea of the differences in living standards across countries.

The world's high-income nations—including the United States, Canada, the Western European countries, and Japan—typically have GDP per capita in the range of $20,000 to $50,000. Middle-income countries, which include much of Latin America, Eastern Europe, and some countries in East Asia, have GDP per capita in the range of $6,000 to $12,000. The world's low-income countries, many of them located in Africa and Asia, often have GDP per capita of less than $2,000 per year.

# 6.5 | How Well GDP Measures the Well-Being of Society

By the end of this section, you will be able to:
- Discuss how productivity influences the standard of living
- Explain the limitations of GDP as a measure of the standard of living
- Analyze the relationship between GDP data and fluctuations in the standard of living

The level of GDP per capita clearly captures some of what we mean by the phrase "standard of living." Most of the migration in the world, for example, involves people who are moving from countries with relatively low GDP per capita to countries with relatively high GDP per capita.

"Standard of living" is a broader term than GDP. While GDP focuses on production that is bought and sold in markets, **standard of living** includes all elements that affect people's well-being, whether they are bought and sold in the market or not. To illuminate the difference between GDP and standard of living, it is useful to spell out some things that GDP does not cover that are clearly relevant to standard of living.

## Limitations of GDP as a Measure of the Standard of Living

While GDP includes spending on recreation and travel, it does not cover leisure time. Clearly, however, there is a substantial difference between an economy that is large because people work long hours, and an economy that is just as large because people are more productive with their time so they do not have to work as many hours. The GDP per capita of the U.S. economy is larger than the GDP per capita of Germany, as **Table 6.9** showed, but does that prove that the standard of living in the United States is higher? Not necessarily, since it is also true that the average U.S. worker works several hundred hours more per year more than the average German worker. Calculating GDP does not account for the German worker's extra vacation weeks.

While GDP includes what a country spends on environmental protection, healthcare, and education, it does not include actual levels of environmental cleanliness, health, and learning. GDP includes the cost of buying pollution-control equipment, but it does not address whether the air and water are actually cleaner or dirtier. GDP includes spending on medical care, but does not address whether life expectancy or infant mortality have risen or fallen. Similarly, it counts spending on education, but does not address directly how much of the population can read, write, or do basic mathematics.

GDP includes production that is exchanged in the market, but it does not cover production that is not exchanged in the market. For example, hiring someone to mow your lawn or clean your house is part of GDP, but doing these tasks yourself is not part of GDP. One remarkable change in the U.S. economy in recent decades is the growth in women's participation in the labor force. As of 1970, only about 42% of women participated in the paid labor force. By the second decade of the 2000s, nearly 60% of women participated in the paid labor force according to the Bureau of Labor Statistics. As women are now in the labor force, many of the services they used to produce in the non-market economy like food preparation and child care have shifted to some extent into the market economy, which makes the GDP appear larger even if people actually are not consuming more services.

GDP has nothing to say about the level of inequality in society. GDP per capita is only an average. When GDP per capita rises by 5%, it could mean that GDP for everyone in the society has risen by 5%, or that GDP of some groups has risen by more while that of others has risen by less—or even declined. GDP also has nothing in particular to say about the amount of variety available. If a family buys 100 loaves of bread in a year, GDP does not care whether they are all white bread, or whether the family can choose from wheat, rye, pumpernickel, and many others—it just looks at the total amount the family spends on bread.

Likewise, GDP has nothing much to say about what technology and products are available. The standard of living in, for example, 1950 or 1900 was not affected only by how much money people had—it was also affected by what they could buy. No matter how much money you had in 1950, you could not buy an iPhone or a personal computer.

In certain cases, it is not clear that a rise in GDP is even a good thing. If a city is wrecked by a hurricane, and then experiences a surge of rebuilding construction activity, it would be peculiar to claim that the hurricane was therefore economically beneficial. If people are led by a rising fear of crime, to pay for installing bars and burglar alarms on all their windows, it is hard to believe that this increase in GDP has made them better off. Similarly, some people would argue that sales of certain goods, like pornography or extremely violent movies, do not represent a gain to society's standard of living.

## Does a Rise in GDP Overstate or Understate the Rise in the Standard of Living?

The fact that GDP per capita does not fully capture the broader idea of standard of living has led to a concern that the increases in GDP over time are illusory. It is theoretically possible that while GDP is rising, the standard of living could be falling if human health, environmental cleanliness, and other factors that are not included in GDP are worsening. Fortunately, this fear appears to be overstated.

In some ways, the rise in GDP understates the actual rise in the standard of living. For example, the typical workweek for a U.S. worker has fallen over the last century from about 60 hours per week to less than 40 hours per week. Life expectancy and health have risen dramatically, and so has the average level of education. Since 1970, the air and water in the United States have generally been getting cleaner. Companies have developed new technologies for entertainment, travel, information, and health. A much wider variety of basic products like food and clothing is available today than several decades ago. Because GDP does not capture leisure, health, a cleaner environment, the possibilities that new technology creates, or an increase in variety, the actual rise in the standard of living for Americans in recent decades has exceeded the rise in GDP.

On the other side, crime rates, traffic congestion levels, and income inequality are higher in the United States now than they were in the 1960s. Moreover, a substantial number of services that women primarily provided in the non-market economy are now part of the market economy that GDP counts. By ignoring these factors, GDP would tend to overstate the true rise in the standard of living.

# Link It Up

Visit this website (http://openstaxcollege.org/l/amdreamvalue) to read about the American Dream and standards of living.

## GDP is Rough, but Useful

A high level of GDP should not be the only goal of macroeconomic policy, or government policy more broadly. Even though GDP does not measure the broader standard of living with any precision, it does measure production well and it does indicate when a country is materially better or worse off in terms of jobs and incomes. In most countries, a significantly higher GDP per capita occurs hand in hand with other improvements in everyday life along many dimensions, like education, health, and environmental protection.

No single number can capture all the elements of a term as broad as "standard of living." Nonetheless, GDP per capita is a reasonable, rough-and-ready measure of the standard of living.

# Bring it Home

## How is the Economy Doing? How Does One Tell?

To determine the state of the economy, one needs to examine economic indicators, such as GDP. To calculate GDP is quite an undertaking. It is the broadest measure of a nation's economic activity and we owe a debt to Simon Kuznets, the creator of the measurement, for that.

The sheer size of the U.S. economy as measured by GDP is huge—as of the fourth quarter of 2016, $18.9 trillion worth of goods and services were produced annually. Real GDP informed us that the 2008–2009 recession was severe and that the recovery from that recession has been slow, but the economy is improving. GDP per capita gives a rough estimate of a nation's standard of living. This chapter is the building block for other chapters that explore more economic indicators such as unemployment, inflation, or interest rates, and perhaps more importantly, will explain how they are related and what causes them to rise or fall.

# KEY TERMS

**business cycle** the economy's relatively short-term movement in and out of recession

**depreciation** the process by which capital ages over time and therefore loses its value

**depression** an especially lengthy and deep decline in output

**double counting** a potential mistake to avoid in measuring GDP, in which output is counted more than once as it travels through the stages of production

**durable good** long-lasting good like a car or a refrigerator

**exchange rate** the price of one currency in terms of another currency

**final good and service** output used directly for consumption, investment, government, and trade purposes; contrast with "intermediate good"

**GDP per capita** GDP divided by the population

**gross domestic product (GDP)** the value of the output of all goods and services produced within a country in a year

**gross national product (GNP)** includes what is produced domestically and what is produced by domestic labor and business abroad in a year

**intermediate good** output provided to other businesses at an intermediate stage of production, not for final users; contrast with "final good and service"

**inventory** good that has been produced, but not yet been sold

**national income** includes all income earned: wages, profits, rent, and profit income

**net national product (NNP)** GDP minus depreciation

**nominal value** the economic statistic actually announced at that time, not adjusted for inflation; contrast with real value

**nondurable good** short-lived good like food and clothing

**peak** during the business cycle, the highest point of output before a recession begins

**real value** an economic statistic after it has been adjusted for inflation; contrast with nominal value

**recession** a significant decline in national output

**service** product which is intangible (in contrast to goods) such as entertainment, healthcare, or education

**standard of living** all elements that affect people's happiness, whether people buy or sell these elements in the market or not

**structure** building used as residence, factory, office building, retail store, or for other purposes

**trade balance** gap between exports and imports

**trade deficit** exists when a nation's imports exceed its exports and it calculates them as imports −exports

**trade surplus** exists when a nation's exports exceed its imports and it calculates them as exports − imports

**trough** during the business cycle, the lowest point of output in a recession, before a recovery begins

# KEY CONCEPTS AND SUMMARY

### 6.1 Measuring the Size of the Economy: Gross Domestic Product

Economists generally express the size of a nation's economy as its gross domestic product (GDP), which measures the value of the output of all goods and services produced within the country in a year. Economists measure GDP by taking the quantities of all goods and services produced, multiplying them by their prices, and summing the total. Since GDP measures what is bought and sold in the economy, we can measure it either by the sum of what is purchased in the economy or what is produced.

We can divide demand into consumption, investment, government, exports, and imports. We can divide what is produced in the economy into durable goods, nondurable goods, services, structures, and inventories. To avoid double counting, GDP counts only final output of goods and services, not the production of intermediate goods or the value of labor in the chain of production.

### 6.2 Adjusting Nominal Values to Real Values

The nominal value of an economic statistic is the commonly announced value. The real value is the value after adjusting for changes in inflation. To convert nominal economic data from several different years into real, inflation-adjusted data, the starting point is to choose a base year arbitrarily and then use a price index to convert the measurements so that economists measure them in the money prevailing in the base year.

### 6.3 Tracking Real GDP over Time

Over the long term, U.S. real GDP have increased dramatically. At the same time, GDP has not increased the same amount each year. The speeding up and slowing down of GDP growth represents the business cycle. When GDP declines significantly, a recession occurs. A longer and deeper decline is a depression. Recessions begin at the business cycle's peak and end at the trough.

### 6.4 Comparing GDP among Countries

Since we measure GDP in a country's currency, in order to compare different countries' GDPs, we need to convert them to a common currency. One way to do that is with the exchange rate, which is the price of one country's currency in terms of another. Once we express GDPs in a common currency, we can compare each country's GDP per capita by dividing GDP by population. Countries with large populations often have large GDPs, but GDP alone can be a misleading indicator of a nation's wealth. A better measure is GDP per capita.

### 6.5 How Well GDP Measures the Well-Being of Society

GDP is an indicator of a society's standard of living, but it is only a rough indicator. GDP does not directly take account of leisure, environmental quality, levels of health and education, activities conducted outside the market, changes in inequality of income, increases in variety, increases in technology, or the (positive or negative) value that society may place on certain types of output.

# SELF-CHECK QUESTIONS

**1.** Country A has export sales of $20 billion, government purchases of $1,000 billion, business investment is $50 billion, imports are $40 billion, and consumption spending is $2,000 billion. What is the dollar value of GDP?

**2.** Which of the following are included in GDP, and which are not?
- a. The cost of hospital stays
- b. The rise in life expectancy over time
- c. Child care provided by a licensed day care center
- d. Child care provided by a grandmother
- e. A used car sale
- f. A new car sale
- g. The greater variety of cheese available in supermarkets
- h. The iron that goes into the steel that goes into a refrigerator bought by a consumer.

**3.** Using data from **Table 6.5** how much of the nominal GDP growth from 1980 to 1990 was real GDP and how much was inflation?

**4.** Without looking at **Table 6.7**, return to **Figure 6.10**. If we define a recession as a significant decline in national output, can you identify any post-1960 recessions in addition to the 2008-2009 recession? (This requires a judgment call.)

**5.** According to **Table 6.7**, how often have recessions occurred since the end of World War II (1945)?

**6.** According to **Table 6.7**, how long has the average recession lasted since the end of World War II?

**7.** According to **Table 6.7**, how long has the average expansion lasted since the end of World War II?

**8.** Is it possible for GDP to rise while at the same time per capita GDP is falling? Is it possible for GDP to fall while per capita GDP is rising?

**9.** The Central African Republic has a GDP of 1,107,689 million CFA francs and a population of 4.862 million. The exchange rate is 284.681CFA francs per dollar. Calculate the GDP per capita of Central African Republic.

**10.** Explain briefly whether each of the following would cause GDP to overstate or understate the degree of change in the broad standard of living.
    a. The environment becomes dirtier
    b. The crime rate declines
    c. A greater variety of goods become available to consumers
    d. Infant mortality declines

## REVIEW QUESTIONS

**11.** What are the main components of measuring GDP with what is demanded?

**12.** What are the main components of measuring GDP with what is produced?

**13.** Would you usually expect GDP as measured by what is demanded to be greater than GDP measured by what is supplied, or the reverse?

**14.** Why must you avoid double counting when measuring GDP?

**15.** What is the difference between a series of economic data over time measured in nominal terms versus the same data series over time measured in real terms?

**16.** How do you convert a series of nominal economic data over time to real terms?

**17.** What are typical GDP patterns for a high-income economy like the United States in the long run and the short run?

**18.** What are the two main difficulties that arise in comparing different countries's GDP?

**19.** List some of the reasons why economists should not consider GDP an effective measure of the standard of living in a country.

## CRITICAL THINKING QUESTIONS

**20.** U.S. macroeconomic data are among the best in the world. Given what you learned in the **Clear It Up** "How do statisticians measure GDP?", does this surprise you, or does this simply reflect the complexity of a modern economy?

**21.** What does GDP not tell us about the economy?

**22.** Should people typically pay more attention to their real income or their nominal income? If you choose the latter, why would that make sense in today's world? Would your answer be the same for the 1970s?

**23.** Why do you suppose that U.S. GDP is so much higher today than 50 or 100 years ago?

**24.** Why do you think that GDP does not grow at a steady rate, but rather speeds up and slows down?

**25.** Cross country comparisons of GDP per capita typically use purchasing power parity equivalent exchange rates, which are a measure of the long run equilibrium value of an exchange rate. In fact, we used PPP equivalent exchange rates in this module. Why could using market exchange rates, which sometimes change dramatically in a short period of time, be misleading?

## PROBLEMS

**28.** Last year, a small nation with abundant forests cut down $200 worth of trees. It then turned $100 worth of trees into $150 worth of lumber. It used $100 worth of that lumber to produce $250 worth of bookshelves. Assuming the country produces no other outputs, and there are no other inputs used in producing trees, lumber, and bookshelves, what is this nation's GDP? In other words, what is the value of the final goods the nation produced including trees, lumber and bookshelves?

**29.** The "prime" interest rate is the rate that banks charge their best customers. Based on the nominal interest rates and inflation rates in **Table 6.10**, in which of the years would it have been best to be a lender? Based on the nominal interest rates and inflation rates in **Table 6.10**, in which of the years given would it have been best to be a borrower?

| Year | Prime Interest Rate | Inflation Rate |
|------|---------------------|----------------|
| 1970 | 7.9% | 5.7% |
| 1974 | 10.8% | 11.0% |
| 1978 | 9.1% | 7.6% |
| 1981 | 18.9% | 10.3% |

**Table 6.10**

**26.** Why might per capita GDP be only an imperfect measure of a country's standard of living?

**27.** How might you measure a "green" GDP?

**30.** A mortgage loan is a loan that a person makes to purchase a house. **Table 6.11** provides a list of the mortgage interest rate for several different years and the rate of inflation for each of those years. In which years would it have been better to be a person borrowing money from a bank to buy a home? In which years would it have been better to be a bank lending money?

| Year | Mortgage Interest Rate | Inflation Rate |
|------|------------------------|----------------|
| 1984 | 12.4% | 4.3% |
| 1990 | 10% | 5.4% |
| 2001 | 7.0% | 2.8% |

**Table 6.11**

**31.** Ethiopia has a GDP of $8 billion (measured in U.S. dollars) and a population of 55 million. Costa Rica has a GDP of $9 billion (measured in U.S. dollars) and a population of 4 million. Calculate the per capita GDP for each country and identify which one is higher.

**32.** In 1980, Denmark had a GDP of $70 billion (measured in U.S. dollars) and a population of 5.1 million. In 2000, Denmark had a GDP of $160 billion (measured in U.S. dollars) and a population of 5.3 million. By what percentage did Denmark's GDP per capita rise between 1980 and 2000?

**33.** The Czech Republic has a GDP of 1,800 billion koruny. The exchange rate is 25 koruny/U.S. dollar. The Czech population is 20 million. What is the GDP per capita of the Czech Republic expressed in U.S. dollars?

# 7 | Economic Growth

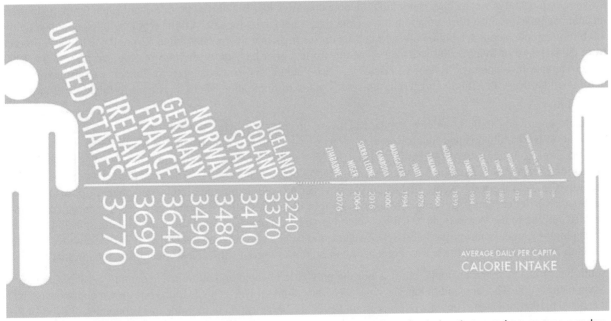

**Figure 7.1 Average Daily Calorie Consumption**  Not only has the number of calories that people consume per day increased, so has the amount of food calories that people are able to afford based on their working wages. (Credit: modification of work by Lauren Manning/Flickr Creative Commons)

## Bring it Home

### Calories and Economic Growth

On average, humans need about 2,500 calories a day to survive, depending on height, weight, and gender. The economist Brad DeLong estimates that the average worker in the early 1600s earned wages that could afford him 2,500 food calories. This worker lived in Western Europe. Two hundred years later, that same worker could afford 3,000 food calories. However, between 1800 and 1875, just a time span of just 75 years, economic growth was so rapid that western European workers could purchase 5,000 food calories a day. By 2012, a low skilled worker in an affluent Western European/North American country could afford to purchase 2.4 million food calories per day.

What caused such a rapid rise in living standards between 1800 and 1875 and thereafter? Why is it that many countries, especially those in Western Europe, North America, and parts of East Asia, can feed their populations more than adequately, while others cannot? We will look at these and other questions as we examine long-run economic growth.

## Introduction to Economic Growth

In this chapter, you will learn about:

- The Relatively Recent Arrival of Economic Growth

- Labor Productivity and Economic Growth

- Components of Economic Growth

- Economic Convergence

Every country worries about economic growth. In the United States and other high-income countries, the question is whether economic growth continues to provide the same remarkable gains in our standard of living as it did during the twentieth century. Meanwhile, can middle-income countries like Brazil, Egypt, or Poland catch up to the higher-income countries, or must they remain in the second tier of per capita income? Of the world's population of roughly 7.5 billion people, about 1.1 billion are scraping by on incomes that average less than $2 per day, not that different from the standard of living 2,000 years ago. Can the world's poor be lifted from their fearful poverty? As the 1995 Nobel laureate in economics, Robert E. Lucas Jr., once noted: "The consequences for human welfare involved in questions like these are simply staggering: Once one starts to think about them, it is hard to think about anything else."

Dramatic improvements in a nation's standard of living are possible. After the Korean War in the late 1950s, the Republic of Korea, often called South Korea, was one of the poorest economies in the world. Most South Koreans worked in peasant agriculture. According to the British economist Angus Maddison, who devoted life's work to measuring GDP and population in the world economy, GDP per capita in 1990 international dollars was $854 per year. From the 1960s to the early twenty-first century, a time period well within the lifetime and memory of many adults, the South Korean economy grew rapidly. Over these four decades, GDP per capita increased by more than 6% per year. According to the World Bank, GDP for South Korea now exceeds $30,000 in nominal terms, placing it firmly among high-income countries like Italy, New Zealand, and Israel. Measured by total GDP in 2015, South Korea is the eleventh-largest economy in the world. For a nation of 50 million people, this transformation is extraordinary.

South Korea is a standout example, but it is not the only case of rapid and sustained economic growth. Other East Asian nations, like Thailand and Indonesia, have seen very rapid growth as well. China has grown enormously since it enacted market-oriented economic reforms around 1980. GDP per capita in high-income economies like the United States also has grown dramatically albeit over a longer time frame. Since the Civil War, the U.S. economy has transformed from a primarily rural and agricultural economy to an economy based on services, manufacturing, and technology.

# 7.1 | The Relatively Recent Arrival of Economic Growth

By the end of this section, you will be able to:
- Explain the conditions that have allowed for modern economic growth in the last two centuries
- Analyze the influence of public policies on an economy's long-run economic growth

Let's begin with a brief overview of spectacular economic growth patterns around the world in the last two centuries. We commonly refer to this as the period of **modern economic growth**. (Later in the chapter we will discuss lower economic growth rates and some key ingredients for economic progress.) Rapid and sustained economic growth is a relatively recent experience for the human race. Before the last two centuries, although rulers, nobles, and conquerors could afford some extravagances and although economies rose above the subsistence level, the average person's standard of living had not changed much for centuries.

Progressive, powerful economic and institutional changes started to have a significant effect in the late eighteenth and early nineteenth centuries. According to the Dutch economic historian Jan Luiten van Zanden, slavery-based societies, favorable demographics, global trading routes, and standardized trading institutions that spread with different empires set the stage for the Industrial Revolution to succeed. The **Industrial Revolution** refers to the widespread use of power-driven machinery and the economic and social changes that resulted in the first half of the 1800s. Ingenious machines—the steam engine, the power loom, and the steam locomotive—performed tasks that otherwise would have taken vast numbers of workers to do. The Industrial Revolution began in Great Britain, and soon spread to the United States, Germany, and other countries.

The jobs for ordinary people working with these machines were often dirty and dangerous by modern standards, but the alternative jobs of that time in peasant agriculture and small-village industry were often dirty and dangerous, too. The new jobs of the Industrial Revolution typically offered higher pay and a chance for social mobility. A self-reinforcing cycle began: New inventions and investments generated profits, the profits provided funds for more new investment and inventions, and the investments and inventions provided opportunities for further profits. Slowly, a group of national economies in Europe and North America emerged from centuries of sluggishness into a period of rapid modern growth. During the last two centuries, the average GDP growth rate per capita in the leading industrialized countries has been about 2% per year. What were times like before then? Read the following Clear It Up feature for the answer.

## What were economic conditions like before 1870?

Angus Maddison, a quantitative economic historian, led the most systematic inquiry into national incomes before 1870. Economists recently have refined and used his methods to compile GDP per capita estimates from year 1 C.E. to 1348. Table 7.1 is an important counterpoint to most of the narrative in this chapter. It shows that nations can decline as well as rise. A wide array of forces, such as epidemics, natural and weather-related disasters, the inability to govern large empires, and the remarkably slow pace of technological and institutional progress explain declines in income. Institutions are the traditions and laws by which people in a community agree to behave and govern themselves. Such institutions include marriage, religion, education, and laws of governance. Institutional progress is the development and codification of these institutions to reinforce social order, and thus, economic growth.

One example of such an institution is the Magna Carta (Great Charter), which the English nobles forced King John to sign in 1215. The Magna Carta codified the principles of due process, whereby a free man could not be penalized unless his peers had made a lawful judgment against him. The United States in its own constitution later adopted this concept. This social order may have contributed to England's GDP per capita in 1348, which was second to that of northern Italy.

In studying economic growth, a country's institutional framework plays a critical role. Table 7.1 also shows relative global equality for almost 1,300 years. After this, we begin to see significant divergence in income (not in the table).

| Year | Northern Italy | Spain | England | Holland | Byzantium | Iraq | Egypt | Japan |
|------|---------|-------|---------|---------|-----------|------|-------|-------|
| 1 | $800 | $600 | $600 | $600 | $700 | $700 | $700 | - |
| 730 | - | - | - | - | - | $920 | $730 | $402 |
| 1000 | | - | - | - | $600 | $820 | $600 | - |
| 1150 | - | - | - | - | $580 | $680 | $660 | $520 |
| 1280 | - | - | - | - | - | - | $670 | $527 |
| 1300 | $1,588 | $864 | $892 | - | - | - | $610 | - |
| 1348 | $1,486 | $907 | $919 | - | - | - | - | - |

Table 7.1 GDP Per Capita Estimates in Current International Dollars from AD 1 to 1348 (Source: Bolt and van Zanden. "The First Update of the Maddison Project. Re-Estimating Growth Before 1820." 2013)

Another fascinating and underreported fact is the high levels of income, compared to others at that time, attained by the Islamic Empire Abbasid Caliphate—which was founded in present-day Iraq in 730 C.E. At its height, the empire spanned large regions of the Middle East, North Africa, and Spain until its gradual decline over 200 years.

The Industrial Revolution led to increasing inequality among nations. Some economies took off, whereas others, like many of those in Africa or Asia, remained close to a subsistence standard of living. General calculations show that the 17 countries of the world with the most-developed economies had, on average, 2.4 times the GDP per capita of the world's poorest economies in 1870. By 1960, the most developed economies had 4.2 times the GDP per capita of the poorest economies.

However, by the middle of the twentieth century, some countries had shown that catching up was possible. Japan's economic growth took off in the 1960s and 1970s, with a growth rate of real GDP per capita averaging 11% per year during those decades. Certain countries in Latin America experienced a boom in economic growth in the 1960s as well. In Brazil, for example, GDP per capita expanded by an average annual rate of 11.1% from 1968 to 1973. In the 1970s, some East Asian economies, including South Korea, Thailand, and Taiwan, saw rapid growth. In these countries, growth rates of 11% to 12% per year in GDP per capita were not uncommon. More recently, China, with its population of nearly 1.4 billion people, grew at a per capita rate 9% per year from 1984 into the 2000s. India, with a population of 1.3 billion, has shown promising signs of economic growth, with growth in GDP per capita of about 4% per year during the 1990s and climbing toward 7% to 8% per year in the 2000s.

# Link It Up

Visit this website (http://openstaxcollege.org/l/asiadevbank) to read about the Asian Development Bank.

These waves of catch-up economic growth have not reached all shores. In certain African countries like Niger, Tanzania, and Sudan, for example, GDP per capita at the start of the 2000s was still less than $300, not much higher than it was in the nineteenth century and for centuries before that. In the context of the overall situation of low-income people around the world, the good economic news from China (population: 1.4 billion) and India (population: 1.3 billion) is, nonetheless, astounding and heartening.

Economic growth in the last two centuries has made a striking change in the human condition. Richard Easterlin, an economist at the University of Southern California, wrote in 2000:

> By many measures, a revolution in the human condition is sweeping the world. Most people today are better fed, clothed, and housed than their predecessors two centuries ago. They are healthier, live longer, and are better educated. Women's lives are less centered on reproduction and political democracy has gained a foothold. Although Western Europe and its offshoots have been the leaders of this advance, most of the less developed nations have joined in during the 20th century, with the newly emerging nations of sub-Saharan Africa the latest to participate. Although the picture is not one of universal progress, it is the greatest advance in the human condition of the world's population ever achieved in such a brief span of time.

## Rule of Law and Economic Growth

Economic growth depends on many factors. Key among those factors is adherence to the **rule of law** and protection of property rights and **contractual rights** by a country's government so that markets can work effectively and efficiently. Laws must be clear, public, fair, enforced, and equally applicable to all members of society. Property rights, as you might recall from **Environmental Protection and Negative Externalities (http://cnx.org/content/m63688/latest/)** are the rights of individuals and firms to own property and use it as they see fit. If you have $100, you have the right to use that money, whether you spend it, lend it, or keep it in a jar. It is your property. The definition of property includes physical property as well as the right to your training and experience, especially since your training is what determines your livelihood. Using this property includes the right to enter into contracts with other parties with your property. Individuals or firms must own the property to enter into a contract.

Contractual rights, then, are based on property rights and they allow individuals to enter into agreements with others regarding the use of their property providing recourse through the legal system in the event of noncompliance. One example is the employment agreement: a skilled surgeon operates on an ill person and expects payment. Failure to pay would constitute property theft by the patient. The theft is property the services that the surgeon provided. In a society with strong property rights and contractual rights, the terms of the patient–surgeon contract will be fulfilled, because the surgeon would have recourse through the court system to extract payment from that individual. Without a legal system that enforces contracts, people would not be likely to enter into contracts for current or future services because of the risk of non-payment. This would make it difficult to transact business and would slow economic growth.

The World Bank considers a country's legal system effective if it upholds property rights and contractual rights. The World Bank has developed a ranking system for countries' legal systems based on effective protection of property rights and rule-based governance using a scale from 1 to 6, with 1 being the lowest and 6 the highest rating. In 2013, the world average ranking was 2.9. The three countries with the lowest ranking of 1.5 were Afghanistan, the Central African Republic, and Zimbabwe. Their GDP per capita was $679, $333, and $1,007 respectively. The World Bank cites Afghanistan as having a low standard of living, weak government structure, and lack of adherence to the rule of law, which has stymied its economic growth. The landlocked Central African Republic has poor economic resources as well as political instability and is a source of children used in human trafficking. Zimbabwe has had declining and often negative growth for much of the period since 1998. Land redistribution and price controls have disrupted the economy, and corruption and violence have dominated the political process. Although global economic growth has increased, those countries lacking a clear system of property rights and an independent court system free from corruption have lagged far behind.

# 7.2 | Labor Productivity and Economic Growth

By the end of this section, you will be able to:

- Identify the role of labor productivity in promoting economic growth
- Analyze the sources of economic growth using the aggregate production function
- Measure an economy's rate of productivity growth
- Evaluate the power of sustained growth

Sustained long-term economic growth comes from increases in worker productivity, which essentially means how well we do things. In other words, how efficient is your nation with its time and workers? **Labor productivity** is the value that each employed person creates per unit of his or her input. The easiest way to comprehend labor productivity is to imagine a Canadian worker who can make 10 loaves of bread in an hour versus a U.S. worker who in the same hour can make only two loaves of bread. In this fictional example, the Canadians are more productive. More productivity essentially means you can do more in the same amount of time. This in turn frees up resources for workers to use elsewhere.

What determines how productive workers are? The answer is pretty intuitive. The first determinant of labor productivity is human capital. **Human capital** is the accumulated knowledge (from education and experience), skills, and expertise that the average worker in an economy possesses. Typically the higher the average level of education in an economy, the higher the accumulated human capital and the higher the labor productivity.

The second factor that determines labor productivity is technological change. **Technological change** is a combination of **invention**—advances in knowledge—and **innovation**, which is putting those advances to use in a new product or service. For example, the transistor was invented in 1947. It allowed us to miniaturize the footprint of electronic devices and use less power than the tube technology that came before it. Innovations since then have produced smaller and better transistors that are ubiquitous in products as varied as smart-phones, computers, and escalators. Developing the transistor has allowed workers to be anywhere with smaller devices. People can use these devices to communicate with other workers, measure product quality or do any other task in less time, improving worker productivity.

The third factor that determines labor productivity is economies of scale. Recall that economies of scale are the cost advantages that industries obtain due to size. (Read more about economies of scale in **Production, Cost and Industry Structure (http://cnx.org/content/m63680/latest/)** .) Consider again the case of the fictional

Canadian worker who could produce 10 loaves of bread in an hour. If this difference in productivity was due only to economies of scale, it could be that the Canadian worker had access to a large industrial-size oven while the U.S. worker was using a standard residential size oven.

Now that we have explored the determinants of worker productivity, let's turn to how economists measure economic growth and productivity.

## Sources of Economic Growth: The Aggregate Production Function

To analyze the sources of economic growth, it is useful to think about a **production function**, which is the technical relationship by which economic inputs like labor, machinery, and raw materials are turned into outputs like goods and services that consumers use. A microeconomic production function describes a firm's or perhaps an industry's inputs and outputs. In macroeconomics, we call the connection from inputs to outputs for the entire economy an **aggregate production function**.

## Components of the Aggregate Production Function

Economists construct different production functions depending on the focus of their studies. **Figure 7.2** presents two examples of aggregate production functions. In the first production function in **Figure 7.2** (a), the output is GDP. The inputs in this example are workforce, human capital, physical capital, and technology. We discuss these inputs further in the module, Components of Economic Growth.

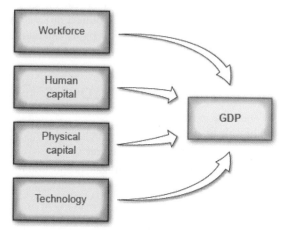

(a) Aggregate production function with GDP as its output

(b) Aggregate production function with GDP per capita as its output

**Figure 7.2 Aggregate Production Functions**   An aggregate production function shows what goes into producing the output for an overall economy. (a) This aggregate production function has GDP as its output. (b) This aggregate production function has GDP per capita as its output. Because we calculate it on a per-person basis, we already figure the labor input into the other factors and we do not need to list it separately.

## Measuring Productivity

An economy's rate of productivity growth is closely linked to the growth rate of its GDP per capita, although the two are not identical. For example, if the percentage of the population who holds jobs in an economy increases, GDP per capita will increase but the productivity of individual workers may not be affected. Over the long term, the only way that GDP per capita can grow continually is if the productivity of the average worker rises or if there are complementary increases in capital.

A common measure of U.S. productivity per worker is dollar value per hour the worker contributes to the employer's output. This measure excludes government workers, because their output is not sold in the market and so their productivity is hard to measure. It also excludes farming, which accounts for only a relatively small share of the U.S. economy. **Figure 7.3** shows an index of output per hour, with 2009 as the base year (when the index equals 100). The index equaled about 106 in 2014. In 1972, the index equaled 50, which shows that workers have more than doubled their productivity since then.

**Figure 7.3 Output per Hour Worked in the U.S. Economy, 1947–2011**  Output per hour worked is a measure of worker productivity. In the U.S. economy, worker productivity rose more quickly in the 1960s and the mid-1990s compared with the 1970s and 1980s. However, these growth-rate differences are only a few percentage points per year. Look carefully to see them in the changing slope of the line. The average U.S. worker produced over twice as much per hour in 2014 than he did in the early 1970s. (Source: U.S. Department of Labor, Bureau of Labor Statistics.)

According to the Department of Labor, U.S. productivity growth was fairly strong in the 1950s but then declined in the 1970s and 1980s before rising again in the second half of the 1990s and the first half of the 2000s. In fact, the rate of productivity measured by the change in output per hour worked averaged 3.2% per year from 1950 to 1970; dropped to 1.9% per year from 1970 to 1990; and then climbed back to over 2.3% from 1991 to the present, with another modest slowdown after 2001. **Figure 7.4** shows average annual rates of productivity growth averaged over time since 1950.

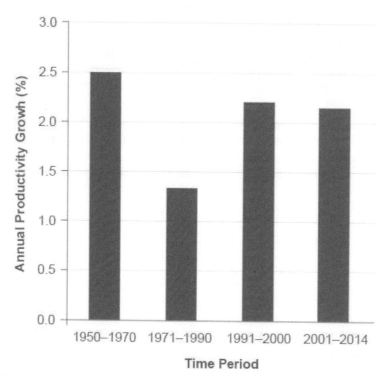

**Figure 7.4 Productivity Growth Since 1950**  U.S. growth in worker productivity was very high between 1950 and 1970. It then declined to lower levels in the 1970s and the 1980s. The late 1990s and early 2000s saw productivity rebound, but then productivity sagged a bit in the 2000s. Some think the productivity rebound of the late 1990s and early 2000s marks the start of a "new economy" built on higher productivity growth, but we cannot determine this until more time has passed. (Source: U.S. Department of Labor, Bureau of Labor Statistics.)

## The "New Economy" Controversy

In recent years a controversy has been brewing among economists about the resurgence of U.S. productivity in the second half of the 1990s. One school of thought argues that the United States had developed a "new economy" based on the extraordinary advances in communications and information technology of the 1990s. The most optimistic proponents argue that it would generate higher average productivity growth for decades to come. The pessimists, alternatively, argue that even five or ten years of stronger productivity growth does not prove that higher productivity will last for the long term. It is hard to infer anything about long-term productivity trends during the later part of the 2000s, because the steep 2008-2009 recession, with its sharp but not completely synchronized declines in output and employment, complicates any interpretation. While productivity growth was high in 2009 and 2010 (around 3%), it has slowed down since then.

Productivity growth is also closely linked to the average level of wages. Over time, the amount that firms are willing to pay workers will depend on the value of the output those workers produce. If a few employers tried to pay their workers less than what those workers produced, then those workers would receive offers of higher wages from other profit-seeking employers. If a few employers mistakenly paid their workers more than what those workers produced, those employers would soon end up with losses. In the long run, productivity per hour is the most important determinant of the average wage level in any economy. To learn how to compare economies in this regard, follow the steps in the following Work It Out feature.

## Comparing the Economies of Two Countries

The Organization for Economic Co-operation and Development (OECD) tracks data on the annual growth rate of real GDP per hour worked. You can find these data on the OECD data webpage "Growth in GDP per capita, productivity and ULC" at **this** (http://stats.oecd.org/Index.aspx?DataSetCode=PDB_GR) website.

Step 1. Visit the OECD website given above and select two countries to compare.

Step 2. On the drop-down menu "Subject," select " GDP per capita, constant prices," and under "Measure," select "Annual growth/change." Then record the data for the countries you have chosen for the five most recent years.

Step 3. Go back to the drop-down "Subject" menu and select "GDP per hour worked, constant prices," and under "Measure" again select "Annual growth/change." Select data for the same years for which you selected GDP per capita data.

Step 4. Compare real GDP growth for both countries. **Table 7.2** provides an example of a comparison between Belgium and Canada.

| **Australia** | **2011** | **2012** | **2013** | **2014** | **2015** |
|---|---|---|---|---|---|
| Real GDP/Capita Growth (%) | 2.3% | 1.5% | 1.3% | 1.4 | 0.1% |
| Real GDP Growth/Hours Worked (%) | 1.7% | −0.1% | 1.4% | 2.2% | −0.2% |
| **Belgium** | **2011** | **2012** | **2013** | **2014** | **2015** |
| Real GDP/Capita Growth (%) | 0.9 | −0.6 | −0.5 | 1.2 | 1.0 |
| Real GDP Growth/Hours Worked (%) | −0.5 | −0.3 | 0.4 | 1.4 | 0.9 |

Table 7.2

Step 5. For both measures, growth in Canada is greater than growth in Belgium for the first four years. In addition, there are year-to-year fluctuations. Many factors can affect growth. For example, one factor that may have contributed to Canada's stronger growth may be its larger inflows of immigrants, who generally contribute to economic growth.

## The Power of Sustained Economic Growth

Nothing is more important for people's standard of living than sustained economic growth. Even small changes in the rate of growth, when sustained and compounded over long periods of time, make an enormous difference in the standard of living. Consider **Table 7.3**, in which the rows of the table show several different rates of growth in GDP per capita and the columns show different periods of time. Assume for simplicity that an economy starts with a GDP per capita of 100. The table then applies the following formula to calculate what GDP will be at the given growth rate in the future:

$$\text{GDP at starting date} \times (1 + \text{growth rate of GDP})^{\text{years}} = \text{GDP at end date}$$

For example, an economy that starts with a GDP of 100 and grows at 3% per year will reach a GDP of 209 after 25 years; that is, $100\,(1.03)^{25} = 209$.

The slowest rate of GDP per capita growth in the table, just 1% per year, is similar to what the United States experienced during its weakest years of productivity growth. The second highest rate, 3% per year, is close to what the U.S. economy experienced during the strong economy of the late 1990s and into the 2000s. Higher rates of per capita growth, such as 5% or 8% per year, represent the experience of rapid growth in economies like Japan, Korea, and China.

**Table 7.3** shows that even a few percentage points of difference in economic growth rates will have a profound effect if sustained and compounded over time. For example, an economy growing at a 1% annual rate over 50 years will see its GDP per capita rise by a total of 64%, from 100 to 164 in this example. However, a country growing at a 5% annual rate will see (almost) the same amount of growth—from 100 to 163—over just 10 years. Rapid rates of economic growth can bring profound transformation. (See the following Clear It Up feature on the relationship between compound growth rates and compound interest rates.) If the rate of growth is 8%, young adults starting at age 20 will see the average standard of living in their country more than double by the time they reach age 30, and grow nearly sixfold by the time they reach age 45.

| Growth Rate | Value of an original 100 in 10 Years | Value of an original 100 in 25 Years | Value of an original 100 in 50 Years |
|---|---|---|---|
| 1% | 110 | 128 | 164 |
| 3% | 134 | 209 | 438 |
| 5% | 163 | 339 | 1,147 |
| 8% | 216 | 685 | 4,690 |

**Table 7.3 Growth of GDP over Different Time Horizons**

# Clear It Up

## How are compound growth rates and compound interest rates related?

The formula for GDP growth rates over different periods of time, as Figure 7.3 shows, is exactly the same as the formula for how a given amount of financial savings grows at a certain interest rate over time, as presented in Choice in a World of Scarcity. Both formulas have the same ingredients:

- an original starting amount, in one case GDP and in the other case an amount of financial saving;

- a percentage increase over time, in one case the GDP growth rate and in the other case an interest rate;

- and an amount of time over which this effect happens.

Recall that compound interest is interest that is earned on past interest. It causes the total amount of financial savings to grow dramatically over time. Similarly, compound rates of economic growth, or the **compound growth rate**, means that we multiply the rate of growth by a base that includes past GDP growth, with dramatic effects over time.

For example, in 2013, the Central Intelligence Agency's World Fact Book reported that South Korea had a GDP of $1.67 trillion with a growth rate of 2.8%. We can estimate that at that growth rate, South Korea's GDP will be $1.92 trillion in five years. If we apply the growth rate to each year's ending GDP for the next five years, we will calculate that at the end of year one, GDP is $1.72 trillion. In year two, we start with the end-of-year one value of $1.72 and increase it by 2.8%. Year three starts with the end-of-year two GDP, and we increase it by 2.8% and so on, as Table 7.4 depicts.

| Year | Starting GDP | Growth Rate 2% | Year-End Amount |
|---|---|---|---|
| 1 | $1.67 Trillion × | (1+0.028) | $1.72 Trillion |
| 2 | $1.72 Trillion × | (1+0.028) | $1.76 Trillion |
| 3 | $1.76 Trillion × | (1+0.028) | $1.81 Trillion |
| 4 | $1.81 Trillion × | (1+0.028) | $1.87 Trillion |
| 5 | $1.87 Trillion × | (1+0.028) | $1.92 Trillion |

Table 7.4

Another way to calculate the growth rate is to apply the following formula:

$$\text{Future Value} = \text{Present Value} \times (1 + g)^n$$

Where "future value" is the value of GDP five years hence, "present value" is the starting GDP amount of $1.67 trillion, "g" is the growth rate of 2.8%, and "n" is the number of periods for which we are calculating growth.

$$\text{Future Value} = 1.67 \times (1+0.028)^5 = \$1.92 \text{ trillion}$$

# 7.3 | Components of Economic Growth

By the end of this section, you will be able to:

- Discuss the components of economic growth, including physical capital, human capital, and technology
- Explain capital deepening and its significance
- Analyze the methods employed in economic growth accounting studies
- Identify factors that contribute to a healthy climate for economic growth

Over decades and generations, seemingly small differences of a few percentage points in the annual rate of economic growth make an enormous difference in GDP per capita. In this module, we discuss some of the components of economic growth, including physical capital, human capital, and technology.

The category of **physical capital** includes the plant and equipment that firms use as well as things like roads (also called **infrastructure**). Again, greater physical capital implies more output. Physical capital can affect productivity in two ways: (1) an increase in the *quantity* of physical capital (for example, more computers of the same quality); and (2) an increase in the *quality* of physical capital (same number of computers but the computers are faster, and so on). **Human capital** refers to the skills and knowledge that make workers productive. Human capital and physical capital accumulation are similar: In both cases, investment now pays off in higher productivity in the future.

The category of **technology** is the "joker in the deck." Earlier we described it as the combination of invention and innovation. When most people think of new technology, the invention of new products like the laser, the smartphone, or some new wonder drug come to mind. In food production, developing more drought-resistant seeds is another example of technology. Technology, as economists use the term, however, includes still more. It includes new ways of organizing work, like the invention of the assembly line, new methods for ensuring better quality of output in factories, and innovative institutions that facilitate the process of converting inputs into output. In short, technology comprises all the advances that make the existing machines and other inputs produce more, and at higher quality, as well as altogether new products.

It may not make sense to compare the GDPs of China and say, Benin, simply because of the great difference in population size. To understand economic growth, which is really concerned with the growth in living standards of an average person, it is often useful to focus on GDP per capita. Using GDP per capita also makes it easier to compare countries with smaller numbers of people, like Belgium, Uruguay, or Zimbabwe, with countries that have larger populations, like the United States, the Russian Federation, or Nigeria.

To obtain a per capita production function, divide each input in **Figure 7.2**(a) by the population. This creates a second aggregate production function where the output is GDP per capita (that is, GDP divided by population). The inputs are the average level of human capital per person, the average level of physical capital per person, and the level of technology per person—see **Figure 7.2**(b). The result of having population in the denominator is mathematically appealing. Increases in population lower per capita income. However, increasing population is important for the average person only if the rate of income growth exceeds population growth. A more important reason for constructing a per capita production function is to understand the contribution of human and physical capital.

## Capital Deepening

When society increases the level of capital per person, we call the result **capital deepening**. The idea of capital deepening can apply both to additional human capital per worker and to additional physical capital per worker.

Recall that one way to measure human capital is to look at the average levels of education in an economy. **Figure 7.5** illustrates the human capital deepening for U.S. workers by showing that the proportion of the U.S. population with a high school and a college degree is rising. As recently as 1970, for example, only about half of U.S. adults had at least a high school diploma. By the start of the twenty-first century, more than 80% of adults had graduated from high school. The idea of human capital deepening also applies to the years of experience that workers have, but the average experience level of U.S. workers has not changed much in recent decades. Thus, the key dimension for deepening human capital in the U.S. economy focuses more on additional education and training than on a higher average level of work experience.

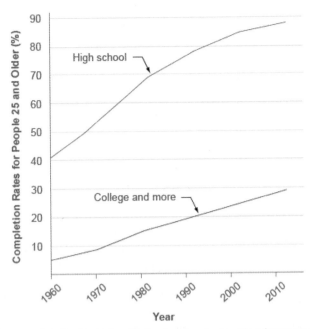

**Figure 7.5 Human Capital Deepening in the U.S.** Rising levels of education for persons 25 and older show the deepening of human capital in the U.S. economy. Even today, under one-third of U.S. adults have completed a four-year college degree. There is clearly room for additional deepening of human capital to occur. (Source: US Department of Education, National Center for Education Statistics)

**Figure 7.6** shows physical capital deepening in the U.S. economy. The average U.S. worker in the late 2000s was working with physical capital worth almost three times as much as that of the average worker of the early 1950s.

**Figure 7.6 Physical Capital per Worker in the United States** The value of the physical capital, measured by plant and equipment, used by the average worker in the U.S. economy has risen over the decades. The increase may have leveled off a bit in the 1970s and 1980s, which were, not coincidentally, times of slower-than-usual growth in worker productivity. We see a renewed increase in physical capital per worker in the late 1990s, followed by a flattening in the early 2000s. (Source: Center for International Comparisons of Production, Income and Prices, University of Pennsylvania)

Not only does the current U.S. economy have better-educated workers with more and improved physical capital than it did several decades ago, but these workers have access to more advanced technologies. Growth in technology is impossible to measure with a simple line on a graph, but evidence that we live in an age of technological marvels is all around us—discoveries in genetics and in the structure of particles, the wireless internet, and other inventions almost too numerous to count. The U.S. Patent and Trademark Office typically has issued more than 150,000 patents annually in recent years.

This recipe for economic growth—investing in labor productivity, with investments in human capital and technology, as well as increasing physical capital—also applies to other economies. South Korea, for example, already achieved universal enrollment in primary school (the equivalent of kindergarten through sixth grade in the United States) by 1965, when Korea's GDP per capita was still near its rock bottom low. By the late 1980s, Korea had achieved almost universal secondary school education (the equivalent of a high school education in the United States). With regard to physical capital, Korea's rates of investment had been about 15% of GDP at the start of the 1960s, but doubled to 30–35% of GDP by the late 1960s and early 1970s. With regard to technology, South Korean students went to universities and colleges around the world to obtain scientific and technical training, and South Korean firms reached out to study and form partnerships with firms that could offer them technological insights. These factors combined to foster South Korea's high rate of economic growth.

## Growth Accounting Studies

Since the late 1950s, economists have conducted growth accounting studies to determine the extent to which physical and human capital deepening and technology have contributed to growth. The usual approach uses an aggregate production function to estimate how much of per capita economic growth can be attributed to growth in physical capital and human capital. We can measure these two inputs at least roughly. The part of growth that is unexplained by measured inputs, called the residual, is then attributed to growth in technology. The exact numerical estimates differ from study to study and from country to country, depending on how researchers measured these three main factors and over what time horizons. For studies of the U.S. economy, three lessons commonly emerge from growth accounting studies.

First, technology is typically the most important contributor to U.S. economic growth. Growth in human capital and physical capital often explains only half or less than half of the economic growth that occurs. New ways of doing things are tremendously important.

Second, while investment in physical capital is essential to growth in labor productivity and GDP per capita, building human capital is at least as important. Economic growth is not just a matter of more machines and buildings. One vivid example of the power of human capital and technological knowledge occurred in Europe in the years after World War II (1939–1945). During the war, a large share of Europe's physical capital, such as factories, roads, and vehicles, was destroyed. Europe also lost an overwhelming amount of human capital in the form of millions of men, women, and children who died during the war. However, the powerful combination of skilled workers and technological knowledge, working within a market-oriented economic framework, rebuilt Europe's productive capacity to an even higher level within less than two decades.

A third lesson is that these three factors of human capital, physical capital, and technology work together. Workers with a higher level of education and skills are often better at coming up with new technological innovations. These technological innovations are often ideas that cannot increase production until they become a part of new investment in physical capital. New machines that embody technological innovations often require additional training, which builds worker skills further. If the recipe for economic growth is to succeed, an economy needs all the ingredients of the aggregate production function. See the following Clear It Up feature for an example of how human capital, physical capital, and technology can combine to significantly impact lives.

## How do girls' education and economic growth relate in low-income countries?

In the early 2000s, according to the World Bank, about 110 million children between the ages of 6 and 11 were not in school—and about two-thirds of them were girls. In Afghanistan, for example, the literacy rate for those aged 15-24 for the period 2005-2014 was 62% for males and only 32% for females. In Benin, in West Africa, it was 55% for males and 31% for females. In Nigeria, Africa's most populous country, it was 76% for males and 58 percent for females.

Whenever any child does not receive a basic education, it is both a human and an economic loss. In low-income countries, wages typically increase by an average of 10 to 20% with each additional year of education. There is, however, some intriguing evidence that helping girls in low-income countries to close the education gap with boys may be especially important, because of the social role that many of the girls will play as mothers and homemakers.

Girls in low-income countries who receive more education tend to grow up to have fewer, healthier, better-educated children. Their children are more likely to be better nourished and to receive basic health care like immunizations. Economic research on women in low-income economies backs up these findings. When 20 women obtain one additional year of schooling, as a group they will, on average, have one less child. When 1,000 women obtain one additional year of schooling, on average one to two fewer women from that group will die in childbirth. When a woman stays in school an additional year, that factor alone means that, on average, each of her children will spend an additional half-year in school. Education for girls is a good investment because it is an investment in economic growth with benefits beyond the current generation.

## A Healthy Climate for Economic Growth

While physical and human capital deepening and better technology are important, equally important to a nation's well-being is the climate or system within which these inputs are cultivated. Both the type of market economy and a legal system that governs and sustains property rights and contractual rights are important contributors to a healthy economic climate.

A healthy economic climate usually involves some sort of market orientation at the microeconomic, individual, or firm decision-making level. Markets that allow personal and business rewards and incentives for increasing human and physical capital encourage overall macroeconomic growth. For example, when workers participate in a competitive and well-functioning labor market, they have an incentive to acquire additional human capital, because additional education and skills will pay off in higher wages. Firms have an incentive to invest in physical capital and in training workers, because they expect to earn higher profits for their shareholders. Both individuals and firms look for new technologies, because even small inventions can make work easier or lead to product improvement. Collectively, such individual and business decisions made within a market structure add up to macroeconomic growth. Much of the rapid growth since the late nineteenth century has come from harnessing the power of competitive markets to allocate resources. This market orientation typically reaches beyond national borders and includes openness to international trade.

A general orientation toward markets does not rule out important roles for government. There are times when markets fail to allocate capital or technology in a manner that provides the greatest benefit for society as a whole. The government's role is to correct these failures. In addition, government can guide or influence markets toward certain outcomes. The following examples highlight some important areas that governments around the world have chosen to invest in to facilitate capital deepening and technology:

- Education. The Danish government requires all children under 16 to attend school. They can choose to attend a public school (*Folkeskole*) or a private school. Students do not pay tuition to attend *Folkeskole*. Thirteen percent of primary/secondary (elementary/high) school is private, and the government supplies vouchers to citizens who choose private school.

- Savings and Investment. In the United States, as in other countries, the government taxes gains from private investment. Low capital gains taxes encourage investment and so also economic growth.

- Infrastructure. The Japanese government in the mid-1990s undertook significant infrastructure projects to improve roads and public works. This in turn increased the stock of physical capital and ultimately economic growth.

- Special Economic Zones. The island of Mauritius is one of the few African nations to encourage international trade in government-supported **special economic zones (SEZ)**. These are areas of the country, usually with access to a port where, among other benefits, the government does not tax trade. As a result of its SEZ, Mauritius has enjoyed above-average economic growth since the 1980s. Free trade does not have to occur in an SEZ however. Governments can encourage international trade across the board, or surrender to protectionism.

- Scientific Research. The European Union has strong programs to invest in scientific research. The researchers Abraham García and Pierre Mohnen demonstrate that firms which received support from the Austrian government actually increased their research intensity and had more sales. Governments can support scientific research and technical training that helps to create and spread new technologies. Governments can also provide a legal environment that protects the ability of inventors to profit from their inventions.

There are many more ways in which the government can play an active role in promoting economic growth. We explore them in other chapters and in particular in **Macroeconomic Policy Around the World**. A healthy climate for growth in GDP per capita and labor productivity includes human capital deepening, physical capital deepening, and technological gains, operating in a market-oriented economy with supportive government policies.

# 7.4 | Economic Convergence

By the end of this section, you will be able to:
- Explain economic convergence
- Analyze various arguments for and against economic convergence
- Evaluate the speed of economic convergence between high-income countries and the rest of the world

Some low-income and middle-income economies around the world have shown a pattern of **convergence**, in which their economies grow faster than those of high-income countries. GDP increased by an average rate of 2.7% per year in the 1990s and 2.3% per year from 2000 to 2008 in the high-income countries of the world, which include the

United States, Canada, the European Union countries, Japan, Australia, and New Zealand.

**Table 7.5** lists 10 countries that belong to an informal "fast growth club." These countries averaged GDP growth (after adjusting for inflation) of at least 5% per year in both the time periods from 1990 to 2000 and from 2000 to 2008. Since economic growth in these countries has exceeded the average of the world's high-income economies, these countries may converge with the high-income countries. The second part of **Table 7.5** lists the "slow growth club," which consists of countries that averaged GDP growth of 2% per year or less (after adjusting for inflation) during the same time periods. The final portion of **Table 7.5** shows GDP growth rates for the countries of the world divided by income.

| Country | Average Growth Rate of Real GDP 1990–2000 | Average Growth Rate of Real GDP 2000–2008 |
|---|---|---|
| *Fast Growth Club (5% or more per year in both time periods)* | | |
| Cambodia | 7.1% | 9.1% |
| China | 10.6% | 9.9% |
| India | 6.0% | 7.1% |
| Ireland | 7.5% | 5.1% |
| Jordan | 5.0% | 6.3% |
| Laos | 6.5% | 6.8 % |
| Mozambique | 6.4% | 7.3% |
| Sudan | 5.4% | 7.3% |
| Uganda | 7.1% | 7.3% |
| Vietnam | 7.9% | 7.3% |
| *Slow Growth Club (2% or less per year in both time periods)* | | |
| Central African Republic | 2.0% | 0.8% |
| France | 2.0% | 1.8% |
| Germany | 1.8% | 1.3% |
| Guinea-Bissau | 1.2% | 0.2% |
| Haiti | −1.5% | 0.3% |
| Italy | 1.6% | 1.2% |
| Jamaica | 0.9% | 1.4% |
| Japan | 1.3% | 1.3% |
| Switzerland | 1.0% | 2.0% |
| United States (for reference) | 3.2% | 2.2% |

**Table 7.5 Economic Growth around the World**   (Source: http://databank.worldbank.org/data/views/ variableSelection/selectvariables.aspx?source=world-development-indicators#c_u)

| Country | Average Growth Rate of Real GDP 1990–2000 | Average Growth Rate of Real GDP 2000–2008 |
|---|---|---|
| *World Overview* | | |
| High income | 2.7% | 2.3% |
| Low income | 3.8% | 5.6% |
| Middle income | 4.7% | 6.1% |

**Table 7.5 Economic Growth around the World**   (Source: http://databank.worldbank.org/data/views/variableSelection/selectvariables.aspx?source=world-development-indicators#c_u)

Each of the countries in **Table 7.5** has its own unique story of investments in human and physical capital, technological gains, market forces, government policies, and even lucky events, but an overall pattern of convergence is clear. The low-income countries have GDP growth that is faster than that of the middle-income countries, which in turn have GDP growth that is faster than that of the high-income countries. Two prominent members of the fast-growth club are China and India, which between them have nearly 40% of the world's population. Some prominent members of the slow-growth club are high-income countries like France, Germany, Italy, and Japan.

Will this pattern of economic convergence persist into the future? This is a controversial question among economists that we will consider by looking at some of the main arguments on both sides.

## Arguments Favoring Convergence

Several arguments suggest that low-income countries might have an advantage in achieving greater worker productivity and economic growth in the future.

A first argument is based on diminishing marginal returns. Even though deepening human and physical capital will tend to increase GDP per capita, the law of diminishing returns suggests that as an economy continues to increase its human and physical capital, the marginal gains to economic growth will diminish. For example, raising the average education level of the population by two years from a tenth-grade level to a high school diploma (while holding all other inputs constant) would produce a certain increase in output. An additional two-year increase, so that the average person had a two-year college degree, would increase output further, but the marginal gain would be smaller. Yet another additional two-year increase in the level of education, so that the average person would have a four-year-college bachelor's degree, would increase output still further, but the marginal increase would again be smaller. A similar lesson holds for physical capital. If the quantity of physical capital available to the average worker increases, by, say, $5,000 to $10,000 (again, while holding all other inputs constant), it will increase the level of output. An additional increase from $10,000 to $15,000 will increase output further, but the marginal increase will be smaller.

Low-income countries like China and India tend to have lower levels of human capital and physical capital, so an investment in capital deepening should have a larger marginal effect in these countries than in high-income countries, where levels of human and physical capital are already relatively high. Diminishing returns implies that low-income economies could converge to the levels that the high-income countries achieve.

A second argument is that low-income countries may find it easier to improve their technologies than high-income countries. High-income countries must continually invent new technologies, whereas low-income countries can often find ways of applying technology that has already been invented and is well understood. The economist Alexander Gerschenkron (1904–1978) gave this phenomenon a memorable name: "the advantages of backwardness." Of course, he did not literally mean that it is an advantage to have a lower standard of living. He was pointing out that a country that is behind has some extra potential for catching up.

Finally, optimists argue that many countries have observed the experience of those that have grown more quickly and have learned from it. Moreover, once the people of a country begin to enjoy the benefits of a higher standard of living, they may be more likely to build and support the market-friendly institutions that will help provide this standard of living.

## Arguments That Convergence Is neither Inevitable nor Likely

If the economy's growth depended only on the deepening of human capital and physical capital, then we would expect that economy's growth rate to slow down over the long run because of diminishing marginal returns. However, there is another crucial factor in the aggregate production function: technology.

Developing new technology can provide a way for an economy to sidestep the diminishing marginal returns of capital deepening. **Figure 7.7** shows how. The figure's horizontal axis measures the amount of capital deepening, which on this figure is an overall measure that includes deepening of both physical and human capital. The amount of human and physical capital per worker increases as you move from left to right, from $C_1$ to $C_2$ to $C_3$. The diagram's vertical axis measures per capita output. Start by considering the lowest line in this diagram, labeled Technology 1. Along this aggregate production function, the level of technology is held constant, so the line shows only the relationship between capital deepening and output. As capital deepens from $C_1$ to $C_2$ to $C_3$ and the economy moves from R to U to W, per capita output does increase—but the way in which the line starts out steeper on the left but then flattens as it moves to the right shows the diminishing marginal returns, as additional marginal amounts of capital deepening increase output by ever-smaller amounts. The shape of the aggregate production line (Technology 1) shows that the ability of capital deepening, by itself, to generate sustained economic growth is limited, since diminishing returns will eventually set in.

**Figure 7.7 Capital Deepening and New Technology** Imagine that the economy starts at point R, with the level of physical and human capital $C_1$ and the output per capita at $G_1$. If the economy relies only on capital deepening, while remaining at the technology level shown by the Technology 1 line, then it would face diminishing marginal returns as it moved from point R to point U to point W. However, now imagine that capital deepening is combined with improvements in technology. Then, as capital deepens from $C_1$ to $C_2$, technology improves from Technology 1 to Technology 2, and the economy moves from R to S. Similarly, as capital deepens from $C_2$ to $C_3$, technology increases from Technology 2 to Technology 3, and the economy moves from S to T. With improvements in technology, there is no longer any reason that economic growth must necessarily slow down.

Now, bring improvements in technology into the picture. Improved technology means that with a given set of inputs, more output is possible. The production function labeled Technology 1 in the figure is based on one level of technology, but Technology 2 is based on an improved level of technology, so for every level of capital deepening on the horizontal axis, it produces a higher level of output on the vertical axis. In turn, production function Technology 3 represents a still higher level of technology, so that for every level of inputs on the horizontal axis, it produces a higher level of output on the vertical axis than either of the other two aggregate production functions.

Most healthy, growing economies are deepening their human and physical capital and increasing technology at the same time. As a result, the economy can move from a choice like point R on the Technology 1 aggregate production line to a point like S on Technology 2 and a point like T on the still higher aggregate production line (Technology 3). With the combination of technology and capital deepening, the rise in GDP per capita in high-income countries does not need to fade away because of diminishing returns. The gains from technology can offset the diminishing returns involved with capital deepening.

Will technological improvements themselves run into diminishing returns over time? That is, will it become continually harder and more costly to discover new technological improvements? Perhaps someday, but, at least over the last two centuries since the beginning of the Industrial Revolution, improvements in technology have not run into diminishing marginal returns. Modern inventions, like the internet or discoveries in genetics or materials science, do not seem to provide smaller gains to output than earlier inventions like the steam engine or the railroad. One reason that technological ideas do not seem to run into diminishing returns is that we often can apply widely the ideas of new technology at a marginal cost that is very low or even zero. A specific worker or group of workers must use a specific additional machine, or an additional year of education. Many workers across the economy can use a new technology or invention at very low marginal cost.

The argument that it is easier for a low-income country to copy and adapt existing technology than it is for a high-income country to invent new technology is not necessarily true, either. When it comes to adapting and using new technology, a society's performance is not necessarily guaranteed, but is the result of whether the country's economic, educational, and public policy institutions are supportive. In theory, perhaps, low-income countries have many opportunities to copy and adapt technology, but if they lack the appropriate supportive economic infrastructure and institutions, the theoretical possibility that backwardness might have certain advantages is of little practical relevance.

# Link It Up ∞

Visit this website (http://openstaxcollege.org/l/Indiapoverty) to read more about economic growth in India.

## The Slowness of Convergence

Although economic convergence between the high-income countries and the rest of the world seems possible and even likely, it will proceed slowly. Consider, for example, a country that starts off with a GDP per capita of $40,000, which would roughly represent a typical high-income country today, and another country that starts out at $4,000, which is roughly the level in low-income but not impoverished countries like Indonesia, Guatemala, or Egypt. Say that the rich country chugs along at a 2% annual growth rate of GDP per capita, while the poorer country grows at the aggressive rate of 7% per year. After 30 years, GDP per capita in the rich country will be $72,450 (that is, $40,000 $(1 + 0.02)^{30}$) while in the poor country it will be $30,450 (that is, $4,000 $(1 + 0.07)^{30}$). Convergence has occurred. The rich country used to be 10 times as wealthy as the poor one, and now it is only about 2.4 times as wealthy. Even after 30 consecutive years of very rapid growth, however, people in the low-income country are still likely to feel quite poor compared to people in the rich country. Moreover, as the poor country catches up, its opportunities for catch-up growth are reduced, and its growth rate may slow down somewhat.

The slowness of convergence illustrates again that small differences in annual rates of economic growth become huge differences over time. The high-income countries have been building up their advantage in standard of living over decades—more than a century in some cases. Even in an optimistic scenario, it will take decades for the low-income countries of the world to catch up significantly.

# Bring it Home

## Calories and Economic Growth

We can tell the story of modern economic growth by looking at calorie consumption over time. The dramatic rise in incomes allowed the average person to eat better and consume more calories. How did these incomes increase? The neoclassical growth consensus uses the aggregate production function to suggest that the period of modern economic growth came about because of increases in inputs such as technology and physical and human capital. Also important was the way in which technological progress combined with physical and human capital deepening to create growth and convergence. The issue of distribution of income notwithstanding, it is clear that the average worker can afford more calories in 2017 than in 1875.

Aside from increases in income, there is another reason why the average person can afford more food. Modern agriculture has allowed many countries to produce more food than they need. Despite having more than enough food, however, many governments and multilateral agencies have not solved the food distribution problem. In fact, food shortages, famine, or general food insecurity are caused more often by the failure of government macroeconomic policy, according to the Nobel Prize-winning economist Amartya Sen. Sen has conducted extensive research into issues of inequality, poverty, and the role of government in improving standards of living. Macroeconomic policies that strive toward stable inflation, full employment, education of women, and preservation of property rights are more likely to eliminate starvation and provide for a more even distribution of food.

Because we have more food per capita, global food prices have decreased since 1875. The prices of some foods, however, have decreased more than the prices of others. For example, researchers from the University of Washington have shown that in the United States, calories from zucchini and lettuce are 100 times more expensive than calories from oil, butter, and sugar. Research from countries like India, China, and the United States suggests that as incomes rise, individuals want more calories from fats and protein and fewer from carbohydrates. This has very interesting implications for global food production, obesity, and environmental consequences. Affluent urban India has an obesity problem much like many parts of the United States. The forces of convergence are at work.

## KEY TERMS

**aggregate production function**  the process whereby an economy as a whole turns economic inputs such as human capital, physical capital, and technology into output measured as GDP per capita

**capital deepening**  an increase by society in the average level of physical and/or human capital per person

**compound growth rate**  the rate of growth when multiplied by a base that includes past GDP growth

**contractual rights**  the rights of individuals to enter into agreements with others regarding the use of their property providing recourse through the legal system in the event of noncompliance

**convergence**  pattern in which economies with low per capita incomes grow faster than economies with high per capita incomes

**human capital**  the accumulated skills and education of workers

**Industrial Revolution**  the widespread use of power-driven machinery and the economic and social changes that occurred in the first half of the 1800s

**infrastructure**  a component of physical capital such as roads and rail systems

**innovation**  putting advances in knowledge to use in a new product or service

**invention**  advances in knowledge

**labor productivity**  the value of what is produced per worker, or per hour worked (sometimes called worker productivity)

**modern economic growth**  the period of rapid economic growth from 1870 onward

**physical capital**  the plant and equipment that firms use in production; this includes infrastructure

**production function**  the process whereby a firm turns economic inputs like labor, machinery, and raw materials into outputs like goods and services that consumers use

**rule of law**  the process of enacting laws that protect individual and entity rights to use their property as they see fit. Laws must be clear, public, fair, and enforced, and applicable to all members of society

**special economic zone (SEZ)**  area of a country, usually with access to a port where, among other benefits, the government does not tax trade

**technological change**  a combination of invention—advances in knowledge—and innovation

**technology**  all the ways in which existing inputs produce more or higher quality, as well as different and altogether new products

## KEY CONCEPTS AND SUMMARY

### 7.1 The Relatively Recent Arrival of Economic Growth

Since the early nineteenth century, there has been a spectacular process of long-run economic growth during which the world's leading economies—mostly those in Western Europe and North America—expanded GDP per capita at an average rate of about 2% per year. In the last half-century, countries like Japan, South Korea, and China have shown the potential to catch up. The Industrial Revolution facilitated the extensive process of economic growth, that economists often refer to as modern economic growth. This increased worker productivity and trade, as well as the development of governance and market institutions.

## 7.2 Labor Productivity and Economic Growth
We can measure productivity, the value of what is produced per worker, or per hour worked, as the level of GDP per worker or GDP per hour. The United States experienced a productivity slowdown between 1973 and 1989. Since then, U.S. productivity has rebounded for the most part, but annual growth in productivity in the nonfarm business sector has been less than one percent each year between 2011 and 2016. It is not clear what productivity growth will be in the coming years. The rate of productivity growth is the primary determinant of an economy's rate of long-term economic growth and higher wages. Over decades and generations, seemingly small differences of a few percentage points in the annual rate of economic growth make an enormous difference in GDP per capita. An aggregate production function specifies how certain inputs in the economy, like human capital, physical capital, and technology, lead to the output measured as GDP per capita.

Compound interest and compound growth rates behave in the same way as productivity rates. Seemingly small changes in percentage points can have big impacts on income over time.

## 7.3 Components of Economic Growth
Over decades and generations, seemingly small differences of a few percentage points in the annual rate of economic growth make an enormous difference in GDP per capita. Capital deepening refers to an increase in the amount of capital per worker, either human capital per worker, in the form of higher education or skills, or physical capital per worker. Technology, in its economic meaning, refers broadly to all new methods of production, which includes major scientific inventions but also small inventions and even better forms of management or other types of institutions. A healthy climate for growth in GDP per capita consists of improvements in human capital, physical capital, and technology, in a market-oriented environment with supportive public policies and institutions.

## 7.4 Economic Convergence
When countries with lower GDP levels per capita catch up to countries with higher GDP levels per capita, we call the process convergence. Convergence can occur even when both high- and low-income countries increase investment in physical and human capital with the objective of growing GDP. This is because the impact of new investment in physical and human capital on a low-income country may result in huge gains as new skills or equipment combine with the labor force. In higher-income countries, however, a level of investment equal to that of the low income country is not likely to have as big an impact, because the more developed country most likely already has high levels of capital investment. Therefore, the marginal gain from this additional investment tends to be successively less and less. Higher income countries are more likely to have diminishing returns to their investments and must continually invent new technologies. This allows lower-income economies to have a chance for convergent growth. However, many high-income economies have developed economic and political institutions that provide a healthy economic climate for an ongoing stream of technological innovations. Continuous technological innovation can counterbalance diminishing returns to investments in human and physical capital.

# SELF-CHECK QUESTIONS

1. Explain what the Industrial Revolution was and where it began.

2. Explain the difference between property rights and contractual rights. Why do they matter to economic growth?

3. Are there other ways in which we can measure productivity besides the amount produced per hour of work?

4. Assume there are two countries: South Korea and the United States. South Korea grows at 4% and the United States grows at 1%. For the sake of simplicity, assume they both start from the same fictional income level, $10,000. What will the incomes of the United States and South Korea be in 20 years? By how many multiples will each country's income grow in 20 years?

5. What do the growth accounting studies conclude are the determinants of growth? Which is more important, the determinants or how they are combined?

6. What policies can the government of a free-market economy implement to stimulate economic growth?

**7.** List the areas where government policy can help economic growth.

**8.** Use an example to explain why, after periods of rapid growth, a low-income country that has not caught up to a high-income country may feel poor.

**9.** Would the following events usually lead to capital deepening? Why or why not?
   a. A weak economy in which businesses become reluctant to make long-term investments in physical capital.
   b. A rise in international trade.
   c. A trend in which many more adults participate in continuing education courses through their employers and at colleges and universities.

**10.** What are the "advantages of backwardness" for economic growth?

**11.** Would you expect capital deepening to result in diminished returns? Why or why not? Would you expect improvements in technology to result in diminished returns? Why or why not?

**12.** Why does productivity growth in high-income economies not slow down as it runs into diminishing returns from additional investments in physical capital and human capital? Does this show one area where the theory of diminishing returns fails to apply? Why or why not?

## REVIEW QUESTIONS

**13.** How did the Industrial Revolution increase the economic growth rate and income levels in the United States?

**14.** How much should a nation be concerned if its rate of economic growth is just 2% slower than other nations?

**15.** How is GDP per capita calculated differently from labor productivity?

**16.** How do gains in labor productivity lead to gains in GDP per capita?

**17.** What is an aggregate production function?

**18.** What is capital deepening?

**19.** What do economists mean when they refer to improvements in technology?

**20.** For a high-income economy like the United States, what aggregate production function elements are most important in bringing about growth in GDP per capita? What about a middle-income country such as Brazil? A low-income country such as Niger?

**21.** List some arguments for and against the likelihood of convergence.

## CRITICAL THINKING QUESTIONS

**22.** Over the past 50 years, many countries have experienced an annual growth rate in real GDP per capita greater than that of the United States. Some examples are China, Japan, South Korea, and Taiwan. Does that mean the United States is regressing relative to other countries? Does that mean these countries will eventually overtake the United States in terms of the growth rate of real GDP per capita? Explain.

**23. Labor Productivity and Economic Growth** outlined the logic of how increased productivity is associated with increased wages. Detail a situation where this is not the case and explain why it is not.

**24.** Change in labor productivity is one of the most watched international statistics of growth. Visit the St. Louis Federal Reserve website and find the data section (http://research.stlouisfed.org). Find international comparisons of labor productivity, listed under the FRED Economic database (Growth Rate of Total Labor Productivity), and compare two countries in the recent past. State what you think the reasons for differences in labor productivity could be.

**25.** Refer back to the **Work It Out** about Comparing the Economies of Two Countries and examine the data for the two countries you chose. How are they similar? How are they different?

**26.** Education seems to be important for human capital deepening. As people become better educated and more knowledgeable, are there limits to how much additional benefit more education can provide? Why or why not?

**27.** Describe some of the political and social tradeoffs that might occur when a less developed country adopts a strategy to promote labor force participation and economic growth via investment in girls' education.

**28.** Why is investing in girls' education beneficial for growth?

**29.** How is the concept of technology, as defined with the aggregate production function, different from our everyday use of the word?

**30.** What sorts of policies can governments implement to encourage convergence?

**31.** As technological change makes us more sedentary and food costs increase, obesity is likely. What factors do you think may limit obesity?

## PROBLEMS

**32.** An economy starts off with a GDP per capita of $5,000. How large will the GDP per capita be if it grows at an annual rate of 2% for 20 years? 2% for 40 years? 4% for 40 years? 6% for 40 years?

**33.** An economy starts off with a GDP per capita of 12,000 euros. How large will the GDP per capita be if it grows at an annual rate of 3% for 10 years? 3% for 30 years? 6% for 30 years?

**34.** Say that the average worker in Canada has a productivity level of $30 per hour while the average worker in the United Kingdom has a productivity level of $25 per hour (both measured in U.S. dollars). Over the next five years, say that worker productivity in Canada grows at 1% per year while worker productivity in the UK grows 3% per year. After five years, who will have the higher productivity level, and by how much?

**35.** Say that the average worker in the U.S. economy is eight times as productive as an average worker in Mexico. If the productivity of U.S. workers grows at 2% for 25 years and the productivity of Mexico's workers grows at 6% for 25 years, which country will have higher worker productivity at that point?

# 8 | Unemployment

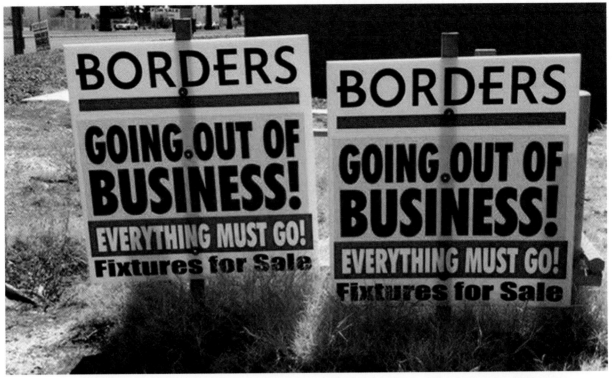

**Figure 8.1 Out of Business**  Borders was one of the many companies unable to recover from the 2008-2009 economic recession. (Credit: modification of work by Luis Villa del Campo/Flickr Creative Commons)

## Bring it Home

### Unemployment and the Great Recession

Nearly eight million U.S. jobs were lost as a consequence of the Great Recession, which lasted from December 2007 to June 2009. At the outset of the recession, the unemployment rate was 5.0%. The rate began rising several months after the recession began, and it peaked at 10.0% in October 2009, several months after the recession ended, according to the Bureau of Labor Statistics (BLS). The job loss represented a huge number of positions gone. Subsequently, the recovery was tepid. Companies added some positions, but as of summer 2013, four years after the end of the recession, unemployment was about 7.5%, well above the pre-recession rate. Employment began increasing at the outset of 2010, and reached its pre-recession level in mid-2014. However, because of population and labor force growth, the unemployment rate at that point was still slightly above 6%. The economy only returned to an unemployment rate of 5.0% in September 2015, and it has remained at or slightly below that level since then, up through January 2017.

This brief overview of unemployment during and after the Great Recession highlights a few important points. First, unemployment is a lagging indicator of business activity. It didn't begin to increase until a few months after the onset of the recession, and it didn't begin to decline until several months after the recovery. Second, the decline in the unemployment rate was quite slow, with the pre-recession unemployment rate only reaching a higher level than six years after the recession ended. This reflects a combination of slow increase in the number of jobs and ongoing increases in the size of the population and the labor force.

It turns out that recent recessions, going back to the early 1990s, have been characterized by longer periods of recovery than their predecessors. We will return to this point at the end of the chapter. However, first we need to examine unemployment. What constitutes it, and how do we measure it?

# Introduction to Unemployment

In this chapter, you will learn about:

- How Economists Define and Compute Unemployment Rate
- Patterns of Unemployment
- What Causes Changes in Unemployment over the Short Run
- What Causes Changes in Unemployment over the Long Run

Unemployment can be a terrible and wrenching life experience—like a serious automobile accident or a messy divorce—whose consequences only someone who has gone through it can fully understand. For unemployed individuals and their families, there is the day-to-day financial stress of not knowing from where the next paycheck is coming. There are painful adjustments, like watching your savings account dwindle, selling a car and buying a cheaper one, or moving to a less expensive place to live. Even when the unemployed person finds a new job, it may pay less than the previous one. For many people, their job is an important part of their self worth. When unemployment separates people from the workforce, it can affect family relationships as well as mental and physical health.

The human costs of unemployment alone would justify making a low level of unemployment an important public policy priority. However, unemployment also includes economic costs to the broader society. When millions of unemployed but willing workers cannot find jobs, economic resource are unused. An economy with high unemployment is like a company operating with a functional but unused factory. The opportunity cost of unemployment is the output that the unemployed workers could have produced.

This chapter will discuss how economists define and compute the unemployment rate. It will examine the patterns of unemployment over time, for the U.S. economy as a whole, for different demographic groups in the U.S. economy, and for other countries. It will then consider an economic explanation for unemployment, and how it explains the patterns of unemployment and suggests public policies for reducing it.

# 8.1 | How Economists Define and Compute Unemployment Rate

By the end of this section, you will be able to:
- Calculate the labor force participation rate and the unemployment rate
- Explain hidden unemployment and what it means to be in or out of the labor force
- Evaluate the collection and interpretation of unemployment data

Newspaper or television reports typically describe unemployment as a percentage or a rate. A recent report might have said, for example, *from August 2009 to November 2009, the U.S. unemployment rate rose from 9.7% to 10.0%, but by June 2010, it had fallen to 9.5%.* At a glance, the changes between the percentages may seem small. However, remember that the U.S. economy has about 160 million adults (as of the beginning of 2017) who either have jobs or are looking for them. A rise or fall of just 0.1% in the unemployment rate of 160 million potential workers translates into 160,000 people, which is roughly the total population of a city like Syracuse, New York, Brownsville, Texas, or Pasadena, California. Large rises in the unemployment rate mean large numbers of job losses. In November 2009, at the peak of the recession, about 15 million people were out of work. Even with the unemployment rate now at 4.8% as of January 2017, about 7.6 million people who would like to have jobs are out of work.

# Link It Up

The Bureau of Labor Statistics (http://openstaxcollege.org/l/BLS1) tracks and reports all data related to unemployment.

## Who's In or Out of the Labor Force?

Should we count everyone without a job as unemployed? Of course not. For example, we should not count children as unemployed. Surely, we should not count the retired as unemployed. Many full-time college students have only a part-time job, or no job at all, but it seems inappropriate to count them as suffering the pains of unemployment. Some people are not working because they are rearing children, ill, on vacation, or on parental leave.

The point is that we do not just divide the adult population into employed and unemployed. A third group exists: people who do not have a job, and for some reason—retirement, looking after children, taking a voluntary break before a new job—are not interested in having a job, either. It also includes those who do want a job but have quit looking, often due to discouragement due to their inability to find suitable employment. Economists refer to this third group of those who are not working and not looking for work as **out of the labor force** or not in the labor force.

The U.S. unemployment rate, which is based on a monthly survey carried out by the U.S. Bureau of the Census, asks a series of questions to divide the adult population into employed, unemployed, or not in the labor force. To be classified as unemployed, a person must be without a job, currently available to work, and actively looking for work in the previous four weeks. Thus, a person who does not have a job but who is not currently available to work or has not actively looked for work in the last four weeks is counted as out of the labor force.

Employed: currently working for pay

Unemployed: Out of work and actively looking for a job

Out of the labor force: Out of paid work and not actively looking for a job

Labor force: the number of employed plus the unemployed

## Calculating the Unemployment Rate

**Figure 8.2** shows the three-way division of the 16-and-over population. In January 2017, about 62.9% of the adult population was "in the labor force"; that is, people are either employed or without a job but looking for work. We can divide those in the labor force into the employed and the unemployed. **Table 8.1** shows those values. The **unemployment rate** is not the percentage of the total adult population without jobs, but rather the percentage of adults who are in the labor force but who do not have jobs:

$$\text{Unemployment rate} \quad = \quad \frac{\text{Unemployed people}}{\text{Total labor force}} \times 100$$

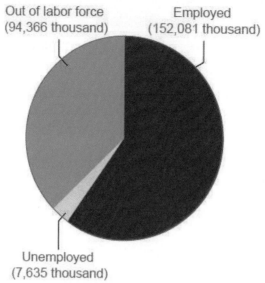

**Figure 8.2 Employed, Unemployed, and Out of the Labor Force Distribution of Adult Population (age 16 and older), January 2017** The total adult, working-age population in January 2017 was 254.1 million. Out of this total population, 152.1 were classified as employed, and 7.6 million were classified as unemployed. The remaining 94.4 were classified as out of the labor force. As you will learn, however, this seemingly simple chart does not tell the whole story.

| Total adult population over the age of 16 | 254.082 million |
|---|---|
| In the labor force | 159.716 million (62.9%) |
| Employed | 152.081 million |
| Unemployed | 7.635 million |
| Out of the labor force | 94.366 million (37.1%) |

**Table 8.1 U.S. Employment and Unemployment, January 2017** (Source: https://data.bls.gov)

In this example, we can calculate the unemployment rate as 7.635 million unemployed people divided by 159.716 million people in the labor force, which works out to a 4.8% rate of unemployment. The following Work It Out feature will walk you through the steps of this calculation.

# Work It Out ─○─○─○

## Calculating Labor Force Percentages

How do economists arrive at the percentages in and out of the labor force and the unemployment rate? We will use the values in **Table 8.1** to illustrate the steps.

To determine the percentage in the labor force:

Step 1. Divide the number of people in the labor force (159.716 million) by the total adult (working-age) population (254.082 million).

Step 2. Multiply by 100 to obtain the percentage.

$$\text{Percentage in the labor force} = \frac{159.716}{254.082}$$

$$= 0.6286$$

$$= 62.9\%$$

To determine the percentage out of the labor force:

Step 1. Divide the number of people out the labor force (94.366 million) by the total adult (working-age) population (254.082 million).

Step 2. Multiply by 100 to obtain the percentage.

$$\text{Percentage in the labor force} = \frac{94.366}{254.082}$$

$$= 0.3714$$

$$= 37.1\%$$

To determine the unemployment rate:

Step 1. Divide the number of unemployed people (7.635 million) by the total labor force (157 million).

Step 2. Multiply by 100 to obtain the rate.

$$\text{Unemployment rate} = \frac{7.635}{159.716}$$

$$= 0.0478$$

$$= 4.8\%$$

## Hidden Unemployment

Even with the "out of the labor force" category, there are still some people who are mislabeled in the categorization of employed, unemployed, or out of the labor force. There are some people who have only part time or temporary jobs, and they are looking for full time and permanent employment that are counted as employed, although they are not employed in the way they would like or need to be. Additionally, there are individuals who are **underemployed**. This includes those who are trained or skilled for one type or level of work but are working in a lower paying job or one that does not utilize their skills. For example, we would consider an individual with a college degree in finance who is working as a sales clerk underemployed. They are, however, also counted in the employed group. All of these individuals fall under the umbrella of the term "hidden unemployment." **Discouraged workers**, those who have stopped looking for employment and, hence, are no longer counted in the unemployed also fall into this group

## Labor Force Participation Rate

Another important statistic is the **labor force participation rate**. This is the percentage of adults in an economy who are either employed or who are unemployed and looking for a job. Using the data in **Figure 8.2** and **Table 8.1**, those included in this calculation would be the 159.716 million individuals in the labor force. We calculate the rate by taking the number of people in the labor force, that is, the number employed and the number unemployed, divided by the total adult population and multiplying by 100 to get the percentage. For the data from January 2017, the labor force participation rate is 62.9%. Historically, the civilian labor force participation rate in the United States climbed beginning in the 1960s as women increasingly entered the workforce, and it peaked at just over 67% in late 1999 to early 2000. Since then, the labor force participation rate has steadily declined, slowly to about 66% in 2008, early in the Great Recession, and then more rapidly during and after that recession, reaching its present level, where it has remained stable, near the end of 2013.

## The Establishment Payroll Survey

When the unemployment report comes out each month, the Bureau of Labor Statistics (BLS) also reports on the number of jobs created—which comes from the establishment payroll survey. The payroll survey is based on a survey of about 147,000 businesses and government agencies throughout the United States. It generates payroll employment estimates by the following criteria: all employees, average weekly hours worked, and average hourly, weekly, and overtime earnings. One of the criticisms of this survey is that it does not count the self-employed. It also does not make a distinction between new, minimum wage, part time or temporary jobs and full time jobs with "decent" pay.

## How Does the U.S. Bureau of Labor Statistics Collect the U.S.

## Unemployment Data?

The unemployment rate announced by the U.S. Bureau of Labor Statistics on the first Friday of each month for the previous month is based on the Current Population Survey (CPS), which the Bureau has carried out every month since 1940. The Bureau takes great care to make this survey representative of the country as a whole. The country is first divided into 3,137 areas. The U.S. Bureau of the Census then selects 729 of these areas to survey. It divides the 729 areas into districts of about 300 households each, and divides each district into clusters of about four dwelling units. Every month, Census Bureau employees call about 15,000 of the four-household clusters, for a total of 60,000 households. Employees interview households for four consecutive months, then rotate them out of the survey for eight months, and then interview them again for the same four months the following year, before leaving the sample permanently.

Based on this survey, state, industry, urban and rural areas, gender, age, race or ethnicity, and level of education statistics comprise components that contribute to unemployment rates. A wide variety of other information is available, too. For example, how long have people been unemployed? Did they become unemployed because they quit, or were laid off, or their employer went out of business? Is the unemployed person the only wage earner in the family? The Current Population Survey is a treasure trove of information about employment and unemployment. If you are wondering what the difference is between the CPS and EPS, read the following Clear it Up feature.

## What is the difference between CPS and EPS?

The United States Census Bureau conducts the Current Population Survey (CPS), which measures the percentage of the labor force that is unemployed. The Bureau of Labor Statistics' establishment payroll survey (EPS) is a payroll survey that measures the net change in jobs created for the month.

## Criticisms of Measuring Unemployment

There are always complications in measuring the number of unemployed. For example, what about people who do not have jobs and would be available to work, but are discouraged by the lack of available jobs in their area and stopped looking? Such people, and their families, may be suffering the pains of unemployment. However, the survey counts them as out of the labor force because they are not actively looking for work. Other people may tell the Census Bureau that they are ready to work and looking for a job but, truly, they are not that eager to work and are not looking very hard at all. They are counted as unemployed, although they might more accurately be classified as out of the labor force. Still other people may have a job, perhaps doing something like yard work, child care, or cleaning houses, but are not reporting the income earned to the tax authorities. They may report being unemployed, when they actually are working.

Although the unemployment rate gets most of the public and media attention, economic researchers at the Bureau of Labor Statistics publish a wide array of surveys and reports that try to measure these kinds of issues and to develop a more nuanced and complete view of the labor market. It is not exactly a hot news flash that economic statistics are imperfect. Even imperfect measures like the unemployment rate, however, can still be quite informative, when interpreted knowledgeably and sensibly.

## Link It Up

Click here (http://openstaxcollege.org/l/BLS_CPS) to learn more about the CPS and to read frequently asked questions about employment and labor.

# 8.2 | Patterns of Unemployment

By the end of this section, you will be able to:
- Explain historical patterns of unemployment in the U.S.
- Identify trends of unemployment based on demographics
- Evaluate global unemployment rates

Let's look at how unemployment rates have changed over time and how various groups of people are affected by unemployment differently.

## The Historical U.S. Unemployment Rate

**Figure 8.3** shows the historical pattern of U.S. unemployment since 1955.

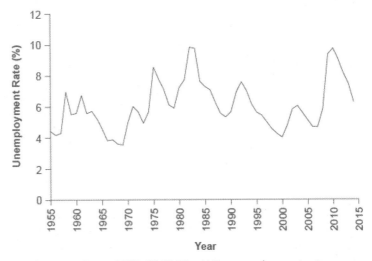

**Figure 8.3 The U.S. Unemployment Rate, 1955–2015** The U.S. unemployment rate moves up and down as the economy moves in and out of recessions. However, over time, the unemployment rate seems to return to a range of 4% to 6%. There does not seem to be a long-term trend toward the rate moving generally higher or generally lower. (Source: Federal Reserve Economic Data (FRED) https://research.stlouisfed.org/fred2/series/LRUN64TTUSA156S0)

As we look at this data, several patterns stand out:

1. Unemployment rates do fluctuate over time. During the deep recessions of the early 1980s and of 2007–2009, unemployment reached roughly 10%. For comparison, during the 1930s Great Depression, the unemployment rate reached almost 25% of the labor force.

2. Unemployment rates in the late 1990s and into the mid-2000s were rather low by historical standards. The unemployment rate was below 5% from 1997 to 2000, and near 5% during almost all of 2006–2007, and 5% or slightly less from September 2015 through January 2017 (the latest date for which data are available as of this writing). The previous time unemployment had been less than 5% for three consecutive years was three

decades earlier, from 1968 to 1970.

3. The unemployment rate never falls all the way to zero. It almost never seems to get below 3%—and it stays that low only for very short periods. (We discuss reasons why this is the case later in this chapter.)

4. The timing of rises and falls in unemployment matches fairly well with the timing of upswings and downswings in the overall economy, except that unemployment tends to lag changes in economic activity, and especially so during upswings of the economy following a recession. During periods of recession and depression, unemployment is high. During periods of economic growth, unemployment tends to be lower.

5. No significant upward or downward trend in unemployment rates is apparent. This point is especially worth noting because the U.S. population more than quadrupled from 76 million in 1900 to over 324 million by 2017. Moreover, a higher proportion of U.S. adults are now in the paid workforce, because women have entered the paid labor force in significant numbers in recent decades. Women comprised 18% of the paid workforce in 1900 and nearly half of the paid workforce in 2017. However, despite the increased number of workers, as well as other economic events like globalization and the continuous invention of new technologies, the economy has provided jobs without causing any long-term upward or downward trend in unemployment rates.

## Unemployment Rates by Group

Unemployment is not distributed evenly across the U.S. population. **Figure 8.4** shows unemployment rates broken down in various ways: by gender, age, and race/ethnicity.

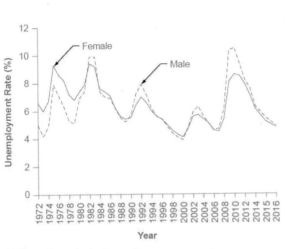

(a) Unemployment rates by gender

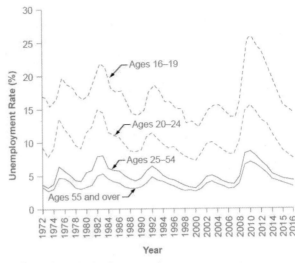

(b) Unemployment rates for women, by age

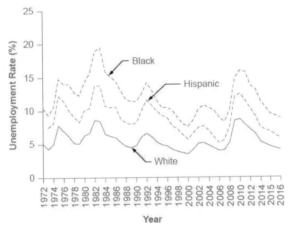

(c) Unemployment rates by race and ethnicity

**Figure 8.4 Unemployment Rate by Demographic Group** (a) By gender, 1972–2016. Unemployment rates for men used to be lower than unemployment rates for women, but in recent decades, the two rates have been very close, often– and especially during and soon after the Great Recession – with the unemployment rate for men somewhat higher. (b) By age, 1972–2016. Unemployment rates are highest for the very young and become lower with age. (c) By race and ethnicity, 1972–2016. Although unemployment rates for all groups tend to rise and fall together, the unemployment rate for blacks is typically about twice as high as that for whites, while the unemployment rate for Hispanics is in between. (Source: www.bls.gov)

The unemployment rate for women had historically tended to be higher than the unemployment rate for men, perhaps reflecting the historical pattern that women were seen as "secondary" earners. By about 1980, however, the unemployment rate for women was essentially the same as that for men, as **Figure 8.4** (a) shows. During the 2008-2009 recession and in the immediate aftermath, the unemployment rate for men exceeded the unemployment rate for women. Subsequently, however, the gap has narrowed.

# Link It Up ⚭

Read this report (http://openstaxcollege.org/l/BLS_recession) for detailed information on the 2008–2009 recession. It also provides some very useful information on the statistics of unemployment.

Younger workers tend to have higher unemployment, while middle-aged workers tend to have lower unemployment, probably because the middle-aged workers feel the responsibility of needing to have a job more heavily. Younger workers move in and out of jobs more than middle-aged workers, as part of the process of matching of workers and jobs, and this contributes to their higher unemployment rates. In addition, middle-aged workers are more likely to feel the responsibility of needing to have a job more heavily. Elderly workers have extremely low rates of unemployment, because those who do not have jobs often exit the labor force by retiring, and thus are not counted in the unemployment statistics. **Figure 8.4** (b) shows unemployment rates for women divided by age. The pattern for men is similar.

The unemployment rate for African-Americans is substantially higher than the rate for other racial or ethnic groups, a fact that surely reflects, to some extent, a pattern of discrimination that has constrained blacks' labor market opportunities. However, the gaps between unemployment rates for whites and for blacks and Hispanics diminished in the 1990s, as **Figure 8.4** (c) shows. In fact, unemployment rates for blacks and Hispanics were at the lowest levels for several decades in the mid-2000s before rising during the recent Great Recession.

Finally, those with less education typically suffer higher unemployment. In January 2017, for example, the unemployment rate for those with a college degree was 2.5%; for those with some college but not a four year degree, the unemployment rate was 3.8%; for high school graduates with no additional degree, the unemployment rate was 5.3%; and for those without a high school diploma, the unemployment rate was 7.7%. This pattern arises because additional education typically offers better connections to the labor market and higher demand. With less attractive labor market opportunities for low-skilled workers compared to the opportunities for the more highly-skilled, including lower pay, low-skilled workers may be less motivated to find jobs.

## Breaking Down Unemployment in Other Ways

The Bureau of Labor Statistics also gives information about the reasons for unemployment, as well as the length of time individuals have been unemployed. **Table 8.2**, for example, shows the four reasons for unemployment and the percentages of the currently unemployed that fall into each category. **Table 8.3** shows the length of unemployment. For both of these, the data is from January 2017.(bls.gov)

| Reason | Percentage |
|---|---|
| New Entrants | 10.8% |
| Re-entrants | 28.7% |
| Job Leavers | 11.4% |
| Job Losers: Temporary | 14.0% |
| Job Losers: Non Temporary | 35.1% |

**Table 8.2 Reasons for Unemployment, January 2017**

| Length of Time | Percentage |
|---|---|
| Under 5 weeks | 32.5% |
| 5 to 14 weeks | 27.5% |
| 15 to 26 weeks | 15.7% |
| Over 27 weeks | 27.4% |

Table 8.3 Length of Unemployment, January 2017

# Link It Up

Watch this speech (http://openstaxcollege.org/l/droids) on the impact of droids on the labor market.

## International Unemployment Comparisons

From an international perspective, the U.S. unemployment rate typically has looked a little better than average. Table 8.4 compares unemployment rates for 1991, 1996, 2001, 2006 (just before the recession), and 2012 (somewhat after the recession) from several other high-income countries.

| Country | 1991 | 1996 | 2001 | 2006 | 2012 |
|---|---|---|---|---|---|
| United States | 6.8% | 5.4% | 4.8% | 4.4% | 8.1% |
| Canada | 9.8% | 8.8% | 6.4% | 6.2% | 6.3% |
| Japan | 2.1% | 3.4% | 5.1% | 4.5% | 3.9% |
| France | 9.5% | 12.5% | 8.7% | 10.1% | 10.0% |
| Germany | 5.6% | 9.0% | 8.9% | 9.8% | 5.5% |
| Italy | 6.9% | 11.7% | 9.6% | 7.8% | 10.8% |
| Sweden | 3.1% | 9.9% | 5.0% | 5.2% | 7.9% |
| United Kingdom | 8.8% | 8.1% | 5.1% | 5.5% | 8.0% |

Table 8.4 International Comparisons of Unemployment Rates

However, we need to treat cross-country comparisons of unemployment rates with care, because each country has slightly different definitions of unemployment, survey tools for measuring unemployment, and also different labor markets. For example, Japan's unemployment rates appear quite low, but Japan's economy has been mired in slow growth and recession since the late 1980s, and Japan's unemployment rate probably paints too rosy a picture of its labor market. In Japan, workers who lose their jobs are often quick to exit the labor force and not look for a new job, in which case they are not counted as unemployed. In addition, Japanese firms are often quite reluctant to fire workers, and so firms have substantial numbers of workers who are on reduced hours or officially employed, but doing very little. We can view this Japanese pattern as an unusual method for society to provide support for the unemployed, rather than a sign of a healthy economy.

# Link It Up

We hear about the Chinese economy in the news all the time. The value of the Chinese yuan in comparison to the U.S. dollar is likely to be part of the nightly business report, so why is the Chinese economy not included in this discussion of international unemployment? The lack of reliable statistics is the reason. This article (http://openstaxcollege.org/l/ChinaEmployment) explains why.

Comparing unemployment rates in the United States and other high-income economies with unemployment rates in Latin America, Africa, Eastern Europe, and Asia is very difficult. One reason is that the statistical agencies in many poorer countries lack the resources and technical capabilities of the U.S. Bureau of the Census. However, a more difficult problem with international comparisons is that in many low-income countries, most workers are not involved in the labor market through an employer who pays them regularly. Instead, workers in these countries are engaged in short-term work, subsistence activities, and barter. Moreover, the effect of unemployment is very different in high-income and low-income countries. Unemployed workers in the developed economies have access to various government programs like unemployment insurance, welfare, and food stamps. Such programs may barely exist in poorer countries. Although unemployment is a serious problem in many low-income countries, it manifests itself in a different way than in high-income countries.

# 8.3 | What Causes Changes in Unemployment over the Short Run

By the end of this section, you will be able to:
- Analyze cyclical unemployment
- Explain the relationship between sticky wages and employment using various economic arguments
- Apply supply and demand models to unemployment and wages

We have seen that unemployment varies across times and places. What causes changes in unemployment? There are different answers in the short run and in the long run. Let's look at the short run first.

## Cyclical Unemployment

Let's make the plausible assumption that in the short run, from a few months to a few years, the quantity of hours that the average person is willing to work for a given wage does not change much, so the labor supply curve does not shift much. In addition, make the standard *ceteris paribus* assumption that there is no substantial short-term change in the age structure of the labor force, institutions and laws affecting the labor market, or other possibly relevant factors.

One primary determinant of the demand for labor from firms is how they perceive the state of the macro economy. If firms believe that business is expanding, then at any given wage they will desire to hire a greater quantity of labor, and the labor demand curve shifts to the right. Conversely, if firms perceive that the economy is slowing down or entering a recession, then they will wish to hire a lower quantity of labor at any given wage, and the labor demand curve will shift to the left. Economists call the variation in unemployment that the economy causes moving from expansion to recession or from recession to expansion (i.e. the business cycle) **cyclical unemployment**.

From the standpoint of the supply-and-demand model of competitive and flexible labor markets, unemployment represents something of a puzzle. In a supply-and-demand model of a labor market, as **Figure 8.5** illustrates, the labor market should move toward an equilibrium wage and quantity. At the equilibrium wage (We), the equilibrium quantity (Qe) of labor supplied by workers should be equal to the quantity of labor demanded by employers.

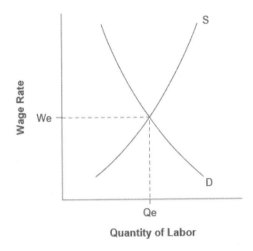

**Figure 8.5 The Unemployment and Equilibrium in the Labor Market**  In a labor market with flexible wages, the equilibrium will occur at wage We and quantity Qe, where the number of people who want jobs (shown by S) equals the number of jobs available (shown by D).

One possibility for unemployment is that people who are unemployed are those who are not willing to work at the current equilibrium wage, say $10 an hour, but would be willing to work at a higher wage, like $20 per hour. The monthly Current Population Survey would count these people as unemployed, because they say they are ready and looking for work (at $20 per hour). However, from an economist's perspective, these people are choosing to be unemployed.

Probably a few people are unemployed because of unrealistic expectations about wages, but they do not represent the majority of the unemployed. Instead, unemployed people often have friends or acquaintances of similar skill levels who are employed, and the unemployed would be willing to work at the jobs and wages similar to what those people are receiving. However, the employers of their friends and acquaintances do not seem to be hiring. In other words, these people are involuntarily unemployed. What causes involuntary unemployment?

## Why Wages Might Be Sticky Downward

If a labor market model with flexible wages does not describe unemployment very well—because it predicts that anyone willing to work at the going wage can always find a job—then it may prove useful to consider economic models in which wages are not flexible or adjust only very slowly. In particular, even though wage increases may occur with relative ease, wage decreases are few and far between.

One set of reasons why wages may be "sticky downward," as economists put it, involves economic laws and institutions. For low-skilled workers receiving minimum wage, it is illegal to reduce their wages. For union workers operating under a multiyear contract with a company, wage cuts might violate the contract and create a labor dispute or a strike. However, minimum wages and union contracts are not a sufficient reason why wages would be sticky downward for the U.S. economy as a whole. After all, out of the 150 million or so employed workers in the U.S. economy, only about 2.6 million—less than 2% of the total—do not receive compensation above the minimum wage. Similarly, labor unions represent only about 11% of American wage and salary workers. In other high-income countries, more workers may have their wages determined by unions or the minimum wage may be set at a level that applies to a larger share of workers. However, for the United States, these two factors combined affect only about 15% or less of the labor force.

Economists looking for reasons why wages might be sticky downwards have focused on factors that may characterize most labor relationships in the economy, not just a few. Many have proposed a number of different theories, but they share a common tone.

One argument is that even employees who are not union members often work under an **implicit contract**, which is that the employer will try to keep wages from falling when the economy is weak or the business is having trouble, and the employee will not expect huge salary increases when the economy or the business is strong. This wage-setting behavior acts like a form of insurance: the employee has some protection against wage declines in bad times, but pays for that protection with lower wages in good times. Clearly, this sort of implicit contract means that firms will be hesitant to cut wages, lest workers feel betrayed and work less hard or even leave the firm.

**Efficiency wage theory** argues that workers' productivity depends on their pay, and so employers will often find it worthwhile to pay their employees somewhat more than market conditions might dictate. One reason is that employees who receive better pay than others will be more productive because they recognize that if they were to lose their current jobs, they would suffer a decline in salary. As a result, they are motivated to work harder and to stay with the current employer. In addition, employers know that it is costly and time-consuming to hire and train new employees, so they would prefer to pay workers a little extra now rather than to lose them and have to hire and train new workers. Thus, by avoiding wage cuts, the employer minimizes costs of training and hiring new workers, and reaps the benefits of well-motivated employees.

The **adverse selection of wage cuts argument** points out that if an employer reacts to poor business conditions by reducing wages for all workers, then the best workers, those with the best employment alternatives at other firms, are the most likely to leave. The least attractive workers, with fewer employment alternatives, are more likely to stay. Consequently, firms are more likely to choose which workers should depart, through layoffs and firings, rather than trimming wages across the board. Sometimes companies that are experiencing difficult times can persuade workers to take a pay cut for the short term, and still retain most of the firm's workers. However, it is far more typical for companies to lay off some workers, rather than to cut wages for everyone.

The **insider-outsider model** of the labor force, in simple terms, argues that those already working for firms are "insiders," while new employees, at least for a time, are "outsiders." A firm depends on its insiders to keep the organization running smoothly, to be familiar with routine procedures, and to train new employees. However, cutting wages will alienate the insiders and damage the firm's productivity and prospects.

Finally, the **relative wage coordination argument** points out that even if most workers were hypothetically willing to see a decline in their own wages in bad economic times as long as everyone else also experiences such a decline, there is no obvious way for a decentralized economy to implement such a plan. Instead, workers confronted with the possibility of a wage cut will worry that other workers will not have such a wage cut, and so a wage cut means being worse off both in absolute terms and relative to others. As a result, workers fight hard against wage cuts.

These theories of why wages tend not to move downward differ in their logic and their implications, and figuring out the strengths and weaknesses of each theory is an ongoing subject of research and controversy among economists. All tend to imply that wages will decline only very slowly, if at all, even when the economy or a business is having tough times. When wages are inflexible and unlikely to fall, then either short-run or long-run unemployment can result. **Figure 8.6** illustrates this.

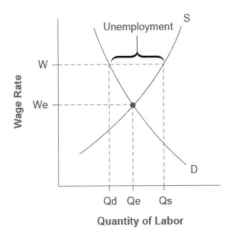

**Figure 8.6 Sticky Wages in the Labor Market** Because the wage rate is stuck at W, above the equilibrium, the number of those who want jobs (Qs) is greater than the number of job openings (Qd). The result is unemployment, shown by the bracket in the figure.

**Figure 8.7** shows the interaction between shifts in labor demand and wages that are sticky downward. **Figure 8.7** (a) illustrates the situation in which the demand for labor shifts to the right from $D_0$ to $D_1$. In this case, the equilibrium wage rises from $W_0$ to $W_1$ and the equilibrium quantity of labor hired increases from $Q_0$ to $Q_1$. It does not hurt employee morale at all for wages to rise.

**Figure 8.7** (b) shows the situation in which the demand for labor shifts to the left, from $D_0$ to $D_1$, as it would tend to do in a recession. Because wages are sticky downward, they do not adjust toward what would have been the new equilibrium wage ($W_1$), at least not in the short run. Instead, after the shift in the labor demand curve, the same quantity of workers is willing to work at that wage as before; however, the quantity of workers demanded at that wage has declined from the original equilibrium ($Q_0$) to $Q_2$. The gap between the original equilibrium quantity ($Q_0$) and the new quantity demanded of labor ($Q_2$) represents workers who would be willing to work at the going wage but cannot find jobs. The gap represents the economic meaning of unemployment.

(a) Rising demand for labor, wages rise

(b) Falling demand for labor, sticky wages, and unemployment

**Figure 8.7 Rising Wage and Low Unemployment: Where Is the Unemployment in Supply and Demand?** (a) In a labor market where wages are able to rise, an increase in the demand for labor from $D_0$ to $D_1$ leads to an increase in equilibrium quantity of labor hired from $Q_0$ to $Q_1$ and a rise in the equilibrium wage from $W_0$ to $W_1$. (b) In a labor market where wages do not decline, a fall in the demand for labor from $D_0$ to $D_1$ leads to a decline in the quantity of labor demanded at the original wage ($W_0$) from $Q_0$ to $Q_2$. These workers will want to work at the prevailing wage ($W_0$), but will not be able to find jobs.

This analysis helps to explain the connection that we noted earlier: that unemployment tends to rise in recessions and to decline during expansions. The overall state of the economy shifts the labor demand curve and, combined with wages that are sticky downwards, unemployment changes. The rise in unemployment that occurs because of a recession is cyclical unemployment.

## Link It Up

The St. Louis Federal Reserve Bank is the best resource for macroeconomic time series data, known as the Federal Reserve Economic Data (FRED). FRED (http://openstaxcollege.org/l/FRED_employment) provides complete data sets on various measures of the unemployment rate as well as the monthly Bureau of Labor Statistics report on the results of the household and employment surveys.

# 8.4 | What Causes Changes in Unemployment over the Long Run

By the end of this section, you will be able to:
- Explain frictional and structural unemployment
- Assess relationships between the natural rate of employment and potential real GDP, productivity, and public policy
- Identify recent patterns in the natural rate of employment
- Propose ways to combat unemployment

Cyclical unemployment explains why unemployment rises during a recession and falls during an economic expansion, but what explains the remaining level of unemployment even in good economic times? Why is the unemployment rate never zero? Even when the U.S. economy is growing strongly, the unemployment rate only rarely dips as low as 4%. Moreover, the discussion earlier in this chapter pointed out that unemployment rates in many European countries like Italy, France, and Germany have often been remarkably high at various times in the last few decades. Why does some level of unemployment persist even when economies are growing strongly? Why are unemployment rates continually higher in certain economies, through good economic years and bad? Economists have a term to describe the remaining level of unemployment that occurs even when the economy is healthy: they call it the **natural rate of unemployment**.

## The Long Run: The Natural Rate of Unemployment

The natural rate of unemployment is not "natural" in the sense that water freezes at 32 degrees Fahrenheit or boils at 212 degrees Fahrenheit. It is not a physical and unchanging law of nature. Instead, it is only the "natural" rate because it is the unemployment rate that would result from the combination of economic, social, and political factors that exist at a time—assuming the economy was neither booming nor in recession. These forces include the usual pattern of companies expanding and contracting their workforces in a dynamic economy, social and economic forces that affect the labor market, or public policies that affect either the eagerness of people to work or the willingness of businesses to hire. Let's discuss these factors in more detail.

## Frictional Unemployment

In a market economy, some companies are always going broke for a variety of reasons: old technology; poor management; good management that happened to make bad decisions; shifts in tastes of consumers so that less of the firm's product is desired; a large customer who went broke; or tough domestic or foreign competitors. Conversely, other companies will be doing very well for just the opposite reasons and looking to hire more employees. In a perfect world, all of those who lost jobs would immediately find new ones. However, in the real world, even if the number of job seekers is equal to the number of job vacancies, it takes time to find out about new jobs, to interview and figure out if the new job is a good match, or perhaps to sell a house and buy another in proximity to a new job. Economists call the unemployment that occurs in the meantime, as workers move between jobs, **frictional unemployment**. Frictional unemployment is not inherently a bad thing. It takes time on part of both the employer and the individual to match those looking for employment with the correct job openings. For individuals and companies to be successful and productive, you want people to find the job for which they are best suited, not just the first job offered.

In the mid-2000s, before the 2008–2009 recession, it was true that about 7% of U.S. workers saw their jobs disappear in any three-month period. However, in periods of economic growth, these destroyed jobs are counterbalanced for the economy as a whole by a larger number of jobs created. In 2005, for example, there were typically about 7.5 million unemployed people at any given time in the U.S. economy. Even though about two-thirds of those unemployed people found a job in 14 weeks or fewer, the unemployment rate did not change much during the year, because those who found new jobs were largely offset by others who lost jobs.

Of course, it would be preferable if people who were losing jobs could immediately and easily move into newly created jobs, but in the real world, that is not possible. Someone who is laid off by a textile mill in South Carolina cannot turn around and immediately start working for a textile mill in California. Instead, the adjustment process happens in ripples. Some people find new jobs near their old ones, while others find that they must move to new locations. Some people can do a very similar job with a different company, while others must start new career paths. Some people may be near retirement and decide to look only for part-time work, while others want an employer that offers a long-term career path. The frictional unemployment that results from people moving between jobs in a dynamic economy may account for one to two percentage points of total unemployment.

The level of frictional unemployment will depend on how easy it is for workers to learn about alternative jobs, which may reflect the ease of communications about job prospects in the economy. The extent of frictional unemployment will also depend to some extent on how willing people are to move to new areas to find jobs—which in turn may depend on history and culture.

Frictional unemployment and the natural rate of unemployment also seem to depend on the age distribution of the population. **Figure 8.4** (b) showed that unemployment rates are typically lower for people between 25–54 years of age or aged 55 and over than they are for those who are younger. "Prime-age workers," as those in the 25–54 age bracket are sometimes called, are typically at a place in their lives when they want to have a job and income arriving at all times. In addition, older workers who lose jobs may prefer to opt for retirement. By contrast, it is likely that a relatively high proportion of those who are under 25 will be trying out jobs and life options, and this leads to greater job mobility and hence higher frictional unemployment. Thus, a society with a relatively high proportion of young workers, like the U.S. beginning in the mid-1960s when Baby Boomers began entering the labor market, will tend to have a higher unemployment rate than a society with a higher proportion of its workers in older ages.

## Structural Unemployment

Another factor that influences the natural rate of unemployment is the amount of **structural unemployment**. The structurally unemployed are individuals who have no jobs because they lack skills valued by the labor market, either because demand has shifted away from the skills they do have, or because they never learned any skills. An example of the former would be the unemployment among aerospace engineers after the U.S. space program downsized in the 1970s. An example of the latter would be high school dropouts.

Some people worry that technology causes structural unemployment. In the past, new technologies have put lower skilled employees out of work, but at the same time they create demand for higher skilled workers to use the new technologies. Education seems to be the key in minimizing the amount of structural unemployment. Individuals who have degrees can be retrained if they become structurally unemployed. For people with no skills and little education, that option is more limited.

## Natural Unemployment and Potential Real GDP

The natural unemployment rate is related to two other important concepts: full employment and potential real GDP. Economists consider the economy to be at full employment when the actual unemployment rate is equal to the natural unemployment rate. When the economy is at full employment, real GDP is equal to potential real GDP. By contrast, when the economy is below full employment, the unemployment rate is greater than the natural unemployment rate and real GDP is less than potential. Finally, when the economy is above full employment, then the unemployment rate is less than the natural unemployment rate and real GDP is greater than potential. Operating above potential is only possible for a short while, since it is analogous to all workers working overtime.

## Productivity Shifts and the Natural Rate of Unemployment

Unexpected shifts in productivity can have a powerful effect on the natural rate of unemployment. Over time, workers' productivity determines the level of wages in an economy. After all, if a business paid workers more than could be justified by their productivity, the business will ultimately lose money and go bankrupt. Conversely, if a business tries to pay workers less than their productivity then, in a competitive labor market, other businesses will find it worthwhile to hire away those workers and pay them more.

However, adjustments of wages to productivity levels will not happen quickly or smoothly. Employers typically review wages only once or twice a year. In many modern jobs, it is difficult to measure productivity at the individual level. For example, how precisely would one measure the quantity produced by an accountant who is one of many people working in the tax department of a large corporation? Because productivity is difficult to observe, employers often determine wage increases based on recent experience with productivity. If productivity has been rising at, say, 2% per year, then wages rise at that level as well. However, when productivity changes unexpectedly, it can affect the natural rate of unemployment for a time.

The U.S. economy in the 1970s and 1990s provides two vivid examples of this process. In the 1970s, productivity growth slowed down unexpectedly (as we discussed in **Economic Growth**). For example, output per hour of U.S. workers in the business sector increased at an annual rate of 3.3% per year from 1960 to 1973, but only 0.8% from 1973 to 1982. **Figure 8.8** (a) illustrates the situation where the demand for labor—that is, the quantity of labor that business is willing to hire at any given wage—has been shifting out a little each year because of rising productivity, from $D_0$ to $D_1$ to $D_2$. As a result, equilibrium wages have been rising each year from $W_0$ to $W_1$ to $W_2$. However, when productivity unexpectedly slows down, the pattern of wage increases does not adjust right away. Wages keep rising each year from $W_2$ to $W_3$ to $W_4$, but the demand for labor is no longer shifting up. A gap opens where the quantity of labor supplied at wage level $W_4$ is greater than the quantity demanded. The natural rate of unemployment rises. In the aftermath of this unexpectedly low productivity in the 1970s, the national unemployment rate did not fall below 7% from May, 1980 until 1986. Over time, the rise in wages will adjust to match the slower gains in productivity, and the unemployment rate will ease back down, but this process may take years.

(a) Productivity rises, and then stops rising          (b) Productivity doesn't change, and then rises

**Figure 8.8 Unexpected Productivity Changes and Unemployment**   (a) Productivity is rising, increasing the demand for labor. Employers and workers become used to the pattern of wage increases. Then productivity suddenly stops increasing. However, the expectations of employers and workers for wage increases do not shift immediately, so wages keep rising as before. However, the demand for labor has not increased, so at wage $W_4$, unemployment exists where the quantity supplied of labor exceeds the quantity demanded. (b) The rate of productivity increase has been zero for a time, so employers and workers have come to accept the equilibrium wage level (W). Then productivity increases unexpectedly, shifting demand for labor from $D_0$ to $D_1$. At the wage (W), this means that the quantity demanded of labor exceeds the quantity supplied, and with job offers plentiful, the unemployment rate will be low.

The late 1990s provide an opposite example: instead of the surprise decline in productivity that occurred in the 1970s, productivity unexpectedly rose in the mid-1990s. The annual growth rate of real output per hour of labor increased from 1.7% from 1980–1995, to an annual rate of 2.6% from 1995–2001. Let's simplify the situation a bit, so that the economic lesson of the story is easier to see graphically, and say that productivity had not been increasing at all in earlier years, so the intersection of the labor market was at point E in **Figure 8.8** (b), where the demand curve for labor ($D_0$) intersects the supply curve for labor. As a result, real wages were not increasing. Now, productivity jumps upward, which shifts the demand for labor out to the right, from $D_0$ to $D_1$. At least for a time, however, wages are still set according to the earlier expectations of no productivity growth, so wages do not rise. The result is that at the prevailing wage level (W), the quantity of labor demanded (Qd) will for a time exceed the quantity of labor supplied (Qs), and unemployment will be very low—actually below the natural level of unemployment for a time. This pattern of unexpectedly high productivity helps to explain why the unemployment rate stayed below 4.5%—quite a low level by historical standards—from 1998 until after the U.S. economy had entered a recession in 2001.

Levels of unemployment will tend to be somewhat higher on average when productivity is unexpectedly low, and conversely, will tend to be somewhat lower on average when productivity is unexpectedly high. However, over time, wages do eventually adjust to reflect productivity levels.

## Public Policy and the Natural Rate of Unemployment

Public policy can also have a powerful effect on the natural rate of unemployment. On the supply side of the labor market, public policies to assist the unemployed can affect how eager people are to find work. For example, if a worker who loses a job is guaranteed a generous package of unemployment insurance, welfare benefits, food stamps, and government medical benefits, then the opportunity cost of unemployment is lower and that worker will be less eager to seek a new job.

What seems to matter most is not just the amount of these benefits, but how long they last. A society that provides generous help for the unemployed that cuts off after, say, six months, may provide less of an incentive for unemployment than a society that provides less generous help that lasts for several years. Conversely, government assistance for job search or retraining can in some cases encourage people back to work sooner. See the Clear it Up to learn how the U.S. handles unemployment insurance.

## How does U.S. unemployment insurance work?

Unemployment insurance is a joint federal–state program that the federal government enacted in 1935. While the federal government sets minimum standards for the program, state governments conduct most of the administration.

The funding for the program is a federal tax collected from employers. The federal government requires tax collection on the first $7,000 in wages paid to each worker; however, states can choose to collect the tax on a higher amount if they wish, and 41 states have set a higher limit. States can choose the length of time that they pay benefits, although most states limit unemployment benefits to 26 weeks—with extensions possible in times of especially high unemployment. The states then use the fund to pay benefits to those who become unemployed. Average unemployment benefits are equal to about one-third of the wage that the person earned in his or her previous job, but the level of unemployment benefits varies considerably across states.

| Bottom 10 States That Pay the Lowest Benefit per Week | | Top 10 States That Pay the Highest Benefit per Week | |
|---|---|---|---|
| Delaware | $330 | Massachusetts | $672 |
| Georgia | $330 | Minnesota | $683 |
| South Carolina | $326 | Washington | $681 |
| Missouri | $320 | New Jersey | $657 |
| Florida | $275 | North Dakota | $633 |
| Tennessee | $275 | Connecticut | $598 |
| Alabama | $265 | Oregon | $590 |
| Louisiana | $247 | Pennsylvania | $573 |
| Arizona | $240 | Colorado | $568 |
| Mississippi | $235 | Rhode Island | $566 |

Table 8.5 Maximum Weekly Unemployment Benefits by State in 2017  (Source: http://www.savingtoinvest.com/maximum-weekly-unemployment-benefits-by-state/)

One other interesting thing to note about the classifications of unemployment—an individual does not have to collect unemployment benefits to be classified as unemployed. While there are statistics kept and studied relating to how many people are collecting unemployment insurance, this is not the source of unemployment rate information.

## Link It Up

View this article (http://openstaxcollege.org/l/NYT_Benefits) for an explanation of exactly who is eligible for unemployment benefits.

On the demand side of the labor market, government rules, social institutions, and the presence of unions can affect the willingness of firms to hire. For example, if a government makes it hard for businesses to start up or to expand, by wrapping new businesses in bureaucratic red tape, then businesses will become more discouraged about hiring. Government regulations can make it harder to start a business by requiring that a new business obtain many permits and pay many fees, or by restricting the types and quality of products that a company can sell. Other government regulations, like zoning laws, may limit where companies can conduct business, or whether businesses are allowed to be open during evenings or on Sunday.

Whatever defenses may be offered for such laws in terms of social value—like the value some Christians place on not working on Sunday, or Orthodox Jews or highly observant Muslims on Saturday—these kinds of restrictions impose a barrier between some willing workers and other willing employers, and thus contribute to a higher natural rate of unemployment. Similarly, if government makes it difficult to fire or lay off workers, businesses may react by trying not to hire more workers than strictly necessary—since laying these workers off would be costly and difficult. High minimum wages may discourage businesses from hiring low-skill workers. Government rules may encourage and support powerful unions, which can then push up wages for union workers, but at a cost of discouraging businesses from hiring those workers.

## The Natural Rate of Unemployment in Recent Years

The underlying economic, social, and political factors that determine the natural rate of unemployment can change over time, which means that the natural rate of unemployment can change over time, too.

Estimates by economists of the natural rate of unemployment in the U.S. economy in the early 2000s run at about 4.5 to 5.5%. This is a lower estimate than earlier. We outline three of the common reasons that economists propose for this change below.

1. The internet has provided a remarkable new tool through which job seekers can find out about jobs at different companies and can make contact with relative ease. An internet search is far easier than trying to find a list of local employers and then hunting up phone numbers for all of their human resources departments, and requesting a list of jobs and application forms. Social networking sites such as LinkedIn have changed how people find work as well.

2. The growth of the temporary worker industry has probably helped to reduce the natural rate of unemployment. In the early 1980s, only about 0.5% of all workers held jobs through temp agencies. By the early 2000s, the figure had risen above 2%. Temp agencies can provide jobs for workers while they are looking for permanent work. They can also serve as a clearinghouse, helping workers find out about jobs with certain employers and getting a tryout with the employer. For many workers, a temp job is a stepping-stone to a permanent job that they might not have heard about or obtained any other way, so the growth of temp jobs will also tend to reduce frictional unemployment.

3. The aging of the "baby boom generation"—the especially large generation of Americans born between 1946 and 1964—meant that the proportion of young workers in the economy was relatively high in the 1970s, as the boomers entered the labor market, but is relatively low today. As we noted earlier, middle-aged and older workers are far more likely to experience low unemployment than younger workers, a factor that tends to reduce the natural rate of unemployment as the baby boomers age.

The combined result of these factors is that the natural rate of unemployment was on average lower in the 1990s and the early 2000s than in the 1980s. The 2008–2009 Great Recession pushed monthly unemployment rates up to 10% in late 2009. However, even at that time, the Congressional Budget Office was forecasting that by 2015, unemployment rates would fall back to about 5%. During the last four months of 2015 the unemployment rate held steady at 5.0%. Throughout 2016 and up through January 2017, the unemployment rate has remained at or slightly below 5%. As of the first quarter of 2017, the Congressional Budget Office estimates the natural rate to be 4.74%, and the measured unemployment rate for January 2017 is 4.8%.

## The Natural Rate of Unemployment in Europe

By the standards of other high-income economies, the natural rate of unemployment in the U.S. economy appears relatively low. Through good economic years and bad, many European economies have had unemployment rates hovering near 10%, or even higher, since the 1970s. European rates of unemployment have been higher not because recessions in Europe have been deeper, but rather because the conditions underlying supply and demand for labor have been different in Europe, in a way that has created a much higher natural rate of unemployment.

Many European countries have a combination of generous welfare and unemployment benefits, together with nests of rules that impose additional costs on businesses when they hire. In addition, many countries have laws that require firms to give workers months of notice before laying them off and to provide substantial severance or retraining packages after laying them off. The legally required notice before laying off a worker can be more than three months in Spain, Germany, Denmark, and Belgium, and the legally required severance package can be as high as a year's salary or more in Austria, Spain, Portugal, Italy, and Greece. Such laws will surely discourage laying off or firing current workers. However, when companies know that it will be difficult to fire or lay off workers, they also become hesitant about hiring in the first place.

We can attribute the typically higher levels of unemployment in many European countries in recent years, which have prevailed even when economies are growing at a solid pace, to the fact that the sorts of laws and regulations that lead to a high natural rate of unemployment are much more prevalent in Europe than in the United States.

## A Preview of Policies to Fight Unemployment

The **Government Budgets and Fiscal Policy** and **Macroeconomic Policy Around the World** chapters provide a detailed discussion of how to fight unemployment, when we can discuss these policies in the context of the full array of macroeconomic goals and frameworks for analysis. However, even at this preliminary stage, it is useful to preview the main issues concerning policies to fight unemployment.

The remedy for unemployment will depend on the diagnosis. Cyclical unemployment is a short-term problem, caused because the economy is in a recession. Thus, the preferred solution will be to avoid or minimize recessions. As **Government Budgets and Fiscal Policy** discusses, governments can enact this policy by stimulating the overall buying power in the economy, so that firms perceive that sales and profits are possible, which makes them eager to hire.

Dealing with the natural rate of unemployment is trickier. In a market-oriented economy, firms will hire and fire workers. Governments cannot control this. Furthermore, the evolving age structure of the economy's population, or unexpected shifts in productivity are beyond a government's control and, will affect the natural rate of unemployment for a time. However, as the example of high ongoing unemployment rates for many European countries illustrates, government policy clearly can affect the natural rate of unemployment that will persist even when GDP is growing.

When a government enacts policies that will affect workers or employers, it must examine how these policies will affect the information and incentives employees and employers have to find one another. For example, the government may have a role to play in helping some of the unemployed with job searches. Governments may need to rethink the design of their programs that offer assistance to unemployed workers and protections to employed workers so that they will not unduly discourage the supply of labor. Similarly, governments may need to reassess rules that make it difficult for businesses to begin or to expand so that they will not unduly discourage the demand for labor. The message is not that governments should repeal all laws affecting labor markets, but only that when they enact such laws, a society that cares about unemployment will need to consider the tradeoffs involved.

# Bring it Home

## Unemployment and the Great Recession

In the review of unemployment during and after the Great Recession at the outset of this chapter, we noted that unemployment tends to be a lagging indicator of business activity. This has historically been the case, and it is evident for all recessions that have taken place since the end of World War II. In brief, this results from the costs to employers of recruitment, hiring, and training workers. Those costs represent investments by firms in their work forces.

At the outset of a recession, when a firm realizes that demand for its product or service is not as strong as anticipated, it has an incentive to lay off workers. However, doing so runs the risk of losing those workers, and if the weak demand proves to be only temporary, the firm will be obliged to recruit, hire, and train new workers. Thus, firms tend to retain workers initially in a downturn. Similarly, as business begins to pick up when a recession is over, firms are not sure if the improvement will last. Rather than incur the costs of hiring and training new workers, they will wait, and perhaps resort to overtime work for existing workers, until they are confident that the recession is over.

Another point that we noted at the outset is that the duration of recoveries in employment following recessions has been longer following the last three recessions (going back to the early 1990s) than previously. Nir Jaimovich and Henry Siu have argued that these "jobless recoveries" are a consequence of job polarization – the disappearance of employment opportunities focused on "routine" tasks. Job polarization refers to the increasing concentration of employment in the highest- and lowest-wage occupations, as jobs in middle-skill occupations disappear. Job polarization is an outcome of technological progress in robotics, computing, and information and communication technology. The result of this progress is a decline in demand for labor in occupations that perform "routine" tasks – tasks that are limited in scope and can be performed by following a well-defined set of procedures – and hence a decline in the share of total employment that is composed of routine occupations. Jaimovich and Siu have shown that job polarization characterizes the aftermath of the last three recessions, and this appears to be responsible for the jobless recoveries.

# KEY TERMS

**adverse selection of wage cuts argument** if employers reduce wages for all workers, the best will leave

**cyclical unemployment** unemployment closely tied to the business cycle, like higher unemployment during a recession

**discouraged workers** those who have stopped looking for employment due to the lack of suitable positions available

**efficiency wage theory** the theory that the productivity of workers, either individually or as a group, will increase if the employer pays them more

**frictional unemployment** unemployment that occurs as workers move between jobs

**implicit contract** an unwritten agreement in the labor market that the employer will try to keep wages from falling when the economy is weak or the business is having trouble, and the employee will not expect huge salary increases when the economy or the business is strong

**insider-outsider model** those already working for the firm are "insiders" who know the procedures; the other workers are "outsiders" who are recent or prospective hires

**labor force participation rate** this is the percentage of adults in an economy who are either employed or who are unemployed and looking for a job

**natural rate of unemployment** the unemployment rate that would exist in a growing and healthy economy from the combination of economic, social, and political factors that exist at a given time

**out of the labor force** those who are not working and not looking for work—whether they want employment or not; also termed "not in the labor force"

**relative wage coordination argument** across-the-board wage cuts are hard for an economy to implement, and workers fight against them

**structural unemployment** unemployment that occurs because individuals lack skills valued by employers

**underemployed** individuals who are employed in a job that is below their skills

**unemployment rate** the percentage of adults who are in the labor force and thus seeking jobs, but who do not have jobs

# KEY CONCEPTS AND SUMMARY

### 8.1 How Economists Define and Compute Unemployment Rate

Unemployment imposes high costs. Unemployed individuals suffer from loss of income and from stress. An economy with high unemployment suffers an opportunity cost of unused resources. We can divide the adult population into those in the labor force and those out of the labor force. In turn, we divide those in the labor force into employed and unemployed. A person without a job must be willing and able to work and actively looking for work to be counted as unemployed; otherwise, a person without a job is counted as out of the labor force. Economists define the unemployment rate as the number of unemployed persons divided by the number of persons in the labor force (not the overall adult population). The Current Population Survey (CPS) conducted by the United States Census Bureau measures the percentage of the labor force that is unemployed. The establishment payroll survey by the Bureau of Labor Statistics measures the net change in jobs created for the month.

### 8.2 Patterns of Unemployment

The U.S. unemployment rate rises during periods of recession and depression, but falls back to the range of 4% to

6% when the economy is strong. The unemployment rate never falls to zero. Despite enormous growth in the size of the U.S. population and labor force in the twentieth century, along with other major trends like globalization and new technology, the unemployment rate shows no long-term rising trend.

Unemployment rates differ by group: higher for African-Americans and Hispanics than for whites; higher for less educated than more educated; higher for the young than the middle-aged. Women's unemployment rates used to be higher than men's, but in recent years men's and women's unemployment rates have been very similar. In recent years, unemployment rates in the United States have compared favorably with unemployment rates in most other high-income economies.

### 8.3 What Causes Changes in Unemployment over the Short Run

Cyclical unemployment rises and falls with the business cycle. In a labor market with flexible wages, wages will adjust in such a market so that quantity demanded of labor always equals the quantity supplied of labor at the equilibrium wage. Economists have proposed many theories for why wages might not be flexible, but instead may adjust only in a "sticky" way, especially when it comes to downward adjustments: implicit contracts, efficiency wage theory, adverse selection of wage cuts, insider-outsider model, and relative wage coordination.

### 8.4 What Causes Changes in Unemployment over the Long Run

The natural rate of unemployment is the rate of unemployment that the economic, social, and political forces in the economy would cause even when the economy is not in a recession. These factors include the frictional unemployment that occurs when people either choose to change jobs or are put out of work for a time by the shifts of a dynamic and changing economy. They also include any laws concerning conditions of hiring and firing that have the undesired side effect of discouraging job formation. They also include structural unemployment, which occurs when demand shifts permanently away from a certain type of job skill.

## SELF-CHECK QUESTIONS

**1.** Suppose the adult population over the age of 16 is 237.8 million and the labor force is 153.9 million (of whom 139.1 million are employed). How many people are "not in the labor force?" What are the proportions of employed, unemployed and not in the labor force in the population? *Hint*: Proportions are percentages.

**2.** Using the above data, what is the unemployment rate? These data are U.S. statistics from 2010. How does it compare to the February 2015 unemployment rate computed earlier?

**3.** Over the long term, has the U.S. unemployment rate generally trended up, trended down, or remained at basically the same level?

**4.** Whose unemployment rates are commonly higher in the U.S. economy:
   a. Whites or nonwhites?
   b. The young or the middle-aged?
   c. College graduates or high school graduates?

**5.** Beginning in the 1970s and continuing for three decades, women entered the U.S. labor force in a big way. If we assume that wages are sticky in a downward direction, but that around 1970 the demand for labor equaled the supply of labor at the current wage rate, what do you imagine happened to the wage rate, employment, and unemployment as a result of increased labor force participation?

**6.** Is the increase in labor force participation rates among women better thought of as causing an increase in cyclical unemployment or an increase in the natural rate of unemployment? Why?

**7.** Many college students graduate from college before they have found a job. When graduates begin to look for a job, they are counted as what category of unemployed?

# REVIEW QUESTIONS

**8.** What is the difference between being unemployed and being out of the labor force?

**9.** How do you calculate the unemployment rate? How do you calculate the labor force participation rate?

**10.** Are all adults who do not hold jobs counted as unemployed?

**11.** If you are out of school but working part time, are you considered employed or unemployed in U.S. labor statistics? If you are a full time student and working 12 hours a week at the college cafeteria are you considered employed or not in the labor force? If you are a senior citizen who is collecting social security and a pension and working as a greeter at Wal-Mart are you considered employed or not in the labor force?

**12.** What happens to the unemployment rate when unemployed workers are reclassified as discouraged workers?

**13.** What happens to the labor force participation rate when employed individuals are reclassified as unemployed? What happens when they are reclassified as discouraged workers?

**14.** What are some of the problems with using the unemployment rate as an accurate measure of overall joblessness?

**15.** What criteria do the BLS use to count someone as employed? As unemployed?

**16.** Assess whether the following would be counted as "unemployed" in the Current Employment Statistics survey.

    a. A husband willingly stays home with children while his wife works.

    b. A manufacturing worker whose factory just closed down.

    c. A college student doing an unpaid summer internship.

    d. A retiree.

    e. Someone who has been out of work for two years but keeps looking for a job.

    f. Someone who has been out of work for two months but isn't looking for a job.

    g. Someone who hates her present job and is actively looking for another one.

    h. Someone who decides to take a part time job because she could not find a full time position.

**17.** Are U.S. unemployment rates typically higher, lower, or about the same as unemployment rates in other high-income countries?

**18.** Are U.S. unemployment rates distributed evenly across the population?

**19.** When would you expect cyclical unemployment to be rising? Falling?

**20.** Why is there unemployment in a labor market with flexible wages?

**21.** Name and explain some of the reasons why wages are likely to be sticky, especially in downward adjustments.

**22.** What term describes the remaining level of unemployment that occurs even when the economy is healthy?

**23.** What forces create the natural rate of unemployment for an economy?

**24.** Would you expect the natural rate of unemployment to be roughly the same in different countries?

**25.** Would you expect the natural rate of unemployment to remain the same within one country over the long run of several decades?

**26.** What is frictional unemployment? Give examples of frictional unemployment.

**27.** What is structural unemployment? Give examples of structural unemployment.

**28.** After several years of economic growth, would you expect the unemployment in an economy to be mainly cyclical or mainly due to the natural rate of unemployment? Why?

**29.** What type of unemployment (cyclical, frictional, or structural) applies to each of the following:

a. landscapers laid off in response to a drop in new housing construction during a recession.

b. coal miners laid off due to EPA regulations that shut down coal fired power

c. a financial analyst who quits his/her job in Chicago and is pursing similar work in Arizona

d. printers laid off due to drop in demand for printed catalogues and flyers as firms go the internet to promote an advertise their products.

e. factory workers in the U.S. laid off as the plants shut down and move to Mexico and Ireland.

## CRITICAL THINKING QUESTIONS

**30.** Using the definition of the unemployment rate, is an increase in the unemployment rate necessarily a bad thing for a nation?

**31.** Is a decrease in the unemployment rate necessarily a good thing for a nation? Explain.

**32.** If many workers become discouraged from looking for jobs, explain how the number of jobs could decline but the unemployment rate could fall at the same time.

**33.** Would you expect hidden unemployment to be higher, lower, or about the same when the unemployment rate is high, say 10%, versus low, say 4%? Explain.

**34.** Is the higher unemployment rates for minority workers necessarily an indication of discrimination? What could be some other reasons for the higher unemployment rate?

**35.** While unemployment is highly negatively correlated with the level of economic activity, in the real world it responds with a lag. In other words, firms do not immediately lay off workers in response to a sales decline. They wait a while before responding. Similarly, firms do not immediately hire workers when sales pick up. What do you think accounts for the lag in response time?

**36.** Why do you think that unemployment rates are lower for individuals with more education?

**37.** Do you think it is rational for workers to prefer sticky wages to wage cuts, when the consequence of sticky wages is unemployment for some workers? Why or why not? How do the reasons for sticky wages explained in this section apply to your argument?

**38.** Under what condition would a decrease in unemployment be bad for the economy?

**39.** Under what condition would an increase in the unemployment rate be a positive sign?

**40.** As the baby boom generation retires, the ratio of retirees to workers will increase noticeably. How will this affect the Social Security program? How will this affect the standard of living of the average American?

**41.** Unemployment rates have been higher in many European countries in recent decades than in the United States. Is the main reason for this long-term difference in unemployment rates more likely to be cyclical unemployment or the natural rate of unemployment? Explain briefly.

**42.** Is it desirable to pursue a goal of zero unemployment? Why or why not?

**43.** Is it desirable to eliminate natural unemployment? Why or why not? *Hint*: Think about what our economy would look like today and what assumptions would have to be met to have a zero rate of natural unemployment.

**44.** The U.S. unemployment rate increased from 4.6% in July 2001 to 5.9% by June 2002. Without studying the subject in any detail, would you expect that a change of this kind is more likely to be due to cyclical unemployment or a change in the natural rate of unemployment? Why?

## PROBLEMS

**45.** A country with a population of eight million adults has five million employed, 500,000 unemployed, and the rest of the adult population is out of the labor force. What's the unemployment rate? What share of population is in the labor force? Sketch a pie chart that divides the adult population into these three groups.

**46.** A government passes a family-friendly law that no companies can have evening, nighttime, or weekend hours, so that everyone can be home with their families during these times. Analyze the effect of this law using a demand and supply diagram for the labor market: first assuming that wages are flexible, and then assuming that wages are sticky downward.

**47.** As the baby boomer generation retires, what should happen to wages and employment? Can you show this graphically?

# 9 | Inflation

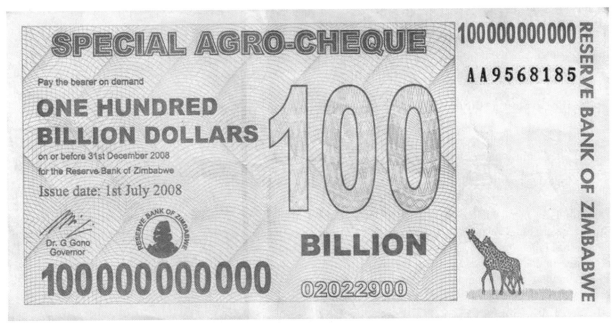

**Figure 9.1 Big Bucks in Zimbabwe** This bill was worth 100 billion Zimbabwean dollars when issued in 2008. There were even bills issued with a face value of 100 trillion Zimbabwean dollars. The bills had $100,000,000,000,000 written on them. Unfortunately, they were almost worthless. At one point, 621,984,228 Zimbabwean dollars were equal to one U.S. dollar. Eventually, the country abandoned its own currency and allowed people to use foreign currency for purchases. (Credit: modification of work by Samantha Marx/Flickr Creative Commons)

## Bring it Home

### A $550 Million Loaf of Bread?

If you were born within the last three decades in the United States, Canada, or many other countries in the developed world, you probably have no real experience with a high rate of inflation. Inflation is when most prices in an entire economy are rising. However, there is an extreme form of inflation called hyperinflation. This occurred in Germany between 1921 and 1928, and more recently in Zimbabwe between 2008 and 2009. In November 2008, Zimbabwe had an inflation rate of 79.6 billion percent. In contrast, in 2014, the United States had an average annual rate of inflation of 1.6%.

Zimbabwe's inflation rate was so high it is difficult to comprehend, so let's put it into context. It is equivalent to price increases of 98% per day. This means that, from one day to the next, prices essentially double. What is life like in an economy afflicted with hyperinflation? Most of you reading this will have never experienced this phenomenon. The government adjusted prices for commodities in Zimbabwean dollars several times *each day*. There was no desire to hold on to currency since it lost value by the minute. The people there spent a great deal of time getting rid of any cash they acquired by purchasing whatever food or other commodities they could find. At one point, a loaf of bread cost 550 million Zimbabwean dollars. Teachers' salaries were in the trillions a month; however, this was equivalent to only one U.S. dollar a day. At its height, it took 621,984,228 Zimbabwean dollars to purchase one U.S. dollar.

Government agencies had no money to pay their workers so they started printing money to pay their bills rather than raising taxes. Rising prices caused the government to enact price controls on private businesses, which led to shortages and the emergence of black markets. In 2009, the country abandoned its currency and allowed people to use foreign currencies for purchases.

How does this happen? How can both government and the economy fail to function at the most basic level? Before we consider these extreme cases of hyperinflation, let's first look at inflation itself.

# Introduction to Inflation

In this chapter, you will learn about:

- Tracking Inflation

- How to Measure Changes in the Cost of Living

- How the U.S. and Other Countries Experience Inflation

- The Confusion Over Inflation

- Indexing and Its Limitations

**Inflation** is a general and ongoing rise in the level of prices in an entire economy. Inflation does not refer to a change in relative prices. A relative price change occurs when you see that the price of tuition has risen, but the price of laptops has fallen. Inflation, on the other hand, means that there is pressure for prices to rise in most markets in the economy. In addition, price increases in the supply-and-demand model were one-time events, representing a shift from a previous equilibrium to a new one. Inflation implies an ongoing rise in prices. If inflation happened for one year and then stopped, then it would not be inflation any more.

This chapter begins by showing how to combine prices of individual goods and services to create a measure of overall inflation. It discusses the historical and recent experience of inflation, both in the United States and in other countries around the world. Other chapters have sometimes included a note under an exhibit or a parenthetical reminder in the text saying that the numbers have been adjusted for inflation. In this chapter, it is time to show how to use inflation statistics to adjust other economic variables, so that you can tell how much of, for example, we can attribute the rise in GDP over different periods of time to an actual increase in the production of goods and services and how much we should attribute to the fact that prices for most items have risen.

Inflation has consequences for people and firms throughout the economy, in their roles as lenders and borrowers, wage-earners, taxpayers, and consumers. The chapter concludes with a discussion of some imperfections and biases in the inflation statistics, and a preview of policies for fighting inflation that we will discuss in other chapters.

# 9.1 | Tracking Inflation

By the end of this section, you will be able to:
- Calculate the annual rate of inflation
- Explain and use index numbers and base years when simplifying the total quantity spent over a year for products
- Calculate inflation rates using index numbers

Dinner table conversations where you might have heard about inflation usually entail reminiscing about when "everything seemed to cost so much less. You used to be able to buy three gallons of gasoline for a dollar and then go see an afternoon movie for another dollar." **Table 9.1** compares some prices of common goods in 1970 and 2017. Of course, the average prices in this table may not reflect the prices where you live. The cost of living in New York City is much higher than in Houston, Texas, for example. In addition, certain products have evolved over recent decades. A new car in 2017, loaded with antipollution equipment, safety gear, computerized engine controls, and many other technological advances, is a more advanced machine (and more fuel efficient) than your typical 1970s car. However, put details like these to one side for the moment, and look at the overall pattern. The primary reason behind the price rises in **Table 9.1**—and all the price increases for the other products in the economy—is not specific to the market for housing or cars or gasoline or movie tickets. Instead, it is part of a general rise in the level of all prices. At the beginning of 2017, $1 had about the same purchasing power in overall terms of goods and services as 18 cents did in

1972, because of the amount of inflation that has occurred over that time period.

| Items | 1970 | 2017 |
|---|---|---|
| Pound of ground beef | $0.66 | $3.62 |
| Pound of butter | $0.87 | $2.03 |
| Movie ticket | $1.55 | $8.65 |
| Sales price of new home (median) | $22,000 | $312,900 |
| New car | $3,000 | $4,077 |
| Gallon of gasoline | $0.36 | $2.35 |
| Average hourly wage for a manufacturing worker | $3.23 | $20.65 |
| Per capita GDP | $5,069 | $57,294 |

Table 9.1 Price Comparisons, 1970 and 2017   (Sources: See chapter References at end of book.)

Moreover, the power of inflation does not affect just goods and services, but wages and income levels, too. The second-to-last row of Table 9.1 shows that the average hourly wage for a manufacturing worker increased nearly six-fold from 1970 to 2017. The average worker in 2017 is better educated and more productive than the average worker in 1970—but not six times more productive. Per capita GDP increased substantially from 1970 to 2017, but is the average person in the U.S. economy really more than eleven times better off in just 47 years? Not likely.

A modern economy has millions of goods and services whose prices are continually quivering in the breezes of supply and demand. How can all of these shifts in price attribute to a single inflation rate? As with many problems in economic measurement, the conceptual answer is reasonably straightforward: Economists combine prices of a variety of goods and services into a single price level. The inflation rate is simply the percentage change in the price level. Applying the concept, however, involves some practical difficulties.

## The Price of a Basket of Goods

To calculate the price level, economists begin with the concept of a **basket of goods and services**, consisting of the different items individuals, businesses, or organizations typically buy. The next step is to look at how the prices of those items change over time. In thinking about how to combine individual prices into an overall price level, many people find that their first impulse is to calculate the average of the prices. Such a calculation, however, could easily be misleading because some products matter more than others.

Changes in the prices of goods for which people spend a larger share of their incomes will matter more than changes in the prices of goods for which people spend a smaller share of their incomes. For example, an increase of 10% in the rental rate on housing matters more to most people than whether the price of carrots rises by 10%. To construct an overall measure of the price level, economists compute a weighted average of the prices of the items in the basket, where the weights are based on the actual quantities of goods and services people buy. The following Work It Out feature walks you through the steps of calculating the annual rate of inflation based on a few products.

# Work It Out ━O━O━O

## Calculating an Annual Rate of Inflation

Consider the simple basket of goods with only three items, represented in Table 9.2. Say that in any given month, a college student spends money on 20 hamburgers, one bottle of aspirin, and five movies. The table provides prices for these items over four years through each time period (Pd). Prices of some goods in the basket may rise while others fall. In this example, the price of aspirin does not change over the four years, while movies increase in price and hamburgers bounce up and down. The table shows the cost of buying the given basket of goods at the prices prevailing at that time.

| Items | Hamburger | Aspirin | Movies | Total | Inflation Rate |
|---|---|---|---|---|---|
| Qty | 20 | 1 bottle | 5 | - | - |
| (Pd 1) Price | $3.00 | $10.00 | $6.00 | - | - |
| (Pd 1) Amount Spent | $60.00 | $10.00 | $30.00 | $100.00 | - |
| (Pd 2) Price | $3.20 | $10.00 | $6.50 | - | - |
| (Pd 2) Amount Spent | $64.00 | $10.00 | $32.50 | $106.50 | 6.5% |
| (Pd 3) Price | $3.10 | $10.00 | $7.00 | - | - |
| (Pd 3) Amount Spent | $62.00 | $10.00 | $35.00 | $107.00 | 0.5% |
| (Pd 4) Price | $3.50 | $10.00 | $7.50 | - | - |
| (Pd 4) Amount Spent | $70.00 | $10.00 | $37.50 | $117.50 | 9.8% |

Table 9.2 A College Student's Basket of Goods

To calculate the annual rate of inflation in this example:

Step 1. Find the percentage change in the cost of purchasing the overall basket of goods between the time periods. The general equation for percentage changes between two years, whether in the context of inflation or in any other calculation, is:

$$\frac{(\text{Level in new year} - \text{Level in previous year})}{\text{Level in previous year}} \times 100 = \text{Percentage change}$$

Step 2. From period 1 to period 2, the total cost of purchasing the basket of goods in Table 9.2 rises from $100 to $106.50. Therefore, the percentage change over this time—the inflation rate—is:

$$\frac{(106.50 - 100)}{100.0} = 0.065 = 6.5\%$$

Step 3. From period 2 to period 3, the overall change in the cost of purchasing the basket rises from $106.50 to $107. Thus, the inflation rate over this time, again calculated by the percentage change, is approximately:

$$\frac{(107 - 106.50)}{106.50} = 0.0047 = 0.47\%$$

Step 4. From period 3 to period 4, the overall cost rises from $107 to $117.50. The inflation rate is thus:

$$\frac{(117.50 - 107)}{107} = 0.098 = 9.8\%$$

This calculation of the change in the total cost of purchasing a basket of goods accounts for how much a student spends on each good. Hamburgers are the lowest-priced good in this example, and aspirin is the highest-priced. If an individual buys a greater quantity of a low-price good, then it makes sense that changes in the price of that good should have a larger impact on the buying power of that person's money. The larger impact of hamburgers shows up in the "amount spent" row, where, in all time periods, hamburgers are the largest item within the amount spent row.

## Index Numbers

The numerical results of a calculation based on a basket of goods can get a little messy. The simplified example in Table 9.2 has only three goods and the prices are in even dollars, not numbers like 79 cents or $124.99. If the list of products were much longer, and we used more realistic prices, the total quantity spent over a year might be some messy-looking number like \$17,147.51 or \$27,654.92.

To simplify the task of interpreting the price levels for more realistic and complex baskets of goods, economists typically report the price level in each period as an **index number**, rather than as the dollar amount for buying the basket of goods. Economists create price indices to calculate an overall average change in relative prices over time. To convert the money spent on the basket to an index number, economists arbitrarily choose one year to be the **base year**, or starting point from which we measure changes in prices. The base year, by definition, has an index number equal to 100. This sounds complicated, but it is really a simple math trick. In the example above, say that we choose time period 3 as the base year. Since the total amount of spending in that year is \$107, we divide that amount by itself (\$107) and multiply by 100. Again, this is because the index number in the base year *always* has to have a value of 100. Then, to figure out the values of the index number for the other years, we divide the dollar amounts for the other years by 1.07 as well. Note also that the dollar signs cancel out so that index numbers have no units.

Table 9.3 shows calculations for the other values of the index number, based on the example in Table 9.2. Because we calculate the index numbers so that they are in exactly the same proportion as the total dollar cost of purchasing the basket of goods, we can calculate the inflation rate based on the index numbers, using the percentage change formula. Thus, the inflation rate from period 1 to period 2 would be

$$\frac{(99.5 - 93.4)}{93.4} \ = \ 0.065 \ = \ 6.5\%$$

This is the same answer that we derived when measuring inflation based on the dollar cost of the basket of goods for the same time period.

| | Total Spending | Index Number | Inflation Rate Since Previous Period |
|---|---|---|---|
| **Period 1** | \$100 | $\frac{100}{1.07} = 93.4$ | |
| **Period 2** | \$106.50 | $\frac{106.50}{1.07} = 99.5$ | $\frac{(99.5 - 93.4)}{93.4} = 0.065 = 6.5\%$ |
| **Period 3** | \$107 | $\frac{107}{1.07} = 100.0$ | $\frac{100 - 99.5}{99.5} = 0.005 = 0.5\%$ |
| **Period 4** | \$117.50 | $\frac{117.50}{1.07} = 109.8$ | $\frac{109.8 - 100}{100} = 0.098 = 9.8\%$ |

Table 9.3 Calculating Index Numbers When Period 3 is the Base Year

If the inflation rate is the same whether it is based on dollar values or index numbers, then why bother with the index numbers? The advantage is that indexing allows easier eyeballing of the inflation numbers. If you glance at two index numbers like 107 and 110, you know automatically that the rate of inflation between the two years is about, but not quite exactly equal to, 3%. By contrast, imagine that we express the price levels in absolute dollars of a large basket of goods, so that when you looked at the data, the numbers were \$19,493.62 and \$20,040.17. Most people find it difficult to eyeball those kinds of numbers and say that it is a change of about 3%. However, the two numbers expressed in absolute dollars are exactly in the same proportion of 107 to 110 as the previous example. If you're wondering why simple subtraction of the index numbers wouldn't work, read the following Clear It Up feature.

# Clear It Up

## Why do you not just subtract index numbers?

A word of warning: When a price index moves from, say, 107 to 110, the rate of inflation is not *exactly* 3%. Remember, the inflation rate is not derived by subtracting the index numbers, but rather through the percentage-change calculation. We calculate the precise inflation rate as the price index moves from 107 to

110 as 100 x (110 − 107) / 107 = 100 x 0.028 = 2.8%. When the base year is fairly close to 100, a quick subtraction is not a terrible shortcut to calculating the inflation rate—but when precision matters down to tenths of a percent, subtracting will not give the right answer.

Two final points about index numbers are worth remembering. First, index numbers have no dollar signs or other units attached to them. Although we can use index numbers to calculate a percentage inflation rate, the index numbers themselves do not have percentage signs. Index numbers just mirror the proportions that we find in other data. They transform the other data so that it is easier to work with the data.

Second, the choice of a base year for the index number—that is, the year that is automatically set equal to 100—is arbitrary. We choose it as a starting point from which we can track changes in prices. In the official inflation statistics, it is common to use one base year for a few years, and then to update it, so that the base year of 100 is relatively close to the present. However, any base year that we choose for the index numbers will result in exactly the same inflation rate. To see this in the previous example, imagine that period 1 is the base year when total spending was $100, and we assign it an index number of 100. At a glance, you can see that the index numbers would now exactly match the dollar figures, and the inflation rate in the first period would be 6.5%.

Now that we see how indexes work to track inflation, the next module will show us how economists measure the cost of living.

## Link It Up @☾☾

Watch this video (http://openstaxcollege.org/l/Duck_Tales) from the cartoon *Duck Tales* to view a mini-lesson on inflation.

# 9.2 | How to Measure Changes in the Cost of Living

By the end of this section, you will be able to:
- Use the Consumer Price Index (CPI) to calculate U.S. inflation rates
- Identify several ways the Bureau of Labor Statistics avoids biases in the Consumer Price Index (CPI)
- Differentiate among the Consumer Price Index (CPI), the Producer Price Index (PPI), the International Price Index, the Employment Cost Index, and the GDP deflator.

The most commonly cited measure of inflation in the United States is the **Consumer Price Index (CPI)**. Government statisticians at the U.S. Bureau of Labor Statistics calculate the CPI based on the prices in a fixed basket of goods and services that represents the purchases of the average family of four. In recent years, the statisticians have paid considerable attention to a subtle problem: that the change in the total cost of buying a fixed basket of goods and services over time is conceptually not quite the same as the change in the cost of living, because the cost of living represents how much it costs for a person to feel that his or her consumption provides an equal level of satisfaction or utility.

To understand the distinction, imagine that over the past 10 years, the cost of purchasing a fixed basket of goods increased by 25% and your salary also increased by 25%. Has your personal standard of living held constant? If you do not necessarily purchase an identical fixed basket of goods every year, then an inflation calculation based on the cost of a fixed basket of goods may be a misleading measure of how your cost of living has changed. Two problems arise here: substitution bias and quality/new goods bias.

When the price of a good rises, consumers tend to purchase less of it and to seek out substitutes instead. Conversely, as the price of a good falls, people will tend to purchase more of it. This pattern implies that goods with generally rising prices should tend over time to become less important in the overall basket of goods used to calculate inflation, while goods with falling prices should tend to become more important. Consider, as an example, a rise in the price of peaches by $100 per pound. If consumers were utterly inflexible in their demand for peaches, this would lead to a big rise in the price of food for consumers. Alternatively, imagine that people are utterly indifferent to whether they have peaches or other types of fruit. Now, if peach prices rise, people completely switch to other fruit choices and the average price of food does not change at all. A fixed and unchanging basket of goods assumes that consumers are locked into buying exactly the same goods, regardless of price changes—not a very likely assumption. Thus, **substitution bias**—the rise in the price of a fixed basket of goods over time—tends to overstate the rise in a consumer's true cost of living, because it does not take into account that the person can substitute away from goods whose relative prices have risen.

The other major problem in using a fixed basket of goods as the basis for calculating inflation is how to deal with the arrival of improved versions of older goods or altogether new goods. Consider the problem that arises if a cereal is improved by adding 12 essential vitamins and minerals—and also if a box of the cereal costs 5% more. It would clearly be misleading to count the entire resulting higher price as inflation, because the new price reflects a higher quality (or at least different) product. Ideally, one would like to know how much of the higher price is due to the quality change, and how much of it is just a higher price. The Bureau of Labor Statistics, which is responsible for computing the Consumer Price Index, must deal with these difficulties in adjusting for quality changes.

# Link It Up

Visit this website (http://openstax.org/l/Fords) to view a list of Ford car prices between 1909 and 1927. Consider how these prices compare to today's models. Is the product today of a different quality?

We can think of a new product as an extreme improvement in quality—from something that did not exist to something that does. However, the basket of goods that was fixed in the past obviously does not include new goods created since then. The basket of goods and services in the Consumer Price Index (CPI) is revised and updated over time, and so new products are gradually included. However, the process takes some time. For example, room air conditioners were widely sold in the early 1950s, but were not introduced into the basket of goods behind the Consumer Price Index until 1964. The VCR and personal computer were available in the late 1970s and widely sold by the early 1980s, but did not enter the CPI basket of goods until 1987. By 1996, there were more than 40 million cellular phone subscribers in the United States—but cell phones were not yet part of the CPI basket of goods. The parade of inventions has continued, with the CPI inevitably lagging a few years behind.

The arrival of new goods creates problems with respect to the accuracy of measuring inflation. The reason people buy new goods, presumably, is that the new goods offer better value for money than existing goods. Thus, if the price index leaves out new goods, it overlooks one of the ways in which the cost of living is improving. In addition, the price of a new good is often higher when it is first introduced and then declines over time. If the new good is not included in the CPI for some years, until its price is already lower, the CPI may miss counting this price decline altogether. Taking these arguments together, the **quality/new goods bias** means that the rise in the price of a fixed basket of goods over time tends to overstate the rise in a consumer's true cost of living, because it does not account for how improvements in the quality of existing goods or the invention of new goods improves the standard of living. The following Clear It Up feature is a must-read on how statisticians comprise and calculate the CPI.

## How do U.S. government statisticians measure the Consumer Price Index?

When the U.S. Bureau of Labor Statistics (BLS) calculates the Consumer Price Index, the first task is to decide on a basket of goods that is representative of the purchases of the average household. We do this by using the Consumer Expenditure Survey, a national survey of about 7,000 households, which provides detailed information on spending habits. Statisticians divide consumer expenditures into eight major groups (seen below), which in turn they divide into more than 200 individual item categories. The BLS currently uses 1982–1984 as the base period.

For each of the 200 individual expenditure items, the BLS chooses several hundred very specific examples of that item and looks at the prices of those examples. In figuring out the "breakfast cereal" item under the overall category of "foods and beverages," the BLS picks several hundred examples of breakfast cereal. One example might be the price of a 24-oz. box of a particular brand of cereal sold at a particular store. The BLS statistically selects specific products and sizes and stores to reflect what people buy and where they shop. The basket of goods in the Consumer Price Index thus consists of about 80,000 products; that is, several hundred specific products in over 200 broad-item categories. Statisticians rotate about one-quarter of these 80,000 specific products of the sample each year, and replace them with a different set of products.

The next step is to collect data on prices. Data collectors visit or call about 23,000 stores in 87 urban areas all over the United States every month to collect prices on these 80,000 specific products. The BLS also conducts a survey of 50,000 landlords or tenants to collect information about rents.

Statisticians then calculate the Consumer Price Index by taking the 80,000 prices of individual products and combining them, using weights (see **Figure 9.2**) determined by the quantities of these products that people buy and allowing for factors like substitution between goods and quality improvements, into price indices for the 200 or so overall items. Then, the statisticians combine the price indices for the 200 items into an overall Consumer Price Index. According the Consumer Price Index website, there are eight categories that data collectors use:

**The Eight Major Categories in the Consumer Price Index**

1. Food and beverages (breakfast cereal, milk, coffee, chicken, wine, full-service meals, and snacks)

2. Housing (renter's cost of housing, homeowner's cost of housing, fuel oil, bedroom furniture)

3. Apparel (men's shirts and sweaters, women's dresses, jewelry)

4. Transportation (new vehicles, airline fares, gasoline, motor vehicle insurance)

5. Medical care (prescription drugs and medical supplies, physicians' services, eyeglasses and eye care, hospital services)

6. Recreation (televisions, cable television, pets and pet products, sports equipment, admissions)

7. Education and communication (college tuition, postage, telephone services, computer software and accessories)

8. Other goods and services (tobacco and smoking products, haircuts and other personal services, funeral expenses)

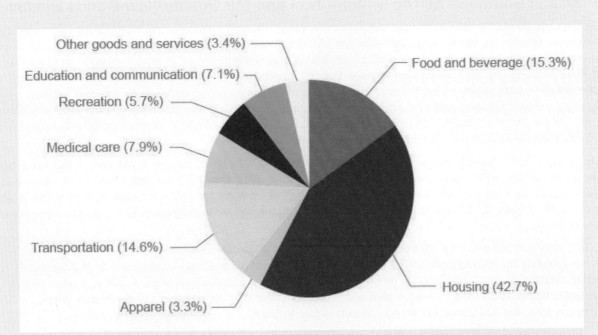

**Figure 9.2 The Weighting of CPI Components**   Of the eight categories used to generate the Consumer Price Index, housing is the highest at 42.7%. The next highest category, food and beverage at 15.3%, is less than half the size of housing. Other goods and services, and apparel, are the lowest at 3.4% and 3.3%, respectively. (Source: www.bls.gov/cpi)

## The CPI and Core Inflation Index

Imagine if you were driving a company truck across the country- you probably would care about things like the prices of available roadside food and motel rooms as well as the truck's operating condition. However, the manager of the firm might have different priorities. He would care mostly about the truck's on-time performance and much less so about the food you were eating and the places you were staying. In other words, the company manager would be paying attention to the firm's production, while ignoring transitory elements that impacted you, but did not affect the company's bottom line.

In a sense, a similar situation occurs with regard to measures of inflation. As we've learned, CPI measures prices as they affect everyday household spending. Economists typically calculate a **core inflation index** by taking the CPI and excluding volatile economic variables. In this way, economists have a better sense of the underlying trends in prices that affect the cost of living.

Examples of excluded variables include energy and food prices, which can jump around from month to month because of the weather. According to an article by Kent Bernhard, during Hurricane Katrina in 2005, a key supply point for the nation's gasoline was nearly knocked out. Gas prices quickly shot up across the nation, in some places by up to 40 cents a gallon in one day. This was not the cause of an economic policy but rather a short-lived event until the pumps were restored in the region. In this case, the CPI that month would register the change as a cost of living event to households, but the core inflation index would remain unchanged. As a result, the Federal Reserve's decisions on interest rates would not be influenced. Similarly, droughts can cause world-wide spikes in food prices that, if temporary, do not affect the nation's economic capability.

As former Chairman of the Federal Reserve Ben Bernanke noted in 1999 about the core inflation index, "It provide(s) a better guide to monetary policy than the other indices, since it measures the more persistent underlying inflation rather than transitory influences on the price level." Bernanke also noted that it helps communicate that the Federal Reserve does not need to respond to every inflationary shock since some price changes are transitory and not part of a structural change in the economy.

In sum, both the CPI and the core inflation index are important, but serve different audiences. The CPI helps households understand their overall cost of living from month to month, while the core inflation index is a preferred gauge from which to make important government policy changes.

## Practical Solutions for the Substitution and the Quality/New Goods Biases

By the early 2000s, the Bureau of Labor Statistics was using alternative mathematical methods for calculating the Consumer Price Index, more complicated than just adding up the cost of a fixed basket of goods, to allow for some substitution between goods. It was also updating the basket of goods behind the CPI more frequently, so that it could include new and improved goods more rapidly. For certain products, the BLS was carrying out studies to try to measure the quality improvement. For example, with computers, an economic study can try to adjust for changes in speed, memory, screen size, and other product characteristics, and then calculate the change in price after accounting for these product changes. However, these adjustments are inevitably imperfect, and exactly how to make these adjustments is often a source of controversy among professional economists.

By the early 2000s, the substitution bias and quality/new goods bias had been somewhat reduced, so that since then the rise in the CPI probably overstates the true rise in inflation by only about 0.5% per year. Over one or a few years, this is not much. Over a period of a decade or two, even half of a percent per year compounds to a more significant amount. In addition, the CPI tracks prices from physical locations, and not at online sites like Amazon, where prices can be lower.

When measuring inflation (and other economic statistics, too), a tradeoff arises between simplicity and interpretation. If we calculate the inflation rate with a basket of goods that is fixed and unchanging, then the calculation of an inflation rate is straightforward, but the problems of substitution bias and quality/new goods bias will arise. However, when the basket of goods is allowed to shift and evolve to reflect substitution toward lower relative prices, quality improvements, and new goods, the technical details of calculating the inflation rate grow more complex.

## Additional Price Indices: PPI, GDP Deflator, and More

The basket of goods behind the Consumer Price Index represents an average hypothetical U.S. household's consumption, which is to say that it does not exactly capture anyone's personal experience. When the task is to calculate an average level of inflation, this approach works fine. What if, however, you are concerned about inflation experienced by a certain group, like the elderly, or the poor, or single-parent families with children, or Hispanic-Americans? In specific situations, a price index based on the buying power of the average consumer may not feel quite right.

This problem has a straightforward solution. If the Consumer Price Index does not serve the desired purpose, then invent another index, based on a basket of goods appropriate for the group of interest. The Bureau of Labor Statistics publishes a number of experimental price indices: some for particular groups like the elderly or the poor, some for different geographic areas, and some for certain broad categories of goods like food or housing.

The BLS also calculates several price indices that are not based on baskets of consumer goods. For example, the **Producer Price Index (PPI)** is based on prices paid for supplies and inputs by producers of goods and services. We can break it down into price indices for different industries, commodities, and stages of processing (like finished goods, intermediate goods, or crude materials for further processing). There is an **International Price Index** based on the prices of merchandise that is exported or imported. An **Employment Cost Index** measures wage inflation in the labor market. The **GDP deflator**, which the Bureau of Economic Analysis measures, is a price index that includes all the GDP components (that is, consumption plus investment plus government plus exports minus imports). Unlike the CPI, its baskets are not fixed but re-calculate what that year's GDP would have been worth using the base-year's prices. MIT's Billion Prices Project is a more recent alternative attempt to measure prices: economists collect data online from retailers and then put them into an index that they compare to the CPI (Source: http://bpp.mit.edu/usa/).

What's the best measure of inflation? If one is concerned with the most accurate measure of inflation, one should use the GDP deflator as it picks up the prices of goods and services produced. However, it is not a good measure of the cost of living as it includes prices of many products not purchased by households (for example, aircraft, fire engines, factory buildings, office complexes, and bulldozers). If one wants the most accurate measure of inflation as it impacts households, one should use the CPI, as it only picks up prices of products purchased by households. That is why economists sometimes refer to the CPI as the cost-of-living index. As the Bureau of Labor Statistics states on its website: "The 'best' measure of inflation for a given application depends on the intended use of the data."

# 9.3 | How the U.S. and Other Countries Experience Inflation

By the end of this section, you will be able to:
- Identify patterns of inflation for the United States using data from the Consumer Price Index
- Identify patterns of inflation on an international level

In the last three decades, inflation has been relatively low in the U.S. economy, with the Consumer Price Index typically rising 2% to 4% per year. Looking back over the twentieth century, there have been several periods where inflation caused the price level to rise at double-digit rates, but nothing has come close to hyperinflation.

## Historical Inflation in the U.S. Economy

**Figure 9.3** (a) shows the level of prices in the Consumer Price Index stretching back to 1913. In this case, the base years (when the CPI is defined as 100) are set for the average level of prices that existed from 1982 to 1984. **Figure 9.3** (b) shows the annual percentage changes in the CPI over time, which is the inflation rate.

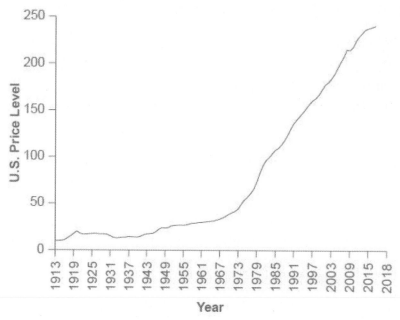

(a) U.S. price level 1913-2016

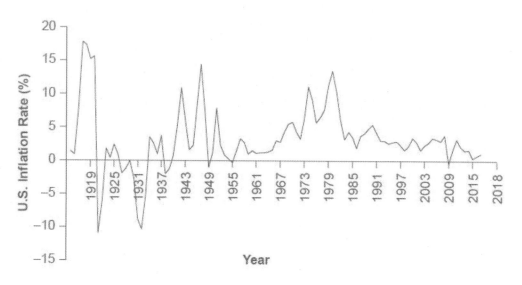

(b) U.S. inflation rate 1913-2016

**Figure 9.3 U.S. Price Level and Inflation Rates since 1913**   Graph a shows the trends in the U.S. price level from the year 1913 to 2016. In 1913, the graph starts out close to 10, rises to around 20 in 1920, stays around 16 or 17 until 1931, then falls to 13 or 14 until 1940. It gradually increases until about 1973, then increases more rapidly through the remainder of the 1970s and beyond, with periodic dips, until 2016, when it reached around 240. Graph b shows the trends in U.S. inflation rates from the year 1914 to 2016. In 1916, the graph starts out with inflation at almost 8%, jumps to about 17% in 1917, drops drastically to close to –11% in 1921, goes up and down periodically, with peaks in the 1940s and the 1970s, until settling to around 1.3% in 2016.

The first two waves of inflation are easy to characterize in historical terms: they are right after World War I and World War II. However, there are also two periods of severe negative inflation—called **deflation**—in the early decades of the twentieth century: one following the deep 1920-21 recession of and the other during the 1930s Great Depression of the 1930s. (Since inflation is a time when the buying power of money in terms of goods and services is reduced, deflation will be a time when the buying power of money in terms of goods and services increases.) For the period from 1900 to about 1960, the major inflations and deflations nearly balanced each other out, so the average annual rate of inflation over these years was only about 1% per year. A third wave of more severe inflation arrived in the

1970s and departed in the early 1980s.

# Link It Up

Visit this website (http://openstax.org/l/CPI_calculator) to use an inflation calculator and discover how prices have changed in the last 100 years.

Times of recession or depression often seem to be times when the inflation rate is lower, as in the recession of 1920–1921, the Great Depression, the recession of 1980–1982, and the Great Recession in 2008–2009. There were a few months in 2009 that were deflationary, but not at an annual rate. High levels of unemployment typically accompany recessions, and the total demand for goods falls, pulling the price level down. Conversely, the rate of inflation often, but not always, seems to start moving up when the economy is growing very strongly, like right after wartime or during the 1960s. The frameworks for macroeconomic analysis, that we developed in other chapters, will explain why recession often accompanies higher unemployment and lower inflation, while rapid economic growth often brings lower unemployment but higher inflation.

## Inflation around the World

Around the rest of the world, the pattern of inflation has been very mixed; **Figure 9.4** shows inflation rates over the last several decades. Many industrialized countries, not just the United States, had relatively high inflation rates in the 1970s. For example, in 1975, Japan's inflation rate was over 8% and the inflation rate for the United Kingdom was almost 25%. In the 1980s, inflation rates came down in the United States and in Europe and have largely stayed down.

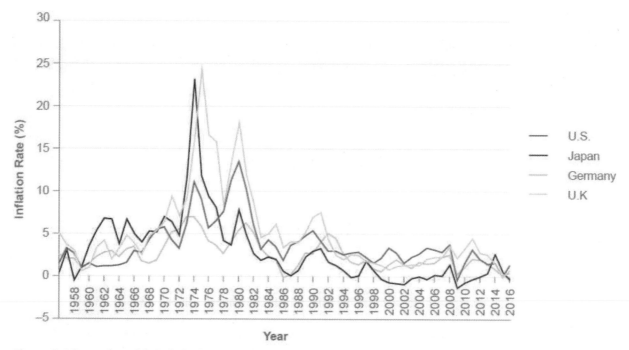

**Figure 9.4 Countries with Relatively Low Inflation Rates, 1960–2016** This chart shows the annual percentage change in consumer prices compared with the previous year's consumer prices in the United States, the United Kingdom, Japan, and Germany.

Countries with controlled economies in the 1970s, like the Soviet Union and China, historically had very low rates of measured inflation—because prices were forbidden to rise by law, except for the cases where the government deemed a price increase to be due to quality improvements. However, these countries also had perpetual shortages of goods, since forbidding prices to rise acts like a price ceiling and creates a situation where quantity demanded often exceeds quantity supplied. As Russia and China made a transition toward more market-oriented economies, they also experienced outbursts of inflation, although we should regard the statistics for these economies as somewhat shakier. Inflation in China averaged about 10% per year for much of the 1980s and early 1990s, although it has dropped off since then. Russia experienced **hyperinflation**—an outburst of high inflation—of 2,500% per year in the early 1990s, although by 2006 Russia's consumer price inflation had dipped below 10% per year, as **Figure 9.5** shows. The closest the United States has ever reached hyperinflation was during the 1860–1865 Civil War, in the Confederate states.

(a) Inflation rates 1980-1995

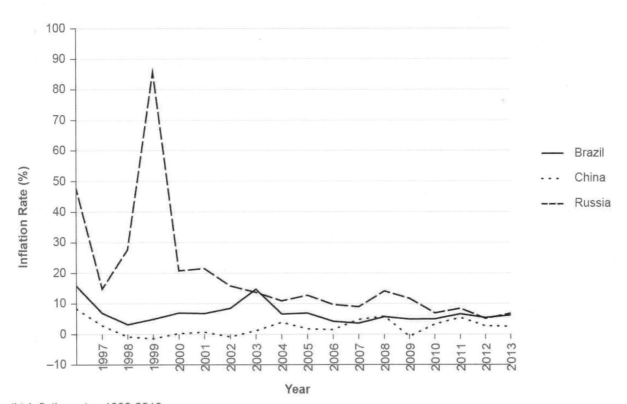

(b) Inflation rates 1996-2013

**Figure 9.5 Countries with Relatively High Inflation Rates, 1980–2016** These charts show the percentage change in consumer prices compared with the previous year's consumer prices in Brazil, China, and Russia. (a) Of these, Brazil and Russia experienced very high inflation at some point between the late-1980s and late-1990s. (b) Though not as high, China also had high inflation rates in the mid-1990s. Even though their inflation rates have come down over the last two decades, several of these countries continue to see significant inflation rates. (Sources: http://www.inflation.eu/inflation-rates; http://research.stlouisfed.org/fred2/series/FPCPITOTLZGBRA; http://research.stlouisfed.org/fred2/series/CHNCPIALLMINMEI; http://research.stlouisfed.org/fred2/series/FPCPITOTLZGRUS)

Many countries in Latin America experienced raging inflation during the 1980s and early 1990s, with inflation rates often well above 100% per year. In 1990, for example, both Brazil and Argentina saw inflation climb above 2000%. Certain countries in Africa experienced extremely high rates of inflation, sometimes bordering on hyperinflation, in the 1990s. Nigeria, the most populous country in Africa, had an inflation rate of 75% in 1995.

In the early 2000s, the problem of inflation appears to have diminished for most countries, at least in comparison to the worst times of recent decades. As we noted in this earlier Bring it Home feature, in recent years, the world's worst example of hyperinflation was in Zimbabwe, where at one point the government was issuing bills with a face value of $100 trillion (in Zimbabwean dollars)—that is, the bills had $100,000,000,000,000 written on the front, but were almost worthless. In many countries, the memory of double-digit, triple-digit, and even quadruple-digit inflation is not very far in the past.

# 9.4 | The Confusion Over Inflation

By the end of this section, you will be able to:
- Explain how inflation can cause redistributions of purchasing power
- Identify ways inflation can blur the perception of supply and demand
- Explain the economic benefits and challenges of inflation

Economists usually oppose high inflation, but they oppose it in a milder way than many non-economists. Robert Shiller, one of 2013's Nobel Prize winners in economics, carried out several surveys during the 1990s about attitudes toward inflation. One of his questions asked, "Do you agree that preventing high inflation is an important national priority, as important as preventing drug abuse or preventing deterioration in the quality of our schools?" Answers were on a scale of 1–5, where 1 meant "Fully agree" and 5 meant "Completely disagree." For the U.S. population as a whole, 52% answered "Fully agree" that preventing high inflation was a highly important national priority and just 4% said "Completely disagree." However, among professional economists, only 18% answered "Fully agree," while the same percentage of 18% answered "Completely disagree."

## The Land of Funny Money

What are the economic problems caused by inflation, and why do economists often regard them with less concern than the general public? Consider a very short story: "The Land of Funny Money."

One morning, everyone in the Land of Funny Money awakened to find that everything denominated in money had increased by 20%. The change was completely unexpected. Every price in every store was 20% higher. Paychecks were 20% higher. Interest rates were 20 % higher. The amount of money, everywhere from wallets to savings accounts, was 20% larger. This overnight inflation of prices made newspaper headlines everywhere in the Land of Funny Money. However, the headlines quickly disappeared, as people realized that in terms of what they could actually buy with their incomes, this inflation had no economic impact. Everyone's pay could still buy exactly the same set of goods as it did before. Everyone's savings were still sufficient to buy exactly the same car, vacation, or retirement that they could have bought before. Equal levels of inflation in all wages and prices ended up not mattering much at all.

When the people in Robert Shiller's surveys explained their concern about inflation, one typical reason was that they feared that as prices rose, they would not be able to afford to buy as much. In other words, people were worried because they did not live in a place like the Land of Funny Money, where all prices and wages rose simultaneously. Instead, people live here on Planet Earth, where prices might rise while wages do not rise at all, or where wages rise more slowly than prices.

Economists note that over most periods, the inflation level in prices is roughly similar to the inflation level in wages, and so they reason that, on average, over time, people's economic status is not greatly changed by inflation. If all prices, wages, and interest rates adjusted automatically and immediately with inflation, as in the Land of Funny Money, then no one's purchasing power, profits, or real loan payments would change. However, if other economic variables do not move exactly in sync with inflation, or if they adjust for inflation only after a time lag, then inflation can cause three types of problems: unintended redistributions of purchasing power, blurred price signals, and difficulties in long-term planning.

## Unintended Redistributions of Purchasing Power

Inflation can cause redistributions of purchasing power that hurt some and help others. People who are hurt by inflation include those who are holding considerable cash, whether it is in a safe deposit box or in a cardboard box under the bed. When inflation happens, the buying power of cash diminishes. However, cash is only an example of a more general problem: anyone who has financial assets invested in a way that the nominal return does not keep up with inflation will tend to suffer from inflation. For example, if a person has money in a bank account that pays 4% interest, but inflation rises to 5%, then the real rate of return for the money invested in that bank account is negative 1%.

The problem of a good-looking nominal interest rate transforming into an ugly-looking real interest rate can be worsened by taxes. The U.S. income tax is charged on the nominal interest received in dollar terms, without an adjustment for inflation. Thus, the government taxes a person who invests $10,000 and receives a 5% nominal rate of interest on the $500 received—no matter whether the inflation rate is 0%, 5%, or 10%. If inflation is 0%, then the real interest rate is 5% and all $500 is a gain in buying power. However, if inflation is 5%, then the real interest rate is zero and the person had no real gain—but owes income tax on the nominal gain anyway. If inflation is 10%, then the real interest rate is *negative* 5% and the person is actually falling behind in buying power, but would still owe taxes on the $500 in nominal gains.

Inflation can cause unintended redistributions for wage earners, too. Wages do typically creep up with inflation over time, eventually. The last row of **Table 9.1** at the start of this chapter showed that the average hourly wage in manufacturing in the U.S. economy increased from $3.23 in 1970 to $20.65 in 2017, which is an increase by a factor of more than six. Over that time period, the Consumer Price Index increased by an almost identical amount. However, increases in wages may lag behind inflation for a year or two, since wage adjustments are often somewhat sticky and occur only once or twice a year. Moreover, the extent to which wages keep up with inflation creates insecurity for workers and may involve painful, prolonged conflicts between employers and employees. If the government adjusts minimum wage for inflation only infrequently, minimum wage workers are losing purchasing power from their nominal wages, as **Figure 9.6** shows.

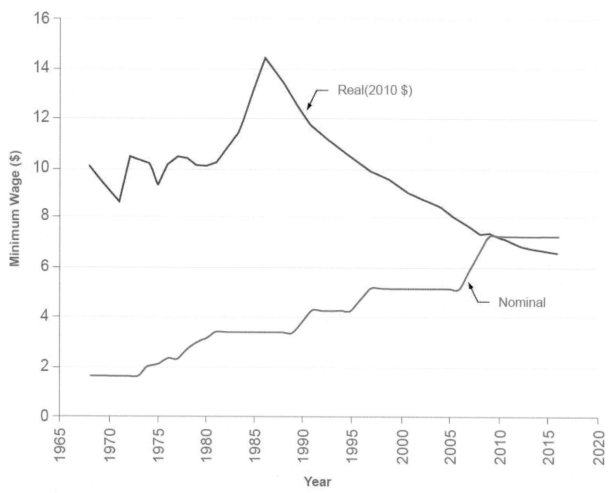

**Figure 9.6 U.S. Minimum Wage and Inflation**   After adjusting for inflation, the federal minimum wage dropped more than 30 percent from 1967 to 2010, even though the nominal figure climbed from $1.40 to $7.25 per hour. Increases in the minimum wage in between 2008 and 2010 kept the decline from being worse—as it would have been if the wage had remained the same as it did from 1997 through 2007. Since 2010, the real minimum wage has continued to decline. (Sources: http://www.dol.gov/whd/minwage/chart.htm; http://data.bls.gov/cgi-bin/surveymost?cu)

One sizable group of people has often received a large share of their income in a form that does not increase over time: retirees who receive a private company pension. Most pensions have traditionally been set as a fixed nominal dollar amount per year at retirement. For this reason, economists call pensions "defined benefits" plans. Even if inflation is low, the combination of inflation and a fixed income can create a substantial problem over time. A person who retires on a fixed income at age 65 will find that losing just 1% to 2% of buying power per year to inflation compounds to a considerable loss of buying power after a decade or two.

Fortunately, pensions and other defined benefits retirement plans are increasingly rare, replaced instead by "defined contribution" plans, such as 401(k)s and 403(b)s. In these plans, the employer contributes a fixed amount to the worker's retirement account on a regular basis (usually every pay check). The employee often contributes as well. The worker invests these funds in a wide range of investment vehicles. These plans are tax deferred, and they are portable so that if the individual takes a job with a different employer, their 401(k) comes with them. To the extent that the investments made generate real rates of return, retirees do not suffer from the inflation costs of traditional pensioners.

However, ordinary people can sometimes benefit from the unintended redistributions of inflation. Consider someone who borrows $10,000 to buy a car at a fixed interest rate of 9%. If inflation is 3% at the time the loan is made, then he or she must repay the loan at a real interest rate of 6%. However, if inflation rises to 9%, then the real interest rate on the loan is zero. In this case, the borrower's benefit from inflation is the lender's loss. A borrower paying a fixed interest rate, who benefits from inflation, is just the flip side of an investor receiving a fixed interest rate, who suffers from inflation. The lesson is that when interest rates are fixed, rises in the rate of inflation tend to penalize suppliers of financial capital, who receive repayment in dollars that are worth less because of inflation, while demanders of financial capital end up better off, because they can repay their loans in dollars that are worth less than originally expected.

The unintended redistributions of buying power that inflation causes may have a broader effect on society. America's widespread acceptance of market forces rests on a perception that people's actions have a reasonable connection to market outcomes. When inflation causes a retiree who built up a pension or invested at a fixed interest rate to suffer, however, while someone who borrowed at a fixed interest rate benefits from inflation, it is hard to believe that this outcome was deserved in any way. Similarly, when homeowners benefit from inflation because the price of their homes rises, while renters suffer because they are paying higher rent, it is hard to see any useful incentive effects. One of the reasons that the general public dislikes inflation is a sense that it makes economic rewards and penalties more arbitrary—and therefore likely to be perceived as unfair – even dangerous, as the next Clear It Up feature shows.

# Clear It Up

## Is there a connection between German hyperinflation and Hitler's rise to power?

Germany suffered an intense hyperinflation of its currency, the Mark, in the years after World War I, when the Weimar Republic in Germany resorted to printing money to pay its bills and the onset of the Great Depression created the social turmoil that Adolf Hitler was able to take advantage of in his rise to power. Shiller described the connection this way in a National Bureau of Economic Research 1996 Working Paper:

> A fact that is probably little known to young people today, even in Germany, is that the final collapse of the Mark in 1923, the time when the Mark's inflation reached astronomical levels (inflation of 35,974.9% in November 1923 alone, for an annual rate that month of $4.69 \times 10^{28}\%$), came in the same month as did Hitler's Beer Hall Putsch, his Nazi Party's armed attempt to overthrow the German government. This failed putsch resulted in Hitler's imprisonment, at which time he wrote his book *Mein Kampf*, setting forth an inspirational plan for Germany's future, suggesting plans for world domination. . .

> . . . Most people in Germany today probably do not clearly remember these events; this lack of attention to it may be because its memory is blurred by the more dramatic events that succeeded it (the Nazi seizure of power and World War II). However, to someone living through these historical events in sequence . . . [the putsch] may have been remembered as vivid evidence of the potential effects of inflation.

## Blurred Price Signals

Prices are the messengers in a market economy, conveying information about conditions of demand and supply. Inflation blurs those price messages. Inflation means that we perceive price signals more vaguely, like a radio program received with considerable static. If the static becomes severe, it is hard to tell what is happening.

In Israel, when inflation accelerated to an annual rate of 500% in 1985, some stores stopped posting prices directly on items, since they would have had to put new labels on the items or shelves every few days to reflect inflation. Instead, a shopper just took items from a shelf and went up to the checkout register to find out the price for that day. Obviously, this situation makes comparing prices and shopping for the best deal rather difficult. When the levels and changes of prices become uncertain, businesses and individuals find it harder to react to economic signals. In a world where inflation is at a high rate, but bouncing up and down to some extent, does a higher price of a good mean that inflation has risen, or that supply of that good has decreased, or that demand for that good has increased? Should a buyer of the good take the higher prices as an economic hint to start substituting other products—or have the prices of the substitutes risen by an equal amount? Should a seller of the good take a higher price as a reason to increase production—or is the higher price only a sign of a general inflation in which the prices of all inputs to production are rising as well? The true story will presumably become clear over time, but at a given moment, who can say?

High and variable inflation means that the incentives in the economy to adjust in response to changes in prices are weaker. Markets will adjust toward their equilibrium prices and quantities more erratically and slowly, and many individual markets will experience a greater chance of surpluses and shortages.

## Problems of Long-Term Planning

Inflation can make long-term planning difficult. In discussing unintended redistributions, we considered the case of someone trying to plan for retirement with a pension that is fixed in nominal terms and a high rate of inflation. Similar problems arise for all people trying to save for retirement, because they must consider what their money will really buy several decades in the future when we cannot know the rate of future inflation.

Inflation, especially at moderate or high levels, will pose substantial planning problems for businesses, too. A firm can make money from inflation—for example, by paying bills and wages as late as possible so that it can pay in inflated dollars, while collecting revenues as soon as possible. A firm can also suffer losses from inflation, as in the case of a retail business that gets stuck holding too much cash, only to see inflation eroding the value of that cash. However, when a business spends its time focusing on how to profit by inflation, or at least how to avoid suffering from it, an inevitable tradeoff strikes: less time is spent on improving products and services or on figuring out how to make existing products and services more cheaply. An economy with high inflation rewards businesses that have found clever ways of profiting from inflation, which are not necessarily the businesses that excel at productivity, innovation, or quality of service.

In the short term, low or moderate levels of inflation may not pose an overwhelming difficulty for business planning, because costs of doing business and sales revenues may rise at similar rates. If, however, inflation varies substantially over the short or medium term, then it may make sense for businesses to stick to shorter-term strategies. The evidence as to whether relatively low rates of inflation reduce productivity is controversial among economists. There is some evidence that if inflation can be held to moderate levels of less than 3% per year, it need not prevent a nation's real economy from growing at a healthy pace. For some countries that have experienced hyperinflation of several thousand percent per year, an annual inflation rate of 20–30% may feel basically the same as zero. However, several economists have pointed to the suggestive fact that when U.S. inflation heated up in the early 1970s—to 10%—U.S. growth in productivity slowed down, and when inflation slowed down in the 1980s, productivity edged up again not long thereafter, as **Figure 9.7** shows.

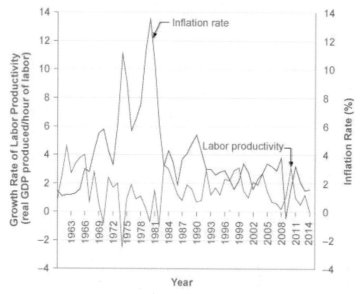

**Figure 9.7 U.S. Inflation Rate and U.S. Labor Productivity, 1961–2014**   Over the last several decades in the United States, there have been times when rising inflation rates have been closely followed by lower productivity rates and lower inflation rates have corresponded to increasing productivity rates. As the graph shows, however, this correlation does not always exist.

## Any Benefits of Inflation?

Although the economic effects of inflation are primarily negative, two countervailing points are worth noting. First, the impact of inflation will differ considerably according to whether it is creeping up slowly at 0% to 2% per year, galloping along at 10% to 20% per year, or racing to the point of hyperinflation at, say, 40% per month. Hyperinflation can rip an economy and a society apart. An annual inflation rate of 2%, 3%, or 4%, however, is a long way from a national crisis. Low inflation is also better than deflation which occurs with severe recessions.

Second, economists sometimes argue that moderate inflation may help the economy by making wages in labor markets more flexible. The discussion in **Unemployment** pointed out that wages tend to be sticky in their downward movements and that unemployment can result. A little inflation could nibble away at real wages, and thus help real wages to decline if necessary. In this way, even if a moderate or high rate of inflation may act as sand in the gears of the economy, perhaps a low rate of inflation serves as oil for the gears of the labor market. This argument is controversial. A full analysis would have to account for all the effects of inflation. It does, however, offer another reason to believe that, all things considered, very low rates of inflation may not be especially harmful.

# 9.5 | Indexing and Its Limitations

By the end of this section, you will be able to:
- Explain the relationship between indexing and inflation
- Identify three ways the government can control inflation through macroeconomic policy

When a price, wage, or interest rate is adjusted automatically with inflation, economists use the term **indexed**. An indexed payment increases according to the index number that measures inflation. Those in private markets and government programs observe a wide range of indexing arrangements. Since the negative effects of inflation depend in large part on having inflation unexpectedly affect one part of the economy but not another—say, increasing the prices that people pay but not the wages that workers receive—indexing will take some of the sting out of inflation.

## Indexing in Private Markets

In the 1970s and 1980s, labor unions commonly negotiated wage contracts that had **cost-of-living adjustments (COLAs)** which guaranteed that their wages would keep up with inflation. These contracts were sometimes written as, for example, COLA plus 3%. Thus, if inflation was 5%, the wage increase would automatically be 8%, but if inflation rose to 9%, the wage increase would automatically be 12%. COLAs are a form of indexing applied to wages.

Loans often have built-in inflation adjustments, too, so that if the inflation rate rises by two percentage points, then the interest rate that a financial institution charges on the loan rises by two percentage points as well. An **adjustable-rate mortgage (ARM)** is a type of loan that one can use to purchase a home in which the interest rate varies with the rate of inflation. Often, a borrower will be able receive a lower interest rate if borrowing with an ARM, compared to a fixed-rate loan. The reason is that with an ARM, the lender is protected against the risk that higher inflation will reduce the real loan payments, and so the risk premium part of the interest rate can be correspondingly lower.

A number of ongoing or long-term business contracts also have provisions that prices will adjust automatically according to inflation. Sellers like such contracts because they are not locked into a low nominal selling price if inflation turns out higher than expected. Buyers like such contracts because they are not locked into a high buying price if inflation turns out to be lower than expected. A contract with automatic adjustments for inflation in effect agrees on a real price for the borrower to pay, rather than a nominal price.

## Indexing in Government Programs

Many government programs are indexed to inflation. The U.S. income tax code is designed so that as a person's income rises above certain levels, the tax rate on the marginal income earned rises as well. That is what the expression "move into a higher tax bracket" means. For example, according to the basic tax tables from the Internal Revenue Service, in 2017 a single person owed 10% of all taxable income from $0 to $9,325; 15% of all income from $9,326 to $37,950; 25% of all taxable income from $37,951 to $91,900; 28% of all taxable income from $91,901 to $191,650; 33% of all taxable income from $191,651 to $416,700; 35% of all taxable income from $416,701 to $418,400; and 39.6% of all income from $418,401 and above.

Because of the many complex provisions in the rest of the tax code, it is difficult to determine exactly the taxes an individual owes the government based on these numbers, but the numbers illustrate the basic theme that tax rates rise as the marginal dollar of income rises. Until the late 1970s, if nominal wages increased along with inflation, people were moved into higher tax brackets and owed a higher proportion of their income in taxes, even though their real income had not risen. In 1981, the government eliminated this "bracket creep". Now, the income levels where higher tax rates kick in are indexed to rise automatically with inflation.

The Social Security program offers two examples of indexing. Since the passage of the Social Security Indexing Act of 1972, the level of Social Security benefits increases each year along with the Consumer Price Index. Also, Social Security is funded by payroll taxes, which the government imposes on the income earned up to a certain amount—$117,000 in 2014. The government adjusts this level of income upward each year according to the rate of inflation, so that an indexed increase in the Social Security tax base accompanies the indexed rise in the benefit level.

As yet another example of a government program affected by indexing, in 1996 the U.S., government began offering indexed bonds. Bonds are means by which the U.S. government (and many private-sector companies as well) borrows money; that is, investors buy the bonds, and then the government repays the money with interest. Traditionally, government bonds have paid a fixed rate of interest. This policy gave a government that had borrowed an incentive to encourage inflation, because it could then repay its past borrowing in inflated dollars at a lower real interest rate. However, indexed bonds promise to pay a certain real rate of interest above whatever inflation rate occurs. In the case of a retiree trying to plan for the long term and worried about the risk of inflation, for example, indexed bonds that guarantee a rate of return higher than inflation—no matter the level of inflation—can be a very comforting investment.

## Might Indexing Reduce Concern over Inflation?

Indexing may seem like an obviously useful step. After all, when individuals, firms, and government programs are indexed against inflation, then people can worry less about arbitrary redistributions and other effects of inflation.

However, some of the fiercest opponents of inflation express grave concern about indexing. They point out that indexing is always partial. Not every employer will provide COLAs for workers. Not all companies can assume that costs and revenues will rise in lockstep with the general rates of inflation. Not all interest rates for borrowers and savers will change to match inflation exactly. However, as partial inflation indexing spreads, the political opposition to inflation may diminish. After all, older people whose Social Security benefits are protected against inflation, or banks that have loaned their money with adjustable-rate loans, no longer have as much reason to care whether inflation heats up. In a world where some people are indexed against inflation and some are not, financially savvy businesses and investors may seek out ways to be protected against inflation, while the financially unsophisticated and small businesses may suffer from it most.

## A Preview of Policy Discussions of Inflation

This chapter has focused on how economists measure inflation, historical experience with inflation, how to adjust nominal variables into real ones, how inflation affects the economy, and how indexing works. We have barely hinted at the causes of inflation, and we have not addressed government policies to deal with inflation. We will examine these issues in depth in other chapters. However, it is useful to offer a preview here.

We can sum up the cause of inflation in one phrase: Too many dollars chasing too few goods. The great surges of inflation early in the twentieth century came after wars, which are a time when government spending is very high, but consumers have little to buy, because production is going to the war effort. Governments also commonly impose price controls during wartime. After the war, the price controls end and pent-up buying power surges forth, driving up inflation. Otherwise, if too few dollars are chasing too many goods, then inflation will decline or even turn into deflation. Therefore, we typically associate slowdowns in economic activity, as in major recessions and the Great Depression, with a reduction in inflation or even outright deflation.

The policy implications are clear. If we are to avoid inflation, the amount of purchasing power in the economy must grow at roughly the same rate as the production of goods. Macroeconomic policies that the government can use to affect the amount of purchasing power—through taxes, spending, and regulation of interest rates and credit—can thus cause inflation to rise or reduce inflation to lower levels.

# Bring it Home

## A $550 Million Loaf of Bread?

As we will learn in **Money and Banking**, the existence of money provides enormous benefits to an economy. In a real sense, money is the lubrication that enhances the workings of markets. Money makes transactions easier. It allows people to find employment producing one product, then use the money earned to purchase the other products they need to live. However, too much money in circulation can lead to inflation. Extreme cases of governments recklessly printing money lead to hyperinflation. Inflation reduces the value of money. Hyperinflation, because money loses value so quickly, ultimately results in people no longer using money. The economy reverts to barter, or it adopts another country's more stable currency, like U.S. dollars. In the meantime, the economy literally falls apart as people leave jobs and fend for themselves because it is not worth the time to work for money that will be worthless in a few days.

Only national governments have the power to cause hyperinflation. Hyperinflation typically happens when government faces extraordinary demands for spending, which it cannot finance by taxes or borrowing. The only option is to print money—more and more of it. With more money in circulation chasing the same amount (or even fewer) goods and services, the only result is increasingly higher prices until the economy and/or the government collapses. This is why economists are generally wary of letting inflation spiral out of control.

# KEY TERMS

**adjustable-rate mortgage (ARM)** a loan a borrower uses to purchase a home in which the interest rate varies with market interest rates

**base year** arbitrary year whose value as an index number economists define as 100; inflation from the base year to other years can easily be seen by comparing the index number in the other year to the index number in the base year—for example, 100; so, if the index number for a year is 105, then there has been exactly 5% inflation between that year and the base year

**basket of goods and services** a hypothetical group of different items, with specified quantities of each one meant to represent a "typical" set of consumer purchases, used as a basis for calculating how the price level changes over time

**Consumer Price Index (CPI)** a measure of inflation that U.S. government statisticians calculate based on the price level from a fixed basket of goods and services that represents the average consumer's purchases

**core inflation index** a measure of inflation typically calculated by taking the CPI and excluding volatile economic variables such as food and energy prices to better measure the underlying and persistent trend in long-term prices

**cost-of-living adjustments (COLAs)** a contractual provision that wage increases will keep up with inflation

**deflation** negative inflation; most prices in the economy are falling

**Employment Cost Index** a measure of inflation based on wages paid in the labor market

**GDP deflator** a measure of inflation based on the prices of all the GDP components

**hyperinflation** an outburst of high inflation that often occurs (although not exclusively) when economies shift from a controlled economy to a market-oriented economy

**index number** a unit-free number derived from the price level over a number of years, which makes computing inflation rates easier, since the index number has values around 100

**indexed** a price, wage, or interest rate is adjusted automatically for inflation

**inflation** a general and ongoing rise in price levels in an economy

**International Price Index** a measure of inflation based on the prices of merchandise that is exported or imported

**Producer Price Index (PPI)** a measure of inflation based on prices paid for supplies and inputs by producers of goods and services

**quality/new goods bias** inflation calculated using a fixed basket of goods over time tends to overstate the true rise in cost of living, because it does not account for improvements in the quality of existing goods or the invention of new goods

**substitution bias** an inflation rate calculated using a fixed basket of goods over time tends to overstate the true rise in the cost of living, because it does not take into account that the person can substitute away from goods whose prices rise considerably

# KEY CONCEPTS AND SUMMARY

### 9.1 Tracking Inflation

Economists measure the price level by using a basket of goods and services and calculating how the total cost of buying that basket of goods will increase over time. Economists often express the price level in terms of index numbers, which transform the cost of buying the basket of goods and services into a series of numbers in the same proportion to each other, but with an arbitrary base year of 100. We measure the inflation rate as the percentage change between price levels or index numbers over time.

## 9.2 How to Measure Changes in the Cost of Living

Measuring price levels with a fixed basket of goods will always have two problems: the substitution bias, by which a fixed basket of goods does not allow for buying more of what becomes relatively less expensive and less of what becomes relatively more expensive; and the quality/new goods bias, by which a fixed basket cannot account for improvements in quality and the advent of new goods. These problems can be reduced in degree—for example, by allowing the basket of goods to evolve over time—but we cannot totally eliminate them. The most commonly cited measure of inflation is the Consumer Price Index (CPI), which is based on a basket of goods representing what the typical consumer buys. The Core Inflation Index further breaks down the CPI by excluding volatile economic commodities. Several price indices are not based on baskets of consumer goods. The GDP deflator is based on all GDP components. The Producer Price Index is based on prices of supplies and inputs bought by producers of goods and services. An Employment Cost Index measures wage inflation in the labor market. An International Price Index is based on the prices of merchandise that is exported or imported.

## 9.3 How the U.S. and Other Countries Experience Inflation

In the U.S. economy, the annual inflation rate in the last two decades has typically been around 2% to 4%. The periods of highest inflation in the United States in the twentieth century occurred during the years after World Wars I and II, and in the 1970s. The period of lowest inflation—actually, with deflation—was the 1930s Great Depression.

## 9.4 The Confusion Over Inflation

Unexpected inflation will tend to hurt those whose money received, in terms of wages and interest payments, does not rise with inflation. In contrast, inflation can help those who owe money that they can pay in less valuable, inflated dollars. Low rates of inflation have relatively little economic impact over the short term. Over the medium and the long term, even low rates of inflation can complicate future planning. High rates of inflation can muddle price signals in the short term and prevent market forces from operating efficiently, and can vastly complicate long-term savings and investment decisions.

## 9.5 Indexing and Its Limitations

A payment is indexed if it is automatically adjusted for inflation. Examples of indexing in the private sector include wage contracts with cost-of-living adjustments (COLAs) and loan agreements like adjustable-rate mortgages (ARMs). Examples of indexing in the public sector include tax brackets and Social Security payments.

## SELF-CHECK QUESTIONS

**1.** Table 9.4 shows the fruit prices that the typical college student purchased from 2001 to 2004. What is the amount spent each year on the "basket" of fruit with the quantities shown in column 2?

| Items | Qty | (2001) Price | (2001) Amount Spent | (2002) Price | (2002) Amount Spent | (2003) Price | (2003) Amount Spent | (2004) Price | (2004) Amount Spent |
|---|---|---|---|---|---|---|---|---|---|
| Apples | 10 | $0.50 | | $0.75 | | $0.85 | | $0.88 | |
| Bananas | 12 | $0.20 | | $0.25 | | $0.25 | | $0.29 | |
| Grapes | 2 | $0.65 | | $0.70 | | $0.90 | | $0.95 | |
| Raspberries | 1 | $2.00 | | $1.90 | | $2.05 | | $2.13 | $2.13 |
| Total | | | | | | | | | |

Table 9.4

**2.** Construct the price index for a "fruit basket" in each year using 2003 as the base year.

**3.** Compute the inflation rate for fruit prices from 2001 to 2004.

**4.** Edna is living in a retirement home where most of her needs are taken care of, but she has some discretionary spending. Based on the basket of goods in Table 9.5, by what percentage does Edna's cost of living increase between time 1 and time 2?

| Items | Quantity | (Time 1) Price | (Time 2) Price |
|---|---|---|---|
| Gifts for grandchildren | 12 | $50 | $60 |
| Pizza delivery | 24 | $15 | $16 |
| Blouses | 6 | $60 | $50 |
| Vacation trips | 2 | $400 | $420 |

Table 9.5

**5. How to Measure Changes in the Cost of Living** introduced a number of different price indices. Which price index would be best to use to adjust your paycheck for inflation?

**6.** The Consumer Price Index is subject to the substitution bias and the quality/new goods bias. Are the Producer Price Index and the GDP Deflator also subject to these biases? Why or why not?

**7.** Go to this **website (http://www.measuringworth.com/ppowerus/)** for the Purchasing Power Calculator at MeasuringWorth.com. How much money would it take today to purchase what one dollar would have bought in the year of your birth?

**8.** If inflation rises unexpectedly by 5%, would a state government that had recently borrowed money to pay for a new highway benefit or lose?

**9.** How should an increase in inflation affect the interest rate on an adjustable-rate mortgage?

**10.** A fixed-rate mortgage has the same interest rate over the life of the loan, whether the mortgage is for 15 or 30 years. By contrast, an adjustable-rate mortgage changes with market interest rates over the life of the mortgage. If inflation falls unexpectedly by 3%, what would likely happen to a homeowner with an adjustable-rate mortgage?

## REVIEW QUESTIONS

**11.** How do economists use a basket of goods and services to measure the price level?

**12.** Why do economists use index numbers to measure the price level rather than dollar value of goods?

**13.** What is the difference between the price level and the rate of inflation?

**14.** Why does "substitution bias" arise if we calculate the inflation rate based on a fixed basket of goods?

**15.** Why does the "quality/new goods bias" arise if we calculate the inflation rate based on a fixed basket of goods?

**16.** What has been a typical range of inflation in the U.S. economy in the last decade or so?

**17.** Over the last century, during what periods was the U.S. inflation rate highest and lowest?

**18.** What is deflation?

**19.** Identify several parties likely to be helped and hurt by inflation.

**20.** What is indexing?

**21.** Name several forms of indexing in the private and public sector.

## CRITICAL THINKING QUESTIONS

**22.** Inflation rates, like most statistics, are imperfect measures. Can you identify some ways that the inflation rate for fruit does not perfectly capture the rising price of fruit?

**23.** Given the federal budget deficit in recent years, some economists have argued that by adjusting Social Security payments for inflation using the CPI, Social Security is overpaying recipients. What is their argument, and do you agree or disagree with it?

**24.** Why is the GDP deflator not an accurate measure of inflation as it impacts a household?

**25.** Imagine that the government statisticians who calculate the inflation rate have been updating the basic basket of goods once every 10 years, but now they decide to update it every five years. How will this change affect the amount of substitution bias and quality/new goods bias?

**26.** Describe a situation, either a government policy situation, an economic problem, or a private sector situation, where using the CPI to convert from nominal to real would be more appropriate than using the GDP deflator.

**27.** Describe a situation, either a government policy situation, an economic problem, or a private sector situation, where using the GDP deflator to convert from nominal to real would be more appropriate than using the CPI.

**28.** Why do you think the U.S. experience with inflation over the last 50 years has been so much milder than in many other countries?

**29.** If, over time, wages and salaries on average rise at least as fast as inflation, why do people worry about how inflation affects incomes?

**30.** Who in an economy is the big winner from inflation?

**31.** If a government gains from unexpected inflation when it borrows, why would it choose to offer indexed bonds?

**32.** Do you think perfect indexing is possible? Why or why not?

# PROBLEMS

**33.** The index number representing the price level changes from 110 to 115 in one year, and then from 115 to 120 the next year. Since the index number increases by five each year, is five the inflation rate each year? Is the inflation rate the same each year? Explain your answer.

**34.** The total price of purchasing a basket of goods in the United Kingdom over four years is: year 1=£940, year 2=£970, year 3=£1000, and year 4=£1070. Calculate two price indices, one using year 1 as the base year (set equal to 100) and the other using year 4 as the base year (set equal to 100). Then, calculate the inflation rate based on the first price index. If you had used the other price index, would you get a different inflation rate? If you are unsure, do the calculation and find out.

**35.** Within 1 or 2 percentage points, what has the U.S. inflation rate been during the last 20 years? Draw a graph to show the data.

**36.** If inflation rises unexpectedly by 5%, indicate for each of the following whether the economic actor is helped, hurt, or unaffected:
a. A union member with a COLA wage contract
b. Someone with a large stash of cash in a safe deposit box
c. A bank lending money at a fixed rate of interest
d. A person who is not due to receive a pay raise for another 11 months

**37.** Rosalie the Retiree knows that when she retires in 16 years, her company will give her a one-time payment of $20,000. However, if the inflation rate is 6% per year, how much buying power will that $20,000 have when measured in today's dollars? *Hint*: Start by calculating the rise in the price level over the 16 years.

# 10 | The International Trade and Capital Flows

**Figure 10.1 A World of Money**   We are all part of the global financial system, which includes many different currencies. (Credit: modification of work by epSos.de/Flickr Creative Commons)

## Bring it Home

### More than Meets the Eye in the Congo

How much do you interact with the global financial system? Do you think not much? Think again. Suppose you take out a student loan, or you deposit money into your bank account. You just affected domestic savings and borrowing. Now say you are at the mall and buy two T-shirts "made in China," and later contribute to a charity that helps refugees. What is the impact? You affected how much money flows into and out of the United States. If you open an IRA savings account and put money in an international mutual fund, you are involved in the flow of money overseas. While your involvement may not seem as influential as that of someone like the president, who can increase or decrease foreign aid and, thereby, have a huge impact on money flows in and out of the country, you do interact with the global financial system on a daily basis.

The balance of payments—a term you will meet soon—seems like a huge topic, but once you learn the specific components of trade and money, it all makes sense. Along the way, you may have to give up some common misunderstandings about trade and answer some questions: If a country is running a trade deficit, is that bad? Is a trade surplus good? For example, look at the Democratic Republic of the Congo (often referred to as "Congo"), a large country in Central Africa. In 2013, it ran a trade surplus of $1 billion, so it must be doing well, right? In contrast, the trade deficit in the United States was $508 billion in 2013. Do these figures suggest that the United States economy is performing worse than the Congolese economy? Not necessarily. The U.S. trade deficit tends to worsen as the economy strengthens. In contrast, high poverty rates in the Congo persist, and these rates are not going down even with the positive trade balance. Clearly, it is more complicated than simply asserting that running a trade deficit is bad for the economy. You will learn more about these issues and others in this chapter.

# Introduction to International Trade and Capital Flows

In this chapter, you will learn about:

- Measuring Trade Balances
- Trade Balances in Historical and International Context
- Trade Balances and Flows of Financial Capital
- The National Saving and Investment Identity
- The Pros and Cons of Trade Deficits and Surpluses
- The Difference between Level of Trade and the Trade Balance

The **balance of trade** (or trade balance) is any gap between a nation's dollar value of its exports, or what its producers sell abroad, and a nation's dollar value of imports, or the foreign-made products and services that households and businesses purchase. Recall from **The Macroeconomic Perspective** that if exports exceed imports, the economy has a trade surplus. If imports exceed exports, the economy has a trade deficit. If exports and imports are equal, then trade is balanced, but what happens when trade is out of balance and large trade surpluses or deficits exist?

Germany, for example, has had substantial trade surpluses in recent decades, in which exports have greatly exceeded imports. According to the Central Intelligence Agency's The World Factbook, in 2016, Germany ran a trade surplus of $295 billion. In contrast, the U.S. economy in recent decades has experienced large trade deficits, in which imports have considerably exceeded exports. In 2016, for example, U.S. imports exceeded exports by $502 billion.

A series of financial crises triggered by unbalanced trade can lead economies into deep recessions. These crises begin with large trade deficits. At some point, foreign investors become pessimistic about the economy and move their money to other countries. The economy then drops into deep recession, with real GDP often falling up to 10% or more in a single year. This happened to Mexico in 1995 when their GDP fell 8.1%. A number of countries in East Asia—Thailand, South Korea, Malaysia, and Indonesia—succumbed to the same economic illness in 1997–1998 (called the Asian Financial Crisis). In the late 1990s and into the early 2000s, Russia and Argentina had the identical experience. What are the connections between imbalances of trade in goods and services and the flows of international financial capital that set off these economic avalanches?

We will start by examining the balance of trade in more detail, by looking at some patterns of trade balances in the United States and around the world. Then we will examine the intimate connection between international flows of goods and services and international flows of financial capital, which to economists are really just two sides of the same coin. People often assume that trade surpluses like those in Germany must be a positive sign for an economy, while trade deficits like those in the United States must be harmful. As it turns out, both trade surpluses and deficits can be either good or bad. We will see why in this chapter.

# 10.1 | Measuring Trade Balances

By the end of this section, you will be able to:

- Explain merchandise trade balance, current account balance, and unilateral transfers
- Identify components of the U.S. current account balance
- Calculate the merchandise trade balance and current account balance using import and export data for a country

A few decades ago, it was common to track the solid or physical items that planes, trains, and trucks transported between countries as a way of measuring the balance of trade. Economists call this measurement is called the

**merchandise trade balance**. In most high-income economies, including the United States, goods comprise less than half of a country's total production, while services comprise more than half. The last two decades have seen a surge in international trade in services, powered by technological advances in telecommunications and computers that have made it possible to export or import customer services, finance, law, advertising, management consulting, software, construction engineering, and product design. Most global trade still takes the form of goods rather than services, and the government announces and the media prominently report the merchandise trade balance. Old habits are hard to break. Economists, however, typically rely on broader measures such as the balance of trade or the **current account balance** which includes other international flows of income and foreign aid.

## Components of the U.S. Current Account Balance

**Table 10.1** breaks down the four main components of the U.S. current account balance for the last quarter of 2015 (seasonally adjusted). The first line shows the merchandise trade balance; that is, exports and imports of goods. Because imports exceed exports, the trade balance in the final column is negative, showing a merchandise trade deficit. We can explain how the government collects this trade information in the following Clear It Up feature.

| | Value of Exports (money flowing into the United States) | Value of Imports (money flowing out of the United States) | Balance |
|---|---|---|---|
| Goods | $410.0 | $595.5 | –$185.3 |
| Services | $180.4 | $122.3 | $58.1 |
| Income receipts and payments | $203.0 | $152.4 | $50.6 |
| Unilateral transfers | $27.3 | $64.4 | –$37.1 |
| **Current account balance** | $820.7 | $934.4 | –$113.7 |

Table 10.1 Components of the U.S. Current Account Balance for 2015 (in billions)

## How does the U.S. government collect trade statistics?

Do not confuse the balance of trade (which tracks imports and exports), with the current account balance, which includes not just exports and imports, but also income from investment and transfers.

The Bureau of Economic Analysis (BEA) within the U.S. Department of Commerce compiles statistics on the balance of trade using a variety of different sources. Merchandise importers and exporters must file monthly documents with the Census Bureau, which provides the basic data for tracking trade. To measure international trade in services—which can happen over a telephone line or computer network without shipping any physical goods—the BEA carries out a set of surveys. Another set of BEA surveys tracks investment flows, and there are even specific surveys to collect travel information from U.S. residents visiting Canada and Mexico. For measuring unilateral transfers, the BEA has access to official U.S. government spending on aid, and then also carries out a survey of charitable organizations that make foreign donations.

The BEA then cross-checks this information on international flows of goods and capital against other available data. For example, the Census Bureau also collects data from the shipping industry, which it can use to check the data on trade in goods. All companies involved in international flows of capital—including banks and companies making financial investments like stocks—must file reports, which the U.S. Department of the Treasury ultimately checks. The BEA also can cross check information on foreign trade by looking at data collected by other countries on their foreign trade with the United States, and also at the data collected by various international organizations. Take these data sources, stir carefully, and you have the U.S. balance of trade statistics. Much of the statistics that we cite in this chapter come from these sources.

The second row of **Table 10.1** provides data on trade in services. Here, the U.S. economy is running a surplus. Although the level of trade in services is still relatively small compared to trade in goods, the importance of services has expanded substantially over the last few decades. For example, U.S. exports of services were equal to about one-half of U.S. exports of goods in 2015, compared to one-fifth in 1980.

The third component of the current account balance, labeled "income payments," refers to money that U.S. financial investors received on their foreign investments (money flowing into the United States) and payments to foreign investors who had invested their funds here (money flowing out of the United States). The reason for including this money on foreign investment in the overall measure of trade, along with goods and services, is that, from an economic perspective, income is just as much an economic transaction as car, wheat, or oil shipments: it is just trade that is happening in the financial capital market.

The final category of the current account balance is **unilateral transfers**, which are payments that government, private charities, or individuals make in which they send money abroad without receiving any direct good or service. Economic or military assistance from the U.S. government to other countries fits into this category, as does spending abroad by charities to address poverty or social inequalities. When an individual in the United States sends money overseas, as is the case with some immigrants, it is also counted in this category. The current account balance treats these unilateral payments like imports, because they also involve a stream of payments leaving the country. For the U.S. economy, unilateral transfers are almost always negative. This pattern, however, does not always hold. In 1991, for example, when the United States led an international coalition against Saddam Hussein's Iraq in the Gulf War, many other nations agreed that they would make payments to the United States to offset the U.S. war expenses. These payments were large enough that, in 1991, the overall U.S. balance on unilateral transfers was a positive $10 billion.

The following Work It Out feature steps you through the process of using the values for goods, services, and income payments to calculate the merchandise balance and the current account balance.

# Work It Out ─O─O─O

## Calculating the Merchandise Balance and the Current Account Balance

| | Exports (in $ billions) | Imports (in $ billions) | Balance |
|---|---|---|---|
| Goods | | | |
| Services | | | |
| Income payments | | | |
| Unilateral transfers | | | |
| Current account balance | | | |

Table 10.2 Calculating Merchandise Balance and Current Account Balance

Use the information given below to fill in **Table 10.2**, and then calculate:

- The merchandise balance
- The current account balance

Known information:

- Unilateral transfers: $130
- Exports in goods: $1,046
- Exports in services: $509
- Imports in goods: $1,562
- Imports in services: $371
- Income received by U.S. investors on foreign stocks and bonds: $561
- Income received by foreign investors on U.S. assets: $472

Step 1. Focus on goods and services first. Enter the dollar amount of exports of both goods and services under the Export column.

Step 2. Enter imports of goods and services under the Import column.

Step 3. Under the Export column and in the row for Income payments, enter the financial flows of money coming back to the United States. U.S. investors are earning this income from abroad.

Step 4. Under the Import column and in the row for Income payments, enter the financial flows of money going out of the United States to foreign investors. Foreign investors are earning this money on U.S. assets, like stocks.

Step 5. Unilateral transfers are money flowing out of the United States in the form of, for example, military aid, foreign aid, and global charities. Because the money leaves the country, enter it under Imports and in the final column as well, as a negative.

Step 6. Calculate the trade balance by subtracting imports from exports in both goods and services. Enter this in the final Balance column. This can be positive or negative.

Step 7. Subtract the income payments flowing out of the country (under Imports) from the money coming back to the United States (under Exports) and enter this amount under the Balance column.

Step 8. Enter unilateral transfers as a negative amount under the Balance column.

Step 9. The merchandise trade balance is the difference between exports of goods and imports of goods—the first number under Balance.

Step 10. Now sum up your columns for Exports, Imports, and Balance. The final balance number is the current account balance.

The merchandise balance of trade is the difference between exports and imports. In this case, it is equal to $1,046 − $1,562, a trade deficit of −$516 billion. The current account balance is −$419 billion. See the completed Table 10.3.

| | Value of Exports (money flowing into the United States) | Value of Imports (money flowing out of the United States) | Balance |
|---|---|---|---|
| Goods | $1,510.3 | $2,272.9 | −$762.6 |
| Services | $750.9 | $488.7 | $262.2 |
| Income receipts and payments | $782.9 | $600.5 | $182.4 |
| Unilateral transfers | $128.6 | $273.6 | −$145.0 |

|  | Value of Exports (money flowing into the United States) | Value of Imports (money flowing out of the United States) | Balance |
|---|---|---|---|
| **Current account balance** | $3,172.7 | $3,635.7 | −$463.0 |

**Table 10.3 Completed Merchandise Balance and Current Account Balance**

# 10.2 | Trade Balances in Historical and International Context

By the end of this section, you will be able to:
- Analyze graphs of the current account balance and the merchandise trade balance
- Identify patterns in U.S. trade surpluses and deficits
- Compare the U.S. trade surpluses and deficits to other countries' trade surpluses and deficits

We present the history of the U.S. current account balance in recent decades in several different ways. **Figure 10.2** (a) shows the current account balance and the merchandise trade balance in dollar terms. **Figure 10.2** (b) shows the current account balance and merchandise account balance yet again, this time as a share of the GDP for that year. By dividing the trade deficit in each year by GDP in that year, **Figure 10.2** (b) factors out both inflation and growth in the real economy.

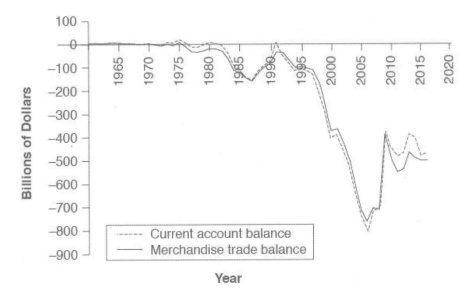

(a) The current account and merchandise trade balance in nominal dollars

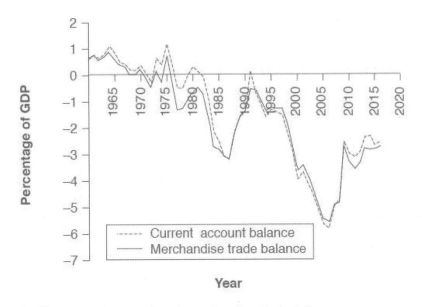

(b) The current account and merchandise trade balance as a percentage of GDP

**Figure 10.2 Current Account Balance and Merchandise Trade Balance, 1960–2015** (a) The current account balance and the merchandise trade balance in billions of dollars from 1960 to 2015. If the lines are above zero dollars, the United States was running a positive trade balance and current account balance. If the lines fall below zero dollars, the United States is running a trade deficit and a deficit in its current account balance. (b) This shows the same items—trade balance and current account balance—in relationship to the size of the U.S. economy, or GDP, from 1960 to 2015.

By either measure, the U.S. balance of trade pattern is clear. From the 1960s into the 1970s, the U.S. economy had mostly small trade surpluses—that is, the graphs in **Figure 10.2** show positive numbers. However, starting in the 1980s, the trade deficit increased rapidly, and after a tiny surplus in 1991, the current account trade deficit became even larger in the late 1990s and into the mid-2000s. However, the trade deficit declined in 2009 after the recession had taken hold, then rebounded partially in 2010 and has remained stable up through 2016.

**Table 10.4** shows the U.S. trade picture in 2013 compared with some other economies from around the world. While the U.S. economy has consistently run trade deficits in recent years, Japan and many European nations, among them France and Germany, have consistently run trade surpluses. Some of the other countries listed include Brazil, the largest economy in Latin America; Nigeria, along with South Africa competing to be the largest economy in Africa; and China, India, and Korea. The first column offers one measure of an economy's globalization: **exports of goods and services as a percentage of GDP**. The second column shows the trade balance. Usually, most countries have trade surpluses or deficits that are less than 5% of GDP. As you can see, the U.S. current account balance is –2.6% of GDP, while Germany's is 8.4% of GDP.

|  | Exports of Goods and Services | Current Account Balance |
|---|---|---|
| United States | 17.6% | –2.6% |
| Japan | 16.2% | 3.1% |
| Germany | 46.8% | 8.4% |
| United Kingdom | 27.2% | –5.4% |
| Canada | 31.5% | –3.2% |
| Sweden | 45.6% | 5.2% |
| Korea | 45.9% | 7.7% |
| Mexico | 35.4% | –2.9% |
| Brazil | 13.0% | –3.3% |
| China | 22.1% | 3.0% |
| India | 19.9% | –1.1% |
| Nigeria | 10.7% | -3.3% |
| World | - | 0.0% |

Table 10.4 Level and Balance of Trade in 2015 (figures as a percentage of GDP, Source: http://data.worldbank.org/indicator/BN.CAB.XOKA.GD.ZS)

# 10.3 | Trade Balances and Flows of Financial Capital

By the end of this section, you will be able to:

- Explain the connection between trade balances and financial capital flows
- Calculate comparative advantage
- Explain balanced trade in terms of investment and capital flows

As economists see it, trade surpluses can be either good or bad, depending on circumstances, and trade deficits can be good or bad, too. The challenge is to understand how the international flows of goods and services are connected with international flows of **financial capital**. In this module we will illustrate the intimate connection between trade balances and flows of financial capital in two ways: a parable of trade between Robinson Crusoe and Friday, and a circular flow diagram representing flows of trade and payments.

## A Two-Person Economy: Robinson Crusoe and Friday

To understand how economists view trade deficits and surpluses, consider a parable based on the story of Robinson Crusoe. Crusoe, as you may remember from the classic novel by Daniel Defoe first published in 1719, was shipwrecked on a desert island. After living alone for some time, he is joined by a second person, whom he names Friday. Think about the balance of trade in a two-person economy like that of Robinson and Friday.

Robinson and Friday trade goods and services. Perhaps Robinson catches fish and trades them to Friday for coconuts, or Friday weaves a hat out of tree fronds and trades it to Robinson for help in carrying water. For a period of time, each individual trade is self-contained and complete. Because each trade is voluntary, both Robinson and Friday must feel that they are receiving fair value for what they are giving. As a result, each person's exports are always equal to his imports, and trade is always in balance between the two. Neither person experiences either a trade deficit or a trade surplus.

However, one day Robinson approaches Friday with a proposition. Robinson wants to dig ditches for an irrigation system for his garden, but he knows that if he starts this project, he will not have much time left to fish and gather coconuts to feed himself each day. He proposes that Friday supply him with a certain number of fish and coconuts for several months, and then after that time, he promises to repay Friday out of the extra produce that he will be able to grow in his irrigated garden. If Friday accepts this offer, then a trade imbalance comes into being. For several months, Friday will have a trade surplus: that is, he is exporting to Robinson more than he is importing. More precisely, he is giving Robinson fish and coconuts, and at least for the moment, he is receiving nothing in return. Conversely, Robinson will have a trade deficit, because he is importing more from Friday than he is exporting.

This parable raises several useful issues in thinking about what a trade deficit and a trade surplus really mean in economic terms. The first issue that this story of Robinson and Friday raises is this: Is it better to have a trade surplus or a trade deficit? The answer, as in any voluntary market interaction, is that if both parties agree to the transaction, then they may both be better off. Over time, if Robinson's irrigated garden is a success, it is certainly possible that both Robinson and Friday can benefit from this agreement.

The parable raises a second issue: What can go wrong? Robinson's proposal to Friday introduces an element of uncertainty. Friday is, in effect, making a loan of fish and coconuts to Robinson, and Friday's happiness with this arrangement will depend on whether Robinson repays that loan as planned, in full and on time. Perhaps Robinson spends several months loafing and never builds the irrigation system, or perhaps Robinson has been too optimistic about how much he will be able to grow with the new irrigation system, which turns out not to be very productive. Perhaps, after building the irrigation system, Robinson decides that he does not want to repay Friday as much as he previously agreed. Any of these developments will prompt a new round of negotiations between Friday and Robinson. Why the repayment failed is likely to shape Friday's attitude toward these renegotiations. If Robinson worked very hard and the irrigation system just did not increase production as intended, Friday may have some sympathy. If Robinson loafed or if he just refuses to pay, Friday may become irritated.

A third issue that the parable raises is that an intimate relationship exists between a trade deficit and international borrowing, and between a trade surplus and international lending. The size of Friday's trade surplus is exactly how much he is lending to Robinson. The size of Robinson's trade deficit is exactly how much he is borrowing from Friday. To economists, a trade surplus literally means the same thing as an outflow of financial capital, and a trade deficit literally means the same thing as an inflow of financial capital. This last insight is worth exploring in greater detail, which we will do in the following section.

The story of Robinson and Friday also provides a good opportunity to consider the law of comparative advantage, which you learn more about in the **International Trade** chapter. The following Work It Out feature steps you through calculating comparative advantage for the wheat and cloth traded between the United States and Great Britain in the 1800s.

# Work It Out —O—O—O

## Calculating Comparative Advantage

In the 1800s, the United States and Britain traded wheat and cloth. **Table 10.5** shows the varying hours of labor per unit of output.

| | Wheat (in bushels) | Cloth (in yards) | Relative labor cost of wheat (Pw/Pc) | Relative labor cost of cloth (Pc/Pw) |
|---|---|---|---|---|
| United States | 8 | 9 | 8/9 | 9/8 |
| Britain | 4 | 3 | 4/3 | 3/4 |

**Table 10.5**

Step 1. Observe from **Table 10.5** that, in the United States, it takes eight hours to supply a bushel of wheat and nine hours to supply a yard of cloth. In contrast, it takes four hours to supply a bushel of wheat and three hours to supply a yard of cloth in Britain.

Step 2. Recognize the difference between absolute advantage and comparative advantage. Britain has an absolute advantage (lowest cost) in each good, since it takes a lower amount of labor to make each good in Britain. Britain also has a comparative advantage in the production of cloth (lower opportunity cost in cloth (3/4 versus 9/8)). The United States has a comparative advantage in wheat production (lower opportunity cost of 8/9 versus 4/3).

Step 3. Determine the relative price of one good in terms of the other good. The price of wheat, in this example, is the amount of cloth you have to give up. To find this price, convert the hours per unit of wheat and cloth into units per hour. To do so, observe that in the United States it takes eight hours to make a bushel of wheat, so workers can process 1/8 of a bushel of wheat in an hour. It takes nine hours to make a yard of cloth in the United States, so workers can produce 1/9 of a yard of cloth in an hour. If you divide the amount of cloth (1/9 of a yard) by the amount of wheat you give up (1/8 of a bushel) in an hour, you find the price (8/9) of one good (wheat) in terms of the other (cloth).

## The Balance of Trade as the Balance of Payments

The connection between trade balances and international flows of financial capital is so close that economists sometimes describe the balance of trade as the balance of payments. Each category of the current account balance involves a corresponding flow of payments between a given country and the rest of the world economy.

**Figure 10.3** shows the flow of goods and services and payments between one country—the United States in this example—and the rest of the world. The top line shows U.S. exports of goods and services, while the second line shows financial payments from purchasers in other countries back to the U.S. economy. The third line then shows U.S. imports of goods, services, and investment, and the fourth line shows payments from the home economy to the rest of the world. Flow of goods and services (lines one and three) show up in the current account, while we find flow of funds (lines two and four) in the financial account.

The bottom four lines in **Figure 10.3** show the flows of investment income. In the first of the bottom lines, we see investments made abroad with funds flowing from the home country to the rest of the world. Investment income stemming from an investment abroad then runs in the other direction from the rest of the world to the home country. Similarly, we see on the bottom third line, an investment from the rest of the world into the home country and investment income (bottom fourth line) flowing from the home country to the rest of the world. We find the investment income (bottom lines two and four) in the current account, while investment to the rest of the world or into the home country (lines one and three) is in the financial account. This figure does not show unilateral transfers, the fourth item in the current account.

**Figure 10.3 Flow of Investment Goods and Capital**   Each element of the current account balance involves a flow of financial payments between countries. The top line shows exports of goods and services leaving the home country; the second line shows the money that the home country receives for those exports. The third line shows imports that the home country receives; the fourth line shows the payments that the home country sent abroad in exchange for these imports.

A current account deficit means that, the country is a net borrower from abroad. Conversely, a positive current account balance means a country is a net lender to the rest of the world. Just like the parable of Robinson and Friday, the lesson is that a trade surplus means an overall outflow of financial investment capital, as domestic investors put their funds abroad, while a deficit in the current account balance is exactly equal to the overall or net inflow of foreign investment capital from abroad.

It is important to recognize that an inflow and outflow of foreign capital does not necessarily refer to a debt that governments owe to other governments, although government debt may be part of the picture. Instead, these international flows of financial capital refer to all of the ways in which private investors in one country may invest in another country—by buying real estate, companies, and financial investments like stocks and bonds.

# 10.4 | The National Saving and Investment Identity

By the end of this section, you will be able to:
- Explain the determinants of trade and current account balance
- Identify and calculate supply and demand for financial capital
- Explain how a nation's own level of domestic saving and investment determines a nation's balance of trade
- Predict the rising and falling of trade deficits based on a nation's saving and investment identity

The close connection between trade balances and international flows of savings and investments leads to a macroeconomic analysis. This approach views trade balances—and their associated flows of financial capital—in the context of the overall levels of savings and financial investment in the economy.

## Understanding the Determinants of the Trade and Current Account Balance

The **national saving and investment identity** provides a useful way to understand the determinants of the trade and current account balance. In a nation's financial capital market, the quantity of financial capital supplied at any given time must equal the quantity of financial capital demanded for purposes of making investments. What is on the supply and demand sides of financial capital? See the following Clear It Up feature for the answer to this question.

## What comprises the supply and demand of financial capital?

A country's national savings is the total of its domestic savings by household and companies (private savings) as well as the government (public savings). If a country is running a trade deficit, it means money from abroad is entering the country and the government considers it part of the supply of financial capital.

The demand for financial capital (money) represents groups that are borrowing the money. Businesses need to borrow to finance their investments in factories, materials, and personnel. When the federal government runs a budget deficit, it is also borrowing money from investors by selling Treasury bonds. Therefore, both business investment and the federal government can demand (or borrow) the supply of savings.

There are two main sources for the supply of financial capital in the U.S. economy: saving by individuals and firms, called S, and the inflow of financial capital from foreign investors, which is equal to the trade deficit (M – X), or imports minus exports. There are also two main sources of demand for financial capital in the U.S. economy: private sector investment, I, and government borrowing, where the government needs to borrow when government spending, G, is higher than the taxes collected, T. We can express this national savings and investment identity in algebraic terms:

$$\text{Supply of financial capital} = \text{Demand for financial capital}$$
$$S + (M - X) = I + (G - T)$$

Again, in this equation, S is private savings, T is taxes, G is government spending, M is imports, X is exports, and I is investment. This relationship is true as a matter of definition because, for the macro economy, the quantity supplied of financial capital must be equal to the quantity demanded.

However, certain components of the national savings and investment identity can switch between the supply side and the demand side. Some countries, like the United States in most years since the 1970s, have budget deficits, which mean the government is spending more than it collects in taxes, and so the government needs to borrow funds. In this case, the government term would be G – T > 0, showing that spending is larger than taxes, and the government would be a demander of financial capital on the left-hand side of the equation (that is, a borrower), not a supplier of financial capital on the right-hand side. However, if the government runs a budget surplus so that the taxes exceed spending, as the U.S. government did from 1998 to 2001, then the government in that year was contributing to the supply of financial capital (T – G > 0), and would appear on the left (saving) side of the national savings and investment identity.

Similarly, if a national economy runs a trade surplus, the trade sector will involve an outflow of financial capital to other countries. A trade surplus means that the domestic financial capital is in surplus within a country and can be invested in other countries.

The fundamental notion that total quantity of financial capital demanded equals total quantity of financial capital supplied must always remain true. Domestic savings will always appear as part of the supply of financial capital and domestic investment will always appear as part of the demand for financial capital. However, the government and trade balance elements of the equation can move back and forth as either suppliers or demanders of financial capital, depending on whether government budgets and the trade balance are in surplus or deficit.

## Domestic Saving and Investment Determine the Trade Balance

One insight from the national saving and investment identity is that a nation's own levels of domestic saving and investment determine a nation's balance of trade. To understand this point, rearrange the identity to put the balance of trade all by itself on one side of the equation. Consider first the situation with a trade deficit, and then the situation with a trade surplus.

In the case of a trade deficit, the national saving and investment identity can be rewritten as:

$$\text{Trade deficit} = \text{Domestic investment} - \text{Private domestic saving} - \text{Government (or public) savings}$$
$$(M - X) = I - S - (T - G)$$

In this case, domestic investment is higher than domestic saving, including both private and government saving. The only way that domestic investment can exceed domestic saving is if capital is flowing into a country from abroad. After all, that extra financial capital for investment has to come from someplace.

Now consider a trade *surplus* from the standpoint of the national saving and investment identity:

$$\text{Trade surplus} = \text{Private domestic saving} + \text{Public saving} - \text{Domestic investment}$$
$$(X - M) = S + (T - G) - I$$

In this case, domestic savings (both private and public) is higher than domestic investment. That extra financial capital will be invested abroad.

This connection of domestic saving and investment to the trade balance explains why economists view the balance of trade as a fundamentally macroeconomic phenomenon. As the national saving and investment identity shows, the performance of certain sectors of an economy, like cars or steel, do not determine the trade balance. Further, whether the nation's trade laws and regulations encourage free trade or protectionism also does not determine the trade balance (see **Globalization and Protectionism**).

## Exploring Trade Balances One Factor at a Time

The national saving and investment identity also provides a framework for thinking about what will cause trade deficits to rise or fall. Begin with the version of the identity that has domestic savings and investment on the left and the trade deficit on the right:

$$\text{Domestic investment} - \text{Private domestic savings} - \text{Public domestic savings} = \text{Trade deficit}$$
$$I - S - (T - G) = (M - X)$$

Now, consider the factors on the left-hand side of the equation one at a time, while holding the other factors constant.

As a first example, assume that the level of domestic investment in a country rises, while the level of private and public saving remains unchanged. **Table 10.6** shows the result in the first row under the equation. Since the equality of the national savings and investment identity must continue to hold—it is, after all, an identity that must be true by definition—the rise in domestic investment will mean a higher trade deficit. This situation occurred in the U.S. economy in the late 1990s. Because of the surge of new information and communications technologies that became available, business investment increased substantially. A fall in private saving during this time and a rise in government saving more or less offset each other. As a result, the financial capital to fund that business investment came from abroad, which is one reason for the very high U.S. trade deficits of the late 1990s and early 2000s.

| Domestic Investment | − | Private Domestic Savings | − | Public Domestic Savings | = | Trade Deficit |
|---|---|---|---|---|---|---|
| I | − | S | − | (T − G) | = | (M − X) |
| Up | | No change | | No change | | Then M − X must rise |
| No change | | Up | | No change | | Then M − X must fall |
| No change | | No change | | Down | | Then M − X must rise |

Table 10.6 Causes of a Changing Trade Balance

As a second scenario, assume that the level of domestic savings rises, while the level of domestic investment and public savings remain unchanged. In this case, the trade deficit would decline. As domestic savings rises, there would be less need for foreign financial capital to meet investment needs. For this reason, a policy proposal often made for reducing the U.S. trade deficit is to increase private saving—although exactly how to increase the overall rate of saving has proven controversial.

As a third scenario, imagine that the government budget deficit increased dramatically, while domestic investment and private savings remained unchanged. This scenario occurred in the U.S. economy in the mid-1980s. The federal budget deficit increased from $79 billion in 1981 to $221 billion in 1986—an increase in the demand for financial capital of $142 billion. The current account balance collapsed from a surplus of $5 billion in 1981 to a deficit of $147 billion in 1986—an increase in the supply of financial capital from abroad of $152 billion. The connection at that time is clear: a sharp increase in government borrowing increased the U.S. economy's demand for financial capital, and foreign investors through the trade deficit primarily supplied that increase. The following Work It Out feature walks you through a scenario in which private domestic savings has to rise by a certain amount to reduce a trade deficit.

# Work It Out ─○─○─○

## Solving Problems with the Saving and Investment Identity

Use the saving and investment identity to answer the following question: Country A has a trade deficit of $200 billion, private domestic savings of $500 billion, a government deficit of $200 billion, and private domestic investment of $500 billion. To reduce the $200 billion trade deficit by $100 billion, by how much does private domestic savings have to increase?

Step 1. Write out the savings investment formula solving for the trade deficit or surplus on the left:

$$(X - M) \ = \ S + (T - G) - I$$

Step 2. In the formula, put the amount for the trade deficit in as a negative number (X − M). The left side of your formula is now:

$$-200 \ = \ S + (T - G) - I$$

Step 3. Enter the private domestic savings (S) of $500 in the formula:

$$-200 \ = \ 500 + (T - G) - I$$

Step 4. Enter the private domestic investment (I) of $500 into the formula:

$$-200 \ = \ 500 + (T - G) - 500$$

Step 5. The government budget surplus or balance is represented by (T − G). Enter a budget deficit amount for (T − G) of −200:

$$-200 \ = \ 500 + (-200) - 500$$

Step 6. Your formula now is:

$$(X - M) \ = \ S + (T - G) - I$$
$$-200 \ = \ 500 + (-200) - 500$$

The question is: To reduce your trade deficit (X − M) of −200 to −100 (in billions of dollars), by how much will savings have to rise?

$$(X - M) \ = \ S + (T - G) - I$$
$$-100 \ = \ S + (-200) - 500$$
$$600 \ = \ S$$

Step 7. Summarize the answer: Private domestic savings needs to rise by $100 billion, to a total of $600 billion, for the two sides of the equation to remain equal (−100 = −100).

## Short-Term Movements in the Business Cycle and the Trade Balance

In the short run, whether an economy is in a recession or on the upswing can affect trade imbalances. A recession tends to make a trade deficit smaller, or a trade surplus larger, while a period of strong economic growth tends to make a trade deficit larger, or a trade surplus smaller.

As an example, note in **Figure 10.2** that the U.S. trade deficit declined by almost half from 2006 to 2009. One primary reason for this change is that during the recession, as the U.S. economy slowed down, it purchased fewer of all goods, including fewer imports from abroad. However, buying power abroad fell less, and so U.S. exports did not fall by as much.

Conversely, in the mid-2000s, when the U.S. trade deficit became very large, a contributing short-term reason is that the U.S. economy was growing. As a result, there was considerable aggressive buying in the U.S. economy, including the buying of imports. Thus, a trade deficit (or a much lower trade surplus) often accompanies a rapidly growing domestic economy, while a trade surplus (or a much lower trade deficit) accompanies a slowing or recessionary domestic economy.

When the trade deficit rises, it necessarily means a greater net inflow of foreign financial capital. The national saving and investment identity teaches that the rest of the economy can absorb this inflow of foreign financial capital in several different ways. For example, reduced private savings could offset the additional inflow of financial capital from abroad, leaving domestic investment and public saving unchanged. Alternatively, the inflow of foreign financial capital could result in higher domestic investment, leaving private and public saving unchanged. Yet another possibility is that greater government borrowing could absorb the inflow of foreign financial capital, leaving domestic saving and investment unchanged. The national saving and investment identity does not specify which of these scenarios, alone or in combination, will occur—only that one of them must occur.

# 10.5 | The Pros and Cons of Trade Deficits and Surpluses

By the end of this section, you will be able to:

- Identify three ways in which borrowing money or running a trade deficit can result in a healthy economy
- Identify three ways in which borrowing money or running a trade deficit can result in a weaker economy

Because flows of trade always involve flows of financial payments, flows of international trade are actually the same as flows of international financial capital. The question of whether trade deficits or surpluses are good or bad for an economy is, in economic terms, exactly the same question as whether it is a good idea for an economy to rely on net inflows of financial capital from abroad or to make net investments of financial capital abroad. Conventional wisdom often holds that borrowing money is foolhardy, and that a prudent country, like a prudent person, should always rely on its own resources. While it is certainly possible to borrow too much—as anyone with an overloaded credit card can testify—borrowing at certain times can also make sound economic sense. For both individuals and countries, there is no economic merit in a policy of abstaining from participation in financial capital markets.

It makes economic sense to borrow when you are buying something with a long-run payoff; that is, when you are making an investment. For this reason, it can make economic sense to borrow for a college education, because the education will typically allow you to earn higher wages, and so to repay the loan and still come out ahead. It can also make sense for a business to borrow in order to purchase a machine that will last 10 years, as long as the machine will increase output and profits by more than enough to repay the loan. Similarly, it can make economic sense for a national economy to borrow from abroad, as long as it wisely invests the money in ways that will tend to raise the nation's economic growth over time. Then, it will be possible for the national economy to repay the borrowed money over time and still end up better off than before.

One vivid example of a country that borrowed heavily from abroad, invested wisely, and did perfectly well is the United States during the nineteenth century. The United States ran a trade deficit in 40 of the 45 years from 1831 to 1875, which meant that it was importing capital from abroad over that time. However, that financial capital was mostly invested in projects like railroads that brought a substantial economic payoff. (See the following Clear It Up feature for more on this.)

A more recent example along these lines is the experience of South Korea, which had trade deficits during much of the 1970s—and so was an importer of capital over that time. However, South Korea also had high rates of investment in physical plant and equipment, and its economy grew rapidly. From the mid-1980s into the mid-1990s, South Korea often had trade surpluses—that is, it was repaying its past borrowing by sending capital abroad.

In contrast, some countries have run large trade deficits, borrowed heavily in global capital markets, and ended up in all kinds of trouble. Two specific sorts of trouble are worth examining. First, a borrower nation can find itself in a bind if it does not invest the incoming funds from abroad in a way that leads to increased productivity. Several of

Latin America's large economies, including Mexico and Brazil, ran large trade deficits and borrowed heavily from abroad in the 1970s, but the inflow of financial capital did not boost productivity sufficiently, which meant that these countries faced enormous troubles repaying the money borrowed when economic conditions shifted during the 1980s. Similarly, it appears that a number of African nations that borrowed foreign funds in the 1970s and 1980s did not invest in productive economic assets. As a result, several of those countries later faced large interest payments, with no economic growth to show for the borrowed funds.

## Are trade deficits always harmful?

For most years of the nineteenth century, U.S. imports exceeded exports and the U.S. economy had a trade deficit. Yet the string of trade deficits did not hold back the economy at all. Instead, the trade deficits contributed to the strong economic growth that gave the U.S. economy the highest per capita GDP in the world by around 1900.

The U.S. trade deficits meant that the U.S. economy was receiving a net inflow of foreign capital from abroad. Much of that foreign capital flowed into two areas of investment—railroads and public infrastructure like roads, water systems, and schools—which were important to helping the U.S. economy grow.

We should not overstate the effect of foreign investment capital on U.S. economic growth. In most years the foreign financial capital represented no more than 6–10% of the funds that the government used for overall physical investment in the economy. Nonetheless, the trade deficit and the accompanying investment funds from abroad were clearly a help, not a hindrance, to the U.S. economy in the nineteenth century.

A second "trouble" is: What happens if the foreign money flows in, and then suddenly flows out again? We raised this scenario at the start of the chapter. In the mid-1990s, a number of countries in East Asia—Thailand, Indonesia, Malaysia, and South Korea—ran large trade deficits and imported capital from abroad. However, in 1997 and 1998 many foreign investors became concerned about the health of these economies, and quickly pulled their money out of stock and bond markets, real estate, and banks. The extremely rapid departure of that foreign capital staggered the banking systems and economies of these countries, plunging them into deep recession. We investigate and discuss the links between international capital flows, banks, and recession in **The Impacts of Government Borrowing**.

While a trade deficit is not always harmful, there is no guarantee that running a trade surplus will bring robust economic health. For example, Germany and Japan ran substantial trade surpluses for most of the last three decades. Regardless of their persistent trade surpluses, both countries have experienced occasional recessions and neither country has had especially robust annual growth in recent years. Read more about Japan's trade surplus in the next Clear It Up feature.

# Link It Up

Watch this video (http://openstaxcollege.org/l/tradedeficit) on whether or not trade deficit is good for the economy.

The sheer size and persistence of the U.S. trade deficits and inflows of foreign capital since the 1980s are a legitimate cause for concern. The huge U.S. economy will not be destabilized by an outflow of international capital as easily as, say, the comparatively tiny economies of Thailand and Indonesia were in 1997–1998. Even an economy that is not knocked down, however, can still be shaken. American policymakers should certainly be paying attention to those cases where a pattern of extensive and sustained current account deficits and foreign borrowing has gone badly—if only as a cautionary tale.

### Are trade surpluses always beneficial? Considering Japan since the 1990s.

Perhaps no economy around the world is better known for its trade surpluses than Japan. Since 1990, the size of these surpluses has often been near $100 billion per year. When Japan's economy was growing vigorously in the 1960s and 1970s, many, especially non-economists, described its large trade surpluses either a cause or a result of its robust economic health. However, from a standpoint of economic growth, Japan's economy has been teetering in and out of recession since 1990, with real GDP growth averaging only about 1% per year, and an unemployment rate that has been creeping higher. Clearly, a whopping trade surplus is no guarantee of economic good health.

Instead, Japan's trade surplus reflects that Japan has a very high rate of domestic savings, more than the Japanese economy can invest domestically, and so it invests the extra funds abroad. In Japan's slow economy, consumption of imports is relatively low, and the growth of consumption is relatively slow. Thus, Japan's exports continually exceed its imports, leaving the trade surplus continually high. Recently, Japan's trade surpluses began to deteriorate. In 2013, Japan ran a trade deficit due to the high cost of imported oil. By 2015, Japan again had a surplus.

## 10.6 | The Difference between Level of Trade and the Trade Balance

By the end of this section, you will be able to:
- Identify three factors that influence a country's level of trade
- Differentiate between balance of trade and level of trade

A nation's *level* of trade may at first sound like much the same issue as the *balance* of trade, but these two are actually quite separate. It is perfectly possible for a country to have a very high level of trade—measured by its exports of goods and services as a share of its GDP—while it also has a near-balance between exports and imports. A high level of trade indicates that the nation exports a good portion of its production. It is also possible for a country's trade to be a relatively low share of GDP, relative to global averages, but for the imbalance between its exports and its imports to be quite large. We emphasized this general theme earlier in **Measuring Trade Balances**, which offered some illustrative figures on trade levels and balances.

A country's level of trade tells how much of its production it exports. We measure this by the percent of exports out of GDP. It indicates the degree of an economy's globalization. Some countries, such as Germany, have a high level of trade—they export almost 50% of their total production. The balance of trade tells us if the country is running a trade surplus or trade deficit. A country can have a low level of trade but a high trade deficit. (For example, the United States only exports 13% of GDP, but it has a trade deficit of over $500 billion.)

Three factors strongly influence a nation's level of trade: the size of its economy, its geographic location, and its history of trade. Large economies like the United States can do much of their trading internally, while small economies like Sweden have less ability to provide what they want internally and tend to have higher ratios of exports and imports to GDP. Nations that are neighbors tend to trade more, since costs of transportation and communication are lower. Moreover, some nations have long and established patterns of international trade, while others do not.

Consequently, a relatively small economy like Sweden, with many nearby trading partners across Europe and a long history of foreign trade, has a high level of trade. Brazil and India, which are fairly large economies that have often sought to inhibit trade in recent decades, have lower levels of trade; whereas, the United States and Japan are extremely large economies that have comparatively few nearby trading partners. Both countries actually have quite low levels of trade by world standards. The ratio of exports to GDP in either the United States or in Japan is about half of the world average.

The balance of trade is a separate issue from the level of trade. The United States has a low level of trade, but had enormous trade deficits for most years from the mid-1980s into the 2000s. Japan has a low level of trade by world standards, but has typically shown large trade surpluses in recent decades. Nations like Germany and the United Kingdom have medium to high levels of trade by world standards, but Germany had a moderate trade surplus in 2015, while the United Kingdom had a moderate trade deficit. Their trade picture was roughly in balance in the late 1990s. Sweden had a high level of trade and a moderate trade surplus in 2015, while Mexico had a high level of trade and a moderate trade deficit that same year.

In short, it is quite possible for nations with a relatively low level of trade, expressed as a percentage of GDP, to have relatively large trade deficits. It is also quite possible for nations with a near balance between exports and imports to worry about the consequences of high levels of trade for the economy. It is not inconsistent to believe that a high level of trade is potentially beneficial to an economy, because of the way it allows nations to play to their comparative advantages, and to also be concerned about any macroeconomic instability caused by a long-term pattern of large trade deficits. The following Clear It Up feature discusses how this sort of dynamic played out in Colonial India.

## Are trade surpluses always beneficial? Considering Colonial India.

India was formally under British rule from 1858 to 1947. During that time, India consistently had trade surpluses with Great Britain. Anyone who believes that trade surpluses are a sign of economic strength and dominance while trade deficits are a sign of economic weakness must find this pattern odd, since it would mean that colonial India was successfully dominating and exploiting Great Britain for almost a century—which was not true.

Instead, India's trade surpluses with Great Britain meant that each year there was an overall flow of financial capital from India to Great Britain. In India, many heavily criticized this financial capital flow as the "drain," and they viewed eliminating the financial capital drain as one of the many reasons why India would benefit from achieving independence.

## Final Thoughts about Trade Balances

Trade deficits can be a good or a bad sign for an economy, and trade surpluses can be a good or a bad sign. Even a trade balance of zero—which just means that a nation is neither a net borrower nor lender in the international economy—can be either a good or bad sign. The fundamental economic question is not whether a nation's economy is borrowing or lending at all, but whether the particular borrowing or lending in the particular economic conditions of that country makes sense.

It is interesting to reflect on how public attitudes toward trade deficits and surpluses might change if we could somehow change the labels that people and the news media affix to them. If we called a trade deficit "attracting foreign financial capital"—which accurately describes what a trade deficit means—then trade deficits might look more attractive. Conversely, if we called a trade surplus "shipping financial capital abroad"—which accurately captures what a trade surplus does—then trade surpluses might look less attractive. Either way, the key to understanding trade balances is to understand the relationships between flows of trade and flows of international payments, and what these relationships imply about the causes, benefits, and risks of different kinds of trade balances. The first step along this journey of understanding is to move beyond knee-jerk reactions to terms like "trade surplus," "trade balance," and "trade deficit."

## Bring it Home

### More than Meets the Eye in the Congo

Now that you see the big picture, you undoubtedly realize that all of the economic choices you make, such as depositing savings or investing in an international mutual fund, do influence the flow of goods and services as well as the flows of money around the world.

You now know that a trade surplus does not necessarily tell us whether an economy is performing well or not. The Democratic Republic of the Congo ran a trade surplus in 2013, as we learned in the beginning of the chapter. Yet its current account balance was –$2.8 billion. However, the return of political stability and the rebuilding in the aftermath of the civil war there has meant a flow of investment and financial capital into the country. In this case, a negative current account balance means the country is being rebuilt—and that is a good thing.

# KEY TERMS

**balance of trade (trade balance)** the gap, if any, between a nation's exports and imports

**current account balance** a broad measure of the balance of trade that includes trade in goods and services, as well as international flows of income and foreign aid

**exports of goods and services as a percentage of GDP** the dollar value of exports divided by the dollar value of a country's GDP

**financial capital** the international flows of money that facilitates trade and investment

**merchandise trade balance** the balance of trade looking only at goods

**national savings and investment identity** the total of private savings and public savings (a government budget surplus)

**unilateral transfers** "one-way payments" that governments, private entities, or individuals make that they sent abroad with nothing received in return

# KEY CONCEPTS AND SUMMARY

### 10.1 Measuring Trade Balances

The trade balance measures the gap between a country's exports and its imports. In most high-income economies, goods comprise less than half of a country's total production, while services comprise more than half. The last two decades have seen a surge in international trade in services; however, most global trade still takes the form of goods rather than services. The current account balance includes the trade in goods, services, and money flowing into and out of a country from investments and unilateral transfers.

### 10.2 Trade Balances in Historical and International Context

The United States developed large trade surpluses in the early 1980s, swung back to a tiny trade surplus in 1991, and then had even larger trade deficits in the late 1990s and early 2000s. As we will see below, a trade deficit necessarily means a net inflow of financial capital from abroad, while a trade surplus necessarily means a net outflow of financial capital from an economy to other countries.

### 10.3 Trade Balances and Flows of Financial Capital

International flows of goods and services are closely connected to the international flows of financial capital. A current account deficit means that, after taking all the flows of payments from goods, services, and income together, the country is a net borrower from the rest of the world. A current account surplus is the opposite and means the country is a net lender to the rest of the world.

### 10.4 The National Saving and Investment Identity

The national saving and investment identity is based on the relationship that the total quantity of financial capital supplied from all sources must equal the total quantity of financial capital demanded from all sources. If S is private saving, T is taxes, G is government spending, M is imports, X is exports, and I is investment, then for an economy with a current account deficit and a budget deficit:

$$\text{Supply of financial capital} = \text{Demand for financial capital}$$
$$S + (M - X) = I + (G - T)$$

A recession tends to increase the trade balance (meaning a higher trade surplus or lower trade deficit), while economic boom will tend to decrease the trade balance (meaning a lower trade surplus or a larger trade deficit).

## 10.5 The Pros and Cons of Trade Deficits and Surpluses

Trade surpluses are no guarantee of economic health, and trade deficits are no guarantee of economic weakness. Either trade deficits or trade surpluses can work out well or poorly, depending on whether a government wisely invests the corresponding flows of financial capital.

## 10.6 The Difference between Level of Trade and the Trade Balance

There is a difference between the level of a country's trade and the balance of trade. The government measures its level of trade by the percentage of exports out of GDP, or the size of the economy. Small economies that have nearby trading partners and a history of international trade will tend to have higher levels of trade. Larger economies with few nearby trading partners and a limited history of international trade will tend to have lower levels of trade. The level of trade is different from the trade balance. The level of trade depends on a country's history of trade, its geography, and the size of its economy. A country's balance of trade is the dollar difference between its exports and imports.

Trade deficits and trade surpluses are not necessarily good or bad—it depends on the circumstances. Even if a country is borrowing, if it invests that money in productivity-boosting investments it can lead to an improvement in long-term economic growth.

# SELF-CHECK QUESTIONS

**1.** If foreign investors buy more U.S. stocks and bonds, how would that show up in the current account balance?

**2.** If the trade deficit of the United States increases, how is the current account balance affected?

**3.** State whether each of the following events involves a financial flow to the Mexican economy or a financial flow out of the Mexican economy:
   a. Mexico imports services from Japan
   b. Mexico exports goods to Canada
   c. U.S. investors receive a return from past financial investments in Mexico

**4.** In what way does comparing a country's exports to GDP reflect its degree of globalization?

**5.** At one point Canada's GDP was $1,800 billion and its exports were $542 billion. What was Canada's export ratio at this time?

**6.** The GDP for the United States is $18,036 billion and its current account balance is –$484 billion. What percent of GDP is the current account balance?

**7.** Why does the trade balance and the current account balance track so closely together over time?

**8.** State whether each of the following events involves a financial flow to the U.S. economy or away from the U.S. economy:
   a. Export sales to Germany
   b. Returns paid on past U.S. financial investments in Brazil
   c. Foreign aid from the U.S. government to Egypt
   d. Imported oil from the Russian Federation
   e. Japanese investors buying U.S. real estate

**9.** How does the bottom portion of **Figure 10.3**, showing the international flow of investments and capital, differ from the upper portion?

**10.** Explain the relationship between a current account deficit or surplus and the flow of funds.

**11.** Using the national savings and investment identity, explain how each of the following changes (*ceteris paribus*) will increase or decrease the trade balance:
   a. A lower domestic savings rate
   b. The government changes from running a budget surplus to running a budget deficit
   c. The rate of domestic investment surges

**12.** If a country is running a government budget surplus, why is (T – G) on the left side of the saving-investment identity?

**13.** What determines the size of a country's trade deficit?

**14.** If domestic investment increases, and there is no change in the amount of private and public saving, what must happen to the size of the trade deficit?

**15.** Why does a recession cause a trade deficit to increase?

**16.** Both the United States and global economies are booming. Will U.S. imports and/or exports increase?

**17.** For each of the following, indicate which type of government spending would justify a budget deficit and which would not.
   a. Increased federal spending on Medicare
   b. Increased spending on education
   c. Increased spending on the space program
   d. Increased spending on airports and air traffic control

**18.** How did large trade deficits hurt the East Asian countries in the mid 1980s? (Recall that trade deficits are equivalent to inflows of financial capital from abroad.)

**19.** Describe a scenario in which a trade surplus benefits an economy and one in which a trade surplus is occurring in an economy that performs poorly. What key factor or factors are making the difference in the outcome that results from a trade surplus?

**20.** The United States exports 14% of GDP while Germany exports about 50% of its GDP. Explain what that means.

**21.** Explain briefly whether each of the following would be more likely to lead to a higher level of trade for an economy, or a greater imbalance of trade for an economy.
   a. Living in an especially large country
   b. Having a domestic investment rate much higher than the domestic savings rate
   c. Having many other large economies geographically nearby
   d. Having an especially large budget deficit
   e. Having countries with a tradition of strong protectionist legislation shutting out imports

## REVIEW QUESTIONS

**22.** If imports exceed exports, is it a trade deficit or a trade surplus? What about if exports exceed imports?

**23.** What is included in the current account balance?

**24.** In recent decades, has the U.S. trade balance usually been in deficit, surplus, or balanced?

**25.** Does a trade surplus mean an overall inflow of financial capital to an economy, or an overall outflow of financial capital? What about a trade deficit?

**26.** What are the two main sides of the national savings and investment identity?

**27.** What are the main components of the national savings and investment identity?

**28.** When is a trade deficit likely to work out well for an economy? When is it likely to work out poorly?

**29.** Does a trade surplus help to guarantee strong economic growth?

**30.** What three factors will determine whether a nation has a higher or lower share of trade relative to its GDP?

**31.** What is the difference between trade deficits and balance of trade?

# CRITICAL THINKING QUESTIONS

**32.** Occasionally, a government official will argue that a country should strive for both a trade surplus and a healthy inflow of capital from abroad. Explain why such a statement is economically impossible.

**33.** A government official announces a new policy. The country wishes to eliminate its trade deficit, but will strongly encourage financial investment from foreign firms. Explain why such a statement is contradictory.

**34.** If a country is a big exporter, is it more exposed to global financial crises?

**35.** If countries reduced trade barriers, would the international flows of money increase?

**36.** Is it better for your country to be an international lender or borrower?

**37.** Many think that the size of a trade deficit is due to a lack of competitiveness of domestic sectors, such as autos. Explain why this is not true.

**38.** If you observed a country with a rapidly growing trade surplus over a period of a year or so, would you be more likely to believe that the country's economy was in a period of recession or of rapid growth? Explain.

**39.** Occasionally, a government official will argue that a country should strive for both a trade surplus and a healthy inflow of capital from abroad. Is this possible?

**40.** What is more important, a country's current account balance or GDP growth? Why?

**41.** Will nations that are more involved in foreign trade tend to have higher trade imbalances, lower trade imbalances, or is the pattern unpredictable?

**42.** Some economists warn that the persistent trade deficits and a negative current account balance that the United States has run will be a problem in the long run. Do you agree or not? Explain your answer.

# PROBLEMS

**43.** In 2001, the United Kingdom's economy exported goods worth £192 billion and services worth another £77 billion. It imported goods worth £225 billion and services worth £66 billion. Receipts of income from abroad were £140 billion while income payments going abroad were £131 billion. Government transfers from the United Kingdom to the rest of the world were £23 billion, while various U.K government agencies received payments of £16 billion from the rest of the world.

    a. Calculate the U.K. merchandise trade deficit for 2001.

    b. Calculate the current account balance for 2001.

    c. Explain how you decided whether payments on foreign investment and government transfers counted on the positive or the negative side of the current account balance for the United Kingdom in 2001.

**44.** Imagine that the U.S. economy finds itself in the following situation: a government budget deficit of $100 billion, total domestic savings of $1,500 billion, and total domestic physical capital investment of $1,600 billion. According to the national saving and investment identity, what will be the current account balance? What will be the current account balance if investment rises by $50 billion, while the budget deficit and national savings remain the same?

**45.** **Table 10.7** provides some hypothetical data on macroeconomic accounts for three countries represented by A, B, and C and measured in billions of currency units. In **Table 10.7**, private household saving is SH, tax revenue is T, government spending is G, and investment spending is I.

|     | A   | B   | C   |
| --- | --- | --- | --- |
| SH  | 700 | 500 | 600 |
| T   | 00  | 500 | 500 |
| G   | 600 | 350 | 650 |
| I   | 800 | 400 | 450 |

Table 10.7 Macroeconomic Accounts

a. Calculate the trade balance and the net inflow of foreign saving for each country.
b. State whether each one has a trade surplus or deficit (or balanced trade).
c. State whether each is a net lender or borrower internationally and explain.

**46.** Imagine that the economy of Germany finds itself in the following situation: the government budget has a surplus of 1% of Germany's GDP; private savings is 20% of GDP; and physical investment is 18% of GDP.

a. Based on the national saving and investment identity, what is the current account balance?
b. If the government budget surplus falls to zero, how will this affect the current account balance?

# 11 | The Aggregate Demand/ Aggregate Supply Model

**Figure 11.1 New Home Construction**  At the peak of the housing bubble, many people across the country were able to secure the loans necessary to build new houses. (Credit: modification of work by Tim Pierce/Flickr Creative Commons)

## Bring it Home

### From Housing Bubble to Housing Bust

The United States experienced rising home ownership rates for most of the last two decades. Between 1990 and 2006, the U.S. housing market grew. Homeownership rates grew from 64% to a high of over 69% between 2004 and 2005. For many people, this was a period in which they could either buy first homes or buy a larger and more expensive home. During this time mortgage values tripled. Housing became more accessible to Americans and was considered to be a safe financial investment. Figure 11.2 shows how new single family home sales peaked in 2005 at 107,000 units.

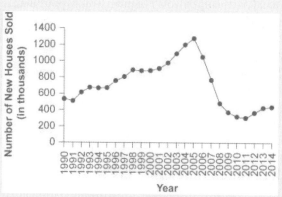

**Figure 11.2 New Single Family Houses Sold** From the early 1990s up through 2005, the number of new single family houses sold rose steadily. In 2006, the number dropped dramatically and this dramatic decline continued through 2011. By 2014, the number of new houses sold had begun to climb back up, but the levels are still lower than those of 1990. (Source: U.S. Census Bureau)

The housing bubble began to show signs of bursting in 2005, as delinquency and late payments began to grow and an oversupply of new homes on the market became apparent. Dropping home values contributed to a decrease in the overall wealth of the household sector and caused homeowners to pull back on spending. Several mortgage lenders were forced to file for bankruptcy because homeowners were not making their payments, and by 2008 the problem had spread throughout the financial markets. Lenders clamped down on credit and the housing bubble burst. Financial markets were now in crisis and unable or unwilling to even extend credit to credit-worthy customers.

The housing bubble and the crisis in the financial markets were major contributors to the Great Recession that led to unemployment rates over 10% and falling GDP. While the United States is still recovering from the impact of the Great Recession, it has made substantial progress in restoring financial market stability through implementing aggressive fiscal and monetary policy.

The economic history of the United States is cyclical in nature with recessions and expansions. Some of these fluctuations are severe, such as the economic downturn that occurred during the Great Depression in the 1930s which lasted several years. Why does the economy grow at different rates in different years? What are the causes of the cyclical behavior of the economy? This chapter will introduce an important model, the aggregate demand–aggregate supply model, to begin our understanding of why economies expand and contract over time.

# Introduction to the Aggregate Supply–Aggregate Demand Model

In this chapter, you will learn about:

- Macroeconomic Perspectives on Demand and Supply

- Building a Model of Aggregate Supply and Aggregate Demand

- Shifts in Aggregate Supply

- Shifts in Aggregate Demand

- How the AS–AD Model Incorporates Growth, Unemployment, and Inflation

- Keynes' Law and Say's Law in the AS–AD Model

A key part of macroeconomics is the use of models to analyze macro issues and problems. How is the rate of economic growth connected to changes in the unemployment rate? Is there a reason why unemployment and inflation seem to move in opposite directions: lower unemployment and higher inflation from 1997 to 2000, higher unemployment and lower inflation in the early 2000s, lower unemployment and higher inflation in the mid-2000s, and then higher unemployment and lower inflation in 2009? Why did the current account deficit rise so high, but then decline in 2009?

To analyze questions like these, we must move beyond discussing macroeconomic issues one at a time, and begin building economic models that will capture the relationships and interconnections between them. The next three chapters take up this task. This chapter introduces the macroeconomic model of aggregate supply and aggregate demand, how the two interact to reach a macroeconomic equilibrium, and how shifts in aggregate demand or aggregate supply will affect that equilibrium. This chapter also relates the model of aggregate supply and aggregate demand to the three goals of economic policy (growth, unemployment, and inflation), and provides a framework for thinking about many of the connections and tradeoffs between these goals. The chapter on **The Keynesian Perspective** focuses on the macroeconomy in the short run, where aggregate demand plays a crucial role. The chapter on **The Neoclassical Perspective** explores the macroeconomy in the long run, where aggregate supply plays a crucial role.

# 11.1 | Macroeconomic Perspectives on Demand and Supply

By the end of this section, you will be able to:
- Explain Say's Law and understand why it primarily applies in the long run
- Explain Keynes' Law and understand why it primarily applies in the short run

Macroeconomists over the last two centuries have often divided into two groups: those who argue that supply is the most important determinant of the size of the macroeconomy while demand just tags along, and those who argue that demand is the most important factor in the size of the macroeconomy while supply just tags along.

## Say's Law and the Macroeconomics of Supply

Those economists who emphasize the role of supply in the macroeconomy often refer to the work of a famous early nineteenth century French economist named Jean-Baptiste Say (1767–1832). **Say's law** is: "Supply creates its own demand." As a matter of historical accuracy, it seems clear that Say never actually wrote down this law and that it oversimplifies his beliefs, but the law lives on as useful shorthand for summarizing a point of view.

The intuition behind Say's law is that each time a good or service is produced and sold, it generates income that is earned for someone: a worker, a manager, an owner, or those who are workers, managers, and owners at firms that supply inputs along the chain of production. We alluded to this earlier in our discussion of the National Income approach to measuring GDP. The forces of supply and demand in individual markets will cause prices to rise and fall. The bottom line remains, however, that every sale represents income to someone, and so, Say's law argues, a given value of supply must create an equivalent value of demand somewhere else in the economy. Because Jean-Baptiste Say, Adam Smith, and other economists writing around the turn of the nineteenth century who discussed this view were known as "classical" economists, modern economists who generally subscribe to the Say's law view on the importance of supply for determining the size of the macroeconomy are called **neoclassical economists**.

If supply always creates exactly enough demand at the macroeconomic level, then (as Say himself recognized) it is hard to understand why periods of recession and high unemployment should ever occur. To be sure, even if total supply always creates an equal amount of total demand, the economy could still experience a situation of some firms earning profits while other firms suffer losses. Nevertheless, a recession is not a situation where all business failures are exactly counterbalanced by an offsetting number of successes. A recession is a situation in which the economy as a whole is shrinking in size, business failures outnumber the remaining success stories, and many firms end up suffering losses and laying off workers.

Say's law that supply creates its own demand does seem a good approximation for the long run. Over periods of some years or decades, as the productive power of an economy to supply goods and services increases, total demand in the economy grows at roughly the same pace. However, over shorter time horizons of a few months or even years, recessions or even depressions occur in which firms, as a group, seem to face a lack of demand for their products.

## Keynes' Law and the Macroeconomics of Demand

The alternative to Say's law, with its emphasis on supply, is **Keynes' law**: "Demand creates its own supply." As a matter of historical accuracy, just as Jean-Baptiste Say never wrote down anything as simpleminded as Say's law, John Maynard Keynes never wrote down Keynes' law, but the law is a useful simplification that conveys a certain point of view.

When Keynes wrote his influential work *The General Theory of Employment, Interest, and Money* during the 1930s Great Depression, he pointed out that during the Depression, the economy's capacity to supply goods and services had not changed much. U.S. unemployment rates soared higher than 20% from 1933 to 1935, but the number of possible workers had not increased or decreased much. Factories closed, but machinery and equipment had not disappeared. Technologies that had been invented in the 1920s were not un-invented and forgotten in the 1930s. Thus, Keynes argued that the Great Depression—and many ordinary recessions as well—were not caused by a drop in the ability of the economy to supply goods as measured by labor, physical capital, or technology. He argued the economy often produced less than its full potential, not because it was technically impossible to produce more with the existing workers and machines, but because a lack of demand in the economy as a whole led to inadequate incentives for firms to produce. In such cases, he argued, the level of GDP in the economy was not primarily determined by the potential of what the economy could supply, but rather by the amount of total demand.

Keynes' law seems to apply fairly well in the short run of a few months to a few years, when many firms experience either a drop in demand for their output during a recession or so much demand that they have trouble producing enough during an economic boom. However, demand cannot tell the whole macroeconomic story, either. After all, if demand was all that mattered at the macroeconomic level, then the government could make the economy as large as it wanted just by pumping up total demand through a large increase in the government spending component or by legislating large tax cuts to push up the consumption component. Economies do, however, face genuine limits to how much they can produce, limits determined by the quantity of labor, physical capital, technology, and the institutional and market structures that bring these factors of production together. These constraints on what an economy can supply at the macroeconomic level do not disappear just because of an increase in demand.

## Combining Supply and Demand in Macroeconomics

Two insights emerge from this overview of Say's law with its emphasis on macroeconomic supply and Keynes' law with its emphasis on macroeconomic demand. The first conclusion, which is not exactly a hot news flash, is that an economic approach focused only on the supply side or only on the demand side can be only a partial success. We need to take into account both supply and demand. The second conclusion is that since Keynes' law applies more accurately in the short run and Say's law applies more accurately in the long run, the tradeoffs and connections between the three goals of macroeconomics may be different in the short run and the long run.

# 11.2 | Building a Model of Aggregate Demand and Aggregate Supply

By the end of this section, you will be able to:
- Explain the aggregate supply curve and how it relates to real GDP and potential GDP
- Explain the aggregate demand curve and how it is influenced by price levels
- Interpret the aggregate demand/aggregate supply model
- Identify the point of equilibrium in the aggregate demand/aggregate supply model
- Define short run aggregate supply and long run aggregate supply

To build a useful macroeconomic model, we need a model that shows what determines total supply or total demand for the economy, and how total demand and total supply interact at the macroeconomic level. We call this the **aggregate demand/aggregate supply model**. This module will explain aggregate supply, aggregate demand, and the equilibrium between them. The following modules will discuss the causes of shifts in aggregate supply and aggregate demand.

## The Aggregate Supply Curve and Potential GDP

Firms make decisions about what quantity to supply based on the profits they expect to earn. They determine profits, in turn, by the price of the outputs they sell and by the prices of the inputs, like labor or raw materials, that they need to buy. **Aggregate supply (AS)** refers to the total quantity of output (i.e. real GDP) firms will produce and sell. The

**aggregate supply (AS) curve** shows the total quantity of output (i.e. real GDP) that firms will produce and sell at each price level.

**Figure 11.3** shows an aggregate supply curve. In the following paragraphs, we will walk through the elements of the diagram one at a time: the horizontal and vertical axes, the aggregate supply curve itself, and the meaning of the potential GDP vertical line.

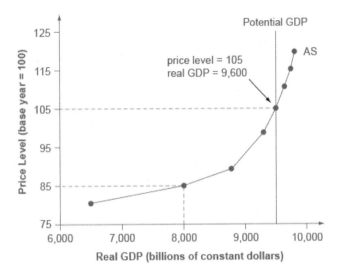

**Figure 11.3 The Aggregate Supply Curve** Aggregate supply (AS) slopes up, because as the price level for outputs rises, with the price of inputs remaining fixed, firms have an incentive to produce more to earn higher profits. The potential GDP line shows the maximum that the economy can produce with full employment of workers and physical capital.

The diagram's horizontal axis shows real GDP—that is, the level of GDP adjusted for inflation. The vertical axis shows the price level, which measures the average price of all goods and services produced in the economy. In other words, the price level in the AD-AS model is what we called the GDP Deflator in **The Macroeconomic Perspective**. Remember that the price level is different from the inflation rate. Visualize the price level as an index number, like the Consumer Price Index, while the inflation rate is the percentage change in the price level over time.

As the price level rises, real GDP rises as well. Why? The price level on the vertical axis represents prices for final goods or outputs bought in the economy—i.e. the GDP deflator—not the price level for intermediate goods and services that are inputs to production. Thus, the AS curve describes how suppliers will react to a higher price level for final outputs of goods and services, while holding the prices of inputs like labor and energy constant. If firms across the economy face a situation where the price level of what they produce and sell is rising, but their costs of production are not rising, then the lure of higher profits will induce them to expand production. In other words, an aggregate supply curve shows how producers as a group will respond to an increase in aggregate demand.

An AS curve's slope changes from nearly flat at its far left to nearly vertical at its far right. At the far left of the aggregate supply curve, the level of output in the economy is far below **potential GDP**, which we define as the amount of real GDP an economy can produce by fully employing its existing levels of labor, physical capital, and technology, in the context of its existing market and legal institutions. At these relatively low levels of output, levels of unemployment are high, and many factories are running only part-time, or have closed their doors. In this situation, a relatively small increase in the prices of the outputs that businesses sell—while assuming no rise in input prices—can encourage a considerable surge in the quantity of aggregate supply because so many workers and factories are ready to swing into production.

As the GDP increases, however, some firms and industries will start running into limits: perhaps nearly all of the expert workers in a certain industry will have jobs or factories in certain geographic areas or industries will be running at full speed. In the AS curve's intermediate area, a higher price level for outputs continues to encourage a greater quantity of output—but as the increasingly steep upward slope of the aggregate supply curve shows, the increase in real GDP in response to a given rise in the price level will not be as large. (Read the following Clear It Up feature to learn why the AS curve crosses potential GDP.)

## Why does AS cross potential GDP?

Economists typically draw the aggregate supply curve to cross the potential GDP line. This shape may seem puzzling: How can an economy produce at an output level which is higher than its "potential" or "full employment" GDP? The economic intuition here is that if prices for outputs were high enough, producers would make fanatical efforts to produce: all workers would be on double-overtime, all machines would run 24 hours a day, seven days a week. Such hyper-intense production would go beyond using potential labor and physical capital resources fully, to using them in a way that is not sustainable in the long term. Thus, it is possible for production to sprint above potential GDP, but only in the short run.

At the far right, the aggregate supply curve becomes nearly vertical. At this quantity, higher prices for outputs cannot encourage additional output, because even if firms want to expand output, the inputs of labor and machinery in the economy are fully employed. In this example, the vertical line in the exhibit shows that potential GDP occurs at a total output of 9,500. When an economy is operating at its potential GDP, machines and factories are running at capacity, and the unemployment rate is relatively low—at the natural rate of unemployment. For this reason, potential GDP is sometimes also called **full-employment GDP**.

## The Aggregate Demand Curve

**Aggregate demand (AD)** refers to the amount of total spending on domestic goods and services in an economy. (Strictly speaking, AD is what economists call total planned expenditure. We will further explain this distinction in the appendix **The Expenditure-Output Model** . For now, just think of aggregate demand as total spending.) It includes all four components of demand: consumption, investment, government spending, and net exports (exports minus imports). This demand is determined by a number of factors, but one of them is the price level—recall though, that the price level is an index number such as the GDP deflator that measures the average price of the things we buy. The **aggregate demand (AD) curve** shows the total spending on domestic goods and services at each price level.

**Figure 11.4** presents an aggregate demand (AD) curve. Just like the aggregate supply curve, the horizontal axis shows real GDP and the vertical axis shows the price level. The AD curve slopes down, which means that increases in the price level of outputs lead to a lower quantity of total spending. The reasons behind this shape are related to how changes in the price level affect the different components of aggregate demand. The following components comprise aggregate demand: consumption spending (C), investment spending (I), government spending (G), and spending on exports (X) minus imports (M): C + I + G + X – M.

**Figure 11.4 The Aggregate Demand Curve** Aggregate demand (AD) slopes down, showing that, as the price level rises, the amount of total spending on domestic goods and services declines.

The wealth effect holds that as the price level increases, the buying power of savings that people have stored up in bank accounts and other assets will diminish, eaten away to some extent by inflation. Because a rise in the price level reduces people's wealth, consumption spending will fall as the price level rises.

The interest rate effect is that as prices for outputs rise, the same purchases will take more money or credit to accomplish. This additional demand for money and credit will push interest rates higher. In turn, higher interest rates will reduce borrowing by businesses for investment purposes and reduce borrowing by households for homes and cars—thus reducing consumption and investment spending.

The foreign price effect points out that if prices rise in the United States while remaining fixed in other countries, then goods in the United States will be relatively more expensive compared to goods in the rest of the world. U.S. exports will be relatively more expensive, and the quantity of exports sold will fall. U.S. imports from abroad will be relatively cheaper, so the quantity of imports will rise. Thus, a higher domestic price level, relative to price levels in other countries, will reduce net export expenditures.

Among economists all three of these effects are controversial, in part because they do not seem to be very large. For this reason, the aggregate demand curve in **Figure 11.4** slopes downward fairly steeply. The steep slope indicates that a higher price level for final outputs reduces aggregate demand for all three of these reasons, but that the change in the quantity of aggregate demand as a result of changes in price level is not very large.

Read the following Work It Out feature to learn how to interpret the AD/AS model. In this example, aggregate supply, aggregate demand, and the price level are given for the imaginary country of Xurbia.

# Work It Out ⊢○─○─○

## Interpreting the AD/AS Model

**Table 11.1** shows information on aggregate supply, aggregate demand, and the price level for the imaginary country of Xurbia. What information does **Table 11.1** tell you about the state of the Xurbia's economy? Where is the equilibrium price level and output level (this is the SR macroequilibrium)? Is Xurbia risking inflationary pressures or facing high unemployment? How can you tell?

| Price Level | Aggregate Demand | Aggregate Supply |
|:---:|:---:|:---:|
| 110 | $700 | $600 |
| 120 | $690 | $640 |
| 130 | $680 | $680 |
| 140 | $670 | $720 |
| 150 | $660 | $740 |
| 160 | $650 | $760 |
| 170 | $640 | $770 |

**Table 11.1 Price Level: Aggregate Demand/Aggregate Supply**

To begin to use the AD/AS model, it is important to plot the AS and AD curves from the data provided. What is the equilibrium?

Step 1. Draw your x- and y-axis. Label the x-axis Real GDP and the y-axis Price Level.

Step 2. Plot AD on your graph.

Step 3. Plot AS on your graph.

Step 4. Look at **Figure 11.5** which provides a visual to aid in your analysis.

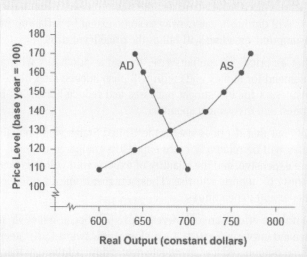

**Figure 11.5 The AD/AS Curves** AD and AS curves created from the data in Table 11.1.

Step 5. Determine where AD and AS intersect. This is the equilibrium with price level at 130 and real GDP at $680.

Step 6. Look at the graph to determine where equilibrium is located. We can see that this equilibrium is fairly far from where the AS curve becomes near-vertical (or at least quite steep) which seems to start at about $750 of real output. This implies that the economy is not close to potential GDP. Thus, unemployment will be high. In the relatively flat part of the AS curve, where the equilibrium occurs, changes in the price level will not be a major concern, since such changes are likely to be small.

Step 7. Determine what the steep portion of the AS curve indicates. Where the AS curve is steep, the economy is at or close to potential GDP.

Step 8. Draw conclusions from the given information:

- If equilibrium occurs in the flat range of AS, then economy is not close to potential GDP and will be experiencing unemployment, but stable price level.

- If equilibrium occurs in the steep range of AS, then the economy is close or at potential GDP and will be experiencing rising price levels or inflationary pressures, but will have a low unemployment rate.

## Equilibrium in the Aggregate Demand/Aggregate Supply Model

The intersection of the aggregate supply and aggregate demand curves shows the equilibrium level of real GDP and the equilibrium price level in the economy. At a relatively low price level for output, firms have little incentive to produce, although consumers would be willing to purchase a large quantity of output. As the price level rises, aggregate supply rises and aggregate demand falls until the equilibrium point is reached.

Figure 11.6 combines the AS curve from Figure 11.3 and the AD curve from Figure 11.4 and places them both on a single diagram. In this example, the equilibrium point occurs at point E, at a price level of 90 and an output level of 8,800.

**Figure 11.6 Aggregate Supply and Aggregate Demand** The equilibrium, where aggregate supply (AS) equals aggregate demand (AD), occurs at a price level of 90 and an output level of 8,800.

Confusion sometimes arises between the aggregate supply and aggregate demand model and the microeconomic analysis of demand and supply in particular markets for goods, services, labor, and capital. Read the following Clear It Up feature to gain an understanding of whether AS and AD are macro or micro.

## Are AS and AD macro or micro?

These aggregate supply and demand models and the microeconomic analysis of demand and supply in particular markets for goods, services, labor, and capital have a superficial resemblance, but they also have many underlying differences.

For example, the vertical and horizontal axes have distinctly different meanings in macroeconomic and microeconomic diagrams. The vertical axis of a microeconomic demand and supply diagram expresses a price (or wage or rate of return) for an individual good or service. This price is implicitly relative: it is intended to be compared with the prices of other products (for example, the price of pizza relative to the price of fried chicken). In contrast, the vertical axis of an aggregate supply and aggregate demand diagram expresses the level of a price index like the Consumer Price Index or the GDP deflator—combining a wide array of prices from across the economy. The price level is absolute: it is not intended to be compared to any other prices since it is essentially the average price of all products in an economy. The horizontal axis of a microeconomic supply and demand curve measures the quantity of a particular good or service. In contrast, the horizontal axis of the aggregate demand and aggregate supply diagram measures GDP, which is the sum of all the final goods and services produced in the economy, not the quantity in a specific market.

In addition, the economic reasons for the shapes of the curves in the macroeconomic model are different from the reasons behind the shapes of the curves in microeconomic models. Demand curves for individual goods or services slope down primarily because of the existence of substitute goods, not the wealth effects, interest rate, and foreign price effects associated with aggregate demand curves. The slopes of individual supply and demand curves can have a variety of different slopes, depending on the extent to which quantity demanded and quantity supplied react to price in that specific market, but the slopes of the AS and AD curves are much the same in every diagram (although as we shall see in later chapters, short-run and long-run perspectives will emphasize different parts of the AS curve).

In short, just because the AD/AS diagram has two lines that cross, do not assume that it is the same as every other diagram where two lines cross. The intuitions and meanings of the macro and micro diagrams are only distant cousins from different branches of the economics family tree.

## Defining SRAS and LRAS

In the Clear It Up feature titled "Why does AS cross potential GDP?" we differentiated between short run changes in aggregate supply which the AS curve shows and long run changes in aggregate supply which the vertical line at potential GDP defines. In the short run, if demand is too low (or too high), it is possible for producers to supply less GDP (or more GDP) than potential. In the long run, however, producers are limited to producing at potential GDP. For this reason, we may also refer to what we have been calling the AS curve as the **short run aggregate supply (SRAS) curve**. We may also refer to the vertical line at potential GDP as the **long run aggregate supply (LRAS) curve**.

# 11.3 | Shifts in Aggregate Supply

By the end of this section, you will be able to:
- Explain how productivity growth changes the aggregate supply curve
- Explain how changes in input prices change the aggregate supply curve

The original equilibrium in the AD/AS diagram will shift to a new equilibrium if the AS or AD curve shifts. When the aggregate supply curve shifts to the right, then at every price level, producers supply a greater quantity of real GDP. When the AS curve shifts to the left, then at every price level, producers supply a lower quantity of real GDP. This module discusses two of the most important factors that can lead to shifts in the AS curve: productivity growth and changes in input prices.

## How Productivity Growth Shifts the AS Curve

In the long run, the most important factor shifting the AS curve is productivity growth. Productivity means how much output can be produced with a given quantity of labor. One measure of this is output per worker or GDP per capita. Over time, productivity grows so that the same quantity of labor can produce more output. Historically, the real growth in GDP per capita in an advanced economy like the United States has averaged about 2% to 3% per year, but productivity growth has been faster during certain extended periods like the 1960s and the late 1990s through the early 2000s, or slower during periods like the 1970s. A higher level of productivity shifts the AS curve to the right, because with improved productivity, firms can produce a greater quantity of output at every price level. **Figure 11.7** (a) shows an outward shift in productivity over two time periods. The AS curve shifts out from $SRAS_0$ to $SRAS_1$ to $SRAS_2$, and the equilibrium shifts from $E_0$ to $E_1$ to $E_2$. Note that with increased productivity, workers can produce more GDP. Thus, full employment corresponds to a higher level of potential GDP, which we show as a rightward shift in LRAS from $LRAS_0$ to $LRAS_1$ to $LRAS_2$.

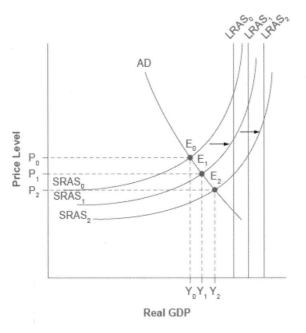

(a) Productivity growth shifts AS to the right

(b) Higher prices for key inputs shifts AS to the left

**Figure 11.7 Shifts in Aggregate Supply** (a) The rise in productivity causes the SRAS curve to shift to the right. The original equilibrium $E_0$ is at the intersection of AD and $SRAS_0$. When SRAS shifts right, then the new equilibrium $E_1$ is at the intersection of AD and $SRAS_1$, and then yet another equilibrium, $E_2$, is at the intersection of AD and $SRAS_2$. Shifts in SRAS to the right, lead to a greater level of output and to downward pressure on the price level. (b) A higher price for inputs means that at any given price level for outputs, a lower real GDP will be produced so aggregate supply will shift to the left from $SRAS_0$ to $SRAS_1$. The new equilibrium, $E_1$, has a reduced quantity of output and a higher price level than the original equilibrium ($E_0$).

A shift in the SRAS curve to the right will result in a greater real GDP and downward pressure on the price level, if aggregate demand remains unchanged. However, if this shift in SRAS results from gains in productivity growth, which we typically measure in terms of a few percentage points per year, the effect will be relatively small over a few months or even a couple of years. Recall how in **Choice in a World of Scarcity**, we said that a nation's production possibilities frontier is fixed in the short run, but shifts out in the long run? This is the same phenomenon using a different model.

## How Changes in Input Prices Shift the AS Curve

Higher prices for inputs that are widely used across the entire economy can have a macroeconomic impact on aggregate supply. Examples of such widely used inputs include labor and energy products. Increases in the price of such inputs will cause the SRAS curve to shift to the left, which means that at each given price level for outputs, a higher price for inputs will discourage production because it will reduce the possibilities for earning profits. **Figure 11.7** (b) shows the aggregate supply curve shifting to the left, from $SRAS_0$ to $SRAS_1$, causing the equilibrium to move from $E_0$ to $E_1$. The movement from the original equilibrium of $E_0$ to the new equilibrium of $E_1$ will bring a nasty set of effects: reduced GDP or recession, higher unemployment because the economy is now further away from potential GDP, and an inflationary higher price level as well. For example, the U.S. economy experienced recessions in 1974–1975, 1980–1982, 1990–91, 2001, and 2007–2009 that were each preceded or accompanied by a rise in the key input of oil prices. In the 1970s, this pattern of a shift to the left in SRAS leading to a stagnant economy with high unemployment and inflation was nicknamed **stagflation**.

Conversely, a decline in the price of a key input like oil will shift the SRAS curve to the right, providing an incentive for more to be produced at every given price level for outputs. From 1985 to 1986, for example, the average price of crude oil fell by almost half, from $24 a barrel to $12 a barrel. Similarly, from 1997 to 1998, the price of a barrel of crude oil dropped from $17 per barrel to $11 per barrel. In both cases, the plummeting oil price led to a situation like that which we presented earlier in **Figure 11.7** (a), where the outward shift of SRAS to the right allowed the economy to expand, unemployment to fall, and inflation to decline.

Along with energy prices, two other key inputs that may shift the SRAS curve are the cost of labor, or wages, and the cost of imported goods that we use as inputs for other products. In these cases as well, the lesson is that lower prices for inputs cause SRAS to shift to the right, while higher prices cause it to shift back to the left. Note that, unlike changes in productivity, changes in input prices do not generally cause LRAS to shift, only SRAS.

### Other Supply Shocks

The aggregate supply curve can also shift due to shocks to input goods or labor. For example, an unexpected early freeze could destroy a large number of agricultural crops, a shock that would shift the AS curve to the left since there would be fewer agricultural products available at any given price.

Similarly, shocks to the labor market can affect aggregate supply. An extreme example might be an overseas war that required a large number of workers to cease their ordinary production in order to go fight for their country. In this case, SRAS and LRAS would both shift to the left because there would be fewer workers available to produce goods at any given price.

# 11.4 | Shifts in Aggregate Demand

By the end of this section, you will be able to:

- Explain how imports influence aggregate demand
- Identify ways in which business confidence and consumer confidence can affect aggregate demand
- Explain how government policy can change aggregate demand
- Evaluate why economists disagree on the topic of tax cuts

As we mentioned previously, the components of aggregate demand are consumption spending (C), investment spending (I), government spending (G), and spending on exports (X) minus imports (M). (Read the following Clear It Up feature for explanation of why imports are subtracted from exports and what this means for aggregate demand.) A shift of the AD curve to the right means that at least one of these components increased so that a greater amount of total spending would occur at every price level. A shift of the AD curve to the left means that at least one of these components decreased so that a lesser amount of total spending would occur at every price level. **The Keynesian Perspective** will discuss the components of aggregate demand and the factors that affect them. Here, the discussion will sketch two broad categories that could cause AD curves to shift: changes in consumer or firm behavior and changes in government tax or spending policy.

## Do imports diminish aggregate demand?

We have seen that the formula for aggregate demand is AD = C + I + G + X - M, where M is the total value of imported goods. Why is there a minus sign in front of imports? Does this mean that more imports will result in a lower level of aggregate demand? The short answer is yes, because aggregate demand is defined as total demand for domestically produced goods and services.

When an American buys a foreign product, for example, it gets counted along with all the other consumption. Thus, the income generated does not go to American producers, but rather to producers in another country. It would be wrong to count this as part of domestic demand. Therefore, imports added in consumption are subtracted back out in the M term of the equation.

Because of the way in which we write the demand equation, it is easy to make the mistake of thinking that imports are bad for the economy. Just keep in mind that every negative number in the M term has a corresponding positive number in the C or I or G term, and they always cancel out.

## How Changes by Consumers and Firms Can Affect AD

When consumers feel more confident about the future of the economy, they tend to consume more. If business confidence is high, then firms tend to spend more on investment, believing that the future payoff from that investment will be substantial. Conversely, if consumer or business confidence drops, then consumption and investment spending decline.

The University of Michigan publishes a survey of consumer confidence and constructs an index of consumer confidence each month. The survey results are then reported at **http://www.sca.isr.umich.edu (http://www.sca.isr.umich.edu/)** , which break down the change in consumer confidence among different income levels. According to that index, consumer confidence averaged around 90 prior to the Great Recession, and then it fell to below 60 in late 2008, which was the lowest it had been since 1980. Since then, confidence has climbed from a 2011 low of 55.8 back to a level in the low 80s, which economists consider close to a healthy state.

The Organization for Economic Development and Cooperation (OECD) publishes one measure of business confidence: the "business tendency surveys". The OECD collects business opinion survey data for 21 countries on future selling prices and employment, among other business climate elements. After sharply declining during the Great Recession, the measure has risen above zero again and is back to long-term averages (the indicator dips below zero when business outlook is weaker than usual). Of course, either of these survey measures is not very precise. They can however, suggest when confidence is rising or falling, as well as when it is relatively high or low compared to the past.

Because economists associate a rise in confidence with higher consumption and investment demand, it will lead to an outward shift in the AD curve, and a move of the equilibrium, from $E_0$ to $E_1$, to a higher quantity of output and a higher price level, as **Figure 11.8** (a) shows.

Consumer and business confidence often reflect macroeconomic realities; for example, confidence is usually high when the economy is growing briskly and low during a recession. However, economic confidence can sometimes rise or fall for reasons that do not have a close connection to the immediate economy, like a risk of war, election results, foreign policy events, or a pessimistic prediction about the future by a prominent public figure. U.S. presidents, for example, must be careful in their public pronouncements about the economy. If they offer economic pessimism, they risk provoking a decline in confidence that reduces consumption and investment and shifts AD to the left, and in a self-fulfilling prophecy, contributes to causing the recession that the president warned against in the first place. **Figure 11.8** (b) shows a shift of AD to the left, and the corresponding movement of the equilibrium, from $E_0$ to $E_1$, to a lower quantity of output and a lower price level.

## Link It Up @

Visit this website (http://openstaxcollege.org/l/consumerconfid) for data on consumer confidence.

## Link It Up @

Visit this website (http://openstaxcollege.org/l/businessconfid) for data on business confidence.

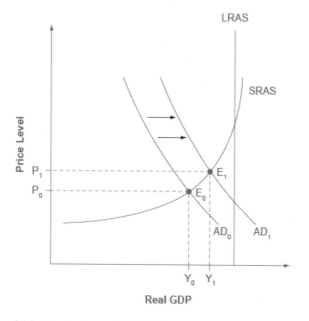

(a) Aggregate demand shifts right

(b) Aggregate demand shifts left

**Figure 11.8 Shifts in Aggregate Demand** (a) An increase in consumer confidence or business confidence can shift AD to the right, from $AD_0$ to $AD_1$. When AD shifts to the right, the new equilibrium ($E_1$) will have a higher quantity of output and also a higher price level compared with the original equilibrium ($E_0$). In this example, the new equilibrium ($E_1$) is also closer to potential GDP. An increase in government spending or a cut in taxes that leads to a rise in consumer spending can also shift AD to the right. (b) A decrease in consumer confidence or business confidence can shift AD to the left, from $AD_0$ to $AD_1$. When AD shifts to the left, the new equilibrium ($E_1$) will have a lower quantity of output and also a lower price level compared with the original equilibrium ($E_0$). In this example, the new equilibrium ($E_1$) is also farther below potential GDP. A decrease in government spending or higher taxes that leads to a fall in consumer spending can also shift AD to the left.

## How Government Macroeconomic Policy Choices Can Shift AD

Government spending is one component of AD. Thus, higher government spending will cause AD to shift to the right, as in **Figure 11.8** (a), while lower government spending will cause AD to shift to the left, as in **Figure 11.8** (b). For example, in the United States, government spending declined by 3.2% of GDP during the 1990s, from 21% of GDP in 1991, and to 17.8% of GDP in 1998. However, from 2005 to 2009, the peak of the Great Recession, government spending increased from 19% of GDP to 21.4% of GDP. If changes of a few percentage points of GDP seem small to you, remember that since GDP was about $14.4 trillion in 2009, a seemingly small change of 2% of GDP is equal to close to $300 billion.

Tax policy can affect consumption and investment spending, too. Tax cuts for individuals will tend to increase consumption demand, while tax increases will tend to diminish it. Tax policy can also pump up investment demand by offering lower tax rates for corporations or tax reductions that benefit specific kinds of investment. Shifting C or I will shift the AD curve as a whole.

During a recession, when unemployment is high and many businesses are suffering low profits or even losses, the U.S. Congress often passes tax cuts. During the 2001 recession, for example, the U.S. Congress enacted a tax cut into law. At such times, the political rhetoric often focuses on how people experiencing hard times need relief from taxes. The aggregate supply and aggregate demand framework, however, offers a complementary rationale, as **Figure 11.9** illustrates. The original equilibrium during a recession is at point $E_0$, relatively far from the full employment level of output. The tax cut, by increasing consumption, shifts the AD curve to the right. At the new equilibrium ($E_1$), real GDP rises and unemployment falls and, because in this diagram the economy has not yet reached its potential or full employment level of GDP, any rise in the price level remains muted. Read the following Clear It Up feature to consider the question of whether economists favor tax cuts or oppose them.

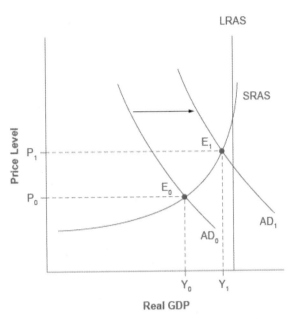

**Figure 11.9 Recession and Full Employment in the AD/AS Model** Whether the economy is in a recession is illustrated in the AD/AS model by how close the equilibrium is to the potential GDP line as indicated by the vertical LRAS line. In this example, the level of output $Y_0$ at the equilibrium $E_0$ is relatively far from the potential GDP line, so it can represent an economy in recession, well below the full employment level of GDP. In contrast, the level of output $Y_1$ at the equilibrium $E_1$ is relatively close to potential GDP, and so it would represent an economy with a lower unemployment rate.

# Clear It Up

## Do economists favor tax cuts or oppose them?

One of the most fundamental divisions in American politics over the last few decades has been between those who believe that the government should cut taxes substantially and those who disagree. Ronald Reagan rode into the presidency in 1980 partly because of his promise, soon carried out, to enact a substantial tax cut. George Bush lost his bid for reelection against Bill Clinton in 1992 partly because he had broken his 1988 promise: "Read my lips! No new taxes!" In the 2000 presidential election, both George W. Bush and Al Gore advocated substantial tax cuts and Bush succeeded in pushing a tax cut package through Congress early in 2001. More recently in 2017, Donald Trump has pushed for tax cuts to stimulate the economy. Disputes over tax cuts often ignite at the state and local level as well.

What side do economists take? Do they support broad tax cuts or oppose them? The answer, unsatisfying to zealots on both sides, is that it depends. One issue is whether equally large government spending cuts accompany the tax cuts. Economists differ, as does any broad cross-section of the public, on how large government spending should be and what programs the government might cut back. A second issue, more relevant to the discussion in this chapter, concerns how close the economy is to the full employment output level. In a recession, when the AD and AS curves intersect far below the full employment level, tax cuts can make sense as a way of shifting AD to the right. However, when the economy is already performing extremely well, tax cuts may shift AD so far to the right as to generate inflationary pressures, with little gain to GDP.

With the AD/AS framework in mind, many economists might readily believe that the 1981 Reagan tax cuts, which took effect just after two serious recessions, were beneficial economic policy. Similarly, Congress enacted the 2001 Bush tax cuts and the 2009 Obama tax cuts during recessions. However, some of the same economists who favor tax cuts during recession would be much more dubious about identical tax cuts at a time the economy is performing well and cyclical unemployment is low.

Government spending and tax rate changes can be useful tools to affect aggregate demand. We will discuss these in greater detail in the **Government Budgets and Fiscal Policy** chapter and **The Impacts of Government Borrowing**. Other policy tools can shift the aggregate demand curve as well. For example, as we will discus in the **Monetary Policy and Bank Regulation** chapter, the Federal Reserve can affect interest rates and credit availability. Higher interest rates tend to discourage borrowing and thus reduce both household spending on big-ticket items like houses and cars and investment spending by business. Conversely, lower interest rates will stimulate consumption and investment demand. Interest rates can also affect exchange rates, which in turn will have effects on the export and import components of aggregate demand.

Clarifying the details of these alternative policies and how they affect the components of aggregate demand can wait for **The Keynesian Perspective** chapter. Here, the key lesson is that a shift of the aggregate demand curve to the right leads to a greater real GDP and to upward pressure on the price level. Conversely, a shift of aggregate demand to the left leads to a lower real GDP and a lower price level. Whether these changes in output and price level are relatively large or relatively small, and how the change in equilibrium relates to potential GDP, depends on whether the shift in the AD curve is happening in the AS curve's relatively flat or relatively steep portion.

# 11.5 | How the AD/AS Model Incorporates Growth, Unemployment, and Inflation

By the end of this section, you will be able to:
- Use the aggregate demand/aggregate supply model to show periods of economic growth and recession
- Explain how unemployment and inflation impact the aggregate demand/aggregate supply model
- Evaluate the importance of the aggregate demand/aggregate supply model

The AD/AS model can convey a number of interlocking relationships between the three macroeconomic goals of growth, unemployment, and low inflation. Moreover, the AD/AS framework is flexible enough to accommodate both the Keynes' law approach that focuses on aggregate demand and the short run, while also including the Say's law approach that focuses on aggregate supply and the long run. These advantages are considerable. Every model is a simplified version of the deeper reality and, in the context of the AD/AS model, the three macroeconomic goals arise in ways that are sometimes indirect or incomplete. In this module, we consider how the AD/AS model illustrates the three macroeconomic goals of economic growth, low unemployment, and low inflation.

## Growth and Recession in the AD/AS Diagram

In the AD/AS diagram, long-run economic growth due to productivity increases over time will be represented by a gradual shift to the right of aggregate supply. The vertical line representing potential GDP (or the "full employment level of GDP") will gradually shift to the right over time as well. Earlier **Figure 11.7** (a) showed a pattern of economic growth over three years, with the AS curve shifting slightly out to the right each year. However, the factors that determine the speed of this long-term economic growth rate—like investment in physical and human capital, technology, and whether an economy can take advantage of catch-up growth—do not appear directly in the AD/AS diagram.

In the short run, GDP falls and rises in every economy, as the economy dips into recession or expands out of recession.

The AD/AS diagram illustrates recessions when the equilibrium level of real GDP is substantially below potential GDP, as we see at the equilibrium point $E_0$ in **Figure 11.9**. From another standpoint, in years of resurgent economic growth the equilibrium will typically be close to potential GDP, as equilibrium point $E_1$ in that earlier figure shows.

## Unemployment in the AD/AS Diagram

We described two types of unemployment in the **Unemployment** chapter. Short run variations in unemployment (cyclical unemployment) are caused by the business cycle as the economy expands and contracts. Over the long run, in the United States, the unemployment rate typically hovers around 5% (give or take one percentage point or so), when the economy is healthy. In many of the national economies across Europe, the unemployment rate in recent decades has only dropped to about 10% or a bit lower, even in good economic years. We call this baseline level of unemployment that occurs year-in and year-out the natural rate of unemployment and we determine it by how well the structures of market and government institutions in the economy lead to a matching of workers and employers in the labor market. Potential GDP can imply different unemployment rates in different economies, depending on the natural rate of unemployment for that economy.

The AD/AS diagram shows cyclical unemployment by how close the economy is to the potential or full GDP employment level. Returning to **Figure 11.9**, relatively low cyclical unemployment for an economy occurs when the level of output is close to potential GDP, as in the equilibrium point $E_1$. Conversely, high cyclical unemployment arises when the output is substantially to the left of potential GDP on the AD/AS diagram, as at the equilibrium point $E_0$. Although we do not show the factors that determine the natural rate of unemployment separately in the AD/AS model, they are implicitly part of what determines potential GDP or full employment GDP in a given economy.

## Inflationary Pressures in the AD/AS Diagram

Inflation fluctuates in the short run. Higher inflation rates have typically occurred either during or just after economic booms: for example, the biggest spurts of inflation in the U.S. economy during the twentieth century followed the wartime booms of World War I and World War II. Conversely, rates of inflation generally decline during recessions. As an extreme example, inflation actually became negative—a situation called "deflation"—during the Great Depression. Even during the relatively short 1991-1992 recession, the inflation rate declined from 5.4% in 1990 to 3.0% in 1992. During the relatively short 2001 recession, the rate of inflation declined from 3.4% in 2000 to 1.6% in 2002. During the deep recession of 2007–2009, the inflation rate declined from 3.8% in 2008 to –0.4% in 2009. Some countries have experienced bouts of high inflation that lasted for years. In the U.S. economy since the mid–1980s, inflation does not seem to have had any long-term trend to be substantially higher. Instead, it has stayed in the 1–5% range annually.

The AD/AS framework implies two ways that inflationary pressures may arise. One possible trigger is if aggregate demand continues to shift to the right when the economy is already at or near potential GDP and full employment, thus pushing the macroeconomic equilibrium into the AS curve's steep portion. In **Figure 11.10** (a), there is a shift of aggregate demand to the right. The new equilibrium $E_1$ is clearly at a higher price level than the original equilibrium $E_0$. In this situation, the aggregate demand in the economy has soared so high that firms in the economy are not capable of producing additional goods, because labor and physical capital are fully employed, and so additional increases in aggregate demand can only result in a rise in the price level.

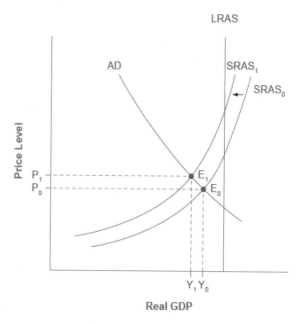

(a) Inflationary pressure from a shift in AD

(b) Inflationary pressure from a shift in AS

**Figure 11.10 Sources of Inflationary Pressure in the AD/AS Model** (a) A shift in aggregate demand, from $AD_0$ to $AD_1$, when it happens in the area of the SRAS curve that is near potential GDP, will lead to a higher price level and to pressure for a higher price level and inflation. The new equilibrium (E1) is at a higher price level (P1) than the original equilibrium. (b) A shift in aggregate supply, from $SRAS_0$ to $SRAS_1$, will lead to a lower real GDP and to pressure for a higher price level and inflation. The new equilibrium ($E_1$) is at a higher price level ($P_1$), while the original equilibrium ($E_0$) is at the lower price level ($P_0$).

An alternative source of inflationary pressures can occur due to a rise in input prices that affects many or most firms across the economy—perhaps an important input to production like oil or labor—and causes the aggregate supply curve to shift back to the left. In **Figure 11.10** (b), the SRAS curve's shift to the left also increases the price level from $P_0$ at the original equilibrium ($E_0$) to a higher price level of $P_1$ at the new equilibrium ($E_1$). In effect, the rise in input prices ends up, after the final output is produced and sold, passing along in the form of a higher price level for outputs.

The AD/AS diagram shows only a one-time shift in the price level. It does not address the question of what would cause inflation either to vanish after a year, or to sustain itself for several years. There are two explanations for why inflation may persist over time. One way that continual inflationary price increases can occur is if the government continually attempts to stimulate aggregate demand in a way that keeps pushing the AD curve when it is already in the SRAS curve's steep portion. A second possibility is that, if inflation has been occurring for several years, people might begin to expect a certain level of inflation. If they do, then these expectations will cause prices, wages and interest rates to increase annually by the amount of the inflation expected. These two reasons are interrelated, because if a government fosters a macroeconomic environment with inflationary pressures, then people will grow to expect inflation. However, the AD/AS diagram does not show these patterns of ongoing or expected inflation in a direct way.

## Importance of the Aggregate Demand/Aggregate Supply Model

Macroeconomics takes an overall view of the economy, which means that it needs to juggle many different concepts. For example, start with the three macroeconomic goals of growth, low inflation, and unemployment. Aggregate demand has four elements: consumption, investment, government spending, and exports less imports. Aggregate supply reveals how businesses throughout the economy will react to a higher price level for outputs. Finally, a wide array of economic events and policy decisions can affect aggregate demand and aggregate supply, including government tax and spending decisions; consumer and business confidence; changes in prices of key inputs like oil; and technology that brings higher levels of productivity.

The aggregate demand/aggregate supply model is one of the fundamental diagrams in this course (like the budget constraint diagram that we introduced in the **Choice in a World of Scarcity** chapter and the supply and demand diagram in the **Demand and Supply** chapter) because it provides an overall framework for bringing these factors together in one diagram. Some version of the AD/AS model will appear in every chapter in the rest of this book.

# 11.6 | Keynes' Law and Say's Law in the AD/AS Model

By the end of this section, you will be able to:
- Identify the neoclassical zone, the intermediate zone, and the Keynesian zone in the aggregate demand/aggregate supply model
- Use an aggregate demand/aggregate supply model as a diagnostic test to understand the current state of the economy

We can use the AD/AS model to illustrate both Say's law that supply creates its own demand and Keynes' law that demand creates its own supply. Consider the SRAS curve's three zones which **Figure 11.11** identifies: the Keynesian zone, the neoclassical zone, and the intermediate zone.

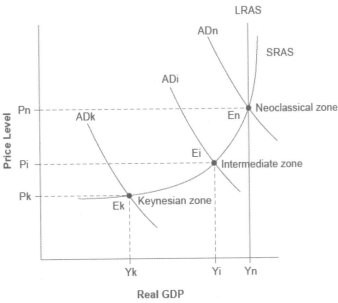

**Figure 11.11 Keynes, Neoclassical, and Intermediate Zones in the Aggregate Supply Curve** Near the equilibrium Ek, in the Keynesian zone at the far left of the SRAS curve, small shifts in AD, either to the right or the left, will affect the output level Yk, but will not much affect the price level. In the Keynesian zone, AD largely determines the quantity of output. Near the equilibrium En, in the neoclassical zone at the SRAS curve's far right, small shifts in AD, either to the right or the left, will have relatively little effect on the output level Yn, but instead will have a greater effect on the price level. In the neoclassical zone, the near-vertical SRAS curve close to the level of potential GDP largely determines the quantity of output. In the intermediate zone around equilibrium Ei, movement in AD to the right will increase both the output level and the price level, while a movement in AD to the left would decrease both the output level and the price level.

Focus first on the **Keynesian zone**, that portion of the SRAS curve on the far left which is relatively flat. If the AD curve crosses this portion of the SRAS curve at an equilibrium point like Ek, then certain statements about the economic situation will follow. In the Keynesian zone, the equilibrium level of real GDP is far below potential GDP, the economy is in recession, and cyclical unemployment is high. If aggregate demand shifted to the right or left in the Keynesian zone, it will determine the resulting level of output (and thus unemployment). However, inflationary price pressure is not much of a worry in the Keynesian zone, since the price level does not vary much in this zone.

Now, focus your attention on the **neoclassical zone** of the SRAS curve, which is the near-vertical portion on the right-hand side. If the AD curve crosses this portion of the SRAS curve at an equilibrium point like En where output is at or near potential GDP, then the size of potential GDP pretty much determines the level of output in the economy.

Since the equilibrium is near potential GDP, cyclical unemployment is low in this economy, although structural unemployment may remain an issue. In the neoclassical zone, shifts of aggregate demand to the right or the left have little effect on the level of output or employment. The only way to increase the size of the real GDP in the neoclassical zone is for AS to shift to the right. However, shifts in AD in the neoclassical zone will create pressures to change the price level.

Finally, consider the SRAS curve's **intermediate zone** in **Figure 11.11**. If the AD curve crosses this portion of the SRAS curve at an equilibrium point like Ei, then we might expect unemployment and inflation to move in opposing directions. For instance, a shift of AD to the right will move output closer to potential GDP and thus reduce unemployment, but will also lead to a higher price level and upward pressure on inflation. Conversely, a shift of AD to the left will move output further from potential GDP and raise unemployment, but will also lead to a lower price level and downward pressure on inflation.

This approach of dividing the SRAS curve into different zones works as a diagnostic test that we can apply to an economy, like a doctor checking a patient for symptoms. First, figure out in what zone the economy is. This will clarify the economic issues, tradeoffs, and policy choices. Some economists believe that the economy is strongly predisposed to be in one zone or another. Thus, hard-line Keynesian economists believe that the economies are in the Keynesian zone most of the time, and so they view the neoclassical zone as a theoretical abstraction. Conversely, hard-line neoclassical economists argue that economies are in the neoclassical zone most of the time and that the Keynesian zone is a distraction. **The Keynesian Perspective** and **The Neoclassical Perspective** should help to clarify the underpinnings and consequences of these contrasting views of the macroeconomy.

## Bring it Home

### From Housing Bubble to Housing Bust

We can explain economic fluctuations, whether those experienced during the 1930s Great Depression, the 1970s stagflation, or the 2008-2009 Great Recession, can be explained using the AD/AS diagram. Short-run fluctuations in output occur due to shifts of the SRAS curve, the AD curve, or both. In the case of the housing bubble, rising home values caused the AD curve to shift to the right as more people felt that rising home values increased their overall wealth. Many homeowners took on mortgages that exceeded their ability to pay because, as home values continued to rise, the increased value would pay off any debt outstanding. Increased wealth due to rising home values lead to increased home equity loans and increased spending. All these activities pushed AD to the right, contributing to low unemployment rates and economic growth in the United States. When the housing bubble burst, overall wealth dropped dramatically, wiping out the recent gains. This drop in home values was a demand shock to the U.S. economy because of its impact directly on the wealth of the household sector, and its contagion into the financial that essentially locked up new credit. The AD curve shifted to the left as evidenced by the Great Recession's rising unemployment.

Understanding the source of these macroeconomic fluctuations provided monetary and fiscal policy makers with insight about what policy actions to take to mitigate the impact of the housing crisis. From a monetary policy perspective, the Federal Reserve lowered short-term interest rates to between 0% and 0.25 %, to loosen up credit throughout the financial system. Discretionary fiscal policy measures included the passage of the Emergency Economic Stabilization Act of 2008 that allowed for the purchase of troubled assets, such as mortgages, from financial institutions and the American Recovery and Reinvestment Act of 2009 that increased government spending on infrastructure, provided for tax cuts, and increased transfer payments. In combination, both monetary and fiscal policy measures were designed to help stimulate aggregate demand in the U.S. economy, pushing the AD curve to the right.

While most economists agree on the usefulness of the AD/AS diagram in analyzing the sources of these fluctuations, there is still some disagreement about the effectiveness of policy decisions that are useful in stabilizing these fluctuations. We discuss the possible policy actions and the differences among economists about their effectiveness in more detail in **The Keynesian Perspective**, **Monetary Policy and Bank Regulation**, and **Government Budgets and Fiscal Policy**.

# KEY TERMS

**aggregate demand (AD)**  the amount of total spending on domestic goods and services in an economy

**aggregate demand (AD) curve**  the total spending on domestic goods and services at each price level

**aggregate demand/aggregate supply model**  a model that shows what determines total supply or total demand for the economy, and how total demand and total supply interact at the macroeconomic level

**aggregate supply (AS)**  the total quantity of output (i.e. real GDP) firms will produce and sell

**aggregate supply (AS) curve**  the total quantity of output (i.e. real GDP) that firms will produce and sell at each price level

**full-employment GDP**  another name for potential GDP, when the economy is producing at its potential and unemployment is at the natural rate of unemployment

**intermediate zone**  portion of the SRAS curve where GDP is below potential but not so far below as in the Keynesian zone; the SRAS curve is upward-sloping, but not vertical in the intermediate zone

**Keynesian zone**  portion of the SRAS curve where GDP is far below potential and the SRAS curve is flat

**Keynes' law**  "demand creates its own supply"

**long run aggregate supply (LRAS) curve**  vertical line at potential GDP showing no relationship between the price level for output and real GDP in the long run

**neoclassical economists**  economists who generally emphasize the importance of aggregate supply in determining the size of the macroeconomy over the long run

**neoclassical zone**  portion of the SRAS curve where GDP is at or near potential output where the SRAS curve is steep

**potential GDP**  the maximum quantity that an economy can produce given full employment of its existing levels of labor, physical capital, technology, and institutions

**Say's law**  "supply creates its own demand"

**short run aggregate supply (SRAS) curve**  positive short run relationship between the price level for output and real GDP, holding the prices of inputs fixed

**stagflation**  an economy experiences stagnant growth and high inflation at the same time

# KEY CONCEPTS AND SUMMARY

### 11.1 Macroeconomic Perspectives on Demand and Supply
Neoclassical economists emphasize Say's law, which holds that supply creates its own demand. Keynesian economists emphasize Keynes' law, which holds that demand creates its own supply. Many mainstream economists take a Keynesian perspective, emphasizing the importance of aggregate demand, for the short run, and a neoclassical perspective, emphasizing the importance of aggregate supply, for the long run.

### 11.2 Building a Model of Aggregate Demand and Aggregate Supply
The upward-sloping short run aggregate supply (SRAS) curve shows the positive relationship between the price level and the level of real GDP in the short run. Aggregate supply slopes up because when the price level for outputs increases, while the price level of inputs remains fixed, the opportunity for additional profits encourages more production. The aggregate supply curve is near-horizontal on the left and near-vertical on the right. In the long run,

we show the aggregate supply by a vertical line at the level of potential output, which is the maximum level of output the economy can produce with its existing levels of workers, physical capital, technology, and economic institutions.

The downward-sloping aggregate demand (AD) curve shows the relationship between the price level for outputs and the quantity of total spending in the economy. It slopes down because of: (a) the wealth effect, which means that a higher price level leads to lower real wealth, which reduces the level of consumption; (b) the interest rate effect, which holds that a higher price level will mean a greater demand for money, which will tend to drive up interest rates and reduce investment spending; and (c) the foreign price effect, which holds that a rise in the price level will make domestic goods relatively more expensive, discouraging exports and encouraging imports.

## 11.3 Shifts in Aggregate Supply

The aggregate demand/aggregate supply (AD/AS) diagram shows how AD and AS interact. The intersection of the AD and AS curves shows the equilibrium output and price level in the economy. Movements of either AS or AD will result in a different equilibrium output and price level. The aggregate supply curve will shift out to the right as productivity increases. It will shift back to the left as the price of key inputs rises, and will shift out to the right if the price of key inputs falls. If the AS curve shifts back to the left, the combination of lower output, higher unemployment, and higher inflation, called stagflation, occurs. If AS shifts out to the right, a combination of lower inflation, higher output, and lower unemployment is possible.

## 11.4 Shifts in Aggregate Demand

The AD curve will shift out as the components of aggregate demand—C, I, G, and X–M—rise. It will shift back to the left as these components fall. These factors can change because of different personal choices, like those resulting from consumer or business confidence, or from policy choices like changes in government spending and taxes. If the AD curve shifts to the right, then the equilibrium quantity of output and the price level will rise. If the AD curve shifts to the left, then the equilibrium quantity of output and the price level will fall. Whether equilibrium output changes relatively more than the price level or whether the price level changes relatively more than output is determined by where the AD curve intersects with the AS curve.

The AD/AS diagram superficially resembles the microeconomic supply and demand diagram on the surface, but in reality, what is on the horizontal and vertical axes and the underlying economic reasons for the shapes of the curves are very different. We can illustrate long-term economic growth in the AD/AS framework by a gradual shift of the aggregate supply curve to the right. We illustrate a recession when the intersection of AD and AS is substantially below potential GDP, while we illustrate an expanding economy when the intersection of AS and AD is near potential GDP.

## 11.5 How the AD/AS Model Incorporates Growth, Unemployment, and Inflation

Cyclical unemployment is relatively large in the AD/AS framework when the equilibrium is substantially below potential GDP. Cyclical unemployment is small in the AD/AS framework when the equilibrium is near potential GDP. The natural rate of unemployment, as determined by the labor market institutions of the economy, is built into what economists mean by potential GDP, but does not otherwise appear in an AD/AS diagram. The AD/AS framework shows pressures for inflation to rise or fall when the movement from one equilibrium to another causes the price level to rise or to fall. The balance of trade does not appear directly in the AD/AS diagram, but it appears indirectly in several ways. Increases in exports or declines in imports can cause shifts in AD. Changes in the price of key imported inputs to production, like oil, can cause shifts in AS. The AD/AS model is the key model we use in this book to understand macroeconomic issues.

## 11.6 Keynes' Law and Say's Law in the AD/AS Model

We can divide the SRAS curve into three zones. Keynes' law says demand creates its own supply, so that changes in aggregate demand cause changes in real GDP and employment. We can show Keynes' law on the horizontal Keynesian zone of the aggregate supply curve. The Keynesian zone occurs at the left of the SRAS curve where it is fairly flat, so movements in AD will affect output, but have little effect on the price level. Say's law says supply creates its own demand. Changes in aggregate demand have no effect on real GDP and employment, only on the price level. We can show Say's law on the vertical neoclassical zone of the aggregate supply curve. The neoclassical zone occurs at the right of the SRAS curve where it is fairly vertical, and so movements in AD will affect the price level, but have little impact on output. The intermediate zone in the middle of the SRAS curve is upward-sloping, so a rise in AD will cause higher output and price level, while a fall in AD will lead to a lower output and price level.

## SELF-CHECK QUESTIONS

**1.** Describe the mechanism by which supply creates its own demand.

**2.** Describe the mechanism by which demand creates its own supply.

**3.** The short run aggregate supply curve was constructed assuming that as the price of outputs increases, the price of inputs stays the same. How would an increase in the prices of important inputs, like energy, affect aggregate supply?

**4.** In the AD/AS model, what prevents the economy from achieving equilibrium at potential output?

**5.** Suppose the U.S. Congress passes significant immigration reform that makes it more difficult for foreigners to come to the United States to work. Use the AD/AS model to explain how this would affect the equilibrium level of GDP and the price level.

**6.** Suppose concerns about the size of the federal budget deficit lead the U.S. Congress to cut all funding for research and development for ten years. Assuming this has an impact on technology growth, what does the AD/AS model predict would be the likely effect on equilibrium GDP and the price level?

**7.** How would a dramatic increase in the value of the stock market shift the AD curve? What effect would the shift have on the equilibrium level of GDP and the price level?

**8.** Suppose Mexico, one of our largest trading partners and purchaser of a large quantity of our exports, goes into a recession. Use the AD/AS model to determine the likely impact on our equilibrium GDP and price level.

**9.** A policymaker claims that tax cuts led the economy out of a recession. Can we use the AD/AS diagram to show this?

**10.** Many financial analysts and economists eagerly await the press releases for the reports on the home price index and consumer confidence index. What would be the effects of a negative report on both of these? What about a positive report?

**11.** What impact would a decrease in the size of the labor force have on GDP and the price level according to the AD/AS model?

**12.** Suppose, after five years of sluggish growth, the European Union's economy picks up speed. What would be the likely impact on the U.S. trade balance, GDP, and employment?

**13.** Suppose the Federal Reserve begins to increase the supply of money at an increasing rate. What impact would that have on GDP, unemployment, and inflation?

**14.** If the economy is operating in the neoclassical zone of the SRAS curve and aggregate demand falls, what is likely to happen to real GDP?

**15.** If the economy is operating in the Keynesian zone of the SRAS curve and aggregate demand falls, what is likely to happen to real GDP?

## REVIEW QUESTIONS

**16.** What is Say's law?

**17.** What is Keynes' law?

**18.** Do neoclassical economists believe in Keynes' law or Say's law?

**19.** Does Say's law apply more accurately in the long run or the short run? What about Keynes' law?

**20.** What is on the horizontal axis of the AD/AS diagram? What is on the vertical axis?

**21.** What is the economic reason why the SRAS curve slopes up?

**22.** What are the components of the aggregate demand (AD) curve?

**23.** What are the economic reasons why the AD curve slopes down?

**24.** Briefly explain the reason for the near-horizontal shape of the SRAS curve on its far left.

**25.** Briefly explain the reason for the near-vertical shape of the SRAS curve on its far right.

**26.** What is potential GDP?

**27.** Name some factors that could cause the SRAS curve to shift, and say whether they would shift SRAS to the right or to the left.

**28.** Will the shift of SRAS to the right tend to make the equilibrium quantity and price level higher or lower? What about a shift of SRAS to the left?

**29.** What is stagflation?

**30.** Name some factors that could cause AD to shift, and say whether they would shift AD to the right or to the left.

**31.** Would a shift of AD to the right tend to make the equilibrium quantity and price level higher or lower? What about a shift of AD to the left?

**32.** How is long-term growth illustrated in an AD/AS model?

**33.** How is recession illustrated in an AD/AS model?

**34.** How is cyclical unemployment illustrated in an AD/AS model?

**35.** How is the natural rate of unemployment illustrated in an AD/AS model?

**36.** How is pressure for inflationary price increases shown in an AD/AS model?

**37.** What are some of the ways in which exports and imports can affect the AD/AS model?

**38.** What is the Keynesian zone of the SRAS curve? How much is the price level likely to change in the Keynesian zone?

**39.** What is the neoclassical zone of the SRAS curve? How much is the output level likely to change in the neoclassical zone?

**40.** What is the intermediate zone of the SRAS curve? Will a rise in output be accompanied by a rise or a fall in the price level in this zone?

# CRITICAL THINKING QUESTIONS

**41.** Why would an economist choose either the neoclassical perspective or the Keynesian perspective, but not both?

**42.** On a microeconomic demand curve, a decrease in price causes an increase in quantity demanded because the product in question is now relatively less expensive than substitute products. Explain why aggregate demand does not increase for the same reason in response to a decrease in the aggregate price level. In other words, what causes total spending to increase if it is not because goods are now cheaper?

**43.** Economists expect that as the labor market continues to tighten going into the latter part of 2015 that workers should begin to expect wage increases in 2015 and 2016. Assuming this occurs and it was the only development in the labor market that year, how would this affect the AS curve? What if it was also accompanied by an increase in worker productivity?

**44.** If new government regulations require firms to use a cleaner technology that is also less efficient than what they previously used, what would the effect be on output, the price level, and employment using the AD/AS diagram?

**45.** During spring 2016 the Midwestern United States, which has a large agricultural base, experiences above-average rainfall. Using the AD/AS diagram, what is the effect on output, the price level, and employment?

**46.** Hydraulic fracturing (fracking) has the potential to significantly increase the amount of natural gas produced in the United States. If a large percentage of factories and utility companies use natural gas, what will happen to output, the price level, and employment as fracking becomes more widely used?

**47.** Some politicians have suggested tying the minimum wage to the consumer price index (CPI). Using the AD/AS diagram, what effects would this policy most likely have on output, the price level, and employment?

**48.** If households decide to save a larger portion of their income, what effect would this have on the output, employment, and price level in the short run? What about the long run?

**49.** If firms become more optimistic about the future of the economy and, at the same time, innovation in 3-D printing makes most workers more productive, what is the combined effect on output, employment, and the price-level?

**50.** If Congress cuts taxes at the same time that businesses become more pessimistic about the economy, what is the combined effect on output, the price level, and employment using the AD/AS diagram?

**51.** Suppose the level of structural unemployment increases. How would you illustrate the increase in structural unemployment in the AD/AS model? *Hint*: How does structural unemployment affect potential GDP?

**52.** If foreign wealth-holders decide that the United States is the safest place to invest their savings, what would the effect be on the economy here? Show graphically using the AD/AS model.

**53.** The AD/AS model is static. It shows a snapshot of the economy at a given point in time. Both economic growth and inflation are dynamic phenomena. Suppose economic growth is 3% per year and aggregate demand is growing at the same rate. What does the AD/AS model say the inflation rate should be?

**54.** Explain why the short-run aggregate supply curve might be fairly flat in the Keynesian zone of the SRAS curve. How might we tell if we are in the Keynesian zone of the AS?

**55.** Explain why the short-run aggregate supply curve might be vertical in the neoclassical zone of the SRAS curve. How might we tell if we are in the neoclassical zone of the AS?

**56.** Why might it be important for policymakers to know which in zone of the SRAS curve the economy is?

**57.** In your view, is the economy currently operating in the Keynesian, intermediate or neoclassical portion of the economy's aggregate supply curve?

**58.** Are Say's law and Keynes' law necessarily mutually exclusive?

# PROBLEMS

**59.** Review the problem in the **Work It Out** titled "Interpreting the AD/AS Model." Like the information provided in that feature, **Table 11.2** shows information on aggregate supply, aggregate demand, and the price level for the imaginary country of Xurbia.

| Price Level | AD | AS |
|---|---|---|
| 110 | 700 | 600 |
| 120 | 690 | 640 |
| 130 | 680 | 680 |
| 140 | 670 | 720 |
| 150 | 660 | 740 |
| 160 | 650 | 760 |
| 170 | 640 | 770 |

Table 11.2 Price Level: AD/AS

a. Plot the AD/AS diagram from the data. Identify the equilibrium.
b. Imagine that, as a result of a government tax cut, aggregate demand becomes higher by 50 at every price level. Identify the new equilibrium.
c. How will the new equilibrium alter output? How will it alter the price level? What do you think will happen to employment?

**60.** The imaginary country of Harris Island has the aggregate supply and aggregate demand curves as **Table 11.3** shows.

| Price Level | AD | AS |
|---|---|---|
| 100 | 700 | 200 |
| 120 | 600 | 325 |
| 140 | 500 | 500 |
| 160 | 400 | 570 |
| 180 | 300 | 620 |

Table 11.3 Price Level: AD/AS

a. Plot the AD/AS diagram. Identify the equilibrium.
b. Would you expect unemployment in this economy to be relatively high or low?
c. Would you expect concern about inflation in this economy to be relatively high or low?
d. Imagine that consumers begin to lose confidence about the state of the economy, and so AD becomes lower by 275 at every price level. Identify the new aggregate equilibrium.
e. How will the shift in AD affect the original output, price level, and employment?

**61.** Table 11.4 describes Santher's economy.

| Price Level | AD | AS |
|---|---|---|
| 50 | 1,000 | 250 |
| 60 | 950 | 580 |
| 70 | 900 | 750 |
| 80 | 850 | 850 |
| 90 | 800 | 900 |

Table 11.4 Price Level: AD/AS

a. Plot the AD/AS curves and identify the equilibrium.

b. Would you expect unemployment in this economy to be relatively high or low?

c. Would you expect prices to be a relatively large or small concern for this economy?

d. Imagine that input prices fall and so AS shifts to the right by 150 units. Identify the new equilibrium.

e. How will the shift in AS affect the original output, price level, and employment?

# 12 | The Keynesian Perspective

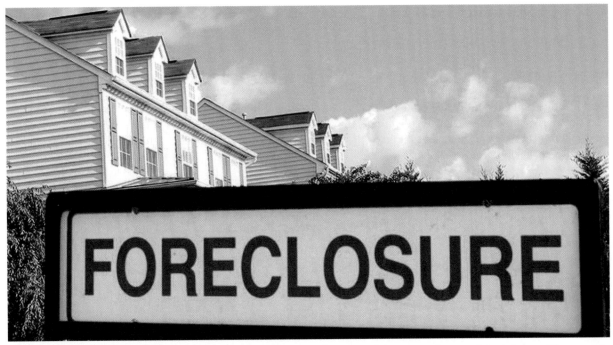

**Figure 12.1 Signs of a Recession** Home foreclosures were just one of the many signs and symptoms of the recent Great Recession. During that time, many businesses closed and many people lost their jobs. (Credit: modification of work by Taber Andrew Bain/Flickr Creative Commons)

## Bring it Home

### The Great Recession

The 2008-2009 Great Recession hit the U.S. economy hard. According to the Bureau of Labor Statistics (BLS), the number of unemployed Americans rose from 6.8 million in May 2007 to 15.4 million in October 2009. During that time, the U.S. Census Bureau estimated that approximately 170,000 small businesses closed. Mass layoffs peaked in February 2009 when employers gave 326,392 workers notice. U.S. productivity and output fell as well. Job losses, declining home values, declining incomes, and uncertainty about the future caused consumption expenditures to decrease. According to the BLS, household spending dropped by 7.8%.

Home foreclosures and the meltdown in U.S. financial markets called for immediate action by Congress, the President, and the Federal Reserve Bank. For example, the government implemented programs such as the American Restoration and Recovery Act to help millions of people by providing tax credits for homebuyers, paying "cash for clunkers," and extending unemployment benefits. From cutting back on spending, filing for unemployment, and losing homes, millions of people were affected by the recession. While the United States is now on the path to recovery, people will feel the impact for many years to come.

What caused this recession and what prevented the economy from spiraling further into another depression? Policymakers looked to the lessons learned from the 1930s Great Depression and to John Maynard Keynes' models to analyze the causes and find solutions to the country's economic woes. The Keynesian perspective is the subject of this chapter.

# Introduction to the Keynesian Perspective

In this chapter, you will learn about:

- Aggregate Demand in Keynesian Analysis

- The Building Blocks of Keynesian Analysis

- The Phillips Curve

- The Keynesian Perspective on Market Forces

We have learned that the level of economic activity, for example output, employment, and spending, tends to grow over time. In **The Keynesian Perspective** we learned the reasons for this trend. **The Macroeconomic Perspective** pointed out that the economy tends to cycle around the long-run trend. In other words, the economy does not always grow at its average growth rate. Sometimes economic activity grows at the trend rate, sometimes it grows more than the trend, sometimes it grows less than the trend, and sometimes it actually declines. You can see this cyclical behavior in **Figure 12.2**.

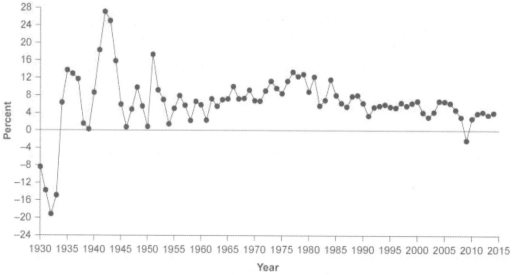

**Figure 12.2 U.S. Gross Domestic Product, Percent Changes 1930–2014** The chart tracks the percent change in GDP since 1930. The magnitude of both recessions and peaks was quite large between 1930 and 1945. (Source: Bureau of Economic Analysis, "National Economic Accounts")

This empirical reality raises two important questions: How can we explain the cycles, and to what extent can we moderate them? This chapter (on the Keynesian perspective) and **The Neoclassical Perspective** explore those questions from two different points of view, building on what we learned in **The Aggregate Demand/Aggregate Supply Model**.

# 12.1 | Aggregate Demand in Keynesian Analysis

By the end of this section, you will be able to:
- Explain real GDP, recessionary gaps, and inflationary gaps
- Recognize the Keynesian AD/AS model
- Identify the determining factors of both consumption expenditure and investment expenditure
- Analyze the factors that determine government spending and net exports

The Keynesian perspective focuses on aggregate demand. The idea is simple: firms produce output only if they expect it to sell. Thus, while the availability of the factors of production determines a nation's potential GDP, the amount of goods and services that actually sell, known as **real GDP**, depends on how much demand exists across the economy. **Figure 12.3** illustrates this point.

**Figure 12.3 The Keynesian AD/AS Model** The Keynesian View of the AD/AS Model uses an SRAS curve, which is horizontal at levels of output below potential and vertical at potential output. Thus, when beginning from potential output, any decrease in AD affects only output, but not prices. Any increase in AD affects only prices, not output.

Keynes argued that, for reasons we explain shortly, aggregate demand is not stable—that it can change unexpectedly. Suppose the economy starts where AD intersects SRAS at $P_0$ and Yp. Because Yp is potential output, the economy is at full employment. Because AD is volatile, it can easily fall. Thus, even if we start at Yp, if AD falls, then we find ourselves in what Keynes termed a **recessionary gap**. The economy is in equilibrium but with less than full employment, as $Y_1$ in **Figure 12.3** shows. Keynes believed that the economy would tend to stay in a recessionary gap, with its attendant unemployment, for a significant period of time.

In the same way (although we do not show it in the figure), if AD increases, the economy could experience an **inflationary gap**, where demand is attempting to push the economy past potential output. Consequently, the economy experiences inflation. The key policy implication for either situation is that government needs to step in and close the gap, increasing spending during recessions and decreasing spending during booms to return aggregate demand to match potential output.

Recall from **The Aggregate Supply-Aggregate Demand Model** that aggregate demand is total spending, economy-wide, on domestic goods and services. (Aggregate demand (AD) is actually what economists call total planned expenditure. Read the appendix on **The Expenditure-Output Model** for more on this.) You may also remember that aggregate demand is the sum of four components: consumption expenditure, investment expenditure, government spending, and spending on net exports (exports minus imports). In the following sections, we will examine each component through the Keynesian perspective.

## What Determines Consumption Expenditure?

Consumption expenditure is spending by households and individuals on durable goods, nondurable goods, and services. Durable goods are items that last and provide value over time, such as automobiles. Nondurable goods are things like groceries—once you consume them, they are gone. Recall from **The Macroeconomic Perspective** that services are intangible things consumers buy, like healthcare or entertainment.

Keynes identified three factors that affect consumption:

- Disposable income: For most people, the single most powerful determinant of how much they consume is how much income they have in their take-home pay, also known as **disposable income**, which is income after taxes.

- Expected future income: Consumer expectations about future income also are important in determining consumption. If consumers feel optimistic about the future, they are more likely to spend and increase overall aggregate demand. News of recession and troubles in the economy will make them pull back on consumption.

- Wealth or credit: When households experience a rise in wealth, they may be willing to consume a higher share of their income and to save less. When the U.S. stock market rose dramatically in the late 1990s, for example, U.S. savings rates declined, probably in part because people felt that their wealth had increased and there was less need to save. How do people spend beyond their income, when they perceive their wealth increasing? The answer is borrowing. On the other side, when the U.S. stock market declined about 40% from March 2008 to

March 2009, people felt far greater uncertainty about their economic future, so savings rates increased while consumption declined.

Finally, Keynes noted that a variety of other factors combine to determine how much people save and spend. If household preferences about saving shift in a way that encourages consumption rather than saving, then AD will shift out to the right.

# Link It Up

Visit this website (http://openstaxcollege.org/l/Diane_Rehm) for more information about how the recession affected various groups of people.

## What Determines Investment Expenditure?

We call spending on new capital goods investment expenditure. Investment falls into four categories: producer's durable equipment and software, nonresidential structures (such as factories, offices, and retail locations), changes in inventories, and residential structures (such as single-family homes, townhouses, and apartment buildings). Businesses conduct the first three types of investment, while households conduct the last.

Keynes's treatment of investment focuses on the key role of expectations about the future in influencing business decisions. When a business decides to make an investment in physical assets, like plants or equipment, or in intangible assets, like skills or a research and development project, that firm considers both the expected investment benefits (future profit expectations) and the investment costs (interest rates).

- Expectations of future profits: The clearest driver of investment benefits is expectations for future profits. When we expect an economy to grow, businesses perceive a growing market for their products. Their higher degree of business confidence will encourage new investment. For example, in the second half of the 1990s, U.S. investment levels surged from 18% of GDP in 1994 to 21% in 2000. However, when a recession started in 2001, U.S. investment levels quickly sank back to 18% of GDP by 2002.

- Interest rates also play a significant role in determining how much investment a firm will make. Just as individuals need to borrow money to purchase homes, so businesses need financing when they purchase big ticket items. The cost of investment thus includes the interest rate. Even if the firm has the funds, the interest rate measures the opportunity cost of purchasing business capital. Lower interest rates stimulate investment spending and higher interest rates reduce it.

Many factors can affect the expected profitability on investment. For example, if the energy prices decline, then investments that use energy as an input will yield higher profits. If government offers special incentives for investment (for example, through the tax code), then investment will look more attractive; conversely, if government removes special investment incentives from the tax code, or increases other business taxes, then investment will look less attractive. As Keynes noted, business investment is the most variable of all the components of aggregate demand.

## What Determines Government Spending?

The third component of aggregate demand is federal, state, and local government spending. Although we usually view the United States as a market economy, government still plays a significant role in the economy. As we discuss in **Environmental Protection and Negative Externalities (http://cnx.org/content/m63688/latest/)** and **Positive Externalitites and Public Goods (http://cnx.org/content/m63697/latest/)** , government provides important public services such as national defense, transportation infrastructure, and education.

Keynes recognized that the government budget offered a powerful tool for influencing aggregate demand. Not only could more government spending stimulate AD (or less government spending reduce it), but lowering or raising tax rates could influence consumption and investment spending. Keynes concluded that during extreme times like deep recessions, only the government had the power and resources to move aggregate demand.

## What Determines Net Exports?

Recall that exports are domestically produced products that sell abroad while imports are foreign produced products that consumers purchase domestically. Since we define aggregate demand as spending on domestic goods and services, export expenditures add to AD, while import expenditures subtract from AD.

Two sets of factors can cause shifts in export and import demand: changes in relative growth rates between countries and changes in relative prices between countries. What is happening in the countries' economies that would be purchasing those exports heavily affects the level of demand for a nation's exports. For example, if major importers of American-made products like Canada, Japan, and Germany have recessions, exports of U.S. products to those countries are likely to decline. Conversely, the amount of income in the domestic economy directly affects the quantity of a nation's imports: more income will bring a higher level of imports.

Relative prices of goods in domestic and international markets can also affect exports and imports. If U.S. goods are relatively cheaper compared with goods made in other places, perhaps because a group of U.S. producers has mastered certain productivity breakthroughs, then U.S. exports are likely to rise. If U.S. goods become relatively more expensive, perhaps because a change in the exchange rate between the U.S. dollar and other currencies has pushed up the price of inputs to production in the United States, then exports from U.S. producers are likely to decline.

**Table 12.1** summarizes the reasons we have explained for changes in aggregate demand.

| Reasons for a Decrease in Aggregate Demand | Reasons for an Increase in Aggregate Demand |
|---|---|
| **Consumption** | **Consumption** |
| • Rise in taxes | • Decrease in taxes |
| • Fall in income | • Increase in income |
| • Rise in interest rates | • Fall in interest rates |
| • Desire to save more | • Desire to save less |
| • Decrease in wealth | • Rise in wealth |
| • Fall in future expected income | • Rise in future expected income |
| **Investment** | **Investment** |
| • Fall in expected rate of return | • Rise in expected rate of return |
| • Rise in interest rates | • Drop in interest rates |
| • Drop in business confidence | • Rise in business confidence |
| **Government** | **Government** |
| • Reduction in government spending | • Increase in government spending |
| • Increase in taxes | • Decrease in taxes |
| **Net Exports** | **Net Exports** |
| • Decrease in foreign demand | • Increase in foreign demand |
| • Relative price increase of U.S. goods | • Relative price drop of U.S. goods |

Table 12.1 Determinants of Aggregate Demand

# 12.2 | The Building Blocks of Keynesian Analysis

By the end of this section, you will be able to:
- Evaluate the Keynesian view of recessions through an understanding of sticky wages and prices and the importance of aggregate demand
- Explain the coordination argument, menu costs, and macroeconomic externality
- Analyze the impact of the expenditure multiplier

Now that we have a clear understanding of what constitutes aggregate demand, we return to the Keynesian argument using the model of aggregate demand/aggregate supply (AD/AS). (For a similar treatment using Keynes' income-expenditure model, see the appendix on **The Expenditure-Output Model**.)

Keynesian economics focuses on explaining why recessions and depressions occur and offering a policy prescription for minimizing their effects. The Keynesian view of recession is based on two key building blocks. First, aggregate demand is not always automatically high enough to provide firms with an incentive to hire enough workers to reach full employment. Second, the macroeconomy may adjust only slowly to shifts in aggregate demand because of **sticky wages and prices**, which are wages and prices that do not respond to decreases or increases in demand. We will consider these two claims in turn, and then see how they are represented in the AD/AS model.

The first building block of the Keynesian diagnosis is that recessions occur when the level of demand for goods and services is less than what is produced when labor is fully employed. In other words, the intersection of aggregate supply and aggregate demand occurs at a level of output less than the level of GDP consistent with full employment. Suppose the stock market crashes, as in 1929, or suppose the housing market collapses, as in 2008. In either case, household wealth will decline, and consumption expenditure will follow. Suppose businesses see that consumer spending is falling. That will reduce expectations of the profitability of investment, so businesses will decrease investment expenditure.

This seemed to be the case during the Great Depression, since the physical capacity of the economy to supply goods did not alter much. No flood or earthquake or other natural disaster ruined factories in 1929 or 1930. No outbreak of disease decimated the ranks of workers. No key input price, like the price of oil, soared on world markets. The U.S. economy in 1933 had just about the same factories, workers, and state of technology as it had had four years earlier in 1929—and yet the economy had shrunk dramatically. This also seems to be what happened in 2008.

As Keynes recognized, the events of the Depression contradicted Say's law that "supply creates its own demand." Although production capacity existed, the markets were not able to sell their products. As a result, real GDP was less than potential GDP.

## Link It Up

Visit this website (http://openstaxcollege.org/l/expenditures) for raw data used to calculate GDP.

## Wage and Price Stickiness

Keynes also pointed out that although AD fluctuated, prices and wages did not immediately respond as economists often expected. Instead, prices and wages are "sticky," making it difficult to restore the economy to full employment and potential GDP. Keynes emphasized one particular reason why wages were sticky: the **coordination argument**. This argument points out that, even if most people would be willing—at least hypothetically—to see a decline in their own wages in bad economic times as long as everyone else also experienced such a decline, a market-oriented economy has no obvious way to implement a plan of coordinated wage reductions. **Unemployment** proposed a number of reasons why wages might be sticky downward, most of which center on the argument that businesses avoid wage cuts because they may in one way or another depress morale and hurt the productivity of the existing workers.

Some modern economists have argued in a Keynesian spirit that, along with wages, other prices may be sticky, too. Many firms do not change their prices every day or even every month. When a firm considers changing prices, it must consider two sets of costs. First, changing prices uses company resources: managers must analyze the competition and market demand and decide the new prices, they must update sales materials, change billing records, and redo product and price labels. Second, frequent price changes may leave customers confused or angry—especially if they discover that a product now costs more than they expected. These costs of changing prices are called **menu costs**—like the costs of printing a new set of menus with different prices in a restaurant. Prices do respond to forces of supply and demand, but from a macroeconomic perspective, the process of changing all prices throughout the economy takes time.

To understand the effect of sticky wages and prices in the economy, consider **Figure 12.4** (a) illustrating the overall labor market, while **Figure 12.4** (b) illustrates a market for a specific good or service. The original equilibrium ($E_0$) in each market occurs at the intersection of the demand curve ($D_0$) and supply curve ($S_0$). When aggregate demand declines, the demand for labor shifts to the left (to $D_1$) in **Figure 12.4** (a) and the demand for goods shifts to the left (to $D_1$) in **Figure 12.4** (b). However, because of sticky wages and prices, the wage remains at its original level ($W_0$) for a period of time and the price remains at its original level ($P_0$).

As a result, a situation of excess supply—where the quantity supplied exceeds the quantity demanded at the existing wage or price—exists in markets for both labor and goods, and $Q_1$ is less than $Q_0$ in both **Figure 12.4** (a) and **Figure 12.4** (b). When many labor markets and many goods markets all across the economy find themselves in this position, the economy is in a recession; that is, firms cannot sell what they wish to produce at the existing market price and do not wish to hire all who are willing to work at the existing market wage. The Clear It Up feature discusses this problem in more detail.

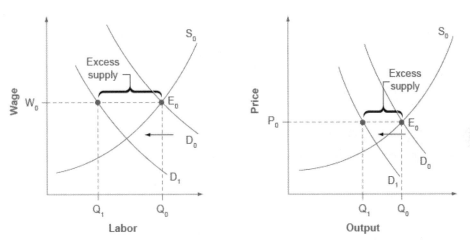

(a) Sticky wages in the labor market                      (b) Sticky prices in the goods market

**Figure 12.4 Sticky Prices and Falling Demand in the Labor and Goods Market** In both (a) and (b), demand shifts left from $D_0$ to $D_1$. However, the wage in (a) and the price in (b) do not immediately decline. In (a), the quantity demanded of labor at the original wage ($W_0$) is $Q_0$, but with the new demand curve for labor ($D_1$), it will be $Q_1$. Similarly, in (b), the quantity demanded of goods at the original price ($P_0$) is $Q_0$, but at the new demand curve ($D_1$) it will be $Q_1$. An excess supply of labor will exist, which we call unemployment. An excess supply of goods will also exist, where the quantity demanded is substantially less than the quantity supplied. Thus, sticky wages and sticky prices, combined with a drop in demand, bring about unemployment and recession.

## Why Is the Pace of Wage Adjustments Slow?

The recovery after the Great Recession in the United States has been slow, with wages stagnant, if not declining. In fact, many low-wage workers at McDonalds, Dominos, and Walmart have threatened to strike for higher wages. Their plight is part of a larger trend in job growth and pay in the post–recession recovery.

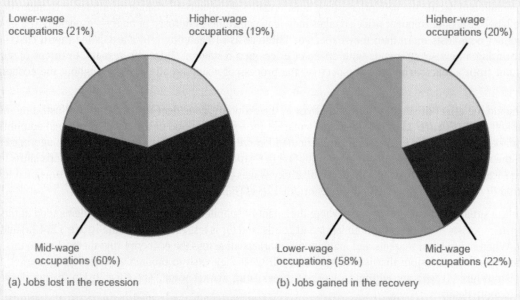

**Figure 12.5 Jobs Lost/Gained in the Recession/Recovery** Data in the aftermath of the Great Recession suggests that jobs lost were in mid-wage occupations, while jobs gained were in low-wage occupations.

The National Employment Law Project compiled data from the Bureau of Labor Statistics and found that, during the Great Recession, 60% of job losses were in medium-wage occupations. Most of them were replaced during the recovery period with lower-wage jobs in the service, retail, and food industries. **Figure 12.5** illustrates this data.

Wages in the service, retail, and food industries are at or near minimum wage and tend to be both downwardly and upwardly "sticky." Wages are downwardly sticky due to minimum wage laws. They may be upwardly sticky if insufficient competition in low-skilled labor markets enables employers to avoid raising wages that would reduce their profits. At the same time, however, the Consumer Price Index increased 11% between 2007 and 2012, pushing real wages down.

## The Two Keynesian Assumptions in the AD/AS Model

**Figure 12.6** is the AD/AS diagram which illustrates these two Keynesian assumptions—the importance of aggregate demand in causing recession and the stickiness of wages and prices. Note that because of the stickiness of wages and prices, the aggregate supply curve is flatter than either supply curve (labor or specific good). In fact, if wages and prices were so sticky that they did not fall at all, the aggregate supply curve would be completely flat below potential GDP, as **Figure 12.6** shows. This outcome is an important example of a **macroeconomic externality**, where what happens at the macro level is different from and inferior to what happens at the micro level. For example, a firm should respond to a decrease in demand for its product by cutting its price to increase sales. However, if all firms experience a decrease in demand for their products, sticky prices in the aggregate prevent aggregate demand from rebounding (which we would show as a movement along the AD curve in response to a lower price level).

The original equilibrium of this economy occurs where the aggregate demand function ($AD_0$) intersects with AS. Since this intersection occurs at potential GDP (Yp), the economy is operating at full employment. When aggregate demand shifts to the left, all the adjustment occurs through decreased real GDP. There is no decrease in the price level. Since the equilibrium occurs at $Y_1$, the economy experiences substantial unemployment.

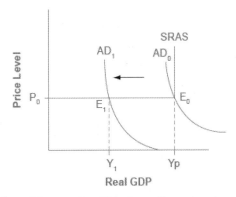

**Figure 12.6 A Keynesian Perspective of Recession** This figure illustrates the two key assumptions behind Keynesian economics. A recession begins when aggregate demand declines from $AD_0$ to $AD_1$. The recession persists because of the assumption of fixed wages and prices, which makes the SRAS flat below potential GDP. If that were not the case, the price level would fall also, raising GDP and limiting the recession. Instead the intersection $E_1$ occurs in the flat portion of the SRAS curve where GDP is less than potential.

## The Expenditure Multiplier

A key concept in Keynesian economics is the **expenditure multiplier**. The expenditure multiplier is the idea that not only does spending affect the equilibrium level of GDP, but that spending is powerful. More precisely, it means that a change in spending causes a more than proportionate change in GDP.

$$\frac{\Delta Y}{\Delta \text{Spending}} > 1$$

The reason for the expenditure multiplier is that one person's spending becomes another person's income, which leads to additional spending and additional income so that the cumulative impact on GDP is larger than the initial increase in spending. The appendix on **The Expenditure-Output Model** provides the details of the multiplier process, but the concept is important enough for us to summarize here. While the multiplier is important for understanding the effectiveness of fiscal policy, it occurs whenever any autonomous increase in spending occurs. Additionally, the multiplier operates in a negative as well as a positive direction. Thus, when investment spending collapsed during the Great Depression, it caused a much larger decrease in real GDP. The size of the multiplier is critical and was a key element in discussions of the effectiveness of the Obama administration's fiscal stimulus package, officially titled the American Recovery and Reinvestment Act of 2009.

# 12.3 | The Phillips Curve

By the end of this section, you will be able to:
- Explain the Phillips curve, noting its impact on the theories of Keynesian economics
- Graph a Phillips curve
- Identify factors that cause the instability of the Phillips curve
- Analyze the Keynesian policy for reducing unemployment and inflation

The simplified AD/AS model that we have used so far is fully consistent with Keynes's original model. More recent research, though, has indicated that in the real world, an aggregate supply curve is more curved than the right angle that we used in this chapter. Rather, the real-world AS curve is very flat at levels of output far below potential ("the Keynesian zone"), very steep at levels of output above potential ("the neoclassical zone") and curved in between ("the intermediate zone"). **Figure 12.7** illustrates this. The typical aggregate supply curve leads to the concept of the Phillips curve.

**Figure 12.7 Keynes, Neoclassical, and Intermediate Zones in the Aggregate Supply Curve** Near the equilibrium Ek, in the Keynesian zone at the SRAS curve's far left, small shifts in AD, either to the right or the left, will affect the output level Yk, but will not much affect the price level. In the Keynesian zone, AD largely determines the quantity of output. Near the equilibrium En, in the neoclassical zone, at the SRAS curve's far right, small shifts in AD, either to the right or the left, will have relatively little effect on the output level Yn, but instead will have a greater effect on the price level. In the neoclassical zone, the near-vertical SRAS curve close to the level of potential GDP (as represented by the LRAS line) largely determines the quantity of output. In the intermediate zone around equilibrium Ei, movement in AD to the right will increase both the output level and the price level, while a movement in AD to the left would decrease both the output level and the price level.

## The Discovery of the Phillips Curve

In the 1950s, A.W. Phillips, an economist at the London School of Economics, was studying the Keynesian analytical framework. The Keynesian theory implied that during a recession inflationary pressures are low, but when the level of output is at or even pushing beyond potential GDP, the economy is at greater risk for inflation. Phillips analyzed 60 years of British data and did find that tradeoff between unemployment and inflation, which became known as the **Phillips curve. Figure 12.8** shows a theoretical Phillips curve, and the following Work It Out feature shows how the pattern appears for the United States.

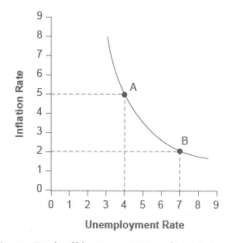

**Figure 12.8 A Keynesian Phillips Curve Tradeoff between Unemployment and Inflation** A Phillips curve illustrates a tradeoff between the unemployment rate and the inflation rate. If one is higher, the other must be lower. For example, point A illustrates a 5% inflation rate and a 4% unemployment. If the government attempts to reduce inflation to 2%, then it will experience a rise in unemployment to 7%, as point B shows.

# Work It Out ⊢○─○─○

## The Phillips Curve for the United States

Step 1. Go to this website (http://1.usa.gov/1c3psdL) to see the 2005 *Economic Report of the President.*

Step 2. Scroll down and locate Table B-63 in the Appendices. This table is titled "Changes in special consumer price indexes, 1960–2004."

Step 3. Download the table in Excel by selecting the XLS option and then selecting the location in which to save the file.

Step 4. Open the downloaded Excel file.

Step 5. View the third column (labeled "Year to year"). This is the inflation rate, measured by the percentage change in the Consumer Price Index.

Step 6. Return to the website and scroll to locate the Appendix Table B-42 "Civilian unemployment rate, 1959–2004.

Step 7. Download the table in Excel.

Step 8. Open the downloaded Excel file and view the second column. This is the overall unemployment rate.

Step 9. Using the data available from these two tables, plot the Phillips curve for 1960–69, with unemployment rate on the x-axis and the inflation rate on the y-axis. Your graph should look like Figure 12.9.

**Figure 12.9 The Phillips Curve from 1960–1969** This chart shows the negative relationship between unemployment and inflation.

Step 10. Plot the Phillips curve for 1960–1979. What does the graph look like? Do you still see the tradeoff between inflation and unemployment? Your graph should look like Figure 12.10.

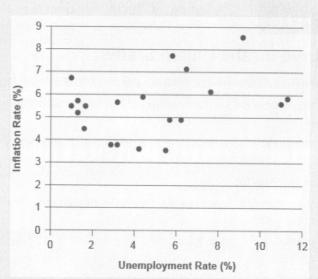

**Figure 12.10 U.S. Phillips Curve, 1960–1979** The tradeoff between unemployment and inflation appeared to break down during the 1970s as the Phillips Curve shifted out to the right.

Over this longer period of time, the Phillips curve appears to have shifted out. There is no tradeoff any more.

## The Instability of the Phillips Curve

During the 1960s, economists viewed the Phillips curve as a policy menu. A nation could choose low inflation and high unemployment, or high inflation and low unemployment, or anywhere in between. Economies could use fiscal and monetary policy to move up or down the Phillips curve as desired. Then a curious thing happened. When policymakers tried to exploit the tradeoff between inflation and unemployment, the result was an increase in both inflation and unemployment. What had happened? The Phillips curve shifted.

The U.S. economy experienced this pattern in the deep recession from 1973 to 1975, and again in back-to-back recessions from 1980 to 1982. Many nations around the world saw similar increases in unemployment and inflation. This pattern became known as stagflation. (Recall from **The Aggregate Demand/Aggregate Supply Model** that stagflation is an unhealthy combination of high unemployment and high inflation.) Perhaps most important, stagflation was a phenomenon that traditional Keynesian economics could not explain.

Economists have concluded that two factors cause the Phillips curve to shift. The first is supply shocks, like the mid-1970s oil crisis, which first brought stagflation into our vocabulary. The second is changes in people's expectations about inflation. In other words, there may be a tradeoff between inflation and unemployment when people expect no inflation, but when they realize inflation is occurring, the tradeoff disappears. Both factors (supply shocks and changes in inflationary expectations) cause the aggregate supply curve, and thus the Phillips curve, to shift.

In short, we should interpret a downward-sloping Phillips curve as valid for short-run periods of several years, but over longer periods, when aggregate supply shifts, the downward-sloping Phillips curve can shift so that unemployment and inflation are both higher (as in the 1970s and early 1980s) or both lower (as in the early 1990s or first decade of the 2000s).

## Keynesian Policy for Fighting Unemployment and Inflation

Keynesian macroeconomics argues that the solution to a recession is **expansionary fiscal policy**, such as tax cuts to stimulate consumption and investment, or direct increases in government spending that would shift the aggregate demand curve to the right. For example, if aggregate demand was originally at ADr in **Figure 12.11**, so that the economy was in recession, the appropriate policy would be for government to shift aggregate demand to the right from ADr to ADf, where the economy would be at potential GDP and full employment.

Keynes noted that while it would be nice if the government could spend additional money on housing, roads, and other amenities, he also argued that if the government could not agree on how to spend money in practical ways, then it could spend in impractical ways. For example, Keynes suggested building monuments, like a modern equivalent of the Egyptian pyramids. He proposed that the government could bury money underground, and let mining companies start digging up the money again. These suggestions were slightly tongue-in-cheek, but their purpose was to emphasize that a Great Depression is no time to quibble over the specifics of government spending programs and tax cuts when the goal should be to pump up aggregate demand by enough to lift the economy to potential GDP.

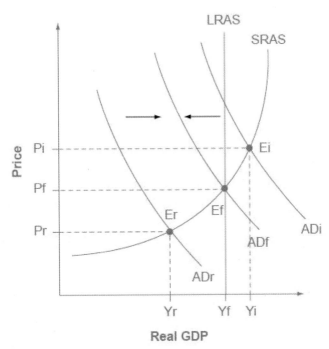

**Figure 12.11 Fighting Recession and Inflation with Keynesian Policy** If an economy is in recession, with an equilibrium at Er, then the Keynesian response would be to enact a policy to shift aggregate demand to the right from ADr toward ADf. If an economy is experiencing inflationary pressures with an equilibrium at Ei, then the Keynesian response would be to enact a policy response to shift aggregate demand to the left, from ADi toward ADf.

The other side of Keynesian policy occurs when the economy is operating above potential GDP. In this situation, unemployment is low, but inflationary rises in the price level are a concern. The Keynesian response would be **contractionary fiscal policy**, using tax increases or government spending cuts to shift AD to the left. The result would be downward pressure on the price level, but very little reduction in output or very little rise in unemployment. If aggregate demand was originally at ADi in **Figure 12.11**, so that the economy was experiencing inflationary rises in the price level, the appropriate policy would be for government to shift aggregate demand to the left, from ADi toward ADf, which reduces the pressure for a higher price level while the economy remains at full employment.

In the Keynesian economic model, too little aggregate demand brings unemployment and too much brings inflation. Thus, you can think of Keynesian economics as pursuing a "Goldilocks" level of aggregate demand: not too much, not too little, but looking for what is just right.

# 12.4 | The Keynesian Perspective on Market Forces

By the end of this section, you will be able to:
- Explain the Keynesian perspective on market forces
- Analyze the role of government policy in economic management

Ever since the birth of Keynesian economics in the 1930s, controversy has simmered over the extent to which government should play an active role in managing the economy. In the aftermath of the human devastation and misery of the Great Depression, many people—including many economists—became more aware of vulnerabilities within the market-oriented economic system. Some supporters of Keynesian economics advocated a high degree of government planning in all parts of the economy.

However, Keynes himself was careful to separate the issue of aggregate demand from the issue of how well individual markets worked. He argued that individual markets for goods and services were appropriate and useful, but that sometimes that level of aggregate demand was just too low. When 10 million people are willing and able to work, but one million of them are unemployed, he argued, individual markets may be doing a perfectly good job of allocating the efforts of the nine million workers—the problem is that insufficient aggregate demand exists to support jobs for all 10 million. Thus, he believed that, while government should ensure that overall level of aggregate demand is sufficient for an economy to reach full employment, this task did not imply that the government should attempt to set prices and wages throughout the economy, nor to take over and manage large corporations or entire industries directly.

Even if one accepts the Keynesian economic theory, a number of practical questions remain. In the real world, can government economists identify potential GDP accurately? Is a desired increase in aggregate demand better accomplished by a tax cut or by an increase in government spending? Given the inevitable delays and uncertainties as governments enact policies into law, is it reasonable to expect that the government can implement Keynesian economics? Can fixing a recession really be just as simple as pumping up aggregate demand? **Government Budgets and Fiscal Policy** will probe these issues. The Keynesian approach, with its focus on aggregate demand and sticky prices, has proved useful in understanding how the economy fluctuates in the short run and why recessions and cyclical unemployment occur. In **The Neoclassical Perspective**, we will consider some of the shortcomings of the Keynesian approach and why it is not especially well-suited for long-run macroeconomic analysis.

## Bring it Home

### The Great Recession

The lessons learned during the 1930s Great Depression and the aggregate expenditure model that John Maynard Keynes proposed gave the modern economists and policymakers of today the tools to effectively navigate the treacherous economy in the latter half of the 2000s. In "How the Great Recession Was Brought to an End", Alan S. Blinder and Mark Zandi wrote that the actions taken by today's policymakers stand in sharp contrast to those of the early years of the Great Depression. Today's economists and policymakers were not content to let the markets recover from recession without taking proactive measures to support consumption and investment. The Federal Reserve actively lowered short-term interest rates and developed innovative ways to pump money into the economy so that credit and investment would not dry up. Both Presidents Bush and Obama and Congress implemented a variety of programs ranging from tax rebates to "Cash for Clunkers" to the Troubled Asset Relief Program to stimulate and stabilize household consumption and encourage investment. Although these policies came under harsh criticism from the public and many politicians, they lessened the impact of the economic downturn and may have saved the country from a second Great Depression.

# KEY TERMS

**contractionary fiscal policy** tax increases or cuts in government spending designed to decrease aggregate demand and reduce inflationary pressures

**coordination argument** downward wage and price flexibility requires perfect information about the level of lower compensation acceptable to other laborers and market participants

**disposable income** income after taxes

**expansionary fiscal policy** tax cuts or increases in government spending designed to stimulate aggregate demand and move the economy out of recession

**expenditure multiplier** Keynesian concept that asserts that a change in autonomous spending causes a more than proportionate change in real GDP

**inflationary gap** equilibrium at a level of output above potential GDP

**macroeconomic externality** occurs when what happens at the macro level is different from and inferior to what happens at the micro level; an example would be where upward sloping supply curves for firms become a flat aggregate supply curve, illustrating that the price level cannot fall to stimulate aggregate demand

**menu costs** costs firms face in changing prices

**Phillips curve** the tradeoff between unemployment and inflation

**real GDP** the amount of goods and services actually sold in a nation

**recessionary gap** equilibrium at a level of output below potential GDP

**sticky wages and prices** a situation where wages and prices do not fall in response to a decrease in demand, or do not rise in response to an increase in demand

# KEY CONCEPTS AND SUMMARY

## 12.1 Aggregate Demand in Keynesian Analysis
Aggregate demand is the sum of four components: consumption, investment, government spending, and net exports. Consumption will change for a number of reasons, including movements in income, taxes, expectations about future income, and changes in wealth levels. Investment will change in response to its expected profitability, which in turn is shaped by expectations about future economic growth, the creation of new technologies, the price of key inputs, and tax incentives for investment. Investment will also change when interest rates rise or fall. Political considerations determine government spending and taxes. Exports and imports change according to relative growth rates and prices between two economies.

## 12.2 The Building Blocks of Keynesian Analysis
Keynesian economics is based on two main ideas: (1) aggregate demand is more likely than aggregate supply to be the primary cause of a short-run economic event like a recession; (2) wages and prices can be sticky, and so, in an economic downturn, unemployment can result. The latter is an example of a macroeconomic externality. While surpluses cause prices to fall at the micro level, they do not necessarily at the macro level. Instead the adjustment to a decrease in demand occurs only through decreased quantities. One reason why prices may be sticky is menu costs, the costs of changing prices. These include internal costs a business faces in changing prices in terms of labeling, recordkeeping, and accounting, and also the costs of communicating the price change to (possibly unhappy) customers. Keynesians also believe in the existence of the expenditure multiplier—the notion that a change in autonomous expenditure causes a more than proportionate change in GDP.

## 12.3 The Phillips Curve

A Phillips curve shows the tradeoff between unemployment and inflation in an economy. From a Keynesian viewpoint, the Phillips curve should slope down so that higher unemployment means lower inflation, and vice versa. However, a downward-sloping Phillips curve is a short-term relationship that may shift after a few years.

Keynesian macroeconomics argues that the solution to a recession is expansionary fiscal policy, such as tax cuts to stimulate consumption and investment, or direct increases in government spending that would shift the aggregate demand curve to the right. The other side of Keynesian policy occurs when the economy is operating above potential GDP. In this situation, unemployment is low, but inflationary rises in the price level are a concern. The Keynesian response would be contractionary fiscal policy, using tax increases or government spending cuts to shift AD to the left.

## 12.4 The Keynesian Perspective on Market Forces

The Keynesian prescription for stabilizing the economy implies government intervention at the macroeconomic level—increasing aggregate demand when private demand falls and decreasing aggregate demand when private demand rises. This does not imply that the government should be passing laws or regulations that set prices and quantities in microeconomic markets.

## SELF-CHECK QUESTIONS

**1.** In the Keynesian framework, which of the following events might cause a recession? Which might cause inflation? Sketch AD/AS diagrams to illustrate your answers.
   a. A large increase in the price of the homes people own.
   b. Rapid growth in the economy of a major trading partner.
   c. The development of a major new technology offers profitable opportunities for business.
   d. The interest rate rises.
   e. The good imported from a major trading partner become much less expensive.

**2.** In a Keynesian framework, using an AD/AS diagram, which of the following government policy choices offer a possible solution to recession? Which offer a possible solution to inflation?
   a. A tax increase on consumer income.
   b. A surge in military spending.
   c. A reduction in taxes for businesses that increase investment.
   d. A major increase in what the U.S. government spends on healthcare.

**3.** Use the AD/AS model to explain how an inflationary gap occurs, beginning from the initial equilibrium in **Figure 12.6**.

**4.** Suppose the U.S. Congress cuts federal government spending in order to balance the Federal budget. Use the AD/AS model to analyze the likely impact on output and employment. *Hint*: revisit **Figure 12.6**.

**5.** How would a decrease in energy prices affect the Phillips curve?

**6.** Does Keynesian economics require government to set controls on prices, wages, or interest rates?

**7.** List three practical problems with the Keynesian perspective.

## REVIEW QUESTIONS

**8.** Name some economic events not related to government policy that could cause aggregate demand to shift.

**9.** Name some government policies that could cause aggregate demand to shift.

**10.** From a Keynesian point of view, which is more likely to cause a recession: aggregate demand or aggregate supply, and why?

**11.** Why do sticky wages and prices increase the impact of an economic downturn on unemployment and recession?

**12.** Explain what economists mean by "menu costs."

**13.** What tradeoff does a Phillips curve show?

**14.** Would you expect to see long-run data trace out a stable downward-sloping Phillips curve?

**15.** What is the Keynesian prescription for recession? For inflation?

**16.** How did the Keynesian perspective address the economic market failure of the Great Depression?

## CRITICAL THINKING QUESTIONS

**17.** In its recent report, The Conference Board's *Global Economic Outlook 2015*, updated November 2014 (http://www.conference-board.org/data/ globaloutlook.cfm), projects China's growth between 2015 and 2019 to be about 5.5%. *International Business Times* (http://www.ibtimes.com/us-exports-china-have-grown-294-over-past-decade-1338693) reports that China is the United States' third largest export market, with exports to China growing 294% over the last ten years. Explain what impact China has on the U.S. economy.

**18.** What may happen if growth in China continues or contracts?

**19.** Does it make sense that wages would be sticky downwards but not upwards? Why or why not?

**20.** Suppose the economy is operating at potential GDP when it experiences an increase in export demand. How might the economy increase production of exports to meet this demand, given that the economy is already at full employment?

**21.** Do you think the Phillips curve is a useful tool for analyzing the economy today? Why or why not?

**22.** Return to the table from the *Economic Report of the President* in the earlier **Work It Out** feature titled "The Phillips Curve for the United States." How would you expect government spending to have changed over the last six years?

**23.** Explain what types of policies the federal government may have implemented to restore aggregate demand and the potential obstacles policymakers may have encountered.

# 13 | The Neoclassical Perspective

**Figure 13.1 Impact of the Great Recession** We can see the impact of the Great Recession in many areas of the economy that impact our daily lives. One of the most visible signs was in the housing market where many people were forced to abandon their homes and other buildings, including ones midway through construction. (Credit: modification of work by A McLin/Flickr Creative Commons)

## Bring it Home

### Navigating Unchartered Waters

The Great Recession ended in June 2009 after 18 months, according to the National Bureau of Economic Research (NBER). The NBER examines a variety of measures of economic activity to gauge the economy's overall health. These measures include real income, wholesale and retail sales, employment, and industrial production. In the years since the official end of this historic economic downturn, it has become clear that the Great Recession was two-pronged, hitting the U.S. economy with the collapse of the housing market and the failure of the financial system's credit institutions, further contaminating global economies. While the stock market rapidly lost trillions of dollars of value, consumer spending dried up, and companies began cutting jobs, economic policymakers were struggling with how to best combat and prevent a national, and even global economic collapse. In the end, policymakers used a number of controversial monetary and fiscal policies to support the housing market and domestic industries as well as to stabilize the financial sector. Some of these initiatives included:

- Federal Reserve Bank purchase of both traditional and nontraditional assets off banks' balance sheets. By doing this, the Fed injected money into the banking system and increased the amounts of funds available to lend to the business sector and consumers. This also dropped short-term interest rates to as low as zero percent, which had the effect of devaluing U.S. dollars in the global market and boosting exports.

- The Congress and the President also passed several pieces of legislation that would stabilize the financial market. The Troubled Asset Relief Program (TARP), passed in late 2008, allowed the government to inject cash into troubled banks and other financial institutions and help support General Motors and Chrysler as they faced bankruptcy and threatened job losses throughout their supply chain. The American Recovery and Reinvestment Act in early 2009 provided tax rebates to low- and middle-income households to encourage consumer spending.

Four years after the end of the Great Recession, the economy has yet to return to its pre-recession levels of productivity and growth. Annual productivity increased only 1.9% between 2009 and 2012 compared to its 2.7% annual growth rate between 2000 and 2007, unemployment remains above the natural rate, and real GDP continues to lag behind potential growth. The actions the government has taken to stabilize the economy are still under scrutiny and debate about their effectiveness continues. In this chapter, we will discuss the neoclassical perspective on economics and compare it to the Keynesian perspective. At the end of the chapter, we will use the neoclassical perspective to analyze the actions the government has taken in the Great Recession.

# Introduction to the Neoclassical Perspective

In this chapter, you will learn about:

- The Building Blocks of Neoclassical Analysis

- The Policy Implications of the Neoclassical Perspective

- Balancing Keynesian and Neoclassical Models

In Chicago, Illinois, the highest recorded temperature was 105° in July 1995, while the lowest recorded temperature was 27° below zero in January 1958. Understanding why these extreme weather patterns occurred would be interesting. However, if you wanted to understand the typical weather pattern in Chicago, instead of focusing on one-time extremes, you would need to look at the entire pattern of data over time.

A similar lesson applies to the study of macroeconomics. It is interesting to study extreme situations, like the 1930s Great Depression or what many have called the 2008-2009 Great Recession. If you want to understand the whole picture, however, you need to look at the long term. Consider the unemployment rate. The unemployment rate has fluctuated from as low as 3.5% in 1969 to as high as 9.7% in 1982 and 9.6% in 2009. Even as the U.S. unemployment rate rose during recessions and declined during expansions, it kept returning to the general neighborhood of 5.0–5.5%. When the nonpartisan Congressional Budget Office carried out its long-range economic forecasts in 2010, it assumed that from 2015 to 2020, after the recession has passed, the unemployment rate would be 5.0%. From a long-run perspective, the economy seems to keep adjusting back to this rate of unemployment.

As the name "neoclassical" implies, this perspective of how the macroeconomy works is a "new" view of the "old" classical model of the economy. The classical view, the predominant economic philosophy until the Great Depression, was that short-term fluctuations in economic activity would rather quickly, with flexible prices, adjust back to full employment. This view of the economy implied a vertical aggregate supply curve at full employment GDP, and prescribed a "hands off" policy approach. For example, if the economy were to slip into recession (a leftward shift of the aggregate demand curve), it would temporarily exhibit a surplus of goods. Falling prices would eliminate this surplus, and the economy would return to full employment level of GDP. No active fiscal or monetary policy was needed. In fact, the classical view was that expansionary fiscal or monetary policy would only cause inflation, rather than increase GDP. The deep and lasting impact of the Great Depression changed this thinking and Keynesian economics, which prescribed active fiscal policy to alleviate weak aggregate demand, became the more mainstream perspective.

# 13.1 | The Building Blocks of Neoclassical Analysis

By the end of this section, you will be able to:

- Explain the importance of potential GDP in the long run
- Analyze the role of flexible prices
- Interpret a neoclassical model of aggregate demand and aggregate supply
- Evaluate different ways for measuring the speed of macroeconomic adjustment

The **neoclassical perspective** on macroeconomics holds that, in the long run, the economy will fluctuate around its potential GDP and its natural rate of unemployment. This chapter begins with two building blocks of neoclassical economics: (1) potential GDP determines the economy's the size and (2) wages and prices will adjust in a flexible manner so that the economy will adjust back to its potential GDP level of output. The key policy implication is this: The government should focus more on long-term growth and on controlling inflation than on worrying about recession or cyclical unemployment. This focus on long-run growth rather than the short-run fluctuations in the business cycle means that neoclassical economics is more useful for long-run macroeconomic analysis and Keynesian economics is more useful for analyzing the macroeconomic short run. Let's consider the two neoclassical building blocks in turn, and how we can embody them in the aggregate demand/aggregate supply model.

## The Importance of Potential GDP in the Long Run

Over the long run, the level of potential GDP determines the size of real GDP. When economists refer to "potential GDP" they are referring to that level of output that an economy can achieve when all resources (land, labor, capital, and entrepreneurial ability) are fully employed. While the unemployment rate in labor markets will never be zero, full employment in the labor market refers to zero cyclical unemployment. There will still be some level of unemployment due to frictional or structural unemployment, but when the economy is operating with zero cyclical unemployment, economists say that the economy is at the natural rate of unemployment or at full employment.

Economists benchmark actual or real GDP against the potential GDP to determine how well the economy is performing. As explained in **Economic Growth**, we can explain GDP growth by increases and investment in physical capital and human capital per person as well as advances in technology. **Physical capital per person** refers to the amount and kind of machinery and equipment available to help people get work done. Compare, for example, your productivity in typing a term paper on a typewriter to working on your laptop with word processing software. Clearly, you will be able to be more productive using word processing software. The technology and level of capital of your laptop and software has increased your productivity. More broadly, the development of GPS technology and Universal Product Codes (those barcodes on every product we buy) has made it much easier for firms to track shipments, tabulate inventories, and sell and distribute products. These two technological innovations, and many others, have increased a nation's ability to produce goods and services for a given population. Likewise, increasing human capital involves increasing levels of knowledge, education, and skill sets per person through vocational or higher education. Physical and human capital improvements with technological advances will increase overall productivity and, thus, GDP.

To see how these improvements have increased productivity and output at the national level, we should examine evidence from the United States. The United States experienced significant growth in the twentieth century due to phenomenal changes in infrastructure, equipment, and technological improvements in physical capital and human capital. The population more than tripled in the twentieth century, from 76 million in 1900 to over 300 million in 2016. The human capital of modern workers is far higher today because the education and skills of workers have risen dramatically. In 1900, only about one-eighth of the U.S. population had completed high school and just one person in 40 had completed a four-year college degree. By 2010, more than 87% of Americans had a high school degree and over 29% had a four-year college degree as well. In 2014, 40% of working-age Americans had a four-year college degree. The average amount of physical capital per worker has grown dramatically. The technology available to modern workers is extraordinarily better than a century ago: cars, airplanes, electrical machinery, smartphones, computers, chemical and biological advances, materials science, health care—the list of technological advances could run on and on. More workers, higher skill levels, larger amounts of physical capital per worker, and amazingly better technology, and potential GDP for the U.S. economy has clearly increased a great deal since 1900.

This growth has fallen below its potential GDP and, at times, has exceeded its potential. For example from 2008 to

2009, the U.S. economy tumbled into recession and remains below its potential. At other times, like in the late 1990s, the economy ran at potential GDP—or even slightly ahead. **Figure 13.2** shows the actual data for the increase in real GDP since 1960. The slightly smoother line shows the potential GDP since 1960 as estimated by the nonpartisan Congressional Budget Office. Most economic recessions and upswings are times when the economy is 1–3% below or above potential GDP in a given year. Clearly, short-run fluctuations around potential GDP do exist, but over the long run, the upward trend of potential GDP determines the size of the economy.

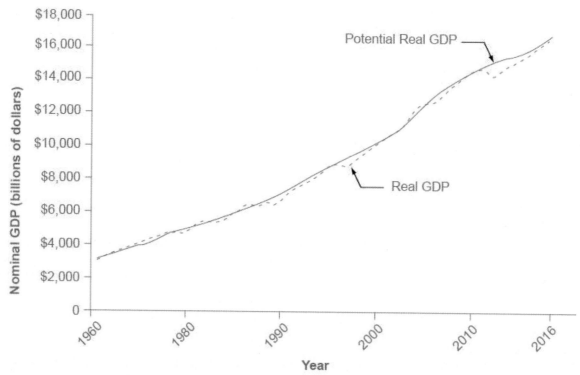

**Figure 13.2 Potential and Actual GDP (in 2009 Dollars)** Actual GDP falls below potential GDP during and after recessions, like the recessions of 1980 and 1981–82, 1990–91, 2001, and 2008–2009 and continues below potential GDP through 2016. In other cases, actual GDP can be above potential GDP for a time, as in the late 1990s.

In the aggregate demand/aggregate supply model, we show potential GDP as a vertical line. Neoclassical economists who focus on potential GDP as the primary determinant of real GDP argue that the long-run aggregate supply curve is located at potential GDP—that is, we draw the long-run aggregate supply curve as a vertical line at the level of potential GDP, as **Figure 13.3** shows. A vertical LRAS curve means that the level of aggregate supply (or potential GDP) will determine the economy's real GDP, regardless of the level of aggregate demand. Over time, increases in the quantity and quality of physical capital, increases in human capital, and technological advancements shift potential GDP and the vertical LRAS curve gradually to the right. Economists often describe this gradual increase in an economy's potential GDP as a nation's long-term economic growth.

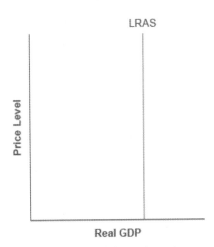

**Figure 13.3 A Vertical AS Curve** In the neoclassical model, we draw the aggregate supply curve as a vertical line at the level of potential GDP. If AS is vertical, then it determines the level of real output, no matter where we draw the aggregate demand curve. Over time, the LRAS curve shifts to the right as productivity increases and potential GDP expands.

## The Role of Flexible Prices

How does the macroeconomy adjust back to its level of potential GDP in the long run? What if aggregate demand increases or decreases? Economists base the neoclassical view of how the macroeconomy adjusts on the insight that even if wages and prices are "sticky", or slow to change, in the short run, they are flexible over time. To understand this better, let's follow the connections from the short-run to the long-run macroeconomic equilibrium.

The aggregate demand and aggregate supply diagram in **Figure 13.4** shows two aggregate supply curves. We draw the original upward sloping aggregate supply curve (SRAS$_0$) is a short-run or Keynesian AS curve. The vertical aggregate supply curve (LRASn) is the long-run or neoclassical AS curve, which is located at potential GDP. The original aggregate demand curve, labeled AD$_0$, so that the original equilibrium occurs at point E$_0$, at which point the economy is producing at its potential GDP.

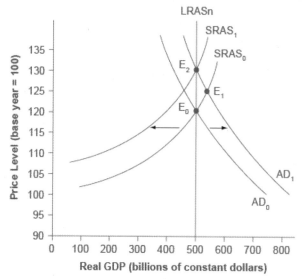

**Figure 13.4 The Rebound to Potential GDP after AD Increases** The original equilibrium ($E_0$), at an output level of 500 and a price level of 120, happens at the intersection of the aggregate demand curve ($AD_0$) and the short-run aggregate supply curve ($SRAS_0$). The output at $E_0$ is equal to potential GDP. Aggregate demand shifts right from $AD_0$ to $AD_1$. The new equilibrium is $E_1$, with a higher output level of 550 and an increase in the price level to 125. With unemployment rates unsustainably low, eager employers bid up wages, which shifts short-run aggregate supply to the left, from $SRAS_0$ to $SRAS_1$. The new equilibrium ($E_2$) is at the same original level of output, 500, but at a higher price level 130. Thus, the long-run aggregate supply curve (LRASn), which is vertical at the level of potential GDP, determines the level of real GDP in this economy in the long run.

Now, imagine that some economic event boosts aggregate demand: perhaps a surge of export sales or a rise in business confidence that leads to more investment, perhaps a policy decision like higher government spending, or perhaps a tax cut that leads to additional aggregate demand. The short-run Keynesian analysis is that the rise in aggregate demand will shift the aggregate demand curve out to the right, from $AD_0$ to $AD_1$, leading to a new equilibrium at point $E_1$ with higher output, lower unemployment, and pressure for an inflationary rise in the price level.

In the long-run neoclassical analysis, however, the chain of economic events is just beginning. As economic output rises above potential GDP, the level of unemployment falls. The economy is now above full employment and there is a labor shortage. Eager employers are trying to bid workers away from other companies and to encourage their current workers to exert more effort and to work longer hours. This high demand for labor will drive up wages. Most employers review their workers salaries only once or twice a year, and so it will take time before the higher wages filter through the economy. As wages do rise, it will mean a leftward shift in the short-run Keynesian aggregate supply curve back to $SRAS_1$, because the price of a major input to production has increased. The economy moves to a new equilibrium ($E_2$). The new equilibrium has the same level of real GDP as did the original equilibrium ($E_0$), but there has been an inflationary increase in the price level.

This description of the short-run shift from $E_0$ to $E_1$ and the long-run shift from $E_1$ to $E_2$ is a step-by-step way of making a simple point: the economy cannot sustain production above its potential GDP in the long run. An economy may produce above its level of potential GDP in the short run, under pressure from a surge in aggregate demand. Over the long run, however, that surge in aggregate demand ends up as an increase in the price level, not as a rise in output.

The rebound of the economy back to potential GDP also works in response to a shift to the left in aggregate demand. **Figure 13.5** again starts with two aggregate supply curves, with $SRAS_0$ showing the original upward sloping short-run Keynesian AS curve and LRASn showing the vertical long-run neoclassical aggregate supply curve. A decrease in aggregate demand—for example, because of a decline in consumer confidence that leads to less consumption and more saving—causes the original aggregate demand curve $AD_0$ to shift back to $AD_1$. The shift from the original equilibrium ($E_0$) to the new equilibrium ($E_1$) results in a decline in output. The economy is now below full employment and there is a surplus of labor. As output falls below potential GDP, unemployment rises. While a lower price level (i.e., deflation) is rare in the United States, it does happen occasionally during very weak periods of economic activity. For practical purposes, we might consider a lower price level in the AD–AS model as indicative of disinflation, which is a decline in the inflation rate. Thus, the long-run aggregate supply curve LRASn, which is vertical at the level of potential GDP, ultimately determines this economy's real GDP.

**Figure 13.5 A Rebound Back to Potential GDP from a Shift to the Left in Aggregate Demand** The original equilibrium ($E_0$), at an output level of 500 and a price level of 120, happens at the intersection of the aggregate demand curve ($AD_0$) and the short-run aggregate supply curve ($SRAS_0$). The output at $E_0$ is equal to potential GDP. Aggregate demand shifts left, from $AD_0$ to $AD_1$. The new equilibrium is at $E_1$, with a lower output level of 450 and downward pressure on the price level of 115. With high unemployment rates, wages are held down. Lower wages are an economy-wide decrease in the price of a key input, which shifts short-run aggregate supply to the right, from $SRAS_0$ to $SRAS_1$. The new equilibrium ($E_2$) is at the same original level of output, 500, but at a lower price level of 110.

Again, from the neoclassical perspective, this short-run scenario is only the beginning of the chain of events. The higher level of unemployment means more workers looking for jobs. As a result, employers can hold down on pay increases—or perhaps even replace some of their higher-paid workers with unemployed people willing to accept a lower wage. As wages stagnate or fall, this decline in the price of a key input means that the short-run Keynesian aggregate supply curve shifts to the right from its original ($SRAS_0$ to $SRAS_1$). The overall impact in the long run, as the macroeconomic equilibrium shifts from $E_0$ to $E_1$ to $E_2$, is that the level of output returns to potential GDP, where it started. There is, however, downward pressure on the price level. Thus, in the neoclassical view, changes in aggregate demand can have a short-run impact on output and on unemployment—but only a short-run impact. In the long run, when wages and prices are flexible, potential GDP and aggregate supply determine real GDP's size.

## How Fast Is the Speed of Macroeconomic Adjustment?

How long does it take for wages and prices to adjust, and for the economy to rebound to its potential GDP? This subject is highly contentious. Keynesian economists argue that if the adjustment from recession to potential GDP takes a very long time, then neoclassical theory may be more hypothetical than practical. In response to John Maynard Keynes' immortal words, "In the long run we are all dead," neoclassical economists respond that even if the adjustment takes as long as, say, ten years the neoclassical perspective remains of central importance in understanding the economy.

One subset of neoclassical economists holds that wage and price adjustment in the macroeconomy might be quite rapid. The theory of **rational expectations** holds that people form the most accurate possible expectations about the future that they can, using all information available to them. In an economy where most people have rational expectations, economic adjustments may happen very quickly.

To understand how rational expectations may affect the speed of price adjustments, think about a situation in the real estate market. Imagine that several events seem likely to push up home values in the neighborhood. Perhaps a local employer announces that it plans to hire many more people or the city announces that it will build a local park or a library in that neighborhood. The theory of rational expectations points out that even though none of the changes will happen immediately, home prices in the neighborhood will rise immediately, because the expectation that homes will be worth more in the future will lead buyers to be willing to pay more in the present. The amount of the immediate increase in home prices will depend on how likely it seems that the announcements about the future will actually happen and on how distant the local jobs and neighborhood improvements are in the future. The key point is that, because of rational expectations, prices do not wait on events, but adjust immediately.

At a macroeconomic level, the theory of rational expectations points out that if the aggregate supply curve is vertical over time, then people should rationally expect this pattern. When a shift in aggregate demand occurs, people and businesses with rational expectations will know that its impact on output and employment will be temporary, while its impact on the price level will be permanent. If firms and workers perceive the outcome of the process in advance, and if all firms and workers know that everyone else is perceiving the process in the same way, then they have no incentive to go through an extended series of short-run scenarios, like a firm first hiring more people when aggregate demand shifts out and then firing those same people when aggregate supply shifts back. Instead, everyone will recognize where this process is heading—toward a change in the price level—and then will act on that expectation. In this scenario, the expected long-run change in the price level may happen very quickly, without a drawn-out zigzag of output and employment first moving one way and then the other.

The theory that people and firms have rational expectations can be a useful simplification, but as a statement about how people and businesses actually behave, the assumption seems too strong. After all, many people and firms are not especially well informed, either about what is happening in the economy or about how the economy works. An alternate assumption is that people and firms act with **adaptive expectations**: they look at past experience and gradually adapt their beliefs and behavior as circumstances change, but are not perfect synthesizers of information and accurate predictors of the future in the sense of rational expectations theory. If most people and businesses have some form of adaptive expectations, then the adjustment from the short run and long run will be traced out in incremental steps that occur over time.

The empirical evidence on the speed of macroeconomic adjustment of prices and wages is not clear-cut. The speed of macroeconomic adjustment probably varies among different countries and time periods. A reasonable guess is that the initial short-run effect of a shift in aggregate demand might last two to five years, before the adjustments in wages and prices cause the economy to adjust back to potential GDP. Thus, one might think of the short run for applying Keynesian analysis as time periods less than two to five years, and the long run for applying neoclassical analysis as longer than five years. For practical purposes, this guideline is frustratingly imprecise, but when analyzing a complex social mechanism like an economy as it evolves over time, some imprecision seems unavoidable.

# 13.2 | The Policy Implications of the Neoclassical Perspective

By the end of this section, you will be able to:
- Discuss why and how economists measure inflation expectations
- Analyze the impacts of fiscal and monetary policy on aggregate supply and aggregate demand
- Explain the neoclassical Phillips curve, noting its tradeoff between inflation and unemployment
- Identify clear distinctions between neoclassical economics and Keynesian economics

To understand the policy recommendations of the neoclassical economists, it helps to start with the Keynesian perspective. Suppose a decrease in aggregate demand causes the economy to go into recession with high unemployment. The Keynesian response would be to use government policy to stimulate aggregate demand and eliminate the recessionary gap. The neoclassical economists believe that the Keynesian response, while perhaps well intentioned, will not have a good outcome for reasons we will discuss shortly. Since the neoclassical economists believe that the economy will correct itself over time, the only advantage of a Keynesian stabilization policy would be to accelerate the process and minimize the time that the unemployed are out of work. Is that the likely outcome?

Keynesian macroeconomic policy requires some optimism about the government's ability to recognize a situation of too little or too much aggregate demand, and to adjust aggregate demand accordingly with the right level of changes in taxes or spending, all enacted in a timely fashion. After all, neoclassical economists argue, it takes government statisticians months to produce even preliminary estimates of GDP so that politicians know whether a recession is occurring—and those preliminary estimates may be revised substantially later. Moreover, there is the question of timely action. The political process can take more months to enact a tax cut or a spending increase. Political or economic considerations may determine the amount of tax or spending changes. Then the economy will take still more months to put into effect changes in aggregate demand through spending and production. When economists and policy makers consider all of these time lags and political realities, active fiscal policy may fail to address the current problem, and could even make the future economy worse. The average U.S. post-World War II recession has lasted only about a year. By the time government policy activates, the recession will likely be over. As a consequence, the only result of government fine-tuning will be to stimulate the economy when it is already recovering (or to contract the economy when it is already falling). In other words, an active macroeconomic policy is likely to exacerbate the cycles rather than dampen them. Some neoclassical economists believe a large part of the business cycles we observe are due to flawed government policy. To learn about this issue further, read the following Clear It Up feature.

## Clear It Up

### Why and how do economists measure inflation expectations?

People take expectations about inflation into consideration every time they make a major purchase, such as a house or a car. As inflation fluctuates, so too does the nominal interest rate on loans to buy these goods. The nominal interest rate is comprised of the real rate, plus an **expected inflation** factor. Expected inflation also tells economists about how the public views the economy's direction. Suppose the public expects inflation to increase. This could be the result of positive demand shock due to an expanding economy and increasing aggregate demand. It could also be the result of a negative supply shock, perhaps from rising energy prices, and decreasing aggregate supply. In either case, the public may expect the central bank to engage in contractionary monetary policy to reduce inflation, and this policy results in higher interest rates. If, however economists expect inflation to decrease, the public may anticipate a recession. In turn, the public may expect expansionary monetary policy, and lower interest rates, in the short run. By monitoring expected inflation, economists garner information about the effectiveness of macroeconomic policies. Additionally, monitoring expected inflation allows for projecting the direction of real interest rates that isolate for the effect of inflation. This information is necessary for making decisions about financing investments.

Expectations about inflation may seem like a highly theoretical concept, but, in fact the Federal Reserve Bank measures, inflation expectations based upon early research conducted by Joseph Livingston, a financial journalist for the *Philadelphia Inquirer*. In 1946, he started a twice-a-year survey of economists about their expectations of inflation. After Livingston's death in 1969, the Federal Reserve Bank and other economic research agencies such as the Survey Research Center at the University of Michigan, the American Statistical Association, and the National Bureau of Economic Research continued the survey.

Current Federal Reserve research compares these expectations to actual inflation that has occurred, and the results, so far, are mixed. Economists' forecasts, however, have become notably more accurate in the last few decades. Economists are actively researching how inflation expectations and other economic variables form and change.

## Link It Up

Visit this website (https://www.clevelandfed.org/newsroom-and-events/publications/economic-commentary/economic-commentary-archives/2009-economic-commentaries/ec-20090809-a-new-approach-to-gauging-inflation-expectations.aspx) to read "The Federal Reserve Bank of Cleveland's Economic Commentary: A New Approach to Gauging Inflation Expectations" by Joseph G. Haubrich for more information about how economists forecast expected inflation.

# The Neoclassical Phillips Curve Tradeoff

**The Keynesian Perspective** introduced the Phillips curve and explained how it is derived from the aggregate supply curve. The short run upward sloping aggregate supply curve implies a downward sloping Phillips curve; thus, there is a tradeoff between inflation and unemployment in the short run. By contrast, a neoclassical long-run aggregate supply curve will imply a vertical shape for the Phillips curve, indicating no long run tradeoff between inflation and unemployment. **Figure 13.6** (a) shows the vertical AS curve, with three different levels of aggregate demand, resulting in three different equilibria, at three different price levels. At every point along that vertical AS curve, potential GDP and the rate of unemployment remains the same. Assume that for this economy, the natural rate of unemployment is 5%. As a result, the long-run Phillips curve relationship, in **Figure 13.6** (b), is a vertical line, rising up from 5% unemployment, at any level of inflation. Read the following Work It Out feature for additional information on how to interpret inflation and unemployment rates.

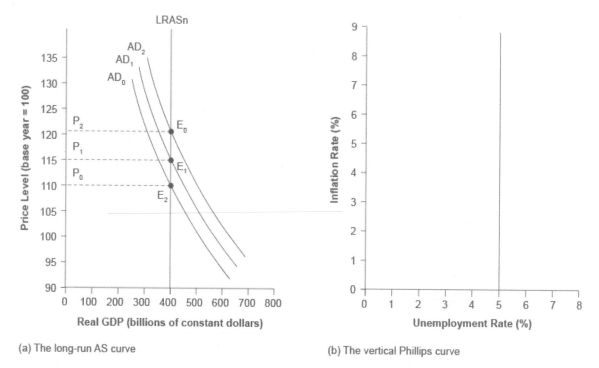

(a) The long-run AS curve                              (b) The vertical Phillips curve

**Figure 13.6 From a Long-Run AS Curve to a Long-Run Phillips Curve** (a) With a vertical LRAS curve, shifts in aggregate demand do not alter the level of output but do lead to changes in the price level. Because output is unchanged between the equilibria $E_0$, $E_1$, and $E_2$, all unemployment in this economy will be due to the natural rate of unemployment. (b) If the natural rate of unemployment is 5%, then the Phillips curve will be vertical. That is, regardless of changes in the price level, the unemployment rate remains at 5%.

# Work It Out ──○──○──○

## Tracking Inflation and Unemployment Rates

Suppose that you have collected data for years on inflation and unemployment rates and recorded them in a table, such as Table 13.1. How do you interpret that information?

| Year | Inflation Rate | Unemployment Rate |
|------|----------------|-------------------|
| 1970 | 2% | 4% |
| 1975 | 3% | 3% |
| 1980 | 2% | 4% |
| 1985 | 1% | 6% |
| 1990 | 1% | 4% |
| 1995 | 4% | 2% |
| 2000 | 5% | 4% |

Table 13.1

Step 1. Plot the data points in a graph with inflation rate on the vertical axis and unemployment rate on the horizontal axis. Your graph will appear similar to Figure 13.7.

Figure 13.7 Inflation Rates

Step 2. What patterns do you see in the data? You should notice that there are years when unemployment falls but inflation rises, and other years where unemployment rises and inflation falls.

Step 3. Can you determine the natural rate of unemployment from the data or from the graph? As you analyze the graph, it appears that the natural rate of unemployment lies at 4%. This is the rate that the economy appears to adjust back to after an apparent change in the economy. For example, in 1975 the economy appeared to have an increase in aggregate demand. The unemployment rate fell to 3% but inflation increased from 2% to 3%. By 1980, the economy had adjusted back to 4% unemployment and the inflation rate had returned to 2%. In 1985, the economy looks to have suffered a recession as unemployment rose to 6% and inflation fell to 1%. This would be consistent with a decrease in aggregate demand. By 1990, the economy recovered back to 4% unemployment, but at a lower inflation rate of 1%. In 1995 the economy again rebounded and unemployment fell to 2%, but inflation increased to 4%, which is consistent with a large increase in aggregate demand. The economy adjusted back to 4% unemployment but at a higher rate of inflation of 5%. Then in 2000, both unemployment and inflation increased to 5% and 4%, respectively.

Step 4. Do you see the Phillips curve(s) in the data? If we trace the downward sloping trend of data points, we could see a short-run Phillips curve that exhibits the inverse tradeoff between higher unemployment and lower inflation rates. If we trace the vertical line of data points, we could see a long-run Phillips curve at the 4% natural rate of unemployment.

The unemployment rate on the long-run Phillips curve will be the natural rate of unemployment. A small inflationary increase in the price level from $AD_0$ to $AD_1$ will have the same natural rate of unemployment as a larger inflationary increase in the price level from $AD_0$ to $AD_2$. The macroeconomic equilibrium along the vertical aggregate supply curve can occur at a variety of different price levels, and the natural rate of unemployment can be consistent with all different rates of inflation. The great economist Milton Friedman (1912–2006) summed up the neoclassical view of the long-term Phillips curve tradeoff in a 1967 speech: "[T]here is always a temporary trade-off between inflation and unemployment; there is no permanent trade-off."

In the Keynesian perspective, the primary focus is on getting the level of aggregate demand right in relationship to an upward-sloping aggregate supply curve. That is, the government should adjust AD so that the economy produces at its potential GDP, not so low that cyclical unemployment results and not so high that inflation results. In the neoclassical perspective, aggregate supply will determine output at potential GDP, the natural rate of unemployment determines unemployment, and shifts in aggregate demand are the primary determinant of changes in the price level.

# Link It Up

Visit this website (http://openstaxcollege.org/l/modeledbehavior) to read about the effects of economic intervention.

## Fighting Unemployment or Inflation?

As we explained in **Unemployment**, economists divide unemployment into two categories: cyclical unemployment and the natural rate of unemployment, which is the sum of frictional and structural unemployment. Cyclical unemployment results from fluctuations in the business cycle and is created when the economy is producing below potential GDP—giving potential employers less incentive to hire. When the economy is producing at potential GDP, cyclical unemployment will be zero. Because of labor market dynamics, in which people are always entering or exiting the labor force, the unemployment rate never falls to 0%, not even when the economy is producing at or even slightly above potential GDP. Probably the best we can hope for is for the number of job vacancies to equal the number of job seekers. We know that it takes time for job seekers and employers to find each other, and this time is the cause of frictional unemployment. Most economists do not consider frictional unemployment to be a "bad" thing. After all, there will always be workers who are unemployed while looking for a job that is a better match for their skills. There will always be employers that have an open position, while looking for a worker that is a better match for the job. Ideally, these matches happen quickly, but even when the economy is very strong there will be some natural unemployment and this is what the natural rate of unemployment measures.

The neoclassical view of unemployment tends to focus attention away from the cyclical unemployment problem—that is, unemployment caused by recession—while putting more attention on the unemployment rate issue that prevails even when the economy is operating at potential GDP. To put it another way, the neoclassical view of unemployment tends to focus on how the government can adjust public policy to reduce the natural rate of unemployment. Such policy changes might involve redesigning unemployment and welfare programs so that they support those in need, but also offer greater encouragement for job-hunting. It might involve redesigning business rules with an eye to whether they are unintentionally discouraging businesses from taking on new employees. It might involve building institutions to improve the flow of information about jobs and the mobility of workers, to help bring workers and employers together more quickly. For those workers who find that their skills are permanently no longer in demand (for example, the structurally unemployed), economists can design policy to provide opportunities for retraining so that these workers can reenter the labor force and seek employment.

Neoclassical economists will not tend to see aggregate demand as a useful tool for reducing unemployment; after all, with a vertical aggregate supply curve determining economic output, then aggregate demand has no long-run effect on unemployment. Instead, neoclassical economists believe that aggregate demand should be allowed to expand only to match the gradual shifts of aggregate supply to the right—keeping the price level much the same and inflationary pressures low.

If aggregate demand rises rapidly in the neoclassical model, in the long run it leads only to inflationary pressures. **Figure 13.8** shows a vertical LRAS curve and three different levels of aggregate demand, rising from $AD_0$ to $AD_1$ to $AD_2$. As the macroeconomic equilibrium rises from $E_0$ to $E_1$ to $E_2$, the price level rises, but real GDP does not budge; nor does the rate of unemployment, which adjusts to its natural rate. Conversely, reducing inflation has no long-term costs, either. Think about **Figure 13.8** in reverse, as the aggregate demand curve shifts from $AD_2$ to $AD_1$ to $AD_0$, and the equilibrium moves from $E_2$ to $E_1$ to $E_0$. During this process, the price level falls, but, in the long run, neither real GDP nor the natural unemployment rate changes.

**Figure 13.8 How Aggregate Demand Determines the Price Level in the Long Run** As aggregate demand shifts to the right, from $AD_0$ to $AD_1$ to $AD_2$, real GDP in this economy and the level of unemployment do not change. However, there is inflationary pressure for a higher price level as the equilibrium changes from $E_0$ to $E_1$ to $E_2$.

# Link It Up ⚭

Visit this website (http://openstaxcollege.org/l/inflatemploy) to read about how inflation and unemployment are related.

## Fighting Recession or Encouraging Long-Term Growth?

Neoclassical economists believe that the economy will rebound out of a recession or eventually contract during an expansion because prices and wage rates are flexible and will adjust either upward or downward to restore the economy to its potential GDP. Thus, the key policy question for neoclassicals is how to promote growth of potential GDP. We know that economic growth ultimately depends on the growth rate of long-term productivity. Productivity measures how effective inputs are at producing outputs. We know that U.S. productivity has grown on average about 2% per year. That means that the same amount of inputs produce 2% more output than the year before. We also know that productivity growth varies a great deal in the short term due to cyclical factors. It also varies somewhat in the long term. From 1953–1972, U.S. labor productivity (as measured by output per hour in the business sector) grew at 3.2% per year. From 1973–1992, productivity growth declined significantly to 1.8% per year. Then, from 1993–2014, productivity growth increased slightly to 2% per year. The neoclassical economists believe the underpinnings of long-run productivity growth to be an economy's investments in human capital, physical capital, and technology, operating together in a market-oriented environment that rewards innovation. Government policy should focus on promoting these factors.

## Summary of Neoclassical Macroeconomic Policy Recommendations

Let's summarize what neoclassical economists recommend for macroeconomic policy. Neoclassical economists do not believe in "fine-tuning" the economy. They believe that a stable economic environment with a low rate of inflation fosters economic growth. Similarly, tax rates should be low and unchanging. In this environment, private economic agents can make the best possible investment decisions, which will lead to optimal investment in physical and human capital as well as research and development to promote improvements in technology.

## Summary of Neoclassical Economics versus Keynesian Economics

Table 13.2 summarizes the key differences between the two schools of thought.

| Summary | Neoclassical Economics | Keynesian Economics |
|---|---|---|
| Focus: long-term or short term | Long-term | Short-term |
| Prices and wages: sticky or flexible? | Flexible | Sticky |
| Economic output: Primarily determined by aggregate demand or aggregate supply? | Aggregate supply | Aggregate demand |
| Aggregate supply: vertical or upward-sloping? | Vertical | Upward-sloping |
| Phillips curve vertical or downward-sloping | Vertical | Downward sloping |

Table 13.2 Neoclassical versus Keynesian Economics

| Summary | Neoclassical Economics | Keynesian Economics |
|---|---|---|
| Is aggregate demand a useful tool for controlling inflation? | Yes | Yes |
| What should be the primary area of policy emphasis for reducing unemployment? | Reform labor market institutions to reduce natural rate of unemployment | Increase aggregate demand to eliminate cyclical unemployment |
| Is aggregate demand a useful tool for ending recession? | At best, only in the short-run temporary sense, but may just increase inflation instead | Yes |

Table 13.2 Neoclassical versus Keynesian Economics

# 13.3 | Balancing Keynesian and Neoclassical Models

By the end of this section, you will be able to:
- Evaluate how neoclassical economists and Keynesian economists react to recessions
- Analyze the interrelationship between the neoclassical and Keynesian economic models

We can compare finding the balance between Keynesian and Neoclassical models to the challenge of riding two horses simultaneously. When a circus performer stands on two horses, with a foot on each one, much of the excitement for the viewer lies in contemplating the gap between the two. As modern macroeconomists ride into the future on two horses—with one foot on the short-term Keynesian perspective and one foot on the long-term neoclassical perspective—the balancing act may look uncomfortable, but there does not seem to be any way to avoid it. Each approach, Keynesian and neoclassical, has its strengths and weaknesses.

The short-term Keynesian model, built on the importance of aggregate demand as a cause of business cycles and a degree of wage and price rigidity, does a sound job of explaining many recessions and why cyclical unemployment rises and falls. By focusing on the short-run aggregate demand adjustments, Keynesian economics risks overlooking the long-term causes of economic growth or the natural rate of unemployment that exist even when the economy is producing at potential GDP.

The neoclassical model, with its emphasis on aggregate supply, focuses on the underlying determinants of output and employment in markets, and thus tends to put more emphasis on economic growth and how labor markets work. However, the neoclassical view is not especially helpful in explaining why unemployment moves up and down over short time horizons of a few years. Nor is the neoclassical model especially helpful when the economy is mired in an especially deep and long-lasting recession, like the 1930s Great Depression. Keynesian economics tends to view inflation as a price that might sometimes be paid for lower unemployment; neoclassical economics tends to view inflation as a cost that offers no offsetting gains in terms of lower unemployment.

Macroeconomics cannot, however, be summed up as an argument between one group of economists who are pure Keynesians and another group who are pure neoclassicists. Instead, many mainstream economists believe both the Keynesian and neoclassical perspectives. Robert Solow, the Nobel laureate in economics in 1987, described the dual approach in this way:

> At short time scales, I think, something sort of 'Keynesian' is a good approximation, and surely better than anything straight 'neoclassical.' At very long time scales, the interesting questions are best studied in a neoclassical framework, and attention to the Keynesian side of things would be a minor distraction. At the five-to-ten-year time scale, we have to piece things together as best we can, and look for a hybrid model that will do the job.

Many modern macroeconomists spend considerable time and energy trying to construct models that blend the most attractive aspects of the Keynesian and neoclassical approaches. It is possible to construct a somewhat complex mathematical model where aggregate demand and sticky wages and prices matter in the short run, but wages, prices, and aggregate supply adjust in the long run. However, creating an overall model that encompasses both short-term Keynesian and long-term neoclassical models is not easy.

# Bring it Home

## Navigating Unchartered Waters

Were the policies that the government implemented to stabilize the economy and financial markets during the Great Recession effective? Many economists from both the Keynesian and neoclassical schools have found that they were, although to varying degrees. Alan Blinder of Princeton University and Mark Zandi for Moody's Analytics found that, without fiscal policy, GDP decline would have been significantly more than its 3.3% in 2008 followed by its 0.1% decline in 2009. They also estimated that there would have been 8.5 million more job losses had the government not intervened in the market with the TARP to support the financial industry and key automakers General Motors and Chrysler. Federal Reserve Bank economists Carlos Carvalho, Stefano Eusip, and Christian Grisse found in their study, *Policy Initiatives in the Global Recession: What Did Forecasters Expect?* that once the government implemented policies, forecasters adapted their expectations to these policies. They were more likely to anticipate increases in investment due to lower interest rates brought on by monetary policy and increased economic growth resulting from fiscal policy.

The difficulty with evaluating the effectiveness of the stabilization policies that the government took in response to the Great Recession is that we will never know what would have happened had the government not implemented those policies. Surely some of the programs were more effective at creating and saving jobs, while other programs were less so. The final conclusion on the effectiveness of macroeconomic policies is still up for debate, and further study will no doubt consider the impact of these policies on the U.S. budget and deficit, as well as the U.S. dollar's value in the financial market.

# KEY TERMS

**adaptive expectations**  the theory that people look at past experience and gradually adapt their beliefs and behavior as circumstances change

**expected inflation**  a future rate of inflation that consumers and firms build into current decision making

**neoclassical perspective**  the philosophy that, in the long run, the business cycle will fluctuate around the potential, or full-employment, level of output

**physical capital per person**  the amount and kind of machinery and equipment available to help a person produce a good or service

**rational expectations**  the theory that people form the most accurate possible expectations about the future that they can, using all information available to them

# KEY CONCEPTS AND SUMMARY

## 13.1 The Building Blocks of Neoclassical Analysis

The neoclassical perspective argues that, in the long run, the economy will adjust back to its potential GDP level of output through flexible price levels. Thus, the neoclassical perspective views the long-run AS curve as vertical. A rational expectations perspective argues that people have excellent information about economic events and how the economy works and that, as a result, price and other economic adjustments will happen very quickly. In adaptive expectations theory, people have limited information about economic information and how the economy works, and so price and other economic adjustments can be slow.

## 13.2 The Policy Implications of the Neoclassical Perspective

Neoclassical economists tend to put relatively more emphasis on long-term growth than on fighting recession, because they believe that recessions will fade in a few years and long-term growth will ultimately determine the standard of living. They tend to focus more on reducing the natural rate of unemployment caused by economic institutions and government policies than the cyclical unemployment caused by recession.

Neoclassical economists also see no social benefit to inflation. With an upward-sloping Keynesian AS curve, inflation can arise because an economy is approaching full employment. With a vertical long-run neoclassical AS curve, inflation does not accompany any rise in output. If aggregate supply is vertical, then aggregate demand does not affect the quantity of output. Instead, aggregate demand can only cause inflationary changes in the price level. A vertical aggregate supply curve, where the quantity of output is consistent with many different price levels, also implies a vertical Phillips curve.

## 13.3 Balancing Keynesian and Neoclassical Models

The Keynesian perspective considers changes to aggregate demand to be the cause of business cycle fluctuations. Keynesians are likely to advocate that policy makers actively attempt to reverse recessionary and inflationary periods because they are not convinced that the self-correcting economy can easily return to full employment.

The neoclassical perspective places more emphasis on aggregate supply. Neoclassical economists believe that long term productivity growth determines the potential GDP level and that the economy typically will return to full employment after a change in aggregate demand. Skeptical of the effectiveness and timeliness of Keynesian policy, neoclassical economists are more likely to advocate a hands-off, or fairly limited, role for active stabilization policy.

While Keynesians would tend to advocate an acceptable tradeoff between inflation and unemployment when counteracting a recession, neoclassical economists argue that no such tradeoff exists. Any short-term gains in lower unemployment will eventually vanish and the result of active policy will only be inflation.

## SELF-CHECK QUESTIONS

**1.** Do rational expectations tend to look back at past experience while adaptive expectations look ahead to the future? Explain your answer.

**2.** Legislation proposes that the government should use macroeconomic policy to achieve an unemployment rate of zero percent, by increasing aggregate demand for as much and as long as necessary to accomplish this goal. From a neoclassical perspective, how will this policy affect output and the price level in the short run and in the long run? Sketch an aggregate demand/aggregate supply diagram to illustrate your answer. *Hint*: revisit **Figure 13.4**.

**3.** Would it make sense to argue that rational expectations economics is an extreme version of neoclassical economics? Explain.

**4.** Summarize the Keynesian and Neoclassical models.

## REVIEW QUESTIONS

**5.** Does neoclassical economics focus on the long term or the short term? Explain your answer.

**6.** Does neoclassical economics view prices and wages as sticky or flexible? Why?

**7.** What shape is the long-run aggregate supply curve? Why does it have this shape?

**8.** What is the difference between rational expectations and adaptive expectations?

**9.** A neoclassical economist and a Keynesian economist are studying the economy of Vineland. It appears that Vineland is beginning to experience a mild recession with a decrease in aggregate demand. Which of these two economists would likely advocate that the government of Vineland take active measures to reverse this decline in aggregate demand? Why?

**10.** Do neoclassical economists tend to focus more on long term economic growth or on recessions? Explain briefly.

**11.** Do neoclassical economists tend to focus more on cyclical unemployment or on inflation? Explain briefly.

**12.** Do neoclassical economists see a value in tolerating a little more inflation if it brings additional economic output? Explain your answer.

**13.** If aggregate supply is vertical, what role does aggregate demand play in determining output? In determining the price level?

**14.** What is the shape of the neoclassical long-run Phillips curve? What assumptions do economists make that lead to this shape?

**15.** When the economy is experiencing a recession, why would a neoclassical economist be unlikely to argue for aggressive policy to stimulate aggregate demand and return the economy to full employment? Explain your answer.

**16.** If the economy is suffering through a rampant inflationary period, would a Keynesian economist advocate for stabilization policy that involves higher taxes and higher interest rates? Explain your answer.

## CRITICAL THINKING QUESTIONS

**17.** If most people have rational expectations, how long will recessions last?

**18.** Explain why the neoclassical economists believe that the government does not need to do much about unemployment. Do you agree or disagree? Explain.

**19.** Economists from all theoretical persuasions criticized the American Recovery and Reinvestment Act. The "Stimulus Package" was arguably a Keynesian measure so why would a Keynesian economist be critical of it? Why would neoclassical economists be critical?

**20.** Is it a logical contradiction to be a neoclassical Keynesian? Explain.

# PROBLEMS

**21.** Use **Table 13.3** to answer the following questions.

| Price Level | Aggregate Supply | Aggregate Demand |
|---|---|---|
| 90 | 3,000 | 3,500 |
| 95 | 3,000 | 3,000 |
| 100 | 3,000 | 2,500 |
| 105 | 3,000 | 2,200 |
| 110 | 3,000 | 2,100 |

**Table 13.3**

    a. Sketch an aggregate supply and aggregate demand diagram.

    b. What is the equilibrium output and price level?

    c. If aggregate demand shifts right, what is equilibrium output?

    d. If aggregate demand shifts left, what is equilibrium output?

    e. In this scenario, would you suggest using aggregate demand to alter the level of output or to control any inflationary increases in the price level?

# 14 | Money and Banking

**Figure 14.1 Cowrie Shell or Money?** Is this an image of a cowrie shell or money? The answer is: Both. For centuries, people used the extremely durable cowrie shell as a medium of exchange in various parts of the world. (Credit: modification of work by "prilfish"/Flickr Creative Commons)

## Bring it Home

### The Many Disguises of Money: From Cowries to Bitcoins

Here is a trivia question: In the history of the world, what item did people use for money over the broadest geographic area and for the longest period of time? The answer is not gold, silver, or any precious metal. It is the cowrie, a mollusk shell found mainly off the Maldives Islands in the Indian Ocean. Cowries served as money as early as 700 B.C. in China. By the 1500s, they were in widespread use across India and Africa. For several centuries after that, cowries were the means for exchange in markets including southern Europe, western Africa, India, and China: everything from buying lunch or a ferry ride to paying for a shipload of silk or rice. Cowries were still acceptable as a way of paying taxes in certain African nations in the early twentieth century.

What made cowries work so well as money? First, they are extremely durable—lasting a century or more. As the late economic historian Karl Polyani put it, they can be "poured, sacked, shoveled, hoarded in heaps" while remaining "clean, dainty, stainless, polished, and milk-white." Second, parties could use cowries either by counting shells of a certain size, or—for large purchases—by measuring the weight or volume of the total shells they would exchange. Third, it was impossible to counterfeit a cowrie shell, but dishonest people could counterfeit gold or silver coins by making copies with cheaper metals. Finally, in the heyday of cowrie money, from the 1500s into the 1800s, governments, first the Portuguese, then the Dutch and English, tightly controlled collecting cowries. As a result, the supply of cowries grew quickly enough to serve the needs of commerce, but not so quickly that they were no longer scarce. Money throughout the ages has taken many different forms and continues to evolve even today. What do you think money is?

# Introduction to Money and Banking

In this chapter, you will learn about:

- Defining Money by Its Functions
- Measuring Money: Currency, M1, and M2
- The Role of Banks
- How Banks Create Money

The discussion of money and banking is a central component in studying macroeconomics. At this point, you should have firmly in mind the main goals of macroeconomics from **Welcome to Economics!**: economic growth, low unemployment, and low inflation. We have yet to discuss money and its role in helping to achieve our macroeconomic goals.

You should also understand Keynesian and neoclassical frameworks for macroeconomic analysis and how we can embody these frameworks in the aggregate demand/aggregate supply (AD/AS) model. With the goals and frameworks for macroeconomic analysis in mind, the final step is to discuss the two main categories of macroeconomic policy: monetary policy, which focuses on money, banking and interest rates; and fiscal policy, which focuses on government spending, taxes, and borrowing. This chapter discusses what economists mean by money, and how money is closely interrelated with the banking system. **Monetary Policy and Bank Regulation** furthers this discussion.

# 14.1 | Defining Money by Its Functions

By the end of this section, you will be able to:
- Explain the various functions of money
- Contrast commodity money and fiat money

Money for the sake of money is not an end in itself. You cannot eat dollar bills or wear your bank account. Ultimately, the usefulness of money rests in exchanging it for goods or services. As the American writer and humorist Ambrose Bierce (1842–1914) wrote in 1911, money is a "blessing that is of no advantage to us excepting when we part with it." Money is what people regularly use when purchasing or selling goods and services, and thus both buyers and sellers must widely accept money. This concept of money is intentionally flexible, because money has taken a wide variety of forms in different cultures.

## Barter and the Double Coincidence of Wants

To understand the usefulness of money, we must consider what the world would be like without money. How would people exchange goods and services? Economies without money typically engage in the barter system. **Barter**—literally trading one good or service for another—is highly inefficient for trying to coordinate the trades in a modern advanced economy. In an economy without money, an exchange between two people would involve a **double coincidence of wants**, a situation in which two people each want some good or service that the other person can provide. For example, if an accountant wants a pair of shoes, this accountant must find someone who has a pair of shoes in the correct size and who is willing to exchange the shoes for some hours of accounting services. Such a trade is likely to be difficult to arrange. Think about the complexity of such trades in a modern economy, with its extensive division of labor that involves thousands upon thousands of different jobs and goods.

Another problem with the barter system is that it does not allow us to easily enter into future contracts for purchasing many goods and services. For example, if the goods are perishable it may be difficult to exchange them for other goods in the future. Imagine a farmer wanting to buy a tractor in six months using a fresh crop of strawberries. Additionally, while the barter system might work adequately in small economies, it will keep these economies from growing. The time that individuals would otherwise spend producing goods and services and enjoying leisure time they spend bartering.

## Functions for Money

Money solves the problems that the barter system creates. (We will get to its definition soon.) First, money serves as a **medium of exchange**, which means that money acts as an intermediary between the buyer and the seller. Instead of exchanging accounting services for shoes, the accountant now exchanges accounting services for money. The accountant then uses this money to buy shoes. To serve as a medium of exchange, people must widely accept money as a method of payment in the markets for goods, labor, and financial capital.

Second, money must serve as a **store of value**. In a barter system, we saw the example of the shoemaker trading shoes for accounting services. However, she risks having her shoes go out of style, especially if she keeps them in a warehouse for future use—their value will decrease with each season. Shoes are not a good store of value. Holding money is a much easier way of storing value. You know that you do not need to spend it immediately because it will still hold its value the next day, or the next year. This function of money does not require that money is a *perfect* store of value. In an economy with inflation, money loses some buying power each year, but it remains money.

Third, money serves as a **unit of account**, which means that it is the ruler by which we measure values. For example, an accountant may charge $100 to file your tax return. That $100 can purchase two pair of shoes at $50 a pair. Money acts as a common denominator, an accounting method that simplifies thinking about trade-offs.

Finally, another function of money is that it must serve as a **standard of deferred payment**. This means that if money is usable today to make purchases, it must also be acceptable to make purchases today that the purchaser will pay in the *future*. Loans and future agreements are stated in monetary terms and the standard of deferred payment is what allows us to buy goods and services today and pay in the future. Thus, **money** serves all of these functions— it is a medium of exchange, store of value, unit of account, and standard of deferred payment.

## Commodity versus Fiat Money

Money has taken a wide variety of forms in different cultures. People have used gold, silver, cowrie shells, cigarettes, and even cocoa beans as money. Although we use these items as **commodity money**, they also have a value from use as something other than money. For example, people have used gold throughout the ages as money although today we do not use it as money but rather value it for its other attributes. Gold is a good conductor of electricity and the electronics and aerospace industry use it. Other industries use gold too, such as to manufacture energy efficient reflective glass for skyscrapers and is used in the medical industry as well. Of course, gold also has value because of its beauty and malleability in creating jewelry.

As commodity money, gold has historically served its purpose as a medium of exchange, a store of value, and as a unit of account. **Commodity-backed currencies** are dollar bills or other currencies with values backed up by gold or other commodities held at a bank. During much of its history, gold and silver backed the money supply in the United States. Interestingly, antique dollars dated as late as 1957, have "Silver Certificate" printed over the portrait of George Washington, as **Figure 14.2** shows. This meant that the holder could take the bill to the appropriate bank and exchange it for a dollar's worth of silver.

**Figure 14.2 A Silver Certificate and a Modern U.S. Bill** Until 1958, silver certificates were commodity-backed money—backed by silver, as indicated by the words "Silver Certificate" printed on the bill. Today, The Federal Reserve backs U.S. bills, but as fiat money (inconvertible paper money made legal tender by a government decree). (Credit: "The.Comedian"/Flickr Creative Commons)

As economies grew and became more global in nature, the use of commodity monies became more cumbersome. Countries moved towards the use of **fiat money**. Fiat money has no intrinsic value, but is declared by a government to be a country's legal tender. The United States' paper money, for example, carries the statement: "THIS NOTE IS LEGAL TENDER FOR ALL DEBTS, PUBLIC AND PRIVATE." In other words, by government decree, if you owe a debt, then legally speaking, you can pay that debt with the U.S. currency, even though it is not backed by a commodity. The only backing of our money is universal faith and trust that the currency has value, and nothing more.

# Link It Up

Watch this video (http://openstaxcollege.org/l/moneyhistory) on the "History of Money."

# 14.2 | Measuring Money: Currency, M1, and M2

By the end of this section, you will be able to:
- Contrast M1 money supply and M2 money supply
- Classify monies as M1 money supply or M2 money supply

Cash in your pocket certainly serves as money; however, what about checks or credit cards? Are they money, too? Rather than trying to state a single way of measuring money, economists offer broader definitions of money based on liquidity. Liquidity refers to how quickly you can use a financial asset to buy a good or service. For example, cash is very liquid. You can use your $10 bill easily to buy a hamburger at lunchtime. However, $10 that you have in your savings account is not so easy to use. You must go to the bank or ATM machine and withdraw that cash to buy your lunch. Thus, $10 in your savings account is *less* liquid.

The Federal Reserve Bank, which is the central bank of the United States, is a bank regulator and is responsible for monetary policy and defines money according to its liquidity. There are two definitions of money: M1 and M2 money supply. **M1 money supply** includes those monies that are very liquid such as cash, checkable (demand) deposits, and traveler's checks **M2 money supply** is less liquid in nature and includes M1 plus savings and time deposits, certificates of deposits, and money market funds.

M1 money supply includes **coins and currency in circulation**—the coins and bills that circulate in an economy that the U.S. Treasury does not hold at the Federal Reserve Bank, or in bank vaults. Closely related to currency are checkable deposits, also known as **demand deposits**. These are the amounts held in checking accounts. They are called demand deposits or checkable deposits because the banking institution must give the deposit holder his money "on demand" when the customer writes a check or uses a debit card. These items together—currency, and checking accounts in banks—comprise the definition of money known as M1, which the Federal Reserve System measures daily.

A broader definition of money, M2 includes everything in M1 but also adds other types of deposits. For example, M2 includes **savings deposits** in banks, which are bank accounts on which you cannot write a check directly, but from which you can easily withdraw the money at an automatic teller machine or bank. Many banks and other financial institutions also offer a chance to invest in **money market funds**, where they pool together the deposits of many individual investors and invest them in a safe way, such as short-term government bonds. Another ingredient of M2 are the relatively small (that is, less than about $100,000) certificates of deposit (CDs) or **time deposits**, which are accounts that the depositor has committed to leaving in the bank for a certain period of time, ranging from a few months to a few years, in exchange for a higher interest rate. In short, all these types of M2 are money that you can withdraw and spend, but which require a greater effort to do so than the items in M1. **Figure 14.3** should help in visualizing the relationship between M1 and M2. Note that M1 is included in the M2 calculation.

**Figure 14.3 The Relationship between M1 and M2 Money**  M1 and M2 money have several definitions, ranging from narrow to broad. M1 = coins and currency in circulation + checkable (demand) deposit + traveler's checks. M2 = M1 + savings deposits + money market funds + certificates of deposit + other time deposits.

The Federal Reserve System is responsible for tracking the amounts of M1 and M2 and prepares a weekly release of information about the money supply. To provide an idea of what these amounts sound like, according to the Federal Reserve Bank's measure of the U.S. money stock, at the end of February 2015, M1 in the United States was $3 trillion, while M2 was $11.8 trillion. **Table 14.1** provides a breakdown of the portion of each type of money that comprised M1 and M2 in February 2015, as provided by the Federal Reserve Bank.

| Components of M1 in the U.S. (February 2015, Seasonally Adjusted) | $ billions |
|---|---|
| Currency | $1,271.8 |
| Traveler's checks | $2.9 |
| Demand deposits and other checking accounts | $1,713.5 |
| Total M1 | $2,988.2 (or $3 trillion) |
| **Components of M2 in the U.S. (February 2015, Seasonally Adjusted)** | **$ billions** |
| M1 money supply | $2,988.2 |
| Savings accounts | $7,712.1 |
| Time deposits | $509.2 |
| Individual money market mutual fund balances | $610.8 |
| Total M2 | $11,820.3 (or $11.8 trillion) |

**Table 14.1 M1 and M2 Federal Reserve Statistical Release, Money Stock Measures** (Source: Federal Reserve Statistical Release, http://www.federalreserve.gov/RELEASES/h6/current/default.htm#t2tg1link)

The lines separating M1 and M2 can become a little blurry. Sometimes businesses do not treat elements of M1 alike. For example, some businesses will not accept personal checks for large amounts, but will accept traveler's checks or cash. Changes in banking practices and technology have made the savings accounts in M2 more similar to the checking accounts in M1. For example, some savings accounts will allow depositors to write checks, use automatic teller machines, and pay bills over the internet, which has made it easier to access savings accounts. As with many other economic terms and statistics, the important point is to know the strengths and limitations of the various definitions of money, not to believe that such definitions are as clear-cut to economists as, say, the definition of nitrogen is to chemists.

Where does "plastic money" like debit cards, credit cards, and smart money fit into this picture? A **debit card**, like a check, is an instruction to the user's bank to transfer money directly and immediately from your bank account to the seller. It is important to note that in our definition of money, it is *checkable deposits* that are money, not the paper check or the debit card. Although you can make a purchase with a **credit card**, the financial institution does not consider it money but rather a short term loan from the credit card company to you. When you make a credit card purchase, the credit card company immediately transfers money from its checking account to the seller, and at the end of the month, the credit card company sends you a bill for what you have charged that month. Until you pay the credit card bill, you have effectively borrowed money from the credit card company. With a **smart card**, you can store a certain value of money on the card and then use the card to make purchases. Some "smart cards" used for specific purposes, like long-distance phone calls or making purchases at a campus bookstore and cafeteria, are not really all that smart, because you can only use them for certain purchases or in certain places.

In short, credit cards, debit cards, and smart cards are different ways to move money when you make a purchase. However, having more credit cards or debit cards does not change the quantity of money in the economy, any more than printing more checks increases the amount of money in your checking account.

One key message underlying this discussion of M1 and M2 is that money in a modern economy is not just paper bills and coins. Instead, money is closely linked to bank accounts. The banking system largely conducts macroeconomic policies concerning money. The next section explains how banks function and how a nation's banking system has the power to create money.

Link It Up ⟨⟨∞⟩⟩

Read a brief article (http://openstaxcollege.org/l/Sweden) on the current monetary challenges in Sweden.

# 14.3 | The Role of Banks

By the end of this section, you will be able to:

- Explain how banks act as intermediaries between savers and borrowers
- Evaluate the relationship between banks, savings and loans, and credit unions
- Analyze the causes of bankruptcy and recessions

Somebody once asked the late bank robber named Willie Sutton why he robbed banks. He answered: "That's where the money is." While this may have been true at one time, from the perspective of modern economists, Sutton is both right and wrong. He is wrong because the overwhelming majority of money in the economy is not in the form of currency sitting in vaults or drawers at banks, waiting for a robber to appear. Most money is in the form of bank accounts, which exist only as electronic records on computers. From a broader perspective, however, the bank robber was more right than he may have known. Banking is intimately interconnected with money and consequently, with the broader economy.

Banks make it far easier for a complex economy to carry out the extraordinary range of transactions that occur in goods, labor, and financial capital markets. Imagine for a moment what the economy would be like if everybody had to make all payments in cash. When shopping for a large purchase or going on vacation you might need to carry hundreds of dollars in a pocket or purse. Even small businesses would need stockpiles of cash to pay workers and to purchase supplies. A bank allows people and businesses to store this money in either a checking account or savings account, for example, and then withdraw this money as needed through the use of a direct withdrawal, writing a check, or using a debit card.

Banks are a critical intermediary in what we call the **payment system**, which helps an economy exchange goods and services for money or other financial assets. Also, those with extra money that they would like to save can store their money in a bank rather than look for an individual who is willing to borrow it from them and then repay them at a later date. Those who want to borrow money can go directly to a bank rather than trying to find someone to lend them cash. **Transaction costs** are the costs associated with finding a lender or a borrower for this money. Thus, banks lower transactions costs and act as financial intermediaries—they bring savers and borrowers together. Along with making transactions much safer and easier, banks also play a key role in creating money.

## Banks as Financial Intermediaries

An "intermediary" is one who stands between two other parties. Banks are a **financial intermediary**—that is, an institution that operates between a saver who deposits money in a bank and a borrower who receives a loan from that bank. Financial intermediaries include other institutions in the financial market such as insurance companies and pension funds, but we will not include them in this discussion because they are not **depository institutions**, which are institutions that accept money *deposits* and then use these to make loans. All the deposited funds mingle in one big pool, which the financial institution then lends. **Figure 14.4** illustrates the position of banks as financial intermediaries, with deposits flowing into a bank and loans flowing out. Of course, when banks make loans to firms, the banks will try to funnel financial capital to healthy businesses that have good prospects for repaying the loans, not to firms that are suffering losses and may be unable to repay.

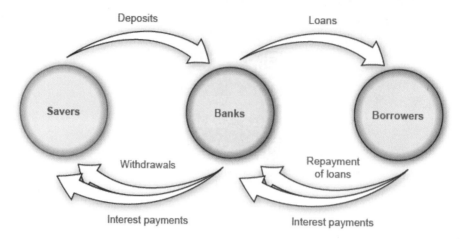

**Figure 14.4 Banks as Financial Intermediaries** Banks act as financial intermediaries because they stand between savers and borrowers. Savers place deposits with banks, and then receive interest payments and withdraw money. Borrowers receive loans from banks and repay the loans with interest. In turn, banks return money to savers in the form of withdrawals, which also include interest payments from banks to savers.

## How are banks, savings and loans, and credit unions related?

Banks have a couple of close cousins: savings institutions and credit unions. Banks, as we explained, receive deposits from individuals and businesses and make loans with the money. Savings institutions are also sometimes called "savings and loans" or "thrifts." They also take loans and make deposits. However, from the 1930s until the 1980s, federal law limited how much interest savings institutions were allowed to pay to depositors. They were also required to make most of their loans in the form of housing-related loans, either to homebuyers or to real-estate developers and builders.

A credit union is a nonprofit financial institution that its members own and run. Members of each credit union decide who is eligible to be a member. Usually, potential members would be everyone in a certain community, or groups of employees, or members of a certain organization. The credit union accepts deposits from members and focuses on making loans back to its members. While there are more credit unions than banks and more banks than savings and loans, the total assets of credit unions are growing.

In 2008, there were 7,085 banks. Due to the bank failures of 2007–2009 and bank mergers, there were 5,571 banks in the United States at the end of the fourth quarter in 2014. According to the Credit Union National Association, as of December 2014 there were 6,535 credit unions with assets totaling $1.1 billion. A day of "Transfer Your Money" took place in 2009 out of general public disgust with big bank bailouts. People were encouraged to transfer their deposits to credit unions. This has grown into the ongoing Move Your Money Project. Consequently, some now hold deposits as large as $50 billion. However, as of 2013, the 12 largest banks (0.2%) controlled 69 percent of all banking assets, according to the Dallas Federal Reserve.

## A Bank's Balance Sheet

A **balance sheet** is an accounting tool that lists assets and liabilities. An **asset** is something of value that you own and you can use to produce something. For example, you can use the cash you own to pay your tuition. If you own a home, this is also an asset. A **liability** is a debt or something you owe. Many people borrow money to buy homes. In this case, a home is the asset, but the mortgage is the liability. The **net worth** is the asset value minus how much is owed (the liability). A bank's balance sheet operates in much the same way. A bank's net worth as **bank capital**. We also refer to a bank has assets such as cash held in its vaults, monies that the bank holds at the Federal Reserve bank (called "reserves"), loans that it makes to customers, and bonds.

**Figure 14.5** illustrates a hypothetical and simplified balance sheet for the Safe and Secure Bank. Because of the two-column format of the balance sheet, with the T-shape formed by the vertical line down the middle and the horizontal line under "Assets" and "Liabilities," we sometimes call it a **T-account**.

| Assets | | Liabilities + Net Worth | |
|---|---|---|---|
| Loans | $5 million | Deposits | $10 million |
| U.S. Government Securities (USGS) | $4 million | | |
| Reserves | $2 million | Net Worth | $1 million |

**Figure 14.5 A Balance Sheet for the Safe and Secure Bank**

The "T" in a T-account separates the assets of a firm, on the left, from its liabilities, on the right. All firms use T-accounts, though most are much more complex. For a bank, the assets are the financial instruments that either the bank is holding (its reserves) or those instruments where other parties owe money to the bank—like loans made by the bank and U.S. Government Securities, such as U.S. treasury bonds purchased by the bank. Liabilities are what the bank owes to others. Specifically, the bank owes any deposits made in the bank to those who have made them. The net worth of the bank is the total assets minus total liabilities. Net worth is included on the liabilities side to have the T account balance to zero. For a healthy business, net worth will be positive. For a bankrupt firm, net worth will be negative. In either case, on a bank's T-account, assets will always equal liabilities plus net worth.

When bank customers deposit money into a checking account, savings account, or a certificate of deposit, the bank views these deposits as liabilities. After all, the bank owes these deposits to its customers, when the customers wish to withdraw their money. In the example in **Figure 14.5**, the Safe and Secure Bank holds $10 million in deposits.

Loans are the first category of bank assets in **Figure 14.5**. Say that a family takes out a 30-year mortgage loan to purchase a house, which means that the borrower will repay the loan over the next 30 years. This loan is clearly an asset from the bank's perspective, because the borrower has a legal obligation to make payments to the bank over time. However, in practical terms, how can we measure the value of the mortgage loan that the borrower is paying over 30 years in the present? One way of measuring the value of something—whether a loan or anything else—is by estimating what another party in the market is willing to pay for it. Many banks issue home loans, and charge various handling and processing fees for doing so, but then sell the loans to other banks or financial institutions who collect the loan payments. We call the market where financial institutions make loans to borrowers the primary loan market, while the market in which financial institutions buy and sell these loans is the secondary loan market.

One key factor that affects what financial institutions are willing to pay for a loan, when they buy it in the secondary loan market, is the perceived riskiness of the loan: that is, given the borrower's characteristics, such as income level and whether the local economy is performing strongly, what proportion of loans of this type will the borrower repay? The greater the risk that a borrower will not repay loan, the less that any financial institution will pay to acquire the loan. Another key factor is to compare the interest rate the financial institution charged on the original loan with the current interest rate in the economy. If the original loan requires the borrower to pay a low interest rate, but current interest rates are relatively high, then a financial institution will pay less to acquire the loan. In contrast, if the original loan requires the borrower to pay a high interest rate, while current interest rates are relatively low, then a financial institution will pay more to acquire the loan. For the Safe and Secure Bank in this example, the total value of its loans if they sold them to other financial institutions in the secondary market is $5 million.

The second category of bank asset is bonds, which are a common mechanism for borrowing, used by the federal and local government, and also private companies, and nonprofit organizations. A bank takes some of the money it has received in deposits and uses the money to buy bonds—typically bonds issued that the U.S. government issues. Government bonds are low-risk because the government is virtually certain to pay off the bond, albeit at a low rate of interest. These bonds are an asset for banks in the same way that loans are an asset: The bank will receive a stream of payments in the future. In our example, the Safe and Secure Bank holds bonds worth a total value of $4 million.

The final entry under assets is **reserves**, which is money that the bank keeps on hand, and that it does not lend or invest in bonds—and thus does not lead to interest payments. The Federal Reserve requires that banks keep a certain percentage of depositors' money on "reserve," which means either in their vaults or at the Federal Reserve Bank. We call this a reserve requirement. (**Monetary Policy and Bank Regulation** will explain how the level of these required reserves are one policy tool that governments have to influence bank behavior.) Additionally, banks may also want to keep a certain amount of reserves on hand in excess of what is required. The Safe and Secure Bank is holding

$2 million in reserves.

We define net worth of a bank as its total assets minus its total liabilities. For the Safe and Secure Bank in **Figure 14.5**, net worth is equal to $1 million; that is, $11 million in assets minus $10 million in liabilities. For a financially healthy bank, the net worth will be positive. If a bank has negative net worth and depositors tried to withdraw their money, the bank would not be able to give all depositors their money.

## Link It Up

For some concrete examples of what banks do, watch this video (http://openstaxcollege.org/l/makingsense) from Paul Solman's "Making Sense of Financial News."

## How Banks Go Bankrupt

A bank that is bankrupt will have a negative net worth, meaning its assets will be worth less than its liabilities. How can this happen? Again, looking at the balance sheet helps to explain.

A well-run bank will assume that a small percentage of borrowers will not repay their loans on time, or at all, and factor these missing payments into its planning. Remember, the calculations of the banks' expenses every year include a factor for loans that borrowers do not repay, and the value of a bank's loans on its balance sheet assumes a certain level of riskiness because some customers will not repay loans. Even if a bank expects a certain number of loan defaults, it will suffer if the number of loan defaults is much greater than expected, as can happen during a recession. For example, if the Safe and Secure Bank in **Figure 14.5** experienced a wave of unexpected defaults, so that its loans declined in value from $5 million to $3 million, then the assets of the Safe and Secure Bank would decline so that the bank had negative net worth.

## Clear It Up

### What led to the 2008–2009 financial crisis?

Many banks make mortgage loans so that people can buy a home, but then do not keep the loans on their books as an asset. Instead, the bank sells the loan. These loans are "securitized," which means that they are bundled together into a financial security that a financial institution sells to investors. Investors in these mortgage-backed securities receive a rate of return based on the level of payments that people make on all the mortgages that stand behind the security.

Securitization offers certain advantages. If a bank makes most of its loans in a local area, then the bank may be financially vulnerable if the local economy declines, so that many people are unable to make their payments. However, if a bank sells its local loans, and then buys a mortgage-backed security based on home loans in many parts of the country, it can avoid exposure to local financial risks. (In the simple example in the text, banks just own "bonds." In reality, banks can own a number of financial instruments, as long as these financial investments are safe enough to satisfy the government bank regulators.) From the standpoint of a local homebuyer, securitization offers the benefit that a local bank does not need to have significant extra funds to make a loan, because the bank is only planning to hold that loan for a short time, before selling the loan so that it can pool it into a financial security.

However, securitization also offers one potentially large disadvantage. If a bank plans to hold a mortgage loan as an asset, the bank has an incentive to scrutinize the borrower carefully to ensure that the customer is likely to repay the loan. However, a bank that plans to sell the loan may be less careful in making the loan in the first place. The bank will be more willing to make what we call "subprime loans," which are loans that have characteristics like low or zero down-payment, little scrutiny of whether the borrower has a reliable income, and sometimes low payments for the first year or two that will be followed by much higher payments. Economists dubbed some financial institutions that made subprime loans in the mid-2000s NINJA loans: loans that financial institutions made even though the borrower had demonstrated No Income, No Job, or Assets.

Financial institutions typically sold these subprime loans and turned them into financial securities—but with a twist. The idea was that if losses occurred on these mortgage-backed securities, certain investors would agree to take the first, say, 5% of such losses. Other investors would agree to take, say, the next 5% of losses. By this approach, still other investors would not need to take any losses unless these mortgage-backed financial securities lost 25% or 30% or more of their total value. These complex securities, along with other economic factors, encouraged a large expansion of subprime loans in the mid-2000s.

The economic stage was now set for a banking crisis. Banks thought they were buying only ultra-safe securities, because even though the securities were ultimately backed by risky subprime mortgages, the banks only invested in the part of those securities where they were protected from small or moderate levels of losses. However, as housing prices fell after 2007, and the deepening recession made it harder for many people to make their mortgage payments, many banks found that their mortgage-backed financial assets could be worth much less than they had expected—and so the banks were faced with staring bankruptcy. In the 2008–2011 period, 318 banks failed in the United States.

The risk of an unexpectedly high level of loan defaults can be especially difficult for banks because a bank's liabilities, namely it customers' deposits. Customers can withdraw funds quickly but many of the bank's assets like loans and bonds will only be repaid over years or even decades. This **asset-liability time mismatch**—the ability for customers to withdraw bank's liabilities in the short term while customers repay its assets in the long term—can cause severe problems for a bank. For example, imagine a bank that has loaned a substantial amount of money at a certain interest rate, but then sees interest rates rise substantially. The bank can find itself in a precarious situation. If it does not raise the interest rate it pays to depositors, then deposits will flow to other institutions that offer the higher interest rates that are now prevailing. However, if the bank raises the interest rates that it pays to depositors, it may end up in a situation where it is paying a higher interest rate to depositors than it is collecting from those past loans that it at lower interest rates. Clearly, the bank cannot survive in the long term if it is paying out more in interest to depositors than it is receiving from borrowers.

How can banks protect themselves against an unexpectedly high rate of loan defaults and against the risk of an asset-liability time mismatch? One strategy is for a bank to **diversify** its loans, which means lending to a variety of customers. For example, suppose a bank specialized in lending to a niche market—say, making a high proportion of its loans to construction companies that build offices in one downtown area. If that one area suffers an unexpected economic downturn, the bank will suffer large losses. However, if a bank loans both to consumers who are buying homes and cars and also to a wide range of firms in many industries and geographic areas, the bank is less exposed to risk. When a bank diversifies its loans, those categories of borrowers who have an unexpectedly large number of defaults will tend to be balanced out, according to random chance, by other borrowers who have an unexpectedly low number of defaults. Thus, diversification of loans can help banks to keep a positive net worth. However, if a widespread recession occurs that touches many industries and geographic areas, diversification will not help.

Along with diversifying their loans, banks have several other strategies to reduce the risk of an unexpectedly large number of loan defaults. For example, banks can sell some of the loans they make in the secondary loan market, as we described earlier, and instead hold a greater share of assets in the form of government bonds or reserves. Nevertheless, in a lengthy recession, most banks will see their net worth decline because customers will not repay a higher share of loans in tough economic times.

# 14.4 | How Banks Create Money

By the end of this section, you will be able to:

- Utilize the money multiplier formulate to determine how banks create money
- Analyze and create T-account balance sheets
- Evaluate the risks and benefits of money and banks

Banks and money are intertwined. It is not just that most money is in the form of bank accounts. The banking system can literally create money through the process of making loans. Let's see how.

## Money Creation by a Single Bank

Start with a hypothetical bank called Singleton Bank. The bank has $10 million in deposits. The T-account balance sheet for Singleton Bank, when it holds all of the deposits in its vaults, is in **Figure 14.6**. At this stage, Singleton Bank is simply storing money for depositors and is using these deposits to make loans. In this simplified example, Singleton Bank cannot earn any interest income from these loans and cannot pay its depositors an interest rate either.

| Assets | | Liabilities + Net Worth | |
|---|---|---|---|
| Reserves | $10 million | Deposits | $10 million |

Figure 14.6 Singleton Bank's Balance Sheet: Receives $10 million in Deposits

The Federal Reserve requires Singleton Bank to keep $1 million on reserve (10% of total deposits). It will loan out the remaining $9 million. By loaning out the $9 million and charging interest, it will be able to make interest payments to depositors and earn interest income for Singleton Bank (for now, we will keep it simple and not put interest income on the balance sheet). Instead of becoming just a storage place for deposits, Singleton Bank can become a financial intermediary between savers and borrowers.

This change in business plan alters Singleton Bank's balance sheet, as **Figure 14.7** shows. Singleton's assets have changed. It now has $1 million in reserves and a loan to Hank's Auto Supply of $9 million. The bank still has $10 million in deposits.

| Assets | | Liabilities + Net Worth | |
|---|---|---|---|
| Reserves | $1 million | Deposits | $10 million |
| Loan to Hank's Auto Supply | $9 million | | |

Figure 14.7 Singleton Bank's Balance Sheet: 10% Reserves, One Round of Loans

Singleton Bank lends $9 million to Hank's Auto Supply. The bank records this loan by making an entry on the balance sheet to indicate that it has made a loan. This loan is an asset, because it will generate interest income for the bank. Of course, the loan officer will not allow let Hank to walk out of the bank with $9 million in cash. The bank issues Hank's Auto Supply a cashier's check for the $9 million. Hank deposits the loan in his regular checking account with First National. The deposits at First National rise by $9 million and its reserves also rise by $9 million, as **Figure 14.8** shows. First National must hold 10% of additional deposits as required reserves but is free to loan out the rest

| Assets | | Liabilities + Net Worth | |
|---|---|---|---|
| Reserves | + $9 million | Deposits | + $9 million |

Figure 14.8 First National Balance Sheet

Making loans that are deposited into a demand deposit account increases the M1 money supply. Remember the definition of M1 includes checkable (demand) deposits, which one can easily use as a medium of exchange to buy goods and services. Notice that the money supply is now $19 million: $10 million in deposits in Singleton bank and $9 million in deposits at First National. Obviously as Hank's Auto Supply writes checks to pay its bills the deposits will draw down. However, the bigger picture is that a bank must hold enough money in reserves to meet its liabilities.

The rest the bank loans out. In this example so far, bank lending has expanded the money supply by $9 million.

Now, First National must hold only 10% as required reserves ($900,000) but can lend out the other 90% ($8.1 million) in a loan to Jack's Chevy Dealership as **Figure 14.9** shows.

| Assets | | Liabilities + Net Worth | |
|---|---|---|---|
| Reserves | $900,000 | Deposits | + $9 million |
| Loans | $8.1 million | | |

**Figure 14.9 First National Balance Sheet**

If Jack's deposits the loan in its checking account at Second National, the money supply just increased by an additional $8.1 million, as **Figure 14.10** shows.

| Assets | | Liabilities + Net Worth | |
|---|---|---|---|
| Reserves | + $8.1 million | Deposits | + $8.1 million |

**Figure 14.10 Second National Bank's Balance Sheet**

How is this money creation possible? It is possible because there are multiple banks in the financial system, they are required to hold only a fraction of their deposits, and loans end up deposited in other banks, which increases deposits and, in essence, the money supply.

# Link It Up

Watch this video (http://openstaxcollege.org/l/createmoney) to learn more about how banks create money.

## The Money Multiplier and a Multi-Bank System

In a system with multiple banks, Singleton Bank deposited the initial excess reserve amount that it decided to lend to Hank's Auto Supply into First National Bank, which is free to loan out $8.1 million. If all banks loan out their excess reserves, the money supply will expand. In a multi-bank system, institutions determine the amount of money that the system can create by using the money multiplier. This tells us by how many times a loan will be "multiplied" as it is spent in the economy and then re-deposited in other banks.

Fortunately, a formula exists for calculating the total of these many rounds of lending in a banking system. The **money multiplier formula** is:

$$\frac{1}{\text{Reserve Requirement}}$$

We then multiply the money multiplier by the change in excess reserves to determine the total amount of M1 money supply created in the banking system. See the Work it Out feature to walk through the multiplier calculation.

# Work It Out ─○─○─○

## Using the Money Multiplier Formula

Using the money multiplier for the example in this text:

Step 1. In the case of Singleton Bank, for whom the reserve requirement is 10% (or 0.10), the money multiplier is 1 divided by .10, which is equal to 10.

Step 2. We have identified that the excess reserves are $9 million, so, using the formula we can determine the total change in the M1 money supply:

$$\text{Total Change in the M1 Money Supply} = \frac{1}{\text{Reserve Requirement}} \times \text{Excess Requirement}$$

$$= \frac{1}{0.10} \times \$9 \text{ million}$$

$$= 10 \times \$9 \text{ million}$$

$$= \$90 \text{ million}$$

Step 3. Thus, we can say that, in this example, the total quantity of money generated in this economy after all rounds of lending are completed will be $90 million.

## Cautions about the Money Multiplier

The money multiplier will depend on the proportion of reserves that the Federal Reserve Band requires banks to hold. Additionally, a bank can also choose to hold extra reserves. Banks may decide to vary how much they hold in reserves for two reasons: macroeconomic conditions and government rules. When an economy is in recession, banks are likely to hold a higher proportion of reserves because they fear that customers are less likely to repay loans when the economy is slow. The Federal Reserve may also raise or lower the required reserves held by banks as a policy move to affect the quantity of money in an economy, as **Monetary Policy and Bank Regulation** will discuss.

The process of how banks create money shows how the quantity of money in an economy is closely linked to the quantity of lending or credit in the economy. All the money in the economy, except for the original reserves, is a result of bank loans that institutions repeatedly re-deposit and loan.

Finally, the money multiplier depends on people re-depositing the money that they receive in the banking system. If people instead store their cash in safe-deposit boxes or in shoeboxes hidden in their closets, then banks cannot recirculate the money in the form of loans. Central banks have an incentive to assure that bank deposits are safe because if people worry that they may lose their bank deposits, they may start holding more money in cash, instead of depositing it in banks, and the quantity of loans in an economy will decline. Low-income countries have what economists sometimes refer to as "mattress savings," or money that people are hiding in their homes because they do not trust banks. When mattress savings in an economy are substantial, banks cannot lend out those funds and the money multiplier cannot operate as effectively. The overall quantity of money and loans in such an economy will decline.

# Link It Up ⚭

Watch a video (http://openstaxcollege.org/l/moneymyth) of Jem Bendell discussing "The Money Myth."

## Money and Banks—Benefits and Dangers

Money and banks are marvelous social inventions that help a modern economy to function. Compared with the alternative of barter, money makes market exchanges vastly easier in goods, labor, and financial markets. Banking makes money still more effective in facilitating exchanges in goods and labor markets. Moreover, the process of banks making loans in financial capital markets is intimately tied to the creation of money.

However, the extraordinary economic gains that are possible through money and banking also suggest some possible corresponding dangers. If banks are not working well, it sets off a decline in convenience and safety of transactions throughout the economy. If the banks are under financial stress, because of a widespread decline in the value of their assets, loans may become far less available, which can deal a crushing blow to sectors of the economy that depend on borrowed money like business investment, home construction, and car manufacturing. The 2008–2009 Great Recession illustrated this pattern.

## Bring it Home

### The Many Disguises of Money: From Cowries to Bit Coins

The global economy has come a long way since it started using cowrie shells as currency. We have moved away from commodity and commodity-backed paper money to fiat currency. As technology and global integration increases, the need for paper currency is diminishing, too. Every day, we witness the increased use of debit and credit cards.

The latest creation and perhaps one of the purest forms of fiat money is the Bitcoin. Bitcoins are a digital currency that allows users to buy goods and services online. Customers can purchase products and services such as videos and books using Bitcoins. This currency is not backed by any commodity nor has any government decreed as legal tender, yet customers use it as a medium of exchange and can store its value (online at least). It is also unregulated by any central bank, but is created online through people solving very complicated mathematics problems and receiving payment afterward. Bitcoin.org is an information source if you are curious. Bitcoins are a relatively new type of money. At present, because it is not sanctioned as a legal currency by any country nor regulated by any central bank, it lends itself for use in illegal as well as legal trading activities. As technology increases and the need to reduce transactions costs associated with using traditional forms of money increases, Bitcoins or some sort of digital currency may replace our dollar bill, just as man replaced the cowrie shell.

# KEY TERMS

**asset**  item of value that a firm or an individual owns

**asset–liability time mismatch**  customers can withdraw a bank's liabilities in the short term while customers repay its assets in the long term

**balance sheet**  an accounting tool that lists assets and liabilities

**bank capital**  a bank's net worth

**barter**  literally, trading one good or service for another, without using money

**coins and currency in circulation**  the coins and bills that circulate in an economy that are not held by the U.S Treasury, at the Federal Reserve Bank, or in bank vaults

**commodity money**  an item that is used as money, but which also has value from its use as something other than money

**commodity-backed currencies**  dollar bills or other currencies with values backed up by gold or another commodity

**credit card**  immediately transfers money from the credit card company's checking account to the seller, and at the end of the month the user owes the money to the credit card company; a credit card is a short-term loan

**debit card**  like a check, is an instruction to the user's bank to transfer money directly and immediately from your bank account to the seller

**demand deposit**  checkable deposit in banks that is available by making a cash withdrawal or writing a check

**depository institution**  institution that accepts money deposits and then uses these to make loans

**diversify**  making loans or investments with a variety of firms, to reduce the risk of being adversely affected by events at one or a few firms

**double coincidence of wants**  a situation in which two people each want some good or service that the other person can provide

**fiat money**  has no intrinsic value, but is declared by a government to be the country's legal tender

**financial intermediary**  an institution that operates between a saver with financial assets to invest and an entity who will borrow those assets and pay a rate of return

**liability**  any amount or debt that a firm or an individual owes

**M1 money supply**  a narrow definition of the money supply that includes currency and checking accounts in banks, and to a lesser degree, traveler's checks.

**M2 money supply**  a definition of the money supply that includes everything in M1, but also adds savings deposits, money market funds, and certificates of deposit

**medium of exchange**  whatever is widely accepted as a method of payment

**money**  whatever serves society in four functions: as a medium of exchange, a store of value, a unit of account, and a standard of deferred payment.

**money market fund**  the deposits of many investors are pooled together and invested in a safe way like short-term government bonds

**money multiplier formula**  total money in the economy divided by the original quantity of money, or change in the total money in the economy divided by a change in the original quantity of money

**net worth** the excess of the asset value over and above the amount of the liability; total assets minus total liabilities

**payment system** helps an economy exchange goods and services for money or other financial assets

**reserves** funds that a bank keeps on hand and that it does not loan out or invest in bonds

**savings deposit** bank account where you cannot withdraw money by writing a check, but can withdraw the money at a bank—or can transfer it easily to a checking account

**smart card** stores a certain value of money on a card and then one can use the card to make purchases

**standard of deferred payment** money must also be acceptable to make purchases today that will be paid in the future

**store of value** something that serves as a way of preserving economic value that one can spend or consume in the future

**T-account** a balance sheet with a two-column format, with the T-shape formed by the vertical line down the middle and the horizontal line under the column headings for "Assets" and "Liabilities"

**time deposit** account that the depositor has committed to leaving in the bank for a certain period of time, in exchange for a higher rate of interest; also called certificate of deposit

**transaction costs** the costs associated with finding a lender or a borrower for money

**unit of account** the common way in which we measure market values in an economy

# KEY CONCEPTS AND SUMMARY

## 14.1 Defining Money by Its Functions
Money is what people in a society regularly use when purchasing or selling goods and services. If money were not available, people would need to barter with each other, meaning that each person would need to identify others with whom they have a double coincidence of wants—that is, each party has a specific good or service that the other desires. Money serves several functions: a medium of exchange, a unit of account, a store of value, and a standard of deferred payment. There are two types of money: commodity money, which is an item used as money, but which also has value from its use as something other than money; and fiat money, which has no intrinsic value, but is declared by a government to be the country's legal tender.

## 14.2 Measuring Money: Currency, M1, and M2
We measure money with several definitions: M1 includes currency and money in checking accounts (demand deposits). Traveler's checks are also a component of M1, but are declining in use. M2 includes all of M1, plus savings deposits, time deposits like certificates of deposit, and money market funds.

## 14.3 The Role of Banks
Banks facilitate using money for transactions in the economy because people and firms can use bank accounts when selling or buying goods and services, when paying a worker or receiving payment, and when saving money or receiving a loan. In the financial capital market, banks are financial intermediaries; that is, they operate between savers who supply financial capital and borrowers who demand loans. A balance sheet (sometimes called a T-account) is an accounting tool which lists assets in one column and liabilities in another. The bank's liabilities are its deposits. The bank's assets include its loans, its ownership of bonds, and its reserves (which it does not loan out). We calculate a bank's net worth by subtracting its liabilities from its assets. Banks run a risk of negative net worth if the value of their assets declines. The value of assets can decline because of an unexpectedly high number of defaults on loans, or if interest rates rise and the bank suffers an asset-liability time mismatch in which the bank is receiving a low interest rate on its long-term loans but must pay the currently higher market interest rate to attract depositors. Banks

can protect themselves against these risks by choosing to diversify their loans or to hold a greater proportion of their assets in bonds and reserves. If banks hold only a fraction of their deposits as reserves, then the process of banks' lending money, re-depositing those loans in banks, and the banks making additional loans will create money in the economy.

### 14.4 How Banks Create Money

We define the money multiplier as the quantity of money that the banking system can generate from each $1 of bank reserves. The formula for calculating the multiplier is 1/reserve ratio, where the reserve ratio is the fraction of deposits that the bank wishes to hold as reserves. The quantity of money in an economy and the quantity of credit for loans are inextricably intertwined. The network of banks making loans, people making deposits, and banks making more loans creates much of the money in an economy.

Given the macroeconomic dangers of a malfunctioning banking system, Monetary Policy and Bank Regulation will discuss government policies for controlling the money supply and for keeping the banking system safe.

## SELF-CHECK QUESTIONS

**1.** In many casinos, a person buys chips to use for gambling. Within the casino's walls, customers often can use these chips to buy food and drink or even a hotel room. Do chips in a gambling casino serve all three functions of money?

**2.** Can you name some item that is a store of value, but does not serve the other functions of money?

**3.** If you are out shopping for clothes and books, what is easiest and most convenient for you to spend: M1 or M2? Explain your answer.

**4.** For the following list of items, indicate if they are in M1, M2, or neither:
  a.  Your $5,000 line of credit on your Bank of America card
  b.  $50 dollars' worth of traveler's checks you have not used yet
  c.  $1 in quarters in your pocket
  d.  $1200 in your checking account
  e.  $2000 you have in a money market account

**5.** Explain why the money listed under assets on a bank balance sheet may not actually be in the bank?

**6.** Imagine that you are in the position of buying loans in the secondary market (that is, buying the right to collect the payments on loans) for a bank or other financial services company. Explain why you would be willing to pay more or less for a given loan if:
  a.  The borrower has been late on a number of loan payments
  b.  Interest rates in the economy as a whole have risen since the bank made the loan
  c.  The borrower is a firm that has just declared a high level of profits
  d.  Interest rates in the economy as a whole have fallen since the bank made the loan

## REVIEW QUESTIONS

**7.** What are the four functions that money serves?

**8.** How does the existence of money simplify the process of buying and selling?

**9.** What is the double-coincidence of wants?

**10.** What components of money do we count as part of M1?

**11.** What components of money do we count in M2?

**12.** Why do we call a bank a financial intermediary?

**13.** What does a balance sheet show?

**14.** What are a bank's assets? What are its liabilities?

**15.** How do you calculate a bank's net worth?

**16.** How can a bank end up with negative net worth?

**17.** What is the asset-liability time mismatch that all banks face?

**18.** What is the risk if a bank does not diversify its loans?

**19.** How do banks create money?

**20.** What is the formula for the money multiplier?

## CRITICAL THINKING QUESTIONS

**21.** The Bring it Home Feature discusses the use of cowrie shells as money. Although we no longer use cowrie shells as money, do you think other forms of commodity monies are possible? What role might technology play in our definition of money?

**22.** Imagine that you are a barber in a world without money. Explain why it would be tricky to obtain groceries, clothing, and a place to live.

**23.** Explain why you think the Federal Reserve Bank tracks M1 and M2.

**24.** The total amount of U.S. currency in circulation divided by the U.S. population comes out to about $3,500 per person. That is more than most of us carry. Where is all the cash?

**25.** Explain the difference between how you would characterize bank deposits and loans as assets and liabilities on your own personal balance sheet and how a bank would characterize deposits and loans as assets and liabilities on its balance sheet.

**26.** Should banks have to hold 100% of their deposits? Why or why not?

**27.** Explain what will happen to the money multiplier process if there is an increase in the reserve requirement?

**28.** What do you think the Federal Reserve Bank did to the reserve requirement during the 2008–2009 Great Recession?

## PROBLEMS

**29.** If you take $100 out of your piggy bank and deposit it in your checking account, how did M1 change? Did M2 change?

**30.** A bank has deposits of $400. It holds reserves of $50. It has purchased government bonds worth $70. It has made loans of $500. Set up a T-account balance sheet for the bank, with assets and liabilities, and calculate the bank's net worth.

**31.** Humongous Bank is the only bank in the economy. The people in this economy have $20 million in money, and they deposit all their money in Humongous Bank.

   a. Humongous Bank decides on a policy of holding 100% reserves. Draw a T-account for the bank.
   b. Humongous Bank is required to hold 5% of its existing $20 million as reserves, and to loan out the rest. Draw a T-account for the bank after it has made its first round of loans.
   c. Assume that Humongous bank is part of a multibank system. How much will money supply increase with that original $19 million loan?

# 15 | Monetary Policy and Bank Regulation

**Figure 15.1 Marriner S. Eccles Federal Reserve Headquarters, Washington D.C.** Some of the most influential decisions regarding monetary policy in the United States are made behind these doors. (Credit: modification of work by "squirrel83"/Flickr Creative Commons)

## Bring it Home

### The Problem of the Zero Percent Interest Rate Lower Bound

Most economists believe that monetary policy (the manipulation of interest rates and credit conditions by a nation's central bank) has a powerful influence on a nation's economy. Monetary policy works when the central bank reduces interest rates and makes credit more available. As a result, business investment and other types of spending increase, causing GDP and employment to grow.

However, what if the interest rates banks pay are close to zero already? They cannot be made negative, can they? That would mean that lenders pay borrowers for the privilege of taking their money. Yet, this was the situation the U.S. Federal Reserve found itself in at the end of the 2008–2009 recession. The federal funds rate, which is the interest rate for banks that the Federal Reserve targets with its monetary policy, was slightly above 5% in 2007. By 2009, it had fallen to 0.16%.

The Federal Reserve's situation was further complicated because fiscal policy, the other major tool for managing the economy, was constrained by fears that the federal budget deficit and the public debt were already too high. What were the Federal Reserve's options? How could the Federal Reserve use monetary policy to stimulate the economy? The answer, as we will see in this chapter, was to change the rules of the game.

# Introduction to Monetary Policy and Bank Regulation

In this chapter, you will learn about:

- The Federal Reserve Banking System and Central Banks

- Bank Regulation

- How a Central Bank Executes Monetary Policy

- Monetary Policy and Economic Outcomes

- Pitfalls for Monetary Policy

Money, loans, and banks are all interconnected. Money is deposited in bank accounts, which is then loaned to businesses, individuals, and other banks. When the interlocking system of money, loans, and banks works well, economic transactions smoothly occur in goods and labor markets and savers are connected with borrowers. If the money and banking system does not operate smoothly, the economy can either fall into recession or suffer prolonged inflation.

The government of every country has public policies that support the system of money, loans, and banking. However, these policies do not always work perfectly. This chapter discusses how monetary policy works and what may prevent it from working perfectly.

# 15.1 | The Federal Reserve Banking System and Central Banks

By the end of this section, you will be able to:
- Explain the structure and organization of the U.S. Federal Reserve
- Discuss how central banks impact monetary policy, promote financial stability, and provide banking services

In making decisions about the money supply, a central bank decides whether to raise or lower interest rates and, in this way, to influence macroeconomic policy, whose goal is low unemployment and low inflation. The central bank is also responsible for regulating all or part of the nation's banking system to protect bank depositors and insure the health of the bank's balance sheet.

We call the organization responsible for conducting monetary policy and ensuring that a nation's financial system operates smoothly the **central bank**. Most nations have central banks or currency boards. Some prominent central banks around the world include the European Central Bank, the Bank of Japan, and the Bank of England. In the United States, we call the central bank the Federal Reserve—often abbreviated as just "the Fed." This section explains the U.S. Federal Reserve's organization and identifies the major central bank's responsibilities.

## Structure/Organization of the Federal Reserve

Unlike most central banks, the Federal Reserve is semi-decentralized, mixing government appointees with representation from private-sector banks. At the national level, it is run by a Board of Governors, consisting of seven members appointed by the President of the United States and confirmed by the Senate. Appointments are for 14-year terms and they are arranged so that one term expires January 31 of every even-numbered year. The purpose of the long and staggered terms is to insulate the Board of Governors as much as possible from political pressure so that governors can make policy decisions based only on their economic merits. Additionally, except when filling an unfinished term, each member only serves one term, further insulating decision-making from politics. The Fed's policy decisions do not require congressional approval, and the President cannot ask for a Federal Reserve Governor to resign as the President can with cabinet positions.

One member of the Board of Governors is designated as the Chair. For example, from 1987 until early 2006, the Chair was Alan Greenspan. From 2006 until 2014, Ben Bernanke held the post. The current Chair, Janet Yellen, has made many headlines already. Why? See the following Clear It Up feature to find out.

## Who has the most immediate economic power in the world?

**Figure 15.2 Chair of the Federal Reserve Board**   Janet L. Yellen is the first woman to hold the position of Chair of the Federal Reserve Board of Governors. (Credit: Board of Governors of the Federal Reserve System)

What individual can make financial market crash or soar just by making a public statement? It is not Bill Gates or Warren Buffett. It is not even the President of the United States. The answer is the Chair of the Federal Reserve Board of Governors. In early 2014, Janet L. Yellen, (Figure 15.2) became the first woman to hold this post. The media had described Yellen as "perhaps the most qualified Fed chair in history." With a Ph.D. in economics from Yale University, Yellen has taught macroeconomics at Harvard, the London School of Economics, and most recently at the University of California at Berkeley. From 2004–2010, Yellen was President of the Federal Reserve Bank of San Francisco. Not an ivory tower economist, Yellen became one of the few economists who warned about a possible bubble in the housing market, more than two years before the financial crisis occurred. Yellen served on the Board of Governors of the Federal Reserve twice, most recently as Vice Chair. She also spent two years as Chair of the President's Council of Economic Advisors. If experience and credentials mean anything, Yellen is likely to be an effective Fed chair.

The Fed Chair is first among equals on the Board of Governors. While he or she has only one vote, the Chair controls the agenda, and is the Fed's public voice, so he or she has more power and influence than one might expect.

## Link It Up @

Visit this website (http://openstaxcollege.org/l/Governors) to see who the current members of the Federal Reserve Board of Governors are. You can follow the links provided for each board member to learn more about their backgrounds, experiences, and when their terms on the board will end.

The Federal Reserve is more than the Board of Governors. The Fed also includes 12 regional Federal Reserve banks, each of which is responsible for supporting the commercial banks and economy generally in its district. **Figure 15.3** shows the Federal Reserve districts and the cities where their regional headquarters are located. The commercial banks in each district elect a Board of Directors for each regional Federal Reserve bank, and that board chooses a president for each regional Federal Reserve district. Thus, the Federal Reserve System includes both federally and private-sector appointed leaders.

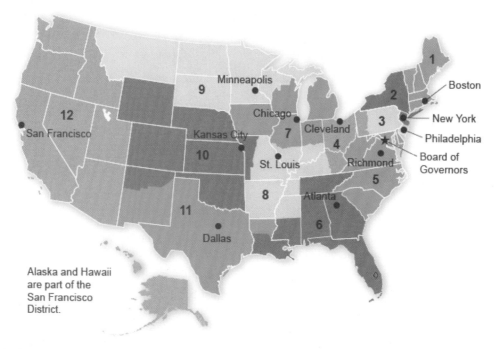

**Figure 15.3 The Twelve Federal Reserve Districts**   There are twelve regional Federal Reserve banks, each with its district.

## What Does a Central Bank Do?

The Federal Reserve, like most central banks, is designed to perform three important functions:

1. To conduct monetary policy

2. To promote stability of the financial system

3. To provide banking services to commercial banks and other depository institutions, and to provide banking services to the federal government.

The first two functions are sufficiently important that we will discuss them in their own modules. The third function we will discuss here.

The Federal Reserve provides many of the same services to banks as banks provide to their customers. For example, all commercial banks have an account at the Fed where they deposit reserves. Similarly, banks can obtain loans from the Fed through the "discount window" facility, which we will discuss in more detail later. The Fed is also responsible for check processing. When you write a check, for example, to buy groceries, the grocery store deposits the check in its bank account. Then, the grocery store's bank returns the physical check (or an image of that actual check) to your bank, after which it transfers funds from your bank account to the grocery store's account. The Fed is responsible for each of these actions.

On a more mundane level, the Federal Reserve ensures that enough currency and coins are circulating through the financial system to meet public demands. For example, each year the Fed increases the amount of currency available in banks around the Christmas shopping season and reduces it again in January.

Finally, the Fed is responsible for assuring that banks are in compliance with a wide variety of consumer protection laws. For example, banks are forbidden from discriminating on the basis of age, race, sex, or marital status. Banks are also required to disclose publicly information about the loans they make for buying houses and how they distribute the loans geographically, as well as by sex and race of the loan applicants.

# 15.2 | Bank Regulation

By the end of this section, you will be able to:
- Discuss the relationship between bank regulation and monetary policy
- Explain bank supervision
- Explain how deposit insurance and lender of last resort are two strategies to protect against bank runs

A safe and stable national financial system is a critical concern of the Federal Reserve. The goal is not only to protect individuals' savings, but to protect the integrity of the financial system itself. This esoteric task is usually behind the scenes, but came into view during the 2008–2009 financial crisis, when for a brief period of time, critical parts of the financial system failed and firms became unable to obtain financing for ordinary parts of their business. Imagine if suddenly you were unable to access the money in your bank accounts because your checks were not accepted for payment and your debit cards were declined. This gives an idea of a failure of the payments/financial system.

Bank regulation is intended to maintain banks' solvency by avoiding excessive risk. Regulation falls into a number of categories, including reserve requirements, capital requirements, and restrictions on the types of investments banks may make. In **Money and Banking**, we learned that banks are required to hold a minimum percentage of their deposits on hand as reserves. "On hand" is a bit of a misnomer because, while a portion of bank reserves are held as cash in the bank, the majority are held in the bank's account at the Federal Reserve, and their purpose is to cover desired withdrawals by depositors. Another part of bank regulation is restrictions on the types of investments banks are allowed to make. Banks are permitted to make loans to businesses, individuals, and other banks. They can purchase U.S. Treasury securities but, to protect depositors, they are not permitted to invest in the stock market or other assets that are perceived as too risky.

Bank capital is the difference between a bank's assets and its liabilities. In other words, it is a bank's net worth. A bank must have positive net worth; otherwise it is insolvent or bankrupt, meaning it would not have enough assets to pay back its liabilities. Regulation requires that banks maintain a minimum net worth, usually expressed as a percent of their assets, to protect their depositors and other creditors.

# Link It Up ⚭

Visit this website (http://openstaxcollege.org/l/bankregulation) to read the brief article, "Stop Confusing Monetary Policy and Bank Regulation."

## Bank Supervision

Several government agencies monitor banks' balance sheets to make sure they have positive net worth and are not taking too high a level of risk. Within the U.S. Department of the Treasury, the Office of the Comptroller of the Currency has a national staff of bank examiners who conduct on-site reviews of the 1,500 or so of the largest national banks. The bank examiners also review any foreign banks that have branches in the United States. The Office of the Comptroller of the Currency also monitors and regulates about 800 savings and loan institutions.

The National Credit Union Administration (NCUA) supervises credit unions, which are nonprofit banks that their members run and own. There are over 6,000 credit unions in the U.S. economy, although the typical credit union is small compared to most banks.

The Federal Reserve also has some responsibility for supervising financial institutions. For example, we call conglomerate firms that own banks and other businesses "bank holding companies." While other regulators like the Office of the Comptroller of the Currency supervises the banks, the Federal Reserve supervises the holding companies.

When bank supervision (and bank-like institutions such as savings and loans and credit unions) works well, most banks will remain financially healthy most of the time. If the bank supervisors find that a bank has low or negative net worth, or is making too high a proportion of risky loans, they can require that the bank change its behavior—or, in extreme cases, even force the bank to close or be sold to a financially healthy bank.

Bank supervision can run into both practical and political questions. The practical question is that measuring the value of a bank's assets is not always straightforward. As we discussed in **Money and Banking**, a bank's assets are its loans, and the value of these assets depends on estimates about the risk that customers will not repay these loans. These issues can become even more complex when a bank makes loans to banks or firms in other countries, or arranges financial deals that are much more complex than a basic loan.

The political question arises because a bank supervisor's decision to require a bank to close or to change its financial investments is often controversial, and the bank supervisor often comes under political pressure from the bank's owners and the local politicians to keep quiet and back off.

For example, many observers have pointed out that Japan's banks were in deep financial trouble through most of the 1990s; however, nothing substantial had been done about it by the early 2000s. A similar unwillingness to confront problems with struggling banks is visible across the rest of the world, in East Asia, Latin America, Eastern Europe, Russia, and elsewhere.

In the United States, the government passed laws in the 1990s requiring that bank supervisors make their findings open and public, and that they act as soon as they identify a problem. However, as many U.S. banks were staggered by the 2008-2009 recession, critics of the bank regulators asked pointed questions about why the regulators had not foreseen the banks' financial shakiness earlier, before such large losses had a chance to accumulate.

## Bank Runs

Back in the nineteenth century and during the first few decades of the twentieth century (around and during the Great Depression), putting your money in a bank could be nerve-wracking. Imagine that the net worth of your bank became negative, so that the bank's assets were not enough to cover its liabilities. In this situation, whoever withdrew their deposits first received all of their money, and those who did not rush to the bank quickly enough, lost their money. We call depositors racing to the bank to withdraw their deposits, as **Figure 15.4** shows a **bank run**. In the movie *It's a Wonderful Life*, the bank manager, played by Jimmy Stewart, faces a mob of worried bank depositors who want to withdraw their money, but manages to allay their fears by allowing some of them to withdraw a portion of their deposits—using the money from his own pocket that was supposed to pay for his honeymoon.

**Figure 15.4 A Run on the Bank**  Bank runs during the Great Depression only served to worsen the economic situation. (Credit: National Archives and Records Administration)

The risk of bank runs created instability in the banking system. Even a rumor that a bank might experience negative net worth could trigger a bank run and, in a bank run, even healthy banks could be destroyed. Because a bank loans out most of the money it receives, and because it keeps only limited reserves on hand, a bank run of any size would quickly drain any of the bank's available cash. When the bank had no cash remaining, it only intensified the fears of remaining depositors that they could lose their money. Moreover, a bank run at one bank often triggered a chain reaction of runs on other banks. In the late nineteenth and early twentieth century, bank runs were typically not the original cause of a recession—but they could make a recession much worse.

## Deposit Insurance

To protect against bank runs, Congress has put two strategies into place: **deposit insurance** and the lender of last resort. Deposit insurance is an insurance system that makes sure depositors in a bank do not lose their money, even if the bank goes bankrupt. About 70 countries around the world, including all of the major economies, have deposit insurance programs. In the United States, the Federal Deposit Insurance Corporation (FDIC) is responsible for deposit insurance. Banks pay an insurance premium to the FDIC. The insurance premium is based on the bank's level of deposits, and then adjusted according to the riskiness of a bank's financial situation. In 2009, for example, a fairly safe bank with a high net worth might have paid 10–20 cents in insurance premiums for every $100 in bank deposits, while a risky bank with very low net worth might have paid 50–60 cents for every $100 in bank deposits.

Bank examiners from the FDIC evaluate the banks' balance sheets, looking at the asset and liability values to determine the risk level. The FDIC provides deposit insurance for about 5,898 banks (as of the end of February 2017). Even if a bank fails, the government guarantees that depositors will receive up to $250,000 of their money in each account, which is enough for almost all individuals, although not sufficient for many businesses. Since the United States enacted deposit insurance in the 1930s, no one has lost any of their insured deposits. Bank runs no longer happen at insured banks.

## Lender of Last Resort

The problem with bank runs is not that insolvent banks will fail; they are, after all, bankrupt and need to be shut down. The problem is that bank runs can cause solvent banks to fail and spread to the rest of the financial system. To prevent this, the Fed stands ready to lend to banks and other financial institutions when they cannot obtain funds from anywhere else. This is known as the **lender of last resort** role. For banks, the central bank acting as a lender of last resort helps to reinforce the effect of deposit insurance and to reassure bank customers that they will not lose their money.

The lender of last resort task can arise in other financial crises, as well. During the 1987 stock market crash panic, when U.S. stock values fell by 25% in a single day, the Federal Reserve made a number of short-term emergency loans so that the financial system could keep functioning. During the 2008-2009 recession, we can interpret the Fed's "quantitative easing" policies (discussed below) as a willingness to make short-term credit available as needed in a time when the banking and financial system was under stress.

# 15.3 | How a Central Bank Executes Monetary Policy

By the end of this section, you will be able to:
- Explain the reason for open market operations
- Evaluate reserve requirements and discount rates
- Interpret and show bank activity through balance sheets

The Federal Reserve's most important function is to conduct the nation's monetary policy. Article I, Section 8 of the U.S. Constitution gives Congress the power "to coin money" and "to regulate the value thereof." As part of the 1913 legislation that created the Federal Reserve, Congress delegated these powers to the Fed. Monetary policy involves managing interest rates and credit conditions, which influences the level of economic activity, as we describe in more detail below.

A central bank has three traditional tools to implement monetary policy in the economy:

- Open market operations
- Changing reserve requirements
- Changing the discount rate

In discussing how these three tools work, it is useful to think of the central bank as a "bank for banks"—that is, each private-sector bank has its own account at the central bank. We will discuss each of these monetary policy tools in the sections below.

## Open Market Operations

The most common monetary policy tool in the U.S. is **open market operations**. These take place when the central bank sells or buys U.S. Treasury bonds in order to influence the quantity of bank reserves and the level of interest rates. The specific interest rate targeted in open market operations is the federal funds rate. The name is a bit of a misnomer since the federal funds rate is the interest rate that commercial banks charge making overnight loans to other banks. As such, it is a very short term interest rate, but one that reflects credit conditions in financial markets very well.

The **Federal Open Market Committee (FOMC)** makes the decisions regarding these open market operations. The FOMC comprises seven members of the Federal Reserve's Board of Governors. It also includes five voting members who the Board draws, on a rotating basis, from the regional Federal Reserve Banks. The New York district president is a permanent FOMC voting member and the Board fills other four spots on a rotating, annual basis, from the other 11 districts. The FOMC typically meets every six weeks, but it can meet more frequently if necessary. The FOMC tries to act by consensus; however, the Federal Reserve's chairman has traditionally played a very powerful role in defining and shaping that consensus. For the Federal Reserve, and for most central banks, open market operations have, over the last few decades, been the most commonly used tool of monetary policy.

# Link It Up 

Visit this website (http://openstaxcollege.org/l/monetarypolicy) for the Federal Reserve to learn more about current monetary policy.

To understand how open market operations affect the money supply, consider the balance sheet of Happy Bank, displayed in **Figure 15.5**. **Figure 15.5** (a) shows that Happy Bank starts with $460 million in assets, divided among reserves, bonds and loans, and $400 million in liabilities in the form of deposits, with a net worth of $60 million. When the central bank purchases $20 million in bonds from Happy Bank, the bond holdings of Happy Bank fall by $20 million and the bank's reserves rise by $20 million, as **Figure 15.5** (b) shows. However, Happy Bank only wants to hold $40 million in reserves (the quantity of reserves with which it started in **Figure 15.5**) (a), so the bank decides to loan out the extra $20 million in reserves and its loans rise by $20 million, as **Figure 15.5**(c) shows. The central bank's open market operation causes Happy Bank to make loans instead of holding its assets in the form of government bonds, which expands the money supply. As the new loans are deposited in banks throughout the economy, these banks will, in turn, loan out some of the deposits they receive, triggering the money multiplier that we discussed in **Money and Banking**.

| Assets | | Liabilities + Net Worth | |
|---|---|---|---|
| Reserves | 40 | Deposits | 400 |
| Bonds | 120 | | |
| Loans | 300 | Net Worth | 60 |

(a) The original balance sheet

| Assets | | Liabilities + Net Worth | |
|---|---|---|---|
| Reserves | 40 + 20 = 60 | Deposits | 400 |
| Bonds | 120 − 20 = 100 | | |
| Loans | 300 | Net Worth | 60 |

(b) The central bank buys bonds

| Assets | | Liabilities + Net Worth | |
|---|---|---|---|
| Reserves | 60 − 20 = 40 | Deposits | 400 |
| Bonds | 100 | | |
| Loans | 300 + 20 = 320 | Net Worth | 60 |

(c) The bank makes additional loans

Figure 15.5

Where did the Federal Reserve get the $20 million that it used to purchase the bonds? A central bank has the power to create money. In practical terms, the Federal Reserve would write a check to Happy Bank, so that Happy Bank can have that money credited to its bank account at the Federal Reserve. In truth, the Federal Reserve created the money to purchase the bonds out of thin air—or with a few clicks on some computer keys.

Open market operations can also reduce the quantity of money and loans in an economy. **Figure 15.6** (a) shows the balance sheet of Happy Bank before the central bank sells bonds in the open market. When Happy Bank purchases $30 million in bonds, Happy Bank sends $30 million of its reserves to the central bank, but now holds an additional $30 million in bonds, as **Figure 15.6** (b) shows. However, Happy Bank wants to hold $40 million in reserves, as in **Figure 15.6** (a), so it will adjust down the quantity of its loans by $30 million, to bring its reserves back to the desired level, as Figure 15.6 (c) shows. In practical terms, a bank can easily reduce its quantity of loans. At any given time, a bank is receiving payments on loans that it made previously and also making new loans. If the bank just slows down or briefly halts making new loans, and instead adds those funds to its reserves, then its overall quantity of loans will decrease. A decrease in the quantity of loans also means fewer deposits in other banks, and other banks reducing their lending as well, as the money multiplier that we discussed in Money and Banking takes effect. What about all those bonds? How do they affect the money supply? Read the following Clear It Up feature for the answer.

| Assets | | Liabilities + Net Worth | |
|---|---|---|---|
| Reserves | 40 | Deposits | 400 |
| Bonds | 120 | | |
| Loans | 300 | Net Worth | 60 |

(a) The original balance sheet

| Assets | | Liabilities + Net Worth | |
|---|---|---|---|
| Reserves | 40 - 30 = 10 | Deposits | 400 |
| Bonds | 120 + 30 = 150 | | |
| Loans | 300 | Net Worth | 60 |

(b) The central bank sells bonds to the bank

| Assets | | Liabilities + Net Worth | |
|---|---|---|---|
| Reserves | 10 + 30 = 40 | Deposits | 400 |
| Bonds | 150 | | |
| Loans | 300 – 30 = 270 | Net Worth | 60 |

(c) The bank makes fewer loans

**Figure 15.6**

## Clear It Up

### Does selling or buying bonds increase the money supply?

Is it a sale of bonds by the central bank which increases bank reserves and lowers interest rates or is it a purchase of bonds by the central bank? The easy way to keep track of this is to treat the central bank as being *outside* the banking system. When a central bank buys bonds, money is flowing from the central bank to individual banks in the economy, increasing the money supply in circulation. When a central bank sells bonds, then money from individual banks in the economy is flowing into the central bank—reducing the quantity of money in the economy.

## Changing Reserve Requirements

A second method of conducting monetary policy is for the central bank to raise or lower the **reserve requirement**, which, as we noted earlier, is the percentage of each bank's deposits that it is legally required to hold either as cash in their vault or on deposit with the central bank. If banks are required to hold a greater amount in reserves, they have less money available to lend out. If banks are allowed to hold a smaller amount in reserves, they will have a greater amount of money available to lend out.

In early 2015, the Federal Reserve required banks to hold reserves equal to 0% of the first $14.5 million in deposits, then to hold reserves equal to 3% of the deposits up to $103.6 million, and 10% of any amount above $103.6 million. The Fed makes small changes in the reserve requirements almost every year. For example, the $103.6 million dividing line is sometimes bumped up or down by a few million dollars. In practice, the Fed rarely uses large changes in reserve requirements to execute monetary policy. A sudden demand that all banks increase their reserves would be extremely disruptive and difficult for them to comply, while loosening requirements too much would create a danger of banks inability to meet withdrawal demands.

## Changing the Discount Rate

The Federal Reserve was founded in the aftermath of the 1907 Financial Panic when many banks failed as a result of bank runs. As mentioned earlier, since banks make profits by lending out their deposits, no bank, even those that are not bankrupt, can withstand a bank run. As a result of the Panic, the Federal Reserve was founded to be the "lender of last resort." In the event of a bank run, sound banks, (banks that were not bankrupt) could borrow as much cash as they needed from the Fed's discount "window" to quell the bank run. We call the interest rate banks pay for such loans the **discount rate**. (They are so named because the bank makes loans against its outstanding loans "at a discount" of their face value.) Once depositors became convinced that the bank would be able to honor their withdrawals, they no longer had a reason to make a run on the bank. In short, the Federal Reserve was originally intended to provide credit passively, but in the years since its founding, the Fed has taken on a more active role with monetary policy.

The third traditional method for conducting monetary policy is to raise or lower the discount rate. If the central bank raises the discount rate, then commercial banks will reduce their borrowing of reserves from the Fed, and instead call in loans to replace those reserves. Since fewer loans are available, the money supply falls and market interest rates rise. If the central bank lowers the discount rate it charges to banks, the process works in reverse.

In recent decades, the Federal Reserve has made relatively few discount loans. Before a bank borrows from the Federal Reserve to fill out its required reserves, the bank is expected to first borrow from other available sources, like other banks. This is encouraged by the Fed charging a higher discount rate than the federal funds rate. Given that most banks borrow little at the discount rate, changing the discount rate up or down has little impact on their behavior. More importantly, the Fed has found from experience that open market operations are a more precise and powerful means of executing any desired monetary policy.

In the Federal Reserve Act, the phrase "...to afford means of rediscounting commercial paper" is contained in its long title. This was the main tool for monetary policy when the Fed was initially created. This illustrates how monetary policy has evolved and how it continues to do so.

# 15.4 | Monetary Policy and Economic Outcomes

By the end of this section, you will be able to:
- Contrast expansionary monetary policy and contractionary monetary policy
- Explain how monetary policy impacts interest rates and aggregate demand
- Evaluate Federal Reserve decisions over the last forty years
- Explain the significance of quantitative easing (QE)

A monetary policy that lowers interest rates and stimulates borrowing is an **expansionary monetary policy** or **loose monetary policy**. Conversely, a monetary policy that raises interest rates and reduces borrowing in the economy is a **contractionary monetary policy** or **tight monetary policy**. This module will discuss how expansionary and contractionary monetary policies affect interest rates and aggregate demand, and how such policies will affect macroeconomic goals like unemployment and inflation. We will conclude with a look at the Fed's monetary policy practice in recent decades.

## The Effect of Monetary Policy on Interest Rates

Consider the market for loanable bank funds in **Figure 15.7**. The original equilibrium ($E_0$) occurs at an 8% interest rate and a quantity of funds loaned and borrowed of $10 billion. An expansionary monetary policy will shift the supply of loanable funds to the right from the original supply curve ($S_0$) to $S_1$, leading to an equilibrium ($E_1$) with a lower 6% interest rate and a quantity $14 billion in loaned funds. Conversely, a contractionary monetary policy will shift the supply of loanable funds to the left from the original supply curve ($S_0$) to $S_2$, leading to an equilibrium ($E_2$) with a higher 10% interest rate and a quantity of $8 billion in loaned funds.

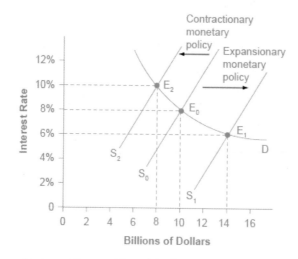

**Figure 15.7 Monetary Policy and Interest Rates**   The original equilibrium occurs at $E_0$. An expansionary monetary policy will shift the supply of loanable funds to the right from the original supply curve ($S_0$) to the new supply curve ($S_1$) and to a new equilibrium of $E_1$, reducing the interest rate from 8% to 6%. A contractionary monetary policy will shift the supply of loanable funds to the left from the original supply curve ($S_0$) to the new supply ($S_2$), and raise the interest rate from 8% to 10%.

How does a central bank "raise" interest rates? When describing the central bank's monetary policy actions, it is common to hear that the central bank "raised interest rates" or "lowered interest rates." We need to be clear about this: more precisely, through open market operations the central bank changes bank reserves in a way which affects the supply curve of loanable funds. As a result, Figure 15.7 shows that interest rates change. If they do not meet the Fed's target, the Fed can supply more or less reserves until interest rates do.

Recall that the specific interest rate the Fed targets is the **federal funds rate**. The Federal Reserve has, since 1995, established its target federal funds rate in advance of any open market operations.

Of course, financial markets display a wide range of interest rates, representing borrowers with different risk premiums and loans that they must repay over different periods of time. In general, when the federal funds rate drops substantially, other interest rates drop, too, and when the federal funds rate rises, other interest rates rise. However, a fall or rise of one percentage point in the federal funds rate—which remember is for borrowing overnight—will typically have an effect of less than one percentage point on a 30-year loan to purchase a house or a three-year loan to purchase a car. Monetary policy can push the entire spectrum of interest rates higher or lower, but the forces of supply and demand in those specific markets for lending and borrowing set the specific interest rates.

## The Effect of Monetary Policy on Aggregate Demand

Monetary policy affects interest rates and the available quantity of loanable funds, which in turn affects several components of aggregate demand. Tight or contractionary monetary policy that leads to higher interest rates and a reduced quantity of loanable funds will reduce two components of aggregate demand. Business investment will decline because it is less attractive for firms to borrow money, and even firms that have money will notice that, with higher interest rates, it is relatively more attractive to put those funds in a financial investment than to make an investment in physical capital. In addition, higher interest rates will discourage consumer borrowing for big-ticket items like houses and cars. Conversely, loose or expansionary monetary policy that leads to lower interest rates and a higher quantity of loanable funds will tend to increase business investment and consumer borrowing for big-ticket items.

If the economy is suffering a recession and high unemployment, with output below potential GDP, expansionary monetary policy can help the economy return to potential GDP. Figure 15.8 (a) illustrates this situation. This example uses a short-run upward-sloping Keynesian aggregate supply curve (SRAS). The original equilibrium during a recession of $E_0$ occurs at an output level of 600. An expansionary monetary policy will reduce interest rates and stimulate investment and consumption spending, causing the original aggregate demand curve ($AD_0$) to shift right to $AD_1$, so that the new equilibrium ($E_1$) occurs at the potential GDP level of 700.

(a) Expansionary monetary policy

(b) Contractionary monetary policy

**Figure 15.8 Expansionary or Contractionary Monetary Policy** (a) The economy is originally in a recession with the equilibrium output and price shown at $E_0$. Expansionary monetary policy will reduce interest rates and shift aggregate demand to the right from $AD_0$ to $AD_1$, leading to the new equilibrium ($E_1$) at the potential GDP level of output with a relatively small rise in the price level. (b) The economy is originally producing above the potential GDP level of output at the equilibrium $E_0$ and is experiencing pressures for an inflationary rise in the price level. Contractionary monetary policy will shift aggregate demand to the left from $AD_0$ to $AD_1$, thus leading to a new equilibrium ($E_1$) at the potential GDP level of output.

Conversely, if an economy is producing at a quantity of output above its potential GDP, a contractionary monetary policy can reduce the inflationary pressures for a rising price level. In **Figure 15.8** (b), the original equilibrium ($E_0$) occurs at an output of 750, which is above potential GDP. A contractionary monetary policy will raise interest rates, discourage borrowing for investment and consumption spending, and cause the original demand curve ($AD_0$) to shift left to $AD_1$, so that the new equilibrium ($E_1$) occurs at the potential GDP level of 700.

These examples suggest that monetary policy should be **countercyclical**; that is, it should act to counterbalance the business cycles of economic downturns and upswings. The Fed should loosen monetary policy when a recession has caused unemployment to increase and tighten it when inflation threatens. Of course, countercyclical policy does pose a danger of overreaction. If loose monetary policy seeking to end a recession goes too far, it may push aggregate demand so far to the right that it triggers inflation. If tight monetary policy seeking to reduce inflation goes too far, it may push aggregate demand so far to the left that a recession begins. **Figure 15.9** (a) summarizes the chain of effects that connect loose and tight monetary policy to changes in output and the price level.

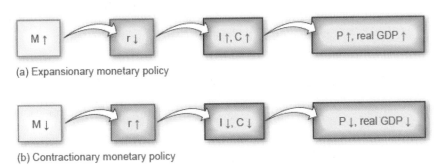

(a) Expansionary monetary policy

(b) Contractionary monetary policy

**Figure 15.9 The Pathways of Monetary Policy** (a) In expansionary monetary policy the central bank causes the supply of money and loanable funds to increase, which lowers the interest rate, stimulating additional borrowing for investment and consumption, and shifting aggregate demand right. The result is a higher price level and, at least in the short run, higher real GDP. (b) In contractionary monetary policy, the central bank causes the supply of money and credit in the economy to decrease, which raises the interest rate, discouraging borrowing for investment and consumption, and shifting aggregate demand left. The result is a lower price level and, at least in the short run, lower real GDP.

# Federal Reserve Actions Over Last Four Decades

For the period from the mid-1970s up through the end of 2007, we can summarize Federal Reserve monetary policy by looking at how it targeted the federal funds interest rate using open market operations.

Of course, telling the story of the U.S. economy since 1975 in terms of Federal Reserve actions leaves out many other macroeconomic factors that were influencing unemployment, recession, economic growth, and inflation over this time. The nine episodes of Federal Reserve action outlined in the sections below also demonstrate that we should consider the central bank as one of the leading actors influencing the macro economy. As we noted earlier, the single person with the greatest power to influence the U.S. economy is probably the Federal Reserve chairperson.

**Figure 15.10** shows how the Federal Reserve has carried out monetary policy by targeting the federal funds interest rate in the last few decades. The graph shows the federal funds interest rate (remember, this interest rate is set through open market operations), the unemployment rate, and the inflation rate since 1975. Different episodes of monetary policy during this period are indicated in the figure.

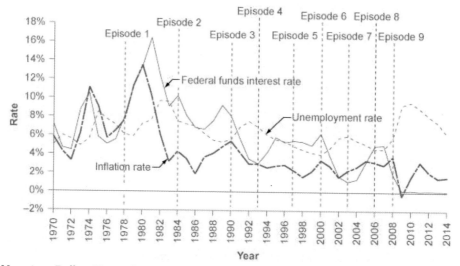

**Figure 15.10 Monetary Policy, Unemployment, and Inflation**   Through the episodes here, the Federal Reserve typically reacted to higher inflation with a contractionary monetary policy and a higher interest rate, and reacted to higher unemployment with an expansionary monetary policy and a lower interest rate.

## Episode 1

Consider Episode 1 in the late 1970s. The rate of inflation was very high, exceeding 10% in 1979 and 1980, so the Federal Reserve used tight monetary policy to raise interest rates, with the federal funds rate rising from 5.5% in 1977 to 16.4% in 1981. By 1983, inflation was down to 3.2%, but aggregate demand contracted sharply enough that back-to-back recessions occurred in 1980 and in 1981–1982, and the unemployment rate rose from 5.8% in 1979 to 9.7% in 1982.

## Episode 2

In Episode 2, when economists persuaded the Federal Reserve in the early 1980s that inflation was declining, the Fed began slashing interest rates to reduce unemployment. The federal funds interest rate fell from 16.4% in 1981 to 6.8% in 1986. By 1986 or so, inflation had fallen to about 2% and the unemployment rate had come down to 7%, and was still falling.

## Episode 3

However, in Episode 3 in the late 1980s, inflation appeared to be creeping up again, rising from 2% in 1986 up toward 5% by 1989. In response, the Federal Reserve used contractionary monetary policy to raise the federal funds rates from 6.6% in 1987 to 9.2% in 1989. The tighter monetary policy stopped inflation, which fell from above 5% in 1990 to under 3% in 1992, but it also helped to cause the 1990-1991 recession, and the unemployment rate rose from 5.3% in 1989 to 7.5% by 1992.

## Episode 4

In Episode 4, in the early 1990s, when the Federal Reserve was confident that inflation was back under control, it reduced interest rates, with the federal funds interest rate falling from 8.1% in 1990 to 3.5% in 1992. As the economy expanded, the unemployment rate declined from 7.5% in 1992 to less than 5% by 1997.

### Episodes 5 and 6

In Episodes 5 and 6, the Federal Reserve perceived a risk of inflation and raised the federal funds rate from 3% to 5.8% from 1993 to 1995. Inflation did not rise, and the period of economic growth during the 1990s continued. Then in 1999 and 2000, the Fed was concerned that inflation seemed to be creeping up so it raised the federal funds interest rate from 4.6% in December 1998 to 6.5% in June 2000. By early 2001, inflation was declining again, but a recession occurred in 2001. Between 2000 and 2002, the unemployment rate rose from 4.0% to 5.8%.

### Episodes 7 and 8

In Episodes 7 and 8, the Federal Reserve conducted a loose monetary policy and slashed the federal funds rate from 6.2% in 2000 to just 1.7% in 2002, and then again to 1% in 2003. They actually did this because of fear of Japan-style deflation. This persuaded them to lower the Fed funds further than they otherwise would have. The recession ended, but, unemployment rates were slow to decline in the early 2000s. Finally, in 2004, the unemployment rate declined and the Federal Reserve began to raise the federal funds rate until it reached 5% by 2007.

### Episode 9

In Episode 9, as the Great Recession took hold in 2008, the Federal Reserve was quick to slash interest rates, taking them down to 2% in 2008 and to nearly 0% in 2009. When the Fed had taken interest rates down to near-zero by December 2008, the economy was still deep in recession. Open market operations could not make the interest rate turn negative. The Federal Reserve had to think "outside the box."

## Quantitative Easing

The most powerful and commonly used of the three traditional tools of monetary policy—open market operations—works by expanding or contracting the money supply in a way that influences the interest rate. In late 2008, as the U.S. economy struggled with recession, the Federal Reserve had already reduced the interest rate to near-zero. With the recession still ongoing, the Fed decided to adopt an innovative and nontraditional policy known as **quantitative easing (QE)**. This is the purchase of long-term government and private mortgage-backed securities by central banks to make credit available so as to stimulate aggregate demand.

Quantitative easing differed from traditional monetary policy in several key ways. First, it involved the Fed purchasing long term Treasury bonds, rather than short term Treasury bills. In 2008, however, it was impossible to stimulate the economy any further by lowering short term rates because they were already as low as they could get. (Read the closing Bring it Home feature for more on this.) Therefore, Chairman Bernanke sought to lower long-term rates utilizing quantitative easing.

This leads to a second way QE is different from traditional monetary policy. Instead of purchasing Treasury securities, the Fed also began purchasing private mortgage-backed securities, something it had never done before. During the financial crisis, which precipitated the recession, mortgage-backed securities were termed "toxic assets," because when the housing market collapsed, no one knew what these securities were worth, which put the financial institutions which were holding those securities on very shaky ground. By offering to purchase mortgage-backed securities, the Fed was both pushing long term interest rates down and also removing possibly "toxic assets" from the balance sheets of private financial firms, which would strengthen the financial system.

Quantitative easing (QE) occurred in three episodes:

1. During $QE_1$, which began in November 2008, the Fed purchased $600 billion in mortgage-backed securities from government enterprises Fannie Mae and Freddie Mac.

2. In November 2010, the Fed began $QE_2$, in which it purchased $600 billion in U.S. Treasury bonds.

3. $QE_3$, began in September 2012 when the Fed commenced purchasing $40 billion of additional mortgage-backed securities per month. This amount was increased in December 2012 to $85 billion per month. The Fed stated that, when economic conditions permit, it will begin tapering (or reducing the monthly purchases). By October 2014, the Fed had announced the final $15 billion bond purchase, ending Quantitative Easing.

We usually think of the quantitative easing policies that the Federal Reserve adopted (as did other central banks around the world) as temporary emergency measures. If these steps are to be temporary, then the Federal Reserve will need to stop making these additional loans and sell off the financial securities it has accumulated. The concern is that the process of quantitative easing may prove more difficult to reverse than it was to enact. The evidence suggests that $QE_1$ was somewhat successful, but that $QE_2$ and $QE_3$ have been less so.

# 15.5 | Pitfalls for Monetary Policy

By the end of this section, you will be able to:
- Analyze whether monetary policy decisions should be made more democratically
- Calculate the velocity of money
- Evaluate the central bank's influence on inflation, unemployment, asset bubbles, and leverage cycles
- Calculate the effects of monetary stimulus

In the real world, effective monetary policy faces a number of significant hurdles. Monetary policy affects the economy only after a time lag that is typically long and of variable length. Remember, monetary policy involves a chain of events: the central bank must perceive a situation in the economy, hold a meeting, and make a decision to react by tightening or loosening monetary policy. The change in monetary policy must percolate through the banking system, changing the quantity of loans and affecting interest rates. When interest rates change, businesses must change their investment levels and consumers must change their borrowing patterns when purchasing homes or cars. Then it takes time for these changes to filter through the rest of the economy.

As a result of this chain of events, monetary policy has little effect in the immediate future. Instead, its primary effects are felt perhaps one to three years in the future. The reality of long and variable time lags does not mean that a central bank should refuse to make decisions. It does mean that central banks should be humble about taking action, because of the risk that their actions can create as much or more economic instability as they resolve.

## Excess Reserves

Banks are legally required to hold a minimum level of reserves, but no rule prohibits them from holding additional **excess reserves** above the legally mandated limit. For example, during a recession banks may be hesitant to lend, because they fear that when the economy is contracting, a high proportion of loan applicants become less likely to repay their loans.

When many banks are choosing to hold excess reserves, expansionary monetary policy may not work well. This may occur because the banks are concerned about a deteriorating economy, while the central bank is trying to expand the money supply. If the banks prefer to hold excess reserves above the legally required level, the central bank cannot force individual banks to make loans. Similarly, sensible businesses and consumers may be reluctant to borrow substantial amounts of money in a recession, because they recognize that firms' sales and employees' jobs are more insecure in a recession, and they do not want to face the need to make interest payments. The result is that during an especially deep recession, an expansionary monetary policy may have little effect on either the price level or the real GDP.

Japan experienced this situation in the 1990s and early 2000s. Japan's economy entered a period of very slow growth, dipping in and out of recession, in the early 1990s. By February 1999, the Bank of Japan had lowered the equivalent of its federal funds rate to 0%. It kept it there most of the time through 2003. Moreover, in the two years from March 2001 to March 2003, the Bank of Japan also expanded the country's money supply by about 50%—an enormous increase. Even this highly expansionary monetary policy, however, had no substantial effect on stimulating aggregate demand. Japan's economy continued to experience extremely slow growth into the mid-2000s.

## Should monetary policy decisions be made more democratically?

Should a nation's Congress or legislature comprised of elected representatives conduct monetary policy or should a politically appointed central bank that is more independent of voters take charge? Here are some of the arguments.

### The Case for Greater Democratic Control of Monetary Policy

Elected representatives pass taxes and spending bills to conduct fiscal policy by passing tax and spending bills. They could handle monetary policy in the same way. They will sometimes make mistakes, but in a democracy, it is better to have elected officials who are accountable to voters make mistakes instead of political appointees. After all, the people appointed to the top governing positions at the Federal Reserve—and to most central banks around the world—are typically bankers and economists. They are not representatives of borrowers like small businesses or farmers nor are they representatives of labor unions. Central banks might not be so quick to raise interest rates if they had to pay more attention to firms and people in the real economy.

### The Case for an Independent Central Bank

Because the central bank has some insulation from day-to-day politics, its members can take a nonpartisan look at specific economic situations and make tough, immediate decisions when necessary. The idea of giving a legislature the ability to create money and hand out loans is likely to end up badly, sooner or later. It is simply too tempting for lawmakers to expand the money supply to fund their projects. The long term result will be rampant inflation. Also, a central bank, acting according to the laws passed by elected officials, can respond far more quickly than a legislature. For example, the U.S. budget takes months to debate, pass, and sign into law, but monetary policy decisions happen much more rapidly. Day-to-day democratic control of monetary policy is impractical and seems likely to lead to an overly expansionary monetary policy and higher inflation.

The problem of excess reserves does not affect contractionary policy. Central bankers have an old saying that monetary policy can be like pulling and pushing on a string: when the central bank pulls on the string and uses contractionary monetary policy, it can definitely raise interest rates and reduce aggregate demand. However, when the central bank tries to push on the string of expansionary monetary policy, the string may sometimes just fold up limp and have little effect, because banks decide not to loan out their excess reserves. Do not take this analogy too literally—expansionary monetary policy usually does have real effects, after that inconveniently long and variable lag. There are also times, like Japan's economy in the late 1990s and early 2000s, when expansionary monetary policy has been insufficient to lift a recession-prone economy.

## Unpredictable Movements of Velocity

Velocity is a term that economists use to describe how quickly money circulates through the economy. We define the **velocity** of money in a year as:

$$\text{Velocity} = \frac{\text{nominal GDP}}{\text{money supply}}$$

Specific measurements of velocity depend on the definition of the money supply used. Consider the velocity of M1, the total amount of currency in circulation and checking account balances. In 2009, for example, M1 was $1.7 trillion and nominal GDP was $14.3 trillion, so the velocity of M1 was 8.4 ($14.3 trillion/$1.7 trillion). A higher velocity of money means that the average dollar circulates more times in a year. A lower velocity means that the average dollar circulates fewer times in a year.

See the following Clear It Up feature for a discussion of how deflation could affect monetary policy.

## What happens during episodes of deflation?

Deflation occurs when the rate of inflation is negative; that is, instead of money having less purchasing power over time, as occurs with inflation, money is worth more. Deflation can make it very difficult for monetary policy to address a recession.

Remember that the real interest rate is the nominal interest rate minus the rate of inflation. If the nominal interest rate is 7% and the rate of inflation is 3%, then the borrower is effectively paying a 4% real interest rate. If the nominal interest rate is 7% and there is *deflation* of 2%, then the real interest rate is actually 9%. In this way, an unexpected deflation raises the real interest payments for borrowers. It can lead to a situation where borrowers do not repay an unexpectedly high number of loans, and banks find that their net worth is decreasing or negative. When banks are suffering losses, they become less able and eager to make new loans. Aggregate demand declines, which can lead to recession.

Then the double-whammy: After causing a recession, deflation can make it difficult for monetary policy to work. Say that the central bank uses expansionary monetary policy to reduce the nominal interest rate all the way to zero—but the economy has 5% deflation. As a result, the real interest rate is 5%, and because a central bank cannot make the nominal interest rate negative, expansionary policy cannot reduce the real interest rate further.

In the U.S. economy during the early 1930s, deflation was 6.7% per year from 1930–1933, which caused many borrowers to default on their loans and many banks to end up bankrupt, which in turn contributed substantially to the Great Depression. Not all episodes of deflation, however, end in economic depression. Japan, for example, experienced deflation of slightly less than 1% per year from 1999–2002, which hurt the Japanese economy, but it still grew by about 0.9% per year over this period. There is at least one historical example of deflation coexisting with rapid growth. The U.S. economy experienced deflation of about 1.1% per year over the quarter-century from 1876–1900, but real GDP also expanded at a rapid clip of 4% per year over this time, despite some occasional severe recessions.

The central bank should be on guard against deflation and, if necessary, use expansionary monetary policy to prevent any long-lasting or extreme deflation from occurring. Except in severe cases like the Great Depression, deflation does not guarantee economic disaster.

Changes in velocity can cause problems for monetary policy. To understand why, rewrite the definition of velocity so that the money supply is on the left-hand side of the equation. That is:

$$\text{Money supply} \times \text{velocity} = \text{Nominal GDP}$$

Recall from **The Macroeconomic Perspective** that

$$\text{Nominal GDP} = \text{Price Level (or GDP Deflator)} \times \text{Real GDP}.$$

Therefore,

$$\text{Money Supply} \times \text{velocity} = \text{Nominal GDP} = \text{Price Level} \times \text{Real GDP}.$$

We sometimes call this equation the **basic quantity equation of money** but, as you can see, it is just the definition of velocity written in a different form. This equation must hold true, by definition.

If velocity is constant over time, then a certain percentage rise in the money supply on the left-hand side of the basic quantity equation of money will inevitably lead to the same percentage rise in nominal GDP—although this change could happen through an increase in inflation, or an increase in real GDP, or some combination of the two. If velocity is changing over time but in a constant and predictable way, then changes in the money supply will continue to have a predictable effect on nominal GDP. If velocity changes unpredictably over time, however, then the effect of changes in the money supply on nominal GDP becomes unpredictable.

Figure 15.11 illustrates the actual velocity of money in the U.S. economy as measured by using M1, the most common definition of the money supply. From 1960 up to about 1980, velocity appears fairly predictable; that is, it is increasing at a fairly constant rate. In the early 1980s, however, velocity as calculated with M1 becomes more variable. The reasons for these sharp changes in velocity remain a puzzle. Economists suspect that the changes in velocity are related to innovations in banking and finance which have changed how we are using money in making economic transactions: for example, the growth of electronic payments; a rise in personal borrowing and credit card usage; and accounts that make it easier for people to hold money in savings accounts, where it is counted as M2, right up to the moment that they want to write a check on the money and transfer it to M1. So far at least, it has proven difficult to draw clear links between these kinds of factors and the specific up-and-down fluctuations in M1. Given many changes in banking and the prevalence of electronic banking, economists now favor M2 as a measure of money rather than the narrower M1.

**Figure 15.11 Velocity Calculated Using M1** Velocity is the nominal GDP divided by the money supply for a given year. We can calculate different measures of velocity by using different measures of the money supply. Velocity, as calculated by using M1, has lacked a steady trend since the 1980s, instead bouncing up and down. (credit: Federal Reserve Bank of St. Louis)

In the 1970s, when velocity as measured by M1 seemed predictable, a number of economists, led by Nobel laureate Milton Friedman (1912–2006), argued that the best monetary policy was for the central bank to increase the money supply at a constant growth rate. These economists argued that with the long and variable lags of monetary policy, and the political pressures on central bankers, central bank monetary policies were as likely to have undesirable as to have desirable effects. Thus, these economists believed that the monetary policy should seek steady growth in the money supply of 3% per year. They argued that a steady monetary growth rate would be correct over longer time periods, since it would roughly match the growth of the real economy. In addition, they argued that giving the central bank less discretion to conduct monetary policy would prevent an overly activist central bank from becoming a source of economic instability and uncertainty. In this spirit, Friedman wrote in 1967: "The first and most important lesson that history teaches about what monetary policy can do—and it is a lesson of the most profound importance—is that monetary policy can prevent money itself from being a major source of economic disturbance."

As the velocity of M1 began to fluctuate in the 1980s, having the money supply grow at a predetermined and unchanging rate seemed less desirable, because as the quantity theory of money shows, the combination of constant growth in the money supply and fluctuating velocity would cause nominal GDP to rise and fall in unpredictable ways. The jumpiness of velocity in the 1980s caused many central banks to focus less on the rate at which the quantity of money in the economy was increasing, and instead to set monetary policy by reacting to whether the economy was experiencing or in danger of higher inflation or unemployment.

## Unemployment and Inflation

If you were to survey central bankers around the world and ask them what they believe should be the primary task of monetary policy, the most popular answer by far would be fighting inflation. Most central bankers believe that the neoclassical model of economics accurately represents the economy over the medium to long term. Remember that in the neoclassical model of the economy, we draw the aggregate supply curve as a vertical line at the level of potential GDP, as **Figure 15.12** shows. In the neoclassical model, economists determine the level of potential GDP (and the natural rate of unemployment that exists when the economy is producing at potential GDP) by real economic factors. If the original level of aggregate demand is $AD_0$, then an expansionary monetary policy that shifts aggregate demand to $AD_1$ only creates an inflationary increase in the price level, but it does not alter GDP or unemployment. From this perspective, all that monetary policy can do is to lead to low inflation or high inflation—and low inflation provides a better climate for a healthy and growing economy. After all, low inflation means that businesses making investments can focus on real economic issues, not on figuring out ways to protect themselves from the costs and risks of inflation. In this way, a consistent pattern of low inflation can contribute to long-term growth.

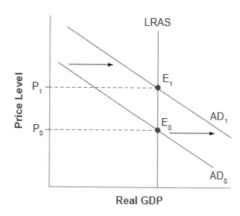

**Figure 15.12 Monetary Policy in a Neoclassical Model**   In a neoclassical view, monetary policy affects only the price level, not the level of output in the economy. For example, an expansionary monetary policy causes aggregate demand to shift from the original $AD_0$ to $AD_1$. However, the adjustment of the economy from the original equilibrium ($E_0$) to the new equilibrium ($E_1$) represents an inflationary increase in the price level from $P_0$ to $P_1$, but has no effect in the long run on output or the unemployment rate. In fact, no shift in AD will affect the equilibrium quantity of output in this model.

This vision of focusing monetary policy on a low rate of inflation is so attractive that many countries have rewritten their central banking laws since in the 1990s to have their bank practice **inflation targeting**, which means that the central bank is legally required to focus primarily on keeping inflation low. By 2014, central banks in 28 countries, including Austria, Brazil, Canada, Israel, Korea, Mexico, New Zealand, Spain, Sweden, Thailand, and the United Kingdom faced a legal requirement to target the inflation rate. A notable exception is the Federal Reserve in the United States, which does not practice inflation-targeting. Instead, the law governing the Federal Reserve requires it to take both unemployment and inflation into account.

Economists have no final consensus on whether a central bank should be required to focus only on inflation or should have greater discretion. For those who subscribe to the inflation targeting philosophy, the fear is that politicians who are worried about slow economic growth and unemployment will constantly pressure the central bank to conduct a loose monetary policy—even if the economy is already producing at potential GDP. In some countries, the central bank may lack the political power to resist such pressures, with the result of higher inflation, but no long-term reduction in unemployment. The U.S. Federal Reserve has a tradition of independence, but central banks in other countries may be under greater political pressure. For all of these reasons—long and variable lags, excess reserves, unstable velocity, and controversy over economic goals—monetary policy in the real world is often difficult. The basic message remains, however, that central banks can affect aggregate demand through the conduct of monetary policy and in that way influence macroeconomic outcomes.

## Asset Bubbles and Leverage Cycles

One long-standing concern about having the central bank focus on inflation and unemployment is that it may be overlooking certain other economic problems that are coming in the future. For example, from 1994 to 2000 during what was known as the "dot-com" boom, the U.S. stock market, which the Dow Jones Industrial Index measures (which includes 30 very large companies from across the U.S. economy), nearly tripled in value. The Nasdaq index, which includes many smaller technology companies, increased in value by a multiple of five from 1994 to 2000. These rates of increase were clearly not sustainable. Stock values as measured by the Dow Jones were almost 20% lower in 2009 than they had been in 2000. Stock values in the Nasdaq index were 50% lower in 2009 than they had been in 2000. The drop-off in stock market values contributed to the 2001 recession and the higher unemployment that followed.

We can tell a similar story about housing prices in the mid-2000s. During the 1970s, 1980s, and 1990s, housing prices increased at about 6% per year on average. During what came to be known as the "housing bubble" from 2003 to 2005, housing prices increased at almost double this annual rate. These rates of increase were clearly not sustainable. When housing prices fell in 2007 and 2008, many banks and households found that their assets were worth less than they expected, which contributed to the recession that started in 2007.

At a broader level, some economists worry about a leverage cycle, where "leverage" is a term financial economists use to mean "borrowing." When economic times are good, banks and the financial sector are eager to lend, and people and firms are eager to borrow. Remember that a money multiplier determines the amount of money and credit in an economy —a process of loans made, money deposited, and more loans made. In good economic times, this surge of lending exaggerates the episode of economic growth. It can even be part of what lead prices of certain assets—like stock prices or housing prices—to rise at unsustainably high annual rates. At some point, when economic times turn bad, banks and the financial sector become much less willing to lend, and credit becomes expensive or unavailable to many potential borrowers. The sharp reduction in credit, perhaps combined with the deflating prices of a dot-com stock price bubble or a housing bubble, makes the economic downturn worse than it would otherwise be.

Thus, some economists have suggested that the central bank should not just look at economic growth, inflation, and unemployment rates, but should also keep an eye on asset prices and leverage cycles. Such proposals are quite controversial. If a central bank had announced in 1997 that stock prices were rising "too fast" or in 2004 that housing prices were rising "too fast," and then taken action to hold down price increases, many people and their elected political representatives would have been outraged. Neither the Federal Reserve nor any other central banks want to take the responsibility of deciding when stock prices and housing prices are too high, too low, or just right. As further research explores how asset price bubbles and leverage cycles can affect an economy, central banks may need to think about whether they should conduct monetary policy in a way that would seek to moderate these effects.

Let's end this chapter with a Work it Out exercise in how the Fed—or any central bank—would stir up the economy by increasing the money supply.

# Work It Out ⊸O⊸O⊸O

## Calculating the Effects of Monetary Stimulus

Suppose that the central bank wants to stimulate the economy by increasing the money supply. The bankers estimate that the velocity of money is 3, and that the price level will increase from 100 to 110 due to the stimulus. Using the quantity equation of money, what will be the impact of an $800 billion dollar increase in the money supply on the quantity of goods and services in the economy given an initial money supply of $4 trillion?

Step 1. We begin by writing the quantity equation of money: $MV = PQ$. We know that initially $V = 3$, $M = 4{,}000$ (billion) and $P = 100$. Substituting these numbers in, we can solve for Q:

$$MV = PQ$$
$$4{,}000 \times 3 = 100 \times Q$$
$$Q = 120$$

Step 2. Now we want to find the effect of the addition $800 billion in the money supply, together with the increase in the price level. The new equation is:

$$MV = PQ$$
$$4{,}800 \times 3 = 110 \times Q$$
$$Q = 130.9$$

Step 3. If we take the difference between the two quantities, we find that the monetary stimulus increased the quantity of goods and services in the economy by 10.9 billion.

The discussion in this chapter has focused on domestic monetary policy; that is, the view of monetary policy within an economy. **Exchange Rates and International Capital Flows** explores the international dimension of monetary policy, and how monetary policy becomes involved with exchange rates and international flows of financial capital.

# Bring it Home

## The Problem of the Zero Percent Interest Rate Lower Bound

In 2008, the U.S. Federal Reserve found itself in a difficult position. The federal funds rate was on its way to near zero, which meant that traditional open market operations, by which the Fed purchases U.S. Treasury Bills to lower short term interest rates, was no longer viable. This so called "zero bound problem," prompted the Fed, under then Chair Ben Bernanke, to attempt some unconventional policies, collectively called quantitative easing. By early 2014, quantitative easing nearly quintupled the amount of bank reserves. This likely contributed to the U.S. economy's recovery, but the impact was muted, probably due to some of the hurdles mentioned in the last section of this module. The unprecedented increase in bank reserves also led to fears of inflation. As of early 2015, however, there have been no serious signs of a boom, with core inflation around a stable 1.7%.

# KEY TERMS

**bank run** when depositors race to the bank to withdraw their deposits for fear that otherwise they would be lost

**basic quantity equation of money** money supply × velocity = nominal GDP

**central bank** institution which conducts a nation's monetary policy and regulates its banking system

**contractionary monetary policy** a monetary policy that reduces the supply of money and loans

**countercyclical** moving in the opposite direction of the business cycle of economic downturns and upswings

**deposit insurance** an insurance system that makes sure depositors in a bank do not lose their money, even if the bank goes bankrupt

**discount rate** the interest rate charged by the central bank on the loans that it gives to other commercial banks

**excess reserves** reserves banks hold that exceed the legally mandated limit

**expansionary monetary policy** a monetary policy that increases the supply of money and the quantity of loans

**federal funds rate** the interest rate at which one bank lends funds to another bank overnight

**inflation targeting** a rule that the central bank is required to focus only on keeping inflation low

**lender of last resort** an institution that provides short-term emergency loans in conditions of financial crisis

**loose monetary policy** see expansionary monetary policy

**open market operations** the central bank selling or buying Treasury bonds to influence the quantity of money and the level of interest rates

**quantitative easing (QE)** the purchase of long term government and private mortgage-backed securities by central banks to make credit available in hopes of stimulating aggregate demand

**reserve requirement** the percentage amount of its total deposits that a bank is legally obligated to to either hold as cash in their vault or deposit with the central bank

**tight monetary policy** see contractionary monetary policy

**velocity** the speed with which money circulates through the economy; calculated as the nominal GDP divided by the money supply

# KEY CONCEPTS AND SUMMARY

## 15.1 The Federal Reserve Banking System and Central Banks

The most prominent task of a central bank is to conduct monetary policy, which involves changes to interest rates and credit conditions, affecting the amount of borrowing and spending in an economy. Some prominent central banks around the world include the U.S. Federal Reserve, the European Central Bank, the Bank of Japan, and the Bank of England.

## 15.2 Bank Regulation

A bank run occurs when there are rumors (possibly true, possibly false) that a bank is at financial risk of having negative net worth. As a result, depositors rush to the bank to withdraw their money and put it someplace safer. Even false rumors, if they cause a bank run, can force a healthy bank to lose its deposits and be forced to close. Deposit insurance guarantees bank depositors that, even if the bank has negative net worth, their deposits will be protected. In the United States, the Federal Deposit Insurance Corporation (FDIC) collects deposit insurance premiums from banks and guarantees bank deposits up to $250,000. Bank supervision involves inspecting the balance sheets of banks to make sure that they have positive net worth and that their assets are not too risky. In the United States, the Office of the Comptroller of the Currency (OCC) is responsible for supervising banks and inspecting savings and loans and the National Credit Union Administration (NCUA) is responsible for inspecting credit unions. The FDIC and the Federal Reserve also play a role in bank supervision.

When a central bank acts as a lender of last resort, it makes short-term loans available in situations of severe financial panic or stress. The failure of a single bank can be treated like any other business failure. Yet if many banks fail, it can reduce aggregate demand in a way that can bring on or deepen a recession. The combination of deposit insurance, bank supervision, and lender of last resort policies help to prevent weaknesses in the banking system from causing recessions.

### 15.3 How a Central Bank Executes Monetary Policy

A central bank has three traditional tools to conduct monetary policy: open market operations, which involves buying and selling government bonds with banks; reserve requirements, which determine what level of reserves a bank is legally required to hold; and discount rates, which is the interest rate charged by the central bank on the loans that it gives to other commercial banks. The most commonly used tool is open market operations.

### 15.4 Monetary Policy and Economic Outcomes

An expansionary (or loose) monetary policy raises the quantity of money and credit above what it otherwise would have been and reduces interest rates, boosting aggregate demand, and thus countering recession. A contractionary monetary policy, also called a tight monetary policy, reduces the quantity of money and credit below what it otherwise would have been and raises interest rates, seeking to hold down inflation. During the 2008–2009 recession, central banks around the world also used quantitative easing to expand the supply of credit.

### 15.5 Pitfalls for Monetary Policy

Monetary policy is inevitably imprecise, for a number of reasons: (a) the effects occur only after long and variable lags; (b) if banks decide to hold excess reserves, monetary policy cannot force them to lend; and (c) velocity may shift in unpredictable ways. The basic quantity equation of money is $MV = PQ$, where M is the money supply, V is the velocity of money, P is the price level, and Q is the real output of the economy. Some central banks, like the European Central Bank, practice inflation targeting, which means that the only goal of the central bank is to keep inflation within a low target range. Other central banks, such as the U.S. Federal Reserve, are free to focus on either reducing inflation or stimulating an economy that is in recession, whichever goal seems most important at the time.

## SELF-CHECK QUESTIONS

**1.** Why is it important for the members of the Board of Governors of the Federal Reserve to have longer terms in office than elected officials, like the President?

**2.** Given the danger of bank runs, why do banks not keep the majority of deposits on hand to meet the demands of depositors?

**3.** Bank runs are often described as "self-fulfilling prophecies." Why is this phrase appropriate to bank runs?

**4.** If the central bank sells $500 in bonds to a bank that has issued $10,000 in loans and is exactly meeting the reserve requirement of 10%, what will happen to the amount of loans and to the money supply in general?

**5.** What would be the effect of increasing the banks' reserve requirements on the money supply?

**6.** Why does contractionary monetary policy cause interest rates to rise?

**7.** Why does expansionary monetary policy causes interest rates to drop?

**8.** Why might banks want to hold excess reserves in time of recession?

**9.** Why might the velocity of money change unexpectedly?

# REVIEW QUESTIONS

**10.** How is a central bank different from a typical commercial bank?

**11.** List the three traditional tools that a central bank has for controlling the money supply.

**12.** How is bank regulation linked to the conduct of monetary policy?

**13.** What is a bank run?

**14.** In a program of deposit insurance as it is operated in the United States, what is being insured and who pays the insurance premiums?

**15.** In government programs of bank supervision, what is being supervised?

**16.** What is the lender of last resort?

**17.** Name and briefly describe the responsibilities of each of the following agencies: FDIC, NCUA, and OCC.

**18.** Explain how to use an open market operation to expand the money supply.

**19.** Explain how to use the reserve requirement to expand the money supply.

**20.** Explain how to use the discount rate to expand the money supply.

**21.** How do the expansionary and contractionary monetary policy affect the quantity of money?

**22.** How do tight and loose monetary policy affect interest rates?

**23.** How do expansionary, tight, contractionary, and loose monetary policy affect aggregate demand?

**24.** Which kind of monetary policy would you expect in response to high inflation: expansionary or contractionary? Why?

**25.** Explain how to use quantitative easing to stimulate aggregate demand.

**26.** Which kind of monetary policy would you expect in response to recession: expansionary or contractionary? Why?

**27.** How might each of the following factors complicate the implementation of monetary policy: long and variable lags, excess reserves, and movements in velocity?

**28.** Define the velocity of the money supply.

**29.** What is the basic quantity equation of money?

**30.** How does a monetary policy of inflation target work?

# CRITICAL THINKING QUESTIONS

**31.** Why do presidents typically reappoint Chairs of the Federal Reserve Board even when they were originally appointed by a president of a different political party?

**32.** In what ways might monetary policy be superior to fiscal policy? In what ways might it be inferior?

**33.** The term "moral hazard" describes increases in risky behavior resulting from efforts to make that behavior safer. How does the concept of moral hazard apply to deposit insurance and other bank regulations?

**34.** Explain what would happen if banks were notified they had to increase their required reserves by one percentage point from, say, 9% to 10% of deposits. What would their options be to come up with the cash?

**35.** A well-known economic model called the Phillips Curve (discussed in **The Keynesian Perspective** chapter) describes the short run tradeoff typically observed between inflation and unemployment. Based on the discussion of expansionary and contractionary monetary policy, explain why one of these variables usually falls when the other rises.

**36.** How does rule-based monetary policy differ from discretionary monetary policy (that is, monetary policy not based on a rule)? What are some of the arguments for each?

**37.** Is it preferable for central banks to primarily target inflation or unemployment? Why?

# PROBLEMS

**38.** Suppose the Fed conducts an open market purchase by buying $10 million in Treasury bonds from Acme Bank. Sketch out the balance sheet changes that will occur as Acme converts the bond sale proceeds to new loans. The initial Acme bank balance sheet contains the following information: Assets – reserves 30, bonds 50, and loans 50; Liabilities – deposits 300 and equity 30.

**39.** Suppose the Fed conducts an open market sale by selling $10 million in Treasury bonds to Acme Bank. Sketch out the balance sheet changes that will occur as Acme restores its required reserves (10% of deposits) by reducing its loans. The initial balance sheet for Acme Bank contains the following information: Assets – reserves 30, bonds 50, and loans 250; Liabilities – deposits 300 and equity 30.

**40.** All other things being equal, by how much will nominal GDP expand if the central bank increases the money supply by $100 billion, and the velocity of money is 3? (Use this information as necessary to answer the following 4 questions.)

**41.** Suppose now that economists expect the velocity of money to increase by 50% as a result of the monetary stimulus. What will be the total increase in nominal GDP?

**42.** If GDP is 1,500 and the money supply is 400, what is velocity?

**43.** If GDP now rises to 1,600, but the money supply does not change, how has velocity changed?

**44.** If GDP now falls back to 1,500 and the money supply falls to 350, what is velocity?

# 16 | Exchange Rates and International Capital Flows

**Figure 16.1 Trade Around the World**   Is a trade deficit between the United States and the European Union good or bad for the U.S. economy? (Credit: modification of work by Milad Mosapoor/Wikimedia Commons)

## Bring it Home

### Is a Stronger Dollar Good for the U.S. Economy?

From 2002 to 2008, the U.S. dollar lost more than a quarter of its value in foreign currency markets. On January 1, 2002, one dollar was worth 1.11 euros. On April 24, 2008 it hit its lowest point with a dollar being worth 0.64 euros. During this period, the trade deficit between the United States and the European Union grew from a yearly total of approximately –85.7 billion dollars in 2002 to 95.8 billion dollars in 2008. Was this a good thing or a bad thing for the U.S. economy?

We live in a global world. U.S. consumers buy trillions of dollars worth of imported goods and services each year, not just from the European Union, but from all over the world. U.S. businesses sell trillions of dollars' worth of exports. U.S. citizens, businesses, and governments invest trillions of dollars abroad every year. Foreign investors, businesses, and governments invest trillions of dollars in the United States each year. Indeed, foreigners are a major buyer of U.S. federal debt.

Many people feel that a weaker dollar is bad for America, that it's an indication of a weak economy, but is it? This chapter will help answer that question.

## Introduction to Exchange Rates and International Capital

# Flows

In this chapter, you will learn about:

- How the Foreign Exchange Market Works

- Demand and Supply Shifts in Foreign Exchange Markets

- Macroeconomic Effects of Exchange Rates

- Exchange Rate Policies

The world has over 150 different currencies, from the Afghanistan afghani and the Albanian lek all the way through the alphabet to the Zambian kwacha and the Zimbabwean dollar. For international economic transactions, households or firms will wish to exchange one currency for another. Perhaps the need for exchanging currencies will come from a German firm that exports products to Russia, but then wishes to exchange the Russian rubles it has earned for euros, so that the firm can pay its workers and suppliers in Germany. Perhaps it will be a South African firm that wishes to purchase a mining operation in Angola, but to make the purchase it must convert South African rand to Angolan kwanza. Perhaps it will be an American tourist visiting China, who wishes to convert U.S. dollars to Chinese yuan to pay the hotel bill.

Exchange rates can sometimes change very swiftly. For example, in the United Kingdom the pound was worth about $1.50 just before the nation voted to leave the European Union (also known as the Brexit vote), but fell to $1.37 just after the vote and continued falling to reach 30-year lows a few months later. For firms engaged in international buying, selling, lending, and borrowing, these swings in exchange rates can have an enormous effect on profits.

This chapter discusses the international dimension of money, which involves conversions from one currency to another at an exchange rate. An exchange rate is nothing more than a price—that is, the price of one currency in terms of another currency—and so we can analyze it with the tools of supply and demand. The first module of this chapter begins with an overview of foreign exchange markets: their size, their main participants, and the vocabulary for discussing movements of exchange rates. The following module uses demand and supply graphs to analyze some of the main factors that cause shifts in exchange rates. A final module then brings the central bank and monetary policy back into the picture. Each country must decide whether to allow the market to determine its exchange rate, or have the central bank intervene. All the choices for exchange rate policy involve distinctive tradeoffs and risks.

# 16.1 | How the Foreign Exchange Market Works

By the end of this section, you will be able to:
- Define "foreign exchange market"
- Describe different types of investments like foreign direct investments (FDI), portfolio investments, and hedging
- Explain how appreciating or depreciating currency affects exchange rates
- Identify who benefits from a stronger currency and benefits from a weaker currency

Most countries have different currencies, but not all. Sometimes small economies use an economically larger neighbor's currency. For example, Ecuador, El Salvador, and Panama have decided to **dollarize**—that is, to use the U.S. dollar as their currency. Sometimes nations share a common currency. A large-scale example of a common currency is the decision by 17 European nations—including some very large economies such as France, Germany, and Italy—to replace their former currencies with the euro. With these exceptions, most of the international economy takes place in a situation of multiple national currencies in which both people and firms need to convert from one currency to another when selling, buying, hiring, borrowing, traveling, or investing across national borders. We call the market in which people or firms use one currency to purchase another currency the **foreign exchange market**.

You have encountered the basic concept of exchange rates in earlier chapters. In **The International Trade and Capital Flows**, for example, we discussed how economists use exchange rates to compare GDP statistics from countries where they measure GDP in different currencies. These earlier examples, however, took the actual exchange rate as given, as if it were a fact of nature. In reality, the exchange rate is a price—the price of one currency expressed in terms of units of another currency. The key framework for analyzing prices, whether in this course, any other economics course, in public policy, or business examples, is the operation of supply and demand in markets.

Visit this website (http://openstax.org/l/exratecalc) for an exchange rate calculator.

## The Extraordinary Size of the Foreign Exchange Markets

The quantities traded in foreign exchange markets are breathtaking. A 2013 Bank of International Settlements survey found that $5.3 trillion *per day* was traded on foreign exchange markets, which makes the foreign exchange market the largest market in the world economy. In contrast, 2013 U.S. real GDP was $15.8 trillion *per year*.

Table 16.1 shows the currencies most commonly traded on foreign exchange markets. The U.S. dollar dominates the foreign exchange market, followed by the euro, the British pound, the Australian dollar, and the Japanese yen.

| Currency | % Daily Share |
|---|---|
| U.S. dollar | 87.6% |
| Euro | 31.3% |
| Japanese yen | 21.6% |
| British pound | 12.8% |
| Australian dollar | 6.9% |
| Canadian dollar | 5.1% |
| Swiss franc | 4.8% |
| Chinese yuan | 2.6% |

Table 16.1 Currencies Traded Most on Foreign Exchange Markets as of April, 2016   (Source: http://www.bis.org/publ/rpfx16fx.pdf)

## Demanders and Suppliers of Currency in Foreign Exchange Markets

In foreign exchange markets, demand and supply become closely interrelated, because a person or firm who demands one currency must at the same time supply another currency—and vice versa. To get a sense of this, it is useful to consider four groups of people or firms who participate in the market: (1) firms that are involved in international trade of goods and services; (2) tourists visiting other countries; (3) international investors buying ownership (or part-ownership) of a foreign firm; (4) international investors making financial investments that do not involve ownership. Let's consider these categories in turn.

Firms that buy and sell on international markets find that their costs for workers, suppliers, and investors are measured in the currency of the nation where their production occurs, but their revenues from sales are measured in the currency of the different nation where their sales happened. Thus, a Chinese firm exporting abroad will earn some other currency—say, U.S. dollars—but will need Chinese yuan to pay the workers, suppliers, and investors who are based in China. In the foreign exchange markets, this firm will be a supplier of U.S. dollars and a demander of Chinese yuan.

International tourists will supply their home currency to receive the currency of the country they are visiting. For example, an American tourist who is visiting China will supply U.S. dollars into the foreign exchange market and demand Chinese yuan.

We often divide financial investments that cross international boundaries, and require exchanging currency into two categories. **Foreign direct investment (FDI)** refers to purchasing a firm (at least ten percent) in another country or starting up a new enterprise in a foreign country For example, in 2008 the Belgian beer-brewing company InBev bought the U.S. beer-maker Anheuser-Busch for $52 billion. To make this purchase, InBev would have to supply euros (the currency of Belgium) to the foreign exchange market and demand U.S. dollars.

The other kind of international financial investment, **portfolio investment**, involves a purely financial investment that does not entail any management responsibility. An example would be a U.S. financial investor who purchased U.K. government bonds, or deposited money in a British bank. To make such investments, the American investor would supply U.S. dollars in the foreign exchange market and demand British pounds.

Business people often link portfolio investment to expectations about how exchange rates will shift. Look at a U.S. financial investor who is considering purchasing U.K. issued bonds. For simplicity, ignore any bond interest payment (which will be small in the short run anyway) and focus on exchange rates. Say that a British pound is currently worth $1.50 in U.S. currency. However, the investor believes that in a month, the British pound will be worth $1.60 in U.S. currency. Thus, as **Figure 16.2** (a) shows, this investor would change $24,000 for 16,000 British pounds. In a month, if the pound is worth $1.60, then the portfolio investor can trade back to U.S. dollars at the new exchange rate, and have $25,600—a nice profit. A portfolio investor who believes that the foreign exchange rate for the pound will work in the opposite direction can also invest accordingly. Say that an investor expects that the pound, now worth $1.50 in U.S. currency, will decline to $1.40. Then, as **Figure 16.2** (b) shows, that investor could start off with £20,000 in British currency (borrowing the money if necessary), convert it to $30,000 in U.S. currency, wait a month, and then convert back to approximately £21,429 in British currency—again making a nice profit. Of course, this kind of investing comes without guarantees, and an investor will suffer losses if the exchange rates do not move as predicted.

(a) An international investor who expects that, in the future, a British pound(£) will buy $1.60 in U.S. currency instead of its current exchange rate of $1.50 may hope for the following chain of events to occur:

(b) An international investor who expects that, in the future, a British pound(£) will buy only $1.40 in U.S. currency instead of its current exchange rate of $1.50 may hope for the following chain of events to occur:

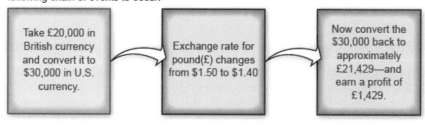

**Figure 16.2 A Portfolio Investor Trying to Benefit from Exchange Rate Movements**   Expectations of a currency's future value can drive its demand and supply in foreign exchange markets.

Many portfolio investment decisions are not as simple as betting that the currency's value will change in one direction or the other. Instead, they involve firms trying to protect themselves from movements in exchange rates. Imagine you are running a U.S. firm that is exporting to France. You have signed a contract to deliver certain products and will receive 1 million euros a year from now. However, you do not know how much this contract will be worth in U.S. dollars, because the dollar/euro exchange rate can fluctuate in the next year. Let's say you want to know for sure what the contract will be worth, and not take a risk that the euro will be worth less in U.S. dollars than it currently is. You can **hedge**, which means using a financial transaction to protect yourself against a risk from one of your investments (in this case, currency risk from the contract). Specifically, you can sign a financial contract and pay a fee that guarantees you a certain exchange rate one year from now—regardless of what the market exchange rate is at that time. Now, it is possible that the euro will be worth more in dollars a year from now, so your hedging contract will be unnecessary, and you will have paid a fee for nothing. However, if the value of the euro in dollars declines, then you are protected by the hedge. When parties wish to enter financial contracts like hedging, they normally rely on a financial institution or brokerage company to handle the hedging. These companies either take a fee or create a spread in the exchange rate in order to earn money through the service they provide.

Both foreign direct investment and portfolio investment involve an investor who supplies domestic currency and demands a foreign currency. With portfolio investment, the client purchases less than ten percent of a company. As such, business players often get involved with portfolio investment with a short term focus. With foreign direct investment the investor purchases more than ten percent of a company and the investor typically assumes some managerial responsibility. Thus, foreign direct investment tends to have a more long-run focus. As a practical matter, an investor can withdraw portfolio investments from a country much more quickly than foreign direct investments. A U.S. portfolio investor who wants to buy or sell U.K. government bonds can do so with a phone call or a few computer keyboard clicks. However, a U.S. firm that wants to buy or sell a company, such as one that manufactures automobile parts in the United Kingdom, will find that planning and carrying out the transaction takes a few weeks, even months. **Table 16.2** summarizes the main categories of currency demanders and suppliers.

| Demand for the U.S. Dollar Comes from… | Supply of the U.S. Dollar Comes from… |
|---|---|
| A U.S. exporting firm that earned foreign currency and is trying to pay U.S.-based expenses | A foreign firm that has sold imported goods in the United States, earned U.S. dollars, and is trying to pay expenses incurred in its home country |
| Foreign tourists visiting the United States | U.S. tourists leaving to visit other countries |
| Foreign investors who wish to make direct investments in the U.S. economy | U.S. investors who want to make foreign direct investments in other countries |
| Foreign investors who wish to make portfolio investments in the U.S. economy | U.S. investors who want to make portfolio investments in other countries |

**Table 16.2 The Demand and Supply Line-ups in Foreign Exchange Markets**

## Participants in the Exchange Rate Market

The foreign exchange market does not involve the ultimate suppliers and demanders of foreign exchange literally seeking each other. If Martina decides to leave her home in Venezuela and take a trip in the United States, she does not need to find a U.S. citizen who is planning to take a vacation in Venezuela and arrange a person-to-person currency trade. Instead, the foreign exchange market works through financial institutions, and it operates on several levels.

Most people and firms who are exchanging a substantial quantity of currency go to a bank, and most banks provide foreign exchange as a service to customers. These banks (and a few other firms), known as dealers, then trade the foreign exchange. This is called the interbank market.

In the world economy, roughly 2,000 firms are foreign exchange dealers. The U.S. economy has less than 100 foreign exchange dealers, but the largest 12 or so dealers carry out more than half the total transactions. The foreign exchange market has no central location, but the major dealers keep a close watch on each other at all times.

The foreign exchange market is huge not because of the demands of tourists, firms, or even foreign direct investment, but instead because of portfolio investment and the actions of interlocking foreign exchange dealers. International tourism is a very large industry, involving about $1 trillion per year. Global exports are about 23% of global GDP; which is about $18 trillion per year. Foreign direct investment totaled about $1.5 trillion in the end of 2013. These quantities are dwarfed, however, by the $5.3 trillion *per day* traded in foreign exchange markets. Most transactions in the foreign exchange market are for portfolio investment—relatively short-term movements of financial capital between currencies—and because of the large foreign exchange dealers' actions as they constantly buy and sell with each other.

## Strengthening and Weakening Currency

When the prices of most goods and services change, the price "rises or "falls". For exchange rates, the terminology is different. When the exchange rate for a currency rises, so that the currency exchanges for more of other currencies, we refer to it as **appreciating** or "strengthening." When the exchange rate for a currency falls, so that a currency trades for less of other currencies, we refer to it as **depreciating** or "weakening."

To illustrate the use of these terms, consider the exchange rate between the U.S. dollar and the Canadian dollar since 1980, in **Figure 16.3** (a). The vertical axis in **Figure 16.3** (a) shows the price of $1 in U.S. currency, measured in terms of Canadian currency. Clearly, exchange rates can move up and down substantially. A U.S. dollar traded for $1.17 Canadian in 1980. The U.S. dollar appreciated or strengthened to $1.39 Canadian in 1986, depreciated or weakened to $1.15 Canadian in 1991, and then appreciated or strengthened to $1.60 Canadian by early in 2002, fell to roughly $1.20 Canadian in 2009, and then had a sharp spike up and decline in 2009 and 2010. In May of 2017, the U.S. dollar stood at $1.36 Canadian. The units in which we measure exchange rates can be confusing, because we measure the exchange rate of the U.S. dollar exchange using a different currency—the Canadian dollar. However, exchange rates always measure the price of one unit of currency by using a different currency.

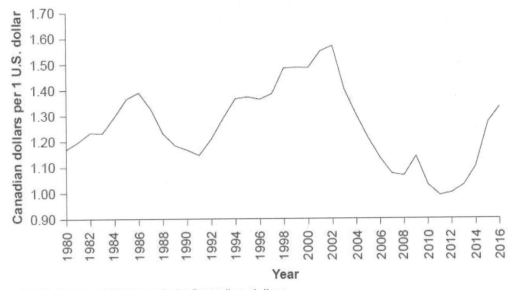

(a) U.S. dollar exchange rate in Canadian dollars

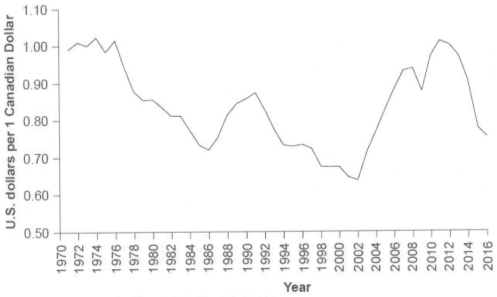

(b) Canadian dollar exchange rate in U.S. dollars

**Figure 16.3 Strengthen or Appreciate vs. Weaken or Depreciate** Exchange rates tend to fluctuate substantially, even between bordering companies such as the United States and Canada. By looking closely at the time values (the years vary slightly on these graphs), it is clear that the values in part (a) are a mirror image of part (b), which demonstrates that the depreciation of one currency correlates to the appreciation of the other and vice versa. This means that when comparing the exchange rates between two countries (in this case, the United States and Canada), the depreciation (or weakening) of one country (the U.S. dollar for this example) indicates the appreciation (or strengthening) of the other currency (which in this example is the Canadian dollar). (Source: Federal Reserve Economic Data (FRED) https://research.stlouisfed.org/fred2/series/EXCAUS)

In looking at the exchange rate between two currencies, the appreciation or strengthening of one currency must mean the depreciation or weakening of the other. **Figure 16.3** (b) shows the exchange rate for the Canadian dollar, measured in terms of U.S. dollars. The exchange rate of the U.S. dollar measured in Canadian dollars, in **Figure 16.3** (a), is a perfect mirror image with the Canadian dollar exchange rate measured in U.S. dollars, in **Figure 16.3** (b). A fall in the Canada $/U.S. $ ratio means a rise in the U.S. $/Canada $ ratio, and vice versa.

With the price of a typical good or service, it is clear that higher prices benefit sellers and hurt buyers, while lower prices benefit buyers and hurt sellers. In the case of exchange rates, where the buyers and sellers are not always intuitively obvious, it is useful to trace how a stronger or weaker currency will affect different market participants. Consider, for example, the impact of a stronger U.S. dollar on six different groups of economic actors, as **Figure 16.4** shows: (1) U.S. exporters selling abroad; (2) foreign exporters (that is, firms selling imports in the U.S. economy); (3) U.S. tourists abroad; (4) foreign tourists visiting the United States; (5) U.S. investors (either foreign direct investment or portfolio investment) considering opportunities in other countries; (6) and foreign investors considering opportunities in the U.S. economy.

**Figure 16.4 How Do Exchange Rate Movements Affect Each Group?**  Exchange rate movements affect exporters, tourists, and international investors in different ways.

For a U.S. firm selling abroad, a stronger U.S. dollar is a curse. A strong U.S. dollar means that foreign currencies are correspondingly weak. When this exporting firm earns foreign currencies through its export sales, and then converts them back to U.S. dollars to pay workers, suppliers, and investors, the stronger dollar means that the foreign currency buys fewer U.S. dollars than if the currency had not strengthened, and that the firm's profits (as measured in dollars) fall. As a result, the firm may choose to reduce its exports, or it may raise its selling price, which will also tend to reduce its exports. In this way, a stronger currency reduces a country's exports.

Conversely, for a foreign firm selling in the U.S. economy, a stronger dollar is a blessing. Each dollar earned through export sales, when traded back into the exporting firm's home currency, will now buy more home currency than expected before the dollar had strengthened. As a result, the stronger dollar means that the importing firm will earn higher profits than expected. The firm will seek to expand its sales in the U.S. economy, or it may reduce prices, which will also lead to expanded sales. In this way, a stronger U.S. dollar means that consumers will purchase more from foreign producers, expanding the country's level of imports.

For a U.S. tourist abroad, who is exchanging U.S. dollars for foreign currency as necessary, a stronger U.S. dollar is a benefit. The tourist receives more foreign currency for each U.S. dollar, and consequently the cost of the trip in U.S. dollars is lower. When a country's currency is strong, it is a good time for citizens of that country to tour abroad. Imagine a U.S. tourist who has saved up $5,000 for a trip to South Africa. In 2010, $1 bought 7.3 South African rand, so the tourist had 36,500 rand to spend. In 2012, $1 bought 8.2 rand, so the tourist had 41,000 rand to spend. By 2015, $1 bought nearly 13 rand. Clearly, more recent years have been better for U.S. tourists to visit South Africa. For foreign visitors to the United States, the opposite pattern holds true. A relatively stronger U.S. dollar means that their own currencies are relatively weaker, so that as they shift from their own currency to U.S. dollars, they have fewer U.S. dollars than previously. When a country's currency is strong, it is not an especially good time for foreign tourists to visit.

A stronger dollar injures the prospects of a U.S. financial investor who has already invested money in another country. A U.S. financial investor abroad must first convert U.S. dollars to a foreign currency, invest in a foreign country, and then later convert that foreign currency back to U.S. dollars. If in the meantime the U.S. dollar becomes stronger and the foreign currency becomes weaker, then when the investor converts back to U.S. dollars, the rate of return on that investment will be less than originally expected at the time it was made.

However, a stronger U.S. dollar boosts the returns of a foreign investor putting money into a U.S. investment. That foreign investor converts from the home currency to U.S. dollars and seeks a U.S. investment, while later planning to switch back to the home currency. If, in the meantime, the dollar grows stronger, then when the time comes to convert from U.S. dollars back to the foreign currency, the investor will receive more foreign currency than expected at the time the original investment was made.

The preceding paragraphs all focus on the case where the U.S. dollar becomes stronger. The first column in **Figure 16.4** illustrates the corresponding happy or unhappy economic reactions. The following Work It Out feature centers the analysis on the opposite: a weaker dollar.

# Work It Out ⚬—⚬—⚬

## Effects of a Weaker Dollar

Let's work through the effects of a weaker dollar on a U.S. exporter, a foreign exporter into the United States, a U.S. tourist going abroad, a foreign tourist coming to the United States, a U.S. investor abroad, and a foreign investor in the United States.

Step 1. Note that the demand for U.S. exports is a function of the price of those exports, which depends on the dollar price of those goods and the exchange rate of the dollar in terms of foreign currency. For example, a Ford pickup truck costs $25,000 in the United States. When it is sold in the United Kingdom, the price is $25,000 / $1.30 per British pound, or £19,231. The dollar affects the price foreigners face who may purchase U.S. exports.

Step 2. Consider that, if the dollar weakens, the pound rises in value. If the pound rises to $2.00 per pound, then the price of a Ford pickup is now $25,000 / $2.00 = £12,500. A weaker dollar means the foreign currency buys more dollars, which means that U.S. exports appear less expensive.

Step 3. Summarize that a weaker U.S. dollar leads to an increase in U.S. exports. For a foreign exporter, the outcome is just the opposite.

Step 4. Suppose a brewery in England is interested in selling its Bass Ale to a grocery store in the United States. If the price of a six pack of Bass Ale is £6.00 and the exchange rate is $1.30 per British pound, the price for the grocery store is 6.00 × $1.30 = $7.80 per six pack. If the dollar weakens to $2.00 per pound, the price of Bass Ale is now 6.00 × $2.00 = $12.

Step 5. Summarize that, from the perspective of U.S. purchasers, a weaker dollar means that foreign currency is more expensive, which means that foreign goods are more expensive also. This leads to a decrease in U.S. imports, which is bad for the foreign exporter.

Step 6. Consider U.S. tourists going abroad. They face the same situation as a U.S. importer—they are purchasing a foreign trip. A weaker dollar means that their trip will cost more, since a given expenditure of foreign currency (e.g., hotel bill) will take more dollars. The result is that the tourist may not stay as long abroad, and some may choose not to travel at all.

Step 7. Consider that, for the foreign tourist to the United States, a weaker dollar is a boon. It means their currency goes further, so the cost of a trip to the United States will be less. Foreigners may choose to take longer trips to the United States, and more foreign tourists may decide to take U.S. trips.

Step 8. Note that a U.S. investor abroad faces the same situation as a U.S. importer—they are purchasing a foreign asset. A U.S. investor will see a weaker dollar as an increase in the "price" of investment, since the same number of dollars will buy less foreign currency and thus less foreign assets. This should decrease the amount of U.S. investment abroad.

Step 9. Note also that foreign investors in the Unites States will have the opposite experience. Since foreign currency buys more dollars, they will likely invest in more U.S. assets.

At this point, you should have a good sense of the major players in the foreign exchange market: firms involved in international trade, tourists, international financial investors, banks, and foreign exchange dealers. The next module shows how players can use the tools of demand and supply in foreign exchange markets to explain the underlying causes of stronger and weaker currencies (we address "stronger" and "weaker" more in the following Clear It Up feature).

## Why is a stronger currency not necessarily better?

One common misunderstanding about exchange rates is that a "stronger" or "appreciating" currency must be better than a "weaker" or "depreciating" currency. After all, is it not obvious that "strong" is better than "weak"? Do not let the terminology confuse you. When a currency becomes stronger, so that it purchases more of other currencies, it benefits some in the economy and injures others. Stronger currency is not necessarily better, it is just different.

# 16.2 | Demand and Supply Shifts in Foreign Exchange Markets

By the end of this section, you will be able to:
- Explain supply and demand for exchange rates
- Define arbitrage
- Explain purchasing power parity's importance when comparing countries.

The foreign exchange market involves firms, households, and investors who demand and supply currencies coming together through their banks and the key foreign exchange dealers. **Figure 16.5** (a) offers an example for the exchange rate between the U.S. dollar and the Mexican peso. The vertical axis shows the exchange rate for U.S. dollars, which in this case is measured in pesos. The horizontal axis shows the quantity of U.S. dollars traded in the foreign exchange market each day. The demand curve (D) for U.S. dollars intersects with the supply curve (S) of U.S. dollars at the equilibrium point (E), which is an exchange rate of 10 pesos per dollar and a total volume of $8.5 billion.

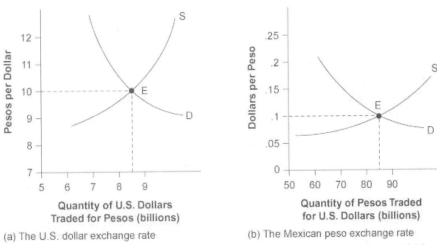

(a) The U.S. dollar exchange rate          (b) The Mexican peso exchange rate

**Figure 16.5 Demand and Supply for the U.S. Dollar and Mexican Peso Exchange Rate** (a) The quantity measured on the horizontal axis is in U.S. dollars, and the exchange rate on the vertical axis is the price of U.S. dollars measured in Mexican pesos. (b) The quantity measured on the horizontal axis is in Mexican pesos, while the price on the vertical axis is the price of pesos measured in U.S. dollars. In both graphs, the equilibrium exchange rate occurs at point E, at the intersection of the demand curve (D) and the supply curve (S).

Figure 16.5 (b) presents the same demand and supply information from the perspective of the Mexican peso. The vertical axis shows the exchange rate for Mexican pesos, which is measured in U.S. dollars. The horizontal axis shows the quantity of Mexican pesos traded in the foreign exchange market. The demand curve (D) for Mexican pesos intersects with the supply curve (S) of Mexican pesos at the equilibrium point (E), which is an exchange rate of 10 cents in U.S. currency for each Mexican peso and a total volume of 85 billion pesos. Note that the two exchange rates are inverses: 10 pesos per dollar is the same as 10 cents per peso (or $0.10 per peso). In the actual foreign exchange market, almost all of the trading for Mexican pesos is for U.S. dollars. What factors would cause the demand or supply to shift, thus leading to a change in the equilibrium exchange rate? We discuss the answer to this question in the following section.

## Expectations about Future Exchange Rates

One reason to demand a currency on the foreign exchange market is the belief that the currency's value is about to increase. One reason to supply a currency—that is, sell it on the foreign exchange market—is the expectation that the currency's value is about to decline. For example, imagine that a leading business newspaper, like the *Wall Street Journal* or the *Financial Times*, runs an article predicting that the Mexican peso will appreciate in value. **Figure 16.6** illustrates the likely effects of such an article. Demand for the Mexican peso shifts to the right, from $D_0$ to $D_1$, as investors become eager to purchase pesos. Conversely, the supply of pesos shifts to the left, from $S_0$ to $S_1$, because investors will be less willing to give them up. The result is that the equilibrium exchange rate rises from 10 cents/peso to 12 cents/peso and the equilibrium exchange rate rises from 85 billion to 90 billion pesos as the equilibrium moves from $E_0$ to $E_1$.

**Figure 16.6 Exchange Rate Market for Mexican Peso Reacts to Expectations about Future Exchange Rates**
An announcement that the peso exchange rate is likely to strengthen in the future will lead to greater demand for the peso in the present from investors who wish to benefit from the appreciation. Similarly, it will make investors less likely to supply pesos to the foreign exchange market. Both the shift of demand to the right and the shift of supply to the left cause an immediate appreciation in the exchange rate.

**Figure 16.6** also illustrates some peculiar traits of supply and demand diagrams in the foreign exchange market. In contrast to all the other cases of supply and demand you have considered, in the foreign exchange market, supply and demand typically both move at the same time. Groups of participants in the foreign exchange market like firms and investors include some who are buyers and some who are sellers. An expectation of a future shift in the exchange rate affects both buyers and sellers—that is, it affects both demand and supply for a currency.

The shifts in demand and supply curves both cause the exchange rate to shift in the same direction. In this example, they both make the peso exchange rate stronger. However, the shifts in demand and supply work in opposing directions on the quantity traded. In this example, the rising demand for pesos is causing the quantity to rise while the falling supply of pesos is causing quantity to fall. In this specific example, the result is a higher quantity. However, in other cases, the result could be that quantity remains unchanged or declines.

This example also helps to explain why exchange rates often move quite substantially in a short period of a few weeks or months. When investors expect a country's currency to strengthen in the future, they buy the currency and cause it to appreciate immediately. The currency's appreciation can lead other investors to believe that future appreciation is likely—and thus lead to even further appreciation. Similarly, a fear that a currency *might* weaken quickly leads to an *actual* weakening of the currency, which often reinforces the belief that the currency will weaken further. Thus, beliefs about the future path of exchange rates can be self-reinforcing, at least for a time, and a large share of the trading in foreign exchange markets involves dealers trying to outguess each other on what direction exchange rates will move next.

## Differences across Countries in Rates of Return

The motivation for investment, whether domestic or foreign, is to earn a return. If rates of return in a country look relatively high, then that country will tend to attract funds from abroad. Conversely, if rates of return in a country look relatively low, then funds will tend to flee to other economies. Changes in the expected rate of return will shift demand and supply for a currency. For example, imagine that interest rates rise in the United States as compared with Mexico. Thus, financial investments in the United States promise a higher return than previously. As a result, more investors will demand U.S. dollars so that they can buy interest-bearing assets and fewer investors will be willing to supply U.S. dollars to foreign exchange markets. Demand for the U.S. dollar will shift to the right, from $D_0$ to $D_1$, and supply will shift to the left, from $S_0$ to $S_1$, as **Figure 16.7** shows. The new equilibrium ($E_1$), will occur at an exchange rate of nine pesos/dollar and the same quantity of $8.5 billion. Thus, a higher interest rate or rate of return relative to other countries leads a nation's currency to appreciate or strengthen, and a lower interest rate relative to other countries leads a nation's currency to depreciate or weaken. Since a nation's central bank can use monetary policy to affect its interest rates, a central bank can also cause changes in exchange rates—a connection that we will discuss in more detail later in this chapter.

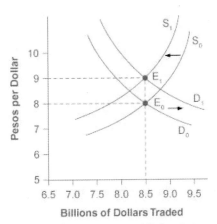

**Figure 16.7 Exchange Rate Market for U.S. Dollars Reacts to Higher Interest Rates** A higher rate of return for U.S. dollars makes holding dollars more attractive. Thus, the demand for dollars in the foreign exchange market shifts to the right, from $D_0$ to $D_1$, while the supply of dollars shifts to the left, from $S_0$ to $S_1$. The new equilibrium ($E_1$) has a stronger exchange rate than the original equilibrium ($E_0$), but in this example, the equilibrium quantity traded does not change.

## Relative Inflation

If a country experiences a relatively high inflation rate compared with other economies, then the buying power of its currency is eroding, which will tend to discourage anyone from wanting to acquire or to hold the currency. **Figure 16.8** shows an example based on an actual episode concerning the Mexican peso. In 1986–87, Mexico experienced an inflation rate of over 200%. Not surprisingly, as inflation dramatically decreased the peso's purchasing power in Mexico. The peso's exchange rate value declined as well. **Figure 16.8** shows that the demand for the peso on foreign exchange markets decreased from $D_0$ to $D_1$, while the peso's supply increased from $S_0$ to $S_1$. The equilibrium exchange rate fell from $2.50 per peso at the original equilibrium ($E_0$) to $0.50 per peso at the new equilibrium ($E_1$). In this example, the quantity of pesos traded on foreign exchange markets remained the same, even as the exchange rate shifted.

**Figure 16.8 Exchange Rate Markets React to Higher Inflation** If a currency is experiencing relatively high inflation, then its buying power is decreasing and international investors will be less eager to hold it. Thus, a rise in inflation in the Mexican peso would lead demand to shift from $D_0$ to $D_1$, and supply to increase from $S_0$ to $S_1$. Both movements in demand and supply would cause the currency to depreciate. Here, we draw the effect on the quantity traded as a decrease, but in truth it could be an increase or no change, depending on the actual movements of demand and supply.

# Link It Up ⟨⟨⟩⟩

Visit this website (http://openstaxcollege.org/l/bigmac) to learn about the Big Mac index.

## Purchasing Power Parity

Over the long term, exchange rates must bear some relationship to the currency's buying power in terms of internationally traded goods. If at a certain exchange rate it was much cheaper to buy internationally traded goods—such as oil, steel, computers, and cars—in one country than in another country, businesses would start buying in the cheap country, selling in other countries, and pocketing the profits.

For example, if a U.S. dollar is worth $1.30 in Canadian currency, then a car that sells for $20,000 in the United States should sell for $26,000 in Canada. If the price of cars in Canada were much lower than $26,000, then at least some U.S. car-buyers would convert their U.S. dollars to Canadian dollars and buy their cars in Canada. If the price of cars were much higher than $26,000 in this example, then at least some Canadian buyers would convert their Canadian dollars to U.S. dollars and go to the United States to purchase their cars. This is known as **arbitrage**, the process of buying and selling goods or currencies across international borders at a profit. It may occur slowly, but over time, it will force prices and exchange rates to align so that the price of internationally traded goods is similar in all countries.

We call the exchange rate that equalizes the prices of internationally traded goods across countries the **purchasing power parity (PPP)** exchange rate. A group of economists at the International Comparison Program, run by the World Bank, have calculated the PPP exchange rate for all countries, based on detailed studies of the prices and quantities of internationally tradable goods.

The purchasing power parity exchange rate has two functions. First, economists often use PPP exchange rates for international comparison of GDP and other economic statistics. Imagine that you are preparing a table showing the size of GDP in many countries in several recent years, and for ease of comparison, you are converting all the values into U.S. dollars. When you insert the value for Japan, you need to use a yen/dollar exchange rate. However, should you use the market exchange rate or the PPP exchange rate? Market exchange rates bounce around. In 2014, the exchange rate was 105 yen/dollar, but in late 2015 the U.S. dollar exchange rate versus the yen was 121 yen/dollar. For simplicity, say that Japan's GDP was ¥500 trillion in both 2014 and 2015. If you use the market exchange rates, then Japan's GDP will be $4.8 trillion in 2014 (that is, ¥500 trillion /(¥105/dollar)) and $4.1 trillion in 2015 (that is, ¥500 trillion /(¥121/dollar)).

The misleading appearance of a changing Japanese economy occurs only because we used the market exchange rate, which often has short-run rises and falls. However, PPP exchange rates stay fairly constant and change only modestly, if at all, from year to year.

The second function of PPP is that exchanges rates will often get closer to it as time passes. It is true that in the short and medium run, as exchange rates adjust to relative inflation rates, rates of return, and to expectations about how interest rates and inflation will shift, the exchange rates will often move away from the PPP exchange rate for a time. However, knowing the PPP will allow you to track and predict exchange rate relationships.

# 16.3 | Macroeconomic Effects of Exchange Rates

By the end of this section you will be able to:
- Explain how exchange rate shifting influences aggregate demand and supply
- Explain how shifting exchange rates also can influence loans and banks

A central bank will be concerned about the exchange rate for multiple reasons: (1) Movements in the exchange rate will affect the quantity of aggregate demand in an economy; (2) frequent substantial fluctuations in the exchange rate can disrupt international trade and cause problems in a nation's banking system–this may contribute to an unsustainable balance of trade and large inflows of international financial capital, which can set up the economy for a deep recession if international investors decide to move their money to another country. Let's discuss these scenarios in turn.

## Exchange Rates, Aggregate Demand, and Aggregate Supply

Foreign trade in goods and services typically involves incurring the costs of production in one currency while receiving revenues from sales in another currency. As a result, movements in exchange rates can have a powerful effect on incentives to export and import, and thus on aggregate demand in the economy as a whole.

For example, in 1999, when the euro first became a currency, its value measured in U.S. currency was $1.06/euro. By the end of 2013, the euro had risen (and the U.S. dollar had correspondingly weakened) to $1.37/euro. However, by the end of February, 2017, the exchange rate was once again $1.06/euro. Consider the situation of a French firm that each year incurs €10 million in costs, and sells its products in the United States for $10 million. In 1999, when this firm converted $10 million back to euros at the exchange rate of $1.06/euro (that is, $10 million × [€1/$1.06]), it received €9.4 million, and suffered a loss. In 2013, when this same firm converted $10 million back to euros at the exchange rate of $1.37/euro (that is, $10 million × [€1 euro/$1.37]), it received approximately €7.3 million and an even larger loss. In the beginning of 2017, with the exchange rate back at $1.06/euro the firm would suffer a loss once again. This example shows how a stronger euro discourages exports by the French firm, because it makes the costs of production in the domestic currency higher relative to the sales revenues earned in another country. From the point of view of the U.S. economy, the example also shows how a weaker U.S. dollar encourages exports.

Since an increase in exports results in more dollars flowing into the economy, and an increase in imports means more dollars are flowing out, it is easy to conclude that exports are "good" for the economy and imports are "bad," but this overlooks the role of exchange rates. If an American consumer buys a Japanese car for $20,000 instead of an American car for $30,000, it may be tempting to argue that the American economy has lost out. However, the Japanese company will have to convert those dollars to yen to pay its workers and operate its factories. Whoever buys those dollars will have to use them to purchase American goods and services, so the money comes right back into the American economy. At the same time, the consumer saves money by buying a less expensive import, and can use the extra money for other purposes.

## Fluctuations in Exchange Rates

Exchange rates can fluctuate a great deal in the short run. As yet one more example, the Indian rupee moved from 39 rupees/dollar in February 2008 to 51 rupees/dollar in March 2009, a decline of more than one-fourth in the value of the rupee on foreign exchange markets. **Figure 16.9** earlier showed that even two economically developed neighboring economies like the United States and Canada can see significant movements in exchange rates over a few years. For firms that depend on export sales, or firms that rely on imported inputs to production, or even purely domestic firms that compete with firms tied into international trade—which in many countries adds up to half or more of a nation's GDP—sharp movements in exchange rates can lead to dramatic changes in profits and losses. A central bank may desire to keep exchange rates from moving too much as part of providing a stable business climate, where firms can focus on productivity and innovation, not on reacting to exchange rate fluctuations.

One of the most economically destructive effects of exchange rate fluctuations can happen through the banking system. Financial institutions measure most international loans are measured in a few large currencies, like U.S. dollars, European euros, and Japanese yen. In countries that do not use these currencies, banks often borrow funds in the currencies of other countries, like U.S. dollars, but then lend in their own domestic currency. The left-hand chain of events in **Figure 16.9** shows how this pattern of international borrowing can work. A bank in Thailand borrows one million in U.S. dollars. Then the bank converts the dollars to its domestic currency—in the case of Thailand, the currency is the baht—at a rate of 40 baht/dollar. The bank then lends the baht to a firm in Thailand. The business repays the loan in baht, and the bank converts it back to U.S. dollars to pay off its original U.S. dollar loan.

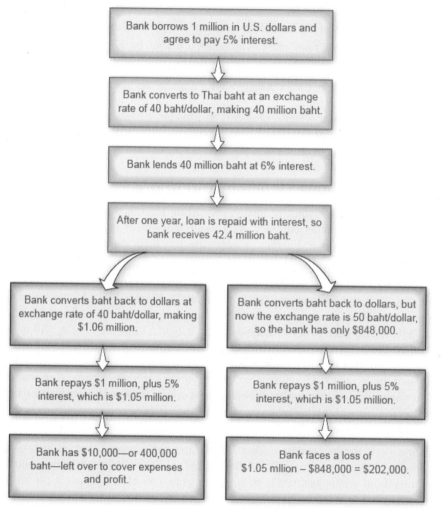

**Figure 16.9 International Borrowing**  The scenario of international borrowing that ends on the left is a success story, but the scenario that ends on the right shows what happens when the exchange rate weakens.

This process of borrowing in a foreign currency and lending in a domestic currency can work just fine, as long as the exchange rate does not shift. In the scenario outlined, if the dollar strengthens and the baht weakens, a problem arises. The right-hand chain of events in **Figure 16.9** illustrates what happens when the baht unexpectedly weakens from 40 baht/dollar to 50 baht/dollar. The Thai firm still repays the loan in full to the bank. However, because of the shift in the exchange rate, the bank cannot repay its loan in U.S. dollars. (Of course, if the exchange rate had changed in the other direction, making the Thai currency stronger, the bank could have realized an unexpectedly large profit.)

In 1997–1998, countries across eastern Asia, like Thailand, Korea, Malaysia, and Indonesia, experienced a sharp depreciation of their currencies, in some cases 50% or more. These countries had been experiencing substantial inflows of foreign investment capital, with bank lending increasing by 20% to 30% per year through the mid-1990s. When their exchange rates depreciated, the banking systems in these countries were bankrupt. Argentina experienced a similar chain of events in 2002. When the Argentine peso depreciated, Argentina's banks found themselves unable to pay back what they had borrowed in U.S. dollars.

Banks play a vital role in any economy in facilitating transactions and in making loans to firms and consumers. When most of a country's largest banks become bankrupt simultaneously, a sharp decline in aggregate demand and a deep recession results. Since the main responsibilities of a central bank are to control the money supply and to ensure that the banking system is stable, a central bank must be concerned about whether large and unexpected exchange rate depreciation will drive most of the country's existing banks into bankruptcy. For more on this concern, return to the chapter on **The International Trade and Capital Flows**.

## Summing Up Public Policy and Exchange Rates

Every nation would prefer a stable exchange rate to facilitate international trade and reduce the degree of risk and uncertainty in the economy. However, a nation may sometimes want a weaker exchange rate to stimulate aggregate demand and reduce a recession, or a stronger exchange rate to fight inflation. The country must also be concerned that rapid movements from a weak to a strong exchange rate may cripple its export industries, while rapid movements from a strong to a weak exchange rate can cripple its banking sector. In short, every choice of an exchange rate—whether it should be stronger or weaker, or fixed or changing—represents potential tradeoffs.

# 16.4 | Exchange Rate Policies

By the end of this section, you will be able to:
- Differentiate among a floating exchange rate, a soft peg, a hard peg, and a merged currency
- Identify the tradeoffs that come with a floating exchange rate, a soft peg, a hard peg, and a merged currency

Exchange rate policies come in a range of different forms listed in **Figure 16.10**: let the foreign exchange market determine the exchange rate; let the market set the value of the exchange rate most of the time, but have the central bank sometimes intervene to prevent fluctuations that seem too large; have the central bank guarantee a specific exchange rate; or share a currency with other countries. Let's discuss each type of exchange rate policy and its tradeoffs.

**Figure 16.10 A Spectrum of Exchange Rate Policies** A nation may adopt one of a variety of exchange rate regimes, from floating rates in which the foreign exchange market determines the rates to pegged rates where governments intervene to manage the exchange rate's value, to a common currency where the nation adopts another country or group of countries' currency.

## Floating Exchange Rates

We refer to a policy which allows the foreign exchange market to set exchange rates as a **floating exchange rate**. The U.S. dollar is a floating exchange rate, as are the currencies of about 40% of the countries in the world economy. The major concern with this policy is that exchange rates can move a great deal in a short time.

Consider the U.S. exchange rate expressed in terms of another fairly stable currency, the Japanese yen, as **Figure 16.11** shows. On January 1, 2002, the exchange rate was 133 yen/dollar. On January 1, 2005, it was 103 yen/dollar. On June 1, 2007, it was 122 yen/dollar, on January 1, 2012, it was 77 yen per dollar, and on March 1, 2015, it was 120 yen per dollar. As investor sentiment swings back and forth, driving exchange rates up and down, exporters, importers, and banks involved in international lending are all affected. At worst, large movements in exchange rates can drive companies into bankruptcy or trigger a nationwide banking collapse. However, even in the moderate case of the yen/dollar exchange rate, these movements of roughly 30 percent back and forth impose stress on both economies as firms must alter their export and import plans to take the new exchange rates into account. Especially in smaller countries where international trade is a relatively large share of GDP, exchange rate movements can rattle their economies.

**Figure 16.11 U.S. Dollar Exchange Rate in Japanese Yen** Even seemingly stable exchange rates such as the Japanese Yen to the U.S. Dollar can vary when closely examined over time. This figure shows a relatively stable rate between 2011 and 2013. In 2013, there was a drastic depreciation of the Yen (relative to the U.S. Dollar) by about 14% and again at the end of the year in 2014 also by about 14%. (Source: Federal Reserve Economic Data (FRED) https://research.stlouisfed.org/fred2/series/DEXJPUS)

However, movements of floating exchange rates have advantages, too. After all, prices of goods and services rise and fall throughout a market economy, as demand and supply shift. If an economy experiences strong inflows or outflows of international financial capital, or has relatively high inflation, or if it experiences strong productivity growth so that purchasing power changes relative to other economies, then it makes economic sense for the exchange rate to shift as well.

Floating exchange rate advocates often argue that if government policies were more predictable and stable, then inflation rates and interest rates would be more predictable and stable. Exchange rates would bounce around less, too. The economist Milton Friedman (1912–2006), for example, wrote a defense of floating exchange rates in 1962 in his book *Capitalism and Freedom*:

> Being in favor of floating exchange rates does not mean being in favor of unstable exchange rates. When we support a free price system [for goods and services] at home, this does not imply that we favor a system in which prices fluctuate wildly up and down. What we want is a system in which prices are free to fluctuate but in which the forces determining them are sufficiently stable so that in fact prices move within moderate ranges. This is equally true in a system of floating exchange rates. The ultimate objective is a world in which exchange rates, while free to vary, are, in fact, highly stable because basic economic policies and conditions are stable.

Advocates of floating exchange rates admit that, yes, exchange rates may sometimes fluctuate. They point out, however, that if a central bank focuses on preventing either high inflation or deep recession, with low and reasonably steady interest rates, then exchange rates will have less reason to vary.

## Using Soft Pegs and Hard Pegs

When a government intervenes in the foreign exchange market so that the currency's exchange rate is different from what the market would have produced, it establishes a "peg" for its currency. A **soft peg** is the name for an exchange rate policy where the government usually allows the market to set exchange rate, but in some cases, especially if the exchange rate seems to be moving rapidly in one direction, the central bank will intervene in the market. With a **hard peg** exchange rate policy, the central bank sets a fixed and unchanging value for the exchange rate. A central bank can implement soft peg and hard peg policies.

Suppose the market exchange rate for the Brazilian currency, the real, would be 35 cents/real with a daily quantity of 15 billion real traded in the market, as the equilibrium $E_0$ in **Figure 16.12** (a) and **Figure 16.12** (b) show. However, Brazil's government decides that the exchange rate should be 30 cents/real, as **Figure 16.12** (a) shows. Perhaps

Brazil sets this lower exchange rate to benefit its export industries. Perhaps it is an attempt to stimulate aggregate demand by stimulating exports. Perhaps Brazil believes that the current market exchange rate is higher than the long-term purchasing power parity value of the real, so it is minimizing fluctuations in the real by keeping it at this lower rate. Perhaps the government set the target exchange rate sometime in the past, and it is now maintaining it for the sake of stability. Whatever the reason, if Brazil's central bank wishes to keep the exchange rate below the market level, it must face the reality that at this weaker exchange rate of 30 cents/real, the quantity demanded of its currency at 17 billion reals is greater than the quantity supplied of 13 billion reals in the foreign exchange market.

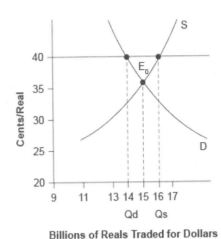

(a) Pegging an exchange rate below equilibrium    (b) Pegging an exchange rate above equilibrium

**Figure 16.12 Pegging an Exchange Rate** (a) If an exchange rate is pegged below what would otherwise be the equilibrium, then the currency's quantity demanded will exceed the quantity supplied. (b) If an exchange rate is pegged above what would otherwise be the equilibrium, then the currency's quantity supplied exceeds the quantity demanded.

The Brazilian central bank could weaken its exchange rate in two ways. One approach is to use an expansionary monetary policy that leads to lower interest rates. In foreign exchange markets, the lower interest rates will reduce demand and increase supply of the real and lead to depreciation. Central banks do not use this technique often because lowering interest rates to weaken the currency may be in conflict with the country's monetary policy goals. Alternatively, Brazil's central bank could trade directly in the foreign exchange market. The central bank can expand the money supply by creating reals, use the reals to purchase foreign currencies, and avoid selling any of its own currency. In this way, it can fill the gap between quantity demanded and quantity supplied of its currency.

**Figure 16.12** (b) shows the opposite situation. Here, the Brazilian government desires a stronger exchange rate of 40 cents/real than the market rate of 35 cents/real. Perhaps Brazil desires the stronger currency to reduce aggregate demand and to fight inflation, or perhaps Brazil believes that that current market exchange rate is temporarily lower than the long-term rate. Whatever the reason, at the higher desired exchange rate, the quantity supplied of 16 billion reals exceeds the quantity demanded of 14 billion reals.

Brazil's central bank can use a contractionary monetary policy to raise interest rates, which will increase demand and reduce currency supply on foreign exchange markets, and lead to an appreciation. Alternatively, Brazil's central bank can trade directly in the foreign exchange market. In this case, with an excess supply of its own currency in foreign exchange markets, the central bank must use reserves of foreign currency, like U.S. dollars, to demand its own currency and thus cause an appreciation of its exchange rate.

Both a soft peg and a hard peg policy require that the central bank intervene in the foreign exchange market. However, a hard peg policy attempts to preserve a fixed exchange rate at all times. A soft peg policy typically allows the exchange rate to move up and down by relatively small amounts in the short run of several months or a year, and to move by larger amounts over time, but seeks to avoid extreme short-term fluctuations.

## Tradeoffs of Soft Pegs and Hard Pegs

When a country decides to alter the market exchange rate, it faces a number of tradeoffs. If it uses monetary policy to alter the exchange rate, it then cannot at the same time use monetary policy to address issues of inflation or recession. If it uses direct purchases and sales of foreign currencies in exchange rates, then it must face the issue of how it will handle its reserves of foreign currency. Finally, a pegged exchange rate can even create additional movements of the exchange rate. For example, even the possibility of government intervention in exchange rate markets will lead to rumors about whether and when the government will intervene, and dealers in the foreign exchange market will react to those rumors. Let's consider these issues in turn.

One concern with pegged exchange rate policies is that they imply a country's monetary policy is no longer focused on controlling inflation or shortening recessions, but now must also take the exchange rate into account. For example, when a country pegs its exchange rate, it will sometimes face economic situations where it would like to have an expansionary monetary policy to fight recession—but it cannot do so because that policy would depreciate its exchange rate and break its hard peg. With a soft peg exchange rate policy, the central bank can sometimes ignore the exchange rate and focus on domestic inflation or recession—but in other cases the central bank may ignore inflation or recession and instead focus on its soft peg exchange rate. With a hard peg policy, domestic monetary policy is effectively no longer determined by domestic inflation or unemployment, but only by what monetary policy is needed to keep the exchange rate at the hard peg.

Another issue arises when a central bank intervenes directly in the exchange rate market. If a central bank ends up in a situation where it is perpetually creating and selling its own currency on foreign exchange markets, it will be buying the currency of other countries, like U.S. dollars or euros, to hold as reserves. Holding large reserves of other currencies has an opportunity cost, and central banks will not wish to boost such reserves without limit.

In addition, a central bank that causes a large increase in the supply of money is also risking an inflationary surge in aggregate demand. Conversely, when a central bank wishes to buy its own currency, it can do so by using its reserves of international currency like the U.S. dollar or the euro. However, if the central bank runs out of such reserves, it can no longer use this method to strengthen its currency. Thus, buying foreign currencies in exchange rate markets can be expensive and inflationary, while selling foreign currencies can work only until a central bank runs out of reserves.

Yet another issue is that when a government pegs its exchange rate, it may unintentionally create another reason for additional fluctuation. With a soft peg policy, foreign exchange dealers and international investors react to every rumor about how or when the central bank is likely to intervene to influence the exchange rate, and as they react to rumors the exchange rate will shift up and down. Thus, even though the goal of a soft peg policy is to reduce short-term fluctuations of the exchange rate, the existence of the policy—when anticipated in the foreign exchange market—may sometimes increase short-term fluctuations as international investors try to anticipate how and when the central bank will act. The following Clear It Up feature discusses the effects of **international capital flows**—capital that flows across national boundaries as either portfolio investment or direct investment.

## How do Tobin taxes control the flow of capital?

Some countries like Chile and Malaysia have sought to reduce movements in exchange rates by limiting international financial capital inflows and outflows. The government can enact this policy either through targeted taxes or by regulations.

Taxes on international capital flows are sometimes known as **Tobin taxes**, named after James Tobin, the 1981 Nobel laureate in economics who proposed such a tax in a 1972 lecture. For example, a government might tax all foreign exchange transactions, or attempt to tax short-term portfolio investment while exempting long-term foreign direct investment. Countries can also use regulation to forbid certain kinds of foreign investment in the first place or to make it difficult for international financial investors to withdraw their funds from a country.

The goal of such policies is to reduce international capital flows, especially short-term portfolio flows, in the hope that doing so will reduce the chance of large movements in exchange rates that can bring macroeconomic disaster.

However, proposals to limit international financial flows have severe practical difficulties. National governments impose taxes, not international ones. If one government imposes a Tobin tax on exchange rate transactions carried out within its territory, a firm based someplace like the Grand Caymans, an island nation in the Caribbean well-known for allowing some financial wheeling and dealing might easily operate the exchange rate market. In an interconnected global economy, if goods and services are allowed to flow across national borders, then payments need to flow across borders, too. It is very difficult—in fact close to impossible—for a nation to allow only the flows of payments that relate to goods and services, while clamping down or taxing other flows of financial capital. If a nation participates in international trade, it must also participate in international capital movements.

Finally, countries all over the world, especially low-income countries, are crying out for foreign investment to help develop their economies. Policies that discourage international financial investment may prevent some possible harm, but they rule out potentially substantial economic benefits as well.

A hard peg exchange rate policy will not allow short-term fluctuations in the exchange rate. If the government first announces a hard peg and then later changes its mind—perhaps the government becomes unwilling to keep interest rates high or to hold high levels of foreign exchange reserves—then the result of abandoning a hard peg could be a dramatic shift in the exchange rate.

In the mid-2000s, about one-third of the countries in the world used a soft peg approach and about one-quarter used a hard peg approach. The general trend in the 1990s was to shift away from a soft peg approach in favor of either floating rates or a hard peg. The concern is that a successful soft peg policy may, for a time, lead to very little variation in exchange rates, so that firms and banks in the economy begin to act as if a hard peg exists. When the exchange rate does move, the effects are especially painful because firms and banks have not planned and hedged against a possible change. Thus, the argument went, it is better either to be clear that the exchange rate is always flexible, or that it is fixed, but choosing an in-between soft peg option may end up being worst of all.

## A Merged Currency

A final approach to exchange rate policy is for a nation to choose a common currency shared with one or more nations is also called a **merged currency**. A merged currency approach eliminates foreign exchange risk altogether. Just as no one worries about exchange rate movements when buying and selling between New York and California, Europeans know that the value of the euro will be the same in Germany and France and other European nations that have adopted the euro.

However, a merged currency also poses problems. Like a hard peg, a merged currency means that a nation has given up altogether on domestic monetary policy, and instead has put its interest rate policies in other hands. When Ecuador uses the U.S. dollar as its currency, it has no voice in whether the Federal Reserve raises or lowers interest rates. The European Central Bank that determines monetary policy for the euro has representatives from all the euro nations. However, from the standpoint of, say, Portugal, there will be times when the decisions of the European Central Bank about monetary policy do not match the decisions that a Portuguese central bank would have made.

The lines between these four different exchange rate policies can blend into each other. For example, a soft peg exchange rate policy in which the government almost never acts to intervene in the exchange rate market will look a great deal like a floating exchange rate. Conversely, a soft peg policy in which the government intervenes often to keep the exchange rate near a specific level will look a lot like a hard peg. A decision to merge currencies with another country is, in effect, a decision to have a permanently fixed exchange rate with those countries, which is like a very hard exchange rate peg. **Table 16.3** summarizes the range of exchange rates policy choices, with their advantages and disadvantages.

| Situation | Floating Exchange Rates | Soft Peg | Hard Peg | Merged Currency |
|---|---|---|---|---|
| Large short-run fluctuations in exchange rates? | Often considerable in the short term | Maybe less in the short run, but still large changes over time | None, unless a change in the fixed rate | None |

**Table 16.3 Tradeoffs of Exchange Rate Policies**

| Situation | Floating Exchange Rates | Soft Peg | Hard Peg | Merged Currency |
|---|---|---|---|---|
| Large long-term fluctuations in exchange rates? | Can often happen | Can often happen | Cannot happen unless hard peg changes, in which case substantial volatility can occur | Cannot happen |
| Power of central bank to conduct countercyclical monetary policy? | Flexible exchange rates make monetary policy stronger | Some power, although conflicts may arise between exchange rate policy and countercyclical policy | Very little; central bank must keep exchange rate fixed | None; nation does not have its own currency |
| Costs of holding foreign exchange reserves? | Do not need to hold reserves | Hold moderate reserves that rise and fall over time | Hold large reserves | No need to hold reserves |
| Risk of ending up with an exchange rate that causes a large trade imbalance and very high inflows or outflows of financial capital? | Adjusts often | Adjusts over the medium term, if not the short term | May end up over time either far above or below the market level | Cannot adjust |

**Table 16.3 Tradeoffs of Exchange Rate Policies**

Global macroeconomics would be easier if the whole world had one currency and one central bank. The exchange rates between different currencies complicate the picture. If financial markets solely set exchange rates, they fluctuate substantially as short-term portfolio investors try to anticipate tomorrow's news. If the government attempts to intervene in exchange rate markets through soft pegs or hard pegs, it gives up at least some of the power to use monetary policy to focus on domestic inflations and recessions, and it risks causing even greater fluctuations in foreign exchange markets.

There is no consensus among economists about which exchange rate policies are best: floating, soft peg, hard peg, or merged currencies. The choice depends both on how well a nation's central bank can implement a specific exchange rate policy and on how well a nation's firms and banks can adapt to different exchange rate policies. A national economy that does a fairly good job at achieving the four main economic goals of growth, low inflation, low unemployment, and a sustainable balance of trade will probably do just fine most of the time with any exchange rate policy. Conversely, no exchange rate policy is likely to save an economy that consistently fails at achieving these goals. Alternatively, a merged currency applied across wide geographic and cultural areas carries with it its own set of problems, such as the ability for countries to conduct their own independent monetary policies.

# Bring it Home

## Is a Stronger Dollar Good for the U.S. Economy?

The foreign exchange value of the dollar is a price and whether a higher price is good or bad depends on where you are standing: sellers benefit from higher prices and buyers are harmed. A stronger dollar is good for U.S. imports (and people working for U.S. importers) and U.S. investment abroad. It is also good for U.S. tourists going to other countries, since their dollar goes further. However, a stronger dollar is bad for U.S. exports (and people working in U.S. export industries); it is bad for foreign investment in the United States (leading, for example, to higher U.S. interest rates); and it is bad for foreign tourists (as well as U.S hotels, restaurants, and others in the tourist industry). In short, whether the U.S. dollar is good or bad is a more complex question than you may have thought. The economic answer is "it depends."

# KEY TERMS

**appreciating** when a currency is worth more in terms of other currencies; also called "strengthening"

**arbitrage** the process of buying a good and selling goods across borders to take advantage of international price differences

**depreciating** when a currency is worth less in terms of other currencies; also called "weakening"

**dollarize** a country that is not the United States uses the U.S. dollar as its currency

**floating exchange rate** a country lets the exchange rate market determine its currency's value

**foreign direct investment (FDI)** purchasing more than ten percent of a firm or starting a new enterprise in another country

**foreign exchange market** the market in which people use one currency to buy another currency

**hard peg** an exchange rate policy in which the central bank sets a fixed and unchanging value for the exchange rate

**hedge** using a financial transaction as protection against risk

**international capital flows** flow of financial capital across national boundaries either as portfolio investment or direct investment

**merged currency** when a nation chooses to use another nation's currency

**portfolio investment** an investment in another country that is purely financial and does not involve any management responsibility

**purchasing power parity (PPP)** the exchange rate that equalizes the prices of internationally traded goods across countries

**soft peg** an exchange rate policy in which the government usually allows the market to set the exchange rate, but in some cases, especially if the exchange rate seems to be moving rapidly in one direction, the central bank will intervene

**Tobin taxes** see international capital flows

# KEY CONCEPTS AND SUMMARY

## 16.1 How the Foreign Exchange Market Works

In the foreign exchange market, people and firms exchange one currency to purchase another currency. The demand for dollars comes from those U.S. export firms seeking to convert their earnings in foreign currency back into U.S. dollars; foreign tourists converting their earnings in a foreign currency back into U.S. dollars; and foreign investors seeking to make financial investments in the U.S. economy. On the supply side of the foreign exchange market for the trading of U.S. dollars are foreign firms that have sold imports in the U.S. economy and are seeking to convert their earnings back to their home currency; U.S. tourists abroad; and U.S. investors seeking to make financial investments in foreign economies. When currency A can buy more of currency B, then currency A has strengthened or appreciated relative to B. When currency A can buy less of currency B, then currency A has weakened or depreciated relative to B. If currency A strengthens or appreciates relative to currency B, then currency B must necessarily weaken or depreciate with regard to currency A. A stronger currency benefits those who are buying with that currency and injures those who are selling. A weaker currency injures those, like importers, who are buying with that currency and benefits those who are selling with it, like exporters.

## 16.2 Demand and Supply Shifts in Foreign Exchange Markets

In the extreme short run, ranging from a few minutes to a few weeks, speculators who are trying to invest in currencies that will grow stronger, and to sell currencies that will grow weaker influence exchange rates. Such speculation can create a self-fulfilling prophecy, at least for a time, where an expected appreciation leads to a stronger currency and vice versa. In the relatively short run, differences in rates of return influence exchange rate markets. Countries with relatively high real rates of return (for example, high interest rates) will tend to experience stronger currencies as they attract money from abroad, while countries with relatively low rates of return will tend to experience weaker exchange rates as investors convert to other currencies.

In the medium run of a few months or a few years, inflation rates influence exchange rate markets. Countries with relatively high inflation will tend to experience less demand for their currency than countries with lower inflation, and thus currency depreciation. Over long periods of many years, exchange rates tend to adjust toward the purchasing power parity (PPP) rate, which is the exchange rate such that the prices of internationally tradable goods in different countries, when converted at the PPP exchange rate to a common currency, are similar in all economies.

## 16.3 Macroeconomic Effects of Exchange Rates

A central bank will be concerned about the exchange rate for several reasons. Exchange rates will affect imports and exports, and thus affect aggregate demand in the economy. Fluctuations in exchange rates may cause difficulties for many firms, but especially banks. The exchange rate may accompany unsustainable flows of international financial capital.

## 16.4 Exchange Rate Policies

In a floating exchange rate policy, a government determines its country's exchange rate in the foreign exchange market. In a soft peg exchange rate policy, the foreign exchange market usually determines a country's exchange rate, but the government sometimes intervenes to strengthen or weaken it. In a hard peg exchange rate policy, the government chooses an exchange rate. A central bank can intervene in exchange markets in two ways. It can raise or lower interest rates to make the currency stronger or weaker. It also can directly purchase or sell its currency in foreign exchange markets. All exchange rates policies face tradeoffs. A hard peg exchange rate policy will reduce exchange rate fluctuations, but means that a country must focus its monetary policy on the exchange rate, not on fighting recession or controlling inflation. When a nation merges its currency with another nation, it gives up on nationally oriented monetary policy altogether.

A soft peg exchange rate may create additional volatility as exchange rate markets try to anticipate when and how the government will intervene. A flexible exchange rate policy allows monetary policy to focus on inflation and unemployment, and allows the exchange rate to change with inflation and rates of return, but also raises a risk that exchange rates may sometimes make large and abrupt movements. The spectrum of exchange rate policies includes: (a) a floating exchange rate, (b) a pegged exchange rate, soft or hard, and (c) a merged currency. Monetary policy can focus on a variety of goals: (a) inflation; (b) inflation or unemployment, depending on which is the most dangerous obstacle; and (c) a long-term rule based policy designed to keep the money supply stable and predictable.

## SELF-CHECK QUESTIONS

1. How will a stronger euro affect the following economic agents?
    a. A British exporter to Germany.
    b. A Dutch tourist visiting Chile.
    c. A Greek bank investing in a Canadian government bond.
    d. A French exporter to Germany.

2. Suppose that political unrest in Egypt leads financial markets to anticipate a depreciation in the Egyptian pound. How will that affect the demand for pounds, supply of pounds, and exchange rate for pounds compared to, say, U.S. dollars?

3. Suppose U.S. interest rates decline compared to the rest of the world. What would be the likely impact on the demand for dollars, supply of dollars, and exchange rate for dollars compared to, say, euros?

**4.** Suppose Argentina gets inflation under control and the Argentine inflation rate decreases substantially. What would likely happen to the demand for Argentine pesos, the supply of Argentine pesos, and the peso/U.S. dollar exchange rate?

**5.** This chapter has explained that "one of the most economically destructive effects of exchange rate fluctuations can happen through the banking system," if banks borrow from abroad to lend domestically. Why is this less likely to be a problem for the U.S. banking system?

**6.** A booming economy can attract financial capital inflows, which promote further growth. However, capital can just as easily flow out of the country, leading to economic recession. Is a country whose economy is booming because it decided to stimulate consumer spending more or less likely to experience capital flight than an economy whose boom is caused by economic investment expenditure?

**7.** How would a contractionary monetary policy affect the exchange rate, net exports, aggregate demand, and aggregate supply?

**8.** A central bank can allow its currency to fall indefinitely, but it cannot allow its currency to rise indefinitely. Why not?

**9.** Is a country for which imports and exports comprise a large fraction of the GDP more likely to adopt a flexible exchange rate or a fixed (hard peg) exchange rate?

## REVIEW QUESTIONS

**10.** What is the foreign exchange market?

**11.** Describe some buyers and some sellers in the market for U.S. dollars.

**12.** What is the difference between foreign direct investment and portfolio investment?

**13.** What does it mean to hedge a financial transaction?

**14.** What does it mean to say that a currency appreciates? Depreciates? Becomes stronger? Becomes weaker?

**15.** Does an expectation of a stronger exchange rate in the future affect the exchange rate in the present? If so, how?

**16.** Does a higher rate of return in a nation's economy, all other things being equal, affect the exchange rate of its currency? If so, how?

**17.** Does a higher inflation rate in an economy, other things being equal, affect the exchange rate of its currency? If so, how?

**18.** What is the purchasing power parity exchange rate?

**19.** What are some of the reasons a central bank is likely to care, at least to some extent, about the exchange rate?

**20.** How can an unexpected fall in exchange rates injure the financial health of a nation's banks?

**21.** What is the difference between a floating exchange rate, a soft peg, a hard peg, and dollarization?

**22.** List some advantages and disadvantages of the different exchange rate policies.

## CRITICAL THINKING QUESTIONS

**23.** Why would a nation "dollarize"—that is, adopt another country's currency instead of having its own?

**24.** Can you think of any major disadvantages to dollarization? How would a central bank work in a country that has dollarized?

**25.** If a country's currency is expected to appreciate in value, what would you think will be the impact of expected exchange rates on yields (e.g., the interest rate paid on government bonds) in that country? *Hint*: Think about how expected exchange rate changes and interest rates affect a currency's demand and supply.

**26.** Do you think that a country experiencing hyperinflation is more or less likely to have an exchange rate equal to its purchasing power parity value when compared to a country with a low inflation rate?

**27.** Suppose a country has an overall balance of trade so that exports of goods and services equal imports of goods and services. Does that imply that the country has balanced trade with *each* of its trading partners?

**28.** We learned that changes in exchange rates and the corresponding changes in the balance of trade amplify monetary policy. From the perspective of a nation's central bank, is this a good thing or a bad thing?

**29.** If a developing country needs foreign capital inflows, management expertise, and technology, how can it encourage foreign investors while at the same time protect itself against capital flight and banking system collapse, as happened during the Asian financial crisis?

**30.** Many developing countries, like Mexico, have moderate to high rates of inflation. At the same time, international trade plays an important role in their economies. What type of exchange rate regime would be best for such a country's currency *vis à vis* the U.S. dollar?

**31.** What would make a country decide to change from a common currency, like the euro, back to its own currency?

## PROBLEMS

**32.** A British pound cost $2.00 in U.S. dollars in 2008, but $1.27 in U.S. dollars in 2017. Was the pound weaker or stronger against the dollar? Did the dollar appreciate or depreciate versus the pound?

# 17 | Government Budgets and Fiscal Policy

**Figure 17.1 Shut Downs and Parks**   Yellowstone National Park is one of the many national parks forced to close down during the government shut down in October 2013. (Credit: modification of work by "daveynin"/flickr Creative Commons)

## Bring it Home

### No Yellowstone Park?

You had trekked all the way to see Yellowstone National Park in the beautiful month of October 2013, only to find it… closed. Closed! Why?

For two weeks in October 2013, the U.S. federal government shut down. Many federal services, like the national parks, closed and 800,000 federal employees were furloughed. Tourists were shocked and so was the rest of the world: Congress and the President could not agree on a budget. Inside the Capitol, Republicans and Democrats argued about spending priorities and whether to increase the national debt limit. Each year's budget, which is over $3 trillion of spending, must be approved by Congress and signed by the President. Two thirds of the budget are entitlements and other mandatory spending which occur without congressional or presidential action once the programs are established. Tied to the budget debate was the issue of increasing the debt ceiling—how high the U.S. government's national debt can be. The House of Representatives refused to sign on to the bills to fund the government unless they included provisions to stop or change the Affordable Health Care Act (more colloquially known as Obamacare). As the days progressed, the United States came very close to defaulting on its debt.

Why does the federal budget create such intense debates? What would happen if the United States actually defaulted on its debt? In this chapter, we will examine the federal budget, taxation, and fiscal policy. We will also look at the annual federal budget deficits and the national debt.

# Introduction to Government Budgets and Fiscal Policy

In this chapter, you will learn about:

- Government Spending

- Taxation

- Federal Deficits and the National Debt

- Using Fiscal Policy to Fight Recessions, Unemployment, and Inflation

- Automatic Stabilizers

- Practical Problems with Discretionary Fiscal Policy

- The Question of a Balanced Budget

All levels of government—federal, state, and local—have budgets that show how much revenue the government expects to receive in taxes and other income and how the government plans to spend it. Budgets, however, can shift dramatically within a few years, as policy decisions and unexpected events disrupt earlier tax and spending plans.

In this chapter, we revisit fiscal policy, which we first covered in **Welcome to Economics!** Fiscal policy is one of two policy tools for fine tuning the economy (the other is monetary policy). While policymakers at the Federal Reserve make monetary policy, Congress and the President make fiscal policy.

The discussion of fiscal policy focuses on how federal government taxing and spending affects aggregate demand. All government spending and taxes affect the economy, but fiscal policy focuses strictly on federal government policies. We begin with an overview of U.S. government spending and taxes. We then discuss fiscal policy from a short-run perspective; that is, how government uses tax and spending policies to address recession, unemployment, and inflation; how periods of recession and growth affect government budgets; and the merits of balanced budget proposals.

# 17.1 | Government Spending

By the end of this section, you will be able to:
- Identify U.S. budget deficit and surplus trends over the past five decades
- Explain the differences between the U.S. federal budget, and state and local budgets

Government spending covers a range of services that the federal, state, and local governments provide. When the federal government spends more money than it receives in taxes in a given year, it runs a **budget deficit**. Conversely, when the government receives more money in taxes than it spends in a year, it runs a **budget surplus**. If government spending and taxes are equal, it has a **balanced budget**. For example, in 2009, the U.S. government experienced its largest budget deficit ever, as the federal government spent $1.4 trillion more than it collected in taxes. This deficit was about 10% of the size of the U.S. GDP in 2009, making it by far the largest budget deficit relative to GDP since the mammoth borrowing the government used to finance World War II.

This section presents an overview of government spending in the United States.

## Total U.S. Government Spending

Federal spending in nominal dollars (that is, dollars not adjusted for inflation) has grown by a multiple of more than 38 over the last four decades, from $93.4 billion in 1960 to $3.9 trillion in 2014. Comparing spending over time in nominal dollars is misleading because it does not take into account inflation or growth in population and the real economy. A more useful method of comparison is to examine government spending as a percent of GDP over time.

The top line in **Figure 17.2** shows the federal spending level since 1960, expressed as a share of GDP. Despite a widespread sense among many Americans that the federal government has been growing steadily larger, the graph shows that federal spending has hovered in a range from 18% to 22% of GDP most of the time since 1960. The other lines in **Figure 17.2** show the major federal spending categories: national defense, Social Security, health programs, and interest payments. From the graph, we see that national defense spending as a share of GDP has generally declined since the 1960s, although there were some upward bumps in the 1980s buildup under President Ronald Reagan and in the aftermath of the terrorist attacks on September 11, 2001. In contrast, Social Security and healthcare have grown steadily as a percent of GDP. Healthcare expenditures include both payments for senior citizens (Medicare), and payments for low-income Americans (Medicaid). State governments also partially fund Medicaid. Interest payments are the final main category of government spending in Figure 30.2.

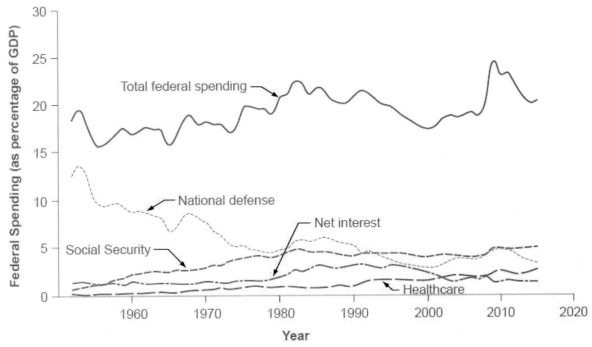

**Figure 17.2 Federal Spending, 1960–2014** Since 1960, total federal spending has ranged from about 18% to 22% of GDP, although it climbed above that level in 2009, but quickly dropped back down to that level by 2013. The share that the government has spent on national defense has generally declined, while the share it has spent on Social Security and on healthcare expenses (mainly Medicare and Medicaid) has increased. (Source: *Economic Report of the President,* Tables B-2 and B-22, http://www.gpo.gov/fdsys/pkg/ERP-2014/content-detail.html)

Each year, the government borrows funds from U.S. citizens and foreigners to cover its budget deficits. It does this by selling securities (Treasury bonds, notes, and bills)—in essence borrowing from the public and promising to repay with interest in the future. From 1961 to 1997, the U.S. government has run budget deficits, and thus borrowed funds, in almost every year. It had budget surpluses from 1998 to 2001, and then returned to deficits.

The interest payments on past federal government borrowing were typically 1–2% of GDP in the 1960s and 1970s but then climbed above 3% of GDP in the 1980s and stayed there until the late 1990s. The government was able to repay some of its past borrowing by running surpluses from 1998 to 2001 and, with help from low interest rates, the interest payments on past federal government borrowing had fallen back to 1.4% of GDP by 2012.

We investigate the government borrowing and debt patterns in more detail later in this chapter, but first we need to clarify the difference between the deficit and the debt. *The deficit is not the debt.* The difference between the deficit and the debt lies in the time frame. The government deficit (or surplus) refers to what happens with the federal government budget each year. The government debt is accumulated over time. It is the sum of all past deficits and surpluses. If you borrow $10,000 per year for each of the four years of college, you might say that your annual deficit was $10,000, but your accumulated debt over the four years is $40,000.

These four categories—national defense, Social Security, healthcare, and interest payments—account for roughly 73% of all federal spending, as **Figure 17.3** shows. The remaining 27% wedge of the pie chart covers all other categories of federal government spending: international affairs; science and technology; natural resources and the environment; transportation; housing; education; income support for the poor; community and regional development; law enforcement and the judicial system; and the administrative costs of running the government.

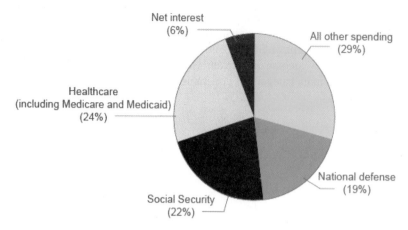

**Figure 17.3 Slices of Federal Spending, 2014** About 73% of government spending goes to four major areas: national defense, Social Security, healthcare, and interest payments on past borrowing. This leaves about 29% of federal spending for all other functions of the U.S. government. (Source: https://www.whitehouse.gov/omb/budget/Historicals/)

## State and Local Government Spending

Although federal government spending often gets most of the media attention, state and local government spending is also substantial—at about $3.1 trillion in 2014. **Figure 17.4** shows that state and local government spending has increased during the last four decades from around 8% to around 14% today. The single biggest item is education, which accounts for about one-third of the total. The rest covers programs like highways, libraries, hospitals and healthcare, parks, and police and fire protection. Unlike the federal government, all states (except Vermont) have balanced budget laws, which means any gaps between revenues and spending must be closed by higher taxes, lower spending, drawing down their previous savings, or some combination of all of these.

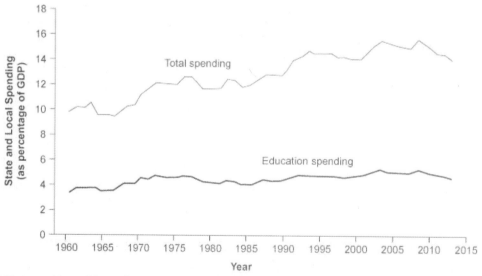

**Figure 17.4 State and Local Spending, 1960–2013** Spending by state and local government increased from about 10% of GDP in the early 1960s to 14–16% by the mid-1970s. It has remained at roughly that level since. The single biggest spending item is education, including both K–12 spending and support for public colleges and universities, which has been about 4–5% of GDP in recent decades. Source: (Source: Bureau of Economic Analysis.)

U.S. presidential candidates often run for office pledging to improve the public schools or to get tough on crime. However, in the U.S. government system, these tasks are primarily state and local government responsibilities. In fiscal year 2014 state and local governments spent about $840 billion per year on education (including K–12 and college and university education), compared to only $100 billion by the federal government, according to usgovernmentspending.com. In other words, about 90 cents of every dollar spent on education happens at the state and local level. A politician who really wants hands-on responsibility for reforming education or reducing crime might do better to run for mayor of a large city or for state governor rather than for president of the United States.

# 17.2 | Taxation

By the end of this section, you will be able to:
- Differentiate among a regressive tax, a proportional tax, and a progressive tax
- Identify major revenue sources for the U.S. federal budget

There are two main categories of taxes: those that the federal government collects and those that the state and local governments collect. What percentage the government collects and for what it uses that revenue varies greatly. The following sections will briefly explain the taxation system in the United States.

## Federal Taxes

Just as many Americans erroneously think that federal spending has grown considerably, many also believe that taxes have increased substantially. The top line of **Figure 17.5** shows total federal taxes as a share of GDP since 1960. Although the line rises and falls, it typically remains within the range of 17% to 20% of GDP, except for 2009, when taxes fell substantially below this level, due to recession.

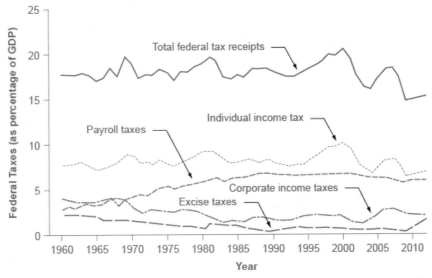

**Figure 17.5 Federal Taxes, 1960–2014** Federal tax revenues have been about 17–20% of GDP during most periods in recent decades. The primary sources of federal taxes are individual income taxes and the payroll taxes that finance Social Security and Medicare. Corporate income taxes and social insurance taxes provide smaller shares of revenue. (Source: *Economic Report of the President, 2015.* Table B-21, https://www.whitehouse.gov/administration/eop/cea/economic-report-of-the-President/2015)

**Figure 17.5** also shows the taxation patterns for the main categories that the federal government taxes: individual income taxes, corporate income taxes, and social insurance and retirement receipts. When most people think of federal government taxes, the first tax that comes to mind is the **individual income tax** that is due every year on April 15 (or the first business day after). The personal income tax is the largest single source of federal government revenue, but it still represents less than half of federal tax revenue.

The second largest source of federal revenue is the **payroll tax** (captured in social insurance and retirement receipts), which provides funds for Social Security and Medicare. Payroll taxes have increased steadily over time. Together, the personal income tax and the payroll tax accounted for about 80% of federal tax revenues in 2014. Although personal income tax revenues account for more total revenue than the payroll tax, nearly three-quarters of households pay more in payroll taxes than in income taxes.

The income tax is a **progressive tax**, which means that the tax rates increase as a household's income increases. Taxes also vary with marital status, family size, and other factors. The **marginal tax rates** (the tax due on all yearly income) for a single taxpayer range from 10% to 35%, depending on income, as the following Clear It Up feature explains.

## How does the marginal rate work?

Suppose that a single taxpayer's income is $35,000 per year. Also suppose that income from $0 to $9,075 is taxed at 10%, income from $9,075 to $36,900 is taxed at 15%, and, finally, income from $36,900 and beyond is taxed at 25%. Since this person earns $35,000, their marginal tax rate is 15%.

The key fact here is that the federal income tax is designed so that tax rates increase as income increases, up to a certain level. The payroll taxes that support Social Security and Medicare are designed in a different way. First, the payroll taxes for Social Security are imposed at a rate of 12.4% up to a certain wage limit, set at $118,500 in 2015. Medicare, on the other hand, pays for elderly healthcare, and is fixed at 2.9%, with no upper ceiling.

In both cases, the employer and the employee split the payroll taxes. An employee only sees 6.2% deducted from his or her paycheck for Social Security, and 1.45% from Medicare. However, as economists are quick to point out, the employer's half of the taxes are probably passed along to the employees in the form of lower wages, so in reality, the worker pays all of the payroll taxes.

We also call the Medicare payroll tax a **proportional tax**; that is, a flat percentage of all wages earned. The Social Security payroll tax is proportional up to the wage limit, but above that level it becomes a **regressive tax**, meaning that people with higher incomes pay a smaller share of their income in tax.

The third-largest source of federal tax revenue, as **Figure 17.5** shows is the **corporate income tax**. The common name for corporate income is "profits." Over time, corporate income tax receipts have declined as a share of GDP, from about 4% in the 1960s to an average of 1% to 2% of GDP in the first decade of the 2000s.

The federal government has a few other, smaller sources of revenue. It imposes an **excise tax**—that is, a tax on a particular good—on gasoline, tobacco, and alcohol. As a share of GDP, the amount the government collects from these taxes has stayed nearly constant over time, from about 2% of GDP in the 1960s to roughly 3% by 2014, according to the nonpartisan Congressional Budget Office. The government also imposes an **estate and gift tax** on people who pass large amounts of assets to the next generation—either after death or during life in the form of gifts. These estate and gift taxes collected about 0.2% of GDP in the first decade of the 2000s. By a quirk of legislation, the government repealed the estate and gift tax in 2010, but reinstated it in 2011. Other federal taxes, which are also relatively small in magnitude, include tariffs the government collects on imported goods and charges for inspections of goods entering the country.

## State and Local Taxes

At the state and local level, taxes have been rising as a share of GDP over the last few decades to match the gradual rise in spending, as **Figure 17.6** illustrates. The main revenue sources for state and local governments are sales taxes, property taxes, and revenue passed along from the federal government, but many state and local governments also levy personal and corporate income taxes, as well as impose a wide variety of fees and charges. The specific sources of tax revenue vary widely across state and local governments. Some states rely more on property taxes, some on sales taxes, some on income taxes, and some more on revenues from the federal government.

**Figure 17.6 State and Local Tax Revenue as a Share of GDP, 1960–2014** State and local tax revenues have increased to match the rise in state and local spending. (Source: *Economic Report of the President, 2015.* Table B-21, https://www.whitehouse.gov/administration/eop/cea/economic-report-of-the-President/2015)

# 17.3 | Federal Deficits and the National Debt

By the end of this section, you will be able to:
- Explain the U.S. federal budget in terms of annual debt and accumulated debt
- Understand how economic growth or decline can influence a budget surplus or budget deficit

Having discussed the revenue (taxes) and expense (spending) side of the budget, we now turn to the annual budget deficit or surplus, which is the difference between the tax revenue collected and spending over a fiscal year, which starts October 1 and ends September 30 of the next year.

**Figure 17.7** shows the pattern of annual federal budget deficits and surpluses, back to 1930, as a share of GDP. When the line is above the horizontal axis, the budget is in surplus. When the line is below the horizontal axis, a budget deficit occurred. Clearly, the biggest deficits as a share of GDP during this time were incurred to finance World War II. Deficits were also large during the 1930s, the 1980s, the early 1990s, and most recently during the 2008-2009 recession.

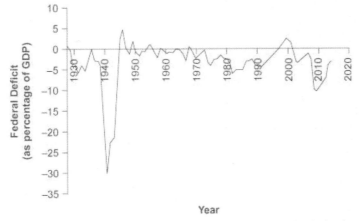

**Figure 17.7 Pattern of Federal Budget Deficits and Surpluses, 1929–2014** The federal government has run budget deficits for decades. The budget was briefly in surplus in the late 1990s, before heading into deficit again in the first decade of the 2000s—and especially deep deficits in the 2008-2009 recession. (Source: Federal Reserve Bank of St. Louis (FRED). http://research.stlouisfed.org/fred2/series/FYFSGDA188S)

## Debt/GDP Ratio

Another useful way to view the budget deficit is through the prism of accumulated debt rather than annual deficits. The **national debt** refers to the total amount that the government has borrowed over time. In contrast, the budget deficit refers to how much the government has borrowed in one particular year. **Figure 17.8** shows the ratio of debt/GDP since 1940. Until the 1970s, the debt/GDP ratio revealed a fairly clear pattern of federal borrowing. The government ran up large deficits and raised the debt/GDP ratio in World War II, but from the 1950s to the 1970s the government ran either surpluses or relatively small deficits, and so the debt/GDP ratio drifted down. Large deficits in the 1980s and early 1990s caused the ratio to rise sharply. When budget surpluses arrived from 1998 to 2001, the debt/GDP ratio declined substantially. The budget deficits starting in 2002 then tugged the debt/GDP ratio higher—with a big jump when the recession took hold in 2008–2009.

**Figure 17.8 Federal Debt as a Percentage of GDP, 1942–2014** Federal debt is the sum of annual budget deficits and surpluses. Annual deficits do not always mean that the debt/GDP ratio is rising. During the 1960s and 1970s, the government often ran small deficits, but since the debt was growing more slowly than the economy, the debt/GDP ratio was declining over this time. In the 2008–2009 recession, the debt/GDP ratio rose sharply. (Source: *Economic Report of the President, Table B-20,* http://www.gpo.gov/fdsys/pkg/ERP-2015/content-detail.html)

The next Clear it Up feature discusses how the government handles the national debt.

## Clear It Up

### What is the national debt?

One year's federal budget deficit causes the federal government to sell Treasury bonds to make up the difference between spending programs and tax revenues. The dollar value of all the outstanding Treasury bonds on which the federal government owes money is equal to the national debt.

## The Path from Deficits to Surpluses to Deficits

Why did the budget deficits suddenly turn to surpluses from 1998 to 2001 and why did the surpluses return to deficits in 2002? Why did the deficit become so large after 2007? **Figure 17.9** suggests some answers. The graph combines the earlier information on total federal spending and taxes in a single graph, but focuses on the federal budget since 1990.

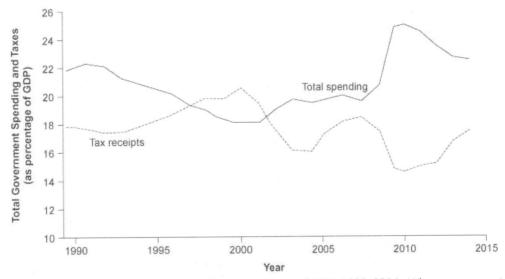

**Figure 17.9 Total Government Spending and Taxes as a Share of GDP, 1990–2014**   When government spending exceeds taxes, the gap is the budget deficit. When taxes exceed spending, the gap is a budget surplus. The recessionary period starting in late 2007 saw higher spending and lower taxes, combining to create a large deficit in 2009. (Source: *Economic Report of the President, Tables B-21 and B-1,*"http://www.gpo.gov/fdsys/pkg/ERP-2015/content-detail.html)

Government spending as a share of GDP declined steadily through the 1990s. The biggest single reason was that defense spending declined from 5.2% of GDP in 1990 to 3.0% in 2000, but interest payments by the federal government also fell by about 1.0% of GDP. However, federal tax collections increased substantially in the later 1990s, jumping from 18.1% of GDP in 1994 to 20.8% in 2000. Powerful economic growth in the late 1990s fueled the boom in taxes. Personal income taxes rise as income goes up; payroll taxes rise as jobs and payrolls go up; corporate income taxes rise as profits go up. At the same time, government spending on transfer payments such as unemployment benefits, foods stamps, and welfare declined with more people working.

This sharp increase in tax revenues and decrease in expenditures on transfer payments was largely unexpected even by experienced budget analysts, and so budget surpluses came as a surprise. However, in the early 2000s, many of these factors started running in reverse. Tax revenues sagged, due largely to the recession that started in March 2001, which reduced revenues. Congress enacted a series of tax cuts and President George W. Bush signed them into law, starting in 2001. In addition, government spending swelled due to increases in defense, healthcare, education, Social Security, and support programs for those who were hurt by the recession and the slow growth that followed. Deficits returned. When the severe recession hit in late 2007, spending climbed and tax collections fell to historically unusual levels, resulting in enormous deficits.

Longer-term U.S. budget forecasts, a decade or more into the future, predict enormous deficits. The higher deficits during the 2008-2009 recession have repercussions, and the demographics will be challenging. The primary reason is the "baby boom"—the exceptionally high birthrates that began in 1946, right after World War II, and lasted for about two decades. Starting in 2010, the front edge of the baby boom generation began to reach age 65, and in the next two decades, the proportion of Americans over the age of 65 will increase substantially. The current level of the payroll taxes that support Social Security and Medicare will fall well short of the projected expenses of these programs, as the following Clear It Up feature shows; thus, the forecast is for large budget deficits. A decision to collect more revenue to support these programs or to decrease benefit levels would alter this long-term forecast.

## What is the long-term budget outlook for Social Security and Medicare?

In 1946, just one American in 13 was over age 65. By 2000, it was one in eight. By 2030, one American in five will be over age 65. Two enormous U.S. federal programs focus on the elderly—Social Security and Medicare. The growing numbers of elderly Americans will increase spending on these programs, as well as on Medicaid. The current payroll tax levied on workers, which supports all of Social Security and the hospitalization insurance part of Medicare, will not be enough to cover the expected costs, so what are the options?

Long-term projections from the Congressional Budget Office in 2009 are that Medicare and Social Security spending combined will rise from 8.3% of GDP in 2009 to about 13% by 2035 and about 20% in 2080. If this rise in spending occurs, without any corresponding rise in tax collections, then some mix of changes must occur: (1) taxes will need to increase dramatically; (2) other spending will need to be cut dramatically; (3) the retirement age and/or age receiving Medicare benefits will need to increase, or (4) the federal government will need to run extremely large budget deficits.

Some proposals suggest removing the cap on wages subject to the payroll tax, so that those with very high incomes would have to pay the tax on the entire amount of their wages. Other proposals suggest moving Social Security and Medicare from systems in which workers pay for retirees toward programs that set up accounts where workers save funds over their lifetimes and then draw out after retirement to pay for healthcare.

The United States is not alone in this problem. Providing the promised level of retirement and health benefits to a growing proportion of elderly with a falling proportion of workers is an even more severe problem in many European nations and in Japan. How to pay promised levels of benefits to the elderly will be a difficult public policy decision.

In the next module we shift to the use of fiscal policy to counteract business cycle fluctuations. In addition, we will explore proposals requiring a balanced budget—that is, for government spending and taxes to be equal each year. **The Impacts of Government Borrowing** will also cover how fiscal policy and government borrowing will affect national saving—and thus affect economic growth and trade imbalances.

# 17.4 | Using Fiscal Policy to Fight Recession, Unemployment, and Inflation

By the end of this section, you will be able to:

- Explain how expansionary fiscal policy can shift aggregate demand and influence the economy
- Explain how contractionary fiscal policy can shift aggregate demand and influence the economy

Fiscal policy is the use of government spending and tax policy to influence the path of the economy over time. Graphically, we see that fiscal policy, whether through changes in spending or taxes, shifts the aggregate demand outward in the case of **expansionary fiscal policy** and inward in the case of **contractionary fiscal policy**. We know from the chapter on economic growth that over time the quantity and quality of our resources grow as the population and thus the labor force get larger, as businesses invest in new capital, and as technology improves. The result of this is regular shifts to the right of the aggregate supply curves, as **Figure 17.10** illustrates.

The original equilibrium occurs at $E_0$, the intersection of aggregate demand curve $AD_0$ and aggregate supply curve $SRAS_0$, at an output level of 200 and a price level of 90. One year later, aggregate supply has shifted to the right to $SRAS_1$ in the process of long-term economic growth, and aggregate demand has also shifted to the right to $AD_1$, keeping the economy operating at the new level of potential GDP. The new equilibrium ($E_1$) is an output level of

206 and a price level of 92. One more year later, aggregate supply has again shifted to the right, now to $SRAS_2$, and aggregate demand shifts right as well to $AD_2$. Now the equilibrium is $E_2$, with an output level of 212 and a price level of 94. In short, the figure shows an economy that is growing steadily year to year, producing at its potential GDP each year, with only small inflationary increases in the price level.

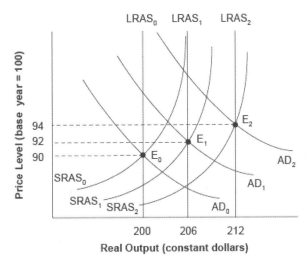

**Figure 17.10 A Healthy, Growing Economy** In this well-functioning economy, each year aggregate supply and aggregate demand shift to the right so that the economy proceeds from equilibrium $E_0$ to $E_1$ to $E_2$. Each year, the economy produces at potential GDP with only a small inflationary increase in the price level. However, if aggregate demand does not smoothly shift to the right and match increases in aggregate supply, growth with deflation can develop.

Aggregate demand and aggregate supply do not always move neatly together. Think about what causes shifts in aggregate demand over time. As aggregate supply increases, incomes tend to go up. This tends to increase consumer and investment spending, shifting the aggregate demand curve to the right, but in any given period it may not shift the same amount as aggregate supply. What happens to government spending and taxes? Government spends to pay for the ordinary business of government- items such as national defense, social security, and healthcare, as **Figure 17.10** shows. Tax revenues, in part, pay for these expenditures. The result may be an increase in aggregate demand more than or less than the increase in aggregate supply. Aggregate demand may fail to increase along with aggregate supply, or aggregate demand may even shift left, for a number of possible reasons: households become hesitant about consuming; firms decide against investing as much; or perhaps the demand from other countries for exports diminishes.

For example, investment by private firms in physical capital in the U.S. economy boomed during the late 1990s, rising from 14.1% of GDP in 1993 to 17.2% in 2000, before falling back to 15.2% by 2002. Conversely, if shifts in aggregate demand run ahead of increases in aggregate supply, inflationary increases in the price level will result. Business cycles of recession and recovery are the consequence of shifts in aggregate supply and aggregate demand. As these occur, the government may choose to use fiscal policy to address the difference.

**Monetary Policy and Bank Regulation** shows us that a central bank can use its powers over the banking system to engage in countercyclical—or "against the business cycle"—actions. If recession threatens, the central bank uses an expansionary monetary policy to increase the money supply, increase the quantity of loans, reduce interest rates, and shift aggregate demand to the right. If inflation threatens, the central bank uses contractionary monetary policy to reduce the money supply, reduce the quantity of loans, raise interest rates, and shift aggregate demand to the left. Fiscal policy is another macroeconomic policy tool for adjusting aggregate demand by using either government spending or taxation policy.

## Expansionary Fiscal Policy

Expansionary fiscal policy increases the level of aggregate demand, through either increases in government spending or reductions in tax rates. Expansionary policy can do this by (1) increasing consumption by raising disposable income through cuts in personal income taxes or payroll taxes; (2) increasing investment spending by raising after-tax profits through cuts in business taxes; and (3) increasing government purchases through increased federal government spending on final goods and services and raising federal grants to state and local governments to increase their expenditures on final goods and services. Contractionary fiscal policy does the reverse: it decreases the level of aggregate demand by decreasing consumption, decreasing investment, and decreasing government spending, either through cuts in government spending or increases in taxes. The aggregate demand/aggregate supply model is useful in judging whether expansionary or contractionary fiscal policy is appropriate.

Consider first the situation in **Figure 17.11**, which is similar to the U.S. economy during the 2008-2009 recession. The intersection of aggregate demand ($AD_0$) and aggregate supply ($SRAS_0$) is occurring below the level of potential GDP as the LRAS curve indicates. At the equilibrium ($E_0$), a recession occurs and unemployment rises. In this case, expansionary fiscal policy using tax cuts or increases in government spending can shift aggregate demand to $AD_1$, closer to the full-employment level of output. In addition, the price level would rise back to the level $P_1$ associated with potential GDP.

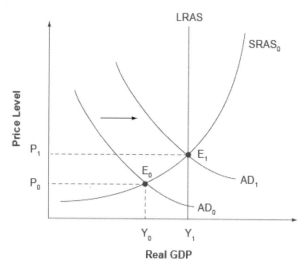

**Figure 17.11 Expansionary Fiscal Policy**   The original equilibrium ($E_0$) represents a recession, occurring at a quantity of output ($Y_0$) below potential GDP. However, a shift of aggregate demand from $AD_0$ to $AD_1$, enacted through an expansionary fiscal policy, can move the economy to a new equilibrium output of $E_1$ at the level of potential GDP which the LRAS curve shows. Since the economy was originally producing below potential GDP, any inflationary increase in the price level from $P_0$ to $P_1$ that results should be relatively small.

Should the government use tax cuts or spending increases, or a mix of the two, to carry out expansionary fiscal policy? During the 2008-2009 Great Recession (which started, actually, in late 2007), the U.S. economy suffered a 3.1% cumulative loss of GDP. That may not sound like much, but it's more than one year's average growth rate of GDP. Over that time frame, the unemployment rate doubled from 5% to 10%. The consensus view is that this was possibly the worst economic downturn in U.S. history since the 1930's Great Depression. The choice between whether to use tax or spending tools often has a political tinge. As a general statement, conservatives and Republicans prefer to see expansionary fiscal policy carried out by tax cuts, while liberals and Democrats prefer that the government implement expansionary fiscal policy through spending increases. In a bipartisan effort to address the extreme situation, the Obama administration and Congress passed an $830 billion expansionary policy in early 2009 involving both tax cuts and increases in government spending. At the same time, however, the federal stimulus was partially offset when state and local governments, whose budgets were hard hit by the recession, began cutting their spending.

The conflict over which policy tool to use can be frustrating to those who want to categorize economics as "liberal" or "conservative," or who want to use economic models to argue against their political opponents. However, advocates of smaller government, who seek to reduce taxes and government spending can use the AD AS model, as well as advocates of bigger government, who seek to raise taxes and government spending. Economic studies of specific taxing and spending programs can help inform decisions about whether the government should change taxes or spending, and in what ways. Ultimately, decisions about whether to use tax or spending mechanisms to implement macroeconomic policy is a political decision rather than a purely economic one.

## Contractionary Fiscal Policy

Fiscal policy can also contribute to pushing aggregate demand beyond potential GDP in a way that leads to inflation.

As **Figure 17.12** shows, a very large budget deficit pushes up aggregate demand, so that the intersection of aggregate demand ($AD_0$) and aggregate supply ($SRAS_0$) occurs at equilibrium $E_0$, which is an output level above potential GDP. Economists sometimes call this an "overheating economy" where demand is so high that there is upward pressure on wages and prices, causing inflation. In this situation, contractionary fiscal policy involving federal spending cuts or tax increases can help to reduce the upward pressure on the price level by shifting aggregate demand to the left, to $AD_1$, and causing the new equilibrium $E_1$ to be at potential GDP, where aggregate demand intersects the LRAS curve.

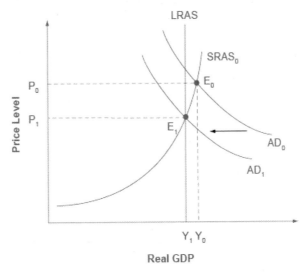

**Figure 17.12 A Contractionary Fiscal Policy** The economy starts at the equilibrium quantity of output $Y_0$, which is above potential GDP. The extremely high level of aggregate demand will generate inflationary increases in the price level. A contractionary fiscal policy can shift aggregate demand down from $AD_0$ to $AD_1$, leading to a new equilibrium output $E_1$, which occurs at potential GDP, where AD1 intersects the LRAS curve.

Again, the AD–AS model does not dictate how the government should carry out this contractionary fiscal policy. Some may prefer spending cuts; others may prefer tax increases; still others may say that it depends on the specific situation. The model only argues that, in this situation, the government needs to reduce aggregate demand.

# 17.5 | Automatic Stabilizers

By the end of this section, you will be able to:
- Describe how the federal government can use discretionary fiscal policy to stabilize the economy
- Identify examples of automatic stabilizers
- Understand how a government can use standardized employment budget to identify automatic stabilizers

The millions of unemployed in 2008–2009 could collect unemployment insurance benefits to replace some of their salaries. Federal fiscal policies include **discretionary fiscal policy**, when the government passes a new law that explicitly changes tax or spending levels. The 2009 stimulus package is an example. Changes in tax and spending levels can also occur automatically, due to **automatic stabilizers**, such as unemployment insurance and food stamps, which are programs that are already laws that stimulate aggregate demand in a recession and hold down aggregate demand in a potentially inflationary boom.

## Counterbalancing Recession and Boom

Consider first the situation where aggregate demand has risen sharply, causing the equilibrium to occur at a level of output above potential GDP. This situation will increase inflationary pressure in the economy. The policy prescription in this setting would be a dose of contractionary fiscal policy, implemented through some combination of higher taxes and lower spending. To some extent, *both* changes happen automatically. On the tax side, a rise in aggregate demand means that workers and firms throughout the economy earn more. Because taxes are based on personal income and corporate profits, a rise in aggregate demand automatically increases tax payments. On the spending side, stronger aggregate demand typically means lower unemployment and fewer layoffs, and so there is less need for government spending on unemployment benefits, welfare, Medicaid, and other programs in the social safety net.

The process works in reverse, too. If aggregate demand were to fall sharply so that a recession occurs, then the prescription would be for expansionary fiscal policy—some mix of tax cuts and spending increases. The lower level of aggregate demand and higher unemployment will tend to pull down personal incomes and corporate profits, an effect that will reduce the amount of taxes owed automatically. Higher unemployment and a weaker economy should lead to increased government spending on unemployment benefits, welfare, and other similar domestic programs. In 2009, the stimulus package included an extension in the time allowed to collect unemployment insurance. In addition, the automatic stabilizers react to a weakening of aggregate demand with expansionary fiscal policy and react to a strengthening of aggregate demand with contractionary fiscal policy, just as the AD/AS analysis suggests.

A combination of automatic stabilizers and discretionary fiscal policy produced the very large budget deficit in 2009. The Great Recession, starting in late 2007, meant less tax-generating economic activity, which triggered the automatic stabilizers that reduce taxes. Most economists, even those who are concerned about a possible pattern of persistently large budget deficits, are much less concerned or even quite supportive of larger budget deficits in the short run of a few years during and immediately after a severe recession.

A glance back at economic history provides a second illustration of the power of automatic stabilizers. Remember that the length of economic upswings between recessions has become longer in the U.S. economy in recent decades (as we discussed in **Unemployment**). The three longest economic booms of the twentieth century happened in the 1960s, the 1980s, and the 1991–2001 time period. One reason why the economy has tipped into recession less frequently in recent decades is that the size of government spending and taxes has increased in the second half of the twentieth century. Thus, the automatic stabilizing effects from spending and taxes are now larger than they were in the first half of the twentieth century. Around 1900, for example, federal spending was only about 2% of GDP. In 1929, just before the Great Depression hit, government spending was still just 4% of GDP. In those earlier times, the smaller size of government made automatic stabilizers far less powerful than in the last few decades, when government spending often hovers at 20% of GDP or more.

## The Standardized Employment Deficit or Surplus

Each year, the nonpartisan Congressional Budget Office (CBO) calculates the **standardized employment budget**—that is, what the budget deficit or surplus would be if the economy were producing at potential GDP, where people who look for work were finding jobs in a reasonable period of time and businesses were making normal profits, with the result that both workers and businesses would be earning more and paying more taxes. In effect, the standardized employment deficit eliminates the impact of the automatic stabilizers. **Figure 17.13** compares the actual budget deficits of recent decades with the CBO's standardized deficit.

# Link It Up

Visit this website (http://openstaxcollege.org/l/CBO) to learn more from the Congressional Budget Office.

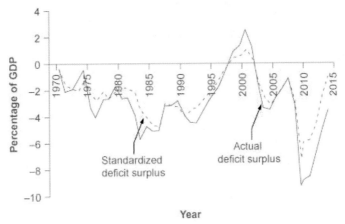

**Figure 17.13 Comparison of Actual Budget Deficits with the Standardized Employment Deficit**   When the economy is in recession, the standardized employment budget deficit is less than the actual budget deficit because the economy is below potential GDP, and the automatic stabilizers are reducing taxes and increasing spending. When the economy is performing extremely well, the standardized employment deficit (or surplus) is higher than the actual budget deficit (or surplus) because the economy is producing about potential GDP, so the automatic stabilizers are increasing taxes and reducing the need for government spending. (Sources: *Actual and Cyclically Adjusted Budget Surpluses/Deficits,* http://www.cbo.gov/publication/43977; and *Economic Report of the President, Table B-1,* http://www.gpo.gov/fdsys/pkg/ERP-2013/content-detail.html)

Notice that in recession years, like the early 1990s, 2001, or 2009, the standardized employment deficit is smaller than the actual deficit. During recessions, the automatic stabilizers tend to increase the budget deficit, so if the economy was instead at full employment, the deficit would be reduced. However, in the late 1990s the standardized employment budget surplus was lower than the actual budget surplus. The gap between the standardized budget deficit or surplus and the actual budget deficit or surplus shows the impact of the automatic stabilizers. More generally, the standardized budget figures allow you to see what the budget deficit would look like with the economy held constant—at its potential GDP level of output.

Automatic stabilizers occur quickly. Lower wages means that a lower amount of taxes is withheld from paychecks right away. Higher unemployment or poverty means that government spending in those areas rises as quickly as people apply for benefits. However, while the automatic stabilizers offset part of the shifts in aggregate demand, they do not offset all or even most of it. Historically, automatic stabilizers on the tax and spending side offset about 10% of any initial movement in the level of output. This offset may not seem enormous, but it is still useful. Automatic stabilizers, like shock absorbers in a car, can be useful if they reduce the impact of the worst bumps, even if they do not eliminate the bumps altogether.

# 17.6 | Practical Problems with Discretionary Fiscal Policy

By the end of this section, you will be able to:
- Understand how fiscal policy and monetary policy are interconnected
- Explain the three lag times that often occur when solving economic problems
- Identify the legal and political challenges of responding to an economic problem

In the early 1960s, many leading economists believed that the problem of the business cycle, and the swings between cyclical unemployment and inflation, were a thing of the past. On the cover of its December 31, 1965, issue, *Time* magazine, then the premier news magazine in the United States, ran a picture of John Maynard Keynes, and the story inside identified Keynesian theories as "the prime influence on the world's economies." The article reported that policymakers have "used Keynesian principles not only to avoid the violent [business] cycles of prewar days but to produce phenomenal economic growth and to achieve remarkably stable prices."

This happy consensus, however, did not last. The U.S. economy suffered one recession from December 1969 to November 1970, a deeper recession from November 1973 to March 1975, and then double-dip recessions from

January to June 1980 and from July 1981 to November 1982. At various times, inflation and unemployment both soared. Clearly, the problems of macroeconomic policy had not been completely solved. As economists began to consider what had gone wrong, they identified a number of issues that make discretionary fiscal policy more difficult than it had seemed in the rosy optimism of the mid-1960s.

## Fiscal Policy and Interest Rates

Because fiscal policy affects the quantity that the government borrows in financial capital markets, it not only affects aggregate demand—it can also affect interest rates. In **Figure 17.14**, the original equilibrium ($E_0$) in the financial capital market occurs at a quantity of $800 billion and an interest rate of 6%. However, an increase in government budget deficits shifts the demand for financial capital from $D_0$ to $D_1$. The new equilibrium ($E_1$) occurs at a quantity of $900 billion and an interest rate of 7%.

A consensus estimate based on a number of studies is that an increase in budget deficits (or a fall in budget surplus) by 1% of GDP will cause an increase of 0.5–1.0% in the long-term interest rate.

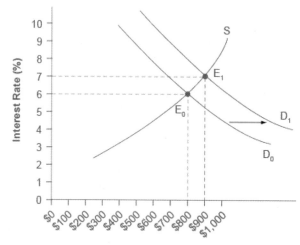

**Figure 17.14 Fiscal Policy and Interest Rates** When a government borrows money in the financial capital market, it causes a shift in the demand for financial capital from $D_0$ to $D_1$. As the equilibrium moves from $E_0$ to $E_1$, the equilibrium interest rate rises from 6% to 7% in this example. In this way, an expansionary fiscal policy intended to shift aggregate demand to the right can also lead to a higher interest rate, which has the effect of shifting aggregate demand back to the left.

A problem arises here. An expansionary fiscal policy, with tax cuts or spending increases, is intended to increase aggregate demand. If an expansionary fiscal policy also causes higher interest rates, then firms and households are discouraged from borrowing and spending (as occurs with tight monetary policy), thus reducing aggregate demand. Even if the direct effect of expansionary fiscal policy on increasing demand is not totally offset by lower aggregate demand from higher interest rates, fiscal policy can end up less powerful than was originally expected. We refer to this as **crowding out**, where government borrowing and spending results in higher interest rates, which reduces business investment and household consumption.

The broader lesson is that the government must coordinate fiscal and monetary policy. If expansionary fiscal policy is to work well, then the central bank can also reduce or keep short-term interest rates low. Conversely, monetary policy can also help to ensure that contractionary fiscal policy does not lead to a recession.

## Long and Variable Time Lags

The government can change monetary policy several times each year, but it takes much longer to enact fiscal policy. Imagine that the economy starts to slow down. It often takes some months before the economic statistics signal clearly that a downturn has started, and a few months more to confirm that it is truly a recession and not just a one- or two-month blip. Economists often call the time it takes to determine that a recession has occurred the **recognition lag**. After this lag, policymakers become aware of the problem and propose fiscal policy bills. The bills go into various congressional committees for hearings, negotiations, votes, and then, if passed, eventually for the president's signature. Many fiscal policy bills about spending or taxes propose changes that would start in the next budget year or would be phased in gradually over time. Economists often refer to the time it takes to pass a bill as the **legislative lag**. Finally, once the government passes the bill it takes some time to disperse the funds to the appropriate agencies to implement the programs. Economists call the time it takes to start the projects the **implementation lag**.

Moreover, the exact level of fiscal policy that the government should implement is never completely clear. Should it increase the budget deficit by 0.5% of GDP? By 1% of GDP? By 2% of GDP? In an AD/AS diagram, it is straightforward to sketch an aggregate demand curve shifting to the potential GDP level of output. In the real world, we only know roughly, not precisely, the actual level of potential output, and exactly how a spending cut or tax increase will affect aggregate demand is always somewhat controversial. Also unknown is the state of the economy at any point in time. During the early days of the Obama administration, for example, no one knew the true extent of the economy's deficit. During the 2008-2009 financial crisis, the rapid collapse of the banking system and automotive sector made it difficult to assess how quickly the economy was collapsing.

Thus, it can take many months or even more than a year to begin an expansionary fiscal policy after a recession has started—and even then, uncertainty will remain over exactly how much to expand or contract taxes and spending. When politicians attempt to use countercyclical fiscal policy to fight recession or inflation, they run the risk of responding to the macroeconomic situation of two or three years ago, in a way that may be exactly wrong for the economy at that time. George P. Schultz, a professor of economics, former Secretary of the Treasury, and Director of the Office of Management and Budget, once wrote: "While the economist is accustomed to the concept of lags, the politician likes instant results. The tension comes because, as I have seen on many occasions, the economist's lag is the politician's nightmare."

## Temporary and Permanent Fiscal Policy

A temporary tax cut or spending increase will explicitly last only for a year or two, and then revert to its original level. A permanent tax cut or spending increase is expected to stay in place for the foreseeable future. The effect of temporary and permanent fiscal policies on aggregate demand can be very different. Consider how you would react if the government announced a tax cut that would last one year and then be repealed, in comparison with how you would react if the government announced a permanent tax cut. Most people and firms will react more strongly to a permanent policy change than a temporary one.

This fact creates an unavoidable difficulty for countercyclical fiscal policy. The appropriate policy may be to have an expansionary fiscal policy with large budget deficits during a recession, and then a contractionary fiscal policy with budget surpluses when the economy is growing well. However, if both policies are explicitly temporary ones, they will have a less powerful effect than a permanent policy.

## Structural Economic Change Takes Time

When an economy recovers from a recession, it does not usually revert to its exact earlier shape. Instead, the economy's internal structure evolves and changes and this process can take time. For example, much of the economic growth of the mid-2000s was in the construction sector (especially of housing) and finance. However, when housing prices started falling in 2007 and the resulting financial crunch led into recession (as we discussed in **Monetary Policy and Bank Regulation**), both sectors contracted. The manufacturing sector of the U.S. economy has been losing jobs in recent years as well, under pressure from technological change and foreign competition. Many of the people who lost work from these sectors in the 2008-2009 Great Recession will never return to the same jobs in the same sectors of the economy. Instead, the economy will need to grow in new and different directions, as the following Clear It Up feature shows. Fiscal policy can increase overall demand, but the process of structural economic change—the expansion of a new set of industries and the movement of workers to those industries—inevitably takes time.

### Why do jobs vanish?

People can lose jobs for a variety of reasons: because of a recession, but also because of longer-run changes in the economy, such as new technology. Productivity improvements in auto manufacturing, for example, can reduce the number of workers needed, and eliminate these jobs in the long run. The internet has created jobs but also caused job loss, from travel agents to book store clerks. Many of these jobs may never come back. Short-run fiscal policy to reduce unemployment can create jobs, but it cannot replace jobs that will never return.

## The Limitations of Fiscal Policy

Fiscal policy can help an economy that is producing below its potential GDP to expand aggregate demand so that it produces closer to potential GDP, thus lowering unemployment. However, fiscal policy cannot help an economy produce at an output level above potential GDP without causing inflation At this point, unemployment becomes so low that workers become scarce and wages rise rapidly.

# Link It Up

Visit this website (http://openstaxcollege.org/l/fiscalpolicy) to read about how fiscal policies are affecting the recovery.

## Political Realties and Discretionary Fiscal Policy

A final problem for discretionary fiscal policy arises out of the difficulties of explaining to politicians how countercyclical fiscal policy that runs against the tide of the business cycle should work. Some politicians have a gut-level belief that when the economy and tax revenues slow down, it is time to hunker down, pinch pennies, and trim expenses. Countercyclical policy, however, says that when the economy has slowed, it is time for the government to stimulate the economy, raising spending, and cutting taxes. This offsets the drop in the economy in the other sectors. Conversely, when economic times are good and tax revenues are rolling in, politicians often feel that it is time for tax cuts and new spending. However, countercyclical policy says that this economic boom should be an appropriate time for keeping taxes high and restraining spending.

Politicians tend to prefer expansionary fiscal policy over contractionary policy. There is rarely a shortage of proposals for tax cuts and spending increases, especially during recessions. However, politicians are less willing to hear the message that in good economic times, they should propose tax increases and spending limits. In the economic upswing of the late 1990s and early 2000s, for example, the U.S. GDP grew rapidly. Estimates from respected government economic forecasters like the nonpartisan Congressional Budget Office and the Office of Management and Budget stated that the GDP was above potential GDP, and that unemployment rates were unsustainably low. However, no mainstream politician took the lead in saying that the booming economic times might be an appropriate time for spending cuts or tax increases. As of February 2017, President Trump has expressed plans to increase spending on national defense by 10% or $54 billion, increase infrastructure investment by $1 trillion, cut corporate and personal income taxes, all while maintaining the existing spending on Social Security and Medicare. The only way this math adds up is with a sizeable increase in the Federal budget deficit.

## Discretionary Fiscal Policy: Summing Up

Expansionary fiscal policy can help to end recessions and contractionary fiscal policy can help to reduce inflation. Given the uncertainties over interest rate effects, time lags, temporary and permanent policies, and unpredictable political behavior, many economists and knowledgeable policymakers had concluded by the mid-1990s that discretionary fiscal policy was a blunt instrument, more like a club than a scalpel. It might still make sense to use it in extreme economic situations, like an especially deep or long recession. For less extreme situations, it was often preferable to let fiscal policy work through the automatic stabilizers and focus on monetary policy to steer short-term countercyclical efforts.

# 17.7 | The Question of a Balanced Budget

By the end of this section, you will be able to:
- Understand the arguments for and against requiring the U.S. federal budget to be balanced
- Consider the long-run and short-run effects of a federal budget deficit

For many decades, going back to the 1930s, various legislators have put forward proposals to require that the U.S. government balance its budget every year. In 1995, a proposed constitutional amendment that would require a balanced budget passed the U.S. House of Representatives by a wide margin, and failed in the U.S. Senate by only a single vote. (For the balanced budget to have become an amendment to the Constitution would have required a two-thirds vote by Congress and passage by three-quarters of the state legislatures.)

Most economists view the proposals for a perpetually balanced budget with bemusement. After all, in the short term, economists would expect the budget deficits and surpluses to fluctuate up and down with the economy and the automatic stabilizers. Economic recessions should automatically lead to larger budget deficits or smaller budget surpluses, while economic booms lead to smaller deficits or larger surpluses. A requirement that the budget be balanced each and every year would prevent these automatic stabilizers from working and would worsen the severity of economic fluctuations.

Some supporters of the balanced budget amendment like to argue that, since households must balance their own budgets, the government should too. However, this analogy between household and government behavior is severely flawed. Most households do not balance their budgets every year. Some years households borrow to buy houses or cars or to pay for medical expenses or college tuition. Other years they repay loans and save funds in retirement accounts. After retirement, they withdraw and spend those savings. Also, the government is not a household for many reasons, one of which is that the government has macroeconomic responsibilities. The argument of Keynesian macroeconomic policy is that the government needs to lean against the wind, spending when times are hard and saving when times are good, for the sake of the overall economy.

There is also no particular reason to expect a government budget to be balanced in the medium term of a few years. For example, a government may decide that by running large budget deficits, it can make crucial long-term investments in human capital and physical infrastructure that will build the country's long-term productivity. These decisions may work out well or poorly, but they are not always irrational. Such policies of ongoing government budget deficits may persist for decades. As the U.S. experience from the end of World War II up to about 1980 shows, it is perfectly possible to run budget deficits almost every year for decades, but as long as the percentage increases in debt are smaller than the percentage growth of GDP, the debt/GDP ratio will decline at the same time.

Nothing in this argument is a claim that budget deficits are always a wise policy. In the short run, a government that runs a very large budget deficit can shift aggregate demand to the right and trigger severe inflation. Additionally, governments may borrow for foolish or impractical reasons. **The Impacts of Government Borrowing** will discuss how large budget deficits, by reducing national saving, can in certain cases reduce economic growth and even contribute to international financial crises. A requirement that the budget be balanced in each calendar year, however, is a misguided overreaction to the fear that in some cases, budget deficits can become too large.

# Bring it Home

## No Yellowstone Park?

The 2013 federal budget shutdown illustrated the many sides to fiscal policy and the federal budget. In 2013, Republicans and Democrats could not agree on which spending policies to fund and how large the government debt should be. Due to the severity of the 2008-2009 recession, the fiscal stimulus, and previous policies, the federal budget deficit and debt was historically high. One way to try to cut federal spending and borrowing was to refuse to raise the legal federal debt limit, or tie on conditions to appropriation bills to stop the Affordable Health Care Act. This disagreement led to a two-week federal government shutdown and got close to the deadline where the federal government would default on its Treasury bonds. Finally, however, a compromise emerged and the government avoided default. This shows clearly how closely fiscal policies are tied to politics.

# KEY TERMS

**automatic stabilizers** tax and spending rules that have the effect of slowing down the rate of decrease in aggregate demand when the economy slows down and restraining aggregate demand when the economy speeds up, without any additional change in legislation

**balanced budget** when government spending and taxes are equal

**budget deficit** when the federal government spends more money than it receives in taxes in a given year

**budget surplus** when the government receives more money in taxes than it spends in a year

**contractionary fiscal policy** fiscal policy that decreases the level of aggregate demand, either through cuts in government spending or increases in taxes

**corporate income tax** a tax imposed on corporate profits

**crowding out** federal spending and borrowing causes interest rates to rise and business investment to fall

**discretionary fiscal policy** the government passes a new law that explicitly changes overall tax or spending levels with the intent of influencing the level or overall economic activity

**estate and gift tax** a tax on people who pass assets to the next generation—either after death or during life in the form of gifts

**excise tax** a tax on a specific good—on gasoline, tobacco, and alcohol

**expansionary fiscal policy** fiscal policy that increases the level of aggregate demand, either through increases in government spending or cuts in taxes

**implementation lag** the time it takes for the funds relating to fiscal policy to be dispersed to the appropriate agencies to implement the programs

**individual income tax** a tax based on the income, of all forms, received by individuals

**legislative lag** the time it takes to get a fiscal policy bill passed

**marginal tax rates** or the tax that must be paid on all yearly income

**national debt** the total accumulated amount the government has borrowed, over time, and not yet paid back

**payroll tax** a tax based on the pay received from employers; the taxes provide funds for Social Security and Medicare

**progressive tax** a tax that collects a greater share of income from those with high incomes than from those with lower incomes

**proportional tax** a tax that is a flat percentage of income earned, regardless of level of income

**recognition lag** the time it takes to determine that a recession has occurred

**regressive tax** a tax in which people with higher incomes pay a smaller share of their income in tax

**standardized employment budget** the budget deficit or surplus in any given year adjusted for what it would have been if the economy were producing at potential GDP

# KEY CONCEPTS AND SUMMARY

## 17.1 Government Spending

Fiscal policy is the set of policies that relate to federal government spending, taxation, and borrowing. In recent decades, the level of federal government spending and taxes, expressed as a share of GDP, has not changed much, typically fluctuating between about 18% to 22% of GDP. However, the level of state spending and taxes, as a share of GDP, has risen from about 12–13% to about 20% of GDP over the last four decades. The four main areas of federal spending are national defense, Social Security, healthcare, and interest payments, which together account for about 70% of all federal spending. When a government spends more than it collects in taxes, it is said to have a budget deficit. When a government collects more in taxes than it spends, it is said to have a budget surplus. If government spending and taxes are equal, it is said to have a balanced budget. The sum of all past deficits and surpluses make up the government debt.

## 17.2 Taxation

The two main federal taxes are individual income taxes and payroll taxes that provide funds for Social Security and Medicare; these taxes together account for more than 80% of federal revenues. Other federal taxes include the corporate income tax, excise taxes on alcohol, gasoline and tobacco, and the estate and gift tax. A progressive tax is one, like the federal income tax, where those with higher incomes pay a higher share of taxes out of their income than those with lower incomes. A proportional tax is one, like the payroll tax for Medicare, where everyone pays the same share of taxes regardless of income level. A regressive tax is one, like the payroll tax (above a certain threshold) that supports Social Security, where those with high income pay a lower share of income in taxes than those with lower incomes.

## 17.3 Federal Deficits and the National Debt

For most of the twentieth century, the U.S. government took on debt during wartime and then paid down that debt slowly in peacetime. However, it took on quite substantial debts in peacetime in the 1980s and early 1990s, before a brief period of budget surpluses from 1998 to 2001, followed by a return to annual budget deficits since 2002, with very large deficits in the recession of 2008 and 2009. A budget deficit or budget surplus is measured annually. Total government debt or national debt is the sum of budget deficits and budget surpluses over time.

## 17.4 Using Fiscal Policy to Fight Recession, Unemployment, and Inflation

Expansionary fiscal policy increases the level of aggregate demand, either through increases in government spending or through reductions in taxes. Expansionary fiscal policy is most appropriate when an economy is in recession and producing below its potential GDP. Contractionary fiscal policy decreases the level of aggregate demand, either through cuts in government spending or increases in taxes. Contractionary fiscal policy is most appropriate when an economy is producing above its potential GDP.

## 17.5 Automatic Stabilizers

Fiscal policy is conducted both through discretionary fiscal policy, which occurs when the government enacts taxation or spending changes in response to economic events, or through automatic stabilizers, which are taxing and spending mechanisms that, by their design, shift in response to economic events without any further legislation. The standardized employment budget is the calculation of what the budget deficit or budget surplus would have been in a given year if the economy had been producing at its potential GDP in that year. Many economists and politicians criticize the use of fiscal policy for a variety of reasons, including concerns over time lags, the impact on interest rates, and the inherently political nature of fiscal policy. We cover the critique of fiscal policy in the next module.

## 17.6 Practical Problems with Discretionary Fiscal Policy

Because fiscal policy affects the quantity of money that the government borrows in financial capital markets, it not only affects aggregate demand—it can also affect interest rates. If an expansionary fiscal policy also causes higher interest rates, then firms and households are discouraged from borrowing and spending, reducing aggregate demand in a situation called crowding out. Given the uncertainties over interest rate effects, time lags (implementation lag, legislative lag, and recognition lag), temporary and permanent policies, and unpredictable political behavior, many economists and knowledgeable policymakers have concluded that discretionary fiscal policy is a blunt instrument and better used only in extreme situations.

## 17.7 The Question of a Balanced Budget

Balanced budget amendments are a popular political idea, but the economic merits behind such proposals are questionable. Most economists accept that fiscal policy needs to be flexible enough to accommodate unforeseen expenditures, such as wars or recessions. While persistent, large budget deficits can indeed be a problem, a balanced budget amendment prevents even small, temporary deficits that might, in some cases, be necessary.

## SELF-CHECK QUESTIONS

1. When governments run budget deficits, how do they make up the differences between tax revenue and spending?

2. When governments run budget surpluses, what is done with the extra funds?

3. Is it possible for a nation to run budget deficits and still have its debt/GDP ratio fall? Explain your answer. Is it possible for a nation to run budget surpluses and still have its debt/GDP ratio rise? Explain your answer.

4. Suppose that gifts were taxed at a rate of 10% for amounts up to $100,000 and 20% for anything over that amount. Would this tax be regressive or progressive?

5. If an individual owns a corporation for which he is the only employee, which different types of federal tax will he have to pay?

6. What taxes would an individual pay if he were self-employed and the business is not incorporated?

7. The social security tax is 6.2% on employees' income earned below $113,000. Is this tax progressive, regressive or proportional?

8. Debt has a certain self-reinforcing quality to it. There is one category of government spending that automatically increases along with the federal debt. What is it?

9. True or False:
    a. Federal spending has grown substantially in recent decades.
    b. By world standards, the U.S. government controls a relatively large share of the U.S. economy.
    c. A majority of the federal government's revenue is collected through personal income taxes.
    d. Education spending is slightly larger at the federal level than at the state and local level.
    e. State and local government spending has not risen much in recent decades.
    f. Defense spending is higher now than ever.
    g. The share of the economy going to federal taxes has increased substantially over time.
    h. Foreign aid is a large portion, although less than half, of federal spending.
    i. Federal deficits have been very large for the last two decades.
    j. The accumulated federal debt as a share of GDP is near an all-time high.

10. What is the main reason for employing contractionary fiscal policy in a time of strong economic growth?

11. What is the main reason for employing expansionary fiscal policy during a recession?

12. In a recession, does the actual budget surplus or deficit fall above or below the standardized employment budget?

13. What is the main advantage of automatic stabilizers over discretionary fiscal policy?

14. Explain how automatic stabilizers work, both on the taxation side and on the spending side, first in a situation where the economy is producing less than potential GDP and then in a situation where the economy is producing more than potential GDP.

15. What would happen if expansionary fiscal policy was implemented in a recession but, due to lag, did not actually take effect until after the economy was back to potential GDP?

**16.** What would happen if contractionary fiscal policy were implemented during an economic boom but, due to lag, it did not take effect until the economy slipped into recession?

**17.** Do you think the typical time lag for fiscal policy is likely to be longer or shorter than the time lag for monetary policy? Explain your answer?

**18.** How would a balanced budget amendment affect a decision by Congress to grant a tax cut during a recession?

**19.** How would a balanced budget amendment change the effect of automatic stabilizer programs?

## REVIEW QUESTIONS

**20.** Give some examples of changes in federal spending and taxes by the government that would be fiscal policy and some that would not.

**21.** Have the spending and taxes of the U.S. federal government generally had an upward or a downward trend in the last few decades?

**22.** What are the main categories of U.S. federal government spending?

**23.** What is the difference between a budget deficit, a balanced budget, and a budget surplus?

**24.** Have spending and taxes by state and local governments in the United States had a generally upward or downward trend in the last few decades?

**25.** What are the main categories of U.S. federal government taxes?

**26.** What is the difference between a progressive tax, a proportional tax, and a regressive tax?

**27.** What has been the general pattern of U.S. budget deficits in recent decades?

**28.** What is the difference between a budget deficit and the national debt?

**29.** What is the difference between expansionary fiscal policy and contractionary fiscal policy?

**30.** Under what general macroeconomic circumstances might a government use expansionary fiscal policy? When might it use contractionary fiscal policy?

**31.** What is the difference between discretionary fiscal policy and automatic stabilizers?

**32.** Why do automatic stabilizers function "automatically?"

**33.** What is the standardized employment budget?

**34.** What are some practical weaknesses of discretionary fiscal policy?

**35.** What are some of the arguments for and against a requirement that the federal government budget be balanced every year?

## CRITICAL THINKING QUESTIONS

**36.** Why is government spending typically measured as a percentage of GDP rather than in nominal dollars?

**37.** Why are expenditures such as crime prevention and education typically done at the state and local level rather than at the federal level?

**38.** Why is spending by the U.S. government on scientific research at NASA fiscal policy while spending by the University of Illinois is not fiscal policy? Why is a cut in the payroll tax fiscal policy whereas a cut in a state income tax is not fiscal policy?

**39.** Excise taxes on tobacco and alcohol and state sales taxes are often criticized for being regressive. Although everyone pays the same rate regardless of income, why might this be so?

**40.** What is the benefit of having state and local taxes on income instead of collecting all such taxes at the federal level?

**41.** In a booming economy, is the federal government more likely to run surpluses or deficits? What are the various factors at play?

**42.** Economist Arthur Laffer famously pointed out that, in some cases, income tax revenue can actually go up when tax rates go down. Why might this be the case?

**43.** Is it possible for a nation to run budget deficits and still have its debt/GDP ratio fall? Explain your answer. Is it possible for a nation to run budget surpluses and still have its debt/GDP ratio rise? Explain your answer.

**44.** How will cuts in state budget spending affect federal expansionary policy?

**45.** Is expansionary fiscal policy more attractive to politicians who believe in larger government or to politicians who believe in smaller government? Explain your answer.

**46.** Is Medicaid (federal government aid to low-income families and individuals) an automatic stabilizer?

**47.** What is a potential problem with a temporary tax increase designed to increase aggregate demand if people know that it is temporary?

**48.** If the government gives a $300 tax cut to everyone in the country, explain the mechanism by which this will cause interest rates to rise.

**49.** Do you agree or disagree with this statement: "It is in the best interest of our economy for Congress and the President to run a balanced budget each year." Explain your answer.

**50.** During the Great Recession of 2008–2009, what actions would have been required of Congress and the President had a balanced budget amendment to the Constitution been ratified? What impact would that have had on the unemployment rate?

## PROBLEMS

**51.** A government starts off with a total debt of $3.5 billion. In year one, the government runs a deficit of $400 million. In year two, the government runs a deficit of $1 billion. In year three, the government runs a surplus of $200 million. What is the total debt of the government at the end of year three?

**52.** If a government runs a budget deficit of $10 billion dollars each year for ten years, then a surplus of $1 billion for five years, and then a balanced budget for another ten years, what is the government debt?

**53.** Specify whether expansionary or contractionary fiscal policy would seem to be most appropriate in response to each of the situations below and sketch a diagram using aggregate demand and aggregate supply curves to illustrate your answer:
   a. A recession.
   b. A stock market collapse that hurts consumer and business confidence.
   c. Extremely rapid growth of exports.
   d. Rising inflation.
   e. A rise in the natural rate of unemployment.
   f. A rise in oil prices.

# 18 | The Impacts of Government Borrowing

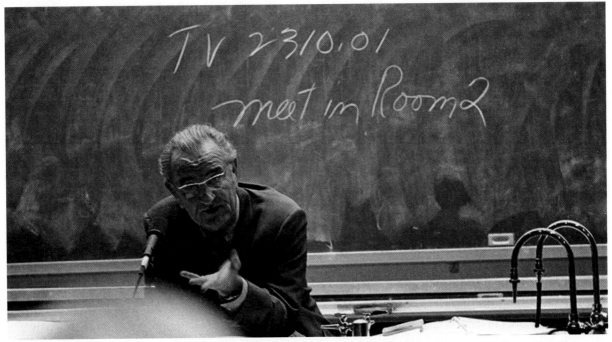

**Figure 18.1 President Lyndon B. Johnson** President Lyndon Johnson played a pivotal role in financing higher education. (Credit: modification of image by LBJ Museum & Library)

## Bring it Home

### Financing Higher Education

On November 8, 1965, President Lyndon B. Johnson signed The Higher Education Act of 1965 into law. With a stroke of the pen, he implemented what we know as the financial aid, work study, and student loan programs to help Americans pay for a college education. In his remarks, the President said:

> Here the seeds were planted from which grew my firm conviction that for the individual, education is the path to achievement and fulfillment; for the Nation, it is a path to a society that is not only free but civilized; and for the world, it is the path to peace—for it is education that places reason over force.

This Act, he said, "is responsible for funding higher education for millions of Americans. It is the embodiment of the United States' investment in 'human capital'." Since Johnson signed the Act into law, the government has renewed it several times.

The purpose of The Higher Education Act of 1965 was to build the country's human capital by creating educational opportunity for millions of Americans. The three criteria that the government uses to judge eligibility are income, full-time or part-time attendance, and the cost of the institution. According to the 2011–2012 National Postsecondary Student Aid Study (NPSAS:12), in the 2011–2012 school year, over 70% of all full-time college students received some form of federal financial aid; 47% received grants; and another 55% received federal government student loans. The budget to support financial aid has increased not only because of more enrollment, but also because of increased tuition and fees for higher education.

The current Trump administration is currently questioning these increases and the entire notion of how the government should deal with higher education. The President and Congress are charged with balancing fiscal responsibility and important government-financed expenditures like investing in human capital.

# Introduction to the Impacts of Government Borrowing

In this chapter, you will learn about:

- How Government Borrowing Affects Investment and the Trade Balance
- Fiscal Policy, Investment, and Economic Growth
- How Government Borrowing Affects Private Saving
- Fiscal Policy and the Trade Balance

Governments have many competing demands for financial support. Any spending should be tempered by fiscal responsibility and by looking carefully at the spending's impact. When a government spends more than it collects in taxes, it runs a budget deficit. It then needs to borrow. When government borrowing becomes especially large and sustained, it can substantially reduce the financial capital available to private sector firms, as well as lead to trade imbalances and even financial crises.

The **Government Budgets and Fiscal Policy** chapter introduced the concepts of deficits and debt, as well as how a government could use fiscal policy to address recession or inflation. This chapter begins by building on the national savings and investment identity, which we first first introduced in **The International Trade and Capital Flows** chapter, to show how government borrowing affects firms' physical capital investment levels and trade balances. A prolonged period of budget deficits may lead to lower economic growth, in part because the funds that the government borrows to fund its budget deficits are typically no longer available for private investment. Moreover, a sustained pattern of large budget deficits can lead to disruptive economic patterns of high inflation, substantial inflows of financial capital from abroad, plummeting exchange rates, and heavy strains on a country's banking and financial system.

# 18.1 | How Government Borrowing Affects Investment and the Trade Balance

By the end of this section, you will be able to:
- Explain the national saving and investment identity in terms of demand and supply
- Evaluate the role of budget surpluses and trade surpluses in national saving and investment identity

When governments are borrowers in financial markets, there are three possible sources for the funds from a macroeconomic point of view: (1) households might save more; (2) private firms might borrow less; and (3) the additional funds for government borrowing might come from outside the country, from foreign financial investors. Let's begin with a review of why one of these three options must occur, and then explore how interest rates and exchange rates adjust to these connections.

## The National Saving and Investment Identity

The national saving and investment identity, which we first introduced in **The International Trade and Capital Flows** chapter, provides a framework for showing the relationships between the sources of demand and supply in financial capital markets. The identity begins with a statement that must always hold true: the quantity of financial capital supplied in the market must equal the quantity of financial capital demanded.

The U.S. economy has two main sources for financial capital: private savings from inside the U.S. economy and public savings.

Total savings = Private savings (S) + Public savings (T – G)

These include the inflow of foreign financial capital from abroad. The inflow of savings from abroad is, by definition, equal to the trade deficit, as we explained in The International Trade and Capital Flows chapter. We can write this inflow of foreign investment capital as imports (M) minus exports (X). There are also two main sources of demand for financial capital: private sector investment (I) and government borrowing. Government borrowing in any given year is equal to the budget deficit, which we can write as the difference between government spending (G) and net taxes (T). Let's call this equation 1.

$$\text{Quantity supplied of financial capital} \; = \; \text{Quantity demanded of financial capital}$$
$$\text{Private savings} + \text{Inflow of foreign savings} \; = \; \text{Private investment} + \text{Government budget deficit}$$
$$S + (M - X) \; = \; I + (G - T)$$

Governments often spend more than they receive in taxes and, therefore, public savings (T – G) is negative. This causes a need to borrow money in the amount of (G – T) instead of adding to the nation's savings. If this is the case, we can view governments as demanders of financial capital instead of suppliers. In algebraic terms, we can rewrite the national savings and investment identity like this:

$$\text{Private investment} \; = \; \text{Private savings} + \; \text{Public savings} \; + \text{Trade deficit}$$
$$I \; = \; S + (T - G) + (M - X)$$

Let's call this equation 2. We must accompany a change in any part of the national saving and investment identity by offsetting changes in at least one other part of the equation because we assume that the equality of quantity supplied and quantity demanded always holds. If the government budget deficit changes, then either private saving or investment or the trade balance—or some combination of the three—must change as well. Figure 18.2 shows the possible effects.

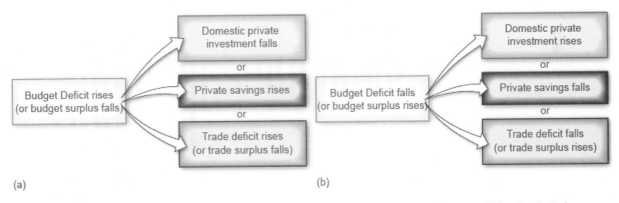

(a)

(b)

Figure 18.2 Effects of Change in Budget Surplus or Deficit on Investment, Savings, and The Trade Balance Chart (a) shows the potential results when the budget deficit rises (or budget surplus falls). Chart (b) shows the potential results when the budget deficit falls (or budget surplus rises).

## What about Budget Surpluses and Trade Surpluses?

The national saving and investment identity must always hold true because, by definition, the quantity supplied and quantity demanded in the financial capital market must always be equal. However, the formula will look somewhat different if the government budget is in deficit rather than surplus or if the balance of trade is in surplus rather than deficit. For example, in 1999 and 2000, the U.S. government had budget surpluses, although the economy was still experiencing trade deficits. When the government was running budget surpluses, it was acting as a saver rather than a borrower, and supplying rather than demanding financial capital. As a result, we would write the national saving and investment identity during this time as:

$$\text{Quantity supplied of financial capital} \; = \; \text{Quantity demanded of financial capital}$$
$$\text{Private savings} + \text{Trade deficit} + \text{Government surplus} \; = \; \text{Private investment}$$
$$S + (M - X) + (T - G) \; = \; I$$

Let's call this equation 3. Notice that this expression is mathematically the same as equation 2 except the savings and investment sides of the identity have simply flipped sides.

During the 1960s, the U.S. government was often running a budget deficit, but the economy was typically running trade surpluses. Since a trade surplus means that an economy is experiencing a net outflow of financial capital, we would write the national saving and investment identity as:

Quantity supplied of financial capital   =   Quantity demanded of financial capital

Private savings   =   Private investment + Outflow of foreign savings + Government budget deficit

$$S = I + (X - M) + (G - T)$$

Instead of the balance of trade representing part of the supply of financial capital, which occurs with a trade deficit, a trade surplus represents an outflow of financial capital leaving the domestic economy and invested elsewhere in the world.

Quantity supplied of financial capital   =   Quantity demanded of financial capital demand

Private savings   =   Private investment + Government budget deficit + Trade surplus

$$S = I + (G - T) + (X - M)$$

We assume that the point to these equations is that the national saving and investment identity always hold. When you write these relationships, it is important to engage your brain and think about what is on the supply and demand side of the financial capital market before you start your calculations.

As you can see in **Figure 18.3**, the Office of Management and Budget shows that the United States has consistently run budget deficits since 1977, with the exception of 1999 and 2000. What is alarming is the dramatic increase in budget deficits that has occurred since 2008, which in part reflects declining tax revenues and increased safety net expenditures due to the Great Recession. (Recall that T is net taxes. When the government must transfer funds back to individuals for safety net expenditures like Social Security and unemployment benefits, budget deficits rise.) These deficits have implications for the future health of the U.S. economy.

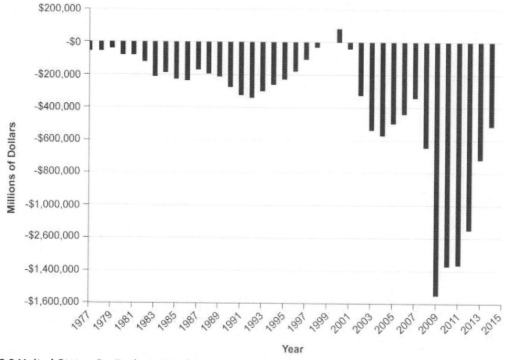

**Figure 18.3 United States On-Budget, Surplus, and Deficit, 1977–2014 ($ millions)**   The United States has run a budget deficit for over 30 years, with the exception of 1999 and 2000. Military expenditures, entitlement programs, and the decrease in tax revenue coupled with increased safety net support during the Great Recession are major contributors to the dramatic increases in the deficit after 2008. (Source: Table 1.1, "Summary of Receipts, Outlays, and Surpluses or Deficits," https://www.whitehouse.gov/omb/budget/Historicals)

A rising budget deficit may result in a fall in domestic investment, a rise in private savings, or a rise in the trade deficit. The following modules discuss each of these possible effects in more detail.

# 18.2 | Fiscal Policy and the Trade Balance

By the end of this section, you will be able to:
- Discuss twin deficits as they related to budget and trade deficit
- Explain the relationship between budget deficits and exchange rates
- Explain the relationship between budget deficits and inflation
- Identify causes of recessions

Government budget balances can affect the trade balance. As **The Keynesian Perspective** chapter discusses, a net inflow of foreign financial investment always accompanies a trade deficit, while a net outflow of financial investment always accompanies a trade surplus. One way to understand the connection from budget deficits to trade deficits is that when government creates a budget deficit with some combination of tax cuts or spending increases, it will increase aggregate demand in the economy, and some of that increase in aggregate demand will result in a higher level of imports. A higher level of imports, with exports remaining fixed, will cause a larger trade deficit. That means foreigners' holdings of dollars increase as Americans purchase more imported goods. Foreigners use those dollars to invest in the United States, which leads to an inflow of foreign investment. One possible source of funding our budget deficit is foreigners buying Treasury securities that the U.S. government sells, thus a trade deficit often accompanies a budget deficit.

## Twin Deficits?

In the mid-1980s, it was common to hear economists and even newspaper articles refer to the twin deficits, as the budget deficit and trade deficit both grew substantially. **Figure 18.4** shows the pattern. The federal budget deficit went from 2.6% of GDP in 1981 to 5.1% of GDP in 1985—a drop of 2.5% of GDP. Over that time, the trade deficit moved from 0.5% in 1981 to 2.9% in 1985—a drop of 2.4% of GDP. In the mid-1980s an inflow of foreign investment capital matched, the considerable increase in government borrowing, so the government budget deficit and the trade deficit moved together.

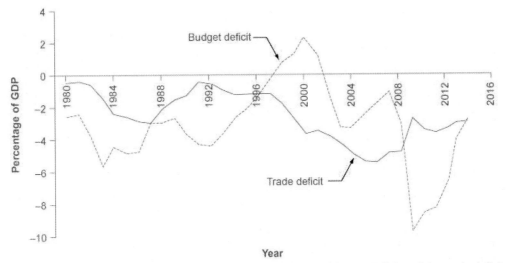

**Figure 18.4 U.S. Budget Deficits and Trade Deficits**  In the 1980s, the budget deficit and the trade deficit declined at the same time. However, since then, the deficits have stopped being twins. The trade deficit grew smaller in the early 1990s as the budget deficit increased, and then the trade deficit grew larger in the late 1990s as the budget deficit turned into a surplus. In the first half of the 2000s, both budget and trade deficits increased. However, in 2009, the trade deficit declined as the budget deficit increased.

Of course, no one should expect the budget deficit and trade deficit to move in lockstep, because the other parts of the national saving and investment identity—investment and private savings—will often change as well. In the late 1990s, for example, the government budget balance turned from deficit to surplus, but the trade deficit remained large and growing. During this time, the inflow of foreign financial investment was supporting a surge of physical capital investment by U.S. firms. In the first half of the 2000s, the budget and trade deficits again increased together, but in

2009, the budget deficit increased while the trade deficit declined. The budget deficit and the trade deficits are related to each other, but they are more like cousins than twins.

## Budget Deficits and Exchange Rates

Exchange rates can also help to explain why budget deficits are linked to trade deficits. **Figure 18.5** shows a situation using the exchange rate for the U.S. dollar, measured in euros. At the original equilibrium ($E_0$), where the demand for U.S. dollars ($D_0$) intersects with the supply of U.S. dollars ($S_0$) on the foreign exchange market, the exchange rate is 0.9 euros per U.S. dollar and the equilibrium quantity traded in the market is $100 billion per day (which was roughly the quantity of dollar–euro trading in exchange rate markets in the mid-2000s). Then the U.S. budget deficit rises and foreign financial investment provides the source of funds for that budget deficit.

International financial investors, as a group, will demand more U.S. dollars on foreign exchange markets to purchase the U.S. government bonds, and they will supply fewer of the U.S. dollars that they already hold in these markets. Demand for U.S. dollars on the foreign exchange market shifts from $D_0$ to $D_1$ and the supply of U.S. dollars falls from $S_0$ to $S_1$. At the new equilibrium ($E_1$), the exchange rate has appreciated to 1.05 euros per dollar while, in this example, the quantity of dollars traded remains the same.

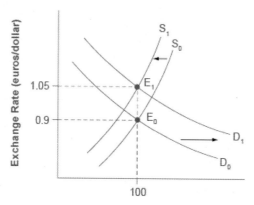

Quantity of Dollars Traded (billions per day)

**Figure 18.5 Budget Deficits and Exchange Rates**   Imagine that the U.S. government increases its borrowing and the funds come from European financial investors. To purchase U.S. government bonds, those European investors will need to demand more U.S. dollars on foreign exchange markets, causing the demand for U.S. dollars to shift to the right from $D_0$ to $D_1$. European financial investors as a group will also be less likely to supply U.S. dollars to the foreign exchange markets, causing the supply of U.S. dollars to shift from $S_0$ to $S_1$. The equilibrium exchange rate strengthens from 0.9 euro/ dollar at $E_0$ to 1.05 euros/dollar at $E_1$.

A stronger exchange rate, of course, makes it more difficult for exporters to sell their goods abroad while making imports cheaper, so a trade deficit (or a reduced trade surplus) results. Thus, a budget deficit can easily result in an inflow of foreign financial capital, a stronger exchange rate, and a trade deficit.

You can also imagine interest rates are driving the exchange rate appreciation. As we explained earlier in **Figure 18.8**, a budget deficit increases demand in markets for domestic financial capital, raising the domestic interest rate. A higher interest rate will attract an inflow of foreign financial capital, and appreciate the exchange rate in response to the increase in demand for U.S. dollars by foreign investors and a decrease in supply of U. S. dollars. Because of higher interest rates in the United States, Americans find U.S. bonds more attractive than foreign bonds. When Americans are buying fewer foreign bonds, they are supplying fewer U.S. dollars. U.S. dollar depreciation leads to a larger trade deficit (or reduced surplus). The connections between inflows of foreign investment capital, interest rates, and exchange rates are all just different ways of drawing the same economic connections: a larger budget deficit can result in a larger trade deficit, although do not expect the connection to be one-to-one.

## From Budget Deficits to International Economic Crisis

We lay out step-by-step the economic story of how an outflow of international financial capital can cause a deep recession in the **Exchange Rates and International Capital Flows** chapter. When international financial investors decide to withdraw their funds from a country like Turkey, they increase the supply of the Turkish lira and reduce the demand for lira, depreciating the lira exchange rate. When firms and the government in a country like

Turkey borrow money in international financial markets, they typically do so in stages. First, banks in Turkey borrow in a widely used currency like U.S. dollars or euros, then convert those U.S. dollars to lira, and then lend the money to borrowers in Turkey. If the lira's exchange rate value depreciates, then Turkey's banks will find it impossible to repay the international loans that are in U.S. dollars or euros.

The combination of less foreign investment capital and banks that are bankrupt can sharply reduce aggregate demand, which causes a deep recession. Many countries around the world have experienced this kind of recession in recent years: along with Turkey in 2002, Mexico followed this general pattern in 1995, Thailand and countries across East Asia in 1997–1998, Russia in 1998, and Argentina in 2002. In many of these countries, large government budget deficits played a role in setting the stage for the financial crisis. A moderate increase in a budget deficit that leads to a moderate increase in a trade deficit and a moderate appreciation of the exchange rate is not necessarily a cause for concern. However, beyond some point that is hard to define in advance, a series of large budget deficits can become a cause for concern among international investors.

One reason for concern is that extremely large budget deficits mean that aggregate demand may shift so far to the right as to cause high inflation. The example of Turkey is a situation where very large budget deficits brought inflation rates well into double digits. In addition, very large budget deficits at some point begin to raise a fear that the government would not repay the borrowing. In the last 175 years, the government of Turkey has been unable to pay its debts and defaulted on its loans six times. Brazil's government has been unable to pay its debts and defaulted on its loans seven times; Venezuela, nine times; and Argentina, five times. The risk of high inflation or a default on repaying international loans will worry international investors, since both factors imply that the rate of return on their investments in that country may end up lower than expected. If international investors start withdrawing the funds from a country rapidly, the scenario of less investment, a depreciated exchange rate, widespread bank failure, and deep recession can occur. The following Clear It Up feature explains other impacts of large deficits.

## What are the risks of chronic large deficits in the United States?

If a government runs large budget deficits for a sustained period of time, what can go wrong? According to a recent Brookings Institution report, a key risk of a large budget deficit is that government debt may grow too high compared to the country's GDP growth. As debt grows, the national savings rate will decline, leaving less available in financial capital for private investment. The impact of chronically large budget deficits is as follows:

- As the population ages, there will be an increasing demand for government services that may cause higher government deficits. Government borrowing and its interest payments will pull resources away from domestic investment in human capital and physical capital that is essential to economic growth.

- Interest rates may start to rise so that the cost of financing government debt will rise as well, creating pressure on the government to reduce its budget deficits through spending cuts and tax increases. These steps will be politically painful, and they will also have a contractionary effect on aggregate demand in the economy.

- Rising percentage of debt to GDP will create uncertainty in the financial and global markets that might cause a country to resort to inflationary tactics to reduce the real value of the debt outstanding. This will decrease real wealth and damage confidence in the country's ability to manage its spending. After all, if the government has borrowed at a fixed interest rate of, say, 5%, and it lets inflation rise above that 5%, then it will effectively be able to repay its debt at a negative real interest rate.

The conventional reasoning suggests that the relationship between sustained deficits that lead to high levels of government debt and long-term growth is negative. How significant this relationship is, how big an issue it is compared to other macroeconomic issues, and the direction of causality, is less clear.

What remains important to acknowledge is that the relationship between debt and growth is negative and that for some countries, the relationship may be stronger than in others. It is also important to acknowledge the direction of causality: does high debt cause slow growth, slow growth cause high debt, or are both high debt and slow growth the result of third factors? In our analysis, we have argued simply that high debt causes slow growth. There may be more to this debate than we have space to discuss here.

## Using Fiscal Policy to Address Trade Imbalances

If a nation is experiencing the inflow of foreign investment capital associated with a trade deficit because foreign investors are making long-term direct investments in firms, there may be no substantial reason for concern. After all, many low-income nations around the world would welcome direct investment by multinational firms that ties them more closely into the global networks of production and distribution of goods and services. In this case, the inflows of foreign investment capital and the trade deficit are attracted by the opportunities for a good rate of return on private sector investment in an economy.

However, governments should beware of a sustained pattern of high budget deficits and high trade deficits. The danger arises in particular when the inflow of foreign investment capital is not funding long-term physical capital investment by firms, but instead is short-term portfolio investment in government bonds. When inflows of foreign financial investment reach high levels, foreign financial investors will be on the alert for any reason to fear that the country's exchange rate may decline or the government may be unable to repay what it has borrowed on time. Just as a few falling rocks can trigger an avalanche; a relatively small piece of bad news about an economy can trigger an enormous outflow of short-term financial capital.

Reducing a nation's budget deficit will not always be a successful method of reducing its trade deficit, because other elements of the national saving and investment identity, like private saving or investment, may change instead. In those cases when the budget deficit is the main cause of the trade deficit, governments should take steps to reduce their budget deficits, lest they make their economy vulnerable to a rapid outflow of international financial capital that could bring a deep recession.

## Bring it Home

### Financing Higher Education

Between 1982 and 2012, the increases in the cost of a college education had far outpaced that of the income of the typical American family. According to President Obama's research staff, the cost of education at a four-year public college increased by 257% compared to an increase in family incomes of only 16% over the prior 30 years. The ongoing debate over a balanced budget and proposed cutbacks accentuated the need to increase investment in human capital to grow the economy versus deepening the already significant debt levels of the U.S. government. In summer 2013, President Obama presented a plan to make college more affordable that included increasing Pell Grant awards and the number of recipients, caps on interest rates for student loans, and providing education tax credits. In addition, the plan includes an accountability method for institutions of higher education that focuses on completion rates and creates a College Scorecard. Whether or not all these initiatives come to fruition remains to be seen, but they are indicative of creative approaches that government can take to meet its obligation from both a public and fiscal policy perspective.

## 18.3 | How Government Borrowing Affects Private Saving

By the end of this section, you will be able to:
- Apply Ricardian equivalence to evaluate how government borrowing affects private saving
- Interpret a graphic representation of Ricardian equivalence

A change in government budgets may impact private saving. Imagine that people watch government budgets and adjust their savings accordingly. For example, whenever the government runs a budget deficit, people might reason: "Well, a higher budget deficit means that I'm just going to owe more taxes in the future to pay off all that government borrowing, so I'll start saving now." If the government runs budget surpluses, people might reason: "With these budget surpluses (or lower budget deficits), interest rates are falling, so that saving is less attractive. Moreover, with a budget surplus the country will be able to afford a tax cut sometime in the future. I won't bother saving as much now."

The theory that rational private households might shift their saving to offset government saving or borrowing is known as **Ricardian equivalence** because the idea has intellectual roots in the writings of the early nineteenth-century economist David Ricardo (1772–1823). If Ricardian equivalence holds completely true, then in the national saving and investment identity, any change in budget deficits or budget surpluses would be completely offset by a corresponding change in private saving. As a result, changes in government borrowing would have no effect at all on either physical capital investment or trade balances.

In practice, the private sector only sometimes and partially adjusts its savings behavior to offset government budget deficits and surpluses. **Figure 18.6** shows the patterns of U.S. government budget deficits and surpluses and the rate of private saving—which includes saving by both households and firms—since 1980. The connection between the two is not at all obvious. In the mid-1980s, for example, government budget deficits were quite large, but there is no corresponding surge of private saving. However, when budget deficits turn to surpluses in the late 1990s, there is a simultaneous decline in private saving. When budget deficits get very large in 2008 and 2009, there is some sign of a rise in saving. A variety of statistical studies based on the U.S. experience suggests that when government borrowing increases by $1, private saving rises by about 30 cents. A World Bank study from the late 1990s, looking at government budgets and private saving behavior in countries around the world, found a similar result.

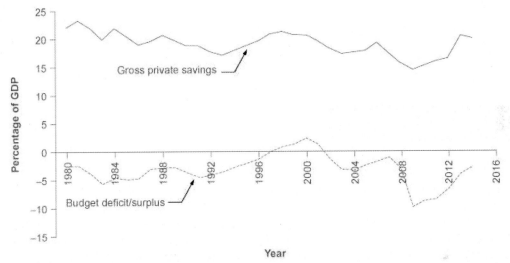

**Figure 18.6 U.S. Budget Deficits and Private Savings** The theory of Ricardian equivalence suggests that additional private saving will offset any increase in government borrowing, while reduced private saving will offset any decrease in government borrowing. Sometimes this theory holds true, and sometimes it does not. (Source: Bureau of Economic Analysis and Federal Reserve Economic Data)

Private saving does increase to some extent when governments run large budget deficits, and private saving falls when governments reduce deficits or run large budget surpluses. However, the offsetting effects of private saving compared to government borrowing are much less than one-to-one. In addition, this effect can vary a great deal from country to country, from time to time, and over the short and the long run.

If the funding for a larger budget deficit comes from international financial investors, then a trade deficit may accompany a budget deficit. In some countries, this pattern of **twin deficits** has set the stage for international financial investors first to send their funds to a country and cause an appreciation of its exchange rate and then to pull their funds out and cause a depreciation of the exchange rate and a financial crisis as well. It depends on whether funding comes from international financial investors.

# 18.4 | Fiscal Policy, Investment, and Economic Growth

By the end of this section, you will be able to:

- Explain crowding out and its effect on physical capital investment
- Explain the relationship between budget deficits and interest rates
- Identify why economic growth is tied to investments in physical capital, human capital, and technology

The underpinnings of economic growth are investments in physical capital, human capital, and technology, all set in an economic environment where firms and individuals can react to the incentives provided by well-functioning markets and flexible prices. Government borrowing can reduce the financial capital available for private firms to invest in physical capital. However, government spending can also encourage certain elements of long-term growth, such as spending on roads or water systems, on education, or on research and development that creates new technology.

## Crowding Out Physical Capital Investment

A larger budget deficit will increase demand for financial capital. If private saving and the trade balance remain the same, then less financial capital will be available for private investment in physical capital. When government borrowing soaks up available financial capital and leaves less for private investment in physical capital, economists call the result crowding out.

To understand the potential impact of crowding out, consider the U.S. economy's situation before the exceptional circumstances of the recession that started in late 2007. In 2005, for example, the budget deficit was roughly 4% of GDP. Private investment by firms in the U.S. economy has hovered in the range of 14% to 18% of GDP in recent decades. However, in any given year, roughly half of U.S. investment in physical capital just replaces machinery and equipment that has worn out or become technologically obsolete. Only about half represents an increase in the total quantity of physical capital in the economy. Investment in new physical capital in any year is about 7% to 9% of GDP. In this situation, even U.S. budget deficits in the range of 4% of GDP can potentially crowd out a substantial share of new investment spending. Conversely, a smaller budget deficit (or an increased budget surplus) increases the pool of financial capital available for private investment.

## Link It Up

Visit this website (http://openstaxcollege.org/l/debtclock) to view the "U.S. Debt Clock."

Figure 18.7 shows the patterns of U.S. budget deficits and private investment since 1980. If greater government deficits lead to less private investment in physical capital, and reduced government deficits or budget surpluses lead to more investment in physical capital, these two lines should move up and down simultaneously. This pattern occurred in the late 1990s and early 2000s. The U.S. federal budget went from a deficit of 2.2% of GDP in 1995 to a budget surplus of 2.4% of GDP in 2000—a swing of 4.6% of GDP. From 1995 to 2000, private investment in physical capital rose from 15% to 18% of GDP—a rise of 3% of GDP. Then, when the U.S. government again started running budget deficits in the early 2000s, less financial capital became available for private investment, and the rate of private investment fell back to about 15% of GDP by 2003.

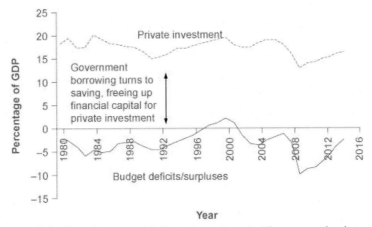

**Figure 18.7 U.S. Budget Deficits/Surpluses and Private Investment**   The connection between private savings and flows of international capital plays a role in budget deficits and surpluses. Consequently, government borrowing and private investment sometimes rise and fall together. For example, the 1990s show a pattern in which reduced government borrowing helped to reduce crowding out so that more funds were available for private investment.

This argument does not claim that a government's budget deficits will exactly shadow its national rate of private investment; after all, we must account for private saving and inflows of foreign financial investment. In the mid-1980s, for example, government budget deficits increased substantially without a corresponding drop off in private investment. In 2009, nonresidential private fixed investment dropped by $300 billion from its previous level of $1,941 billion in 2008, primarily because, during a recession, firms lack both the funds and the incentive to invest. Investment growth between 2009 and 2014 averaged approximately 5.9% to $2,210.5 billion—only slightly above its 2008 level, according to the Bureau of Economic Analysis. During that same period, interest rates dropped from 3.94% to less than a quarter percent as the Federal Reserve took dramatic action to prevent a depression by increasing the money supply through lowering short-term interest rates. The "crowding out" of private investment due to government borrowing to finance expenditures appears to have been suspended during the Great Recession. However, as the economy improves and interest rates rise, government borrowing may potentially create pressure on interest rates.

## The Interest Rate Connection

Assume that government borrowing of substantial amounts will have an effect on the quantity of private investment. How will this affect interest rates in financial markets? In **Figure 18.8**, the original equilibrium ($E_0$) where the demand curve ($D_0$) for financial capital intersects with the supply curve ($S_0$) occurs at an interest rate of 5% and an equilibrium quantity equal to 20% of GDP. However, as the government budget deficit increases, the demand curve for financial capital shifts from $D_0$ to $D_1$. The new equilibrium ($E_1$) occurs at an interest rate of 6% and an equilibrium quantity of 21% of GDP.

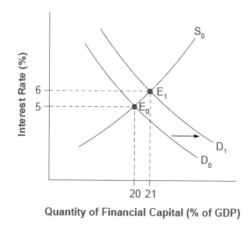

**Figure 18.8 Budget Deficits and Interest Rates**   In the financial market, an increase in government borrowing can shift the demand curve for financial capital to the right from $D_0$ to $D_1$. As the equilibrium interest rate shifts from $E_0$ to $E_1$, the interest rate rises from 5% to 6% in this example. The higher interest rate is one economic mechanism by which government borrowing can crowd out private investment.

A survey of economic studies on the connection between government borrowing and interest rates in the U.S. economy suggests that an increase of 1% in the budget deficit will lead to a rise in interest rates of between 0.5 and 1.0%, other factors held equal. In turn, a higher interest rate tends to discourage firms from making physical capital investments. One reason government budget deficits crowd out private investment, therefore, is the increase in interest rates. There are, however, economic studies that show a limited connection between the two (at least in the United States), but as the budget deficit grows, the dangers of rising interest rates become more real.

At this point, you may wonder about the Federal Reserve. After all, can the Federal Reserve not use expansionary monetary policy to reduce interest rates, or in this case, to prevent interest rates from rising? This useful question emphasizes the importance of considering how fiscal and monetary policies work in relation to each other. Imagine a central bank faced with a government that is running large budget deficits, causing a rise in interest rates and crowding out private investment. If the budget deficits are increasing aggregate demand when the economy is already producing near potential GDP, threatening an inflationary increase in price levels, the central bank may react with a contractionary monetary policy. In this situation, the higher interest rates from the government borrowing would be made even higher by contractionary monetary policy, and the government borrowing might crowd out a great deal of private investment.

Alternatively, if the budget deficits are increasing aggregate demand when the economy is producing substantially less than potential GDP, an inflationary increase in the price level is not much of a danger and the central bank might react with expansionary monetary policy. In this situation, higher interest rates from government borrowing would be largely offset by lower interest rates from expansionary monetary policy, and there would be little crowding out of private investment.

However, even a central bank cannot erase the overall message of the national savings and investment identity. If government borrowing rises, then private investment must fall, or private saving must rise, or the trade deficit must fall. By reacting with contractionary or expansionary monetary policy, the central bank can only help to determine which of these outcomes is likely.

## Public Investment in Physical Capital

Government can invest in physical capital directly: roads and bridges; water supply and sewers; seaports and airports; schools and hospitals; plants that generate electricity, like hydroelectric dams or windmills; telecommunications facilities; and military weapons. In 2014, the U.S. federal government budget for Fiscal Year 2014 shows that the United States spent about $92 billion on transportation, including highways, mass transit, and airports. **Table 18.1** shows the federal government's total outlay for 2014 for major public physical capital investment in the United States. We have omitted physical capital related to the military or to residences where people live from this table, because the focus here is on public investments that have a direct effect on raising output in the private sector.

| Type of Public Physical Capital | Federal Outlays 2014 ($ millions) |
| --- | --- |
| Transportation | $91,915 |
| Community and regional development | $20,670 |
| Natural resources and the environment | $36,171 |
| Education, training, employment, and social services | $90,615 |
| Other | $37,282 |
| Total | $276,653 |

Table 18.1 Grants for Major Physical Capital Investment, 2014

Public physical capital investment of this sort can increase the economy's output and productivity. An economy with reliable roads and electricity will be able to produce more. However, it is hard to quantify how much government investment in physical capital will benefit the economy, because government responds to political as well as economic incentives. When a firm makes an investment in physical capital, it is subject to the discipline of the market: If it does not receive a positive return on investment, the firm may lose money or even go out of business.

In some cases, lawmakers make investments in physical capital as a way of spending money in key politicians' districts. The result may be unnecessary roads or office buildings. Even if a project is useful and necessary, it might be done in a way that is excessively costly, because local contractors who make campaign contributions to politicians appreciate the extra business. Alternatively, governments sometimes do not make the investments they should because a decision to spend on infrastructure does not need to just make economic sense. It must be politically popular as well. Managing public investment cost-effectively can be difficult.

If a government decides to finance an investment in public physical capital with higher taxes or lower government spending in other areas, it need not worry that it is directly crowding out private investment. Indirectly however, higher household taxes could cut down on the level of private savings available and have a similar effect. If a government decides to finance an investment in public physical capital by borrowing, it may end up increasing the quantity of public physical capital at the cost of crowding out investment in private physical capital, which could be more beneficial to the economy.

## Public Investment in Human Capital

In most countries, the government plays a large role in society's investment in human capital through the education system. A highly educated and skilled workforce contributes to a higher rate of economic growth. For the low-income nations of the world, additional investment in human capital seems likely to increase productivity and growth. For the United States, critics have raised tough questions about how much increases in government spending on education will improve the actual level of education.

Among economists, discussions of education reform often begin with some uncomfortable facts. As **Figure 18.9** shows, spending per student for kindergarten through grade 12 (K–12) increased substantially in real dollars through 2010. The U.S. Census Bureau reports that current spending per pupil for elementary and secondary education rose from $5,001 in 1998 to $10,608 in 2012. However, as measured by standardized tests like the SAT, the level of student academic achievement has barely budged in recent decades. On international tests, U.S. students lag behind students from many other countries. (Of course, test scores are an imperfect measure of education for a variety of reasons. It would be difficult, however, to argue that there are not real problems in the U.S. education system and that the tests are just inaccurate.)

**Figure 18.9 Total Spending for Elementary, Secondary, and Vocational Education (1998–2014) in the United States** The graph shows that government spending on education was continually increasing up until 2006 where it leveled off until 2008 when it increased dramatically. Since 2010, spending has steadily decreased. (Source: Office of Management and Budget)

The fact that increased financial resources have not brought greater measurable gains in student performance has led some education experts to question whether the problems may be due to structure, not just to the resources spent.

Other government programs seek to increase human capital either before or after the K–12 education system. Programs for early childhood education, like the federal **Head Start program**, are directed at families where the parents may have limited educational and financial resources. Government also offers substantial support for universities and colleges. For example, in the United States about 60% of students take at least a few college or university classes beyond the high school level. In Germany and Japan, about half of all students take classes beyond the comparable high school level. In the countries of Latin America, only about one student in four takes classes beyond the high school level, and in the nations of sub-Saharan Africa, only about one student in 20.

Not all spending on educational human capital needs to happen through the government: many college students in the United States pay a substantial share of the cost of their education. If low-income countries of the world are going to experience a widespread increase in their education levels for grade-school children, government spending seems likely to play a substantial role. For the U.S. economy, and for other high-income countries, the primary focus at this time is more on how to get a bigger return from existing spending on education and how to improve the performance of the average high school graduate, rather than dramatic increases in education spending.

## How Fiscal Policy Can Improve Technology

Research and development (R&D) efforts are the lifeblood of new technology. According to the National Science Foundation, federal outlays for research, development, and physical plant improvements to various governmental agencies have remained at an average of 8.8% of GDP. About one-fifth of U.S. R&D spending goes to defense and space-oriented research. Although defense-oriented R&D spending may sometimes produce consumer-oriented spinoffs, R&D that is aimed at producing new weapons is less likely to benefit the civilian economy than direct civilian R&D spending.

Fiscal policy can encourage R&D using either direct spending or tax policy. Government could spend more on the R&D that it carries out in government laboratories, as well as expanding federal R&D grants to universities and colleges, nonprofit organizations, and the private sector. By 2014, the federal share of R&D outlays totaled $135.5 billion, or about 4% of the federal government's total budget outlays, according to data from the National Science Foundation. Fiscal policy can also support R&D through tax incentives, which allow firms to reduce their tax bill as they increase spending on research and development.

## Summary of Fiscal Policy, Investment, and Economic Growth

Investment in physical capital, human capital, and new technology is essential for long-term economic growth, as **Table 18.2** summarizes. In a market-oriented economy, private firms will undertake most of the investment in physical capital, and fiscal policy should seek to avoid a long series of outsized budget deficits that might crowd out such investment. We will see the effects of many growth-oriented policies very gradually over time, as students are better educated, we make physical capital investments, and man invents and implements new technologies.

| | Physical Capital | Human Capital | New Technology |
|---|---|---|---|
| Private Sector | New investment in property and equipment | On-the-job training | Research and development |
| Public Sector | Public infrastructure | Public education Job training | Research and development encouraged through private sector incentives and direct spending. |

Table 18.2 Investment Role of Public and Private Sector in a Market Economy

# KEY TERMS

**Head Start program**  a program for early childhood education directed at families with limited educational and financial resources.

**Ricardian equivalence**  the theory that rational private households might shift their saving to offset government saving or borrowing

**twin deficits**  deficits that occur when a country is running both a trade and a budget deficit

# KEY CONCEPTS AND SUMMARY

### 18.1 How Government Borrowing Affects Investment and the Trade Balance

A change in any part of the national saving and investment identity suggests that if the government budget deficit changes, then either private savings, private investment in physical capital, or the trade balance—or some combination of the three—must change as well.

### 18.2 Fiscal Policy and the Trade Balance

The government need not balance its budget every year. However, a sustained pattern of large budget deficits over time risks causing several negative macroeconomic outcomes: a shift to the right in aggregate demand that causes an inflationary increase in the price level; crowding out private investment in physical capital in a way that slows down economic growth; and creating a dependence on inflows of international portfolio investment which can sometimes turn into outflows of foreign financial investment that can be injurious to a macroeconomy.

### 18.3 How Government Borrowing Affects Private Saving

The theory of Ricardian equivalence holds that changes in private saving will offset changes in government borrowing or saving. Thus, greater private saving will offset higher budget deficits, while greater private borrowing will offset larger budget surpluses. If the theory holds true, then changes in government borrowing or saving would have no effect on private investment in physical capital or on the trade balance. However, empirical evidence suggests that the theory holds true only partially.

### 18.4 Fiscal Policy, Investment, and Economic Growth

Economic growth comes from a combination of investment in physical capital, human capital, and technology. Government borrowing can crowd out private sector investment in physical capital, but fiscal policy can also increase investment in publicly owned physical capital, human capital (education), and research and development. Possible methods for improving education and society's investment in human capital include spending more money on teachers and other educational resources, and reorganizing the education system to provide greater incentives for success. Methods for increasing research and development spending to generate new technology include direct government spending on R&D and tax incentives for businesses to conduct additional R&D.

# SELF-CHECK QUESTIONS

**1.**  In a country, private savings equals 600, the government budget surplus equals 200, and the trade surplus equals 100. What is the level of private investment in this economy?

**2.**  Assume an economy has a budget surplus of 1,000, private savings of 4,000, and investment of 5,000.
    a.  Write out a national saving and investment identity for this economy.
    b.  What will be the balance of trade in this economy?
    c.  If the budget surplus changes to a budget deficit of 1000, with private saving and investment unchanged, what is the new balance of trade in this economy?

**3.** In the late 1990s, the U.S. government moved from a budget deficit to a budget surplus and the trade deficit in the U.S. economy grew substantially. Using the national saving and investment identity, what can you say about the direction in which saving and/or investment must have changed in this economy?

**4.** Imagine an economy in which Ricardian equivalence holds. This economy has a budget deficit of 50, a trade deficit of 20, private savings of 130, and investment of 100. If the budget deficit rises to 70, how are the other terms in the national saving and investment identity affected?

**5.** Why have many education experts recently placed an emphasis on altering the incentives that U.S. schools face rather than on increasing their budgets? Without endorsing any of these proposals as especially good or bad, list some of the ways in which incentives for schools might be altered.

**6.** What are some steps the government can take to encourage research and development?

## REVIEW QUESTIONS

**7.** Based on the national saving and investment identity, what are the three ways the macroeconomy might react to greater government budget deficits?

**8.** How would you expect larger budget deficits to affect private sector investment in physical capital? Why?

**9.** Under what conditions will a larger budget deficit cause a trade deficit?

**10.** What is the theory of Ricardian equivalence?

**11.** What does the concept of rationality have to do with Ricardian equivalence?

**12.** What are some of the ways fiscal policy might encourage economic growth?

**13.** What are some fiscal policies for improving a society's human capital?

**14.** What are some fiscal policies for improving the technologies that the economy will have to draw upon in the future?

**15.** Explain how cuts in funding for programs such as Head Start might affect the development of human capital in the United States.

## CRITICAL THINKING QUESTIONS

**16.** Assume there is no discretionary increase in government spending. Explain how an improving economy will affect the budget balance and, in turn, investment and the trade balance.

**17.** Explain how decreased domestic investments that occur due to a budget deficit will affect future economic growth.

**18.** The U.S. government has shut down a number of times in recent history. Explain how a government shutdown will affect the variables in the national investment and savings identity. Could the shutdown affect the government budget deficit?

**19.** Explain how a shift from a government budget deficit to a budget surplus might affect the exchange rate.

**20.** Describe how a plan for reducing the government deficit might affect a college student, a young professional, and a middle-income family.

**21.** Explain whether or not you agree with the premise of the Ricardian equivalence theory that rational people might reason: "Well, a higher budget deficit (surplus) means that I'm just going to owe more (less) taxes in the future to pay off all that government borrowing, so I'll start saving (spending) now." Why or why not?

**22.** Explain why the government might prefer to provide incentives to private firms to do investment or research and development, rather than simply doing the spending itself?

**23.** Under what condition would crowding out not inhibit long-run economic growth? Under what condition would crowding out impede long-run economic growth?

**24.** What must take place for the government to run deficits without any crowding out?

## PROBLEMS

**25.** Sketch a diagram of how a budget deficit causes a trade deficit. (*Hint*: Begin with what will happen to the exchange rate when foreigners demand more U.S. government debt.)

**26.** Sketch a diagram of how sustained budget deficits cause low economic growth.

**27.** Assume that the newly independent government of Tanzania employed you in 1964. Now free from British rule, the Tanzanian parliament has decided that it will spend 10 million shillings on schools, roads, and healthcare for the year. You estimate that the net taxes for the year are eight million shillings. The government will finance the difference by selling 10-year government bonds at 12% interest per year. Parliament must add the interest on outstanding bonds to government expenditure each year. Assume that Parliament places additional taxes to finance this increase in government expenditure so the gap between government spending is always two million. If the school, road, and healthcare budget are unchanged, compute the value of the accumulated debt in 10 years.

**28.** Illustrate the concept of Ricardian equivalence using the demand and supply of financial capital graph.

**29.** During the most recent recession, some economists argued that the change in the interest rates that comes about due to deficit spending implied in the demand and supply of financial capital graph would not occur. A simple reason was that the government was stepping in to invest when private firms were not. Using a graph, explain how the use by government in investment offsets the deficit demand.

# 19 | Macroeconomic Policy Around the World

**Figure 19.1 Looking for Work** Job fairs and job centers are often available to help match people to jobs. This fair took place in the U.S. (Hawaii), a high-income country with policies to keep unemployment levels in check. Unemployment is an issue that has different causes in different countries, and is especially severe in the low- and middle-income economies around the world. (Credit: modification of work by Daniel Ramirez/Flickr Creative Commons)

## Bring it Home

### Youth Unemployment: Three Cases

Chad Harding, a young man from Cape Town, South Africa, completed school having done well on his exams. He had high hopes for the future. Like many young South Africans, however, he had difficulty finding a job. "I was just stuck at home waiting, waiting for something to come up," he said in a BBC interview in 2012. In South Africa 54.6% of young females and 47.2% of males are unemployed. In fact, the problem is not limited to South Africa. Seventy-three million of the world's youth aged 15 to 24 are currently unemployed, according to the International Labour Organization.

According to the *Wall Street Journal,* in India, 60% of the labor force is self-employed, largely because of labor market regulation. A recent World Bank World Development Report says that India's unemployed youth accounted for 9.9% of the youth work force in 2010. In Spain (a far richer country) in the same year, the female/male youth unemployment rate was 39.8% and 43.2% respectively.

Youth unemployment is a significant issue in many parts of the world. However, despite the apparent similarities in rates between South Africa, Spain, and India, macroeconomic policy solutions to decrease youth unemployment in these three countries are different. This chapter will look at macroeconomic policies around the world, specifically those related to reducing unemployment, promoting economic growth, and stable inflation and exchange rates. Then we will look again at the three cases of South Africa, Spain, and India.

# Introduction to Macroeconomic Policy around the World

In this chapter, you will learn about:

- The Diversity of Countries and Economies across the World

- Improving Countries' Standards of Living

- Causes of Unemployment around the World

- Causes of Inflation in Various Countries and Regions

- Balance of Trade Concerns

There are extraordinary differences in the composition and performance of economies across the world. What explains these differences? Are countries motivated by similar goals when it comes to macroeconomic policy? Can we apply the same macroeconomic framework that we developed in this text to understand the performance of these countries? Let's take each of these questions in turn.

*Explaining differences*: Recall from **Unemployment** that we explained the difference in composition and performance of economies by appealing to an aggregate production function. We argued that differences in productivity explain the diversity of average incomes across the world, which in turn were affected by inputs such as capital deepening, human capital, and "technology." Every economy has its own distinctive economic characteristics, institutions, history, and political realities, which imply that access to these "ingredients" will vary by country and so will economic performance.

For example, South Korea invested heavily in education and technology to increase agricultural productivity in the early 1950s. Some of this investment came from its historical relationship with the United States. As a result of these and many other institutions, its economy has managed to converge to the levels of income in leading economies like Japan and the United States.

*Similar goals and frameworks*: Many economies that have performed well in terms of per capita income have—for better or worse—been motivated by a similar goal: to maintain the quality of life of their citizens. Quality of life is a broad term, but as you can imagine it includes but is not limited to such things as low level of unemployment, price stability (low levels of inflation), and the ability to trade. These seem to be universal macroeconomic goals as we discussed in **The Macroeconomic Perspective**. No country would argue against them. To study macroeconomic policy around the world, we begin by comparing standards of living. In keeping with these goals, we also look at indicators such as unemployment, inflation, and the balance of trade policies across countries. Remember that every country has had a diverse set of experiences; therefore although our goals may be similar, each country may well require macroeconomic policies tailored to its circumstances.

# Link It Up

For more reading on the topic of youth unemployment, visit this website (http://openstaxcollege.org/l/genjobless) to read "Generation Jobless" in the *Economist*.

# 19.1 | The Diversity of Countries and Economies across the World

By the end of this section, you will be able to:
- Analyze GDP per capita as a measure of the diversity of international standards of living
- Identify what classifies a country as low-income, middle-income, or high-income
- Explain how geography, demographics, industry structure, and economic institutions influence standards of living

The national economies that comprise the global economy are remarkably diverse. Let us use one key indicator of the standard of living, GDP per capita, to quantify this diversity. You will quickly see that quantifying this diversity is fraught with challenges and limitations. As we explained in **The Macroeconomic Perspective**, we must consider using purchasing power parity or "international dollars" to convert average incomes into comparable units. Purchasing power parity, as we formally defined in **Exchange Rates and International Capital Flows**, takes into account that prices of the same good are different across countries.

**The Macroeconomic Perspective** explained how to measure GDP, the challenges of using GDP to compare standards of living, and the difficulty of confusing economic size with distribution. In China's case, for example, China ranks as the second largest global economy, second to only the United States, with Japan ranking third. However, when we take China's GDP of $9.2 trillion and divide it by its population of 1.4 billion, then the per capita GDP is only $6,900, which is significantly lower than that of Japan, at $38,500, and that of the United States, at $52,800. Measurement issues aside, it's worth repeating that the goal, then, is to not only increase GDP, but to strive toward increased GDP per capita to increase overall living standards for individuals. As we have learned from **Economic Growth**, countries can achieve this at the national level by designing policies that increase worker productivity, deepen capital, and advance technology.

GDP per capita also allows us to rank countries into high-, middle-, or low-income groups. Low-income countries are those with $1,025 per capita GDP per year; middle-income countries have a per capita GDP between $1,025 and $12,475; while high-income countries have over $12,475 per year per capita income. As **Table 19.1** and **Figure 19.2** show, high-income countries earn 68% of world income, but represent just 12% of the global population. Low-income countries earn 1% of total world income, but represent 18.5% of global population.

| Ranking based on GDP/capita | GDP (in billions) | % of Global GDP | Population | % of Global Population |
|---|---|---|---|---|
| Low income ($1,025 or less) | $612.7 | 0.8% | 848,700,000 | 11.8% |
| Middle income ($1,025 - $12,475) | $23,930 | 31.7% | 4,970,000,000 | 69.4% |

**Table 19.1 World Income versus Global Population**   (Source:http://databank.worldbank.org/data/views/reports/tableview.aspx?isshared=true&ispopular=series&pid=20)

| Ranking based on GDP/capita | GDP (in billions) | % of Global GDP | Population | % of Global Population |
|---|---|---|---|---|
| High income (more than $12,475) | $51,090,000,000 | 67.5% | 1,306,000,000 | 18.8% |
| *World Total income* | *$75,592,941* | | *7,162,119,434* | |

Table 19.1 World Income versus Global Population    (Source:http://databank.worldbank.org/data/views/reports/tableview.aspx?isshared=true&ispopular=series&pid=20)

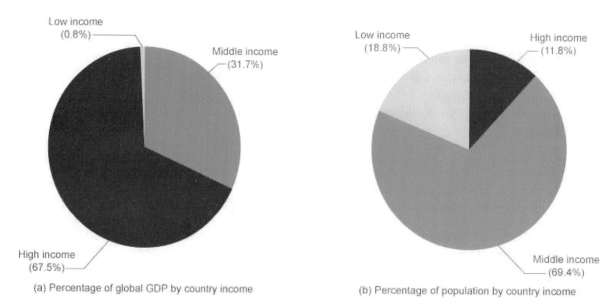

(a) Percentage of global GDP by country income     (b) Percentage of population by country income

**Figure 19.2 Percent of Global GDP and Percent of Population** The pie charts show the GDP (from 2011) for countries categorized into low, middle, or high income. Low-income are those earning less than $1,025 (less than 1% of global income). They represent 18.5% of the world population. Middle-income countries are those with per capita income of $1,025–$12,475 (31.1% of global income). They represent 69.5% of world population. High-income countries have 68.3% of global income and 12% of the world's population. (Source: http://databank.worldbank.org/data/views/reports/tableview.aspx?isshared=true&ispopular=series&pid=20)

An overview of the regional averages of GDP per person for developing countries, measured in comparable international dollars as well as population in 2008 (**Figure 19.3**), shows that the differences across these regions are stark. As **Table 19.2** shows, nominal GDP per capita in 2012 for the 581.4 million people living in Latin America and the Caribbean region was $9,190, which far exceeds that of South Asia and sub-Saharan Africa. In turn, people in the world's high-income nations, such as those who live in the European Union nations or North America, have a per capita GDP three to four times that of the people of Latin America. To put things in perspective, North America and the European Union have slightly more than 9% of the world's population, but they produce and consume close to 70% of the world's GDP.

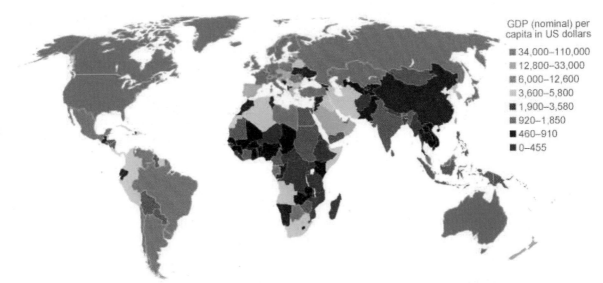

**Figure 19.3 GDP Per Capita in U.S. Dollars (2008)** There is a clear imbalance in the GDP across the world. North America, Australia, and Western Europe have the highest GDPs while large areas of the world have dramatically lower GDPs. Russia and other former Soviet nations, as well as Argentina, Botswana, Brazil, Chile, Gabon, and Mexico, have a mid-tier per capita GDP of about $6,000-12,600. China, though a major economic engine for the world, ranges from $1,900-3,580. Egypt, India, Indonesia, Mongolia, and Sudan are lower at about $920-1,850. (Credit: modification of work by Bsrboy/Wikimedia Commons)

|  | **Population (in millions)** | **GDP Per Capita** |
|---|---|---|
| East Asia and Pacific | 2,006 | $5,536 |
| South Asia | 1,671 | $1,482 |
| Sub-Saharan Africa | 936.1 | $1,657 |
| Latin America and Caribbean | 588 | $9,536 |
| Middle East and North Africa | 345.4 | $3,456 |
| Europe and Central Asia | 272.2 | $7,118 |

**Table 19.2 Regional Comparisons of Nominal GDP per Capita and Population in 2013** (Source: http://databank.worldbank.org/data/home.aspx)

Such comparisons between regions are admittedly rough. After all, per capita GDP cannot fully capture the quality of life. Many other factors have a large impact on the standard of living, like health, education, human rights, crime and personal safety, and environmental quality. These measures also reveal very wide differences in the standard of living across the regions of the world. Much of this is correlated with per capita income, but there are exceptions. For example, life expectancy at birth in many low-income regions approximates those who are more affluent. The data also illustrate that nobody can claim to have perfect standards of living. For instance, despite very high income levels, there is still undernourishment in Europe and North America.

## Link It Up 🔗

Economists know that there are many factors that contribute to your standard of living. People in high-income countries may have very little time due to heavy workloads and may feel disconnected from their community. Lower-income countries may be more community centered, but have little in the way of material wealth. It is hard to measure these characteristics of standard of living. The Organization for Economic Co-Operation and Development has developed the "OECD Better Life Index." Visit this website (http://openstaxcollege.org/l/standofliving) to see how countries measure up to your expected standard of living.

The differences in economic statistics and other measures of well-being, substantial though they are, do not fully capture the reasons for the enormous differences between countries. Aside from the neoclassical determinants of growth, four additional determinants are significant in a wide range of statistical studies and are worth mentioning: geography, demography, industrial structure, and institutions.

### Geographic and Demographic Differences

Countries have geographic differences: some have extensive coastlines, some are landlocked. Some have large rivers that have been a path of commerce for centuries, or mountains that have been a barrier to trade. Some have deserts, some have rain forests. These differences create different positive and negative opportunities for commerce, health, and the environment.

Countries also have considerable differences in the age distribution of the population. Many high-income nations are approaching a situation by 2020 or so in which the elderly will form a much larger share of the population. Most low-income countries still have a higher proportion of youth and young adults, but by about 2050, the elderly populations in these low-income countries are expected to boom as well. These demographic changes will have considerable impact on the standard of living of the young and the old.

### Differences in Industry Structure and Economic Institutions

Countries have differences in industry structure. In the world's high-income economies, only about 2% of GDP comes from agriculture; the average for the rest of the world is 12%. Countries have strong differences in degree of urbanization.

Countries also have strong differences in economic institutions: some nations have economies that are extremely market-oriented, while other nations have command economies. Some nations are open to international trade, while others use tariffs and import quotas to limit the impact of trade. Some nations are torn by long-standing armed conflicts; other nations are largely at peace. There are also differences in political, religious, and social institutions.

No nation intentionally aims for a low standard of living, high rates of unemployment and inflation, or an unsustainable trade imbalance. However, nations will differ in their priorities and in the situations in which they find themselves, and so their policy choices can reasonably vary, too. The next modules will discuss how nations around the world, from high income to low income, approach the four macroeconomic goals of economic growth, low unemployment, low inflation, and a sustainable balance of trade.

# 19.2 | Improving Countries' Standards of Living

By the end of this section, you will be able to:
- Analyze the growth policies of low-income countries seeking to improve standards of living
- Analyze the growth policies of middle-income countries, particularly the East Asian Tigers with their focus on technology and market-oriented incentives
- Analyze the struggles facing economically-challenged countries wishing to enact growth policies
- Evaluate the success of sending aid to low-income countries

Jobs are created in economies that grow. What is the origin of economic growth? According to most economists who believe in the **growth consensus**, economic growth (as we discussed in **Economic Growth**) is built on a foundation of productivity improvements. In turn, productivity increases are the result of greater human and physical capital and technology, all interacting in a market-driven economy. In the pursuit of economic growth, however, some countries and regions start from different levels, as the differences in per capita GDP presented earlier in **Table 19.2** illustrate.

## Growth Policies for the High-Income Countries

For the high-income countries, the challenge of economic growth is to push continually for a more educated workforce that can create, invest in, and apply new technologies. In effect, the goal of their growth-oriented public policy is to shift their aggregate supply curves to the right (refer to **The Aggregate Demand/Aggregate Supply Model**). The main public policies targeted at achieving this goal are fiscal policies focused on investment, including investment in human capital, in technology, and in physical plant and equipment. These countries also recognize that economic growth works best in a stable and market-oriented economic climate. For this reason, they use monetary policy to keep inflation low and stable, and to minimize the risk of exchange rate fluctuations, while also encouraging domestic and international competition.

However, early in the second decade of the 2000s, many high-income countries found themselves more focused on the short term than on the long term. The United States, Western Europe, and Japan all experienced a combination of financial crisis and deep recession, and the after-effects of the recession—like high unemployment rates—seemed likely to linger for several years. Most of these governments took aggressive, and in some cases controversial, steps to jump-start their economies by running very large budget deficits as part of expansionary fiscal policy. These countries must adopt a course that combines lower government spending and higher taxes.

Similarly, many central banks ran highly expansionary monetary policies, with both near-zero interest rates and unconventional loans and investments. For example, in 2012, Shinzo Abe (see **Figure 19.4**), then newly-elected Prime Minister of Japan, unveiled a plan to pull his country out of its two-decade-long slump in economic growth. It included both fiscal stimulus and an increase in the money supply. The plan was quite successful in the short run. However, according to the *Economist*, with public debt "expected to approach 240% of GDP," (as of 2012 it was 226% of GDP) printing money and public-works spending were only short-term solutions.

**Figure 19.4 Japan's Prime Minister, Shinzo Abe** Japan's Prime Minister used fiscal and monetary policies to stimulate his country's economy, which has worked in only the short run. (Credit: modification of work by Chatham House/Flickr Creative Commons)

As we discussed in other chapters, macroeconomics needs to have both a short-run and a long-run focus. The challenge for many of the developed countries in the next few years will be to exit from the short-term policies that they used to correct the 2008–2009 recession. Since the return to growth has been sluggish, it has been politically challenging for these governments to refocus their efforts on new technology, education, and physical capital investment.

## Growth Policies for the Middle-Income Economies

The world's great economic success stories in the last few decades began in the 1970s with that group of nations sometimes known as the **East Asian Tigers**: South Korea, Thailand, Malaysia, Indonesia, and Singapore. The list sometimes includes Hong Kong and Taiwan, although often under international law they are treated as part of China, rather than as separate countries. The economic growth of the Tigers has been phenomenal, typically averaging 5.5% real per capita growth for several decades. In the 1980s, other countries began to show signs of convergence. China began growing rapidly, often at annual rates of 8% to 10% per year. India began growing rapidly, first at rates of about 5% per year in the 1990s, but then higher still in the first decade of the 2000s.

We know the underlying causes of these rapid growth rates:

- China and the East Asian Tigers, in particular, have been among the highest savers in the world, often saving one-third or more of GDP as compared to the roughly one-fifth of GDP, which would be a more typical saving rate in Latin America and Africa. These countries harnessed higher savings for domestic investment to build physical capital.

- These countries had policies that supported heavy investments in human capital, first building up primary-level education and then expanding secondary-level education. Many focused on encouraging math and science education, which is useful in engineering and business.

- Governments made a concerted effort to seek out applicable technology, by sending students and government commissions abroad to look at the most efficient industrial operations elsewhere. They also created policies to support innovative companies that wished to build production facilities to take advantage of the abundant and inexpensive human capital.

- China and India in particular also allowed far greater freedom for market forces, both within their own domestic economies and also in encouraging their firms to participate in world markets.

This combination of technology, human capital, and physical capital, combined with the incentives of a market-oriented economic context, proved an extremely powerful stimulant to growth. Challenges that these middle-income countries faced are a legacy of government economic controls that for political reasons can be dismantled only slowly over time. In many of them, the government heavily regulates the banking and financial sector. Governments have also sometimes selected certain industries to receive low-interest loans or government subsidies. These economies have found that an increased dose of market-oriented incentives for firms and workers has been a critical ingredient in the recipe for faster growth. To learn more about measuring economic growth, read the following Clear It Up feature.

## What is the rule of 72?

It is worth pausing a moment to marvel at the East Asian Tigers' growth rates. If per capita GDP grows at, say, 6% per year, then you can apply the formula for compound growth rates—that is $(1 + 0.06)^{30}$—meaning a nation's level of per capita GDP will rise by a multiple of almost six over 30 years. Another strategy is to apply the rule of 72. The rule of 72 is an approximation to figure out doubling time. We divide the rule number, 72, by the annual growth rate to obtain the approximate number of years it will take for income to double. If we have a 6% growth rate, it will take 72/6, or 12 years, for incomes to double. Using this rule here suggests that a Tiger that grows at 6% will double its GDP every 12 years. In contrast, a technological leader, chugging along with per capita growth rates of about 2% per year, would double its income in 36 years.

## Growth Policies for Economically-Challenged Countries

Many economically-challenged or low-income countries are geographically located in Sub-Saharan Africa. Other pockets of low income are in the former Soviet Bloc, and in parts of Central America and the Caribbean.

There are macroeconomic policies and prescriptions that might alleviate the extreme poverty and low standard of living. However, many of these countries lack the economic and legal stability, along with market-oriented institutions, needed to provide a fertile climate for domestic economic growth and to attract foreign investment. Thus, macroeconomic policies for low income economies are vastly different from those of the high income economies. The World Bank has made it a priority to combat poverty and raise overall income levels through 2030. One of the key obstacles to achieving this is the political instability that seems to be a common feature of low-income countries.

**Figure 19.5** shows the ten lowest income countries as ranked by The World Bank in 2013. These countries share some common traits, the most significant of which is the recent failures of their governments to provide a legal framework for economic growth. Ethiopia and Eritrea recently ended a long-standing war in 2000. Civil and ethnic wars have plagued countries such as Burundi and Liberia. Command economies, corruption, as well as political factionalism and infighting are commonly adopted elements in these low-income countries. The Democratic Republic of the Congo (often referred to as "Congo") is a resource-wealthy country that has not been able to increase its subsistence standard of living due to the political environment.

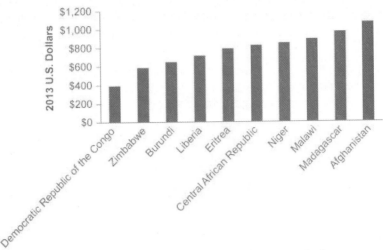

**Figure 19.5 The Ten Lowest Income Countries** This bar chart that shows ten low-income countries, which include, from lowest income to highest: Democratic Republic of the Congo, Zimbabwe, Burundi, Liberia, Eritrea, Central African Republic, Niger, Madagascar, and Afghanistan. (Source: http://databank.worldbank.org/data/views/reports/map.aspx#)

Low-income countries are at a disadvantage because any incomes that people receive are spent immediately on necessities such as food. People in these countries live on less than $1,035 per year, which is less than $100 per month. Lack of saving means a lack of capital accumulation and a lack of loanable funds for investment in physical and human capital. Recent research by two MIT economists, Abhijit Bannerjee and Esther Duflo, has confirmed that the households in these economies are trapped in low incomes because they cannot muster enough investment to push themselves out of poverty.

For example, the average citizen of Burundi, the lowest-income country, subsists on $150 per year (adjusted to 2005 dollars). According to Central Intelligence Agency data in its CIA Factbook, as of 2013, 90% of Burundi's population is agrarian, with coffee and tea as the main income producing crop. Only one in two children attends school and, as **Figure 19.6** shows, many are not in schools comparable to what occurs in developed countries. The CIA Factbook also estimates that 15% of Burundi's population suffers from HIV/AIDS. Political instability has made it difficult for Burundi to make significant headway toward growth, as verified by the electrification of only 2% of households and 42% of its national income coming from foreign aid.

**Figure 19.6 Lack of Funds for Investing in Human Capital** In low-income countries, people often spend all income on necessities for living and cannot accumulate or investe in physical or human capital. The students in this photograph learn in an outside "classroom" void of not only technology, but even chairs and desks. (Credit: Rafaela Printes/Flickr Creative Commons)

## Link It Up

The World Factbook website (http://openstaxcollege.org/l/worldfactbook) is loaded with maps, flags, and other information about countries across the globe.

Other low-income countries share similar stories. These countries have found it difficult to generate investments for themselves or to find foreign investors willing to put up the money for more than the basic needs. Foreign aid and external investment comprise significant portions of the income in these economies, but are not sufficient to allow for the capital accumulation necessary to invest in physical and human capital. However, is foreign aid always a contributor to economic growth? It can be a controversial issue, as the next Clear it Up feature points out.

## Clear It Up

### Does foreign aid to low-income countries work?

According to the Organization of Economic Cooperation and Development (OECD), about $134 billion per year in foreign aid flows from the high-income countries of the world to the low-income ones. Relative to the size of their populations or economies, this is not a large amount for either donors or recipients. For low-income countries, aid averages about 1.3 percent of their GDP. However, even this relatively small amount has been highly controversial.

Supporters of additional foreign aid point to the extraordinary human suffering in the world's low-and middle-income countries. They see opportunities all across Africa, Asia, and Latin America to set up health clinics and schools. They want to help with the task of building economic infrastructure: clean water, plumbing, electricity, and roads. Supporters of this aid include formal state-sponsored institutions like the United Kingdom's Department for International Development (DFID) or independent non-governmental organizations (NGOs) like CARE International that also receive donor government funds. For example, because of an outbreak of meningitis in Ethiopia in 2010, DFID channeled significant funds to the Ethiopian Ministry of Health to train rural health care workers and also for vaccines. These monies helped the Ministry offset shortfalls in their budget.

Opponents of increased aid do not quarrel with the goal of reducing human suffering, but they suggest that foreign aid has often proved a poor tool for advancing that goal. For example, according to an article in the *Attaché Journal of International Affairs*, the Canadian foreign aid organization (CIDA) provided $100 million to Tanzania to grow wheat. The project did produce wheat, but nomadic pastoralists and other villagers who had lived on the land were driven off 100,000 acres of land to make way for the project. The damage in terms of human rights and lost livelihoods was significant. Villagers were beaten and killed because some refused to leave the land. At times, the unintended collateral damage from foreign aid can be significant.

William Easterly, professor of economics at New York University and author of *The White Man's Burden*, argues that countries often receive aid for political reasons and ends up doing more harm than good. If a country's government creates a reasonably stable and market-oriented macroeconomic climate, then foreign investors will be likely to provide funds for many profitable activities. For example, according to *The New York Times*, Facebook is partnering with multiple organizations in a project called Internet.org to provide access in remote and low-income areas of the world, and Google began its own initiative called Project Loon.

Facebook's first forays into providing internet access via mobile phones began in stable, market-oriented countries like India, Brazil, Indonesia, Turkey, and the Philippines.

Policymakers are now wiser about foreign aid limitations than they were a few decades ago. In targeted and specific cases, especially if foreign aid is channeled to long-term investment projects, foreign aid can have a modest role to play in reducing the extreme levels of deprivation that hundreds of millions of people around the world experience.

# Link It Up

Watch this video (http://openstaxcollege.org/l/foodafrica) on the complexities of providing economic aid in Africa.

# 19.3 | Causes of Unemployment around the World

By the end of this section, you will be able to:
- Explain the nature and causes of unemployment
- Analyze the natural rate of unemployment and the factors that affect it
- Identify how undeveloped labor markets can result in the same hardships as unemployment

We can categorize the causes of unemployment in the world's high-income countries in two ways: either cyclical unemployment caused by the economy when in a recession, or the natural rate of unemployment caused by factors in labor markets, such as government regulations regarding hiring and starting businesses.

## Unemployment from a Recession

For unemployment caused by a recession, the Keynesian economic model points out that both monetary and fiscal policy tools are available. The monetary policy prescription for dealing with recession is straightforward: run an expansionary monetary policy to increase the quantity of money and loans, drive down interest rates, and increase aggregate demand. In a recession, there is usually relatively little danger of inflation taking off, and so even a central bank, with fighting inflation as its top priority, can usually justify some reduction in interest rates.

With regard to fiscal policy, the automatic stabilizers that we discussed in Government Budgets and Fiscal Policy should be allowed to work, even if this means larger budget deficits in times of recession. There is less agreement over whether, in addition to automatic stabilizers, governments in a recession should try to adopt discretionary fiscal policy of additional tax cuts or spending increases. In the case of the Great Recession, the case for this kind of extra-aggressive expansionary fiscal policy is stronger, but for a smaller recession, given the time lags of implementing fiscal policy, countries should use discretionary fiscal policy with caution.

However, the aftermath of the Recession emphasizes that expansionary fiscal and monetary policies do not turn off a recession like flipping a switch turns off a lamp. Even after a recession is officially over, and positive growth has returned, it can take some months—or even a couple of years—before private-sector firms believe the economic climate is healthy enough that they can expand their workforce.

## The Natural Rate of Unemployment

Unemployment rates in European nations have typically been higher than in the United States. In 2006, before the start of the Great Recession, the U.S. unemployment rate was 4.6%, compared with 9% in France, 10.4% in Germany, and 7.1% in Sweden. We can attribute the pattern of generally higher unemployment rates in Europe, which dates back to the 1970s, to the fact that European economies have a higher natural rate of unemployment because they have a greater number of rules and restrictions that discourage firms from hiring and unemployed workers from taking jobs.

Addressing the natural rate of unemployment is straightforward in theory but difficult in practice. Government can play a useful role in providing unemployment and welfare payments, for example, by passing rules about where and when businesses can operate, and assuring that the workplace is safe. However, these well-intentioned laws can, in some cases, become so intrusive that businesses decide to place limits on their hiring.

For example, a law that imposes large costs on a business that tries to fire or lay off workers will mean that businesses try to avoid hiring in the first place, as is the case in France. According to *Business Week*, "France has 2.4 times as many companies with 49 employees as with 50 ... according to the French labor code, once a company has at least 50 employees inside France, management must create three worker councils, introduce profit sharing, and submit restructuring plans to the councils if the company decides to fire workers for economic reasons." This labor law essentially limits employment (or raises the natural rate of unemployment).

## Undeveloped Labor Markets

Low-income and middle-income countries face employment issues that go beyond unemployment as it is understood in the high-income economies. A substantial number of workers in these economies provide many of their own needs by farming, fishing, or hunting. They barter and trade with others and may take a succession of short-term or one-day jobs, sometimes receiving pay with food or shelter, sometimes with money. They are not "unemployed" in the sense that we use the term in the United States and Europe, but neither are they employed in a regular wage-paying job.

The starting point of economic activity, as we discussed in **Welcome to Economics!**, is the division of labor, in which workers specialize in certain tasks and trade the fruits of their labor with others. Workers who are not connected to a labor market are often unable to specialize very much. Because these workers are not "officially" employed, they are often not eligible for social benefits like unemployment insurance or old-age payments—if such payments are even available in their country. Helping these workers to become more connected to the labor market and the economy is an important policy goal. Recent research by development economists suggests that one of the key factors in raising people in low-income countries out of the worst kind of poverty is whether they can make a connection to a somewhat regular wage-paying job.

# 19.4 | Causes of Inflation in Various Countries and Regions

By the end of this section, you will be able to:
- Identify the causes and effects of inflation in various economic markets
- Explain the significance of a converging economy

Policymakers of the high-income economies appear to have learned some lessons about fighting inflation. First, whatever happens with aggregate supply and aggregate demand in the short run, countries can use monetary policy to prevent inflation from becoming entrenched in the economy in the medium and long term. Second, there is no long-run gain to letting inflation become established. In fact, allowing inflation to become lasting and persistent poses undesirable risks and tradeoffs. When inflation is high, businesses and individuals need to spend time and effort worrying about protecting themselves against inflation, rather than seeking better ways to serve customers. In short, the high-income economies appear to have both a political consensus to hold inflation low and the economic tools to do so.

In a number of middle- and low-income economies around the world, inflation is far from a solved problem. In the early 2000s, Turkey experienced inflation of more than 50% per year for several years. Belarus had inflation of about 100% per year from 2000 to 2001. From 2008 to 2010, Venezuela and Myanmar had inflation rates of 20% to 30%

per year. Indonesia, Iran, Nigeria, the Russian Federation, and Ukraine all had double-digit inflation for most of the years from 2000 to 2010. Zimbabwe had hyperinflation, with inflation rates that went from more than 100% per year in the mid-2000s to a rate of several million percent in 2008.

In these countries, the problem of very high inflation generally arises from huge budget deficits, which the government finances by printing its domestic currency. This is a case of "too much money chasing too few goods." In the case of Zimbabwe, the government covered its widening deficits by printing ever higher currency notes, including a $100 trillion bill. By late 2008, the money was nearly worthless, which led Zimbabwe to adopt the U.S. dollar, immediately halting their hyperinflation. In some countries, the central bank makes loans to politically favored firms, essentially printing money to do so, and this too leads to higher inflation.

A number of countries have managed to sustain solid levels of economic growth for sustained periods of time with inflation levels that would sound high by recent U.S. standards, like 10% to 30% per year. In such economies, the governments index most contracts, wage levels, and interest rates to inflation. Indexing wage contracts and interest rates means that they will increase when inflation increases to retain purchasing power. When wages do not rise as price levels rise, this leads to a decline in the real wage rate and a decrease in the standard of living. Likewise, interest rates that are not indexed mean that money lenders will receive payment in devalued currency and will also lose purchasing power on monies that they lent. It is clearly possible—and perhaps sometimes necessary—for a **converging economy** (the economy of a country that demonstrates the ability to catch up to the technology leaders) to live with a degree of uncertainty over inflation that would be politically unacceptable in the high-income economies.

# 19.5 | Balance of Trade Concerns

By the end of this section, you will be able to:

- Explain the meaning of trade balance and its implications for the foreign exchange market
- Analyze concerns over international trade in goods and services and international flows of capital
- Identify and evaluate market-oriented economic reforms

In the 1950s and 1960s, and even into the 1970s, low- and middle-income countries often viewed openness to global flows of goods, services, and financial capital in a negative light. These countries feared that foreign trade would mean both economic losses as high-income trading partners "exploited" their economy and they lost domestic political control to powerful business interests and multinational corporations.

These negative feelings about international trade have evolved. After all, the great economic success stories of recent years like Japan, the East Asian Tiger economies, China, and India, all took advantage of opportunities to sell in global markets. European economies thrive with high levels of trade. In the North American Free Trade Agreement (NAFTA), the United States, Canada, and Mexico pledged themselves to reduce trade barriers. Many countries have clearly learned that reducing barriers to trade is at least potentially beneficial to the economy. Many smaller world economies have learned an even tougher lesson: if they do not participate actively in world trade, they are unlikely to join the success stories among the converging economies. There are no examples in world history of small economies that remained apart from the global economy but still attained a high standard of living.

Although almost every country now claims that its goal is to participate in global trade, the possible negative consequences have remained highly controversial. It is useful to divide these possible negative consequences into issues involving trade of goods and services and issues involving international capital flows. These issues are related, but not the same. An economy may have a high level of trade in goods and services relative to GDP, but if exports and imports are balanced, the net flow of foreign investment in and out of the economy will be zero. Conversely, an economy may have only a moderate level of trade relative to GDP, but find that it has a substantial current account trade imbalance. Thus, it is useful to consider the concerns over international trade of goods and services and international flows of financial capital separately.

## Concerns over International Trade in Goods and Services

There is a long list of worries about foreign trade in goods and services: fear of job loss, environmental dangers, unfair labor practices, and many other concerns. We discuss these arguments at some length in the chapter on **The International Trade and Capital Flows**.

Of all of the arguments for limitations on trade, perhaps the most controversial one among economists is the infant industry argument; that is, subsidizing or protecting new industries for a time until they become established. (**Globalization and Protectionism** explains this concept in more detail.) Countries have used such policies with some success at certain points in time, but in the world as a whole, support for key industries is far more often directed at long-established industries with substantial political power that are suffering losses and laying off workers, rather than potentially vibrant new industries that are not yet established. If government intends to favor certain industries, it needs to do so in a way that is temporary and that orients them toward a future of market competition, rather than a future of unending government subsidies and trade protection.

## Concerns over International Flows of Capital

Recall from **The Macroeconomic Perspective** that a trade deficit exists when a nation's imports exceed its exports. In order for a trade deficit to take place, foreign countries must provide loans or investments, which they are willing to do because they expect eventual repayment (that the deficit will become a surplus). A trade surplus, you may remember, exists when a nation's exports exceed its imports. Thus, in order for a trade deficit to switch to a trade surplus, a nation's exports must rise and its imports must fall. Sometimes this happens when the currency decreases in value. For example, if the U.S. had a trade deficit and the dollar depreciated, imports would become more expensive. This would, in turn, benefit the foreign countries that provided the loans or investments.

The expected pattern of trade imbalances in the world economy has been that high-income economies will run trade surpluses, which means they will experience a net outflow of capital to foreign destinations or export more than they import, while low- and middle-income economies will run trade deficits, which means that they will experience a net inflow of foreign capital.

This international investing pattern can benefit all sides. Investors in the high-income countries benefit because they can receive high returns on their investments, and also because they can diversify their investments so that they are at less risk of a downturn in their own domestic economy. The low-income economies that receive an inflow of capital presumably have potential for rapid catch-up economic growth, and they can use the international financial capital inflow to help spur their physical capital investment. In addition, financial capital inflows often come with management abilities, technological expertise, and training.

However, for the last couple of decades, this cheerful scenario has faced two "dark clouds." The first cloud is the very large trade or current account deficits in the U.S. economy. (See **The International Trade and Capital Flows**.) Instead of offering net financial investment abroad, the U.S. economy is soaking up savings from all over the world. These substantial U.S. trade deficits may not be sustainable according to Sebastian Edwards writing for the National Bureau of Economic Research. While trade deficits on their own are not bad, the question is whether governments will reduce them gradually or hastily. In the gradual scenario, U.S. exports could grow more rapidly than imports over a period of years, aided U.S. dollar depreciation. An unintended consequence of the slow growth since the Great Recession has been a decline in the U.S. current account deficit's from 6% pre-recession to 3% most recently.

The other option is that the government could reduce the U.S. trade deficit in a rush. Here is one scenario: if foreign investors became less willing to hold U.S. dollar assets, the dollar exchange rate could weaken. As speculators see this process happening, they might rush to unload their dollar assets, which would drive the dollar down still further.

A lower U.S. dollar would stimulate aggregate demand by making exports cheaper and imports more expensive. It would mean higher prices for imported inputs throughout the economy, shifting the short-term aggregate supply curve to the left. The result could be a burst of inflation and, if the Federal Reserve were to run a tight monetary policy to reduce the inflation, it could also lead to recession. People sometimes talk as if the U.S. economy, with its great size, is invulnerable to this sort of pressure from international markets. While it is difficult to rock, it is not impossible for the $17 trillion U.S. economy to face these international pressures.

The second "dark cloud" is how the smaller world economies should deal with the possibility of sudden foreign financial capital inflows and outflows. Perhaps the most vivid recent example of the potentially destructive forces of international capital movements occurred in the East Asian Tiger economies in 1997–1998. Thanks to their excellent growth performance over the previous few decades, these economies had attracted considerable interest from foreign investors. In the mid-1990s, however, foreign investment into these countries surged even further. Much of this money funneled through banks that borrowed in U.S. dollars and loaned in their national currencies. Bank lending surged at rates of 20% per year or more. This inflow of foreign capital meant that investment in these economies exceeded the level of domestic savings, so that current account deficits in these countries jumped into the 5–10% GDP range.

The surge in bank lending meant that many banks in these East Asian countries did not do an especially good job of screening out safe and unsafe borrowers. Many of the loans—as high as 10% to 15% of all loans in some of these countries—started to turn bad. Fearing losses, foreign investors started pulling out their money. As the foreign money left, the exchange rates of these countries crashed, often falling by 50% or more in a few months. The banks were stuck with a mismatch: even if the rest of their domestic loans were repaid, they could never pay back the U.S. dollars that they owed. The banking sector as a whole went bankrupt. The lack of credit and lending in the economy collapsed aggregate demand, bringing on a deep recession.

If the flow and ebb of international capital markets can flip even the economies of the East Asian Tigers, with their stellar growth records, into a recession, then it is no wonder that other middle- and low-income countries around the world are concerned. Moreover, similar episodes of an inflow and then an outflow of foreign financial capital have rocked a number of economies around the world: for example, in the last few years, economies like Ireland, Iceland, and Greece have all experienced severe shocks when foreign lenders decided to stop extending funds. Especially in Greece, this caused the government to enact austerity measures which led to protests throughout the country (**Figure 19.7**).

**Figure 19.7 Protests in Greece** The economic conditions in Greece have deteriorated from the Great Recession such that the government had to enact austerity measures, (strict rules) cutting wages and increasing taxes on its population. Massive protests are but one byproduct. (Credit: modification of work by Apostolos/Flickr Creative Commons)

Many nations are taking steps to reduce the risk that their economy will be injured if foreign financial capital takes flight, including having their central banks hold large reserves of foreign exchange and stepping up their regulation of domestic banks to avoid a wave of imprudent lending. The most controversial steps in this area involve whether countries should try to take steps to control or reduce the flows of foreign capital. If a country could discourage some speculative short-term capital inflow, and instead only encourage investment capital that it committed for the medium and the long term, then it could be at least somewhat less susceptible to swings in the sentiments of global investors.

If economies participate in the global trade of goods and services, they will also need to participate in international flows of financial payments and investments. These linkages can offer great benefits to an economy. However, any nation that is experiencing a substantial and sustained pattern of trade deficits, along with the corresponding net inflow of international financial capital, has some reason for concern. During the Asian Financial Crisis in the late 1990s, countries that grew dramatically in the years leading up to the crisis as international capital flowed in, saw their economies collapse when the capital very quickly flowed out.

## Market-Oriented Economic Reforms

The standard of living has increased dramatically for billions of people around the world in the last half century. Such increases have occurred not only in the technological leaders like the United States, Canada, the nations of Europe, and Japan, but also in the East Asian Tigers and in many nations of Latin America and Eastern Europe. The challenge for most of these countries is to maintain these growth rates. The economically-challenged regions of the world have stagnated and become stuck in poverty traps. These countries need to focus on the basics: health and education, or human capital development. As **Figure 19.8** illustrates, modern technology allows for the investment in education and human capital development in ways that would have not been possible just a few short years ago.

**Figure 19.8 Solar-powered Technology** Modern technologies, such as solar-power and Wi-Fi, enable students to obtain education even in remote parts of a country without electricity. These students in Ghana are sharing a laptop provided by a van with solar-power. (Credit: EIFL/Flickr Creative Commons)

Other than the issue of economic growth, the other three main goals of macroeconomic policy—that is, low unemployment, low inflation, and a sustainable balance of trade—all involve situations in which, for some reason, the economy fails to coordinate the forces of supply and demand. In the case of cyclical unemployment, for example, the intersection of aggregate supply and aggregate demand occurs at a level of output below potential GDP. In the case of the natural rate of unemployment, government regulations create a situation where otherwise-willing employers become unwilling to hire otherwise-willing workers. Inflation is a situation in which aggregate demand outstrips aggregate supply, at least for a time, so that too much buying power is chasing too few goods. A trade imbalance is a situation where, because of a net inflow or outflow of foreign capital, domestic savings are not aligned with domestic investment. Each of these situations can create a range of easier or harder policy choices.

# Bring it Home

## Youth Unemployment: Three Cases

Spain and South Africa had the same high youth unemployment in 2011, but the reasons for this unemployment are different. Spain's youth unemployment surged due to the 2008-2009 Great Recession and heavy indebtedness on the part of its citizens and its government. Spain's current account balance is negative, which means it is borrowing heavily. To cure cyclical unemployment during a recession, the Keynesian model suggests increases in government spending—fiscal expansion or monetary expansion. Neither option is open to Spain. It currently can borrow at only high interest rates, which will be a real problem in terms of debt service. In addition, the rest of the European Union (EU) has dragged its feet when it comes to debt forgiveness. Monetary expansion is not possible because Spain uses the euro and cannot devalue its currency unless it convinces all of the EU to do so. What can be done? The *Economist*, summarizing some ideas of economists and policymakers, suggests that Spain's only realistic (although painful) option is to reduce government-mandated wages, which would allow it to reduce government spending. As a result, the government would be able to lower tax rates on the working population. With a lower wage or lower tax environment, firms will hire more workers. This will lower unemployment and stimulate the economy. Spain can also encourage greater foreign investment and try to promote policies that encourage domestic savings.

South Africa has more of a natural rate of unemployment problem. It is an interesting case because its youth unemployment is mostly because its young are not ready to work. Economists commonly refer to this as an employability problem. According to interviews of South African firms as reported in the *Economist*, the young are academically smart but lack practical skills for the workplace. Despite a big push to increase investment in human capital, the results have not yet borne fruit. Recently the government unveiled a plan to pay unemployed youth while they were "trained-up" or apprenticed in South African firms. The government has room to increase fiscal expenditure, encourage domestic savings, and continue to fund investment in education, vocational training, and apprentice programs. South Africa can also improve the climate for foreign investment from technology leaders, which would encourage economic growth.

India has a smaller youth employment problem in terms of percentages. However, bear in mind that since this is a populous country, it turns out to be a significant problem in raw numbers. According to Kaushik Basu, writing for the BBC, "there are 45 national laws governing the hiring and firing decisions of firms and close to four times that amount at the state level". These laws make it difficult for companies to fire workers. To stay nimble and responsive to markets, Indian companies respond to these laws by hiring fewer workers. The Indian government can do much to solve this problem by adjusting its labor laws. Essentially, the government has to remove itself from firms' hiring and firing decisions, so that growing Indian firms can freely employ more workers. Indian workers, like those in South Africa, do not have workforce skills. Again, the government can increase its spending on education, vocational training, and workforce readiness programs.

Finally, India has a significant current account deficit. This deficit is mainly a result of short- and long-term capital flows. To solve this deficit, India has experimented by lifting the limitation on domestic savers from investing abroad. This is a step in the right direction that may dampen the growth in the current account deficit. A final policy possibility is to improve domestic capital markets so many self-employed Indians can obtain access to capital to realize their business ideas. If more Indians can obtain access to capital to start businesses, employment might increase.

# KEY TERMS

**converging economy**  economy of a country that has demonstrated the ability to catch up to the technology leaders by investing in both physical and human capital

**East Asian Tigers**  the economies of Taiwan, Singapore, Hong Kong, and South Korea, which maintained high growth rates and rapid export-led industrialization between the early 1960s and 1990 allowing them to converge with the technological leaders in high-income countries

**growth consensus**  a series of studies that show, statistically, that 70% of the differences in income per person across the world is explained by differences in physical capital (savings/investment)

**high-income country**  nation with a per capita income of $12,475 or more; typically has high levels of human and physical capital

**low-income country**  a nation that has a per capita income of less than $1,025; a third of the world's population

**middle-income country**  a nation with per capita income between $1,025 and $12, 475 and that has shown some ability, even if not always sustained, to catch up to the technology leaders in high-income countries

# KEY CONCEPTS AND SUMMARY

## 19.1 The Diversity of Countries and Economies across the World

Macroeconomic policy goals for most countries strive toward low levels of unemployment and inflation, as well as stable trade balances. Economists analyze countries based on their GDP per person and ranked as low-, middle-, and high-income countries. Low-income are those earning less than $1,025 (less than 1%) of global income. They currently have 18.5% of the world population. Middle-income countries are those with per capital income of $1,025–$12,475 (31.1% of global income). They have 69.5% of world population. High-income countries are those with per capita income greater than $12,475 (68.3% of global income). They have 12% of the world's population. Regional comparisons tend to be inaccurate because even countries within those regions tend to differ from each other.

## 19.2 Improving Countries' Standards of Living

The fundamentals of growth are the same in every country: improvements in human capital, physical capital, and technology interacting in a market-oriented economy. Countries that are high-income tend to focus on developing and using new technology. Countries that are middle-income focus on increasing human capital and becoming more connected to technology and global markets. They have charted unconventional paths by relying more on state-led support rather than relying solely on markets. Low-income, economically-challenged countries have many health and human development needs, but they are also challenged by the lack of investment and foreign aid to develop infrastructure like roads. There are some bright spots when it comes to financial development and mobile communications, which suggest that low-income countries can become technology leaders in their own right, but it is too early to claim victory. These countries must do more to connect to the rest of the global economy and find the technologies that work best for them.

## 19.3 Causes of Unemployment around the World

We can address cyclical unemployment by expansionary fiscal and monetary policy. The natural rate of unemployment can be harder to solve, because it involves thinking carefully about the tradeoffs involved in laws that affect employment and hiring. Unemployment is understood differently in high-income countries compared to low- and middle-income countries. People in these countries are not "unemployed" in the sense that we use the term in the United States and Europe, but neither are they employed in a regular wage-paying job. While some may have regular wage-paying jobs, others are part of a barter economy.

## 19.4 Causes of Inflation in Various Countries and Regions

Most high-income economies have learned that their central banks can control inflation in the medium and the long term. In addition, they have learned that inflation has no long-term benefits but potentially substantial long-term costs if it distracts businesses from focusing on real productivity gains. However, smaller economies around the world may face more volatile inflation because their smaller economies can be unsettled by international movements of capital and goods.

## 19.5 Balance of Trade Concerns

There are many legitimate concerns over possible negative consequences of free trade. Perhaps the single strongest response to these concerns is that there are good ways to address them without restricting trade and thus losing its benefits. There are two major issues involving trade imbalances. One is what will happen with the large U.S. trade deficits, and whether they will come down gradually or with a rush. The other is whether smaller countries around the world should take some steps to limit flows of international capital, in the hope that they will not be quite so susceptible to economic whiplash from international financial capital flowing in and out of their economies.

## SELF-CHECK QUESTIONS

**1.** Using the data in **Table 19.3**, rank the seven regions of the world according to GDP and then according to GDP per capita.

| | Population (in millions) | GDP Per Capita | GDP = Population × Per Capita GDP (in millions) |
|---|---|---|---|
| East Asia and Pacific | 2,006 | $5,536 | $10,450,032 |
| South Asia | 1,671 | $1,482 | $2,288,812 |
| Sub-Saharan Africa | 936.1 | $1,657 | $1,287,650 |
| Latin America and Caribbean | 588 | $9,536 | $5,339,390 |
| Middle East and North Africa | 345.4 | $3,456 | $1,541,900 |
| Europe and Central Asia | 272.2 | $7,118 | $1,862,384 |

Table 19.3 GDP and Population of Seven Regions of the World

**2.** What are the drawbacks to analyzing the global economy on a regional basis?

**3.** Create a table that identifies the macroeconomic policies for a high-income country, a middle-income country, and a low-income country.

**4.** Use the data in the text to contrast the policy prescriptions of the high-income, middle-income, and low-income countries.

**5.** What are the different policy tools for dealing with cyclical unemployment?

**6.** Explain how the natural rate of unemployment may be higher in low-income countries.

**7.** How does indexing wage contracts to inflation help workers?

**8.** Use the AD/AS model to show how increases in government spending can lead to more inflation.

**9.** Show, using the AD/AS model, how governments can use monetary policy to decrease the price level.

**10.** What do international flows of capital have to do with trade imbalances?

**11.** Use the demand-and-supply of foreign currency graph to determine what would happen to a small, open economy that experienced capital outflows.

## REVIEW QUESTIONS

**12.** What is the primary way in which economists measure standards of living?

**13.** What are some of the other ways of comparing the standard of living in countries around the world?

**14.** What are the four other factors that determine the economic standard of living around the world?

**15.** What other factors, aside from labor productivity, capital investment, and technology, impact the economic growth of a country? How?

**16.** What strategies did the East Asian Tigers employ to stimulate economic growth?

**17.** What are the two types of unemployment problems?

**18.** In low-income countries, does it make sense to argue that most of the people without long-term jobs are unemployed?

**19.** Is inflation likely to be a severe problem for at least some high-income economies in the near future?

**20.** Is inflation likely to be a problem for at least some low- and middle-income economies in the near future?

**21.** What are the major issues with regard to trade imbalances for the U.S. economy?

**22.** What are the major issues with regard to trade imbalances for low- and middle-income countries?

## CRITICAL THINKING QUESTIONS

**23.** Demography can have important economic effects. The United States has an aging population. Explain one economic benefit and one economic cost of an aging population as well as of a population that is very young.

**24.** Explain why is it difficult to set aside funds for investment when you are in poverty.

**25.** Why do you think it is difficult for high-income countries to achieve high growth rates?

**26.** Is it possible to protect workers from losing their jobs without distorting the labor market?

**27.** Explain what will happen in a nation that tries to solve a structural unemployment problem using expansionary monetary and fiscal policy. Draw one AD/AS diagram, based on the Keynesian model, for what the nation hopes will happen. Then draw a second AD/AS diagram, based on the neoclassical model, for what is more likely to happen.

**28.** Why are inflationary dangers lower in the high-income economies than in low-income and middle-income economies?

**29.** Explain why converging economies may present a strong argument for limiting flows of capital but not for limiting trade.

# PROBLEMS

**30.** Retrieve the following data from The World Bank database (http://databank.worldbank.org/data/home.aspx) for India, Spain, and South Africa for the most recent year available:

- GDP in constant international dollars or PPP
- Population
- GDP per person in constant international dollars
- Mortality rate, infant (per 1,000 live births)
- Health expenditure per capita (current U.S. dollars)
- Life expectancy at birth, total (years)

**31.** Prepare a chart that compares India, Spain, and South Africa based on the data you find. Describe the key differences between the countries. Rank these as high-, medium-, and low-income countries, explain what is surprising or expected about this data.

**32.** Use the Rule of 72 to estimate how long it will take for India, Spain, and South Africa to double their standards of living.

**33.** Using the research skills you have acquired, retrieve the following data from The World Bank database (http://databank.worldbank.org/data/home.aspx) for India, Spain, and South Africa for 2010–2015, if available:

- Telephone lines
- Mobile cellular subscriptions
- Secure Internet servers (per one million people)
- Electricity production (kWh)

Prepare a chart that compares these three countries. Describe the key differences between the countries.

**34.** Retrieve the unemployment data from The World Bank database (http://databank.worldbank.org/data/home.aspx) for India, Spain, and South Africa for 2011-2015. Prepare a chart that compares India, Spain, and South Africa based on the data. Describe the key differences between the countries. Rank these countries as high-, medium-, and low-income countries. Explain what is surprising or expected about this data. How did the Great Recession impact these countries?

**35.** Retrieve inflation data from The World Bank data base (http://databank.worldbank.org/data/home.aspx) for India, Spain, and South Africa for 2011–2015. Prepare a chart that compares India, Spain, and South Africa based on the data. Describe the key differences between the countries. Rank these countries as high-, medium-, and low-income. Explain what is surprising or expected about the data.

# 20 | International Trade

**Figure 20.1 Apple or Samsung iPhone?** While the iPhone is readily recognized as an Apple product, 26% of the component costs in it come from components made by rival phone-maker, Samsung. In international trade, there are often "conflicts" like this as each country or company focuses on what it does best. (Credit: modification of work by Yutaka Tsutano Creative Commons)

## Bring it Home

### Just Whose iPhone Is It?

The iPhone is a global product. Apple does not manufacture the iPhone components, nor does it assemble them. The assembly is done by Foxconn Corporation, a Taiwanese company, at its factory in Sengzhen, China. But, Samsung, the electronics firm and competitor to Apple, actually supplies many of the parts that make up an iPhone—representing about 26% of the costs of production. That means, that Samsung is both the biggest supplier and biggest competitor for Apple. Why do these two firms work together to produce the iPhone? To understand the economic logic behind international trade, you have to accept, as these firms do, that trade is about mutually beneficial exchange. Samsung is one of the world's largest electronics parts suppliers. Apple lets Samsung focus on making the best parts, which allows Apple to concentrate on its strength—designing elegant products that are easy to use. If each company (and by extension each country) focuses on what it does best, there will be gains for all through trade.

## Introduction to International Trade

In this chapter, you will learn about:

- Absolute and Comparative Advantage

- What Happens When a Country Has an Absolute Advantage in All Goods

- Intra-industry Trade between Similar Economies

- The Benefits of Reducing Barriers to International Trade

We live in a global marketplace. The food on your table might include fresh fruit from Chile, cheese from France, and bottled water from Scotland. Your wireless phone might have been made in Taiwan or Korea. The clothes you wear might be designed in Italy and manufactured in China. The toys you give to a child might have come from India. The car you drive might come from Japan, Germany, or Korea. The gasoline in the tank might be refined from crude oil from Saudi Arabia, Mexico, or Nigeria. As a worker, if your job is involved with farming, machinery, airplanes, cars, scientific instruments, or many other technology-related industries, the odds are good that a hearty proportion of the sales of your employer—and hence the money that pays your salary—comes from export sales. We are all linked by international trade, and the volume of that trade has grown dramatically in the last few decades.

The first wave of globalization started in the nineteenth century and lasted up to the beginning of World War I. Over that time, global exports as a share of global GDP rose from less than 1% of GDP in 1820 to 9% of GDP in 1913. As the Nobel Prize-winning economist Paul Krugman of Princeton University wrote in 1995:

> It is a late-twentieth-century conceit that we invented the global economy just yesterday. In fact, world markets achieved an impressive degree of integration during the second half of the nineteenth century. Indeed, if one wants a specific date for the beginning of a truly global economy, one might well choose 1869, the year in which both the Suez Canal and the Union Pacific railroad were completed. By the eve of the First World War steamships and railroads had created markets for standardized commodities, like wheat and wool, that were fully global in their reach. Even the global flow of information was better than modern observers, focused on electronic technology, tend to realize: the first submarine telegraph cable was laid under the Atlantic in 1858, and by 1900 all of the world's major economic regions could effectively communicate instantaneously.

This first wave of globalization crashed to a halt early in the twentieth century. World War I severed many economic connections. During the Great Depression of the 1930s, many nations misguidedly tried to fix their own economies by reducing foreign trade with others. World War II further hindered international trade. Global flows of goods and financial capital were rebuilt only slowly after World War II. It was not until the early 1980s that global economic forces again became as important, relative to the size of the world economy, as they were before World War I.

# 20.1 | Absolute and Comparative Advantage

By the end of this section, you will be able to:
- Define absolute advantage, comparative advantage, and opportunity costs
- Explain the gains of trade created when a country specializes

The American statesman Benjamin Franklin (1706–1790) once wrote: "No nation was ever ruined by trade." Many economists would express their attitudes toward international trade in an even more positive manner. The evidence that international trade confers overall benefits on economies is pretty strong. Trade has accompanied economic growth in the United States and around the world. Many of the national economies that have shown the most rapid growth in the last several decades—for example, Japan, South Korea, China, and India—have done so by dramatically orienting their economies toward international trade. There is no modern example of a country that has shut itself off from world trade and yet prospered. To understand the benefits of trade, or why we trade in the first place, we need to understand the concepts of comparative and absolute advantage.

In 1817, David Ricardo, a businessman, economist, and member of the British Parliament, wrote a treatise called *On the Principles of Political Economy and Taxation*. In this treatise, Ricardo argued that specialization and free trade benefit all trading partners, even those that may be relatively inefficient. To see what he meant, we must be able to distinguish between absolute and comparative advantage.

A country has an **absolute advantage** over another country in producing a good if it uses fewer resources to produce that good. Absolute advantage can be the result of a country's natural endowment. For example, extracting oil in

Saudi Arabia is pretty much just a matter of "drilling a hole." Producing oil in other countries can require considerable exploration and costly technologies for drilling and extraction—if they have any oil at all. The United States has some of the richest farmland in the world, making it easier to grow corn and wheat than in many other countries. Guatemala and Colombia have climates especially suited for growing coffee. Chile and Zambia have some of the world's richest copper mines. As some have argued, "geography is destiny." Chile will provide copper and Guatemala will produce coffee, and they will trade. When each country has a product others need and it can produce it with fewer resources in one country than in another, then it is easy to imagine all parties benefitting from trade. However, thinking about trade just in terms of geography and absolute advantage is incomplete. Trade really occurs because of comparative advantage.

Recall from the chapter **Choice in a World of Scarcity** that a country has a comparative advantage when it can produce a good at a lower cost in terms of other goods. The question each country or company should be asking when it trades is this: "What do we give up to produce this good?" It should be no surprise that the concept of comparative advantage is based on this idea of opportunity cost from **Choice in a World of Scarcity**. For example, if Zambia focuses its resources on producing copper, it cannot use its labor, land and financial resources to produce other goods such as corn. As a result, Zambia gives up the opportunity to produce corn. How do we quantify the cost in terms of other goods? Simplify the problem and assume that Zambia just needs labor to produce copper and corn. The companies that produce either copper or corn tell you that it takes two hours to mine a ton of copper and one hour to harvest a bushel of corn. This means the opportunity cost of producing a ton of copper is two bushels of corn. The next section develops absolute and comparative advantage in greater detail and relates them to trade.

# Link It Up

Visit this website (http://openstaxcollege.org/l/WTO) for a list of articles and podcasts pertaining to international trade topics.

## A Numerical Example of Absolute and Comparative Advantage

Consider a hypothetical world with two countries, Saudi Arabia and the United States, and two products, oil and corn. Further assume that consumers in both countries desire both these goods. These goods are homogeneous, meaning that consumers/producers cannot differentiate between corn or oil from either country. There is only one resource available in both countries, labor hours. Saudi Arabia can produce oil with fewer resources, while the United States can produce corn with fewer resources. **Table 20.1** illustrates the advantages of the two countries, expressed in terms of how many hours it takes to produce one unit of each good.

| Country | Oil (hours per barrel) | Corn (hours per bushel) |
|---|---|---|
| Saudi Arabia | 1 | 4 |
| United States | 2 | 1 |

Table 20.1 How Many Hours It Takes to Produce Oil and Corn

In **Table 20.1**, Saudi Arabia has an absolute advantage in producing oil because it only takes an hour to produce a barrel of oil compared to two hours in the United States. The United States has an absolute advantage in producing corn.

To simplify, let's say that Saudi Arabia and the United States each have 100 worker hours (see **Table 20.2**). **Figure 20.2** illustrates what each country is capable of producing on its own using a production possibility frontier (PPF) graph. Recall from **Choice in a World of Scarcity** that the production possibilities frontier shows the maximum amount that each country can produce given its limited resources, in this case workers, and its level of technology.

| Country | Oil Production using 100 worker hours (barrels) | | Corn Production using 100 worker hours (bushels) |
| --- | --- | --- | --- |
| Saudi Arabia | 100 | or | 25 |
| United States | 50 | or | 100 |

**Table 20.2 Production Possibilities before Trade**

(a) Saudi Arabia

(b) The United States

**Figure 20.2 Production Possibilities Frontiers** (a) Saudi Arabia can produce 100 barrels of oil at maximum and zero corn (point A), or 25 bushels of corn and zero oil (point B). It can also produce other combinations of oil and corn if it wants to consume both goods, such as at point C. Here it chooses to produce/consume 60 barrels of oil, leaving 40 work hours that to allocate to produce 10 bushels of corn, using the data in **Table 20.1**. (b) If the United States produces only oil, it can produce, at maximum, 50 barrels and zero corn (point A'), or at the other extreme, it can produce a maximum of 100 bushels of corn and no oil (point B'). Other combinations of both oil and corn are possible, such as point C'. All points above the frontiers are impossible to produce given the current level of resources and technology.

Arguably Saudi and U.S. consumers desire both oil and corn to live. Let's say that before trade occurs, both countries produce and consume at point C or C'. Thus, before trade, the Saudi Arabian economy will devote 60 worker hours to produce oil, as **Table 20.3** shows. Given the information in **Table 20.1**, this choice implies that it produces/consumes 60 barrels of oil. With the remaining 40 worker hours, since it needs four hours to produce a bushel of corn, it can produce only 10 bushels. To be at point C', the U.S. economy devotes 40 worker hours to produce 20 barrels of oil and it can allocate the remaining worker hours to produce 60 bushels of corn.

| Country | Oil Production (barrels) | Corn Production (bushels) |
| --- | --- | --- |
| Saudi Arabia (C) | 60 | 10 |

**Table 20.3 Production before Trade**

| Country | Oil Production (barrels) | Corn Production (bushels) |
|---|---|---|
| United States (C') | 20 | 60 |
| **Total World Production** | **80** | **70** |

Table 20.3 Production before Trade

The slope of the production possibility frontier illustrates the opportunity cost of producing oil in terms of corn. Using all its resources, the United States can produce 50 barrels of oil *or* 100 bushels of corn; therefore, the opportunity cost of one barrel of oil is two bushels of corn—or the slope is 1/2. Thus, in the U.S. production possibility frontier graph, every increase in oil production of one barrel implies a decrease of two bushels of corn. Saudi Arabia can produce 100 barrels of oil *or* 25 bushels of corn. The opportunity cost of producing one barrel of oil is the loss of 1/4 of a bushel of corn that Saudi workers could otherwise have produced. In terms of corn, notice that Saudi Arabia gives up the least to produce a barrel of oil. **Table 20.4** summarizes these calculations.

| Country | Opportunity cost of one unit — Oil (in terms of corn) | Opportunity cost of one unit — Corn (in terms of oil) |
|---|---|---|
| Saudi Arabia | ¼ | 4 |
| United States | 2 | ½ |

Table 20.4 Opportunity Cost and Comparative Advantage

Again recall that we defined comparative advantage as the opportunity cost of producing goods. Since Saudi Arabia gives up the least to produce a barrel of oil, ($\frac{1}{4} < 2$ in **Table 20.4**) it has a comparative advantage in oil production.

The United States gives up the least to produce a bushel of corn, so it has a comparative advantage in corn production.

In this example, there is symmetry between absolute and comparative advantage. Saudi Arabia needs fewer worker hours to produce oil (absolute advantage, see **Table 20.1**), and also gives up the least in terms of other goods to produce oil (comparative advantage, see **Table 20.4**). Such symmetry is not always the case, as we will show after we have discussed gains from trade fully, but first, read the following Clear It Up feature to make sure you understand why the PPF line in the graphs is straight.

### Can a production possibility frontier be straight?

When you first met the production possibility frontier (PPF) in the chapter on **Choice in a World of Scarcity** we drew it with an outward-bending shape. This shape illustrated that as we transferred inputs from producing one good to another—like from education to health services—there were increasing opportunity costs. In the examples in this chapter, we draw the PPFs as straight lines, which means that opportunity costs are constant. When we transfer a marginal unit of labor away from growing corn and toward producing oil, the decline in the quantity of corn and the increase in the quantity of oil is always the same. In reality this is possible only if the contribution of additional workers to output did not change as the scale of production changed. The linear production possibilities frontier is a less realistic model, but a straight line simplifies calculations. It also illustrates economic themes like absolute and comparative advantage just as clearly.

## Gains from Trade

Consider the trading positions of the United States and Saudi Arabia after they have specialized and traded. Before trade, Saudi Arabia produces/consumes 60 barrels of oil and 10 bushels of corn. The United States produces/ consumes 20 barrels of oil and 60 bushels of corn. Given their current production levels, if the United States can trade an amount of corn fewer than 60 bushels and receives in exchange an amount of oil greater than 20 barrels, it will **gain from trade**. With trade, the United States can consume more of both goods than it did without specialization and trade. (Recall that the chapter **Welcome to Economics!** defined specialization as it applies to workers and firms. Economists also use specialization to describe the occurrence when a country shifts resources to focus on producing a good that offers comparative advantage.) Similarly, if Saudi Arabia can trade an amount of oil less than 60 barrels and receive in exchange an amount of corn greater than 10 bushels, it will have more of both goods than it did before specialization and trade. **Table 20.5** illustrates the range of trades that would benefit both sides.

| The U.S. economy, after specialization, will benefit if it: | The Saudi Arabian economy, after specialization, will benefit if it: |
|---|---|
| Exports no more than 60 bushels of corn | Imports at least 10 bushels of corn |
| Imports at least 20 barrels of oil | Exports less than 60 barrels of oil |

**Table 20.5 The Range of Trades That Benefit Both the United States and Saudi Arabia**

The underlying reason why trade benefits both sides is rooted in the concept of opportunity cost, as the following Clear It Up feature explains. If Saudi Arabia wishes to expand domestic production of corn in a world without international trade, then based on its opportunity costs it must give up four barrels of oil for every one additional bushel of corn. If Saudi Arabia could find a way to give up less than four barrels of oil for an additional bushel of corn (or equivalently, to receive more than one bushel of corn for four barrels of oil), it would be better off.

# Clear It Up

## What are the opportunity costs and gains from trade?

The range of trades that will benefit each country is based on the country's opportunity cost of producing each good. The United States can produce 100 bushels of corn or 50 barrels of oil. For the United States, the opportunity cost of producing one barrel of oil is two bushels of corn. If we divide the numbers above by 50, we get the same ratio: one barrel of oil is equivalent to two bushels of corn, or (100/50 = 2 and 50/50 = 1). In a trade with Saudi Arabia, if the United States is going to give up 100 bushels of corn in exports, it must import at least 50 barrels of oil to be just as well off. Clearly, to gain from trade it needs to be able to gain more than a half barrel of oil for its bushel of corn—or why trade at all?

Recall that David Ricardo argued that if each country specializes in its comparative advantage, it will benefit from trade, and total global output will increase. How can we show gains from trade as a result of comparative advantage and specialization? **Table 20.6** shows the output assuming that each country specializes in its comparative advantage and produces no other good. This is 100% specialization. Specialization leads to an increase in total world production. (Compare the total world production in **Table 20.3** to that in **Table 20.6**.)

| Country | Quantity produced after 100% specialization — Oil (barrels) | Quantity produced after 100% specialization — Corn (bushels) |
|---|---|---|
| Saudi Arabia | 100 | 0 |

**Table 20.6 How Specialization Expands Output**

| Country | Quantity produced after 100% specialization — Oil (barrels) | Quantity produced after 100% specialization — Corn (bushels) |
|---|---|---|
| United States | 0 | 100 |
| **Total World Production** | **100** | **100** |

**Table 20.6 How Specialization Expands Output**

What if we did not have complete specialization, as in **Table 20.6**? Would there still be gains from trade? Consider another example, such as when the United States and Saudi Arabia start at C and C', respectively, as **Figure 20.2** shows. Consider what occurs when trade is allowed and the United States exports 20 bushels of corn to Saudi Arabia in exchange for 20 barrels of oil.

**Figure 20.3 Production Possibilities Frontier in Saudi Arabia**  Trade allows a country to go beyond its domestic production-possibility frontier

Starting at point C, which shows Saudi oil production of 60, reduce Saudi oil domestic oil consumption by 20, since 20 is exported to the United States and exchanged for 20 units of corn. This enables Saudi to reach point D, where oil consumption is now 40 barrels and corn consumption has increased to 30 (see **Figure 20.3**). Notice that even without 100% specialization, if the "trading price," in this case 20 barrels of oil for 20 bushels of corn, is greater than the country's opportunity cost, the Saudis will gain from trade. Since the post-trade consumption point D is beyond its production possibility frontier, Saudi Arabia has gained from trade.

# Link It Up

Visit this website (http://wits.worldbank.org/trade-visualization.aspx) for trade-related data visualizations.

## 20.2 | What Happens When a Country Has an Absolute Advantage in All Goods

By the end of this section, you will be able to:
- Show the relationship between production costs and comparative advantage
- Identify situations of mutually beneficial trade
- Identify trade benefits by considering opportunity costs

What happens to the possibilities for trade if one country has an absolute advantage in everything? This is typical for high-income countries that often have well-educated workers, technologically advanced equipment, and the most up-to-date production processes. These high-income countries can produce all products with fewer resources than a low-income country. If the high-income country is more productive across the board, will there still be gains from trade? Good students of Ricardo understand that trade is about mutually beneficial exchange. Even when one country has an absolute advantage in all products, trade can still benefit both sides. This is because gains from trade come from specializing in one's comparative advantage.

### Production Possibilities and Comparative Advantage

Consider the example of trade between the United States and Mexico described in **Table 20.7**. In this example, it takes four U.S. workers to produce 1,000 pairs of shoes, but it takes five Mexican workers to do so. It takes one U.S. worker to produce 1,000 refrigerators, but it takes four Mexican workers to do so. The United States has an absolute advantage in productivity with regard to both shoes and refrigerators; that is, it takes fewer workers in the United States than in Mexico to produce both a given number of shoes and a given number of refrigerators.

| Country | Number of Workers needed to produce 1,000 units — Shoes | Number of Workers needed to produce 1,000 units — Refrigerators |
|---------|--------------------------------------------------------|----------------------------------------------------------------|
| United States | 4 workers | 1 worker |
| Mexico | 5 workers | 4 workers |

Table 20.7 Resources Needed to Produce Shoes and Refrigerators

Absolute advantage simply compares the productivity of a worker between countries. It answers the question, "How many inputs do I need to produce shoes in Mexico?" Comparative advantage asks this same question slightly differently. Instead of comparing how many workers it takes to produce a good, it asks, "How much am I giving up to produce this good in this country?" Another way of looking at this is that comparative advantage identifies the good for which the producer's absolute advantage is relatively larger, or where the producer's absolute productivity disadvantage is relatively smaller. The United States can produce 1,000 shoes with four-fifths as many workers as Mexico (four versus five), but it can produce 1,000 refrigerators with only one-quarter as many workers (one versus four). So, the comparative advantage of the United States, where its absolute productivity advantage is relatively greatest, lies with refrigerators, and Mexico's comparative advantage, where its absolute productivity disadvantage is least, is in the production of shoes.

## Mutually Beneficial Trade with Comparative Advantage

When nations increase production in their area of comparative advantage and trade with each other, both countries can benefit. Again, the production possibility frontier is a useful tool to visualize this benefit.

Consider a situation where the United States and Mexico each have 40 workers. For example, as **Table 20.8** shows, if the United States divides its labor so that 40 workers are making shoes, then, since it takes four workers in the United States to make 1,000 shoes, a total of 10,000 shoes will be produced. (If four workers can make 1,000 shoes, then 40 workers will make 10,000 shoes). If the 40 workers in the United States are making refrigerators, and each worker can produce 1,000 refrigerators, then a total of 40,000 refrigerators will be produced.

| Country | Shoe Production — using 40 workers | | Refrigerator Production — using 40 workers |
|---|---|---|---|
| United States | 10,000 shoes | or | 40,000 refrigerators |
| Mexico | 8,000 shoes | or | 10,000 refrigerators |

Table 20.8 Production Possibilities before Trade with Complete Specialization

As always, the slope of the production possibility frontier for each country is the opportunity cost of one refrigerator in terms of foregone shoe production–when labor is transferred from producing the latter to producing the former (see **Figure 20.4**).

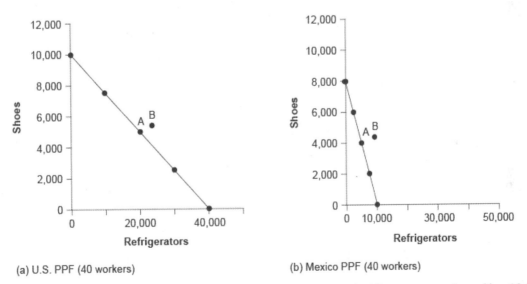

(a) U.S. PPF (40 workers)          (b) Mexico PPF (40 workers)

**Figure 20.4 Production Possibility Frontiers**   (a) With 40 workers, the United States can produce either 10,000 shoes and zero refrigerators or 40,000 refrigerators and zero shoes. (b) With 40 workers, Mexico can produce a maximum of 8,000 shoes and zero refrigerators, or 10,000 refrigerators and zero shoes. All other points on the production possibility line are possible combinations of the two goods that can be produced given current resources. Point A on both graphs is where the countries start producing and consuming before trade. Point B is where they end up after trade.

Let's say that, in the situation before trade, each nation prefers to produce a combination of shoes and refrigerators that is shown at point A. **Table 20.9** shows the output of each good for each country and the total output for the two countries.

| Country | Current Shoe Production | Current Refrigerator Production |
|---|---|---|
| United States | 5,000 | 20,000 |
| Mexico | 4,000 | 5,000 |
| **Total** | **9,000** | **25,000** |

Table 20.9 Total Production at Point A before Trade

Continuing with this scenario, suppose that each country transfers some amount of labor toward its area of comparative advantage. For example, the United States transfers six workers away from shoes and toward producing refrigerators. As a result, U.S. production of shoes decreases by 1,500 units (6/4 × 1,000), while its production of refrigerators increases by 6,000 (that is, 6/1 × 1,000). Mexico also moves production toward its area of comparative advantage, transferring 10 workers away from refrigerators and toward production of shoes. As a result, production of refrigerators in Mexico falls by 2,500 (10/4 × 1,000), but production of shoes increases by 2,000 pairs (10/5 × 1,000). Notice that when both countries shift production toward each of their comparative advantages (what they are relatively better at), their combined production of both goods rises, as shown in **Table 20.10**. The reduction of shoe production by 1,500 pairs in the United States is more than offset by the gain of 2,000 pairs of shoes in Mexico, while the reduction of 2,500 refrigerators in Mexico is more than offset by the additional 6,000 refrigerators produced in the United States.

| Country | Shoe Production | Refrigerator Production |
|---|---|---|
| United States | 3,500 | 26,000 |
| Mexico | 6,000 | 2,500 |
| **Total** | **9,500** | **28,500** |

Table 20.10 Shifting Production Toward Comparative Advantage Raises Total Output

This numerical example illustrates the remarkable insight of comparative advantage: even when one country has an absolute advantage in all goods and another country has an absolute disadvantage in all goods, both countries can still benefit from trade. Even though the United States has an absolute advantage in producing both refrigerators and shoes, it makes economic sense for it to specialize in the good for which it has a comparative advantage. The United States will export refrigerators and in return import shoes.

## How Opportunity Cost Sets the Boundaries of Trade

This example shows that both parties can benefit from specializing in their comparative advantages and trading. By using the opportunity costs in this example, it is possible to identify the range of possible trades that would benefit each country.

Mexico started out, before specialization and trade, producing 4,000 pairs of shoes and 5,000 refrigerators (see **Figure 20.4** and **Table 20.9**). Then, in the numerical example given, Mexico shifted production toward its comparative advantage and produced 6,000 pairs of shoes but only 2,500 refrigerators. Thus, if Mexico can export no more than 2,000 pairs of shoes (giving up 2,000 pairs of shoes) in exchange for imports of at least 2,500 refrigerators (a gain of 2,500 refrigerators), it will be able to consume more of both goods than before trade. Mexico will be unambiguously better off. Conversely, the United States started off, before specialization and trade, producing 5,000 pairs of shoes and 20,000 refrigerators. In the example, it then shifted production toward its comparative advantage, producing only 3,500 shoes but 26,000 refrigerators. If the United States can export no more than 6,000 refrigerators in exchange for imports of at least 1,500 pairs of shoes, it will be able to consume more of both goods and will be unambiguously better off.

The range of trades that can benefit both nations is shown in **Table 20.11**. For example, a trade where the U.S. exports 4,000 refrigerators to Mexico in exchange for 1,800 pairs of shoes would benefit both sides, in the sense that both countries would be able to consume more of both goods than in a world without trade.

| The U.S. economy, after specialization, will benefit if it: | The Mexican economy, after specialization, will benefit if it: |
|---|---|
| *Exports* fewer than 6,000 refrigerators | *Imports* at least 2,500 refrigerators |
| *Imports* at least 1,500 pairs of shoes | *Exports* no more than 2,000 pairs of shoes |

**Table 20.11 The Range of Trades That Benefit Both the United States and Mexico**

Trade allows each country to take advantage of lower opportunity costs in the other country. If Mexico wants to produce more refrigerators without trade, it must face its domestic opportunity costs and reduce shoe production. If Mexico, instead, produces more shoes and then trades for refrigerators made in the United States, where the opportunity cost of producing refrigerators is lower, Mexico can in effect take advantage of the lower opportunity cost of refrigerators in the United States. Conversely, when the United States specializes in its comparative advantage of refrigerator production and trades for shoes produced in Mexico, international trade allows the United States to take advantage of the lower opportunity cost of shoe production in Mexico.

The theory of comparative advantage explains why countries trade: they have different comparative advantages. It shows that the gains from international trade result from pursuing comparative advantage and producing at a lower opportunity cost. The following Work It Out feature shows how to calculate absolute and comparative advantage and the way to apply them to a country's production.

# Work It Out

## Calculating Absolute and Comparative Advantage

In Canada a worker can produce 20 barrels of oil or 40 tons of lumber. In Venezuela, a worker can produce 60 barrels of oil or 30 tons of lumber.

| Country | Oil (barrels) | | Lumber (tons) |
|---|---|---|---|
| Canada | 20 | or | 40 |
| Venezuela | 60 | or | 30 |

**Table 20.12**

    a.  Who has the absolute advantage in the production of oil or lumber? How can you tell?

    b.  Which country has a comparative advantage in the production of oil?

    c.  Which country has a comparative advantage in producing lumber?

    d.  In this example, is absolute advantage the same as comparative advantage, or not?

    e.  In what product should Canada specialize? In what product should Venezuela specialize?

Step 1. Make a table like **Table 20.12**.

Step 2. To calculate absolute advantage, look at the larger of the numbers for each product. One worker in Canada can produce more lumber (40 tons versus 30 tons), so Canada has the absolute advantage in lumber. One worker in Venezuela can produce 60 barrels of oil compared to a worker in Canada who can produce only 20.

Step 3. To calculate comparative advantage, find the opportunity cost of producing one barrel of oil in both countries. The country with the lowest opportunity cost has the comparative advantage. With the same labor time, Canada can produce either 20 barrels of oil or 40 tons of lumber. So in effect, 20 barrels of oil is equivalent to 40 tons of lumber: 20 oil = 40 lumber. Divide both sides of the equation by 20 to calculate the opportunity cost of one barrel of oil in Canada. 20/20 oil = 40/20 lumber. 1 oil = 2 lumber. To produce one additional barrel of oil in Canada has an opportunity cost of 2 lumber. Calculate the same way for Venezuela: 60 oil = 30 lumber. Divide both sides of the equation by 60. One oil in Venezuela has an opportunity cost of 1/2 lumber. Because 1/2 lumber < 2 lumber, Venezuela has the comparative advantage in producing oil.

Step 4. Calculate the opportunity cost of one lumber by reversing the numbers, with lumber on the left side of the equation. In Canada, 40 lumber is equivalent in labor time to 20 barrels of oil: 40 lumber = 20 oil. Divide each side of the equation by 40. The opportunity cost of one lumber is 1/2 oil. In Venezuela, the equivalent labor time will produce 30 lumber or 60 oil: 30 lumber = 60 oil. Divide each side by 30. One lumber has an opportunity cost of two oil. Canada has the lower opportunity cost in producing lumber.

Step 5. In this example, absolute advantage is the same as comparative advantage. Canada has the absolute and comparative advantage in lumber; Venezuela has the absolute and comparative advantage in oil.

Step 6. Canada should specialize in the commodity for which it has a relative lower opportunity cost, which is lumber, and Venezuela should specialize in oil. Canada will be exporting lumber and importing oil, and Venezuela will be exporting oil and importing lumber.

## Comparative Advantage Goes Camping

To build an intuitive understanding of how comparative advantage can benefit all parties, set aside examples that involve national economies for a moment and consider the situation of a group of friends who decide to go camping together. The six friends have a wide range of skills and experiences, but one person in particular, Jethro, has done lots of camping before and is also a great athlete. Jethro has an absolute advantage in all aspects of camping: he is faster at carrying a backpack, gathering firewood, paddling a canoe, setting up tents, making a meal, and washing up. So here is the question: Because Jethro has an absolute productivity advantage in everything, should he do all the work?

Of course not! Even if Jethro is willing to work like a mule while everyone else sits around, he, like all mortals, only has 24 hours in a day. If everyone sits around and waits for Jethro to do everything, not only will Jethro be an unhappy camper, but there will not be much output for his group of six friends to consume. The theory of comparative advantage suggests that everyone will benefit if they figure out their areas of comparative advantage—that is, the area of camping where their productivity disadvantage is least, compared to Jethro. For example, it may be that Jethro is 80% faster at building fires and cooking meals than anyone else, but only 20% faster at gathering firewood and 10% faster at setting up tents. In that case, Jethro should focus on building fires and making meals, and others should attend to the other tasks, each according to where their productivity disadvantage is smallest. If the campers coordinate their efforts according to comparative advantage, they can all gain.

# 20.3 | Intra-industry Trade between Similar Economies

By the end of this section, you will be able to:
- Identify at least two advantages of intra-industry trading
- Explain the relationship between economies of scale and intra-industry trade

Absolute and comparative advantages explain a great deal about global trading patterns. For example, they help to explain the patterns that we noted at the start of this chapter, like why you may be eating fresh fruit from Chile or Mexico, or why lower productivity regions like Africa and Latin America are able to sell a substantial proportion of their exports to higher productivity regions like the European Union and North America. Comparative advantage, however, at least at first glance, does not seem especially well-suited to explain other common patterns of international trade.

## The Prevalence of Intra-industry Trade between Similar Economies

The theory of comparative advantage suggests that trade should happen between economies with large differences in opportunity costs of production. Roughly half of all world trade involves shipping goods between the fairly similar high-income economies of the United States, Canada, the European Union, Japan, Mexico, and China (see **Table 20.13**).

| Country | U.S. Exports Go to ... | U.S. Imports Come from ... |
|---|---|---|
| European Union | 19.0% | 21.0% |
| Canada | 22.0% | 14.0% |
| Japan | 4.0% | 6.0% |
| Mexico | 15.0% | 13.0% |
| China | 8.0% | 20.0% |

**Table 20.13 Where U.S. Exports Go and U.S. Imports Originate (2015)** (Source: https://www.census.gov/foreign-trade/Press-Release/current_press_release/ft900.pdf)

Moreover, the theory of comparative advantage suggests that each economy should specialize to a degree in certain products, and then exchange those products. A high proportion of trade, however, is **intra-industry trade**—that is, trade of goods within the same industry from one country to another. For example, the United States produces and exports autos and imports autos. **Table 20.14** shows some of the largest categories of U.S. exports and imports. In all of these categories, the United States is both a substantial exporter and a substantial importer of goods from the same industry. In 2014, according to the Bureau of Economic Analysis, the United States exported $146 billion worth of autos, and imported $327 billion worth of autos. About 60% of U.S. trade and 60% of European trade is intra-industry trade.

| Some U.S. Exports | Quantity of Exports ($ billions) | Quantity of Imports ($ billions) |
|---|---|---|
| Autos | $146 | $327 |
| Food and beverages | $144 | $126 |
| Capital goods | $550 | $551 |
| Consumer goods | $199 | $558 |
| Industrial supplies | $507 | $665 |
| Other transportation | $45 | $55 |

**Table 20.14 Some Intra-Industry U.S. Exports and Imports in 2014** (Source: http://www.bea.gov/newsreleases/international/trade/tradnewsrelease.htm)

Why do similar high-income economies engage in intra-industry trade? What can be the economic benefit of having workers of fairly similar skills making cars, computers, machinery and other products which are then shipped across the oceans to and from the United States, the European Union, and Japan? There are two reasons: (1) The division of labor leads to learning, innovation, and unique skills; and (2) economies of scale.

## Gains from Specialization and Learning

Consider the category of machinery, where the U.S. economy has considerable intra-industry trade. Machinery comes in many varieties, so the United States may be exporting machinery for manufacturing with wood, but importing machinery for photographic processing. The underlying reason why a country like the United States, Japan, or Germany produces one kind of machinery rather than another is usually not related to U.S., German, or Japanese firms and workers having generally higher or lower skills. It is just that, in working on very specific and particular products, firms in certain countries develop unique and different skills.

Specialization in the world economy can be very finely split. In fact, recent years have seen a trend in international trade, which economists call **splitting up the value chain**. The **value chain** describes how a good is produced in stages. As indicated in the beginning of the chapter, producing the iPhone involves designing and engineering the phone in the United States, supplying parts from Korea, assembling the parts in China, and advertising and marketing in the United States. Thanks in large part to improvements in communication technology, sharing information, and transportation, it has become easier to split up the value chain. Instead of production in a single large factory, different firms operating in various places and even different countries can divide the value chain. Because firms split up the value chain, international trade often does not involve nations trading whole finished products like automobiles or refrigerators. Instead, it involves shipping more specialized goods like, say, automobile dashboards or the shelving that fits inside refrigerators. Intra-industry trade between similar countries produces economic gains because it allows workers and firms to learn and innovate on particular products—and often to focus on very particular parts of the value chain.

## Link It Up @&

Visit this website (http://openstaxcollege.org/l/iphoneassembly) for some interesting information about the assembly of the iPhone.

## Economies of Scale, Competition, Variety

A second broad reason that intra-industry trade between similar nations produces economic gains involves economies of scale. The concept of economies of scale, as we introduced in **Production, Costs and Industry Structure (http://cnx.org/content/m63680/latest/)** , means that as the scale of output goes up, average costs of production decline—at least up to a point. **Figure 20.5** illustrates economies of scale for a plant producing toaster ovens. The horizontal axis of the figure shows the quantity of production by a certain firm or at a certain manufacturing plant. The vertical axis measures the average cost of production. Production plant S produces a small level of output at 30 units and has an average cost of production of $30 per toaster oven. Plant M produces at a medium level of output at 50 units, and has an average cost of production of $20 per toaster oven. Plant L produces 150 units of output with an average cost of production of only $10 per toaster oven. Although plant V can produce 200 units of output, it still has the same unit cost as Plant L.

In this example, a small or medium plant, like S or M, will not be able to compete in the market with a large or a very large plant like L or V, because the firm that operates L or V will be able to produce and sell its output at a lower price. In this example, economies of scale operate up to point L, but beyond point L to V, the additional scale of production does not continue to reduce average costs of production.

**Figure 20.5 Economies of Scale** Production Plant S, has an average cost of production of $30 per toaster oven. Production plant M has an average cost of production of $20 per toaster oven. Production plant L has an average cost of production of only $10 per toaster oven. Production plant V still has an average cost of production of $10 per toaster oven. Thus, production plant M can produce toaster ovens more cheaply than plant S because of economies of scale, and plants L or V can produce more cheaply than S or M because of economies of scale. However, the economies of scale end at an output level of 150. Plant V, despite being larger, cannot produce more cheaply on average than plant L.

The concept of economies of scale becomes especially relevant to international trade when it enables one or two large producers to supply the entire country. For example, a single large automobile factory could probably supply all the cars consumers purchase in a smaller economy like the United Kingdom or Belgium in a given year. However, if a country has only one or two large factories producing cars, and no international trade, then consumers in that country would have relatively little choice between kinds of cars (other than the color of the paint and other nonessential options). Little or no competition will exist between different car manufacturers.

International trade provides a way to combine the lower average production costs that come from economies of scale and still have competition and variety for consumers. Large automobile factories in different countries can make and sell their products around the world. If General Motors, Ford, and Chrysler were the only players in the U.S. automobile market, the level of competition and consumer choice would be considerably lower than when U.S. carmakers must face competition from Toyota, Honda, Suzuki, Fiat, Mitsubishi, Nissan, Volkswagen, Kia, Hyundai, BMW, Subaru, and others. Greater competition brings with it innovation and responsiveness to what consumers want. America's car producers make far better cars now than they did several decades ago, and much of the reason is competitive pressure, especially from East Asian and European carmakers.

## Dynamic Comparative Advantage

The sources of gains from intra-industry trade between similar economies—namely, the learning that comes from a high degree of specialization and splitting up the value chain and from economies of scale—do not contradict the earlier theory of comparative advantage. Instead, they help to broaden the concept.

In intra-industry trade, climate or geography do not determine the level of worker productivity. Even the general level of education or skill does not determine it. Instead, how firms engage in specific learning about specialized products, including taking advantage of economies of scale determine the level of worker productivity. In this vision, comparative advantage can be dynamic—that is, it can evolve and change over time as one develops new skills and as manufacturers split the value chain in new ways. This line of thinking also suggests that countries are not destined to have the same comparative advantage forever, but must instead be flexible in response to ongoing changes in comparative advantage.

# 20.4 | The Benefits of Reducing Barriers to International Trade

By the end of this section, you will be able to:
- Explain tarrifs as barriers to trade
- Identify at least two benefits of reducing barriers to international trade

**Tariffs** are taxes that governments place on imported goods for a variety of reasons. Some of these reasons include protecting sensitive industries, for humanitarian reasons, and protecting against dumping. Traditionally, tariffs were used simply as a political tool to protect certain vested economic, social, and cultural interests. The World Trade Organization (WTO) is committed to lowering barriers to trade. The world's nations meet through the WTO to negotiate how they can reduce barriers to trade, such as tariffs. WTO negotiations happen in "rounds," where all countries negotiate one agreement to encourage trade, take a year or two off, and then start negotiating a new agreement. The current round of negotiations is called the Doha Round because it was officially launched in Doha, the capital city of Qatar, in November 2001. In 2009, economists from the World Bank summarized recent research and found that the Doha round of negotiations would increase the size of the world economy by $160 billion to $385 billion per year, depending on the precise deal that ended up being negotiated.

In the context of a global economy that currently produces more than $30 trillion of goods and services each year, this amount is not huge: it is an increase of 1% or less. But before dismissing the gains from trade too quickly, it is worth remembering two points.

- First, a gain of a few hundred billion dollars is enough money to deserve attention! Moreover, remember that this increase is not a one-time event; it would persist each year into the future.

- Second, the estimate of gains may be on the low side because some of the gains from trade are not measured especially well in economic statistics. For example, it is difficult to measure the potential advantages to consumers of having a variety of products available and a greater degree of competition among producers. Perhaps the most important unmeasured factor is that trade between countries, especially when firms are splitting up the value chain of production, often involves a transfer of knowledge that can involve skills in production, technology, management, finance, and law.

Low-income countries benefit more from trade than high-income countries do. In some ways, the giant U.S. economy has less need for international trade, because it can already take advantage of internal trade within its economy. However, many smaller national economies around the world, in regions like Latin America, Africa, the Middle East, and Asia, have much more limited possibilities for trade inside their countries or their immediate regions. Without international trade, they may have little ability to benefit from comparative advantage, slicing up the value chain, or economies of scale. Moreover, smaller economies often have fewer competitive firms making goods within their economy, and thus firms have less pressure from other firms to provide the goods and prices that consumers want.

The economic gains from expanding international trade are measured in hundreds of billions of dollars, and the gains from international trade as a whole probably reach well into the trillions of dollars. The potential for gains from trade may be especially high among the smaller and lower-income countries of the world.

Link It Up

Visit this website (http://openstaxcollege.org/l/tradebenefits) for a list of some benefits of trade.

## From Interpersonal to International Trade

Most people find it easy to believe that they, personally, would not be better off if they tried to grow and process all of their own food, to make all of their own clothes, to build their own cars and houses from scratch, and so on. Instead, we all benefit from living in economies where people and firms can specialize and trade with each other.

The benefits of trade do not stop at national boundaries, either. Earlier we explained that the division of labor could increase output for three reasons: (1) workers with different characteristics can specialize in the types of production where they have a comparative advantage; (2) firms and workers who specialize in a certain product become more productive with learning and practice; and (3) economies of scale. These three reasons apply from the individual and community level right up to the international level. If it makes sense to you that interpersonal, intercommunity, and interstate trade offer economic gains, it should make sense that international trade offers gains, too.

International trade currently involves about $20 trillion worth of goods and services moving around the globe. Any economic force of that size, even if it confers overall benefits, is certain to cause disruption and controversy. This chapter has only made the case that trade brings economic benefits. Other chapters discuss, in detail, the public policy arguments over whether to restrict international trade.

## Bring it Home

### It's Apple's (Global) iPhone

Apple Corporation uses a global platform to produce the iPhone. Now that you understand the concept of comparative advantage, you can see why the engineering and design of the iPhone is done in the United States. The United States has built up a comparative advantage over the years in designing and marketing products, and sacrifices fewer resources to design high-tech devices relative to other countries. China has a comparative advantage in assembling the phone due to its large skilled labor force. Korea has a comparative advantage in producing components. Korea focuses its production by increasing its scale, learning better ways to produce screens and computer chips, and uses innovation to lower average costs of production. Apple, in turn, benefits because it can purchase these quality products at lower prices. Put the global assembly line together and you have the device with which we are all so familiar.

# KEY TERMS

**absolute advantage**  when one country can use fewer resources to produce a good compared to another country; when a country is more productive compared to another country

**gain from trade**  a country that can consume more than it can produce as a result of specialization and trade

**intra-industry trade**  international trade of goods within the same industry

**splitting up the value chain**  many of the different stages of producing a good happen in different geographic locations

**tariffs**  taxes that governments place on imported goods

**value chain**  how a good is produced in stages

# KEY CONCEPTS AND SUMMARY

## 20.1 Absolute and Comparative Advantage

A country has an absolute advantage in those products in which it has a productivity edge over other countries; it takes fewer resources to produce a product. A country has a comparative advantage when it can produce a good at a lower cost in terms of other goods. Countries that specialize based on comparative advantage gain from trade.

## 20.2 What Happens When a Country Has an Absolute Advantage in All Goods

Even when a country has high levels of productivity in all goods, it can still benefit from trade. Gains from trade come about as a result of comparative advantage. By specializing in a good that it gives up the least to produce, a country can produce more and offer that additional output for sale. If other countries specialize in the area of their comparative advantage as well and trade, the highly productive country is able to benefit from a lower opportunity cost of production in other countries.

## 20.3 Intra-industry Trade between Similar Economies

A large share of global trade happens between high-income economies that are quite similar in having well-educated workers and advanced technology. These countries practice intra-industry trade, in which they import and export the same products at the same time, like cars, machinery, and computers. In the case of intra-industry trade between economies with similar income levels, the gains from trade come from specialized learning in very particular tasks and from economies of scale. Splitting up the value chain means that several stages of producing a good take place in different countries around the world.

## 20.4 The Benefits of Reducing Barriers to International Trade

Tariffs are placed on imported goods as a way of protecting sensitive industries, for humanitarian reasons, and for protection against dumping. Traditionally, tariffs were used as a political tool to protect certain vested economic, social, and cultural interests. The WTO has been, and continues to be, a way for nations to meet and negotiate in order to reduce barriers to trade. The gains of international trade are very large, especially for smaller countries, but are beneficial to all.

# SELF-CHECK QUESTIONS

**1.**  True or False: The source of comparative advantage must be natural elements like climate and mineral deposits. Explain.

**2.**  Brazil can produce 100 pounds of beef or 10 autos. In contrast the United States can produce 40 pounds of beef or 30 autos. Which country has the absolute advantage in beef? Which country has the absolute advantage in producing autos? What is the opportunity cost of producing one pound of beef in Brazil? What is the opportunity cost of producing one pound of beef in the United States?

**3.** In France it takes one worker to produce one sweater, and one worker to produce one bottle of wine. In Tunisia it takes two workers to produce one sweater, and three workers to produce one bottle of wine. Who has the absolute advantage in production of sweaters? Who has the absolute advantage in the production of wine? How can you tell?

**4.** In Germany it takes three workers to make one television and four workers to make one video camera. In Poland it takes six workers to make one television and 12 workers to make one video camera.

    a. Who has the absolute advantage in the production of televisions? Who has the absolute advantage in the production of video cameras? How can you tell?

    b. Calculate the opportunity cost of producing one additional television set in Germany and in Poland. (Your calculation may involve fractions, which is fine.) Which country has a comparative advantage in the production of televisions?

    c. Calculate the opportunity cost of producing one video camera in Germany and in Poland. Which country has a comparative advantage in the production of video cameras?

    d. In this example, is absolute advantage the same as comparative advantage, or not?

    e. In what product should Germany specialize? In what product should Poland specialize?

**5.** How can there be any economic gains for a country from both importing and exporting the same good, like cars?

**6.** Table 20.15 shows how the average costs of production for semiconductors (the "chips" in computer memories) change as the quantity of semiconductors built at that factory increases.

    a. Based on these data, sketch a curve with quantity produced on the horizontal axis and average cost of production on the vertical axis. How does the curve illustrate economies of scale?

    b. If the equilibrium quantity of semiconductors demanded is 90,000, can this economy take full advantage of economies of scale? What about if quantity demanded is 70,000 semiconductors? 50,000 semiconductors? 30,000 semiconductors?

    c. Explain how international trade could make it possible for even a small economy to take full advantage of economies of scale, while also benefiting from competition and the variety offered by several producers.

| Quantity of Semiconductors | Average Total Cost |
|---|---|
| 10,000 | $8 each |
| 20,000 | $5 each |
| 30,000 | $3 each |
| 40,000 | $2 each |
| 100,000 | $2 each |

**Table 20.15**

**7.** If the removal of trade barriers is so beneficial to international economic growth, why would a nation continue to restrict trade on some imported or exported products?

## REVIEW QUESTIONS

**8.** What is absolute advantage? What is comparative advantage?

**9.** Under what conditions does comparative advantage lead to gains from trade?

**10.** What factors does Paul Krugman identify that supported expanding international trade in the 1800s?

**11.** Is it possible to have a comparative advantage in the production of a good but not to have an absolute advantage? Explain.

**12.** How does comparative advantage lead to gains from trade?

**13.** What is intra-industry trade?

**14.** What are the two main sources of economic gains from intra-industry trade?

**15.** What is splitting up the value chain?

**16.** Are the gains from international trade more likely to be relatively more important to large or small countries?

# CRITICAL THINKING QUESTIONS

**17.** Are differences in geography behind the differences in absolute advantages?

**18.** Why does the United States not have an absolute advantage in coffee?

**19.** Look at **Exercise 20.2**. Compute the opportunity costs of producing sweaters and wine in both France and Tunisia. Who has the lowest opportunity cost of producing sweaters and who has the lowest opportunity cost of producing wine? Explain what it means to have a lower opportunity cost.

**20.** You just overheard your friend say the following: "Poor countries like Malawi have no absolute advantages. They have poor soil, low investments in formal education and hence low-skill workers, no capital, and no natural resources to speak of. Because they have no advantage, they cannot benefit from trade." How would you respond?

**21.** Look at **Table 20.9**. Is there a range of trades for which there will be no gains?

**22.** You just got a job in Washington, D.C. You move into an apartment with some acquaintances. All your roommates, however, are slackers and do not clean up after themselves. You, on the other hand, can clean faster than each of them. You determine that you are 70% faster at dishes and 10% faster with vacuuming. All of these tasks have to be done daily. Which jobs should you assign to your roommates to get the most free time overall? Assume you have the same number of hours to devote to cleaning. Now, since you are faster, you seem to get done quicker than your roommate. What sorts of problems may this create? Can you imagine a trade-related analogy to this problem?

**23.** Does intra-industry trade contradict the theory of comparative advantage?

**24.** Do consumers benefit from intra-industry trade?

**25.** Why might intra-industry trade seem surprising from the point of view of comparative advantage?

**26.** In World Trade Organization meetings, what do you think low-income countries lobby for?

**27.** Why might a low-income country put up barriers to trade, such as tariffs on imports?

**28.** Can a nation's comparative advantage change over time? What factors would make it change?

# PROBLEMS

**29.** France and Tunisia both have Mediterranean climates that are excellent for producing/harvesting green beans and tomatoes. In France it takes two hours for each worker to harvest green beans and two hours to harvest a tomato. Tunisian workers need only one hour to harvest the tomatoes but four hours to harvest green beans. Assume there are only two workers, one in each country, and each works 40 hours a week.

   a. Draw a production possibilities frontier for each country. *Hint*: Remember the production possibility frontier is the maximum that all workers can produce at a unit of time which, in this problem, is a week.

   b. Identify which country has the absolute advantage in green beans and which country has the absolute advantage in tomatoes.

   c. Identify which country has the comparative advantage.

   d. How much would France have to give up in terms of tomatoes to gain from trade? How much would it have to give up in terms of green beans?

**30.** In Japan, one worker can make 5 tons of rubber or 80 radios. In Malaysia, one worker can make 10 tons of rubber or 40 radios.

   a. Who has the absolute advantage in the production of rubber or radios? How can you tell?

   b. Calculate the opportunity cost of producing 80 additional radios in Japan and in Malaysia. (Your calculation may involve fractions, which is fine.) Which country has a comparative advantage in the production of radios?

   c. Calculate the opportunity cost of producing 10 additional tons of rubber in Japan and in Malaysia. Which country has a comparative advantage in producing rubber?

   d. In this example, does each country have an absolute advantage and a comparative advantage in the same good?

   e. In what product should Japan specialize? In what product should Malaysia specialize?

**31.** Review the numbers for Canada and Venezuela from **Table 20.12** which describes how many barrels of oil and tons of lumber the workers can produce. Use these numbers to answer the rest of this question.

   a. Draw a production possibilities frontier for each country. Assume there are 100 workers in each country. Canadians and Venezuelans desire both oil and lumber. Canadians want at least 2,000 tons of lumber. Mark a point on their production possibilities where they can get at least 3,000 tons.

   b. Assume that the Canadians specialize completely because they figured out they have a comparative advantage in lumber. They are willing to give up 1,000 tons of lumber. How much oil should they ask for in return for this lumber to be as well off as they were with no trade? How much should they ask for if they want to gain from trading with Venezuela? *Note*: We can think of this "ask" as the relative price or trade price of lumber.

   c. Is the Canadian "ask" you identified in (b) also beneficial for Venezuelans? Use the production possibilities frontier graph for Venezuela to show that Venezuelans can gain from trade.

**32.** In **Exercise 20.31**, is there an "ask" where Venezuelans may say "no thank you" to trading with Canada?

**33.** From earlier chapters you will recall that technological change shifts the average cost curves. Draw a graph showing how technological change could influence intra-industry trade.

**34.** Consider two countries: South Korea and Taiwan. Taiwan can produce one million mobile phones per day at the cost of $10 per phone and South Korea can produce 50 million mobile phones at $5 per phone. Assume these phones are the same type and quality and there is only one price. What is the minimum price at which both countries will engage in trade?

**35.** If trade increases world GDP by 1% per year, what is the global impact of this increase over 10 years? How does this increase compare to the annual GDP of a country like Sri Lanka? Discuss. *Hint*: To answer this question, here are steps you may want to consider. Go to the World Development Indicators (online) published by the World Bank. Find the current level of World GDP in constant international dollars. Also, find the GDP of Sri Lanka in constant international dollars. Once you have these two numbers, compute the amount the additional increase in global incomes due to trade and compare that number to Sri Lanka's GDP.

# 21 | Globalization and Protectionism

**Figure 21.1 Flat Screen Competition** The market for flat-panel displays in the United States is huge. The manufacturers of flat screens in the United States must compete against manufacturers from around the world. (Credit: modification of work by "Jemimus"/Flickr Creative Commons)

## Bring it Home

### What's the Downside of Protection?

Governments are motivated to limit and alter market outcomes for political or social ends. While governments can limit the rise in prices of some products, they cannot control how much people want to buy or how much firms are willing to sell. The laws of demand and supply still hold. Trade policy is an example where regulations can redirect economic forces, but it cannot stop them from manifesting themselves elsewhere.

Flat-panel displays, the displays for laptop computers, tablets, and flat screen televisions, are an example of such an enduring principle. In the early 1990s, the vast majority of flat-panel displays used in U.S.-manufactured laptops were imported, primarily from Japan. The small but politically powerful U.S. flat-panel-display industry filed a dumping complaint with the Commerce Department. They argued that Japanese firms were selling displays at "less than fair value," which made it difficult for U.S. firms to compete. This argument for trade protection is referred to as anti-dumping. Other arguments for protection in this complaint included national security. After a preliminary determination by the Commerce Department that the Japanese firms were dumping, the U.S. International Trade Commission imposed a 63% dumping margin (or tax) on the import of flat-panel displays. Was this a successful exercise of U.S. trade policy? See what you think after reading the chapter.

# Introduction to Globalism and Protectionism

In this chapter, you will learn about:

- Protectionism: An Indirect Subsidy from Consumers to Producers
- International Trade and Its Effects on Jobs, Wages, and Working Conditions
- Arguments in Support of Restricting Imports
- How Trade Policy Is Enacted: Globally, Regionally, and Nationally
- The Tradeoffs of Trade Policy

The world has become more connected on multiple levels, especially economically. In 1970, imports and exports made up 11% of U.S. GDP, while now they make up 32%. However, the United States, due to its size, is less internationally connected than most countries. For example, according to the World Bank, 97% of Botswana's economic activity is connected to trade. This chapter explores trade policy—the laws and strategies a country uses to regulate international trade. This topic is not without controversy.

As the world has become more globally connected, firms and workers in high-income countries like the United States, Japan, or the nations of the European Union, perceive a competitive threat from firms in medium-income countries like Mexico, China, or South Africa, that have lower costs of living and therefore pay lower wages. Firms and workers in low-income countries fear that they will suffer if they must compete against more productive workers and advanced technology in high-income countries.

On a different tack, some environmentalists worry that multinational firms may evade environmental protection laws by moving their production to countries with loose or nonexistent pollution standards, trading a clean environment for jobs. Some politicians worry that their country may become overly dependent on key imported products, like oil, which in a time of war could threaten national security. All of these fears influence governments to reach the same basic policy conclusion: to protect national interests, whether businesses, jobs, or security, imports of foreign products should be restricted. This chapter analyzes such arguments. First, however, it is essential to learn a few key concepts and understand how the demand and supply model applies to international trade.

# 21.1 | Protectionism: An Indirect Subsidy from Consumers to Producers

By the end of this section, you will be able to:
- Explain protectionism and its three main forms
- Analyze protectionism through concepts of demand and supply, noting its effects on equilibrium
- Calculate the effects of trade barriers

When a government legislates policies to reduce or block international trade it is engaging in **protectionism**. Protectionist policies often seek to shield domestic producers and domestic workers from foreign competition. Protectionism takes three main forms: tariffs, import quotas, and nontariff barriers.

Recall from **International Trade** that tariffs are taxes that governments impose on imported goods and services. This makes imports more expensive for consumers, discouraging imports. For example, in recent years large, flat-screen televisions imported to the U.S. from China have faced a 5% tariff rate.

Another way to control trade is through **import quotas**, which are numerical limitations on the quantity of products that a country can import. For instance, during the early 1980s, the Reagan Administration imposed a quota on the import of Japanese automobiles. In the 1970s, many developed countries, including the United States, found themselves with declining textile industries. Textile production does not require highly skilled workers, so producers were able to set up lower-cost factories in developing countries. In order to "manage" this loss of jobs and income, the developed countries established an international Multifiber Agreement that essentially divided the market for textile exports between importers and the remaining domestic producers. The agreement, which ran from 1974 to 2004, specified the exact quota of textile imports that each developed country would accept from each low-income country. A similar story exists for sugar imports into the United States, which are still governed by quotas.

**Nontariff barriers** are all the other ways that a nation can draw up rules, regulations, inspections, and paperwork to make it more costly or difficult to import products. A rule requiring certain safety standards can limit imports just as effectively as high tariffs or low import quotas, for instance. There are also nontariff barriers in the form of "rules-of-origin" regulations; these rules describe the "Made in Country X" label as the one in which the last substantial change in the product took place. A manufacturer wishing to evade import restrictions may try to change the production process so that the last big change in the product happens in his or her own country. For example, certain textiles are made in the United States, shipped to other countries, combined with textiles made in those other countries to make apparel—and then re-exported back to the United States for a final assembly, to escape paying tariffs or to obtain a "Made in the USA" label.

Despite import quotas, tariffs, and nontariff barriers, the share of apparel sold in the United States that is imported rose from about half in 1999 to about three-quarters today. The U.S. Bureau of Labor Statistics (BLS), estimated the number of U.S. jobs in textiles and apparel fell from 666,360 in 2007 to 385,240 in 2012, a 42% decline. Even more U.S. textile industry jobs would have been lost without tariffs. However, domestic jobs that are saved by import quotas come at a cost. Because textile and apparel protectionism adds to the costs of imports, consumers end up paying billions of dollars more for clothing each year.

When the United States eliminates trade barriers in one area, consumers spend the money they save on that product elsewhere in the economy. Thus, while eliminating trade barriers in one sector of the economy will likely result in some job loss in that sector, consumers will spend the resulting savings in other sectors of the economy and hence increase the number of jobs in those other sectors. Of course, workers in some of the poorest countries of the world who would otherwise have jobs producing textiles, would gain considerably if the United States reduced its barriers to trade in textiles. That said, there are good reasons to be wary about reducing barriers to trade. The 2012 and 2013 Bangladeshi fires in textile factories, which resulted in a horrific loss of life, present complications that our simplified analysis in the chapter will not capture.

Realizing the compromises between nations that come about due to trade policy, many countries came together in 1947 to form the General Agreement on Tariffs and Trade (GATT). (We'll cover the GATT in more detail later in the chapter.) This agreement has since been superseded by the **World Trade Organization (WTO)**, whose membership includes about 150 nations and most of the world's economies. It is the primary international mechanism through which nations negotiate their trade rules—including rules about tariffs, quotas, and nontariff barriers. The next section examines the results of such protectionism and develops a simple model to show the impact of trade policy.

## Demand and Supply Analysis of Protectionism

To the non-economist, restricting imports may appear to be nothing more than taking sales from foreign producers and giving them to domestic producers. Other factors are at work, however, because firms do not operate in a vacuum. Instead, firms sell their products either to consumers or to other firms (if they are business suppliers), who are also affected by the trade barriers. A demand and supply analysis of protectionism shows that it is not just a matter of domestic gains and foreign losses, but a policy that imposes substantial domestic costs as well.

Consider two countries, Brazil and the United States, who produce sugar. Each country has a domestic supply and demand for sugar, as **Table 21.1** details and **Figure 21.2** illustrates. In Brazil, without trade, the equilibrium price of sugar is 12 cents per pound and the equilibrium output is 30 tons. When there is no trade in the United States, the equilibrium price of sugar is 24 cents per pound and the equilibrium quantity is 80 tons. We label these equilibrium points as point E in each part of the figure.

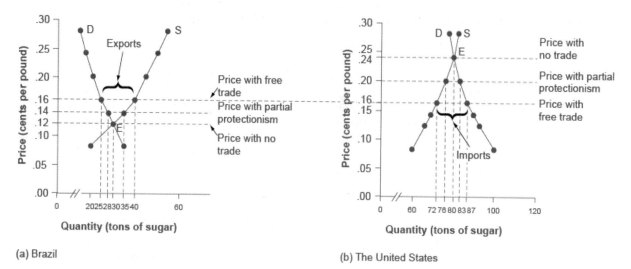

**Figure 21.2 The Sugar Trade between Brazil and the United States** Before trade, the equilibrium price of sugar in Brazil is 12 cents a pound and it is 24 cents per pound in the United States. When trade is allowed, businesses will buy cheap sugar in Brazil and sell it in the United States. This will result in higher prices in Brazil and lower prices in the United States. Ignoring transaction costs, prices should converge to 16 cents per pound, with Brazil exporting 15 tons of sugar and the United States importing 15 tons of sugar. If trade is only partly open between the countries, it will lead to an outcome between the free-trade and no-trade possibilities.

| Price | Brazil: Quantity Supplied (tons) | Brazil: Quantity Demanded (tons) | U.S.: Quantity Supplied (tons) | U.S.: Quantity Demanded (tons) |
|---|---|---|---|---|
| 8 cents | 20 | 35 | 60 | 100 |
| 12 cents | 30 | 30 | 66 | 93 |
| 14 cents | 35 | 28 | 69 | 90 |
| 16 cents | 40 | 25 | 72 | 87 |
| 20 cents | 45 | 21 | 76 | 83 |
| 24 cents | 50 | 18 | 80 | 80 |
| 28 cents | 55 | 15 | 82 | 78 |

**Table 21.1 The Sugar Trade between Brazil and the United States**

If international trade between Brazil and the United States now becomes possible, profit-seeking firms will spot an opportunity: buy sugar cheaply in Brazil, and sell it at a higher price in the United States. As sugar is shipped from Brazil to the United States, the quantity of sugar produced in Brazil will be greater than Brazilian consumption (with the extra production exported), and the amount produced in the United States will be less than the amount of U.S. consumption (with the extra consumption imported). Exports to the United States will reduce the sugar supply in

Brazil, raising its price. Imports into the United States will increase the sugar supply, lowering its price. When the sugar price is the same in both countries, there is no incentive to trade further. As **Figure 21.2** shows, the equilibrium with trade occurs at a price of 16 cents per pound. At that price, the sugar farmers of Brazil supply a quantity of 40 tons, while the consumers of Brazil buy only 25 tons.

The extra 15 tons of sugar production, shown by the horizontal gap between the demand curve and the supply curve in Brazil, is exported to the United States. In the United States, at a price of 16 cents, the farmers produce a quantity of 72 tons and consumers demand a quantity of 87 tons. The excess demand of 15 tons by American consumers, shown by the horizontal gap between demand and domestic supply at the price of 16 cents, is supplied by imported sugar. Free trade typically results in income distribution effects, but the key is to recognize the overall gains from trade, as **Figure 21.3** shows. Building on the concepts that we outlined in **Demand and Supply** and **Demand, Supply, and Efficiency** in terms of consumer and producer surplus, **Figure 21.3** (a) shows that producers in Brazil gain by selling more sugar at a higher price, while **Figure 21.3** (b) shows consumers in the United States benefit from the lower price and greater availability of sugar. Consumers in Brazil are worse off (compare their no-trade consumer surplus with the free-trade consumer surplus) and U.S. producers of sugar are worse off. There are gains from trade—an increase in social surplus in each country. That is, both the United States and Brazil are better off than they would be without trade. The following Clear It Up feature explains how trade policy can influence low-income countries.

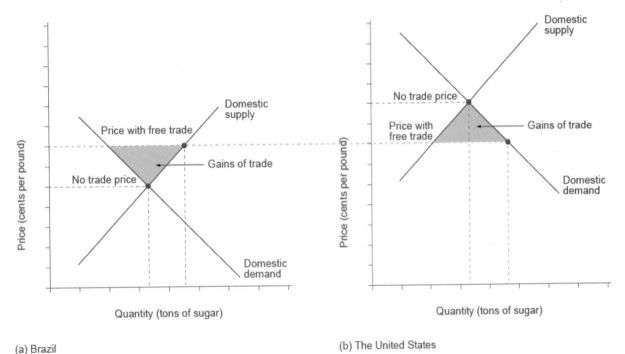

(a) Brazil

(b) The United States

**Figure 21.3 Free Trade of Sugar**  Free trade results in gains from trade. Total surplus increases in both countries, as the two blue-shaded areas show. However, there are clear income distribution effects. Producers gain in the exporting country, while consumers lose; and in the importing country, consumers gain and producers lose.

# Link It Up

Visit this website (http://openstaxcollege.org/l/sugartrade) to read more about the global sugar trade.

## Why are there low-income countries?

Why are the poor countries of the world poor? There are a number of reasons, but one of them will surprise you: the trade policies of the high-income countries. Following is a stark review of social priorities which the international aid organization, Oxfam International has widely publicized.

High-income countries of the world—primarily the United States, Canada, countries of the European Union, and Japan—subsidize their domestic farmers collectively by about $360 billion per year. By contrast, the total amount of foreign aid from these same high-income countries to the poor countries of the world is about $70 billion per year, or less than 20% of the farm subsidies. Why does this matter?

It matters because the support of farmers in high-income countries is devastating to the livelihoods of farmers in low-income countries. Even when their climate and land are well-suited to products like cotton, rice, sugar, or milk, farmers in low-income countries find it difficult to compete. Farm subsidies in the high-income countries cause farmers in those countries to increase the amount they produce. This increase in supply drives down world prices of farm products below the costs of production. As Michael Gerson of the *Washington Post* describes it: "[T]he effects in the cotton-growing regions of West Africa are dramatic . . . keep[ing] millions of Africans on the edge of malnutrition. In some of the poorest countries on Earth, cotton farmers are some of the poorest people, earning about a dollar a day. . . . Who benefits from the current system of subsidies? About 20,000 American cotton producers, with an average annual income of more than $125,000."

As if subsidies were not enough, often, the high-income countries block agricultural exports from low-income countries. In some cases, the situation gets even worse when the governments of high-income countries, having bought and paid for an excess supply of farm products, give away those products in poor countries and drive local farmers out of business altogether.

For example, shipments of excess milk from the European Union to Jamaica have caused great hardship for Jamaican dairy farmers. Shipments of excess rice from the United States to Haiti drove thousands of low-income rice farmers in Haiti out of business. The opportunity costs of protectionism are not paid just by domestic consumers, but also by foreign producers—and for many agricultural products, those foreign producers are the world's poor.

Now, let's look at what happens with protectionism. U.S. sugar farmers are likely to argue that, if only they could be protected from sugar imported from Brazil, the United States would have higher domestic sugar production, more jobs in the sugar industry, and American sugar farmers would receive a higher price. If the United States government sets a high-enough tariff on imported sugar, or sets an import quota at zero, the result will be that the quantity of sugar traded between countries could be reduced to zero, and the prices in each country will return to the levels before trade was allowed.

Blocking only some trade is also possible. Suppose that the United States passed a sugar import quota of seven tons. The United States will import no more than seven tons of sugar, which means that Brazil can export no more than seven tons of sugar to the United States. As a result, the price of sugar in the United States will be 20 cents, which is the price where the quantity demanded is seven tons greater than the domestic quantity supplied. Conversely, if Brazil can export only seven tons of sugar, then the price of sugar in Brazil will be 14 cents per pound, which is the price where the domestic quantity supplied in Brazil is seven tons greater than domestic demand.

In general, when a country sets a low or medium tariff or import quota, the equilibrium price and quantity will be somewhere between those that prevail with no trade and those with completely free trade. The following Work It Out explores the impact of these trade barriers.

# Work It Out ─O─O─O

## Effects of Trade Barriers

Let's look carefully at the effects of tariffs or quotas. If the U.S. government imposes a tariff or quota sufficient to eliminate trade with Brazil, two things occur: U.S. consumers pay a higher price and therefore buy a smaller quantity of sugar. U.S. producers obtain a higher price and they sell a larger quantity of sugar. We can measure the effects of a tariff on producers and consumers in the United States using two concepts that we developed in **Demand, Supply, and Efficiency**: consumer surplus and producer surplus.

**Figure 21.4 U.S. Sugar Supply and Demand**   When there is free trade, the equilibrium is at point A. When there is no trade, the equilibrium is at point E.

Step 1. Look at **Figure 21.4**, which shows a hypothetical version of the demand and supply of sugar in the United States.

Step 2. Note that when there is free trade the sugar market is in equilibrium at point A where Domestic Quantity Demanded (Qd) = Quantity Supplied (Domestic Qs + Imports from Brazil) at a price of $P_{Trade}$.

Step 3. Note, also, that imports are equal to the distance between points C and A.

Step 4. Recall that consumer surplus is the value that consumers get beyond what they paid for when they buy a product. Graphically, it is the area under a demand curve but above the price. In this case, the consumer surplus in the United States is the area of the triangle formed by the points $P_{Trade}$, A, and B.

Step 5. Recall, also, that producer surplus is another name for profit—it is the income producers get above the cost of production, which is shown by the supply curve here. In this case, the producer surplus with trade is the area of the triangle formed by the points $P_{trade}$, C, and D.

Step 6. Suppose that the barriers to trade are imposed, imports are excluded, and the price rises to $P_{NoTrade}$. Look what happens to producer surplus and consumer surplus. At the higher price, the domestic quantity supplied increases from Qs to Q at point E. Because producers are selling more quantity at a higher price, the producer surplus increases to the area of the triangle $P_{NoTrade}$, E, and D.

Step 7. Compare the areas of the two triangles and you will see the increase in the producer surplus.

Step 8. Examine the consumer surplus. Consumers are now paying a higher price to get a lower quantity (Q instead of Qd). Their consumer surplus shrinks to the area of the triangle $P_{NoTrade}$, E, and B.

Step 9. Determine the net effect. The producer surplus increases by the area $P_{trade}$, C, E, $P_{NoTrade}$. The loss of consumer surplus, however, is larger. It is the area $P_{trade}$, A, E, $P_{NoTrade}$. In other words, consumers lose more than producers gain as a result of the trade barriers and the United States has a lower social surplus.

## Who Benefits and Who Pays?

Using the demand and supply model, consider the impact of protectionism on producers and consumers in each of the two countries. For protected producers like U.S. sugar farmers, restricting imports is clearly positive. Without a need to face imported products, these producers are able to sell more, at a higher price. For consumers in the country with the protected good, in this case U.S. sugar consumers, restricting imports is clearly negative. They end up buying a lower quantity of the good and paying a higher price for what they do buy, compared to the equilibrium price and quantity with trade. The following Clear It Up feature considers why a country might outsource jobs even for a domestic product.

### Why are Life Savers, an American product, not made in America?

In 1912, Clarence Crane invented Life Savers, the hard candy with the hole in the middle, in Cleveland, Ohio. Starting in the late 1960s and for 35 years afterward, a plant in Holland, Michigan produced 46 billion Life Savers a year, in 200 million rolls. However, in 2002, the Kraft Company announced that it would close the Michigan plant and move Life Saver production across the border to Montreal, Canada.

One reason is that Canadian workers are paid slightly less, especially in healthcare and insurance costs that are not linked to employment there. Another main reason is that the United States government keeps the sugar price high for the benefit of sugar farmers, with a combination of a government price floor program and strict quotas on imported sugar. According to the Coalition for Sugar Reform, from 2009 to 2012, the price of refined sugar in the United States ranged from 64% to 92% higher than the world price. Life Saver production uses over 100 tons of sugar each day, because the candies are 95% sugar.

A number of other candy companies have also reduced U.S. production and expanded foreign production. From 1997 to 2011, sugar-using industries eliminated some 127,000 jobs, or more than seven times the total employment in sugar production. While the candy industry is especially affected by the cost of sugar, the costs are spread more broadly. U.S. consumers pay roughly $1 billion per year in higher food prices because of elevated sugar costs. Meanwhile, sugar producers in low-income countries are driven out of business. Because of the sugar subsidies to domestic producers and the quotas on imports, they cannot sell their output profitably, or at all, in the United States market.

The fact that protectionism pushes up prices for consumers in the country enacting such protectionism is not always acknowledged openly, but it is not disputed. After all, if protectionism did not benefit domestic producers, there would not be much point in enacting such policies in the first place. Protectionism is simply a method of requiring consumers to subsidize producers. The subsidy is indirect, since consumers pay for it through higher prices, rather than a direct government subsidy paid with money collected from taxpayers. However, protectionism works like a subsidy, nonetheless. The American satirist Ambrose Bierce defined "tariff" this way in his 1911 book, *The Devil's Dictionary*: "Tariff, n. A scale of taxes on imports, designed to protect the domestic producer against the greed of his consumer."

The effect of protectionism on producers and consumers in the foreign country is complex. When a government uses an import quota to impose partial protectionism, Brazilian sugar producers receive a lower price for the sugar they sell in Brazil—but a higher price for the sugar they are allowed to export to the United States. Notice that some of the burden of protectionism, paid by domestic consumers, ends up in the hands of foreign producers in this case. Brazilian sugar consumers seem to benefit from U.S. protectionism, because it reduces the price of sugar that they pay (compared to the free-trade situation). On the other hand, at least some of these Brazilian sugar consumers also work as sugar farmers, so protectionism reduces their incomes and jobs. Moreover, if trade between the countries vanishes, Brazilian consumers would miss out on better prices for imported goods—which do not appear in our single-market example of sugar protectionism.

The effects of protectionism on foreign countries notwithstanding, protectionism requires domestic consumers of a product (consumers may include either households or other firms) to pay higher prices to benefit domestic producers of that product. In addition, when a country enacts protectionism, it loses the economic gains it would have been able to achieve through a combination of comparative advantage, specialized learning, and economies of scale, concepts that we discuss in **International Trade**.

# 21.2 | International Trade and Its Effects on Jobs, Wages, and Working Conditions

By the end of this section, you will be able to:
- Discuss how international trade influences the job market
- Analyze the opportunity cost of protectionism
- Explain how international trade impacts wages, labor standards, and working conditions

In theory at least, imports might injure workers in several different ways: fewer jobs, lower wages, or poor working conditions. Let's consider these in turn.

## Fewer Jobs?

In the early 1990s, the United States was negotiating the North American Free Trade Agreement (NAFTA) with Mexico, an agreement that reduced tariffs, import quotas, and nontariff barriers to trade between the United States, Mexico, and Canada. H. Ross Perot, a 1992 candidate for U.S. president, claimed, in prominent campaign arguments, that if the United States expanded trade with Mexico, there would be a "giant sucking sound" as U.S. employers relocated to Mexico to take advantage of lower wages. After all, average wages in Mexico were, at that time, about one-eighth of those in the United States. NAFTA passed Congress, President Bill Clinton signed it into law, and it took effect in 1995. For the next six years, the United States economy had some of the most rapid job growth and low unemployment in its history. Those who feared that open trade with Mexico would lead to a dramatic decrease in jobs were proven wrong.

This result was no surprise to economists. After all, the trend toward globalization has been going on for decades, not just since NAFTA. If trade did reduce the number of available jobs, then the United States should have been seeing a steady loss of jobs for decades. While the United States economy does experience rises and falls in unemployment rates—according to the Bureau of Labor Statistics, from spring 2007 to late 2009, the unemployment rate rose from 4.4% to 10%. It has since fallen back to under 5% as of the end of 2016—the number of jobs is not falling over extended periods of time. The number of U.S. jobs rose from 71 million in 1970 to 145 million in 2014.

Protectionism certainly saves jobs in the specific industry being protected but, for two reasons, it costs jobs in other unprotected industries. First, if consumers are paying higher prices to the protected industry, they inevitably have less money to spend on goods from other industries, and so jobs are lost in those other industries. Second, if a firm sells the protected product to other firms, so that other firms must now pay a higher price for a key input, then those firms will lose sales to foreign producers who do not need to pay the higher price. Lost sales translate into lost jobs. The hidden opportunity cost of using protectionism to save jobs in one industry is jobs sacrificed in other industries. This is why the United States International Trade Commission, in its study of barriers to trade, predicts that reducing trade barriers would not lead to an overall loss of jobs. Protectionism reshuffles jobs from industries without import protections to industries that are protected from imports, but it does not create more jobs.

Moreover, the costs of saving jobs through protectionism can be very high. A number of different studies have attempted to estimate the cost to consumers in higher prices per job saved through protectionism. **Table 21.2** shows a sample of results, compiled by economists at the Federal Reserve Bank of Dallas. Saving a job through protectionism typically costs much more than the actual worker's salary. For example, a study published in 2002 compiled evidence that using protectionism to save an average job in the textile and apparel industry would cost $199,000 per job saved. In other words, those workers could have been paid $100,000 per year to be unemployed and the cost would only be half of what it is to keep them working in the textile and apparel industry. This result is not unique to textiles and apparel.

| Industry Protected with Import Tariffs or Quotas | Annual Cost per Job Saved |
|---|---|
| Sugar | $826,000 |
| Polyethylene resins | $812,000 |
| Dairy products | $685,000 |
| Frozen concentrated orange juice | $635,000 |
| Ball bearings | $603,000 |
| Machine tools | $479,000 |
| Women's handbags | $263,000 |
| Glassware | $247,000 |
| Apparel and textiles | $199,000 |
| Rubber footwear | $168,000 |
| Women's nonathletic footwear | $139,000 |

Table 21.2 Cost to U.S. Consumers of Saving a Job through Protectionism   (Source: Federal Reserve Bank of Dallas)

Why does it cost so much to save jobs through protectionism? The basic reason is that not all of the extra money that consumers pay because of tariffs or quotas goes to save jobs. For example, if the government imposes tariffs on steel imports so that steel buyers pay a higher price, U.S. steel companies earn greater profits, buy more equipment, pay bigger bonuses to managers, give pay raises to existing employees—and also avoid firing some additional workers. Only part of the higher price of protected steel goes toward saving jobs. Also, when an industry is protected, the economy as a whole loses the benefits of playing to its comparative advantage—in other words, producing what it is best at. Therefore, part of the higher price that consumers pay for protected goods is lost economic efficiency, which we can measure as another deadweight loss, like what we discussed in **Labor and Financial Markets**.

There's a bumper sticker that speaks to the threat some U.S. workers feel from imported products: "Buy American—Save U.S. Jobs." If an economist were driving the car, the sticker might declare: "Block Imports—Save Jobs for Some Americans, Lose Jobs for Other Americans, and Also Pay High Prices."

## Trade and Wages

Even if trade does not reduce the number of jobs, it could affect wages. Here, it is important to separate issues about the average level of wages from issues about whether the wages of certain workers may be helped or hurt by trade.

Because trade raises the amount that an economy can produce by letting firms and workers play to their comparative advantage, trade will also cause the average level of wages in an economy to rise. Workers who can produce more will be more desirable to employers, which will shift the demand for their labor out to the right, and increase wages in the labor market. By contrast, barriers to trade will reduce the average level of wages in an economy.

However, even if trade increases the overall wage level, it will still benefit some workers and hurt others. Workers in industries that are confronted by competition from imported products may find that demand for their labor decreases and shifts back to the left, so that their wages decline with a rise in international trade. Conversely, workers in industries that benefit from selling in global markets may find that demand for their labor shifts out to the right, so that trade raises their wages.

# Link It Up

View this website (http://openstaxcollege.org/l/fairtradecoffee) to read an article on the issues surrounding fair trade coffee.

One concern is that while globalization may be benefiting high-skilled, high-wage workers in the United States, it may also impose costs on low-skilled, low-wage workers. After all, high-skilled U.S. workers presumably benefit from increased sales of sophisticated products like computers, machinery, and pharmaceuticals in which the United States has a comparative advantage. Meanwhile, low-skilled U.S. workers must now compete against extremely low-wage workers worldwide for making simpler products like toys and clothing. As a result, the wages of low-skilled U.S. workers are likely to fall. There are, however, a number of reasons to believe that while globalization has helped some U.S. industries and hurt others, it has not focused its negative impact on the wages of low-skilled Americans. First, about half of U.S. trade is intra-industry trade. That means the U.S. trades similar goods with other high-wage economies like Canada, Japan, Germany, and the United Kingdom. For instance, in 2014 the U.S. exported over 2 million cars, from all the major automakers, and also imported several million cars from other countries.

Most U.S. workers in these industries have above-average skills and wages—and many of them do quite well in the world of globalization. Some evidence suggested that intra-industry trade between similar countries had a small impact on domestic workers but later evidence indicates that it all depends on how flexible the labor market is. In other words, the key is how flexible workers are in finding jobs in different industries. The effect of trade on low-wage workers depends considerably on the structure of labor markets and indirect effects felt in other parts of the economy. For example, in the United States and the United Kingdom, because labor market frictions are low, the impact of trade on low income workers is small.

Second, many low-skilled U.S. workers hold service jobs that imports from low-wage countries cannot replace. For example, we cannot import lawn care services or moving and hauling services or hotel maids from countries long distances away like China or Bangladesh. Competition from imported products is not the primary determinant of their wages.

Finally, while the focus of the discussion here is on wages, it is worth pointing out that low-wage U.S. workers suffer due to protectionism in all the industries—even those in which they do not work. For example, food and clothing are protected industries. These low-wage workers therefore pay higher prices for these basic necessities and as such their dollar stretches over fewer goods.

The benefits and costs of increased trade in terms of its effect on wages are not distributed evenly across the economy. However, the growth of international trade has helped to raise the productivity of U.S. workers as a whole—and thus helped to raise the average level of wages.

## Labor Standards and Working Conditions

Workers in many low-income countries around the world labor under conditions that would be illegal for a worker in the United States. Workers in countries like China, Thailand, Brazil, South Africa, and Poland are often paid less than the United States minimum wage. For example, in the United States, the minimum wage is $7.25 per hour. A typical wage in many low-income countries might be more like $7.25 per day, or often much less. Moreover, working conditions in low-income countries may be extremely unpleasant, or even unsafe. In the worst cases, production may involve the child labor or even workers who are treated nearly like slaves. These concerns over foreign labor standards do not affect most of U.S. trade, which is intra-industry and carried out with other high-income countries that have labor standards similar to the United States, but it is, nonetheless, morally and economically important.

In thinking about labor standards in other countries, it is important to draw some distinctions between what is truly unacceptable and what is painful to think about. Most people, economists included, have little difficulty with the idea that production by six-year-olds confined in factories or by slave labor is morally unacceptable. They would support aggressive efforts to eliminate such practices—including shutting out imported products made with such labor. Many cases, however, are less clear-cut. An opinion article in the *New York Times* several years ago described the case of Ahmed Zia, a 14-year-old boy from Pakistan. He earned $2 per day working in a carpet factory. He dropped out of school in second grade. Should the United States and other countries refuse to purchase rugs made by Ahmed and his co-workers? If the carpet factories were to close, the likely alternative job for Ahmed is farm work, and as Ahmed says of his carpet-weaving job: "This makes much more money and is more comfortable."

Other workers may have even less attractive alternative jobs, perhaps scavenging garbage or prostitution. The real problem for Ahmed and many others in low-income countries is not that globalization has made their lives worse, but rather that they have so few good life alternatives. The United States went through similar situations during the nineteenth and early twentieth centuries.

In closing, there is some irony when the United States government or U.S. citizens take issue with labor standards in low-income countries, because the United States is not a world leader in government laws to protect employees. According to a recent study by the Organization for Economic Cooperation and Development (OECD), the U.S. is the only one of 41 countries that does not provide mandated paid leave for new parents, and among the 40 countries that do mandate paid leave, the minimum duration is about two months. Many European workers receive six weeks or more of paid vacation per year. In the United States, vacations are often one to three weeks per year. If European countries accused the United States of using unfair labor standards to make U.S. products cheaply, and announced that they would shut out all U.S. imports until the United States adopted paid parental leave, added more national holidays, and doubled vacation time, Americans would be outraged. Yet when U.S. protectionists start talking about restricting imports from poor countries because of low wage levels and poor working conditions, they are making a very similar argument. This is not to say that labor conditions in low-income countries are not an important issue. They are. However, linking labor conditions in low-income countries to trade deflects the emphasis from the real question to ask: "What are acceptable and enforceable minimum labor standards and protections to have the world over?"

# 21.3 | Arguments in Support of Restricting Imports

By the end of this section, you will be able to:
- Explain and analyze various arguments that are in support of restricting imports, including the infant industry argument, the anti-dumping argument, the environmental protection argument, the unsafe consumer products argument, and the national interest argument
- Explain dumping and race to the bottom
- Evaluate the significance of countries' perceptions on the benefits of growing trade

As we previously noted, protectionism requires domestic consumers of a product to pay higher prices to benefit domestic producers of that product. Countries that institute protectionist policies lose the economic gains achieved through a combination of comparative advantage, specialized learning, and economies of scale. With these overall costs in mind, let us now consider, one by one, a number of arguments that support restricting imports.

## The Infant Industry Argument

Imagine Bhutan wants to start its own computer industry, but it has no computer firms that can produce at a low enough price and high enough quality to compete in world markets. However, Bhutanese politicians, business leaders, and workers hope that if the local industry had a chance to get established, before it needed to face international competition, then a domestic company or group of companies could develop the skills, management, technology, and economies of scale that it needs to become a successful profit-earning domestic industry. Thus, the infant industry argument for protectionism is to block imports for a limited time, to give the infant industry time to mature, before it starts competing on equal terms in the global economy. (Revisit **Macroeconomic Policy Around the World** for more information on the infant industry argument.)

The infant industry argument is theoretically possible, even sensible: give an industry a short-term indirect subsidy through protection, and then reap the long-term economic benefits of having a vibrant, healthy industry. Implementation, however, is tricky. In many countries, infant industries have gone from babyhood to senility and obsolescence without ever having reached the profitable maturity stage. Meanwhile, the protectionism that was supposed to be short-term often took a very long time to be repealed.

As one example, Brazil treated its computer industry as an infant industry from the late 1970s until about 1990. In an attempt to establish its computer industry in the global economy, Brazil largely barred imports of computer products for several decades. This policy guaranteed increased sales for Brazilian computers. However, by the mid-1980s, due to lack of international competition, Brazil had a backward and out-of-date industry, typically lagging behind world standards for price and performance by three to five years—a long time in this fast-moving industry. After more than a decade, during which Brazilian consumers and industries that would have benefited from up-to-date computers paid the costs and Brazil's computer industry never competed effectively on world markets, Brazil phased out its infant industry policy for the computer industry.

Protectionism for infant industries always imposes costs on domestic users of the product, and typically has provided little benefit in the form of stronger, competitive industries. However, several countries in East Asia offer an exception. Japan, Korea, Thailand, and other countries in this region have sometimes provided a package of indirect and direct subsidies targeted at certain industries, including protection from foreign competition and government loans at interest rates below the market equilibrium. In Japan and Korea, for example, subsidies helped get their domestic steel and auto industries up and running.

Why did the infant industry policy of protectionism and other subsidies work fairly well in East Asia? An early 1990 World Bank study offered three guidelines to countries thinking about infant industry protection:

1. Do not hand out protectionism and other subsidies to all industries, but focus on a few industries where your country has a realistic chance to be a world-class producer.

2. Be very hesitant about using protectionism in areas like computers, where many other industries rely on having the best products available, because it is not useful to help one industry by imposing high costs on many other industries.

3. Have clear guidelines for when the infant industry policy will end.

In Korea in the 1970s and 1980s, a common practice was to link protectionism and subsidies to export sales in global markets. If export sales rose, then the infant industry had succeeded and the government could phase out protectionism. If export sales did not rise, then the infant industry policy had failed and the government could phase out protectionism. Either way, the protectionism would be temporary.

Following these rules is easier said than done. Politics often intrudes, both in choosing which industries will receive the benefits of treatment as "infants" and when to phase out import restrictions and other subsidies. Also, if the country's government wishes to impose costs on its citizens so that it can provide subsidies to a few key industries, it has many tools for doing such as direct government payments, loans, targeted tax reductions, and government support of research and development of new technologies. In other words, protectionism is not the only or even the best way to support key industries.

# Link It Up 🔗

Visit this website (http://openstaxcollege.org/l/integration) to view a presentation by Pankaj Ghemawat questioning how integrated the world really is.

# The Anti-Dumping Argument

**Dumping** refers to selling goods below their cost of production. **Anti-dumping laws** block imports that are sold below the cost of production by imposing tariffs that increase the price of these imports to reflect their cost of production. Since dumping is not allowed under World Trade Organization (WTO) rules, nations that believe they are on the receiving end of dumped goods can file a complaint with the WTO. Anti-dumping complaints have risen in recent years, from about 100 cases per year in the late 1980s to about 200 new cases each year by the late 2000s. Note that dumping cases are countercyclical. During recessions, case filings increase. During economic booms, case filings go down. Individual countries have also frequently started their own anti-dumping investigations. The U.S. government has dozens of anti-dumping orders in place from past investigations. In 2009, for example, some U.S. imports that were under anti-dumping orders included pasta from Turkey, steel pipe fittings from Thailand, pressure-sensitive plastic tape from Italy, preserved mushrooms and lined paper products from India, and cut-to-length carbon steel and non-frozen apple juice concentrate from China.

## Why Might Dumping Occur?

Why would foreign firms export a product at less than its cost of production—which presumably means taking a loss? This question has two possible answers, one innocent and one more sinister.

The innocent explanation is that demand and supply set market prices, not the cost of production. Perhaps demand for a product shifts back to the left or supply shifts out to the right, which drives the market price to low levels—even below the cost of production. When a local store has a going-out-of-business sale, for example, it may sell goods at below the cost of production. If international companies find that there is excess supply of steel or computer chips or machine tools that is driving the market price down below their cost of production—this may be the market in action.

The sinister explanation is that dumping is part of a long-term strategy. Foreign firms sell goods at prices below the cost of production for a short period of time, and when they have driven out the domestic U.S. competition, they then raise prices. Economists sometimes call this scenario predatory pricing, which we discuss in the **Monopoly (http://cnx.org/content/m63911/latest/)** chapter.

## Should Anti-Dumping Cases Be Limited?

Anti-dumping cases pose two questions. How much sense do they make in economic theory? How much sense do they make as practical policy?

In terms of economic theory, the case for anti-dumping laws is weak. In a market governed by demand and supply, the government does not guarantee that firms will be able to make a profit. After all, low prices are difficult for producers, but benefit consumers. Moreover, although there are plenty of cases in which foreign producers have driven out domestic firms, there are zero documented cases in which the foreign producers then jacked up prices. Instead, foreign producers typically continue competing hard against each other and providing low prices to consumers. In short, it is difficult to find evidence of predatory pricing by foreign firms exporting to the United States.

Even if one could make a case that the government should sometimes enact anti-dumping rules in the short term, and then allow free trade to resume shortly thereafter, there is a growing concern that anti-dumping investigations often involve more politics than careful analysis. The U.S. Commerce Department is charged with calculating the appropriate "cost of production," which can be as much an art as a science.

For example, if a company built a new factory two years ago, should it count part of the factory's cost in this year's cost of production? When a company is in a country where the government controls prices, like China for example, how can one measure the true cost of production? When a domestic industry complains loudly enough, government regulators seem very likely to find that unfair dumping has occurred. A common pattern has arisen where a domestic industry files an anti-dumping complaint, the governments meet and negotiate a reduction in imports, and then the domestic producers drop the anti-dumping suit. In such cases, anti-dumping cases often appear to be little more than a cover story for imposing tariffs or import quotas.

In the 1980s, the United States, Canada, the European Union, Australia, and New Zealand implemented almost all the anti-dumping cases. By the 2000s, countries like Argentina, Brazil, South Korea, South Africa, Mexico, and India were filing the majority of the anti-dumping cases before the WTO. As the number of anti-dumping cases has increased, and as countries such as the United States and the European Union feel targeted by the anti-dumping actions of others, the WTO may well propose some additional guidelines to limit the reach of anti-dumping laws.

# The Environmental Protection Argument

The potential for global trade to affect the environment has become controversial. A president of the Sierra Club, an environmental lobbying organization, once wrote: "The consequences of globalization for the environment are not good. ... Globalization, if we are lucky, will raise average incomes enough to pay for cleaning up some of the mess that we have made. But before we get there, globalization could also destroy enough of the planet's basic biological and physical systems that prospects for life itself will be radically compromised."

If free trade meant the destruction of life itself, then even economists would convert to protectionism! While globalization—and economic activity of all kinds—can pose environmental dangers, it seems quite possible that, with the appropriate safeguards in place, we can minimize the environmental impacts of trade. In some cases, trade may even bring environmental benefits.

In general, high-income countries such as the United States, Canada, Japan, and the nations of the European Union have relatively strict environmental standards. In contrast, middle- and low-income countries like Brazil, Nigeria, India, and China have lower environmental standards. The general view of the governments of such countries is that environmental protection is a luxury: as soon as their people have enough to eat, decent healthcare, and longer life expectancies, then they will spend more money on items such as sewage treatment plants, scrubbers to reduce air pollution from factory smokestacks, and national parks to protect wildlife.

This gap in environmental standards between high-income and low-income countries raises two worrisome possibilities in a world of increasing global trade: the "race to the bottom" scenario and the question of how quickly environmental standards will improve in low-income countries.

### The Race to the Bottom Scenario

The **race to the bottom** scenario of global environmental degradation runs like this. Profit-seeking multinational companies shift their production from countries with strong environmental standards to countries with weak standards, thus reducing their costs and increasing their profits. Faced with such behavior, countries reduce their environmental standards to attract multinational firms, which, after all, provide jobs and economic clout. As a result, global production becomes concentrated in countries where firms can pollute the most and environmental laws everywhere "race to the bottom."

Although the race-to-the-bottom scenario sounds plausible, it does not appear to describe reality. In fact, the financial incentive for firms to shift production to poor countries to take advantage of their weaker environmental rules does not seem especially powerful. When firms decide where to locate a new factory, they look at many different factors: the costs of labor and financial capital; whether the location is close to a reliable suppliers of the inputs that they need; whether the location is close to customers; the quality of transportation, communications, and electrical power networks; the level of taxes; and the competence and honesty of the local government. The cost of environmental regulations is a factor, too, but typically environmental costs are no more than 1 to 2% of the costs that a large industrial plant faces. The other factors that determine location are much more important to these companies than trying to skimp on environmental protection costs.

When an international company does choose to build a plant in a low-income country with lax environmental laws, it typically builds a plant similar to those that it operates in high-income countries with stricter environmental standards. Part of the reason for this decision is that designing an industrial plant is a complex and costly task, and so if a plant works well in a high-income country, companies prefer to use the same design everywhere. Also, companies realize that if they create an environmental disaster in a low-income country, it is likely to cost them a substantial amount of money in paying for damages, lost trust, and reduced sales—by building up-to-date plants everywhere they minimize such risks. As a result of these factors, foreign-owned plants in low-income countries often have a better record of compliance with environmental laws than do locally-owned plants.

### Pressuring Low-Income Countries for Higher Environmental Standards

In some cases, the issue is not so much whether globalization will pressure low-income countries to reduce their environmental standards, but instead whether the threat of blocking international trade can pressure these countries into adopting stronger standards. For example, restrictions on ivory imports in high-income countries, along with stronger government efforts to catch elephant poachers, have been credited with helping to reduce the illegal poaching of elephants in certain African countries.

However, it would be highly undemocratic for the well-fed citizens of high-income countries to attempt to dictate to the ill-fed citizens of low-income countries what domestic policies and priorities they must adopt, or how they should balance environmental goals against other priorities for their citizens. Furthermore, if high-income countries want stronger environmental standards in low-income countries, they have many options other than the threat of protectionism. For example, high-income countries could pay for anti-pollution equipment in low-income countries, or could help to pay for national parks. High-income countries could help pay for and carry out the scientific and economic studies that would help environmentalists in low-income countries to make a more persuasive case for the economic benefits of protecting the environment.

After all, environmental protection is vital to two industries of key importance in many low-income countries—agriculture and tourism. Environmental advocates can set up standards for labeling products, like "this tuna caught in a net that kept dolphins safe" or "this product made only with wood not taken from rainforests," so that consumer pressure can reinforce environmentalist values. The United Nations also reinforces these values, by sponsoring treaties to address issues such as climate change and global warming, the preservation of biodiversity, the spread of deserts, and the environmental health of the seabed. Countries that share a national border or are within a region often sign environmental agreements about air and water rights, too. The WTO is also becoming more aware of environmental issues and more careful about ensuring that increases in trade do not inflict environmental damage.

Finally, note that these concerns about the race to the bottom or pressuring low-income countries for more strict environmental standards do not apply very well to the roughly half of all U.S. trade that occurs with other high-income countries. Many European countries have stricter environmental standards in certain industries than the United States.

## The Unsafe Consumer Products Argument

One argument for shutting out certain imported products is that they are unsafe for consumers. Consumer rights groups have sometimes warned that the World Trade Organization would require nations to reduce their health and safety standards for imported products. However, the WTO explains its current agreement on the subject in this way: "It allows countries to set their own standards." It also says "regulations must be based on science. . . . And they should not arbitrarily or unjustifiably discriminate between countries where identical or similar conditions prevail." Thus, for example, under WTO rules it is perfectly legitimate for the United States to pass laws requiring that *all* food products or cars sold in the United States meet certain safety standards approved by the United States government, whether or not other countries choose to pass similar standards. However, such standards must have some scientific basis. It is improper to impose one set of health and safety standards for domestically produced goods but a different set of standards for imports, or one set of standards for imports from Europe and a different set of standards for imports from Latin America.

In 2007, Mattel recalled nearly two million toys imported from China due to concerns about high levels of lead in the paint, as well as some loose parts. It is unclear if other toys were subject to similar standards. More recently, in 2013, Japan blocked imports of U.S. wheat because of concerns that genetically modified (GMO) wheat might be included in the shipments. The science on the impact of GMOs on health is still developing.

## The National Interest Argument

Some argue that a nation should not depend too heavily on other countries for supplies of certain key products, such as oil, or for special materials or technologies that might have national security applications. On closer consideration, this argument for protectionism proves rather weak.

As an example, in the United States, oil provides about 36% of all the energy and 25% of the oil used in the United States economy is imported. Several times in the last few decades, when disruptions in the Middle East have shifted the supply curve of oil back to the left and sharply raised the price, the effects have been felt across the United States economy. This is not, however, a very convincing argument for restricting oil imports. If the United States needs to be protected from a possible cutoff of foreign oil, then a more reasonable strategy would be to import 100% of the petroleum supply now, and save U.S. domestic oil resources for when or if the foreign supply is cut off. It might also be useful to import extra oil and put it into a stockpile for use in an emergency, as the United States government did by starting a Strategic Petroleum Reserve in 1977. Moreover, it may be necessary to discourage people from using oil, and to start a high-powered program to seek out alternatives to oil. A straightforward way to do this would be to raise taxes on oil. Additionally, it makes no sense to argue that because oil is highly important to the United States economy, then the United States should shut out oil imports and use up its domestic supplies more quickly. U.S. domestic oil production is increasing. Shale oil is adding to domestic supply using fracking extraction techniques.

Whether or not to limit certain kinds of imports of key technologies or materials that might be important to national security and weapons systems is a slightly different issue. If weapons' builders are not confident that they can continue to obtain a key product in wartime, they might decide to avoid designing weapons that use this key product, or they can go ahead and design the weapons and stockpile enough of the key high-tech components or materials to last through an armed conflict. There is a U.S. Defense National Stockpile Center that has built up reserves of many materials, from aluminum oxides, antimony, and bauxite to tungsten, vegetable tannin extracts, and zinc (although many of these stockpiles have been reduced and sold in recent years). Think every country is pro-trade? How about the U.S.? The following Clear It Up might surprise you.

## How does the United States really feel about expanding trade?

How do people around the world feel about expanding trade between nations? In summer 2007, the Pew Foundation surveyed 45,000 people in 47 countries. One of the questions asked about opinions on growing trade ties between countries. **Table 21.3** shows the percentages who answered either "very good" or "somewhat good" for some of countries surveyed.

For those who think of the United States as the world's leading supporter of expanding trade, the survey results may be perplexing. When adding up the shares of those who say that growing trade ties between countries is "very good" or "somewhat good," Americans had the least favorable attitude toward increasing globalization, while the Chinese and South Africans ranked highest. In fact, among the 47 countries surveyed, the United States ranked by far the lowest on this measure, followed by Egypt, Italy, and Argentina.

| Country | Very Good | Somewhat Good | Total |
|---|---|---|---|
| China | 38% | 53% | 91% |
| South Africa | 42% | 43% | 87% |
| South Korea | 24% | 62% | 86% |
| Germany | 30% | 55% | 85% |
| Canada | 29% | 53% | 82% |
| United Kingdom | 28% | 50% | 78% |
| Mexico | 22% | 55% | 77% |
| Brazil | 13% | 59% | 72% |
| Japan | 17% | 55% | 72% |
| United States | 14% | 45% | 59% |

**Table 21.3 The Status of Growing Trade Ties between Countries** (Source: http://www.pewglobal.org/files/pdf/258.pdf)

One final reason why economists often treat the **national interest argument** skeptically is that lobbyists and politicians can tout almost any product as vital to national security. In 1954, the United States became worried that it was importing half of the wool required for military uniforms, so it declared wool and mohair to be "strategic materials" and began to give subsidies to wool and mohair farmers. Although the government removed wool from the official list of "strategic" materials in 1960, the subsidies for mohair continued for almost 40 years until the government repealed them in 1993, and then reinstated them in 2002. All too often, the national interest argument has become an excuse for handing out the indirect subsidy of protectionism to certain industries or companies. After all, politicians, not nonpartisan analysts make decisions about what constitutes a key strategic material.

# 21.4 | How Governments Enact Trade Policy: Globally, Regionally, and Nationally

By the end of this section, you will be able to:
- Explain the origin and role of the World Trade Organization (WTO) and General Agreement on Tariffs and Trade (GATT)
- Discuss the significance and provide examples of regional trading agreements
- Analyze trade policy at the national level
- Evaluate long-term trends in barriers to trade

These public policy arguments about how nations should react to globalization and trade are fought out at several levels: at the global level through the World Trade Organization and through regional trade agreements between pairs or groups of countries.

## The World Trade Organization

The World Trade Organization (WTO) was officially born in 1995, but its history is much longer. In the years after the Great Depression and World War II, there was a worldwide push to build institutions that would tie the nations of the world together. The United Nations officially came into existence in 1945. The World Bank, which assists the poorest people in the world, and the International Monetary Fund, which addresses issues raised by international financial transactions, were both created in 1946. The third planned organization was to be an International Trade Organization, which would manage international trade. The United Nations was unable to agree to this. Instead, 27 nations signed the **General Agreement on Tariffs and Trade (GATT)** in Geneva, Switzerland on October 30, 1947 to provide a forum in which nations could come together to negotiate reductions in tariffs and other barriers to trade. In 1995, the GATT transformed into the WTO.

The GATT process was to negotiate an agreement to reduce barriers to trade, sign that agreement, pause for a while, and then start negotiating the next agreement. **Table 21.4** shows rounds of talks in the GATT, and now the WTO. Notice that the early rounds of GATT talks took a relatively short time, included a small number of countries, and focused almost entirely on reducing tariffs. Since the mid-1960s, however, rounds of trade talks have taken years, included a large number of countries, and have included an ever-broadening range of issues.

| Year | Place or Name of Round | Main Subjects | Number of Countries Involved |
|------|------------------------|---------------|------------------------------|
| 1947 | Geneva | Tariff reduction | 23 |
| 1949 | Annecy | Tariff reduction | 13 |
| 1951 | Torquay | Tariff reduction | 38 |
| 1956 | Geneva | Tariff reduction | 26 |
| 1960–61 | Dillon round | Tariff reduction | 26 |
| 1964–67 | Kennedy round | Tariffs, anti-dumping measures | 62 |
| 1973–79 | Tokyo round | Tariffs, nontariff barriers | 102 |

**Table 21.4 The Negotiating Rounds of GATT and the World Trade Organization**

| Year | Place or Name of Round | Main Subjects | Number of Countries Involved |
|---|---|---|---|
| 1986–94 | Uruguay round | Tariffs, nontariff barriers, services, intellectual property, dispute settlement, textiles, agriculture, creation of WTO | 123 |
| 2001– | Doha round | Agriculture, services, intellectual property, competition, investment, environment, dispute settlement | 147 |

**Table 21.4 The Negotiating Rounds of GATT and the World Trade Organization**

The sluggish pace of GATT negotiations led to an old joke that GATT really stood for Gentleman's Agreement to Talk and Talk. The slow pace of international trade talks, however, is understandable, even sensible. Having dozens of nations agree to any treaty is a lengthy process. GATT often set up separate trading rules for certain industries, like agriculture, and separate trading rules for certain countries, like the low-income countries. There were rules, exceptions to rules, opportunities to opt out of rules, and precise wording to be fought over in every case. Like the GATT before it, the WTO is not a world government, with power to impose its decisions on others. The total staff of the WTO in 2014 is 640 people and its annual budget (as of 2014) is $197 million, which makes it smaller in size than many large universities.

## Regional Trading Agreements

There are different types of economic integration across the globe, ranging from **free trade agreements**, in which participants allow each other's imports without tariffs or quotas, to **common markets**, in which participants have a common external trade policy as well as free trade within the group, to full **economic unions**, in which, in addition to a common market, monetary and fiscal policies are coordinated. Many nations belong both to the World Trade Organization and to regional trading agreements.

The best known of these regional trading agreements is the European Union. In the years after World War II, leaders of several European nations reasoned that if they could tie their economies together more closely, they might be more likely to avoid another devastating war. Their efforts began with a free trade association, evolved into a common market, and then transformed into what is now a full economic union, known as the European Union. The EU, as it is often called, has a number of goals. For example, in the early 2000s it introduced a common currency for Europe, the euro, and phased out most of the former national forms of money like the German mark and the French franc, though a few have retained their own currency. Another key element of the union is to eliminate barriers to the mobility of goods, labor, and capital across Europe.

For the United States, perhaps the best-known regional trading agreement is the North American Free Trade Agreement (NAFTA). The United States also participates in some less-prominent regional trading agreements, like the Caribbean Basin Initiative, which offers reduced tariffs for imports from these countries, and a free trade agreement with Israel.

The world has seen a flood of regional trading agreements in recent years. About 100 such agreements are now in place. **Table 21.5** lists a few of the more prominent ones. Some are just agreements to continue talking. Others set specific goals for reducing tariffs, import quotas, and nontariff barriers. One economist described the current trade treaties as a "spaghetti bowl," which is what a map with lines connecting all the countries with trade treaties looks like.

There is concern among economists who favor free trade that some of these regional agreements may promise free trade, but actually act as a way for the countries within the regional agreement to try to limit trade from anywhere else. In some cases, the regional trade agreements may even conflict with the broader agreements of the World Trade Organization.

| Trade Agreements | Participating Countries |
| --- | --- |
| Asia Pacific Economic Cooperation (APEC) | Australia, Brunei, Canada, Chile, People's Republic of China, Hong Kong, China, Indonesia, Japan, Republic of Korea, Malaysia, Mexico, New Zealand, Papua New Guinea, Peru, Philippines, Russia, Singapore, Chinese Taipei, Thailand, United States, Vietnam |
| European Union (EU) | Austria, Belgium, Bulgaria, Cyprus, Czech Republic, Denmark, Estonia, Finland, France, Germany, Greece, Hungary, Ireland, Italy, Latvia, Lithuania, Luxembourg, Malta, Netherlands, Poland, Portugal, Romania, Slovakia, Slovenia, Spain, Sweden, United Kingdom* |
| North America Free Trade Agreement (NAFTA) | Canada, Mexico, United States |
| Latin American Integration Association (LAIA) | Argentina, Bolivia, Brazil, Chile, Columbia, Ecuador, Mexico, Paraguay, Peru, Uruguay, Venezuela |
| Association of Southeast Asian Nations (ASEAN) | Brunei, Cambodia, Indonesia, Laos, Malaysia, Myanmar, Philippines, Singapore, Thailand, Vietnam |
| Southern African Development Community (SADC) | Angola, Botswana, Congo, Lesotho, Madagascar, Malawi, Mauritius, Mozambique, Namibia, Seychelles, South Africa, Swaziland, Tanzania, Zambia, Zimbabwe |

**Table 21.5 Some Regional Trade Agreements** * Following the 2016 referendum vote to leave the European Union, the UK government triggered the withdrawal process on March 29, 2017, setting the date for the UK to leave by April 2019.

## Trade Policy at the National Level

Yet another dimension of trade policy, along with international and regional trade agreements, happens at the national level. The United States, for example, imposes import quotas on sugar, because of a fear that such imports would drive down the price of sugar and thus injure domestic sugar producers. One of the jobs of the United States Department of Commerce is to determine if there is import dumping from other countries. The United States International Trade Commission—a government agency—determines whether the dumping has substantially injured domestic industries, and if so, the president can impose tariffs that are intended to offset the unfairly low price.

In the arena of trade policy, the battle often seems to be between national laws that increase protectionism and international agreements that try to reduce protectionism, like the WTO. Why would a country pass laws or negotiate agreements to shut out certain foreign products, like sugar or textiles, while simultaneously negotiating to reduce trade barriers in general? One plausible answer is that international trade agreements offer a method for countries to restrain their own special interests. A member of Congress can say to an industry lobbying for tariffs or quotas on imports: "Sure would like to help you, but that pesky WTO agreement just won't let me."

# Link It Up ⚭

If consumers are the biggest losers from trade, why do they not fight back? The quick answer is because it is easier to organize a small group of people around a narrow interest (producers) versus a large group that has diffuse interests (consumers). This is a question about trade policy theory. Visit this website (http://openstaxcollege.org/l/tradepolicy) and read the article by Jonathan Rauch.

## Long-Term Trends in Barriers to Trade

In newspaper headlines, trade policy appears mostly as disputes and acrimony. Countries are almost constantly threatening to challenge other nations' "unfair" trading practices. Cases are brought to the dispute settlement procedures of the WTO, the European Union, NAFTA, and other regional trading agreements. Politicians in national legislatures, goaded on by lobbyists, often threaten to pass bills that will "establish a fair playing field" or "prevent unfair trade"—although most such bills seek to accomplish these high-sounding goals by placing more restrictions on trade. Protesters in the streets may object to specific trade rules or to the entire practice of international trade.

Through all the controversy, the general trend in the last 60 years is clearly toward lower barriers to trade. The average level of tariffs on imported products charged by industrialized countries was 40% in 1946. By 1990, after decades of GATT negotiations, it was down to less than 5%. One of the reasons that GATT negotiations shifted from focusing on tariff reduction in the early rounds to a broader agenda was that tariffs had been reduced so dramatically there was not much more to do in that area. U.S. tariffs have followed this general pattern: After rising sharply during the Great Depression, tariffs dropped off to less than 2% by the end of the century. Although measures of import quotas and nontariff barriers are less exact than those for tariffs, they generally appear to be at lower levels than they had been previously, too.

Thus, the last half-century has seen both a dramatic reduction in government-created barriers to trade, such as tariffs, import quotas, and nontariff barriers, and also a number of technological developments that have made international trade easier, like advances in transportation, communication, and information management. The result has been the powerful surge of international trade.

# 21.5 | The Tradeoffs of Trade Policy

By the end of this section, you will be able to:

- Asses the complexity of international trade
- Discuss why a market-oriented economy is so affected by international trade
- Explain disruptive market change

Economists readily acknowledge that international trade is not all sunshine, roses, and happy endings. Over time, the average person gains from international trade, both as a worker who has greater productivity and higher wages because of the benefits of specialization and comparative advantage, and as a consumer who can benefit from shopping all over the world for a greater variety of quality products at attractive prices. The "average person," however, is hypothetical, not real—representing a mix of those who have done very well, those who have done all right, and those who have done poorly. It is a legitimate concern of public policy to focus not just on the average or on the success stories, but also on those who have not been so fortunate. Workers in other countries, the environment, and prospects for new industries and materials that might be of key importance to the national economy are also all legitimate issues.

The common belief among economists is that it is better to embrace the gains from trade, and then deal with the costs and tradeoffs with other policy tools, than it is to cut off trade to avoid the costs and tradeoffs.

To gain a better intuitive understanding for this argument, consider a hypothetical American company called Technotron. Technotron invents a new scientific technology that allows the firm to increase the output and quality of its goods with a smaller number of workers at a lower cost. As a result of this technology, other U.S. firms in this industry will lose money and will also have to lay off workers—and some of the competing firms will even go bankrupt. Should the United States government protect the existing firms and their employees by making it illegal for Technotron to use its new technology? Most people who live in market-oriented economies would oppose trying to block better products that lower the cost of services. Certainly, there is a case for society providing temporary support and assistance for those who find themselves without work. Many would argue for government support of programs that encourage retraining and acquiring additional skills. Government might also support research and development efforts, so that other firms may find ways of outdoing Technotron. Blocking the new technology altogether, however, seems like a mistake. After all, few people would advocate giving up electricity because it caused so much disruption to the kerosene and candle business. Few would suggest holding back on improvements in medical technology because they might cause companies selling leeches and snake oil to lose money. In short, most people view disruptions due to technological change as a necessary cost that is worth bearing.

Now, imagine that Technotron's new "technology" is as simple as this: the company imports what it sells from another country. In other words, think of foreign trade as a type of innovative technology. The objective situation is now exactly the same as before. Because of Technotron's new technology—which in this case is importing goods from another county—other firms in this industry will lose money and lay off workers. Just as it would have been inappropriate and ultimately foolish to respond to the disruptions of new scientific technology by trying to shut it down, it would be inappropriate and ultimately foolish to respond to the disruptions of international trade by trying to restrict trade.

Some workers and firms will suffer because of international trade. In a living, breathing market-oriented economy, some workers and firms will always be experiencing disruptions, for a wide variety of reasons. Corporate management can be better or worse. Workers for a certain firm can be more or less productive. Tough domestic competitors can create just as much disruption as tough foreign competitors. Sometimes a new product is a hit with consumers; sometimes it is a flop. Sometimes a company is blessed by a run of good luck or stricken with a run of bad luck. For some firms, international trade will offer great opportunities for expanding productivity and jobs; for other firms, trade will impose stress and pain. The disruption caused by international trade is not fundamentally different from all the other disruptions caused by the other workings of a market economy.

In other words, the economic analysis of free trade does not rely on a belief that foreign trade is not disruptive or does not pose tradeoffs; indeed, the story of Technotron begins with a particular **disruptive market change**—a new technology—that causes real tradeoffs. In thinking about the disruptions of foreign trade, or any of the other possible costs and tradeoffs of foreign trade discussed in this chapter, the best public policy solutions typically do not involve protectionism, but instead involve finding ways for public policy to address the particular issues resulting from these disruptions, costs, and tradeoffs, while still allowing the benefits of international trade to occur.

## Bring it Home

### What's the Downside of Protection?

The domestic flat-panel display industry employed many workers before the ITC imposed the dumping margin tax. Flat-panel displays make up a significant portion of the cost of producing laptop computers—as much as 50%. Therefore, the antidumping tax would substantially increase the cost, and thus the price, of U.S.-manufactured laptops. As a result of the ITC's decision, Apple moved its domestic manufacturing plant for Macintosh computers to Ireland (where it had an existing plant). Toshiba shut down its U.S. manufacturing plant for laptops. And IBM cancelled plans to open a laptop manufacturing plant in North Carolina, instead deciding to expand production at its plant in Japan. In this case, rather than having the desired effect of protecting U.S. interests and giving domestic manufacturing an advantage over items manufactured elsewhere, it had the unintended effect of driving the manufacturing completely out of the country. Many people lost their jobs and most flat-panel display production now occurs in countries other than the United States.

# KEY TERMS

**anti-dumping laws**  laws that block imports sold below the cost of production and impose tariffs that would increase the price of these imports to reflect their cost of production

**common market**  economic agreement between countries to allow free trade in goods, services, labor, and financial capital between members while having a common external trade policy

**disruptive market change**  innovative new product or production technology which disrupts the status quo in a market, leading the innovators to earn more income and profits and the other firms to lose income and profits, unless they can come up with their own innovations

**dumping**  selling internationally traded goods below their cost of production

**economic union**  economic agreement between countries to allow free trade between members, a common external trade policy, and coordinated monetary and fiscal policies

**free trade agreement**  economic agreement between countries to allow free trade between members

**General Agreement on Tariffs and Trade (GATT)**  forum in which nations could come together to negotiate reductions in tariffs and other barriers to trade; the precursor to the World Trade Organization

**import quotas**  numerical limits on the quantity of products that a country can import

**national interest argument**  the argument that there are compelling national interests against depending on key imports from other nations

**nontariff barriers**  ways a nation can draw up rules, regulations, inspections, and paperwork to make it more costly or difficult to import products

**protectionism**  government policies to reduce or block imports

**race to the bottom**  when production locates in countries with the lowest environmental (or other) standards, putting pressure on all countries to reduce their environmental standards

**World Trade Organization (WTO)**  organization that seeks to negotiate reductions in barriers to trade and to adjudicate complaints about violations of international trade policy; successor to the General Agreement on Tariffs and Trade (GATT)

# KEY CONCEPTS AND SUMMARY

## 21.1 Protectionism: An Indirect Subsidy from Consumers to Producers

There are three tools for restricting the flow of trade: tariffs, import quotas, and nontariff barriers. When a country places limitations on imports from abroad, regardless of whether it uses tariffs, quotas, or nontariff barriers, it is said to be practicing protectionism. Protectionism will raise the price of the protected good in the domestic market, which causes domestic consumers to pay more, but domestic producers to earn more.

## 21.2 International Trade and Its Effects on Jobs, Wages, and Working Conditions

As international trade increases, it contributes to a shift in jobs away from industries where that economy does not have a comparative advantage and toward industries where it does have a comparative advantage. The degree to which trade affects labor markets has much to do with the structure of the labor market in that country and the adjustment process in other industries. Global trade should raise the average level of wages by increasing productivity. However, this increase in average wages may include both gains to workers in certain jobs and industries and losses to others.

In thinking about labor practices in low-income countries, it is useful to draw a line between what is unpleasant to think about and what is morally objectionable. For example, low wages and long working hours in poor countries are unpleasant to think about, but for people in low-income parts of the world, it may well be the best option open to them. Practices like child labor and forced labor are morally objectionable and many countries refuse to import products made using these practices.

## 21.3 Arguments in Support of Restricting Imports

There are a number of arguments that support restricting imports. These arguments are based around industry and competition, environmental concerns, and issues of safety and security.

The infant industry argument for protectionism is that small domestic industries need to be temporarily nurtured and protected from foreign competition for a time so that they can grow into strong competitors. In some cases, notably in East Asia, this approach has worked. Often, however, the infant industries never grow up. On the other hand, arguments against dumping (which is setting prices below the cost of production to drive competitors out of the market), often simply seem to be a convenient excuse for imposing protectionism.

Low-income countries typically have lower environmental standards than high-income countries because they are more worried about immediate basics such as food, education, and healthcare. However, except for a small number of extreme cases, shutting off trade seems unlikely to be an effective method of pursuing a cleaner environment.

Finally, there are arguments involving safety and security. Under the rules of the World Trade Organization, countries are allowed to set whatever standards for product safety they wish, but the standards must be the same for domestic products as for imported products and there must be a scientific basis for the standard. The national interest argument for protectionism holds that it is unwise to import certain key products because if the nation becomes dependent on key imported supplies, it could be vulnerable to a cutoff. However, it is often wiser to stockpile resources and to use foreign supplies when available, rather than preemptively restricting foreign supplies so as not to become dependent on them.

## 21.4 How Governments Enact Trade Policy: Globally, Regionally, and Nationally

Governments determine trade policy at many different levels: administrative agencies within government, laws passed by the legislature, regional negotiations between a small group of nations (sometimes just two), and global negotiations through the World Trade Organization. During the second half of the twentieth century, trade barriers have, in general, declined quite substantially in the United States economy and in the global economy. One reason why countries sign international trade agreements to commit themselves to free trade is to give themselves protection against their own special interests. When an industry lobbies for protection from foreign producers, politicians can point out that, because of the trade treaty, their hands are tied.

## 21.5 The Tradeoffs of Trade Policy

International trade certainly has income distribution effects. This is hardly surprising. All domestic or international competitive market forces are disruptive. They cause companies and industries to rise and fall. Government has a role to play in cushioning workers against the disruptions of the market. However, just as it would be unwise in the long term to clamp down on new technology and other causes of disruption in domestic markets, it would be unwise to clamp down on foreign trade. In both cases, the disruption brings with it economic benefits.

# SELF-CHECK QUESTIONS

**1.** Explain how a tariff reduction causes an increase in the equilibrium quantity of imports and a decrease in the equilibrium price. *Hint:* Consider the **Work It Out** "Effects of Trade Barriers."

**2.** Explain how a subsidy on agricultural goods like sugar adversely affects the income of foreign producers of imported sugar.

**3.** Explain how trade barriers save jobs in protected industries, but only by costing jobs in other industries.

**4.** Explain how trade barriers raise wages in protected industries by reducing average wages economy-wide.

**5.** How does international trade affect working conditions of low-income countries?

**6.** Do the jobs for workers in low-income countries that involve making products for export to high-income countries typically pay these workers more or less than their next-best alternative?

**7.** How do trade barriers affect the average income level in an economy?

**8.** How does the cost of "saving" jobs in protected industries compare to the workers' wages and salaries?

**9.** Explain how predatory pricing could be a motivation for dumping.

**10.** Why do low-income countries like Brazil, Egypt, or Vietnam have lower environmental standards than high-income countries like the Germany, Japan, or the United States?

**11.** Explain the logic behind the "race to the bottom" argument and the likely reason it has not occurred.

**12.** What are the conditions under which a country may use the unsafe products argument to block imports?

**13.** Why is the national security argument not convincing?

**14.** Assume a perfectly competitive market and the exporting country is small. Using a demand and supply diagram, show the impact of increasing standards on a low-income exporter of toys. Show the tariff's impact. Is the effect on toy prices the same or different? Why is a standards policy preferred to tariffs?

**15.** What is the difference between a free trade association, a common market, and an economic union?

**16.** Why would countries promote protectionist laws, while also negotiate for freer trade internationally?

**17.** What might account for the dramatic increase in international trade over the past 50 years?

**18.** How does competition, whether domestic or foreign, harm businesses?

**19.** What are the gains from competition?

# REVIEW QUESTIONS

**20.** Who does protectionism protect? From what does it protect them?

**21.** Name and define three policy tools for enacting protectionism.

**22.** How does protectionism affect the price of the protected good in the domestic market?

**23.** Does international trade, taken as a whole, increase the total number of jobs, decrease the total number of jobs, or leave the total number of jobs about the same?

**24.** Is international trade likely to have roughly the same effect on the number of jobs in each individual industry?

**25.** How is international trade, taken as a whole, likely to affect the average level of wages?

**26.** Is international trade likely to have about the same effect on everyone's wages?

**27.** What are main reasons for protecting "infant industries"? Why is it difficult to stop protecting them?

**28.** What is dumping? Why does prohibiting it often work better in theory than in practice?

**29.** What is the "race to the bottom" scenario?

**30.** Do the rules of international trade require that all nations impose the same consumer safety standards?

**31.** What is the national interest argument for protectionism with regard to certain products?

**32.** Name several of the international treaties where countries negotiate with each other over trade policy.

**33.** What is the general trend of trade barriers over recent decades: higher, lower, or about the same?

**34.** If opening up to free trade would benefit a nation, then why do nations not just eliminate their trade barriers, and not bother with international trade negotiations?

**35.** Who gains and who loses from trade?

**36.** Why is trade a good thing if some people lose?

**37.** What are some ways that governments can help people who lose from trade?

# CRITICAL THINKING QUESTIONS

**38.** Show graphically that for any tariff, there is an equivalent quota that would give the same result. What would be the difference, then, between the two types of trade barriers? *Hint*: It is not something you can see from the graph.

**39.** From the **Work It Out** "Effects of Trade Barriers," you can see that a tariff raises the price of imports. What is interesting is that the price rises by less than the amount of the tariff. Who pays the rest of the tariff amount? Can you show this graphically?

**40.** If trade barriers hurt the average worker in an economy (due to lower wages), why does government create trade barriers?

**41.** Why do you think labor standards and working conditions are lower in the low-income countries of the world than in countries like the United States?

**42.** How would direct subsidies to key industries be preferable to tariffs or quotas?

**43.** How can governments identify good candidates for infant industry protection? Can you suggest some key characteristics of good candidates? Why are industries like computers not good candidates for infant industry protection?

**44.** Microeconomic theory argues that it is economically rationale (and profitable) to sell additional output as long as the price covers the variable costs of production. How is this relevant to the determination of whether dumping has occurred?

**45.** How do you think Americans would feel if other countries began to urge the United States to increase environmental standards?

**46.** Is it legitimate to impose higher safety standards on imported goods that exist in the foreign country where the goods were produced?

**47.** Why might the unsafe consumer products argument be a more effective strategy (from the perspective of the importing country) than using tariffs or quotas to restrict imports?

**48.** Why might a tax on domestic consumption of resources critical for national security be a more efficient approach than barriers to imports?

**49.** Why do you think that the GATT rounds and, more recently, WTO negotiations have become longer and more difficult to resolve?

**50.** An economic union requires giving up some political autonomy to succeed. What are some examples of political power countries must give up to be members of an economic union?

**51.** What are some examples of innovative products that have disrupted their industries for the better?

**52.** In principle, the benefits of international trade to a country exceed the costs, no matter whether the country is importing or exporting. In practice, it is not always possible to compensate the losers in a country, for example, workers who lose their jobs due to foreign imports. In your opinion, does that mean that trade should be inhibited to prevent the losses?

**53.** Economists sometimes say that protectionism is the "second-best" choice for dealing with any particular problem. What they mean is that there is often a policy choice that is more direct or effective for dealing with the problem—a choice that would still allow the benefits of trade to occur. Explain why protectionism is a "second-best" choice for:
   a. helping workers as a group
   b. helping industries stay strong
   c. protecting the environment
   d. advancing national defense

**54.** Trade has income distribution effects. For example, suppose that because of a government-negotiated reduction in trade barriers, trade between Germany and the Czech Republic increases. Germany sells house paint to the Czech Republic. The Czech Republic sells alarm clocks to Germany. Would you expect this pattern of trade to increase or decrease jobs and wages in the paint industry in Germany? The alarm clock industry in Germany? The paint industry in Czech Republic? The alarm clock industry in Czech Republic? What has to happen for there to be no increase in total unemployment in both countries?

# PROBLEMS

**55.** Assume two countries, Thailand (T) and Japan (J), have one good: cameras. The demand (d) and supply (s) for cameras in Thailand and Japan is described by the following functions: $Qd^T = 60 - P$

$$Qs^T = -5 + \frac{1}{4}P \qquad Qd^J = 80 - P$$

$$Qs^J = -10 + \frac{1}{2}P$$

P is the price measured in a common currency used in both countries, such as the Thai Baht.

a. Compute the equilibrium price (P) and quantities (Q) in each country without trade.
b. Now assume that free trade occurs. The free-trade price goes to 56.36 Baht. Who exports and imports cameras and in what quantities?

**56.** You have just been put in charge of trade policy for Malawi. Coffee is a recent crop that is growing well and the Malawian export market is developing. As such, Malawi coffee is an infant industry. Malawi coffee producers come to you and ask for tariff protection from cheap Tanzanian coffee. What sorts of policies will you enact? Explain.

**57.** The country of Pepperland exports steel to the Land of Submarines. Information for the quantity demanded (Qd) and quantity supplied (Qs) in each country, in a world without trade, are given in **Table 21.6** and **Table 21.7**.

| Price ($) | Qd | Qs |
|---|---|---|
| 60 | 230 | 180 |
| 70 | 200 | 200 |
| 80 | 170 | 220 |
| 90 | 150 | 240 |
| 100 | 140 | 250 |

**Table 21.6 Pepperland**

| Price ($) | Qd | Qs |
|---|---|---|
| 60 | 430 | 310 |
| 70 | 420 | 330 |
| 80 | 410 | 360 |
| 90 | 400 | 400 |
| 100 | 390 | 440 |

**Table 21.7 Land of Submarines**

a. What would be the equilibrium price and quantity in each country in a world without trade? How can you tell?
b. What would be the equilibrium price and quantity in each country if trade is allowed to occur? How can you tell?
c. Sketch two supply and demand diagrams, one for each country, in the situation before trade.
d. On those diagrams, show the equilibrium price and the levels of exports and imports in the world after trade.
e. If the Land of Submarines imposes an anti-dumping import quota of 30, explain in general terms whether it will benefit or injure consumers and producers in each country.
f. Does your general answer change if the Land of Submarines imposes an import quota of 70?

# A | The Use of Mathematics in Principles of Economics

(This appendix should be consulted after first reading **Welcome to Economics!**) Economics is not math. There is no important concept in this course that cannot be explained without mathematics. That said, math is a tool that can be used to illustrate economic concepts. Remember the saying a picture is worth a thousand words? Instead of a picture, think of a graph. It is the same thing. Economists use models as the primary tool to derive insights about economic issues and problems. Math is one way of working with (or manipulating) economic models.

There are other ways of representing models, such as text or narrative. But why would you use your fist to bang a nail, if you had a hammer? Math has certain advantages over text. It disciplines your thinking by making you specify exactly what you mean. You can get away with fuzzy thinking in your head, but you cannot when you reduce a model to algebraic equations. At the same time, math also has disadvantages. Mathematical models are necessarily based on simplifying assumptions, so they are not likely to be perfectly realistic. Mathematical models also lack the nuances which can be found in narrative models. The point is that math is one tool, but it is not the only tool or even always the best tool economists can use. So what math will you need for this book? The answer is: little more than high school algebra and graphs. You will need to know:

- What a function is
- How to interpret the equation of a line (i.e., slope and intercept)
- How to manipulate a line (i.e., changing the slope or the intercept)
- How to compute and interpret a growth rate (i.e., percentage change)
- How to read and manipulate a graph

In this text, we will use the easiest math possible, and we will introduce it in this appendix. So if you find some math in the book that you cannot follow, come back to this appendix to review. Like most things, math has diminishing returns. A little math ability goes a long way; the more advanced math you bring in, the less additional knowledge that will get you. That said, if you are going to major in economics, you should consider learning a little calculus. It will be worth your while in terms of helping you learn advanced economics more quickly.

## Algebraic Models

Often economic models (or parts of models) are expressed in terms of mathematical functions. What is a function? A function describes a relationship. Sometimes the relationship is a definition. For example (using words), your professor is Adam Smith. This could be expressed as Professor = Adam Smith. Or Friends = Bob + Shawn + Margaret.

Often in economics, functions describe cause and effect. The variable on the left-hand side is what is being explained ("the effect"). On the right-hand side is what is doing the explaining ("the causes"). For example, suppose your GPA was determined as follows:

$$GPA = 0.25 \times combined\_SAT + 0.25 \times class\_attendance + 0.50 \times hours\_spent\_studying$$

This equation states that your GPA depends on three things: your combined SAT score, your class attendance, and the number of hours you spend studying. It also says that study time is twice as important (0.50) as either combined_SAT score (0.25) or class_attendance (0.25). If this relationship is true, how could you raise your GPA? By not skipping class and studying more. Note that you cannot do anything about your SAT score, since if you are in college, you have (presumably) already taken the SATs.

Of course, economic models express relationships using economic variables, like Budget = money_spent_on_econ_books + money_spent_on_music, assuming that the only things you buy are economics books and music.

Most of the relationships we use in this course are expressed as linear equations of the form:

$$y = b + mx$$

## Expressing Equations Graphically

Graphs are useful for two purposes. The first is to express equations visually, and the second is to display statistics or data. This section will discuss expressing equations visually.

To a mathematician or an economist, a variable is the name given to a quantity that may assume a range of values. In the equation of a line presented above, x and y are the variables, with x on the horizontal axis and y on the vertical axis, and b and m representing factors that determine the shape of the line. To see how this equation works, consider a numerical example:

$$y = 9 + 3x$$

In this equation for a specific line, the b term has been set equal to 9 and the m term has been set equal to 3. **Table A1** shows the values of x and y for this given equation. **Figure A1** shows this equation, and these values, in a graph. To construct the table, just plug in a series of different values for x, and then calculate what value of y results. In the figure, these points are plotted and a line is drawn through them.

| x | y |
|---|---|
| 0 | 9 |
| 1 | 12 |
| 2 | 15 |
| 3 | 18 |
| 4 | 21 |
| 5 | 24 |
| 6 | 27 |

Table A1 Values for the Slope Intercept Equation

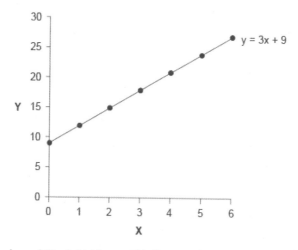

Figure A1 Slope and the Algebra of Straight Lines   This line graph has *x* on the horizontal axis and y on the vertical axis. The y-intercept—that is, the point where the line intersects the y-axis—is 9. The slope of the line is 3; that is, there is a rise of 3 on the vertical axis for every increase of 1 on the horizontal axis. The slope is the same all along a straight line.

This example illustrates how the b and m terms in an equation for a straight line determine the shape of the line. The b term is called the y-intercept. The reason for this name is that, if x = 0, then the b term will reveal where the line intercepts, or crosses, the y-axis. In this example, the line hits the vertical axis at 9. The m term in the equation for the line is the slope. Remember that slope is defined as rise over run; more specifically, the slope of a line from one point to another is the change in the vertical axis divided by the change in the horizontal axis. In this example, each time the x term increases by one (the run), the y term rises by three. Thus, the slope of this line is three. Specifying a y-intercept and a slope—that is, specifying b and m in the equation for a line—will identify a specific line. Although it is rare for real-world data points to arrange themselves as an exact straight line, it often turns out that a straight line can offer a reasonable approximation of actual data.

### Interpreting the Slope

The concept of slope is very useful in economics, because it measures the relationship between two variables. A positive slope means that two variables are positively related; that is, when x increases, so does y, or when x decreases, y decreases also. Graphically, a positive slope means that as a line on the line graph moves from left to right, the line rises. The length-weight relationship, shown in **Figure A3** later in this Appendix, has a positive slope. We will learn in other chapters that price and quantity supplied have a positive relationship; that is, firms will supply more when the price is higher.

A negative slope means that two variables are negatively related; that is, when x increases, y decreases, or when x decreases, y increases. Graphically, a negative slope means that, as the line on the line graph moves from left to right, the line falls. The altitude-air density relationship, shown in **Figure A4** later in this appendix, has a negative slope. We will learn that price and quantity demanded have a negative relationship; that is, consumers will purchase less when the price is higher.

A slope of zero means that there is no relationship between x and y. Graphically, the line is flat; that is, zero rise over the run. **Figure A5** of the unemployment rate, shown later in this appendix, illustrates a common pattern of many line graphs: some segments where the slope is positive, other segments where the slope is negative, and still other segments where the slope is close to zero.

The slope of a straight line between two points can be calculated in numerical terms. To calculate slope, begin by designating one point as the "starting point" and the other point as the "end point" and then calculating the rise over run between these two points. As an example, consider the slope of the air density graph between the points representing an altitude of 4,000 meters and an altitude of 6,000 meters:

Rise: Change in variable on vertical axis (end point minus original point)

$$= \ 0.100 - 0.307$$
$$= \ -0.207$$

Run: Change in variable on horizontal axis (end point minus original point)

$$= \ 6,000 - 4,000$$
$$= \ 2,000$$

Thus, the slope of a straight line between these two points would be that from the altitude of 4,000 meters up to 6,000 meters, the density of the air decreases by approximately 0.1 kilograms/cubic meter for each of the next 1,000 meters.

Suppose the slope of a line were to increase. Graphically, that means it would get steeper. Suppose the slope of a line were to decrease. Then it would get flatter. These conditions are true whether or not the slope was positive or negative to begin with. A higher positive slope means a steeper upward tilt to the line, while a smaller positive slope means a flatter upward tilt to the line. A negative slope that is larger in absolute value (that is, more negative) means a steeper downward tilt to the line. A slope of zero is a horizontal flat line. A vertical line has an infinite slope.

Suppose a line has a larger intercept. Graphically, that means it would shift out (or up) from the old origin, parallel to the old line. If a line has a smaller intercept, it would shift in (or down), parallel to the old line.

### Solving Models with Algebra

Economists often use models to answer a specific question, like: What will the unemployment rate be if the economy grows at 3% per year? Answering specific questions requires solving the "system" of equations that represent the model.

Suppose the demand for personal pizzas is given by the following equation:

$$Qd = 16 - 2P$$

where Qd is the amount of personal pizzas consumers want to buy (i.e., quantity demanded), and P is the price of pizzas. Suppose the supply of personal pizzas is:

$$Qs = 2 + 5P$$

where Qs is the amount of pizza producers will supply (i.e., quantity supplied).

Finally, suppose that the personal pizza market operates where supply equals demand, or

$$Qd = Qs$$

We now have a system of three equations and three unknowns (Qd, Qs, and P), which we can solve with algebra:

Since Qd = Qs, we can set the demand and supply equation equal to each other:

$$\begin{aligned} Qd &= Qs \\ 16 - 2P &= 2 + 5P \end{aligned}$$

Subtracting 2 from both sides and adding 2P to both sides yields:

$$\begin{aligned} 16 - 2P - 2 &= 2 + 5P - 2 \\ 14 - 2P &= 5P \\ 14 - 2P + 2P &= 5P + 2P \\ 14 &= 7P \\ \frac{14}{7} &= \frac{7P}{7} \\ 2 &= P \end{aligned}$$

In other words, the price of each personal pizza will be $2. How much will consumers buy?

Taking the price of $2, and plugging it into the demand equation, we get:

$$\begin{aligned} Qd &= 16 - 2P \\ &= 16 - 2(2) \\ &= 16 - 4 \\ &= 12 \end{aligned}$$

So if the price is $2 each, consumers will purchase 12. How much will producers supply? Taking the price of $2, and plugging it into the supply equation, we get:

$$\begin{aligned} Qs &= 2 + 5P \\ &= 2 + 5(2) \\ &= 2 + 10 \\ &= 12 \end{aligned}$$

So if the price is $2 each, producers will supply 12 personal pizzas. This means we did our math correctly, since Qd = Qs.

### Solving Models with Graphs

If algebra is not your forte, you can get the same answer by using graphs. Take the equations for Qd and Qs and graph them on the same set of axes as shown in **Figure A2**. Since P is on the vertical axis, it is easiest if you solve each equation for P. The demand curve is then $P = 8 - 0.5Qd$ and the supply curve is $P = -0.4 + 0.2Qs$. Note that the vertical intercepts are 8 and −0.4, and the slopes are −0.5 for demand and 0.2 for supply. If you draw the graphs carefully, you will see that where they cross (Qs = Qd), the price is $2 and the quantity is 12, just like the algebra predicted.

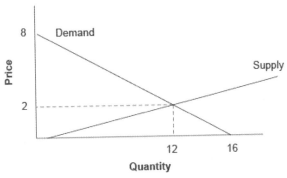

**Figure A2 Supply and Demand Graph**  The equations for Qd and Qs are displayed graphically by the sloped lines.

We will use graphs more frequently in this book than algebra, but now you know the math behind the graphs.

# Growth Rates

Growth rates are frequently encountered in real world economics. A growth rate is simply the percentage change in some quantity. It could be your income. It could be a business's sales. It could be a nation's GDP. The formula for computing a growth rate is straightforward:

$$\text{Percentage change} = \frac{\text{Change in quantity}}{\text{Quantity}}$$

Suppose your job pays $10 per hour. Your boss, however, is so impressed with your work that he gives you a $2 per hour raise. The percentage change (or growth rate) in your pay is $2/$10 = 0.20 or 20%.

To compute the growth rate for data over an extended period of time, for example, the average annual growth in GDP over a decade or more, the denominator is commonly defined a little differently. In the previous example, we defined the quantity as the initial quantity—or the quantity when we started. This is fine for a one-time calculation, but when we compute the growth over and over, it makes more sense to define the quantity as the average quantity over the period in question, which is defined as the quantity halfway between the initial quantity and the next quantity. This is harder to explain in words than to show with an example. Suppose a nation's GDP was $1 trillion in 2005 and $1.03 trillion in 2006. The growth rate between 2005 and 2006 would be the change in GDP ($1.03 trillion – $1.00 trillion) divided by the average GDP between 2005 and 2006 ($1.03 trillion + $1.00 trillion)/2. In other words:

$$= \frac{\$1.03 \text{ trillion} - \$1.00 \text{ trillion}}{(\$1.03 \text{ trillion} + \$1.00 \text{ trillion}) / 2}$$
$$= \frac{0.03}{1.015}$$
$$= 0.0296$$
$$= 2.96\% \text{ growth}$$

Note that if we used the first method, the calculation would be ($1.03 trillion – $1.00 trillion) / $1.00 trillion = 3% growth, which is approximately the same as the second, more complicated method. If you need a rough approximation, use the first method. If you need accuracy, use the second method.

A few things to remember: A positive growth rate means the quantity is growing. A smaller growth rate means the quantity is growing more slowly. A larger growth rate means the quantity is growing more quickly. A negative growth rate means the quantity is decreasing.

The same change over times yields a smaller growth rate. If you got a $2 raise each year, in the first year the growth rate would be $2/$10 = 20%, as shown above. But in the second year, the growth rate would be $2/$12 = 0.167 or 16.7% growth. In the third year, the same $2 raise would correspond to a $2/$14 = 14.2%. The moral of the story is this: To keep the growth rate the same, the change must increase each period.

# Displaying Data Graphically and Interpreting the Graph

Graphs are also used to display data or evidence. Graphs are a method of presenting numerical patterns. They condense detailed numerical information into a visual form in which relationships and numerical patterns can be seen more easily. For example, which countries have larger or smaller populations? A careful reader could examine a long list of numbers representing the populations of many countries, but with over 200 nations in the world, searching through such a list would take concentration and time. Putting these same numbers on a graph can quickly reveal population patterns. Economists use graphs both for a compact and readable presentation of groups of numbers and for building an intuitive grasp of relationships and connections.

Three types of graphs are used in this book: line graphs, pie graphs, and bar graphs. Each is discussed below. We also provide warnings about how graphs can be manipulated to alter viewers' perceptions of the relationships in the data.

**Line Graphs**

The graphs we have discussed so far are called line graphs, because they show a relationship between two variables: one measured on the horizontal axis and the other measured on the vertical axis.

Sometimes it is useful to show more than one set of data on the same axes. The data in Table A2 is displayed in Figure A3 which shows the relationship between two variables: length and median weight for American baby boys and girls during the first three years of life. (The median means that half of all babies weigh more than this and half weigh less.) The line graph measures length in inches on the horizontal axis and weight in pounds on the vertical axis. For example, point A on the figure shows that a boy who is 28 inches long will have a median weight of about 19 pounds. One line on the graph shows the length-weight relationship for boys and the other line shows the relationship for girls. This kind of graph is widely used by healthcare providers to check whether a child's physical development is roughly on track.

**Figure A3 The Length-Weight Relationship for American Boys and Girls**   The line graph shows the relationship between height and weight for boys and girls from birth to 3 years. Point A, for example, shows that a boy of 28 inches in height (measured on the horizontal axis) is typically 19 pounds in weight (measured on the vertical axis). These data apply only to children in the first three years of life.

| Boys from Birth to 36 Months | | Girls from Birth to 36 Months | |
|---|---|---|---|
| Length (inches) | Weight (pounds) | Length (inches) | Weight (pounds) |
| 20.0 | 8.0 | 20.0 | 7.9 |
| 22.0 | 10.5 | 22.0 | 10.5 |

**Table A2 Length to Weight Relationship for American Boys and Girls**

| Boys from Birth to 36 Months | | Girls from Birth to 36 Months | |
|---|---|---|---|
| 24.0 | 13.5 | 24.0 | 13.2 |
| 26.0 | 16.4 | 26.0 | 16.0 |
| 28.0 | 19.0 | 28.0 | 18.8 |
| 30.0 | 21.8 | 30.0 | 21.2 |
| 32.0 | 24.3 | 32.0 | 24.0 |
| 34.0 | 27.0 | 34.0 | 26.2 |
| 36.0 | 29.3 | 36.0 | 28.9 |
| 38.0 | 32.0 | 38.0 | 31.3 |

Table A2 Length to Weight Relationship for American Boys and Girls

Not all relationships in economics are linear. Sometimes they are curves. **Figure A4** presents another example of a line graph, representing the data from **Table A3**. In this case, the line graph shows how thin the air becomes when you climb a mountain. The horizontal axis of the figure shows altitude, measured in meters above sea level. The vertical axis measures the density of the air at each altitude. Air density is measured by the weight of the air in a cubic meter of space (that is, a box measuring one meter in height, width, and depth). As the graph shows, air pressure is heaviest at ground level and becomes lighter as you climb. **Figure A4** shows that a cubic meter of air at an altitude of 500 meters weighs approximately one kilogram (about 2.2 pounds). However, as the altitude increases, air density decreases. A cubic meter of air at the top of Mount Everest, at about 8,828 meters, would weigh only 0.023 kilograms. The thin air at high altitudes explains why many mountain climbers need to use oxygen tanks as they reach the top of a mountain.

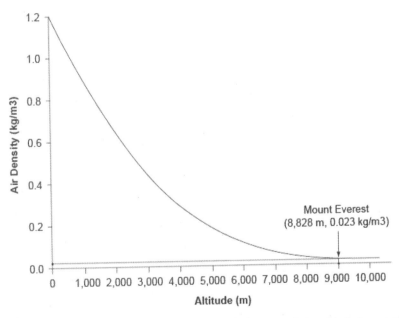

Figure A4 Altitude-Air Density Relationship   This line graph shows the relationship between altitude, measured in meters above sea level, and air density, measured in kilograms of air per cubic meter. As altitude rises, air density declines. The point at the top of Mount Everest has an altitude of approximately 8,828 meters above sea level (the horizontal axis) and air density of 0.023 kilograms per cubic meter (the vertical axis).

| Altitude (meters) | Air Density (kg/cubic meters) |
| --- | --- |
| 0 | 1.200 |
| 500 | 1.093 |
| 1,000 | 0.831 |
| 1,500 | 0.678 |
| 2,000 | 0.569 |
| 2,500 | 0.484 |
| 3,000 | 0.415 |
| 3,500 | 0.357 |
| 4,000 | 0.307 |
| 4,500 | 0.231 |
| 5,000 | 0.182 |
| 5,500 | 0.142 |
| 6,000 | 0.100 |
| 6,500 | 0.085 |
| 7,000 | 0.066 |
| 7,500 | 0.051 |
| 8,000 | 0.041 |
| 8,500 | 0.025 |
| 9,000 | 0.022 |
| 9,500 | 0.019 |
| 10,000 | 0.014 |

**Table A3 Altitude to Air Density Relationship**

The length-weight relationship and the altitude-air density relationships in these two figures represent averages. If you were to collect actual data on air pressure at different altitudes, the same altitude in different geographic locations will have slightly different air density, depending on factors like how far you are from the equator, local weather conditions, and the humidity in the air. Similarly, in measuring the height and weight of children for the previous line graph, children of a particular height would have a range of different weights, some above average and some below. In the real world, this sort of variation in data is common. The task of a researcher is to organize that data in a way that helps to understand typical patterns. The study of statistics, especially when combined with computer statistics and spreadsheet programs, is a great help in organizing this kind of data, plotting line graphs, and looking for typical underlying relationships. For most economics and social science majors, a statistics course will be required at some point.

One common line graph is called a time series, in which the horizontal axis shows time and the vertical axis displays another variable. Thus, a time series graph shows how a variable changes over time. **Figure A5** shows the unemployment rate in the United States since 1975, where unemployment is defined as the percentage of adults who want jobs and are looking for a job, but cannot find one. The points for the unemployment rate in each year are plotted on the graph, and a line then connects the points, showing how the unemployment rate has moved up and down since 1975. The line graph makes it easy to see, for example, that the highest unemployment rate during this time period was slightly less than 10% in the early 1980s and 2010, while the unemployment rate declined from the early 1990s to the end of the 1990s, before rising and then falling back in the early 2000s, and then rising sharply during the recession from 2008–2009.

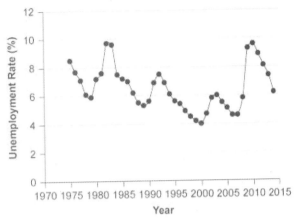

**Figure A5 U.S. Unemployment Rate, 1975–2014** This graph provides a quick visual summary of unemployment data. With a graph like this, it is easy to spot the times of high unemployment and of low unemployment.

## Pie Graphs

A pie graph (sometimes called a pie chart) is used to show how an overall total is divided into parts. A circle represents a group as a whole. The slices of this circular "pie" show the relative sizes of subgroups.

**Figure A6** shows how the U.S. population was divided among children, working age adults, and the elderly in 1970, 2000, and what is projected for 2030. The information is first conveyed with numbers in **Table A4**, and then in three pie charts. The first column of **Table A4** shows the total U.S. population for each of the three years. Columns 2–4 categorize the total in terms of age groups—from birth to 18 years, from 19 to 64 years, and 65 years and above. In columns 2–4, the first number shows the actual number of people in each age category, while the number in parentheses shows the percentage of the total population comprised by that age group.

| Year | Total Population | 19 and Under | 20–64 years | Over 65 |
|------|------------------|--------------|-------------|---------|
| 1970 | 205.0 million | 77.2 (37.6%) | 107.7 (52.5%) | 20.1 (9.8%) |
| 2000 | 275.4 million | 78.4 (28.5%) | 162.2 (58.9%) | 34.8 (12.6%) |
| 2030 | 351.1 million | 92.6 (26.4%) | 188.2 (53.6%) | 70.3 (20.0%) |

Table A4 U.S. Age Distribution, 1970, 2000, and 2030 (projected)

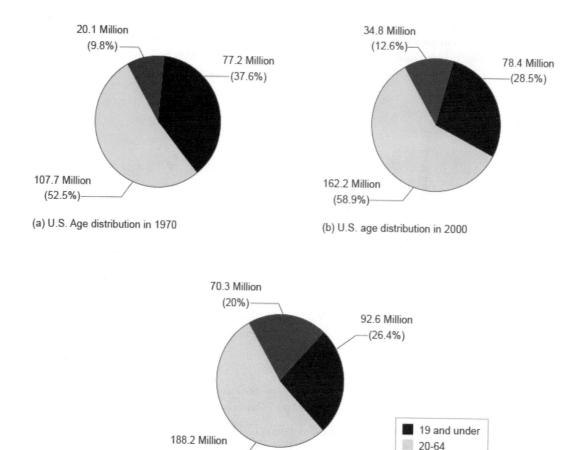

**Figure A6 Pie Graphs of the U.S. Age Distribution (numbers in millions)** The three pie graphs illustrate the division of total population into three age groups for the three different years.

In a pie graph, each slice of the pie represents a share of the total, or a percentage. For example, 50% would be half of the pie and 20% would be one-fifth of the pie. The three pie graphs in **Figure A6** show that the share of the U.S. population 65 and over is growing. The pie graphs allow you to get a feel for the relative size of the different age groups from 1970 to 2000 to 2030, without requiring you to slog through the specific numbers and percentages in the table. Some common examples of how pie graphs are used include dividing the population into groups by age, income level, ethnicity, religion, occupation; dividing different firms into categories by size, industry, number of employees; and dividing up government spending or taxes into its main categories.

**Bar Graphs**

A bar graph uses the height of different bars to compare quantities. **Table A5** lists the 12 most populous countries in the world. **Figure A7** provides this same data in a bar graph. The height of the bars corresponds to the population of each country. Although you may know that China and India are the most populous countries in the world, seeing how the bars on the graph tower over the other countries helps illustrate the magnitude of the difference between the sizes of national populations.

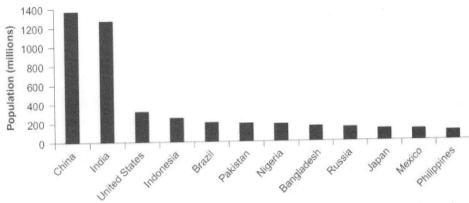

**Figure A7 Leading Countries of the World by Population, 2015 (in millions)** The graph shows the 12 countries of the world with the largest populations. The height of the bars in the bar graph shows the size of the population for each country.

| Country | Population |
|---|---|
| China | 1,369 |
| India | 1,270 |
| United States | 321 |
| Indonesia | 255 |
| Brazil | 204 |
| Pakistan | 190 |
| Nigeria | 184 |
| Bangladesh | 158 |
| Russia | 146 |
| Japan | 127 |
| Mexico | 121 |
| Philippines | 101 |

**Table A5 Leading 12 Countries of the World by Population**

Bar graphs can be subdivided in a way that reveals information similar to that we can get from pie charts. **Figure A8** offers three bar graphs based on the information from **Figure A6** about the U.S. age distribution in 1970, 2000, and 2030. **Figure A8** (a) shows three bars for each year, representing the total number of persons in each age bracket for each year. **Figure A8** (b) shows just one bar for each year, but the different age groups are now shaded inside the bar. In **Figure A8** (c), still based on the same data, the vertical axis measures percentages rather than the number of persons. In this case, all three bar graphs are the same height, representing 100% of the population, with each bar divided according to the percentage of population in each age group. It is sometimes easier for a reader to run his or her eyes across several bar graphs, comparing the shaded areas, rather than trying to compare several pie graphs.

(a) Bars for separate age groups

(b) Bars show total population divided into age groups

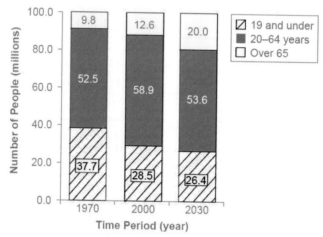

(c) Bars show total population divided into percentages

**Figure A8 U.S. Population with Bar Graphs** Population data can be represented in different ways. (a) Shows three bars for each year, representing the total number of persons in each age bracket for each year. (b) Shows just one bar for each year, but the different age groups are now shaded inside the bar. (c) Sets the vertical axis as a measure of percentages rather than the number of persons. All three bar graphs are the same height and each bar is divided according to the percentage of population in each age group.

**Figure A7** and **Figure A8** show how the bars can represent countries or years, and how the vertical axis can represent a numerical or a percentage value. Bar graphs can also compare size, quantity, rates, distances, and other quantitative categories.

### Comparing Line Graphs with Pie Charts and Bar Graphs

Now that you are familiar with pie graphs, bar graphs, and line graphs, how do you know which graph to use for your data? Pie graphs are often better than line graphs at showing how an overall group is divided. However, if a pie graph has too many slices, it can become difficult to interpret.

Bar graphs are especially useful when comparing quantities. For example, if you are studying the populations of different countries, as in **Figure A7**, bar graphs can show the relationships between the population sizes of multiple countries. Not only can it show these relationships, but it can also show breakdowns of different groups within the population.

A line graph is often the most effective format for illustrating a relationship between two variables that are both changing. For example, time series graphs can show patterns as time changes, like the unemployment rate over time.

Line graphs are widely used in economics to present continuous data about prices, wages, quantities bought and sold, the size of the economy.

**How Graphs Can Be Misleading**

Graphs not only reveal patterns; they can also alter how patterns are perceived. To see some of the ways this can be done, consider the line graphs of **Figure A9**, **Figure A10**, and **Figure A11**. These graphs all illustrate the unemployment rate—but from different perspectives.

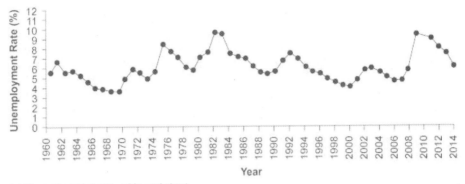

(a) Unemployment rate, wide and short

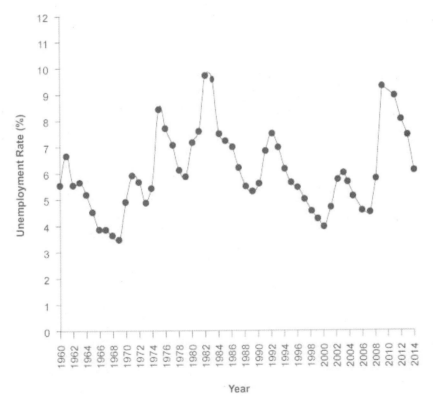

(b) Unemployment rate, narrow and tall

Figure A9

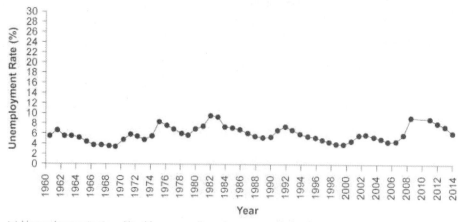

(c) Unemployment rate, with wider range of numbers on vertical axis

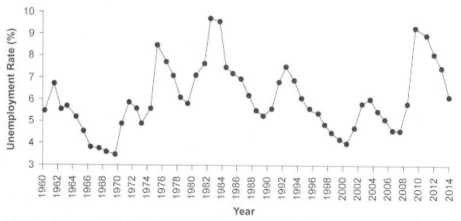

(d) Unemployment rate, with smaller range of numbers on vertical axis

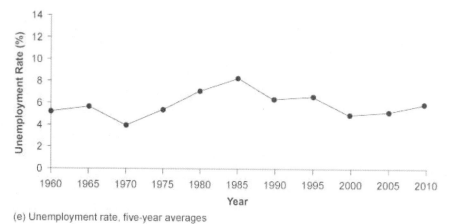

(e) Unemployment rate, five-year averages

**Figure A10 Presenting Unemployment Rates in Different Ways, All of Them Accurate**   Simply changing the width and height of the area in which data is displayed can alter the perception of the data.

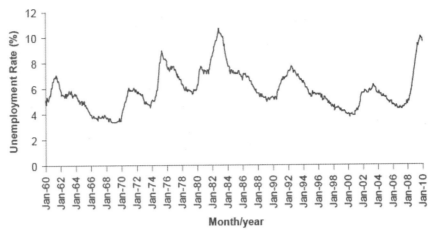

(f) Unemployment rate, monthly data

(g) Unemployment rates, since 1975 only

**Figure A11 Presenting Unemployment Rates in Different Ways, All of Them Accurate** Simply changing the width and height of the area in which data is displayed can alter the perception of the data.

Suppose you wanted a graph which gives the impression that the rise in unemployment in 2009 was not all that large, or all that extraordinary by historical standards. You might choose to present your data as in **Figure A9** (a). **Figure A9** (a) includes much of the same data presented earlier in **Figure A5**, but stretches the horizontal axis out longer relative to the vertical axis. By spreading the graph wide and flat, the visual appearance is that the rise in unemployment is not so large, and is similar to some past rises in unemployment. Now imagine you wanted to emphasize how unemployment spiked substantially higher in 2009. In this case, using the same data, you can stretch the vertical axis out relative to the horizontal axis, as in **Figure A9** (b), which makes all rises and falls in unemployment appear larger.

A similar effect can be accomplished without changing the length of the axes, but by changing the scale on the vertical axis. In **Figure A10** (c), the scale on the vertical axis runs from 0% to 30%, while in **Figure A10** (d), the vertical axis runs from 3% to 10%. Compared to **Figure A5**, where the vertical scale runs from 0% to 12%, **Figure A10** (c) makes the fluctuation in unemployment look smaller, while **Figure A10** (d) makes it look larger.

Another way to alter the perception of the graph is to reduce the amount of variation by changing the number of points plotted on the graph. **Figure A10** (e) shows the unemployment rate according to five-year averages. By averaging out some of the year-to-year changes, the line appears smoother and with fewer highs and lows. In reality, the unemployment rate is reported monthly, and **Figure A11** (f) shows the monthly figures since 1960, which fluctuate more than the five-year average. **Figure A11** (f) is also a vivid illustration of how graphs can compress lots of data. The graph includes monthly data since 1960, which over almost 50 years, works out to nearly 600 data points.

Reading that list of 600 data points in numerical form would be hypnotic. You can, however, get a good intuitive sense of these 600 data points very quickly from the graph.

A final trick in manipulating the perception of graphical information is that, by choosing the starting and ending points carefully, you can influence the perception of whether the variable is rising or falling. The original data show a general pattern with unemployment low in the 1960s, but spiking up in the mid-1970s, early 1980s, early 1990s, early 2000s, and late 2000s. **Figure A11** (g), however, shows a graph that goes back only to 1975, which gives an impression that unemployment was more-or-less gradually falling over time until the 2009 recession pushed it back up to its "original" level—which is a plausible interpretation if one starts at the high point around 1975.

These kinds of tricks—or shall we just call them "presentation choices"— are not limited to line graphs. In a pie chart with many small slices and one large slice, someone must decided what categories should be used to produce these slices in the first place, thus making some slices appear bigger than others. If you are making a bar graph, you can make the vertical axis either taller or shorter, which will tend to make variations in the height of the bars appear more or less.

Being able to read graphs is an essential skill, both in economics and in life. A graph is just one perspective or point of view, shaped by choices such as those discussed in this section. Do not always believe the first quick impression from a graph. View with caution.

## Key Concepts and Summary

Math is a tool for understanding economics and economic relationships can be expressed mathematically using algebra or graphs. The algebraic equation for a line is $y = b + mx$, where $x$ is the variable on the horizontal axis and $y$ is the variable on the vertical axis, the $b$ term is the y-intercept and the $m$ term is the slope. The slope of a line is the same at any point on the line and it indicates the relationship (positive, negative, or zero) between two economic variables.

Economic models can be solved algebraically or graphically. Graphs allow you to illustrate data visually. They can illustrate patterns, comparisons, trends, and apportionment by condensing the numerical data and providing an intuitive sense of relationships in the data. A line graph shows the relationship between two variables: one is shown on the horizontal axis and one on the vertical axis. A pie graph shows how something is allotted, such as a sum of money or a group of people. The size of each slice of the pie is drawn to represent the corresponding percentage of the whole. A bar graph uses the height of bars to show a relationship, where each bar represents a certain entity, like a country or a group of people. The bars on a bar graph can also be divided into segments to show subgroups.

Any graph is a single visual perspective on a subject. The impression it leaves will be based on many choices, such as what data or time frame is included, how data or groups are divided up, the relative size of vertical and horizontal axes, whether the scale used on a vertical starts at zero. Thus, any graph should be regarded somewhat skeptically, remembering that the underlying relationship can be open to different interpretations.

## Review Questions

### Exercise A1

Name three kinds of graphs and briefly state when is most appropriate to use each type of graph.

### Exercise A2

What is slope on a line graph?

### Exercise A3

What do the slices of a pie chart represent?

### Exercise A4

Why is a bar chart the best way to illustrate comparisons?

### Exercise A5

How does the appearance of positive slope differ from negative slope and from zero slope?

# B | The Expenditure-Output Model

(This appendix should be consulted after first reading **The Aggregate Demand/Aggregate Supply Model** and **The Keynesian Perspective**.) The fundamental ideas of Keynesian economics were developed before the AD/AS model was popularized. From the 1930s until the 1970s, Keynesian economics was usually explained with a different model, known as the expenditure-output approach. This approach is strongly rooted in the fundamental assumptions of Keynesian economics: it focuses on the total amount of spending in the economy, with no explicit mention of aggregate supply or of the price level (although as you will see, it is possible to draw some inferences about aggregate supply and price levels based on the diagram).

## The Axes of the Expenditure-Output Diagram

The expenditure-output model, sometimes also called the Keynesian cross diagram, determines the equilibrium level of real GDP by the point where the total or aggregate expenditures in the economy are equal to the amount of output produced. The axes of the Keynesian cross diagram presented in **Figure B1** show real GDP on the horizontal axis as a measure of output and aggregate expenditures on the vertical axis as a measure of spending.

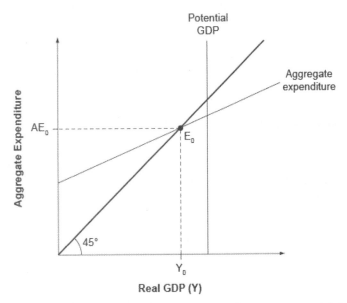

**Figure B1 The Expenditure-Output Diagram**   The aggregate expenditure-output model shows aggregate expenditures on the vertical axis and real GDP on the horizontal axis. A vertical line shows potential GDP where full employment occurs. The 45-degree line shows all points where aggregate expenditures and output are equal. The aggregate expenditure schedule shows how total spending or aggregate expenditure increases as output or real GDP rises. The intersection of the aggregate expenditure schedule and the 45-degree line will be the equilibrium. Equilibrium occurs at $E_0$, where aggregate expenditure $AE_0$ is equal to the output level $Y_0$.

Remember that GDP can be thought of in several equivalent ways: it measures both the value of spending on final goods and also the value of the production of final goods. All sales of the final goods and services that make up GDP will eventually end up as income for workers, for managers, and for investors and owners of firms. The sum of all the income received for contributing resources to GDP is called national income (Y). At some points in the discussion that follows, it will be useful to refer to real GDP as "national income." Both axes are measured in real (inflation-adjusted) terms.

**The Potential GDP Line and the 45-degree Line**

The Keynesian cross diagram contains two lines that serve as conceptual guideposts to orient the discussion. The first is a vertical line showing the level of potential GDP. Potential GDP means the same thing here that it means in the AD/AS diagrams: it refers to the quantity of output that the economy can produce with full employment of its labor and physical capital.

The second conceptual line on the Keynesian cross diagram is the 45-degree line, which starts at the origin and reaches up and to the right. A line that stretches up at a 45-degree angle represents the set of points (1, 1), (2, 2), (3, 3) and so on, where the measurement on the vertical axis is equal to the measurement on the horizontal axis. In this diagram, the 45-degree line shows the set of points where the level of aggregate expenditure in the economy, measured on the vertical axis, is equal to the level of output or national income in the economy, measured by GDP on the horizontal axis.

When the macroeconomy is in equilibrium, it must be true that the aggregate expenditures in the economy are equal to the real GDP—because by definition, GDP is the measure of what is spent on final sales of goods and services in the economy. Thus, the equilibrium calculated with a Keynesian cross diagram will always end up where aggregate expenditure and output are equal—which will only occur along the 45-degree line.

### The Aggregate Expenditure Schedule

The final ingredient of the Keynesian cross or expenditure-output diagram is the aggregate expenditure schedule, which will show the total expenditures in the economy for each level of real GDP. The intersection of the aggregate expenditure line with the 45-degree line—at point $E_0$ in **Figure B1**—will show the equilibrium for the economy, because it is the point where aggregate expenditure is equal to output or real GDP. After developing an understanding of what the aggregate expenditures schedule means, we will return to this equilibrium and how to interpret it.

# Building the Aggregate Expenditure Schedule

Aggregate expenditure is the key to the expenditure-income model. The aggregate expenditure schedule shows, either in the form of a table or a graph, how aggregate expenditures in the economy rise as real GDP or national income rises. Thus, in thinking about the components of the aggregate expenditure line—consumption, investment, government spending, exports and imports—the key question is how expenditures in each category will adjust as national income rises.

### Consumption as a Function of National Income

How do consumption expenditures increase as national income rises? People can do two things with their income: consume it or save it (for the moment, let's ignore the need to pay taxes with some of it). Each person who receives an additional dollar faces this choice. The marginal propensity to consume (MPC), is the share of the additional dollar of income a person decides to devote to consumption expenditures. The marginal propensity to save (MPS) is the share of the additional dollar a person decides to save. It must always hold true that:

$$MPC + MPS = 1$$

For example, if the marginal propensity to consume out of the marginal amount of income earned is 0.9, then the marginal propensity to save is 0.1.

With this relationship in mind, consider the relationship among income, consumption, and savings shown in **Figure B2**. (Note that we use "Aggregate Expenditure" on the vertical axis in this and the following figures, because all consumption expenditures are parts of aggregate expenditures.)

An assumption commonly made in this model is that even if income were zero, people would have to consume something. In this example, consumption would be $600 even if income were zero. Then, the MPC is 0.8 and the MPS is 0.2. Thus, when income increases by $1,000, consumption rises by $800 and savings rises by $200. At an income of $4,000, total consumption will be the $600 that would be consumed even without any income, plus $4,000 multiplied by the marginal propensity to consume of 0.8, or $ 3,200, for a total of $ 3,800. The total amount of consumption and saving must always add up to the total amount of income. (Exactly how a situation of zero income and negative savings would work in practice is not important, because even low-income societies are not literally at zero income, so the point is hypothetical.) This relationship between income and consumption, illustrated in **Figure B2** and **Table B1**, is called the consumption function.

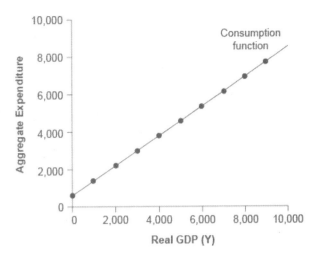

**Figure B2 The Consumption Function**  In the expenditure-output model, how does consumption increase with the level of national income? Output on the horizontal axis is conceptually the same as national income, since the value of all final output that is produced and sold must be income to someone, somewhere in the economy. At a national income level of zero, $600 is consumed. Then, each time income rises by $1,000, consumption rises by $800, because in this example, the marginal propensity to consume is 0.8.

The pattern of consumption shown in **Table B1** is plotted in **Figure B2**. To calculate consumption, multiply the income level by 0.8, for the marginal propensity to consume, and add $600, for the amount that would be consumed even if income was zero. Consumption plus savings must be equal to income.

| Income | Consumption | Savings |
|---|---|---|
| $0 | $600 | –$600 |
| $1,000 | $1,400 | –$400 |
| $2,000 | $2,200 | –$200 |
| $3,000 | $3,000 | $0 |
| $4,000 | $3,800 | $200 |
| $5,000 | $4,600 | $400 |
| $6,000 | $5,400 | $600 |
| $7,000 | $6,200 | $800 |
| $8,000 | $7,000 | $1,000 |
| $9,000 | $7,800 | $1,200 |

**Table B1 The Consumption Function**

However, a number of factors other than income can also cause the entire consumption function to shift. These factors were summarized in the earlier discussion of consumption, and listed in **Table B1**. When the consumption function moves, it can shift in two ways: either the entire consumption function can move up or down in a parallel manner, or the slope of the consumption function can shift so that it becomes steeper or flatter. For example, if a tax cut leads consumers to spend more, but does not affect their marginal propensity to consume, it would cause an upward shift to a new consumption function that is parallel to the original one. However, a change in household preferences for saving that reduced the marginal propensity to save would cause the slope of the consumption function to become steeper: that is, if the savings rate is lower, then every increase in income leads to a larger rise in consumption.

### Investment as a Function of National Income

Investment decisions are forward-looking, based on expected rates of return. Precisely because investment decisions depend primarily on perceptions about future economic conditions, they do *not* depend primarily on the level of GDP in the current year. Thus, on a Keynesian cross diagram, the investment function can be drawn as a horizontal line, at a fixed level of expenditure. **Figure B3** shows an investment function where the level of investment is, for the sake of concreteness, set at the specific level of 500. Just as a consumption function shows the relationship between consumption levels and real GDP (or national income), the investment function shows the relationship between investment levels and real GDP.

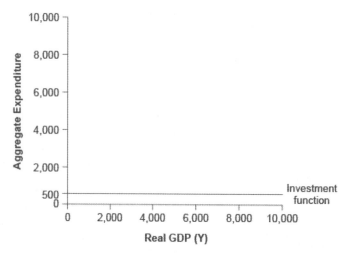

**Figure B3 The Investment Function**   The investment function is drawn as a flat line because investment is based on interest rates and expectations about the future, and so it does not change with the level of current national income. In this example, investment expenditures are at a level of 500. However, changes in factors like technological opportunities, expectations about near-term economic growth, and interest rates would all cause the investment function to shift up or down.

The appearance of the investment function as a horizontal line does not mean that the level of investment never moves. It means only that in the context of this two-dimensional diagram, the level of investment on the vertical aggregate expenditure axis does not vary according to the current level of real GDP on the horizontal axis. However, all the other factors that vary investment—new technological opportunities, expectations about near-term economic growth, interest rates, the price of key inputs, and tax incentives for investment—can cause the horizontal investment function to shift up or down.

### Government Spending and Taxes as a Function of National Income

In the Keynesian cross diagram, government spending appears as a horizontal line, as in **Figure B4**, where government spending is set at a level of 1,300. As in the case of investment spending, this horizontal line does not mean that government spending is unchanging. It means only that government spending changes when Congress decides on a change in the budget, rather than shifting in a predictable way with the current size of the real GDP shown on the horizontal axis.

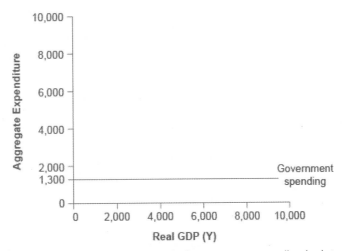

**Figure B4 The Government Spending Function** The level of government spending is determined by political factors, not by the level of real GDP in a given year. Thus, government spending is drawn as a horizontal line. In this example, government spending is at a level of 1,300. Congressional decisions to increase government spending will cause this horizontal line to shift up, while decisions to reduce spending would cause it to shift down.

The situation of taxes is different because taxes often rise or fall with the volume of economic activity. For example, income taxes are based on the level of income earned and sales taxes are based on the amount of sales made, and both income and sales tend to be higher when the economy is growing and lower when the economy is in a recession. For the purposes of constructing the basic Keynesian cross diagram, it is helpful to view taxes as a proportionate share of GDP. In the United States, for example, taking federal, state, and local taxes together, government typically collects about 30–35 % of income as taxes.

**Table B2** revises the earlier table on the consumption function so that it takes taxes into account. The first column shows national income. The second column calculates taxes, which in this example are set at a rate of 30%, or 0.3. The third column shows after-tax income; that is, total income minus taxes. The fourth column then calculates consumption in the same manner as before: multiply after-tax income by 0.8, representing the marginal propensity to consume, and then add $600, for the amount that would be consumed even if income was zero. When taxes are included, the marginal propensity to consume is reduced by the amount of the tax rate, so each additional dollar of income results in a smaller increase in consumption than before taxes. For this reason, the consumption function, with taxes included, is flatter than the consumption function without taxes, as **Figure B5** shows.

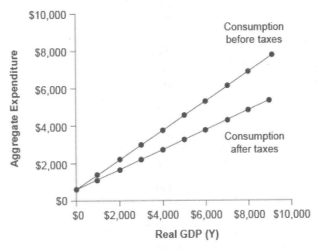

**Figure B5 The Consumption Function Before and After Taxes** The upper line repeats the consumption function from **Figure B2**. The lower line shows the consumption function if taxes must first be paid on income, and then consumption is based on after-tax income.

| Income | Taxes | After-Tax Income | Consumption | Savings |
|--------|-------|------------------|-------------|---------|
| $0 | $0 | $0 | $600 | −$600 |
| $1,000 | $300 | $700 | $1,160 | −$460 |
| $2,000 | $600 | $1,400 | $1,720 | −$320 |
| $3,000 | $900 | $2,100 | $2,280 | −$180 |
| $4,000 | $1,200 | $2,800 | $2,840 | −$40 |
| $5,000 | $1,500 | $3,500 | $3,400 | $100 |
| $6,000 | $1,800 | $4,200 | $3,960 | $240 |
| $7,000 | $2,100 | $4,900 | $4,520 | $380 |
| $8,000 | $2,400 | $5,600 | $5,080 | $520 |
| $9,000 | $2,700 | $6,300 | $5,640 | $660 |

Table B2 The Consumption Function Before and After Taxes

### Exports and Imports as a Function of National Income

The export function, which shows how exports change with the level of a country's own real GDP, is drawn as a horizontal line, as in the example in **Figure B6** (a) where exports are drawn at a level of $840. Again, as in the case of investment spending and government spending, drawing the export function as horizontal does not imply that exports never change. It just means that they do not change because of what is on the horizontal axis—that is, a country's own level of domestic production—and instead are shaped by the level of aggregate demand in other countries. More demand for exports from other countries would cause the export function to shift up; less demand for exports from other countries would cause it to shift down.

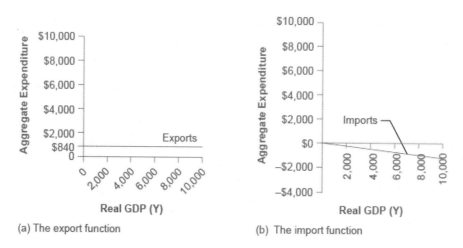

(a) The export function          (b) The import function

**Figure B6 The Export and Import Functions**   (a) The export function is drawn as a horizontal line because exports are determined by the buying power of other countries and thus do not change with the size of the domestic economy. In this example, exports are set at 840. However, exports can shift up or down, depending on buying patterns in other countries. (b) The import function is drawn in negative territory because expenditures on imported products are a subtraction from expenditures in the domestic economy. In this example, the marginal propensity to import is 0.1, so imports are calculated by multiplying the level of income by −0.1.

Imports are drawn in the Keynesian cross diagram as a downward-sloping line, with the downward slope determined by the marginal propensity to import (MPI), out of national income. In **Figure B6** (b), the marginal propensity to import is 0.1. Thus, if real GDP is $5,000, imports are $500; if national income is $6,000, imports are $600, and so on. The import function is drawn as downward sloping and negative, because it represents a subtraction from the aggregate expenditures in the domestic economy. A change in the marginal propensity to import, perhaps as a result of changes in preferences, would alter the slope of the import function.

# Work It Out ─○─○─○

## Using an Algebraic Approach to the Expenditure-Output Model

In the expenditure-output or Keynesian cross model, the equilibrium occurs where the aggregate expenditure line (AE line) crosses the 45-degree line. Given algebraic equations for two lines, the point where they cross can be readily calculated. Imagine an economy with the following characteristics.

Y = Real GDP or national income

T = Taxes = 0.3Y

C = Consumption = 140 + 0.9(Y − T)

I = Investment = 400

G = Government spending = 800

X = Exports = 600

M = Imports = 0.15Y

Step 1. Determine the aggregate expenditure function. In this case, it is:

$$AE = C + I + G + X - M$$
$$AE = 140 + 0.9(Y - T) + 400 + 800 + 600 - 0.15Y$$

Step 2. The equation for the 45-degree line is the set of points where GDP or national income on the horizontal axis is equal to aggregate expenditure on the vertical axis. Thus, the equation for the 45-degree line is: AE = Y.

Step 3. The next step is to solve these two equations for Y (or AE, since they will be equal to each other). Substitute Y for AE:

$$Y = 140 + 0.9(Y - T) + 400 + 800 + 600 - 0.15Y$$

Step 4. Insert the term 0.3Y for the tax rate T. This produces an equation with only one variable, Y.

Step 5. Work through the algebra and solve for Y.

$$
\begin{aligned}
Y &= 140 + 0.9(Y - 0.3Y) + 400 + 800 + 600 - 0.15Y \\
Y &= 140 + 0.9Y - 0.27Y + 1800 - 0.15Y \\
Y &= 1940 + 0.48Y \\
Y - 0.48Y &= 1940 \\
0.52Y &= 1940 \\
\frac{0.52Y}{0.52} &= \frac{1940}{0.52} \\
Y &= 3730
\end{aligned}
$$

This algebraic framework is flexible and useful in predicting how economic events and policy actions will affect real GDP.

Step 6. Say, for example, that because of changes in the relative prices of domestic and foreign goods, the marginal propensity to import falls to 0.1. Calculate the equilibrium output when the marginal propensity to import is changed to 0.1.

$$
\begin{aligned}
Y &= 140 + 0.9(Y - 0.3Y) + 400 + 800 + 600 - 0.1Y \\
Y &= 1940 - 0.53Y \\
0.47Y &= 1940 \\
Y &= 4127
\end{aligned}
$$

Step 7. Because of a surge of business confidence, investment rises to 500. Calculate the equilibrium output.

$$
\begin{aligned}
Y &= 140 + 0.9(Y - 0.3Y) + 500 + 800 + 600 - 0.15Y \\
Y &= 2040 + 0.48Y \\
Y - 0.48Y &= 2040 \\
0.52Y &= 2040 \\
Y &= 3923
\end{aligned}
$$

For issues of policy, the key questions would be how to adjust government spending levels or tax rates so that the equilibrium level of output is the full employment level. In this case, let the economic parameters be:

Y = National income

T = Taxes = 0.3Y

C = Consumption = 200 + 0.9(Y – T)

I = Investment = 600

G = Government spending = 1,000

X = Exports = 600

Y = Imports = 0.1(Y – T)

Step 8. Calculate the equilibrium for this economy (remember Y = AE).

$$
\begin{aligned}
Y &= 200 + 0.9(Y - 0.3Y) + 600 + 1000 + 600 - 0.1(Y - 0.3Y) \\
Y - 0.63Y + 0.07Y &= 2400 \\
0.44Y &= 2400 \\
Y &= 5454
\end{aligned}
$$

Step 9. Assume that the full employment level of output is 6,000. What level of government spending would be necessary to reach that level? To answer this question, plug in 6,000 as equal to Y, but leave G as a variable, and solve for G. Thus:

$$
6000 = 200 + 0.9(6000 - 0.3(6000)) + 600 + G + 600 - 0.1(6000 - 0.3(6000))
$$

Step 10. Solve this problem arithmetically. The answer is: G = 1,240. In other words, increasing government spending by 240, from its original level of 1,000, to 1,240, would raise output to the full employment level of GDP.

Indeed, the question of how much to increase government spending so that equilibrium output will rise from 5,454 to 6,000 can be answered without working through the algebra, just by using the multiplier formula. The multiplier equation in this case is:

$$
\frac{1}{1 - 0.56} = 2.27
$$

Thus, to raise output by 546 would require an increase in government spending of 546/2.27=240, which is the same as the answer derived from the algebraic calculation.

This algebraic framework is highly flexible. For example, taxes can be treated as a total set by political considerations (like government spending) and not dependent on national income. Imports might be based on before-tax income, not after-tax income. For certain purposes, it may be helpful to analyze the economy without exports and imports. A more complicated approach could divide up consumption, investment, government, exports and imports into smaller categories, or to build in some variability in the rates of taxes, savings, and imports. A wise economist will shape the model to fit the specific question under investigation.

## Building the Combined Aggregate Expenditure Function

All the components of aggregate demand—consumption, investment, government spending, and the trade balance—are now in place to build the Keynesian cross diagram. **Figure B7** builds up an aggregate expenditure function, based on the numerical illustrations of C, I, G, X, and M that have been used throughout this text. The first three columns in **Table B3** are lifted from the earlier **Table B2**, which showed how to bring taxes into the consumption function. The first column is real GDP or national income, which is what appears on the horizontal axis of the income-expenditure diagram. The second column calculates after-tax income, based on the assumption, in this case, that 30% of real GDP is collected in taxes. The third column is based on an MPC of 0.8, so that as after-tax income rises by $700 from one row to the next, consumption rises by $560 (700 × 0.8) from one row to the next. Investment, government spending, and exports do not change with the level of current national income. In the previous discussion, investment was $500, government spending was $1,300, and exports were $840, for a total of $2,640. This total is shown in the fourth column. Imports are 0.1 of real GDP in this example, and the level of imports is calculated in the fifth column. The final column, aggregate expenditures, sums up C + I + G + X – M. This aggregate expenditure line is illustrated in **Figure B7**.

**Figure B7 A Keynesian Cross Diagram**   Each combination of national income and aggregate expenditure (after-tax consumption, government spending, investment, exports, and imports) is graphed. The equilibrium occurs where aggregate expenditure is equal to national income; this occurs where the aggregate expenditure schedule crosses the 45-degree line, at a real GDP of $6,000. Potential GDP in this example is $7,000, so the equilibrium is occurring at a level of output or real GDP below the potential GDP level.

| National Income | After-Tax Income | Consumption | Government Spending + Investment + Exports | Imports | Aggregate Expenditure |
|---|---|---|---|---|---|
| $3,000 | $2,100 | $2,280 | $2,640 | $300 | $4,620 |
| $4,000 | $2,800 | $2,840 | $2,640 | $400 | $5,080 |
| $5,000 | $3,500 | $3,400 | $2,640 | $500 | $5,540 |
| $6,000 | $4,200 | $3,960 | $2,640 | $600 | $6,000 |

**Table B3 National Income-Aggregate Expenditure Equilibrium**

| National Income | After-Tax Income | Consumption | Government Spending + Investment + Exports | Imports | Aggregate Expenditure |
|---|---|---|---|---|---|
| $7,000 | $4,900 | $4,520 | $2,640 | $700 | $6,460 |
| $8,000 | $5,600 | $5,080 | $2,640 | $800 | $6,920 |
| $9,000 | $6,300 | $5,640 | $2,640 | $900 | $7,380 |

Table B3 National Income-Aggregate Expenditure Equilibrium

The aggregate expenditure function is formed by stacking on top of each other the consumption function (after taxes), the investment function, the government spending function, the export function, and the import function. The point at which the aggregate expenditure function intersects the vertical axis will be determined by the levels of investment, government, and export expenditures—which do not vary with national income. The upward slope of the aggregate expenditure function will be determined by the marginal propensity to save, the tax rate, and the marginal propensity to import. A higher marginal propensity to save, a higher tax rate, and a higher marginal propensity to import will all make the slope of the aggregate expenditure function flatter—because out of any extra income, more is going to savings or taxes or imports and less to spending on domestic goods and services.

The equilibrium occurs where national income is equal to aggregate expenditure, which is shown on the graph as the point where the aggregate expenditure schedule crosses the 45-degree line. In this example, the equilibrium occurs at 6,000. This equilibrium can also be read off the table under the figure; it is the level of national income where aggregate expenditure is equal to national income.

# Equilibrium in the Keynesian Cross Model

With the aggregate expenditure line in place, the next step is to relate it to the two other elements of the Keynesian cross diagram. Thus, the first subsection interprets the intersection of the aggregate expenditure function and the 45-degree line, while the next subsection relates this point of intersection to the potential GDP line.

### Where Equilibrium Occurs

The point where the aggregate expenditure line that is constructed from C + I + G + X – M crosses the 45-degree line will be the equilibrium for the economy. It is the only point on the aggregate expenditure line where the total amount being spent on aggregate demand equals the total level of production. In **Figure B7**, this point of equilibrium ($E_0$) happens at 6,000, which can also be read off **Table B3**.

The meaning of "equilibrium" remains the same; that is, equilibrium is a point of balance where no incentive exists to shift away from that outcome. To understand why the point of intersection between the aggregate expenditure function and the 45-degree line is a macroeconomic equilibrium, consider what would happen if an economy found itself to the right of the equilibrium point E, say point H in **Figure B8**, where output is higher than the equilibrium. At point H, the level of aggregate expenditure is below the 45-degree line, so that the level of aggregate expenditure in the economy is less than the level of output. As a result, at point H, output is piling up unsold—not a sustainable state of affairs.

**Figure B8 Equilibrium in the Keynesian Cross Diagram** If output was above the equilibrium level, at H, then the real output is greater than the aggregate expenditure in the economy. This pattern cannot hold, because it would mean that goods are produced but piling up unsold. If output was below the equilibrium level at L, then aggregate expenditure would be greater than output. This pattern cannot hold either, because it would mean that spending exceeds the number of goods being produced. Only point E can be at equilibrium, where output, or national income and aggregate expenditure, are equal. The equilibrium (E) must lie on the 45-degree line, which is the set of points where national income and aggregate expenditure are equal.

Conversely, consider the situation where the level of output is at point L—where real output is lower than the equilibrium. In that case, the level of aggregate demand in the economy is above the 45-degree line, indicating that the level of aggregate expenditure in the economy is greater than the level of output. When the level of aggregate demand has emptied the store shelves, it cannot be sustained, either. Firms will respond by increasing their level of production. Thus, the equilibrium must be the point where the amount produced and the amount spent are in balance, at the intersection of the aggregate expenditure function and the 45-degree line.

# Work It Out ─○─○─○

## Finding Equilibrium

Table B4 gives some information on an economy. The Keynesian model assumes that there is some level of consumption even without income. That amount is $236 – $216 = $20. $20 will be consumed when national income equals zero. Assume that taxes are 0.2 of real GDP. Let the marginal propensity to save of after-tax income be 0.1. The level of investment is $70, the level of government spending is $80, and the level of exports is $50. Imports are 0.2 of after-tax income. Given these values, you need to complete Table B4 and then answer these questions:

- What is the consumption function?
- What is the equilibrium?
- Why is a national income of $300 not at equilibrium?
- How do expenditures and output compare at this point?

| National Income | Taxes | After-tax income | Consumption | I + G + X | Imports | Aggregate Expenditures |
|---|---|---|---|---|---|---|
| $300 | | | $236 | | | |
| $400 | | | | | | |
| $500 | | | | | | |
| $600 | | | | | | |
| $700 | | | | | | |

Table B4

Step 1. Calculate the amount of taxes for each level of national income(reminder: GDP = national income) for each level of national income using the following as an example:

$$\begin{array}{ll} \text{National Income (Y)} & \$300 \\ \text{Taxes} = 0.2 \text{ or } 20\% & \times 0.2 \\ \text{Tax amount (T)} & \$60 \end{array}$$

Step 2. Calculate after-tax income by subtracting the tax amount from national income for each level of national income using the following as an example:

$$\begin{array}{ll} \text{National income minus taxes} & \$300 \\ & -\$60 \\ \text{After-tax income} & \$240 \end{array}$$

Step 3. Calculate consumption. The marginal propensity to save is given as 0.1. This means that the marginal propensity to consume is 0.9, since MPS + MPC = 1. Therefore, multiply 0.9 by the after-tax income amount using the following as an example:

$$\begin{array}{ll} \text{After-tax Income} & \$240 \\ \text{MPC} & \times 0.9 \\ \text{Consumption} & \$216 \end{array}$$

Step 4. Consider why the table shows consumption of $236 in the first row. As mentioned earlier, the Keynesian model assumes that there is some level of consumption even without income. That amount is $236 – $216 = $20.

Step 5. There is now enough information to write the consumption function. The consumption function is found by figuring out the level of consumption that will happen when income is zero. Remember that:

$$C = \text{Consumption when national income is zero} + \text{MPC (after-tax income)}$$

Let C represent the consumption function, Y represent national income, and T represent taxes.

$$
\begin{aligned}
C &= \$20 + 0.9(Y - T) \\
&= \$20 + 0.9(\$300 - \$60) \\
&= \$236
\end{aligned}
$$

Step 6. Use the consumption function to find consumption at each level of national income.

Step 7. Add investment (I), government spending (G), and exports (X). Remember that these do not change as national income changes:

Step 8. Find imports, which are 0.2 of after-tax income at each level of national income. For example:

$$
\begin{aligned}
\text{After-tax income} &\quad \$240 \\
\text{Imports of 0.2 or 20\% of Y} - T &\quad \times 0.2 \\
\text{Imports} &\quad \$48
\end{aligned}
$$

Step 9. Find aggregate expenditure by adding C + I + G + X − I for each level of national income. Your completed table should look like **Table B5**.

| National Income (Y) | Tax = 0.2 × Y (T) | After-tax income (Y − T) | Consumption C = \$20 + 0.9(Y − T) | I + G + X | Minus Imports (M) | Aggregate Expenditures AE = C + I + G + X − M |
|---|---|---|---|---|---|---|
| \$300 | \$60 | \$240 | \$236 | \$200 | \$48 | \$388 |
| \$400 | \$80 | \$320 | \$308 | \$200 | \$64 | \$444 |
| *\$500* | *\$100* | *\$400* | *\$380* | *\$200* | *\$80* | *\$500* |
| \$600 | \$120 | \$480 | \$452 | \$200 | \$96 | \$556 |
| \$700 | \$140 | \$560 | \$524 | \$200 | \$112 | \$612 |

**Table B5**

Step 10. Answer the question: What is equilibrium? Equilibrium occurs where AE = Y. **Table B5** shows that equilibrium occurs where national income equals aggregate expenditure at \$500.

Step 11. Find equilibrium mathematically, knowing that national income is equal to aggregate expenditure.

$$
\begin{aligned}
Y &= AE \\
&= C + I + G + X - M \\
&= \$20 + 0.9(Y - T) + \$70 + \$80 + \$50 - 0.2(Y - T) \\
&= \$220 + 0.9(Y - T) - 0.2(Y - T)
\end{aligned}
$$

Since T is 0.2 of national income, substitute T with 0.2 Y so that:

$$
\begin{aligned}
Y &= \$220 + 0.9(Y - 0.2Y) - 0.2(Y - 0.2Y) \\
&= \$220 + 0.9Y - 0.18Y - 0.2Y + 0.04Y \\
&= \$220 + 0.56Y
\end{aligned}
$$

Solve for Y.

$$Y = \$220 + 0.56Y$$
$$Y - 0.56Y = \$220$$
$$0.44Y = \$220$$
$$\frac{0.44Y}{0.44} = \frac{\$220}{0.44}$$
$$Y = \$500$$

Step 12. Answer this question: Why is a national income of $300 not an equilibrium? At national income of $300, aggregate expenditures are $388.

Step 13. Answer this question: How do expenditures and output compare at this point? Aggregate expenditures cannot exceed output (GDP) in the long run, since there would not be enough goods to be bought.

### Recessionary and Inflationary Gaps

In the Keynesian cross diagram, if the aggregate expenditure line intersects the 45-degree line at the level of potential GDP, then the economy is in sound shape. There is no recession, and unemployment is low. But there is no guarantee that the equilibrium will occur at the potential GDP level of output. The equilibrium might be higher or lower.

For example, **Figure B9** (a) illustrates a situation where the aggregate expenditure line intersects the 45-degree line at point $E_0$, which is a real GDP of $6,000, and which is below the potential GDP of $7,000. In this situation, the level of aggregate expenditure is too low for GDP to reach its full employment level, and unemployment will occur. The distance between an output level like $E_0$ that is below potential GDP and the level of potential GDP is called a recessionary gap. Because the equilibrium level of real GDP is so low, firms will not wish to hire the full employment number of workers, and unemployment will be high.

(a) Policy to address a recessionary gap.  (b) Policy to address an inflationary gap.

**Figure B9 Addressing Recessionary and Inflationary Gaps**  (a) If the equilibrium occurs at an output below potential GDP, then a recessionary gap exists. The policy solution to a recessionary gap is to shift the aggregate expenditure schedule up from $AE_0$ to $AE_1$, using policies like tax cuts or government spending increases. Then the new equilibrium $E_1$ occurs at potential GDP. (b) If the equilibrium occurs at an output above potential GDP, then an inflationary gap exists. The policy solution to an inflationary gap is to shift the aggregate expenditure schedule down from $AE_0$ to $AE_1$, using policies like tax increases or spending cuts. Then, the new equilibrium $E_1$ occurs at potential GDP.

What might cause a recessionary gap? Anything that shifts the aggregate expenditure line down is a potential cause of recession, including a decline in consumption, a rise in savings, a fall in investment, a drop in government spending or a rise in taxes, or a fall in exports or a rise in imports. Moreover, an economy that is at equilibrium with a recessionary gap may just stay there and suffer high unemployment for a long time; remember, the meaning of equilibrium is that there is no particular adjustment of prices or quantities in the economy to chase the recession away.

The appropriate response to a recessionary gap is for the government to reduce taxes or increase spending so that the aggregate expenditure function shifts up from $AE_0$ to $AE_1$. When this shift occurs, the new equilibrium $E_1$ now occurs at potential GDP as shown in **Figure B9** (a).

Conversely, **Figure B9** (b) shows a situation where the aggregate expenditure schedule ($AE_0$) intersects the 45-degree line above potential GDP. The gap between the level of real GDP at the equilibrium $E_0$ and potential GDP is called an inflationary gap. The inflationary gap also requires a bit of interpreting. After all, a naïve reading of the Keynesian cross diagram might suggest that if the aggregate expenditure function is just pushed up high enough, real GDP can be as large as desired—even doubling or tripling the potential GDP level of the economy. This implication is clearly wrong. An economy faces some supply-side limits on how much it can produce at a given time with its existing quantities of workers, physical and human capital, technology, and market institutions.

The inflationary gap should be interpreted, not as a literal prediction of how large real GDP will be, but as a statement of how much extra aggregate expenditure is in the economy beyond what is needed to reach potential GDP. An inflationary gap suggests that because the economy cannot produce enough goods and services to absorb this level of aggregate expenditures, the spending will instead cause an inflationary increase in the price level. In this way, even though changes in the price level do not appear explicitly in the Keynesian cross equation, the notion of inflation is implicit in the concept of the inflationary gap.

The appropriate Keynesian response to an inflationary gap is shown in **Figure B9** (b). The original intersection of aggregate expenditure line $AE_0$ and the 45-degree line occurs at \$8,000, which is above the level of potential GDP at \$7,000. If $AE_0$ shifts down to $AE_1$, so that the new equilibrium is at $E_1$, then the economy will be at potential GDP without pressures for inflationary price increases. The government can achieve a downward shift in aggregate expenditure by increasing taxes on consumers or firms, or by reducing government expenditures.

# The Multiplier Effect

The Keynesian policy prescription has one final twist. Assume that for a certain economy, the intersection of the aggregate expenditure function and the 45-degree line is at a GDP of 700, while the level of potential GDP for this economy is \$800. By how much does government spending need to be increased so that the economy reaches the full employment GDP? The obvious answer might seem to be \$800 – \$700 = \$100; so raise government spending by \$100. But that answer is incorrect. A change of, for example, \$100 in government expenditures will have an effect of more than \$100 on the equilibrium level of real GDP. The reason is that a change in aggregate expenditures circles through the economy: households buy from firms, firms pay workers and suppliers, workers and suppliers buy goods from other firms, those firms pay their workers and suppliers, and so on. In this way, the original change in aggregate expenditures is actually spent more than once. This is called the multiplier effect: An initial increase in spending, cycles repeatedly through the economy and has a larger impact than the initial dollar amount spent.

### How Does the Multiplier Work?

To understand how the multiplier effect works, return to the example in which the current equilibrium in the Keynesian cross diagram is a real GDP of \$700, or \$100 short of the \$800 needed to be at full employment, potential GDP. If the government spends \$100 to close this gap, someone in the economy receives that spending and can treat it as income. Assume that those who receive this income pay 30% in taxes, save 10% of after-tax income, spend 10% of total income on imports, and then spend the rest on domestically produced goods and services.

As shown in the calculations in **Figure B10** and **Table B6**, out of the original \$100 in government spending, \$53 is left to spend on domestically produced goods and services. That \$53 which was spent, becomes income to someone, somewhere in the economy. Those who receive that income also pay 30% in taxes, save 10% of after-tax income, and spend 10% of total income on imports, as shown in **Figure B10**, so that an additional \$28.09 (that is, 0.53 × \$53) is spent in the third round. The people who receive that income then pay taxes, save, and buy imports, and the amount spent in the fourth round is \$14.89 (that is, 0.53 × \$28.09).

**Figure B10 The Multiplier Effect** An original increase of government spending of $100 causes a rise in aggregate expenditure of $100. But that $100 is income to others in the economy, and after they save, pay taxes, and buy imports, they spend $53 of that $100 in a second round. In turn, that $53 is income to others. Thus, the original government spending of $100 is multiplied by these cycles of spending, but the impact of each successive cycle gets smaller and smaller. Given the numbers in this example, the original government spending increase of $100 raises aggregate expenditure by $213; therefore, the multiplier in this example is $213/$100 = 2.13.

| Original increase in aggregate expenditure from government spending | 100 |
|---|---|
| Which is income to people throughout the economy: Pay 30% in taxes. Save 10% of after-tax income. Spend 10% of income on imports. Second-round increase of… | 70 – 7 – 10 = 53 |
| Which is $53 of income to people through the economy: Pay 30% in taxes. Save 10% of after-tax income. Spend 10% of income on imports. Third-round increase of… | 37.1 – 3.71 – 5.3 = 28.09 |
| Which is $28.09 of income to people through the economy: Pay 30% in taxes. Save 10% of after-tax income. Spend 10% of income on imports. Fourth-round increase of… | 19.663 – 1.96633 – 2.809 = 14.89 |

**Table B6 Calculating the Multiplier Effect**

Thus, over the first four rounds of aggregate expenditures, the impact of the original increase in government spending of $100 creates a rise in aggregate expenditures of $100 + $53 + $28.09 + $14.89 = $195.98. **Figure B10** shows these total aggregate expenditures after these first four rounds, and then the figure shows the total aggregate expenditures after 30 rounds. The additional boost to aggregate expenditures is shrinking in each round of consumption. After about 10 rounds, the additional increments are very small indeed—nearly invisible to the naked eye. After 30 rounds, the additional increments in each round are so small that they have no practical consequence. After 30 rounds, the cumulative value of the initial boost in aggregate expenditure is approximately $213. Thus, the government spending increase of $100 eventually, after many cycles, produced an increase of $213 in aggregate expenditure and real GDP. In this example, the multiplier is $213/$100 = 2.13.

**Calculating the Multiplier**

Fortunately for everyone who is not carrying around a computer with a spreadsheet program to project the impact of an original increase in expenditures over 20, 50, or 100 rounds of spending, there is a formula for calculating the multiplier.

$$\text{Spending Multiplier} = 1/(1 - \text{MPC} * (1 - \text{tax rate}) + \text{MPI})$$

The data from **Figure B10** and **Table B6** is:

- Marginal Propensity to Save (MPS) = 30%

- Tax rate = 10%

- Marginal Propensity to Import (MPI) = 10%

The MPC is equal to 1 − MPS, or 0.7. Therefore, the spending multiplier is:

$$\text{Spending Multiplier} = \frac{1}{1 - (0.7 - (0.10)(0.7) - 0.10)}$$
$$= \frac{1}{0.47}$$
$$= 2.13$$

A change in spending of $100 multiplied by the spending multiplier of 2.13 is equal to a change in GDP of $213. Not coincidentally, this result is exactly what was calculated in **Figure B10** after many rounds of expenditures cycling through the economy.

The size of the multiplier is determined by what proportion of the marginal dollar of income goes into taxes, saving, and imports. These three factors are known as "leakages," because they determine how much demand "leaks out" in each round of the multiplier effect. If the leakages are relatively small, then each successive round of the multiplier effect will have larger amounts of demand, and the multiplier will be high. Conversely, if the leakages are relatively large, then any initial change in demand will diminish more quickly in the second, third, and later rounds, and the multiplier will be small. Changes in the size of the leakages—a change in the marginal propensity to save, the tax rate, or the marginal propensity to import—will change the size of the multiplier.

### Calculating Keynesian Policy Interventions

Returning to the original question: How much should government spending be increased to produce a total increase in real GDP of $100? If the goal is to increase aggregate demand by $100, and the multiplier is 2.13, then the increase in government spending to achieve that goal would be $100/2.13 = $47. Government spending of approximately $47, when combined with a multiplier of 2.13 (which is, remember, based on the specific assumptions about tax, saving, and import rates), produces an overall increase in real GDP of $100, restoring the economy to potential GDP of $800, as **Figure B11** shows.

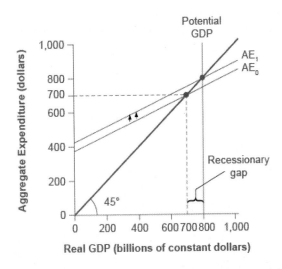

**Figure B11 The Multiplier Effect in an Expenditure-Output Model**   The power of the multiplier effect is that an increase in expenditure has a larger increase on the equilibrium output. The increase in expenditure is the vertical increase from $AE_0$ to $AE_1$. However, the increase in equilibrium output, shown on the horizontal axis, is clearly larger.

The multiplier effect is also visible on the Keynesian cross diagram. **Figure B11** shows the example we have been discussing: a recessionary gap with an equilibrium of $700, potential GDP of $800, the slope of the aggregate expenditure function ($AE_0$) determined by the assumptions that taxes are 30% of income, savings are 0.1 of after-tax income, and imports are 0.1 of before-tax income. At $AE_1$, the aggregate expenditure function is moved up to reach potential GDP.

Now, compare the vertical shift upward in the aggregate expenditure function, which is $47, with the horizontal shift outward in real GDP, which is $100 (as these numbers were calculated earlier). The rise in real GDP is more than double the rise in the aggregate expenditure function. (Similarly, if you look back at **Figure B9**, you will see that the vertical movements in the aggregate expenditure functions are smaller than the change in equilibrium output that is produced on the horizontal axis. Again, this is the multiplier effect at work.) In this way, the power of the multiplier is apparent in the income–expenditure graph, as well as in the arithmetic calculation.

The multiplier does not just affect government spending, but applies to any change in the economy. Say that business confidence declines and investment falls off, or that the economy of a leading trading partner slows down so that export sales decline. These changes will reduce aggregate expenditures, and then will have an even larger effect on real GDP because of the multiplier effect. Read the following Clear It Up feature to learn how the multiplier effect can be applied to analyze the economic impact of professional sports.

## How can the multiplier be used to analyze the economic impact of professional sports?

Attracting professional sports teams and building sports stadiums to create jobs and stimulate business growth is an economic development strategy adopted by many communities throughout the United States. In his recent article, "Public Financing of Private Sports Stadiums," James Joyner of *Outside the Beltway* looked at public financing for NFL teams. Joyner's findings confirm the earlier work of John Siegfried of Vanderbilt University and Andrew Zimbalist of Smith College.

Siegfried and Zimbalist used the multiplier to analyze this issue. They considered the amount of taxes paid and dollars spent locally to see if there was a positive multiplier effect. Since most professional athletes and owners of sports teams are rich enough to owe a lot of taxes, let's say that 40% of any marginal income they earn is paid in taxes. Because athletes are often high earners with short careers, let's assume that they save one-third of their after-tax income.

However, many professional athletes do not live year-round in the city in which they play, so let's say that one-half of the money that they do spend is spent outside the local area. One can think of spending outside a local economy, in this example, as the equivalent of imported goods for the national economy.

Now, consider the impact of money spent at local entertainment venues other than professional sports. While the owners of these other businesses may be comfortably middle-income, few of them are in the economic stratosphere of professional athletes. Because their incomes are lower, so are their taxes; say that they pay only 35% of their marginal income in taxes. They do not have the same ability, or need, to save as much as professional athletes, so let's assume their MPC is just 0.8. Finally, because more of them live locally, they will spend a higher proportion of their income on local goods—say, 65%.

If these general assumptions hold true, then money spent on professional sports will have less local economic impact than money spent on other forms of entertainment. For professional athletes, out of a dollar earned, 40 cents goes to taxes, leaving 60 cents. Of that 60 cents, one-third is saved, leaving 40 cents, and half is spent outside the area, leaving 20 cents. Only 20 cents of each dollar is cycled into the local economy in the first round. For locally-owned entertainment, out of a dollar earned, 35 cents goes to taxes, leaving 65 cents. Of the rest, 20% is saved, leaving 52 cents, and of that amount, 65% is spent in the local area, so that 33.8 cents of each dollar of income is recycled into the local economy.

Siegfried and Zimbalist make the plausible argument that, within their household budgets, people have a fixed amount to spend on entertainment. If this assumption holds true, then money spent attending professional sports events is money that was not spent on other entertainment options in a given metropolitan area. Since the multiplier is lower for professional sports than for other local entertainment options, the arrival of professional sports to a city would reallocate entertainment spending in a way that causes the local economy to shrink, rather than to grow. Thus, their findings seem to confirm what Joyner reports and what newspapers across the country are reporting. A quick Internet search for "economic impact of sports" will yield numerous reports questioning this economic development strategy.

**Multiplier Tradeoffs: Stability versus the Power of Macroeconomic Policy**

Is an economy healthier with a high multiplier or a low one? With a high multiplier, any change in aggregate demand will tend to be substantially magnified, and so the economy will be more unstable. With a low multiplier, by contrast, changes in aggregate demand will not be multiplied much, so the economy will tend to be more stable.

However, with a low multiplier, government policy changes in taxes or spending will tend to have less impact on the equilibrium level of real output. With a higher multiplier, government policies to raise or reduce aggregate expenditures will have a larger effect. Thus, a low multiplier means a more stable economy, but also weaker government macroeconomic policy, while a high multiplier means a more volatile economy, but also an economy in which government macroeconomic policy is more powerful.

# Key Concepts and Summary

The expenditure-output model or Keynesian cross diagram shows how the level of aggregate expenditure (on the vertical axis) varies with the level of economic output (shown on the horizontal axis). Since the value of all macroeconomic output also represents income to someone somewhere else in the economy, the horizontal axis can also be interpreted as national income. The equilibrium in the diagram will occur where the aggregate expenditure line crosses the 45-degree line, which represents the set of points where aggregate expenditure in the economy is equal to output (or national income). Equilibrium in a Keynesian cross diagram can happen at potential GDP, or below or above that level.

The consumption function shows the upward-sloping relationship between national income and consumption. The marginal propensity to consume (MPC) is the amount consumed out of an additional dollar of income. A higher marginal propensity to consume means a steeper consumption function; a lower marginal propensity to consume means a flatter consumption function. The marginal propensity to save (MPS) is the amount saved out of an additional dollar of income. It is necessarily true that MPC + MPS = 1. The investment function is drawn as a flat line, showing that investment in the current year does not change with regard to the current level of national income. However, the investment function will move up and down based on the expected rate of return in the future. Government spending is drawn as a horizontal line in the Keynesian cross diagram, because its level is determined by political considerations, not by the current level of income in the economy. Taxes in the basic Keynesian cross diagram are taken into account by adjusting the consumption function. The export function is drawn as a horizontal line in the Keynesian cross diagram, because exports do not change as a result of changes in domestic income, but they move as a result of changes in foreign income, as well as changes in exchange rates. The import function is drawn as a downward-sloping line, because imports rise with national income, but imports are a subtraction from aggregate demand. Thus, a higher level of imports means a lower level of expenditure on domestic goods.

In a Keynesian cross diagram, the equilibrium may be at a level below potential GDP, which is called a recessionary gap, or at a level above potential GDP, which is called an inflationary gap.

The multiplier effect describes how an initial change in aggregate demand generated several times as much as cumulative GDP. The size of the spending multiplier is determined by three leakages: spending on savings, taxes, and imports. The formula for the multiplier is:

$$\text{Multiplier} = \frac{1}{1 - (\text{MPC} \times (1 - \text{tax rate}) + \text{MPI})}$$

An economy with a lower multiplier is more stable—it is less affected either by economic events or by government policy than an economy with a higher multiplier.

# Self-Check Questions

### Exercise B1

Sketch the aggregate expenditure-output diagram with the recessionary gap.

**Solution**

The following figure shows the aggregate expenditure-output diagram with the recessionary gap.

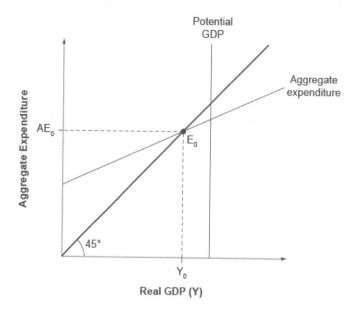

**Figure B12**

Exercise B2

Sketch the aggregate expenditure-output diagram with an inflationary gap.

**Solution**

The following figure shows the aggregate expenditure-output diagram with an inflationary gap.

**Figure B13**

Exercise B3

An economy has the following characteristics:

Y = National income

Taxes = T = 0.25Y

C = Consumption = 400 + 0.85(Y – T)

I = 300

G = 200

X = 500

M = 0.1(Y – T)

Find the equilibrium for this economy. If potential GDP is 3,500, then what change in government spending is needed to achieve this level? Do this problem two ways. First, plug 3,500 into the equations and solve for G. Second, calculate the multiplier and figure it out that way.

## Solution

First, set up the calculation.

$$AE = 400 + 0.85(Y – T) + 300 + 200 + 500 – 0.1(Y – T)$$
$$AE = Y$$

Then insert Y for AE and 0.25Y for T.

$$Y = 400 + 0.85(Y – 0.25Y) + 300 + 200 + 500 – 0.1(Y – 0.25Y)$$
$$Y = 1400 + 0.6375Y – 0.075Y$$
$$0.4375Y = 1400$$
$$Y = 3200$$

If full employment is 3,500, then one approach is to plug in 3,500 for Y throughout the equation, but to leave G as a separate variable.

$$Y = 400 + 0.85(Y – 0.25Y) + 300 + G + 500 + 0.1(Y – 0.25Y)$$
$$3500 = 400 + 0.85(3500 – 0.25(3500)) + 300 + G + 500 – 0.1(3500 – 0.25(3500))$$
$$G = 3500 – 400 – 2231.25 – 1300 – 500 + 262.5$$
$$G = 331.25$$

A G value of 331.25 is an increase of 131.25 from its original level of 200.

Alternatively, the multiplier is that, out of every dollar spent, 0.25 goes to taxes, leaving 0.75, and out of after-tax income, 0.15 goes to savings and 0.1 to imports. Because (0.75)(0.15) = 0.1125 and (0.75)(0.1) = 0.075, this means that out of every dollar spent: 1 –0.25 –0.1125 –0.075 = 0.5625.

Thus, using the formula, the multiplier is:

$$\frac{1}{1 – 0.5625} = 2.2837$$

To increase equilibrium GDP by 300, it will take a boost of 300/2.2837, which again works out to 131.25.

### Exercise B4

**Table B7** represents the data behind a Keynesian cross diagram. Assume that the tax rate is 0.4 of national income; the MPC out of the after-tax income is 0.8; investment is $2,000; government spending is $1,000; exports are $2,000 and imports are 0.05 of after-tax income. What is the equilibrium level of output for this economy?

| National Income | After-tax Income | Consumption | I + G + X | Minus Imports | Aggregate Expenditures |
|---|---|---|---|---|---|
| $8,000 | | $4,340 | | | |
| $9,000 | | | | | |

**Table B7**

| National Income | After-tax Income | Consumption | I + G + X | Minus Imports | Aggregate Expenditures |
|---|---|---|---|---|---|
| $10,000 | | | | | |
| $11,000 | | | | | |
| $12,000 | | | | | |
| $13,000 | | | | | |

Table B7

## Solution

The following table illustrates the completed table. The equilibrium is level is italicized.

| National Income | After-tax Income | Consumption | I + G + X | Minus Imports | Aggregate Expenditures |
|---|---|---|---|---|---|
| $8,000 | $4,800 | $4,340 | $5,000 | $240 | $9,100 |
| $9,000 | $5,400 | $4,820 | $5,000 | $270 | $9,550 |
| *$10,000* | *$6,000* | *$5,300* | *$5,000* | *$300* | *$10,000* |
| $11,000 | $6,600 | $5,780 | $5,000 | $330 | $10,450 |
| $12,000 | $7,200 | $6,260 | $5,000 | $360 | $10,900 |
| $13,000 | $7,800 | $46,740 | $5,000 | $4,390 | $11,350 |

Table B8

The alternative way of determining equilibrium is to solve for Y, where Y = national income, using: Y = AE = C + I + G + X − M

$$Y = \$500 + 0.8(Y - T) + \$2,000 + \$1,000 + \$2,000 - 0.05(Y - T)$$

Solving for Y, we see that the equilibrium level of output is Y = $10,000.

Exercise B5

Explain how the multiplier works. Use an MPC of 80% in an example.

## Solution

The multiplier refers to how many times a dollar will turnover in the economy. It is based on the Marginal Propensity to Consume (MPC) which tells how much of every dollar received will be spent. If the MPC is 80% then this means that out of every one dollar received by a consumer, $0.80 will be spent. This $0.80 is received by another person. In turn, 80% of the $0.80 received, or $0.64, will be spent, and so on. The impact of the multiplier is diluted when the effect of taxes and expenditure on imports is considered. To derive the multiplier, take the 1/1 − F; where F is equal to percent of savings, taxes, and expenditures on imports.

# Review Questions

Exercise B6

What is on the axes of an expenditure-output diagram?

## Exercise B7

What does the 45-degree line show?

## Exercise B8

What determines the slope of a consumption function?

## Exercise B9

What is the marginal propensity to consume, and how is it related to the marginal propensity to import?

## Exercise B10

Why are the investment function, the government spending function, and the export function all drawn as flat lines?

## Exercise B11

Why does the import function slope down? What is the marginal propensity to import?

## Exercise B12

What are the components on which the aggregate expenditure function is based?

## Exercise B13

Is the equilibrium in a Keynesian cross diagram usually expected to be at or near potential GDP?

## Exercise B14

What is an inflationary gap? A recessionary gap?

## Exercise B15

What is the multiplier effect?

## Exercise B16

Why are savings, taxes, and imports referred to as "leakages" in calculating the multiplier effect?

## Exercise B17

Will an economy with a high multiplier be more stable or less stable than an economy with a low multiplier in response to changes in the economy or in government policy?

## Exercise B18

How do economists use the multiplier?

# Critical Thinking Questions

## Exercise B19

What does it mean when the aggregate expenditure line crosses the 45-degree line? In other words, how would you explain the intersection in words?

## Exercise B20

Which model, the AD/AS or the AE model better explains the relationship between rising price levels and GDP? Why?

## Exercise B21

What are some reasons that the economy might be in a recession, and what is the appropriate government action to alleviate the recession?

## Exercise B22

What should the government do to relieve inflationary pressures if the aggregate expenditure is greater than potential GDP?

## Exercise B23

Two countries are in a recession. Country A has an MPC of 0.8 and Country B has an MPC of 0.6. In which country will government spending have the greatest impact?

## Exercise B24

Compare two policies: a tax cut on income or an increase in government spending on roads and bridges. What are both the short-term and long-term impacts of such policies on the economy?

## Exercise B25

What role does government play in stabilizing the economy and what are the tradeoffs that must be considered?

## Exercise B26

If there is a recessionary gap of $100 billion, should the government increase spending by $100 billion to close the gap? Why? Why not?

## Exercise B27

What other changes in the economy can be evaluated by using the multiplier?

# References

Joyner, James. Outside the Beltway. "Public Financing of Private Sports Stadiums." Last modified May 23, 2012. http://www.outsidethebeltway.com/public-financing-of-private-sports-stadiums/.

Siegfried, John J., and Andrew Zimbalist. "The Economics of Sports Facilities and Their Communities." *Journal of Economic Perspectives*. no. 3 (2000): 95-114. http://pubs.aeaweb.org/doi/pdfplus/10.1257/jep.14.3.95.

# ANSWER KEY

## Chapter 1

1. Scarcity means human wants for goods and services exceed the available supply. Supply is limited because resources are limited. Demand, however, is virtually unlimited. Whatever the supply, it seems human nature to want more.

2. 100 people / 10 people per ham = a maximum of 10 hams per month if all residents produce ham. Since consumption is limited by production, the maximum number of hams residents could consume per month is 10.

3. She is very productive at her consulting job, but not very productive growing vegetables. Time spent consulting would produce far more income than it what she could save growing her vegetables using the same amount of time. So on purely economic grounds, it makes more sense for her to maximize her income by applying her labor to what she does best (i.e. specialization of labor).

4. The engineer is better at computer science than at painting. Thus, his time is better spent working for pay at his job and paying a painter to paint his house. Of course, this assumes he does not paint his house for fun!

5. There are many physical systems that would work, for example, the study of planets (micro) in the solar system (macro), or solar systems (micro) in the galaxy (macro).

6. Draw a box outside the original circular flow to represent the foreign country. Draw an arrow from the foreign country to firms, to represents imports. Draw an arrow in the reverse direction representing payments for imports. Draw an arrow from firms to the foreign country to represent exports. Draw an arrow in the reverse direction to represent payments for imports.

7. There are many such problems. Consider the AIDS epidemic. Why are so few AIDS patients in Africa and Southeast Asia treated with the same drugs that are effective in the United States and Europe? It is because neither those patients nor the countries in which they live have the resources to purchase the same drugs.

8. Public enterprise means the factors of production (resources and businesses) are owned and operated by the government.

9. The United States is a large country economically speaking, so it has less need to trade internationally than the other countries mentioned. (This is the same reason that France and Italy have lower ratios than Belgium or Sweden.) One additional reason is that each of the other countries is a member of the European Union, where trade between members occurs without barriers to trade, like tariffs and quotas.

## Chapter 2

1. The opportunity cost of bus tickets is the number of burgers that must be given up to obtain one more bus ticket. Originally, when the price of bus tickets was 50 cents per trip, this opportunity cost was 0.50/2 = .25 burgers. The reason for this is that at the original prices, one burger ($2) costs the same as four bus tickets ($0.50), so the opportunity cost of a burger is four bus tickets, and the opportunity cost of a bus ticket is .25 (the inverse of the opportunity cost of a burger). With the new, higher price of bus tickets, the opportunity cost rises to $1/$2 or 0.50. You can see this graphically since the slope of the new budget constraint is steeper than the original one. If Alphonso spends all of his budget on burgers, the higher price of bus tickets has no impact so the vertical intercept of the budget constraint is the same. If he spends all of his budget on bus tickets, he can now afford only half as many, so the vertical intercept is half as much. In short, the budget constraint rotates clockwise around the vertical intercept, steepening as it goes and the opportunity cost of bus tickets increases.

2. Because of the improvement in technology, the vertical intercept of the PPF would be at a higher level of healthcare. In other words, the PPF would rotate clockwise around the horizontal intercept. This would make the PPF steeper, corresponding to an increase in the opportunity cost of education, since resources devoted to education would now mean forgoing a greater quantity of healthcare.

3. No. Allocative efficiency requires productive efficiency, because it pertains to choices along the production possibilities frontier.

4. Both the budget constraint and the PPF show the constraint that each operates under. Both show a tradeoff between having more of one good but less of the other. Both show the opportunity cost graphically as the slope of the constraint (budget or PPF).

5. When individuals compare cost per unit in the grocery store, or characteristics of one product versus another, they are behaving approximately like the model describes.

6. Since an op-ed makes a case for what should be, it is considered normative.

7. Assuming that the study is not taking an explicit position about whether soft drink consumption is good or bad, but just reporting the science, it would be considered positive.

## Chapter 3

1. Since $1.60 per gallon is above the equilibrium price, the quantity demanded would be lower at 550 gallons and the quantity supplied would be higher at 640 gallons. (These results are due to the laws of demand and supply, respectively.) The outcome of lower Qd and higher Qs would be a surplus in the gasoline market of 640 − 550 = 90 gallons.

2. To make it easier to analyze complex problems. *Ceteris paribus* allows you to look at the effect of one factor at a time on what it is you are trying to analyze. When you have analyzed all the factors individually, you add the results together to get the final answer.

3.

   a. An improvement in technology that reduces the cost of production will cause an increase in supply. Alternatively, you can think of this as a reduction in price necessary for firms to supply any quantity. Either way, this can be shown as a rightward (or downward) shift in the supply curve.

   b. An improvement in product quality is treated as an increase in tastes or preferences, meaning consumers demand more paint at any price level, so demand increases or shifts to the right. If this seems counterintuitive, note that demand in the future for the longer-lasting paint will fall, since consumers are essentially shifting demand from the future to the present.

   c. An increase in need causes an increase in demand or a rightward shift in the demand curve.

   d. Factory damage means that firms are unable to supply as much in the present. Technically, this is an increase in the cost of production. Either way you look at it, the supply curve shifts to the left.

4.

   a. More fuel-efficient cars means there is less need for gasoline. This causes a leftward shift in the demand for gasoline and thus oil. Since the demand curve is shifting down the supply curve, the equilibrium price and quantity both fall.

b. Cold weather increases the need for heating oil. This causes a rightward shift in the demand for heating oil and thus oil. Since the demand curve is shifting up the supply curve, the equilibrium price and quantity both rise.

c. A discovery of new oil will make oil more abundant. This can be shown as a rightward shift in the supply curve, which will cause a decrease in the equilibrium price along with an increase in the equilibrium quantity. (The supply curve shifts down the demand curve so price and quantity follow the law of demand. If price goes down, then the quantity goes up.)

d. When an economy slows down, it produces less output and demands less input, including energy, which is used in the production of virtually everything. A decrease in demand for energy will be reflected as a decrease in the demand for oil, or a leftward shift in demand for oil. Since the demand curve is shifting down the supply curve, both the equilibrium price and quantity of oil will fall.

e. Disruption of oil pumping will reduce the supply of oil. This leftward shift in the supply curve will show a movement up the demand curve, resulting in an increase in the equilibrium price of oil and a decrease in the equilibrium quantity.

f. Increased insulation will decrease the demand for heating. This leftward shift in the demand for oil causes a movement down the supply curve, resulting in a decrease in the equilibrium price and quantity of oil.

g. Solar energy is a substitute for oil-based energy. So if solar energy becomes cheaper, the demand for oil will decrease as consumers switch from oil to solar. The decrease in demand for oil will be shown as a leftward shift in the demand curve. As the demand curve shifts down the supply curve, both equilibrium price and quantity for oil will fall.

h. A new, popular kind of plastic will increase the demand for oil. The increase in demand will be shown as a rightward shift in demand, raising the equilibrium price and quantity of oil.

**5**. Step 1. Draw the graph with the initial supply and demand curves. Label the initial equilibrium price and quantity. Step 2. Did the economic event affect supply or demand? Jet fuel is a cost of producing air travel, so an increase in jet fuel price affects supply. Step 3. An increase in the price of jet fuel caused a decrease in the cost of air travel. We show this as a downward or rightward shift in supply. Step 4. A rightward shift in supply causes a movement down the demand curve, lowering the equilibrium price of air travel and increasing the equilibrium quantity.

**6**. Step 1. Draw the graph with the initial supply and demand curves. Label the initial equilibrium price and quantity. Step 2. Did the economic event affect supply or demand? A tariff is treated like a cost of production, so this affects supply. Step 3. A tariff reduction is equivalent to a decrease in the cost of production, which we can show as a rightward (or downward) shift in supply. Step 4. A rightward shift in supply causes a movement down the demand curve, lowering the equilibrium price and raising the equilibrium quantity.

**7**. A price ceiling (which is below the equilibrium price) will cause the quantity demanded to rise and the quantity supplied to fall. This is why a price ceiling creates a shortage.

**8**. A price ceiling is just a legal restriction. Equilibrium is an economic condition. People may or may not obey the price ceiling, so the actual price may be at or above the price ceiling, but the price ceiling does not change the equilibrium price.

**9**. A price ceiling is a legal maximum price, but a price floor is a legal minimum price and, consequently, it would leave room for the price to rise to its equilibrium level. In other words, a price floor below equilibrium will not be binding and will have no effect.

**10**. Assuming that people obey the price ceiling, the market price will be below equilibrium, which means that Qd will be more than Qs. Buyers can only buy what is offered for sale, so the number of transactions will fall to Qs. This is easy to see graphically. By analogous reasoning, with a price floor the market price will be above the equilibrium price, so Qd will be less than Qs. Since the limit on transactions here is demand, the number of transactions will fall to Qd. Note that because both price floors and price ceilings reduce the number of transactions, social surplus is less.

**11**. Because the losses to consumers are greater than the benefits to producers, so the net effect is negative. Since the lost consumer surplus is greater than the additional producer surplus, social surplus falls.

## Chapter 4

**1.** Changes in the wage rate (the price of labor) cause a movement along the demand curve. A change in anything else that affects demand for labor (e.g., changes in output, changes in the production process that use more or less labor, government regulation) causes a shift in the demand curve.

**2.** Changes in the wage rate (the price of labor) cause a movement along the supply curve. A change in anything else that affects supply of labor (e.g., changes in how desirable the job is perceived to be, government policy to promote training in the field) causes a shift in the supply curve.

**3.** Since a living wage is a suggested minimum wage, it acts like a price floor (assuming, of course, that it is followed). If the living wage is binding, it will cause an excess supply of labor at that wage rate.

**4.** Changes in the interest rate (i.e., the price of financial capital) cause a movement along the demand curve. A change in anything else (non-price variable) that affects demand for financial capital (e.g., changes in confidence about the future, changes in needs for borrowing) would shift the demand curve.

**5.** Changes in the interest rate (i.e., the price of financial capital) cause a movement along the supply curve. A change in anything else that affects the supply of financial capital (a non-price variable) such as income or future needs would shift the supply curve.

**6.** If market interest rates stay in their normal range, an interest rate limit of 35% would not be binding. If the equilibrium interest rate rose above 35%, the interest rate would be capped at that rate, and the quantity of loans would be lower than the equilibrium quantity, causing a shortage of loans.

**7.** b and c will lead to a fall in interest rates. At a lower demand, lenders will not be able to charge as much, and with more available lenders, competition for borrowers will drive rates down.

**8.** a and c will increase the quantity of loans. More people who want to borrow will result in more loans being given, as will more people who want to lend.

**9.** A price floor prevents a price from falling below a certain level, but has no effect on prices above that level. It will have its biggest effect in creating excess supply (as measured by the entire area inside the dotted lines on the graph, from D to S) if it is substantially above the equilibrium price. This is illustrated in the following figure.

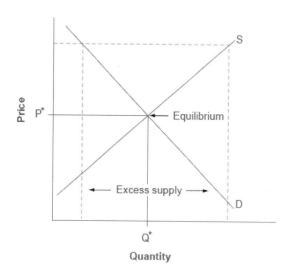

It will have a lesser effect if it is slightly above the equilibrium price. This is illustrated in the next figure.

It will have no effect if it is set either slightly or substantially below the equilibrium price, since an equilibrium price above a price floor will not be affected by that price floor. The following figure illustrates these situations.

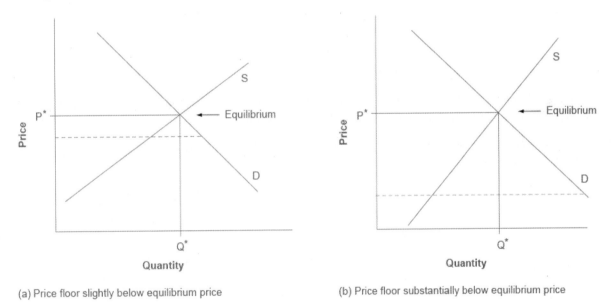

(a) Price floor slightly below equilibrium price                (b) Price floor substantially below equilibrium price

**10**. A price ceiling prevents a price from rising above a certain level, but has no effect on prices below that level. It will have its biggest effect in creating excess demand if it is substantially below the equilibrium price. The following figure illustrates these situations.

(a) Price ceiling substantially below equilibrium price

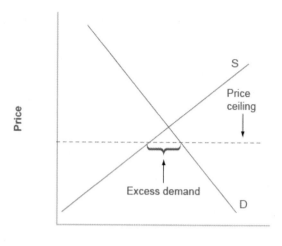

(b) Price ceiling slightly below equilibrium price

When the price ceiling is set substantially or slightly above the equilibrium price, it will have no effect on creating excess demand. The following figure illustrates these situations.

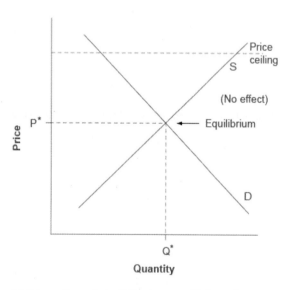

(a) Price ceiling substantially above equilibrium price

(b) Price ceiling slightly above equilibrium price

**11.** Neither. A shift in demand or supply means that at every price, either a greater or a lower quantity is demanded or supplied. A price floor does not shift a demand curve or a supply curve. However, if the price floor is set above the equilibrium, it will cause the quantity supplied on the supply curve to be greater than the quantity demanded on the demand curve, leading to excess supply.

**12.** Neither. A shift in demand or supply means that at every price, either a greater or a lower quantity is demanded or supplied. A price ceiling does not shift a demand curve or a supply curve. However, if the price ceiling is set below the equilibrium, it will cause the quantity demanded on the demand curve to be greater than the quantity supplied on the supply curve, leading to excess demand.

# Chapter 5

**1.** From point B to point C, price rises from \$70 to \$80, and Qd decreases from 2,800 to 2,600. So:

$$\text{\% change in quantity} = \frac{2600 - 2800}{(2600 + 2800) \div 2} \times 100$$

$$= \frac{-200}{2700} \times 100$$

$$= -7.41$$

$$\text{\% change in price} = \frac{80 - 70}{(80 + 70) \div 2} \times 100$$

$$= \frac{10}{75} \times 100$$

$$= 13.33$$

$$\text{Elasticity of Demand} = \frac{-7.41\%}{13.33\%}$$

$$= 0.56$$

The demand curve is inelastic in this area; that is, its elasticity value is less than one. Answer from Point D to point E:

$$\text{\% change in quantity} = \frac{2200 - 2400}{(2200 + 2400) \div 2} \times 100$$

$$= \frac{-200}{2300} \times 100$$

$$= -8.7$$

$$\text{\% change in price} = \frac{100 - 90}{(100 + 90) \div 2} \times 100$$

$$= \frac{10}{95} \times 100$$

$$= 10.53$$

$$\text{Elasticity of Demand} = \frac{-8.7\%}{10.53\%}$$

$$= 0.83$$

The demand curve is inelastic in this area; that is, its elasticity value is less than one. Answer from Point G to point H:

$$\text{\% change in quantity} = \frac{1600 - 1800}{1700} \times 100$$

$$= \frac{-200}{1700} \times 100$$

$$= -11.76$$

$$\text{\% change in price} = \frac{130 - 120}{125} \times 100$$

$$= \frac{10}{125} \times 100$$

$$= 8.00$$

$$\text{Elasticity of Demand} = \frac{-11.76\%}{8.00\%}$$

$$= -1.47$$

The demand curve is elastic in this interval.

**2.** From point J to point K, price rises from \$8 to \$9, and quantity rises from 50 to 70. So:

$$\% \text{ change in quantity} = \frac{70 - 50}{(70 + 50) \div 2} \times 100$$

$$= \frac{20}{60} \times 100$$

$$= 33.33$$

$$\% \text{ change in price} = \frac{\$9 - \$8}{(\$9 + \$8) \div 2} \times 100$$

$$= \frac{1}{8.5} \times 100$$

$$= 11.76$$

$$\text{Elasticity of Supply} = \frac{33.33\%}{11.76\%}$$

$$= 2.83$$

The supply curve is elastic in this area; that is, its elasticity value is greater than one. From point L to point M, the price rises from $10 to $11, while the Qs rises from 80 to 88:

$$\% \text{ change in quantity} = \frac{88 - 80}{(88 + 80) \div 2} \times 100$$

$$= \frac{8}{84} \times 100$$

$$= 9.52$$

$$\% \text{change in price} = \frac{\$11 - \$10}{(\$11 + \$10) \div 2} \times 100$$

$$= \frac{1}{10.5} \times 100$$

$$= 9.52$$

$$\text{Elasticity of Demand} = \frac{9.52\%}{9.52\%}$$

$$= 1.0$$

The supply curve has unitary elasticity in this area. From point N to point P, the price rises from $12 to $13, and Qs rises from 95 to 100:

$$\% \text{ change in quantity} = \frac{100 - 95}{(100 + 95) \div 2} \times 100$$

$$= \frac{5}{97.5} \times 100$$

$$= 5.13$$

$$\% \text{ change in price} = \frac{\$13 - \$12}{(\$13 + \$12) \div 2} \times 100$$

$$= \frac{1}{12.5} \times 100$$

$$= 8.0$$

$$\text{Elasticity of Supply} = \frac{5.13\%}{8.0\%}$$

$$= 0.64$$

The supply curve is inelastic in this region of the supply curve.

3. The demand curve with constant unitary elasticity is concave because the absolute value of declines in price are not identical. The left side of the curve starts with high prices, and then price falls by smaller amounts as it goes down toward the right side. This results in a slope of demand that is steeper on the left but flatter on the right, creating a curved, concave shape.

4. The constant unitary elasticity is a straight line because the curve slopes upward and both price and quantity are increasing proportionally.

5. Carmakers can pass this cost along to consumers if the demand for these cars is inelastic. If the demand for these cars is elastic, then the manufacturer must pay for the equipment.

6. If the elasticity is 1.4 at current prices, you would advise the company to lower its price on the product, since a

decrease in price will be offset by the increase in the amount of the drug sold. If the elasticity were 0.6, then you would advise the company to increase its price. Increases in price will offset the decrease in number of units sold, but increase your total revenue. If elasticity is 1, the total revenue is already maximized, and you would advise that the company maintain its current price level.

7. The percentage change in quantity supplied as a result of a given percentage change in the price of gasoline.

8.

$$
\begin{aligned}
\text{Percentage change in quantity demanded} \quad &= \quad [(\text{change in quantity})/(\text{original quantity})] \times 100 \\
&= \quad [22 - 30]/[(22 + 30)/2] \times 100 \\
&= \quad -8/26 \times 100 \\
&= \quad -30.77 \\
\text{Percentage change in income} \quad &= \quad [(\text{change in income})/(\text{original income})] \times 100 \\
&= \quad [38{,}000 - 25{,}000]/[(38{,}000 + 25{,}000)/2] \times 100 \\
&= \quad 13/31.5 \times 100 \\
&= \quad 41.27
\end{aligned}
$$

In this example, bread is an inferior good because its consumption falls as income rises.

9. The formula for cross-price elasticity is % change in Qd for apples / % change in P of oranges. Multiplying both sides by % change in P of oranges yields: % change in Qd for apples = cross-price elasticity X% change in P of oranges = 0.4 × (–3%) = –1.2%, or a 1.2 % decrease in demand for apples.

## Chapter 6

1. GDP is C + I + G + (X – M). GDP = $2,000 billion + $50 billion + $1,000 billion + ($20 billion – $40 billion) = $3,030

2.
   a.  Hospital stays are part of GDP.
   b.  Changes in life expectancy are not market transactions and not part of GDP.
   c.  Child care that is paid for is part of GDP.
   d.  If Grandma gets paid and reports this as income, it is part of GDP, otherwise not.
   e.  A used car is not produced this year, so it is not part of GDP.
   f.  A new car is part of GDP.
   g.  Variety does not count in GDP, where the cheese could all be cheddar.
   h.  The iron is not counted because it is an intermediate good.

3. From 1980 to 1990, real GDP grew by (8,225.0 – 5,926.5) / (5,926.5) = 39%. Over the same period, prices increased by (72.7 – 48.3) / (48.3/100) = 51%. So about 57% of the growth 51 / (51 + 39) was inflation, and the remainder: 39 / (51 + 39) = 43% was growth in real GDP.

4. Two other major recessions are visible in the figure as slight dips: those of 1973–1975, and 1981–1982. Two other recessions appear in the figure as a flattening of the path of real GDP. These were in 1990–1991 and 2001.

5. 11 recessions in approximately 70 years averages about one recession every six years.

6. The table lists the "Months of Contraction" for each recession. Averaging these figures for the post-WWII recessions gives an average duration of 11 months, or slightly less than a year.

7. The table lists the "Months of Expansion." Averaging these figures for the post-WWII expansions gives an average expansion of 60.5 months, or more than five years.

8. Yes. The answer to both questions depends on whether GDP is growing faster or slower than population. If population grows faster than GDP, GDP increases, while GDP per capita decreases. If GDP falls, but population falls faster, then GDP decreases, while GDP per capita increases.

**9.** Start with Central African Republic's GDP measured in francs. Divide it by the exchange rate to convert to U.S. dollars, and then divide by population to obtain the per capita figure. That is, 1,107,689 million francs / 284.681 francs per dollar / 4.862 million people = $800.28 GDP per capita.

**10.**

  a. A dirtier environment would reduce the broad standard of living, but not be counted in GDP, so a rise in GDP would overstate the standard of living.

  b. A lower crime rate would raise the broad standard of living, but not be counted directly in GDP, and so a rise in GDP would understate the standard of living.

  c. A greater variety of goods would raise the broad standard of living, but not be counted directly in GDP, and so a rise in GDP would understate the rise in the standard of living.

  d. A decline in infant mortality would raise the broad standard of living, but not be counted directly in GDP, and so a rise in GDP would understate the rise in the standard of living.

## Chapter 7

**1.** The Industrial Revolution refers to the widespread use of power-driven machinery and the economic and social changes that resulted in the first half of the 1800s. Ingenious machines—the steam engine, the power loom, and the steam locomotive—performed tasks that would have taken vast numbers of workers to do. The Industrial Revolution began in Great Britain, and soon spread to the United States, Germany, and other countries.

**2.** Property rights are the rights of individuals and firms to own property and use it as they see fit. Contractual rights are based on property rights and they allow individuals to enter into agreements with others regarding the use of their property providing recourse through the legal system in the event of noncompliance. Economic growth occurs when the standard of living increases in an economy, which occurs when output is increasing and incomes are rising. For this to happen, societies must create a legal environment that gives individuals the ability to use their property to their fullest and highest use, including the right to trade or sell that property. Without a legal system that enforces contracts, people would not be likely to enter into contracts for current or future services because of the risk of non-payment. This would make it difficult to transact business and would slow economic growth.

**3.** Yes. Since productivity is output per unit of input, we can measure productivity using GDP (output) per worker (input).

**4.** In 20 years the United States will have an income of $10,000 \times (1 + 0.01)^{20} = \$12,201.90$, and South Korea will have an income of $10,000 \times (1 + 0.04)^{20} = \$21,911.23$. South Korea has grown by a multiple of 2.1 and the United States by a multiple of 1.2.

**5.** Capital deepening and technology are important. What seems to be more important is how they are combined.

**6.** Government can contribute to economic growth by investing in human capital through the education system, building a strong physical infrastructure for transportation and commerce, increasing investment by lowering capital gains taxes, creating special economic zones that allow for reduced tariffs, and investing in research and development.

**7.** Public education, low investment taxes, funding for infrastructure projects, special economic zones

**8.** A good way to think about this is how a runner who has fallen behind in a race feels psychologically and physically as he catches up. Playing catch-up can be more taxing than maintaining one's position at the head of the pack.

**9.**

  a. No. Capital deepening refers to an increase in the amount of capital per person in an economy. A decrease in investment by firms will actually cause the opposite of capital deepening (since the population will grow over time).

  b. There is no direct connection between an increase in international trade and capital deepening. One could imagine particular scenarios where trade could lead to capital deepening (for example, if international capital inflows—which are the counterpart to increasing the trade deficit—lead to an increase in physical capital investment), but in general, no.

    c. Yes. Capital deepening refers to an increase in either physical capital or human capital per person. Continuing education or any time of lifelong learning adds to human capital and thus creates capital deepening.

10. The advantages of backwardness include faster growth rates because of the process of convergence, as well as the ability to adopt new technologies that were developed first in the "leader" countries. While being "backward" is not inherently a good thing, Gerschenkron stressed that there are certain advantages which aid countries trying to "catch up."

11. Capital deepening, by definition, should lead to diminished returns because you're investing more and more but using the same methods of production, leading to the marginal productivity declining. This is shown on a production function as a movement along the curve. Improvements in technology should not lead to diminished returns because you are finding new and more efficient ways of using the same amount of capital. This can be illustrated as a shift upward of the production function curve.

12. Productivity growth from new advances in technology will not slow because the new methods of production will be adopted relatively quickly and easily, at very low marginal cost. Also, countries that are seeing technology growth usually have a vast and powerful set of institutions for training workers and building better machines, which allows the maximum amount of people to benefit from the new technology. These factors have the added effect of making additional technological advances even easier for these countries.

## Chapter 8

1. The population is divided into those "in the labor force" and those "not in the labor force." Thus, the number of adults not in the labor force is 237.8 – 153.9 = 83.9 million. Since the labor force is divided into employed persons and unemployed persons, the number of unemployed persons is 153.9 – 139.1 = 14.8 million. Thus, the adult population has the following proportions:

- 139.1/237.8 = 58.5% employed persons
- 14.8/237.8 = 6.2% unemployed persons
- 83.9/237.8 = 35.3% persons out of the labor force

2. The unemployment rate is defined as the number of unemployed persons as a percentage of the labor force or 14.8/153.9 = 9.6%. This is higher than the February 2015 unemployment rate, computed earlier, of 5.5%.

3. Over the long term, the U.S. unemployment rate has remained basically the same level.

4.
    a. Nonwhites
    b. The young
    c. High school graduates

5. Because of the influx of women into the labor market, the supply of labor shifts to the right. Since wages are sticky downward, the increased supply of labor causes an increase in people looking for jobs (Qs), but no change in the number of jobs available (Qe). As a result, unemployment increases by the amount of the increase in the labor supply. This can be seen in the following figure. Over time, as labor demand grows, the unemployment will decline and eventually wages will begin to increase again. But this increase in labor demand goes beyond the scope of this problem.

**6.** The increase in labor supply was a social demographic trend—it was not caused by the economy falling into a recession. Therefore, the influx of women into the work force increased the natural rate of unemployment.

**7.** New entrants to the labor force, whether from college or otherwise, are counted as frictionally unemployed until they find a job.

## Chapter 9

**1.** To compute the amount spent on each fruit in each year, you multiply the quantity of each fruit by the price.
- 10 apples × 50 cents each = $5.00 spent on apples in 2001.
- 12 bananas × 20 cents each = $2.40 spent on bananas in 2001.
- 2 bunches of grapes at 65 cents each = $1.30 spent on grapes in 2001.
- 1 pint of raspberries at $2 each = $2.00 spent on raspberries in 2001.

Adding up the amounts gives you the total cost of the fruit basket. The total cost of the fruit basket in 2001 was $5.00 + $2.40 + $1.30 + $2.00 = $10.70. The total costs for all the years are shown in the following table.

| 2001 | 2002 | 2003 | 2004 |
|---|---|---|---|
| $10.70 | $13.80 | $15.35 | $16.31 |

**2.** If 2003 is the base year, then the index number has a value of 100 in 2003. To transform the cost of a fruit basket each year, we divide each year's value by $15.35, the value of the base year, and then multiply the result by 100. The price index is shown in the following table.

| 2001 | 2002 | 2003 | 2004 |
|---|---|---|---|
| 69.71 | 89.90 | 100.00 | 106.3 |

Note that the base year has a value of 100; years before the base year have values less than 100; and years after have values more than 100.

**3.** The inflation rate is calculated as the percentage change in the price index from year to year. For example, the inflation rate between 2001 and 2002 is (84.61 − 69.71) / 69.71 = 0.2137 = 21.37%. The inflation rates for all the years are shown in the last row of the following table, which includes the two previous answers.

| Items | Qty | (2001) Price | (2001) Amount Spent | (2002) Price | (2002) Amount Spent | (2003) Price | (2003) Amount Spent | (2004) Price | (2004) Amount Spent |
|---|---|---|---|---|---|---|---|---|---|
| Apples | 10 | $0.50 | $5.00 | $0.75 | $7.50 | $0.85 | $8.50 | $0.88 | $8.80 |
| Bananas | 12 | $0.20 | $2.40 | $0.25 | $3.00 | $0.25 | $3.00 | $0.29 | $3.48 |
| Grapes | 2 | $0.65 | $1.30 | $0.70 | $1.40 | $0.90 | $1.80 | $0.95 | $1.90 |
| Raspberries | 1 | $2.00 | $2.00 | $1.90 | $1.90 | $2.05 | $2.05 | $2.13 | $2.13 |
| Total | | | $10.70 | | $13.80 | | $15.35 | | $16.31 |
| Price Index | | | 69.71 | | 84.61 | | 100.00 | | 106.3 |
| Inflation Rate | | | | | 21.37% | | 18.19% | | 6.3% |

4. Begin by calculating the total cost of buying the basket in each time period, as shown in the following table.

| Items | Quantity | (Time 1) Price | (Time 1) Total Cost | (Time 2) Price | (Time 2) Total Cost |
|---|---|---|---|---|---|
| Gifts | 12 | $50 | $600 | $60 | $720 |
| Pizza | 24 | $15 | $360 | $16 | $384 |
| Blouses | 6 | $60 | $360 | $50 | $300 |
| Trips | 2 | $400 | $800 | $420 | $840 |
| Total Cost | | | $2,120 | | $2,244 |

The rise in cost of living is calculated as the percentage increase: $(2244 - 2120) / 2120 = 0.0585 = 5.85\%$.

5. Since the CPI measures the prices of the goods and services purchased by the typical urban consumer, it measures the prices of things that people buy with their paycheck. For that reason, the CPI would be the best price index to use for this purpose.

6. The PPI is subject to those biases for essentially the same reasons as the CPI is. The GDP deflator picks up prices of what is actually purchased that year, so there are no biases. That is the advantage of using the GDP deflator over the CPI.

7. The calculator requires you to input three numbers:
   - The first year, in this case the year of your birth
   - The amount of money you would want to translate in terms of its purchasing power
   - The last year—now or the most recent year the calculator will accept

My birth year is 1955. The amount is $1. The year 2012 is currently the latest year the calculator will accept. The simple purchasing power calculator shows that $1 of purchases in 1955 would cost $8.57 in 2012. The website also explains how the true answer is more complicated than that shown by the simple purchasing power calculator.

8. The state government would benefit because it would repay the loan in less valuable dollars than it borrowed. Plus, tax revenues for the state government would increase because of the inflation.

9. Higher inflation reduces real interest rates on fixed rate mortgages. Because ARMs can be adjusted, higher inflation

leads to higher interest rates on ARMs.

**10.** Because the mortgage has an adjustable rate, the rate should fall by 3%, the same as inflation, to keep the real interest rate the same.

## Chapter 10

**1.** The stock and bond values will not show up in the current account. However, the dividends from the stocks and the interest from the bonds show up as an import to income in the current account.

**2.** It becomes more negative as imports, which are a negative to the current account, are growing faster than exports, which are a positive.

**3.**
   a. Money flows out of the Mexican economy.
   b. Money flows into the Mexican economy.
   c. Money flows out of the Mexican economy.

**4.** GDP is a dollar value of all production of goods and services. Exports are produced domestically but shipped abroad. The percent ratio of exports to GDP gives us an idea of how important exports are to the national economy out of all goods and services produced. For example, exports represent only 14% of U.S. GDP, but 50% of Germany's GDP

**5.** Divide $542 billion by $1,800 billion.

**6.** Divide –$400 billion by $16,800 billion.

**7.** The trade balance is the difference between exports and imports. The current account balance includes this number (whether it is a trade balance or a trade surplus), but also includes international flows of money from global investments.

**8.**
   a. An export sale to Germany involves a financial flow from Germany to the U.S. economy.
   b. The issue here is not U.S. investments in Brazil, but the return paid on those investments, which involves a financial flow from the Brazilian economy to the U.S. economy.
   c. Foreign aid from the United States to Egypt is a financial flow from the United States to Egypt.
   d. Importing oil from the Russian Federation means a flow of financial payments from the U.S. economy to the Russian Federation.
   e. Japanese investors buying U.S. real estate is a financial flow from Japan to the U.S. economy.

**9.** The top portion tracks the flow of exports and imports and the payments for those. The bottom portion is looking at international financial investments and the outflow and inflow of monies from those investments. These investments can include investments in stocks and bonds or real estate abroad, as well as international borrowing and lending.

**10.** If more monies are flowing out of the country (for example, to pay for imports) it will make the current account more negative or less positive, and if more monies are flowing into the country, it will make the current account less negative or more positive.

**11.** Write out the national savings and investment identity for the situation of the economy implied by this question:

$$\text{Supply of capital} \ = \ \text{Demand for capital}$$
$$S + (M - X) + (T - G) \ = \ I \qquad \text{If domestic savings increases and}$$
$$\text{Savings} + (\text{trade deficit}) + (\text{government budget surplus}) \ = \ \text{Investment}$$

nothing else changes, then the trade deficit will fall. In effect, the economy would be relying more on domestic capital and less on foreign capital. If the government starts borrowing instead of saving, then the trade deficit must rise. In effect, the government is no longer providing savings and so, if nothing else is to change, more investment funds must arrive from abroad. If the rate of domestic investment surges, then, *ceteris paribus*, the trade deficit must also rise, to provide the extra capital. The *ceteris paribus*—or "other things being equal"—assumption is important here. In all of these situations, there is no reason to expect in the real world that the original change will affect only, or primarily, the trade deficit. The identity only says that something will adjust—it does not specify what.

**12.** The government is saving rather than borrowing. The supply of savings, whether private or public, is on the left side of the identity.

**13.** A trade deficit is determined by a country's level of private and public savings and the amount of domestic investment.

**14.** The trade deficit must increase. To put it another way, this increase in investment must be financed by an inflow of financial capital from abroad.

**15.** Incomes fall during a recession, and consumers buy fewer good, including imports.

**16.** A booming economy will increase the demand for goods in general, so import sales will increase. If our trading partners' economies are doing well, they will buy more of our products and so U.S. exports will increase.

**17.**
   a. Increased federal spending on Medicare may not increase productivity, so a budget deficit is not justified.
   b. Increased spending on education will increase productivity and foster greater economic growth, so a budget deficit is justified.
   c. Increased spending on the space program may not increase productivity, so a budget deficit is not justified.
   d. Increased spending on airports and air traffic control will increase productivity and foster greater economic growth, so a budget deficit is justified.

**18.** Foreign investors worried about repayment so they began to pull money out of these countries. The money can be pulled out of stock and bond markets, real estate, and banks.

**19.** A rapidly growing trade surplus could result from a number of factors, so you would not want to be too quick to assume a specific cause. However, if the choice is between whether the economy is in recession or growing rapidly, the answer would have to be recession. In a recession, demand for all goods, including imports, has declined; however, demand for exports from other countries has not necessarily altered much, so the result is a larger trade surplus.

**20.** Germany has a higher level of trade than the United States. The United States has a large domestic economy so it has a large volume of internal trade.

**21.**
   a. A large economy tends to have lower levels of international trade, because it can do more of its trade internally, but this has little impact on its trade imbalance.
   b. An imbalance between domestic physical investment and domestic saving (including government and private saving) will always lead to a trade imbalance, but has little to do with the level of trade.
   c. Many large trading partners nearby geographically increases the level of trade, but has little impact one way or the other on a trade imbalance.
   d. The answer here is not obvious. An especially large budget deficit means a large demand for financial capital which, according to the national saving and investment identity, makes it somewhat more likely that there will be a need for an inflow of foreign capital, which means a trade deficit.
   e. A strong tradition of discouraging trade certainly reduces the level of trade. However, it does not necessarily say much about the balance of trade, since this is determined by both imports and exports, and by national levels of physical investment and savings.

## Chapter 11

**1.** In order to supply goods, suppliers must employ workers, whose incomes increase as a result of their labor. They use this additional income to demand goods of an equivalent value to those they supply.

2. When consumers demand more goods than are available on the market, prices are driven higher and the additional opportunities for profit induce more suppliers to enter the market, producing an equivalent amount to that which is demanded.

3. Higher input prices make output less profitable, decreasing the desired supply. This is shown graphically as a leftward shift in the AS curve.

4. Equilibrium occurs at the level of GDP where AD = AS. Insufficient aggregate demand could explain why the equilibrium occurs at a level of GDP less than potential. A decrease (or leftward shift) in aggregate supply could be another reason.

5. Immigration reform as described should increase the labor supply, shifting SRAS to the right, leading to a higher equilibrium GDP and a lower price level.

6. Given the assumptions made here, the cuts in R&D funding should reduce productivity growth. The model would show this as a leftward shift in the SRAS curve, leading to a lower equilibrium GDP and a higher price level.

7. An increase in the value of the stock market would make individuals feel wealthier and thus more confident about their economic situation. This would likely cause an increase in consumer confidence leading to an increase in consumer spending, shifting the AD curve to the right. The result would be an increase in the equilibrium level of GDP and an increase in the price level.

8. Since imports depend on GDP, if Mexico goes into recession, its GDP declines and so do its imports. This decline in our exports can be shown as a leftward shift in AD, leading to a decrease in our GDP and price level.

9. Tax cuts increase consumer and investment spending, depending on where the tax cuts are targeted. This would shift AD to the right, so if the tax cuts occurred when the economy was in recession (and GDP was less than potential), the tax cuts would increase GDP and "lead the economy out of recession."

10. A negative report on home prices would make consumers feel like the value of their homes, which for most Americans is a major portion of their wealth, has declined. A negative report on consumer confidence would make consumers feel pessimistic about the future. Both of these would likely reduce consumer spending, shifting AD to the left, reducing GDP and the price level. A positive report on the home price index or consumer confidence would do the opposite.

11. A smaller labor force would be reflected in a leftward shift in AS, leading to a lower equilibrium level of GDP and higher price level.

12. Higher EU growth would increase demand for U.S. exports, reducing our trade deficit. The increased demand for exports would show up as a rightward shift in AD, causing GDP to rise (and the price level to rise as well). Higher GDP would require more jobs to fulfill, so U.S. employment would also rise.

13. Expansionary monetary policy shifts AD to the right. A continuing expansionary policy would cause larger and larger shifts (given the parameters of this problem). The result would be an increase in GDP and employment (a decrease in unemployment) and higher prices until potential output was reached. After that point, the expansionary policy would simply cause inflation.

14. Since the SRAS curve is vertical in the neoclassical zone, unless the economy is bordering the intermediate zone, a decrease in AS will cause a decrease in the price level, but no effect on real economic activity (for example, real GDP or employment).

15. Because the SRAS curve is horizontal in the Keynesian zone, a decrease in AD should depress real economic activity but have no effect on prices.

## Chapter 12

1.

    a. An increase in home values will increase consumption spending (due to increased wealth). AD will shift to the right and may cause inflation if it goes beyond potential GDP.

    b. Rapid growth by a major trading partner will increase demand for exports. AD will shift to the right and may cause inflation if it goes beyond potential GDP.

    c. Increased profit opportunities will increase business investment. AD will shift to the right and may cause inflation if it goes beyond potential GDP.

    d. Higher interest rates reduce investment spending. AD will shift to the left and may cause recession if it falls below potential GDP.

    e. Demand for cheaper imports increases, reducing demand for domestic products. AD will shift to the left and may be recessionary.

**2.**

    a. A tax increase on consumer income will cause consumption to fall, pushing the AD curve left, and is a possible solution to inflation.

    b. A surge in military spending is an increase in government spending. This will cause the AD curve to shift to the right. If real GDP is less than potential GDP, then this spending would pull the economy out of a recession. If real GDP is to the right of potential GDP, then the AD curve will shift farther to the right and military spending will be inflationary.

    c. A tax cut focused on business investment will shift AD to the right. If the original macroeconomic equilibrium is below potential GDP, then this policy can help move an economy out of a recession.

    d. Government spending on healthcare will cause the AD curve to shift to the right. If real GDP is less than potential GDP, then this spending would pull the economy out of a recession. If real GDP is to th right of potential GDP, then the AD curve will shift farther to the right and healthcare spending will be inflationary.

**3.** An inflationary gap is the result of an increase in aggregate demand when the economy is at potential output. Since the AS curve is vertical at potential GDP, any increase in AD will lead to a higher price level (i.e. inflation) but no higher real GDP. This is easy to see if you draw $AD_1$ to the right of $AD_0$.

**4.** A decrease in government spending will shift AD to the left.

**5.** A decrease in energy prices, a positive supply shock, would cause the AS curve to shift out to the right, yielding more real GDP at a lower price level. This would shift the Phillips curve down toward the origin, meaning the economy would experience lower unemployment and a lower rate of inflation.

**6.** Keynesian economics does not require microeconomic price controls of any sort. It is true that many Keynesian economic prescriptions were for the government to influence the total amount of aggregate demand in the economy, often through government spending and tax cuts.

**7.** The three problems center on government's ability to estimate potential GDP, decide whether to influence aggregate demand through tax changes or changes in government spending, and the lag time that occurs as Congress and the President attempt to pass legislation.

## Chapter 13

**1.** No, this statement is false. It would be more accurate to say that rational expectations seek to predict the future as accurately as possible, using all of past experience as a guide. Adaptive expectations are largely backward looking; that is, they adapt as experience accumulates, but without attempting to look forward.

**2.** An unemployment rate of zero percent is presumably well below the rate that is consistent with potential GDP and with the natural rate of unemployment. As a result, this policy would be attempting to push AD out to the right. In the short run, it is possible to have unemployment slightly below the natural rate for a time, at a price of higher inflation, as shown by the movement from $E_0$ to $E_1$ along the short-run AS curve. However, over time the extremely low unemployment rates will tend to cause wages to be bid up, and shift the short-run AS curve back to the left. The result would be a higher price level, but an economy still at potential GDP and the natural rate of unemployment, as determined by the long-run AS curve. If the government continues this policy, it will continually be pushing the price level higher and higher, but it will not be able to achieve its goal of zero percent unemployment, because that goal is inconsistent with market forces.

**3.** The statement is accurate. Rational expectations can be thought of as a version of neoclassical economics because it argues that potential GDP and the rate of unemployment are shaped by market forces as wages and prices adjust. However, it is an "extreme" version because it argues that this adjustment takes place very quickly. Other theories, like adaptive expectations, suggest that adjustment to the neoclassical outcome takes a few years.

**4.** The short-term Keynesian model is built on the importance of aggregate demand as a cause of business cycles and a degree of wage and price rigidity, and thus does a sound job of explaining many recessions and why cyclical unemployment rises and falls. The neoclassical model emphasizes aggregate supply by focusing on the underlying determinants of output and employment in markets, and thus tends to put more emphasis on economic growth and how labor markets work.

## Chapter 14

**1.** As long as you remain within the walls of the casino, chips fit the definition of money; that is, they serve as a medium of exchange, a unit of account, and a store of value. Chips do not work very well as money once you leave the casino, but many kinds of money do not work well in other areas. For example, it is hard to spend money from Turkey or Brazil at your local supermarket or at the movie theater.

**2.** Many physical items that a person buys at one time but may sell at another time can serve as an answer to this question. Examples include a house, land, art, rare coins or stamps, and so on.

**3.** The currency and checks in M1 are easiest to spend. It is harder to spend M2 directly, although if there is an automatic teller machine in the shopping mall, you can turn M2 from your savings account into an M1 of currency quite quickly. If your answer is about "credit cards," then you are really talking about spending M1—although it is M1 from the account of the credit card company, which you will repay later when you credit card bill comes due.

**4.**
  a. Neither in M1 or M2
  b. That is part of M1, and because M2 includes M1 it is also part of M2
  c. Currency out in the public hands is part of M1 and M2
  d. Checking deposits are in M1 and M2
  e. Money market accounts are in M2

**5.** A bank's assets include cash held in their vaults, but assets also include monies that the bank holds at the Federal Reserve Bank (called "reserves"), loans that are made to customers, and bonds.

**6.**
  a. A borrower who has been late on a number of loan payments looks perhaps less likely to repay the loan, or to repay it on time, and so you would want to pay less for that loan.
  b. If interest rates generally have risen, then this loan made at a time of relatively lower interest rates looks less attractive, and you would pay less for it.
  c. If the borrower is a firm with a record of high profits, then it is likely to be able to repay the loan, and you would be willing to pay more for the loan.
  d. If interest rates in the economy have fallen, then the loan is worth more.

## Chapter 15

**1.** Longer terms insulate the Board from political forces. Since the presidency can potentially change every four years, the Federal Reserve's independence prevents drastic swings in monetary policy with every new administration and allows policy decisions to be made only on economic grounds.

**2.** Banks make their money from issuing loans and charging interest. The more money that is stored in the bank's vault, the less is available for lending and the less money the bank stands to make.

**3.** The fear and uncertainty created by the suggestion that a bank might fail can lead depositors to withdraw their money. If many depositors do this at the same time, the bank may not be able to meet their demands and will, indeed, fail.

**4.** The bank has to hold $1,000 in reserves, so when it buys the $500 in bonds, it will have to reduce its loans by $500 to make up the difference. The money supply decreases by the same amount.

**5.** An increase in reserve requirements would reduce the supply of money, since more money would be held in banks rather than circulating in the economy.

**6.** Contractionary policy reduces the amount of loanable funds in the economy. As with all goods, greater scarcity leads a greater price, so the interest rate, or the price of borrowing money, rises.

**7.** An increase in the amount of available loanable funds means that there are more people who want to lend. They, therefore, bid the price of borrowing (the interest rate) down.

**8.** In times of economic uncertainty, banks may worry that borrowers will lose the ability to repay their loans. They may also fear that a panic is more likely and they will need the excess reserves to meet their obligations.

**9.** If consumer optimism changes, spending can speed up or slow down. This could also happen in a case where consumers need to buy a large number of items quickly, such as in a situation of national emergency.

## Chapter 16

**1.**
a. The British use the pound sterling, while Germans use the euro, so a British exporter will receive euros from export sales, which will need to be exchanged for pounds. A stronger euro will mean more pounds per euro, so the exporter will be better off. In addition, the lower price for German imports will stimulate demand for British exports. For both these reasons, a stronger euro benefits the British exporter.
b. The Dutch use euros while the Chileans use pesos, so the Dutch tourist needs to turn euros into Chilean pesos. An increase in the euro means that the tourist will get more pesos per euro. As a consequence, the Dutch tourist will have a less expensive vacation than he planned, so the tourist will be better off.
c. The Greek use euros while the Canadians use dollars. An increase in the euro means it will buy more Canadian dollars. As a result, the Greek bank will see a decrease in the cost of the Canadian bonds, so it may purchase more bonds. Either way, the Greek bank benefits.
d. Since both the French and Germans use the euro, an increase in the euro, in terms of other currencies, should have no impact on the French exporter.

**2.** Expected depreciation in a currency will lead people to divest themselves of the currency. We should expect to see an increase in the supply of pounds and a decrease in demand for pounds. The result should be a decrease in the value of the pound *vis à vis* the dollar.

**3.** Lower U.S. interest rates make U.S. assets less desirable compared to assets in the European Union. We should expect to see a decrease in demand for dollars and an increase in supply of dollars in foreign currency markets. As a result, we should expect to see the dollar depreciate compared to the euro.

**4.** A decrease in Argentine inflation relative to other countries should cause an increase in demand for pesos, a decrease in supply of pesos, and an appreciation of the peso in foreign currency markets.

**5.** The problem occurs when banks borrow foreign currency but lend in domestic currency. Since banks' assets (loans they made) are in domestic currency, while their debts (money they borrowed) are in foreign currency, when the domestic currency declines, their debts grow larger. If the domestic currency falls substantially in value, as happened during the Asian financial crisis, then the banking system could fail. This problem is unlikely to occur for U.S. banks because, even when they borrow from abroad, they tend to borrow dollars. Remember, there are trillions of dollars in circulation in the global economy. Since both assets and debts are in dollars, a change in the value of the dollar does not cause banking system failure the way it can when banks borrow in foreign currency.

6. While capital flight is possible in either case, if a country borrows to invest in real capital it is more likely to be able to generate the income to pay back its debts than a country that borrows to finance consumption. As a result, an investment-stimulated economy is less likely to provoke capital flight and economic recession.

7. A contractionary monetary policy, by driving up domestic interest rates, would cause the currency to appreciate. The higher value of the currency in foreign exchange markets would reduce exports, since from the perspective of foreign buyers, they are now more expensive. The higher value of the currency would similarly stimulate imports, since they would now be cheaper from the perspective of domestic buyers. Lower exports and higher imports cause net exports (EX – IM) to fall, which causes aggregate demand to fall. The result would be a decrease in GDP working through the exchange rate mechanism reinforcing the effect contractionary monetary policy has on domestic investment expenditure. However, cheaper imports would stimulate aggregate supply, bringing GDP back to potential, though at a lower price level.

8. For a currency to fall, a central bank need only supply more of its currency in foreign exchange markets. It can print as much domestic currency as it likes. For a currency to rise, a central bank needs to buy its currency in foreign exchange markets, paying with foreign currency. Since no central bank has an infinite amount of foreign currency reserves, it cannot buy its currency indefinitely.

9. Variations in exchange rates, because they change import and export prices, disturb international trade flows. When trade is a large part of a nation's economic activity, government will find it more advantageous to fix exchange rates to minimize disruptions of trade flows.

## Chapter 17

1. The government borrows funds by selling Treasury bonds, notes, and bills.

2. The funds can be used to pay down the national debt or else be refunded to the taxpayers.

3. Yes, a nation can run budget deficits and see its debt/GDP ratio fall. In fact, this is not uncommon. If the deficit is small in a given year, than the addition to debt in the numerator of the debt/GDP ratio will be relatively small, while the growth in GDP is larger, and so the debt/GDP ratio declines. This was the experience of the U.S. economy for the period from the end of World War II to about 1980. It is also theoretically possible, although not likely, for a nation to have a budget surplus and see its debt/GDP ratio rise. Imagine the case of a nation with a small surplus, but in a recession year when the economy shrinks. It is possible that the decline in the nation's debt, in the numerator of the debt/GDP ratio, would be proportionally less than the fall in the size of GDP, so the debt/GDP ratio would rise.

4. Progressive. People who give larger gifts subject to the higher tax rate would typically have larger incomes as well.

5. Corporate income tax on his profits, individual income tax on his salary, and payroll tax taken out of the wages he pays himself.

6. individual income taxes

7. The tax is regressive because wealthy income earners are not taxed at all on income above $113,000. As a percent of total income, the social security tax hits lower income earners harder than wealthier individuals.

8. As debt increases, interest payments also rise, so that the deficit grows even if we keep other government spending constant.

9.
    a. As a share of GDP, this is false. In nominal dollars, it is true.
    b. False.
    c. False.
    d. False. Education spending is much higher at the state level.
    e. False. As a share of GDP, it is up about 50.
    f. As a share of GDP, this is false, and in real dollars, it is also false.

    g.  False.

    h.  False; it's about 1%.

    i.  False. Although budget deficits were large in 2003 and 2004, and continued into the later 2000s, the federal government ran budget surpluses from 1998–2001.

    j.  False.

**10.** To keep prices from rising too much or too rapidly.

**11.** To increase employment.

**12.** It falls below because less tax revenue than expected is collected.

**13.** Automatic stabilizers take effect very quickly, whereas discretionary policy can take a long time to implement.

**14.** In a recession, because of the decline in economic output, less income is earned, and so less in taxes is automatically collected. Many welfare and unemployment programs are designed so that those who fall into certain categories, like "unemployed" or "low income," are eligible for benefits. During a recession, more people fall into these categories and become eligible for benefits automatically. The combination of reduced taxes and higher spending is just what is needed for an economy in recession producing below potential GDP. With an economic boom, average income levels rise in the economy, so more in taxes is automatically collected. Fewer people meet the criteria for receiving government assistance to the unemployed or the needy, so government spending on unemployment assistance and welfare falls automatically. This combination of higher taxes and lower spending is just what is needed if an economy is producing above its potential GDP.

**15.** Prices would be pushed up as a result of too much spending.

**16.** Employment would suffer as a result of too little spending.

**17.** Monetary policy probably has shorter time lags than fiscal policy. Imagine that the data becomes fairly clear that an economy is in or near a recession. Expansionary monetary policy can be carried out through open market operations, which can be done fairly quickly, since the Federal Reserve's Open Market Committee meets six times a year. Also, monetary policy takes effect through interest rates, which can change fairly quickly. However, fiscal policy is carried out through acts of Congress that need to be signed into law by the president. Negotiating such laws often takes months, and even after the laws are negotiated, it takes more months for spending programs or tax cuts to have an effect on the macroeconomy.

**18.** The government would have to make up the revenue either by raising taxes in a different area or cutting spending.

**19.** Programs where the amount of spending is not fixed, but rather determined by macroeconomic conditions, such as food stamps, would lose a great deal of flexibility if spending increases had to be met by corresponding tax increases or spending cuts.

## Chapter 18

**1.** We use the national savings and investment identity to solve this question. In this case, the government has a budget surplus, so the government surplus appears as part of the supply of financial capital. Then:

$$\text{Quantity supplied of financial capital} = \text{Quantity demanded of financial capital}$$
$$S + (T - G) = I + (X - M)$$
$$600 + 200 = I + 100$$
$$I = 700$$

**2.**

    a.  Since the government has a budget surplus, the government budget term appears with the supply of capital. The following shows the national savings and investment identity for this economy.

$$\text{Quantity supplied of financial capital} = \text{Quantity demanded of financial capital}$$
$$S + (T - G) = I + (X - M)$$

b. Plugging the given values into the identity shown in part (a), we find that (X − M) = 0.

c. Since the government has a budget deficit, the government budget term appears with the demand for capital. You do not know in advance whether the economy has a trade deficit or a trade surplus. But when you see that the quantity demanded of financial capital exceeds the quantity supplied, you know that there must be an additional quantity of financial capital supplied by foreign investors, which means a trade deficit of 2000. This example shows that in this case there is a higher budget deficit, and a higher trade deficit.

$$\text{Quantity supplied of financial capital} = \text{Quantity demanded of financial capital}$$
$$S + (M - X) = I + (G - T)$$
$$4000 + 2000 = 5000 + 1000$$

3. In this case, the national saving and investment identity is written in this way:

$$\text{Quantity supplied of financial capital} = \text{Quantity demanded of financial capital}$$
$$(T - G) + (M - X) + S = I$$

The increase in the government budget surplus and the increase in the trade deficit both increased the supply of financial capital. If investment in physical capital remained unchanged, then private savings must go down, and if savings remained unchanged, then investment must go up. In fact, both effects happened; that is, in the late 1990s, in the U.S. economy, savings declined and investment rose.

4. Ricardian equivalence means that private saving changes to offset exactly any changes in the government budget. So, if the deficit increases by 20, private saving increases by 20 as well, and the trade deficit and the budget deficit will not change from their original levels. The original national saving and investment identity is written below. Notice that if any change in the (G − T) term is offset by a change in the S term, then the other terms do not change. So if (G − T) rises by 20, then S must also increase by 20.

$$\text{Quantity supplied of financial capital} = \text{Quantity demanded of financial capital}$$
$$S + (M - X) = I + (G - T)$$
$$130 + 20 = 100 + 50$$

5. In the last few decades, spending per student has climbed substantially. However, test scores have fallen over this time. This experience has led a number of experts to argue that the problem is not resources—or is not just resources by itself—but is also a problem of how schools are organized and managed and what incentives they have for success. There are a number of proposals to alter the incentives that schools face, but relatively little hard evidence on what proposals work well. Without trying to evaluate whether these proposals are good or bad ideas, you can just list some of them: testing students regularly; rewarding teachers or schools that perform well on such tests; requiring additional teacher training; allowing students to choose between public schools; allowing teachers and parents to start new schools; giving student "vouchers" that they can use to pay tuition at either public or private schools.

6. The government can direct government spending to R&D. It can also create tax incentives for business to invest in R&D.

## Chapter 19

1. The answers are shown in the following two tables.

| Region | GDP (in millions) |
|---|---|
| East Asia | $10,450,032 |
| Latin America | $5,339,390 |
| South Asia | $2,288,812 |
| Europe and Central Asia | $1,862,384 |
| Middle East and North Africa | $1,541,900 |

| Region | GDP (in millions) |
|---|---|
| Sub-Saharan Africa | $1,287,650 |

| Region | GDP Per Capita (in millions) |
|---|---|
| East Asia | $5,246 |
| Latin America | $1,388 |
| South Asia | $1,415 |
| Europe and Central Asia | $9,190 |
| Middle East and North Africa | $4,535 |
| Sub-Saharan Africa | $6,847 |

East Asia appears to be the largest economy on GDP basis, but on a per capita basis it drops to third, after Europe and Central Asia and Sub-Saharan Africa.

**2.** A region can have some of high-income countries and some of the low-income countries. Aggregating per capita real GDP will vary widely across countries within a region, so aggregating data for a region has little meaning. For example, if you were to compare per capital real GDP for the United States, Canada, Haiti, and Honduras, it looks much different than if you looked at the same data for North America as a whole. Thus, regional comparisons are broad-based and may not adequately capture an individual country's economic attributes.

**3.** The following table provides a summary of possible answers.

| High-Income Countries | Middle-Income Countries | Low-Income Countries |
|---|---|---|
| • Foster a more educated workforce<br>• Create, invest in, and apply new technologies<br>• Adopt fiscal policies focused on investment, including investment in human capital, in technology, and in physical plant and equipment<br>• Create stable and market-oriented economic climate<br>• Use monetary policy to keep inflation low and stable<br>• Minimize the risk of exchange rate fluctuations, while also encouraging domestic and international competition | • Invest in technology, human capital, and physical capital<br>• Provide incentives of a market-oriented economic context<br>• Work to reduce government economic controls on market activities<br>• Deregulate the banking and financial sector<br>• Reduce protectionist policies | • Eradicate poverty and extreme hunger<br>• Achieve universal primary education<br>• Promote gender equality<br>• Reduce child mortality rates<br>• Improve maternal health<br>• Combat HIV/AIDS, malaria, and other diseases<br>• Ensure environmental sustainability<br>• Develop global partnerships for development |

4. Low-income countries must adopt government policies that are market-oriented and that educate the workforce and population. After this is done, low-income countries should focus on eradicating other social ills that inhibit their growth. The economically challenged are stuck in poverty traps. They need to focus more on health and education and create a stable macroeconomic and political environment. This will attract foreign aid and foreign investment. Middle-income countries strive for increases in physical capital and innovation, while higher-income countries must work to maintain their economies through innovation and technology.

5. If there is a recession and unemployment increases, we can call on an expansionary fiscal policy (lower taxes or increased government spending) or an expansionary monetary policy (increase the money supply and lower interest rates). Both policies stimulate output and decrease unemployment.

6. Aside from a high natural rate of unemployment due to government regulations, subsistence households may be counted as not working.

7. Indexing wage contracts means wages rise when prices rise. This means what you can buy with your wages, your standard of living, remains the same. When wages are not indexed, or rise with inflation, your standard of living falls.

8. An increase in government spending shifts the AD curve to the right, raising both income and price levels.

9. A decrease in the money supply will shift the AD curve leftward and reduce income and price levels. Banks will have less money to lend. Interest rates will increase, affecting consumption and investment, which are both key determinants of aggregate demand.

10. Given the high level of activity in international financial markets, it is typically believed that financial flows across borders are the real reason for trade imbalances. For example, the United States had an enormous trade deficit in

the late 1990s and early 2000s because it was attracting vast inflows of foreign capital. Smaller countries that have attracted such inflows of international capital worry that if the inflows suddenly turn to outflows, the resulting decline in their currency could collapse their banking system and bring on a deep recession.

11. The demand for the country's currency would decrease, lowering the exchange rate.

## Chapter 20

1. False. Anything that leads to different levels of productivity between two economies can be a source of comparative advantage. For example, the education of workers, the knowledge base of engineers and scientists in a country, the part of a split-up value chain where they have their specialized learning, economies of scale, and other factors can all determine comparative advantage.

2. Brazil has the absolute advantage in producing beef and the United States has the absolute advantage in autos. The opportunity cost of producing one pound of beef is 1/10 of an auto; in the United States it is 3/4 of an auto.

3. In answering questions like these, it is often helpful to begin by organizing the information in a table, such as in the following table. Notice that, in this case, the productivity of the countries is expressed in terms of how many workers it takes to produce a unit of a product.

| Country | One Sweater | One Bottle of wine |
|---------|-------------|--------------------|
| France | 1 worker | 1 worker |
| Tunisia | 2 workers | 3 workers |

In this example, France has an absolute advantage in the production of both sweaters and wine. You can tell because it takes France less labor to produce a unit of the good.

4.
  a. In Germany, it takes fewer workers to make either a television or a video camera. Germany has an absolute advantage in the production of both goods.
  b. Producing an additional television in Germany requires three workers. Shifting those three German workers will reduce video camera production by 3/4 of a camera. Producing an additional television set in Poland requires six workers, and shifting those workers from the other good reduces output of video cameras by 6/12 of a camera, or 1/2. Thus, the opportunity cost of producing televisions is lower in Poland, so Poland has the comparative advantage in the production of televisions. *Note*: Do not let the fractions like 3/4 of a camera or 1/2 of a video camera bother you. If either country was to expand television production by a significant amount—that is, lots more than one unit—then we will be talking about whole cameras and not fractional ones. You can also spot this conclusion by noticing that Poland's absolute disadvantage is relatively lower in televisions, because Poland needs twice as many workers to produce a television but three times as many to produce a video camera, so the product with the relatively lower absolute disadvantage is Poland's comparative advantage.
  c. Producing a video camera in Germany requires four workers, and shifting those four workers away from television production has an opportunity cost of 4/3 television sets. Producing a video camera in Poland requires 12 workers, and shifting those 12 workers away from television production has an opportunity cost of two television sets. Thus, the opportunity cost of producing video cameras is lower in Germany, and video cameras will be Germany's comparative advantage.
  d. In this example, absolute advantage differs from comparative advantage. Germany has the absolute advantage in the production of both goods, but Poland has a comparative advantage in the production of televisions.
  e. Germany should specialize, at least to some extent, in the production of video cameras, export video cameras, and import televisions. Conversely, Poland should specialize, at least to some extent, in the production of televisions, export televisions, and import video cameras.

**5.** There are a number of possible advantages of intra-industry trade. Both nations can take advantage of extreme specialization and learning in certain kinds of cars with certain traits, like gas-efficient cars, luxury cars, sport-utility vehicles, higher- and lower-quality cars, and so on. Moreover, nations can take advantage of economies of scale, so that large companies will compete against each other across international borders, providing the benefits of competition and variety to customers. This same argument applies to trade between U.S. states, where people often buy products made by people of other states, even though a similar product is made within the boundaries of their own state. All states—and all countries—can benefit from this kind of competition and trade.

**6.**

    a. Start by plotting the points on a sketch diagram and then drawing a line through them. The following figure illustrates the average costs of production of semiconductors.

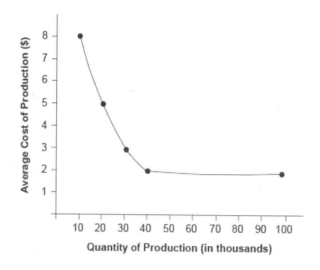

    The curve illustrates economies of scale by showing that as the scale increases—that is, as production at this particular factory goes up—the average cost of production declines. The economies of scale exist up to an output of 40,000 semiconductors; at higher outputs, the average cost of production does not seem to decline any further.

    b. At any quantity demanded above 40,000, this economy can take full advantage of economies of scale; that is, it can produce at the lowest cost per unit. Indeed, if the quantity demanded was quite high, like 500,000, then there could be a number of different factories all taking full advantage of economies of scale and competing with each other. If the quantity demanded falls below 40,000, then the economy by itself, without foreign trade, cannot take full advantage of economies of scale.

    c. The simplest answer to this question is that the small country could have a large enough factory to take full advantage of economies of scale, but then export most of the output. For semiconductors, countries like Taiwan and Korea have recently fit this description. Moreover, this country could also import semiconductors from other countries which also have large factories, thus getting the benefits of competition and variety. A slightly more complex answer is that the country can get these benefits of economies of scale without producing semiconductors, but simply by buying semiconductors made at low cost around the world. An economy, especially a smaller country, may well end up specializing and producing a few items on a large scale, but then trading those items for other items produced on a large scale, and thus gaining the benefits of economies of scale by trade, as well as by direct production.

**7.** A nation might restrict trade on imported products to protect an industry that is important for national security. For example, nation X and nation Y may be geopolitical rivals, each with ambitions of increased political and economic strength. Even if nation Y has comparative advantage in the production of missile defense systems, it is unlikely that nation Y would seek to export those goods to nation X. It is also the case that, for some nations, the production of a particular good is a key component of national identity. In Japan, the production of rice is culturally very important.

It may be difficult for Japan to import rice from a nation like Vietnam, even if Vietnam has a comparative advantage in rice production.

## Chapter 21

**1.** This is the opposite case of the Work It Out feature. A reduced tariff is like a decrease in the cost of production, which is shown by a downward (or rightward) shift in the supply curve.

**2.** A subsidy is like a reduction in cost. This shifts the supply curve down (or to the right), driving the price of sugar down. If the subsidy is large enough, the price of sugar can fall below the cost of production faced by foreign producers, which means they will lose money on any sugar they produce and sell.

**3.** Trade barriers raise the price of goods in protected industries. If those products are inputs in other industries, it raises their production costs and then prices, so sales fall in those other industries. Lower sales lead to lower employment. Additionally, if the protected industries are consumer goods, their customers pay higher prices, which reduce demand for other consumer products and thus employment in those industries.

**4.** Trade based on comparative advantage raises the average wage rate economy-wide, though it can reduce the incomes of import-substituting industries. By moving away from a country's comparative advantage, trade barriers do the opposite: they give workers in protected industries an advantage, while reducing the average wage economy-wide.

**5.** By raising incomes, trade tends to raise working conditions also, even though those conditions may not (yet) be equivalent to those in high-income countries.

**6.** They typically pay more than the next-best alternative. If a Nike firm did not pay workers at least as much as they would earn, for example, in a subsistence rural lifestyle, they many never come to work for Nike.

**7.** Since trade barriers raise prices, real incomes fall. The average worker would also earn less.

**8.** Workers working in other sectors and the protected sector see a decrease in their real wage.

**9.** If imports can be sold at extremely low prices, domestic firms would have to match those prices to be competitive. By definition, matching prices would imply selling under cost and, therefore, losing money. Firms cannot sustain losses forever. When they leave the industry, importers can "take over," raising prices to monopoly levels to cover their short-term losses and earn long-term profits.

**10.** Because low-income countries need to provide necessities—food, clothing, and shelter—to their people. In other words, they consider environmental quality a luxury.

**11.** Low-income countries can compete for jobs by reducing their environmental standards to attract business to their countries. This could lead to a competitive reduction in regulations, which would lead to greater environmental damage. While pollution management is a cost for businesses, it is tiny relative to other costs, like labor and adequate infrastructure. It is also costly for firms to locate far away from their customers, which many low-income countries are.

**12.** The decision should not be arbitrary or unnecessarily discriminatory. It should treat foreign companies the same way as domestic companies. It should be based on science.

**13.** Restricting imports today does not solve the problem. If anything, it makes it worse since it implies using up domestic sources of the products faster than if they are imported. Also, the national security argument can be used to support protection of nearly any product, not just things critical to our national security.

**14.** The effect of increasing standards may increase costs to the small exporting country. The supply curve of toys will shift to the left. Exports will decrease and toy prices will rise. Tariffs also raise prices. So the effect on the price of toys is the same. A tariff is a "second best" policy and also affects other sectors. However, a common standard across countries is a "first best" policy that attacks the problem at its root.

**15.** A free trade association offers free trade between its members, but each country can determine its own trade policy outside the association. A common market requires a common external trade policy in addition to free trade within the group. An economic union is a common market with coordinated fiscal and monetary policy.

**16.** International agreements can serve as a political counterweight to domestic special interests, thereby preventing stronger protectionist measures.

**17.** Reductions in tariffs, quotas, and other trade barriers, improved transportation, and communication media have made people more aware of what is available in the rest of the world.

**18.** Competition from firms with better or cheaper products can reduce a business's profits, and may drive it out of business. Workers would similarly lose income or even their jobs.

**19.** Consumers get better or less expensive products. Businesses with the better or cheaper products increase their profits. Employees of those businesses earn more income. On balance, the gains outweigh the losses to a nation.

# REFERENCES

## Welcome to Economics!

Bureau of Labor Statistics, U.S. Department of Labor. 2015. "The Employment Situation—February 2015." Accessed March 27, 2015. http://www.bls.gov/news.release/pdf/empsit.pdf.

Williamson, Lisa. "US Labor Market in 2012." *Bureau of Labor Statistics*. Accessed December 1, 2013. http://www.bls.gov/opub/mlr/2013/03/art1full.pdf.

The Heritage Foundation. 2015. "2015 Index of Economic Freedom." Accessed March 11, 2015. http://www.heritage.org/index/ranking.

Garling, Caleb. "S.F. plane crash: Reporting, emotions on social media," *The San Francisco Chronicle*. July 7, 2013. http://www.sfgate.com/news/article/S-F-plane-crash-Reporting-emotions-on-social-4651639.php.

Irvine, Jessica. "Social Networking Sites are Factories of Modern Ideas." *The Sydney Morning Herald*. November 25, 2011.http://www.smh.com.au/federal-politics/society-and-culture/social-networking-sites-are-factories-of-modern-ideas-20111124-1nwy3.html#ixzz2YZhPYeME.

Pew Research Center. 2015. "Social Networking Fact Sheet." Accessed March 11, 2015. http://www.pewinternet.org/fact-sheets/social-networking-fact-sheet/.

The World Bank Group. 2015. "World Data Bank." Accessed March 30, 2014. http://databank.worldbank.org/data/.

## Choice in a World of Scarcity

Bureau of Labor Statistics, U.S. Department of Labor. 2015. "Median Weekly Earnings by Educational Attainment in 2014." Accessed March 27, 2015. http://www.bls.gov/opub/ted/2015/median-weekly-earnings-by-education-gender-race-and-ethnicity-in-2014.htm.

Robbins, Lionel. *An Essay on the Nature and Significance of Economic Science*. London: Macmillan. 1932.

United States Department of Transportation. "Total Passengers on U.S Airlines and Foreign Airlines U.S. Flights Increased 1.3% in 2012 from 2011." Accessed October 2013. http://www.rita.dot.gov/bts/press_releases/bts016_13

Smith, Adam. "Of Restraints upon the Importation from Foreign Countries." In *The Wealth of Nations*. London: Methuen & Co., 1904, first pub 1776), I.V. 2.9.

Smith, Adam. "Of the Propriety of Action." In *The Theory of Moral Sentiments*. London: A. Millar, 1759, 1.

## Demand and Supply

Costanza, Robert, and Lisa Wainger. "No Accounting For Nature: How Conventional Economics Distorts the Value of Things." *The Washington Post*. September 2, 1990.

European Commission: Agriculture and Rural Development. 2013. "Overview of the CAP Reform: 2014-2024." Accessed April 13, 205. http://ec.europa.eu/agriculture/cap-post-2013/.

Radford, R. A. "The Economic Organisation of a P.O.W. Camp." *Economica*. no. 48 (1945): 189-201. http://www.jstor.org/stable/2550133.

Landsburg, Steven E. *The Armchair Economist: Economics and Everyday Life*. New York: The Free Press. 2012. specifically Section IV: How Markets Work.

National Chicken Council. 2015. "Per Capita Consumption of Poultry and Livestock, 1965 to Estimated 2015, in Pounds." Accessed April 13, 2015. http://www.nationalchickencouncil.org/about-the-industry/statistics/per-capita-consumption-of-poultry-and-livestock-1965-to-estimated-2012-in-pounds/.

Wessel, David. "Saudi Arabia Fears $40-a-Barrel Oil, Too." *The Wall Street Journal*. May 27, 2004, p. 42. http://online.wsj.com/news/articles/SB108561000087822300.

Pew Research Center. "Pew Research: Center for the People & the Press." http://www.people-press.org/.

## Labor and Financial Markets

American Community Survey. 2012. "School Enrollment and Work Status: 2011." Accessed April 13, 2015. http://www.census.gov/prod/2013pubs/acsbr11-14.pdf.

National Center for Educational Statistics. "Digest of Education Statistics." (2008 and 2010). Accessed December 11, 2013. nces.ed.gov.

CreditCards.com. 2013. http://www.creditcards.com/credit-card-news/credit-card-industry-facts-personal-debt-statistics-1276.php.

## Elasticity

Abkowitz, A. "How Netflix got started: Netflix founder and CEO Reed Hastings tells Fortune how he got the idea for the DVD-by-mail service that now has more than eight million customers." *CNN Money*. Last Modified January 28, 2009. http://archive.fortune.com/2009/01/27/news/newsmakers/hastings_netflix.fortune/index.htm.

Associated Press (a). "Analyst: Coinstar gains from Netflix pricing moves." *Boston Globe Media Partners, LLC*. Accessed June 24, 2013. http://www.boston.com/business/articles/2011/10/12/analyst_coinstar_gains_from_netflix_pricing_moves/.

Associated Press (b). "Netflix loses 800,000 US subscribers in tough 3Q." *ABC Inc*. Accessed June 24, 2013. http://abclocal.go.com/wpvi/story?section=news/business&id=8403368

Baumgardner, James. 2014. "Presentation on Raising the Excise Tax on Cigarettes: Effects on Health and the Federal Budget." Congressional Budget Office. Accessed March 27, 2015. http://www.cbo.gov/sites/default/files/45214-ICA_Presentation.pdf.

Funding Universe. 2015. "Netflix, Inc. History." Accessed March 11, 2015. http://www.fundinguniverse.com/company-histories/netflix-inc-history/.

Laporte, Nicole. "A tale of two Netflix." *Fast Company* 177 (July 2013) 31-32. Accessed December 3 2013. http://www.fastcompany-digital.com/fastcompany/20130708?pg=33#pg33

Liedtke, Michael, The Associated Press. "Investors bash Netflix stock after slower growth forecast - fee hikes expected to take toll on subscribers most likely to shun costly bundled Net, DVD service." *The Seattle Times*. Accessed June 24, 2013 from NewsBank on-line database (Access World News).

Netflix, Inc. 2013. "A Quick Update On Our Streaming Plans And Prices." Netflix (blog). Accessed March 11, 2015. http://blog.netflix.com/2014/05/a-quick-update-on-our-streaming-plans.html.

Organization for Economic Co-Operation and Development (OECC). n.d. "Average annual hours actually worked per worker." Accessed March 11, 2015. https://stats.oecd.org/Index.aspx?DataSetCode=ANHRS.

Savitz, Eric. "Netflix Warns DVD Subs Eroding; Q4 View Weak; Losses Ahead; Shrs Plunge." *Forbes.com*, 2011. Accessed December 3, 2013. http://www.forbes.com/sites/ericsavitz/2011/10/24/netflix-q3-top-ests-but-shares-hit-by-weak-q4-outlook/.

Statistica.com. 2014. "Coffee Export Volumes Worldwide in November 2014, by Leading Countries (in 60-kilo sacks)." Accessed March 27, 2015. http://www.statista.com/statistics/268135/ranking-of-coffee-exporting-countries/.

Stone, Marcie. "Netflix responds to customers angry with price hike; Netflix stock falls 9%." *News & Politics Examiner*, 2011. Clarity Digital Group. Accessed June 24, 2013. http://www.examiner.com/article/netflix-responds-to-customers-angry-with-price-hike-netflix-stock-falls-9.

Weinman, J. (2012). Die hard, hardly dying. Maclean's, 125(18), 44.

The World Bank Group. 2015. "Gross Savings (% of GDP)." Accessed March 11, 2015. http://data.worldbank.org/indicator/NY.GNS.ICTR.ZS.

Yahoo Finance. Retrieved from http://finance.yahoo.com/q?s=NFLX

## The Macroeconomic Perspective

U.S. Department of Commerce: Bureau of Economic Analysis. "National data: National Income and Product Accounts Tables." http://bea.gov/iTable/iTable.cfm?ReqID=9&step=1.

U.S. Department of Commerce: United States Census Bureau. "Census of Governments: 2012 Census of

Governments." http://www.census.gov/govs/cog/.

United States Department of Transportation. "About DOT." Last modified March 2, 2012. http://www.dot.gov/about.

U.S. Department of Energy. "Energy.gov." http://energy.gov/.

U.S. Department of Health & Human Services. "Agency for Healthcare Research and Quality." http://www.ahrq.gov/.

United States Department of Agriculture. "USDA." http://www.usda.gov/wps/portal/usda/usdahome.

Schneider, Friedrich. Department of Economics. "Size and Development of the Shadow Economy of 31 European and 5 other OECD Countries from 2003 to 2013: A Further Decline." *Johannes Kepler University*. Last modified April 5, 2013. http://www.econ.jku.at/members/Schneider/files/publications/2013/ShadEcEurope31_Jan2013.pdf.

The National Bureau of Economic Research. "Information on Recessions and Recoveries, the NBER Business Cycle Dating Committee, and related topics." http://www.nber.org/cycles/main.html.

## Economic Growth

Bolt, Jutta, and Jan Luiten van Zanden. "The Maddison Project: The First Update of the Maddison Project Re-Estimating Growth Before 1820 (Maddison-Project Working Paper WP-4)." *University of Groningen: Groningen Growth and Development Centre*. Last modified January 2013. http://www.ggdc.net/maddison/publications/pdf/wp4.pdf.

Central Intelligence Agency. "The World Factbook: Country Comparison GDP (Purchasing Power Parity)." https://www.cia.gov/library/publications/the-world-factbook/rankorder/2001rank.html.

DeLong, Brad. "Lighting the Rocket of Growth and Lightening the Toil of Work: Another Outtake from My 'Slouching Towards Utopia' MS...." *This is Brad DeLong's Grasping Reality* (blog). September 3, 2013. http://delong.typepad.com/sdj/2013/09/lighting-the-rocket-of-growth-and-lightening-the-toil-of-work-another-outtake-from-my-slouching-towards-utopia-ms.html.

Easterlin, Richard A. "The Worldwide Standard of Living since 1800." *The Journal of Economic Perspectives*. no. 1 (2000): 7–26. http://pubs.aeaweb.org/doi/pdfplus/10.1257/jep.14.1.7.

Maddison, Angus. *Contours of the World Economy 1-2030 AD: Essays in Macro-Economic History*. Oxford: Oxford University Press, 2007.

British Library. "Treasures in Full: Magna Carta." http://www.bl.uk/treasures/magnacarta/.

Rothbard, Murray N. Ludwig von Mises Institute. "Property Rights and the Theory of Contracts." *The Ethics of Liberty*. Last modified June 22, 2007. http://mises.org/daily/2580.

Salois, Matthew J., J. Richard Tiffin, and Kelvin George Balcombe. IDEAS: Research Division of the Federal Reserve Bank of St. Louis. "Impact of Income on Calorie and Nutrient Intakes: A Cross-Country Analysis." Presention at the annual meeting of the Agricultural and Applied Economics Association, Pittsburg, PA, July 24–26, 2011. http://ideas.repec.org/p/ags/aaea11/103647.html.

van Zanden, Jan Luiten. *The Long Road to the Industrial Revolution: The European Economy in a Global Perspective, 1000–1800 (Global Economic History Series)*. Boston: Brill, 2009.

The World Bank. "CPIA Property Rights and Rule-based Governance Rating (1=low to 6=high)." http://data.worldbank.org/indicator/IQ.CPA.PROP.XQ.

Rex A. Hudson, ed. *Brazil: A Country Study*. "Spectacular Growth, 1968–73." Washington: GPO for the Library of Congress, 1997. http://countrystudies.us/brazil/64.htm.

"Women and the World Economy: A Guide to Womenomics." *The Economist*, April 12, 2006. http://www.economist.com/node/6802551.

Farole, Thomas, and Gokhan Akinci, eds. *Special Economic Zones: Progress, Emerging Challenges, and Future Directions*. Washington: The World Bank, 2011. http://publications.worldbank.org/index.php?main_page=product_info&products_id=24138.

Garcia, Abraham, and Pierre Mohnen. United Nations University, Maastricht Economic and Social Research and Training Centre on Innovation and Technology: UNU-MERIT. "Impact of Government Support on R&D and Innovation (Working Paper Series #2010-034)." http://www.merit.unu.edu/publications/wppdf/2010/

wp2010-034.pdf.

Heston, Alan, Robert Summers, and Bettina Aten. "Penn World Table Version 7.1." *Center for International Comparisons of Production, Income and Prices at the University of Pennsylvania*. Last modified July 2012. https://pwt.sas.upenn.edu/php_site/pwt71/pwt71_form.php.

United States Department of Labor: Bureau of Labor Statistics. "Women at Work: A Visual Essay." *Monthly Labor Review*, October 2003, 45–50. http://www.bls.gov/opub/mlr/2003/10/ressum3.pdf.

Central Intelligence Agency. "The World Factbook: Country Comparison: GDP–Real Growth Rate." https://www.cia.gov/library/publications/the-world-factbook/rankorder/2003rank.html.

Sen, Amartya. "Hunger in the Contemporary World (Discussion Paper DEDPS/8)." *The Suntory Centre: London School of Economics and Political Science*. Last modified November 1997. http://sticerd.lse.ac.uk/dps/de/dedps8.pdf.

## Unemployment

Bureau of Labor Statistics. Labor Force Statistics from the Current Population Survey. *Accessed March 6, 2015* http://data.bls.gov/timeseries/LNS14000000.

Cappelli, P. (20 June 2012). "Why Good People Can't Get Jobs: Chasing After the Purple Squirrel." http://knowledge.wharton.upenn.edu/article.cfm?articleid=3027.

## Inflation

Sources for **Table 9.1**:
http://www.eia.gov/dnav/pet/pet_pri_gnd_a_epmr_pte_dpgal_w.htm
http://data.bls.gov/cgi-bin/surveymost?ap
http://www.bls.gov/ro3/apmw.htm
http://www.autoblog.com/2014/03/12/who-can-afford-the-average-car-price-only-folks-in-washington/
https://www.census.gov/construction/nrs/pdf/uspricemon.pdf
http://www.bls.gov/news.release/empsit.t24.htm
http://variety.com/2015/film/news/movie-ticket-prices-increased-in-2014-1201409670/

US Inflation Calculator. "Historical Inflation Rates: 1914-2013." Accessed March 4, 2015. http://www.usinflationcalculator.com/inflation/historical-inflation-rates/.

Bernhard, Kent. "Pump Prices Jump Across U.S. after Katrina." *NBC News*, September 1, 2005. http://www.nbcnews.com/id/9146363/ns/business-local_business/t/pump-prices-jump-across-us-after-katrina/#.U00kRfk7um4.

Wynne, Mark A. "Core Inflation, A Review of Some Conceptual Issues." *Federal Reserve Bank of St. Louis*. p. 209. Accessed April 14, 2014. http://research.stlouisfed.org/publications/review/08/05/part2/Wynne.pdf

Shiller, Robert. "Why Do People Dislike Inflation?" *NBER Working Paper Series, National Bureau of Economic Research*, p. 52. 1996.

Wines, Michael. "How Bad is Inflation in Zimbabwe?" *The New York Times*, May 2, 2006. http://www.nytimes.com/2006/05/02/world/africa/02zimbabwe.html?pagewanted=all&_r=0.

Hanke, Steve H. "R.I.P. Zimbabwe Dollar." *CATO Institute*. Accessed December 31, 2013. http://www.cato.org/zimbabwe.

Massachusetts Institute of Technology. 2015. "Billion Prices Project." Accessed March 4, 2015. http://bpp.mit.edu/usa/.

## The International Trade and Capital Flows

Central Intelligence Agency. "The World Factbook." Last modified October 31, 2013. https://www.cia.gov/library/publications/the-world-factbook/geos/gm.html.

U.S. Department of Commerce. "Bureau of Economic Analysis." Last modified December 1, 2013. http://www.bea.gov/.

U.S. Department of Commerce. "United States Census Bureau." http://www.census.gov/.

Tabuchi, Hiroko. "Japan Reports a $78 Billion Trade Deficit for 2012." *The New York Times*, January 23, 2013. http://www.nytimes.com/2013/01/24/business/global/japan-reports-a-78-billion-trade-deficit-for-2012.html?_r=0.

World Bank. 2014. "Exports of Goods and Services (% of GDP)." Accesed April 13, 2015. http://data.worldbank.org/indicator/NE.EXP.GNFS.ZS/countries.

## The Aggregate Demand/Aggregate Supply Model

Keynes, John Maynard. *The General Theory of Employment, Interest and Money*. London: Palgrave Macmillan, 1936.

U.S. Department of Commerce: United States Census Bureau. "New Residential Sales: Historical Data." http://www.census.gov/construction/nrs/historical_data/.

Library of Economics and Liberty. "The Concise Encyclopedia of Economics: Jean-Baptiste Say." http://www.econlib.org/library/Enc/bios/Say.html.

Library of Economics and Liberty. "The Concise Encyclopedia of Economics: John Maynard Keynes." http://www.econlib.org/library/Enc/bios/Keynes.html.

Organization for Economic Cooperation and Development. 2015. "Business Tendency Surveys: Construction." Accessed March 4, 2015. http://stats.oecd.org/mei/default.asp?lang=e&subject=6.

University of Michigan. 2015. "Surveys of Consumers." Accessed March 4, 2015. http://www.sca.isr.umich.edu/tables.html.

## The Keynesian Perspective

Mahapatra, Lisa. "US Exports To China Have Grown 294% Over The Past Decade." *International Business Times*. Last modified July 09, 2013. http://www.ibtimes.com/us-exports-china-have-grown-294-over-past-decade-1338693.

The Conference Board, Inc. "Global Economic Outlook 2014, November 2013." http://www.conference-board.org/data/globaloutlook.cfm.

Thomas, G. Scott. "Recession claimed 170,000 small businesses in two years." *The Business Journals*. Last modified July 24, 2012. http://www.bizjournals.com/bizjournals/on-numbers/scott-thomas/2012/07/recession-claimed-170000-small.html.

United States Department of Labor: Bureau of Labor Statistics. "Top Picks." http://data.bls.gov/cgi-bin/surveymost?bls.

Harford, Tim. "What Price Supply and Demand?" http://timharford.com/2014/01/what-price-supply-and-demand/?utm_source=dlvr.it&utm_medium=twitter.

National Employment Law Project. "Job Creation and Economic Recovery." http://www.nelp.org/index.php/content/content_issues/category/job_creation_and_economic_recovery/.

Hoover, Kevin. "Phillips Curve." *The Concise Encyclopedia of Economics*. http://www.econlib.org/library/Enc/PhillipsCurve.html.

U.S. Government Printing Office. "Economic Report of the President." http://1.usa.gov/1c3psdL.

Blinder, Alan S., and Mark Zandi. "How the Great Recession Was Brought to an End." Last modified July 27, 2010. http://www.princeton.edu/~blinder/End-of-Great-Recession.pdf.

## The Neoclassical Perspective

Lumina Foundation. 2014. "A Stronger Nation Through Higher Education." Accessed March 4, 2015. http://www.luminafoundation.org/publications/A_stronger_nation_through_higher_education-2014.pdf.

The National Bureau of Economic Research. http://www.nber.org/.

U.S. Department of Commerce: United States Census Bureau. "The 2012 Statistical Abstract." http://www.census.gov/compendia/statab/cats/education.html.

U.S. Department of the Treasury. "TARP Programs." Last modified December 12, 2013. http://www.treasury.gov/initiatives/financial-stability/TARP-Programs/Pages/default.aspx.

United States Government. "Recovery.gov: Track the Money." Last modified October 30, 2013. http://www.recovery.gov/Pages/default.aspx.

American Statistical Association. "ASA Headlines." http://www.amstat.org/.

Haubrich, Joseph G., George Pennacchi, and Peter Ritchken. "Working Paper 11-07: Inflation Expectations, Real Rates, and Risk Premia: Evidence from Inflation Swaps." *Federal Reserve Bank of Cleveland*. Last modified March 2011. http://www.clevelandfed.org/research/workpaper/2011/wp1107.pdf.

University of Michigan: Institute for Social Research. "Survey Research Center." http://www.src.isr.umich.edu/.

Carvalho, Carlos, Stefano Eusepi, and Christian Grisse. "Policy Initiatives in the Global Recession: What Did Forecasters Expect?" *Federal Reserve Bank of New York: Current Issues in Economics and Finance*, 18, no. 2 (2012). http://www.newyorkfed.org/research/current_issues/ci18-2.pdf.

## Money and Banking

Hogendorn, Jan and Marion Johnson. *The Shell Money of the Slave Trade*. Cambridge University Press, 2003. 6.

Federal Reserve Statistical Release. November 23, 2013. http://www.federalreserve.gov/RELEASES/h6/current/default.htm#t2tg1link.

Credit Union National Association. 2014. "Monthly Credit Union Estimates." Last accessed March 4, 2015. http://www.cuna.org/Research-And-Strategy/Credit-Union-Data-And-Statistics/.

Dallas Federal Reserve. 2013. "Ending `Too Big To Fail': A Proposal for Reform Before It's Too Late". Accessed March 4, 2015. http://www.dallasfed.org/news/speeches/fisher/2013/fs130116.cfm.

Richard W. Fisher. "Ending 'Too Big to Fail': A Proposal for Reform Before It's Too Late (With Reference to Patrick Henry, Complexity and Reality) Remarks before the Committee for the Republic, Washington, D.C. Dallas Federal Reserve. January 16, 2013.

"Commercial Banks in the U.S." Federal Reserve Bank of St. Louis. Accessed November 2013. http://research.stlouisfed.org/fred2/series/USNUM.

Bitcoin. 2013. www.bitcoin.org.

National Public Radio. *Lawmakers and Regulators Take Closer Look at Bitcoin*. November 19, 2013. http://thedianerehmshow.org/shows/2013-11-19/lawmakers-and-regulators-take-closer-look-bitcoin.

## Monetary Policy and Bank Regulation

Matthews, Dylan. "Nine amazing facts about Janet Yellen, our next Fed chair." Wonkblog. *The Washington Post*. Posted October 09, 2013. http://www.washingtonpost.com/blogs/wonkblog/wp/2013/10/09/nine-amazing-facts-about-janet-yellen-our-next-fed-chair/.

Appelbaum, Binyamin. "Divining the Regulatory Goals of Fed Rivals." *The New York Times*. Posted August 14, 2013. http://www.nytimes.com/2013/08/14/business/economy/careers-of-2-fed-contenders-reveal-little-on-regulatory-approach.html?pagewanted=3.

U.S. Department of the Treasury. "Office of the Comptroller of the Currency." Accessed November 2013. http://www.occ.gov/.

National Credit Union Administration. "About NCUA." Accessed November 2013. http://www.ncua.gov/about/Pages/default.aspx.

Board of Governors of the Federal Reserve System. "Federal Open Market Committee." Accessed September 3, 2013. http://www.federalreserve.gov/monetarypolicy/fomc.htm.

Board of Governors of the Federal Reserve System. "Reserve Requirements." Accessed November 5, 2013. http://www.federalreserve.gov/monetarypolicy/reservereq.htm.

Cox, Jeff. 2014. "Fed Completes the Taper." Accessed March 31, 2015. http://www.cnbc.com/id/102132961.

Jahan, Sarwat. n.d. "Inflation Targeting: Holding the Line." International Monetary Fund. Accessed March 31, 2015. http://www.imf.org/external/pubs/ft/fandd/basics/target.htm.

Tobin, James. "The Concise Encyclopedia of Economics: Monetary Policy." *Library of Economics and Liberty*. Accessed November 2013. http://www.econlib.org/library/Enc/MonetaryPolicy.html.

Federal Reserve Bank of New York. "The Founding of the Fed." Accessed November 2013. http://www.newyorkfed.org/aboutthefed/history_article.html.

## Exchange Rates and International Capital Flows

Friedman, Milton. *Capitalism and Freedom*. Chicago: University of Chicago Press, 1962.

## Government Budgets and Fiscal Policy

Kramer, Mattea, et. al. *A People's Guide to the Federal Budget*. National Priorities Project. Northampton: Interlink Books, 2012.

Kurtzleben, Danielle. "10 States With The Largest Budget Shortfalls." *U.S. News & World Report*. Januray 14, 2011. http://www.usnews.com/news/articles/2011/01/14/10-states-with-the-largest-budget-shortfalls.

Miller, Rich, and William Selway. "U.S. Cities and States Start Spending Again." *BloombergBusinessweek*, January 10, 2013. http://www.businessweek.com/articles/2013-01-10/u-dot-s-dot-cities-and-states-start-spending-again.

Weisman, Jonathan. "After Year of Working Around Federal Cuts, Agencies Face Fewer Options." *The New York Times*, October 26, 2013. http://www.nytimes.com/2013/10/27/us/politics/after-year-of-working-around-federal-cuts-agencies-face-fewer-options.html?_r=0.

Chantrill, Christopher. USGovernmentSpending.com. "Government Spending Details: United States Federal State and Local Government Spending, Fiscal Year 2013." http://www.usgovernmentspending.com/year_spending_2013USbn_15bs2n_20.

Burman, Leonard E., and Joel Selmrod. *Taxes in America: What Everyone Needs to Know*. New York: Oxford University Press, 2012.

Hall, Robert E., and Alvin Rabushka. *The Flat Tax (Hoover Classics)*. Stanford: Hoover Institution Press, 2007.

Kliff, Sarah. "How Congress Paid for Obamacare (in Two Charts)." *The Washington Post: WonkBlog* (blog), August 30, 2012. http://www.washingtonpost.com/blogs/wonkblog/wp/2012/08/30/how-congress-paid-for-obamacare-in-two-charts/.

Matthews, Dylan. "America's Taxes are the Most Progressive in the World. Its Government is Among the Least." *The Washington Post: WonkBlog* (blog). April 5, 2013. http://www.washingtonpost.com/blogs/wonkblog/wp/2013/04/05/americas-taxes-are-the-most-progressive-in-the-world-its-government-is-among-the-least/.

Eisner, Robert. *The Great Deficit Scares: The Federal Budget, Trade, and Social Security*. New York: Priority Press Publications, 1997.

Weisman, Jonathan, and Ashley Parker. "Republicans Back Down, Ending Crisis Over Shutdown and Debt Limit." *The New York Times*, October 16, 2013. http://www.nytimes.com/2013/10/17/us/congress-budget-debate.html.

Wessel, David. *Red Ink: Inside the High-Stakes Politics of Federal Budget*. New York: Crown Publishing Group, 2013.

Alesina, Alberto, and Francesco Giavazzi. *Fiscal Policy after the Financial Crisis (National Bureau of Economic Research Conference Report)*. Chicago: University Of Chicago Press, 2013.

Martin, Fernando M. "Fiscal Policy in the Great Recession and Lessons from the Past." Federal Reserve Bank of St. Louis: *Economic Synopses*. no. 1 (2012). http://research.stlouisfed.org/publications/es/12/ES_2012-01-06.pdf.

Bivens, Josh, Andrew Fieldhouse, and Heidi Shierholz. "From Free-fall to Stagnation: Five Years After the Start of the Great Recession, Extraordinary Policy Measures Are Still Needed, But Are Not Forthcoming." *Economic Policy Institute*. Last modified February 14, 2013. http://www.epi.org/publication/bp355-five-years-after-start-of-great-recession/.

Lucking, Brian, and Dan Wilson. Federal Reserve Bank of San Francisco, "FRBSF Economic Letter—U.S. Fiscal Policy: Headwind or Tailwind?" Last modified July 2, 2012. http://www.frbsf.org/economic-research/publications/economic-letter/2012/july/us-fiscal-policy/.

Greenstone, Michael, and Adam Looney. Brookings. "The Role of Fiscal Stimulus in the Ongoing Recovery." Last modified July 6, 2012. http://www.brookings.edu/blogs/jobs/posts/2012/07/06-jobs-greenstone-looney.

Leduc, Sylvain, and Daniel Wilson. Federal Reserve Bank of San Francisco: Working Paper Series. "Are State

Governments Roadblocks to Federal Stimulus? Evidence from Highway Grants in the 2009 Recovery Act. (Working Paper 2013-16)." Last modified July 2013. http://www.frbsf.org/economic-research/files/wp2013-16.pdf.

Lucking, Brian, and Daniel Wilson. "FRBSF Economic Letter-Fiscal Headwinds: Is the Other Shoe About to Drop?" *Federal Reserve Bank of San Francisco*. Last modified June 3, 2013. http://www.frbsf.org/economic-research/publications/economic-letter/2013/june/fiscal-headwinds-federal-budget-policy/.

Recovery.gov. "Track the Money." http://www.recovery.gov/Pages/default.aspx.

Bastagli, Francesca, David Coady, and Sanjeev Gupta. International Monetary Fund. "IMF Staff Discussion Note: Income Inequality and Fiscal Policy." Last modified June 28, 2012. http://www.imf.org/external/pubs/ft/sdn/2012/sdn1208.pdf.

## The Impacts of Government Borrowing

The White House. "This is why it's time to make college more affordable." Last modified August 20, 2013. http://www.whitehouse.gov/share/college-affordability.

Rubin, Robert E., Peter R. Orszag, and Allen Sinai. "Sustained Budget Deficits: Longer-Run U.S. Economic Performance and the Risk of Financial and Fiscal Disarray." Last modified January 4, 2004. http://www.brookings.edu/~/media/research/files/papers/2004/1/05budgetdeficit%20orszag/20040105.pdf.

U.S. Department of Commerce: Bureau of Economic Analysis. "National Data: National Income and Product Accounts Tables." Accessed December 1, 2013. http://www.bea.gov/iTable/iTable.cfm?ReqID=9&step=1#reqid=9&step=3&isuri=1&910=X&911=0&903=146&904=2008&905=2013&906=A.

Board of Governors of the Federal Reserve System, "Selected Interest Rates (Daily) – H.15." Accessed December 10, 2013. http://www.federalreserve.gov/releases/h15/data.htm.

The White House. "Fiscal Year 2013 Historical Tables: Budget of the U.S. Government." Accessed December 12, 2013. http://www.whitehouse.gov/sites/default/files/omb/budget/fy2013/assets/hist.pdf.

The National Science Foundation. Accessed December 19, 2013. http://www.nsf.gov/.

## Macroeconomic Policy Around the World

International Labour Organization. "Global Employment Trends for Youth 2013." http://www.ilo.org/global/research/global-reports/global-employment-trends/youth/2013/lang--en/index.htm

International Monetary Fund. "World Economic and Financial Surveys: World Economic Outlook—Transitions and Tensions." Last modified October 2013. http://www.imf.org/external/pubs/ft/weo/2013/02/pdf/text.pdf.

Nobelprize.org. "The Prize in Economics 1987 - Press Release." *Nobel Media AB 2013*. Last modified October 21, 1987. http://www.nobelprize.org/nobel_prizes/economic-sciences/laureates/1987/press.html.

Redvers, Louise. BBC News Business. "Youth unemployment: The big question and South Africa." Last modified October 31, 2012. http://www.bbc.co.uk/news/business-20125053.

The World Bank. "The Complete World Development Report Online." http://www.wdronline.worldbank.org/.

The World Bank. "World DataBank." http://databank.worldbank.org/data/home.aspx.

Todaro, Michael P., and Stephen C Smith. *Economic Development (11$^{th}$Edition)*. Boston, MA: Addison-Wesley: Pearson, 2011, chap. 1–2.

"Shinzo Abe's Government Looks Likely to Disappoint on Fiscal Consolidation." *The Economist*, May 4, 2013. http://www.economist.com/news/finance-and-economics/21577080-shinzo-abes-government-looks-likely-disappoint-fiscal-consolidation-dont.

Banerjee, Abhijit V., and Esther Duflo. *Poor Economics*. "About the Book: Overview." http://pooreconomics.com/about-book.

CARE International. "About Us." Accessed January 14, 2014. http://www.care-international.org/about-us.aspx.

Central Intelligence Agency. "The World Factbook: Africa, Burundi." Last modified November 12, 2013. https://www.cia.gov/library/publications/the-world-factbook/geos/by.html.

Central Intelligence Agency. "The World Factbook: Africa, Democratic Republic of the Congo." Last modified

November 12, 2013. https://www.cia.gov/library/publications/the-world-factbook/geos/cg.html.

Easterly, William. *The White Man's Burden: Why the West's Efforts to Aid the Rest Have Done So Much Ill and So Little Good*. Penguin Group (USA), 2006.

Goel, Vindu. "Facebook Leads an Effort to Lower Barriers to Internet Access," *The New York Times*. Last modified August 20, 2013.

Google. "Project Loon." http://www.google.com/loon/.

GOV.UK. "Department for International Development." https://www.gov.uk/government/organisations/department-for-international-development.

The World Bank. "Millennium Development Goals." http://www.worldbank.org/mdgs/.

Todaro, Michael P., and Stephen C Smith. *Economic Development (11$^{th}$ Edition)*. Boston, MA: Addison-Wesley: Pearson, 2011, chap. 3.

Vercillo, Siera. "The Failures of Canadian Foreign Aid: Tied, Mismanaged and Uncoordinated." *The Attaché Journal of International Affairs*. (2010). http://theattachejia.files.wordpress.com/2013/10/the-attache-2010-issue.pdf.

Viscusi, Gregory, and Mark Deen. "Why France Has So Many 49-Employee Companies." *Business Week*. Last modified May 3, 2012. http://www.businessweek.com/articles/2012-05-03/why-france-has-so-many-49-employee-companies.

Edwards, S. (n.d.). "America's Unsustainable Current Account Deficit." *National Bureau of Economic Research Digest*. http://www.nber.org/digest/mar06/w11541.html. http://www.ustr.gov/trade-agreements/free-trade-agreements/north-american-free-trade-agreement-nafta.

New Country Classifications | Data. (n.d.). Accessed January 14, 2014. http://data.worldbank.org/news/new-country-classifications.

Office of the United States Trade Representative: Executive Office of the President. "North American Free Trade Agreement (NAFTA)."

Why India's Labour Laws are a Problem. (2006, May 18). *BBC*. May 18, 2006. http://news.bbc.co.uk/2/hi/south_asia/4984256.stm.

## International Trade

Krugman, Paul R. *Pop Internationalism*. The MIT Press, Cambridge. 1996.

Krugman, Paul R. "What Do Undergrads Need to Know about Trade?" *American Economic Review* 83, no. 2. 1993. 23-26.

Ricardo, David. *On the Principles of Political Economy and Taxation*. London: John Murray, 1817.

Ricardo, David. "On the Principles of Political Economy and Taxation." *Library of Economics and Liberty*. http://www.econlib.org/library/Ricardo/ricP.html.

Bernstein, William J. *A Splendid Exchange: How Trade Shaped the World*. Atlantic Monthly Press. New York. 2008.

U.S. Census Bureau. 2015. "U.S. International Trade in Goods and Services: December 2014." Accessed April 13, 2015. http://www.bea.gov/newsreleases/international/trade/2015/pdf/trad1214.pdf.

U.S. Census Bureau. U.S. Bureau of Economic Analysis. 2015. "U.S. International Trade in Goods and Services February 2015." Accessed April 10, 2015. https://www.census.gov/foreign-trade/Press-Release/current_press_release/ft900.pdf.

Vernengo, Matias. "What Do Undergraduates Really Need to Know About Trade and Finance?" in *Political Economy and Contemporary Capitalism: Radical Perspectives on Economic Theory and Policy*, ed. Ron Baiman, Heather Boushey, and Dawn Saunders. M. E. Sharpe Inc, 2000. Armonk. 177-183.

World Trade Organization. "The Doha Round." Accessed October 2013. http://www.wto.org/english/tratop_e/dda_e/dda_e.htm.

The World Bank. "Data: World Development Indicators." Accessed October 2013. http://data.worldbank.org/data-catalog/world-development-indicators.

## Globalization and Protectionism

Bureau of Labor Statistics. "Industries at a Glance." Accessed December 31, 2013. http://www.bls.gov/iag/.

Oxfam International. Accessed January 6, 2014. http://www.oxfam.org/.

Bureau of Labor Statistics. "Data Retrieval: Employment, Hours, and Earnings (CES)." Last modified February 1, 2013. http://www.bls.gov/webapps/legacy/cesbtab1.htm.

Dhillon, Kiran. 2015. "Why Are U.S. Oil Imports Falling?" Time.com. Accessed April 1, 2015. http://time.com/67163/why-are-u-s-oil-imports-falling/.

Kristof, Nicholas. "Let Them Sweat." *The New York Times*, June 25, 2002. http://www.nytimes.com/2002/06/25/opinion/let-them-sweat.html.

Kohut, Andrew, Richard Wike, and Juliana Horowitz. "The Pew Global Attitudes Project." *Pew Research Center*. Last modified October 4, 2007. http://www.pewglobal.org/files/pdf/258.pdf.

Lutz, Hannah. 2015. "U.S. Auto Exports Hit Record in 2014." Automotive News. Accessed April 1, 2015. http://www.autonews.com/article/20150206/OEM01/150209875/u.s.-auto-exports-hit-record-in-2014.

United States Department of Labor. Bureau of Labor Statistics. 2015. "Employment Situation Summary." Accessed April 1, 2015. http://www.bls.gov/news.release/empsit.nr0.htm.

United States Department of Commerce. "About the Department of Commerce." Accessed January 6, 2014. http://www.commerce.gov/about-department-commerce.

United States International Trade Commission. "About the USITC." Accessed January 6, 2014. http://www.usitc.gov/press_room/about_usitc.htm.

E. Helpman, and O. Itskhoki, "Labour Market Rigidities, Trade and Unemployment," *The Review of Economic Studies*, 77. 3 (2010): 1100-1137.

M.J. Melitz, and D. Trefler. "Gains from Trade when Firms Matter." *The Journal of Economic Perspectives*, 26.2 (2012): 91-118.

Rauch, J. "Was Mancur Olson Wrong?" *The American*, February 15, 2013. http://www.american.com/archive/2013/february/was-mancur-olson-wrong.

Office of the United States Trade Representative. "U.S. Trade Representative Froman Announces FY 2014 WTO Tariff-Rate Quota Allocations for Raw Cane Sugar, Refined and Specialty Sugar and Sugar-Containing Products."Accessed January 6, 2014. http://www.ustr.gov/about-us/press-office/press-releases/2013/september/WTO-trq-for-sugar.

The World Bank. "Merchandise trade (% of GDP)." Accessed January 4, 2014. http://data.worldbank.org/indicator/TG.VAL.TOTL.GD.ZS.

World Trade Organization. 2014. "Annual Report 2014." Accessed April 1, 2015. https://www.wto.org/english/res_e/booksp_e/anrep_e/anrep14_chap10_e.pdf.

# INDEX